Britain and the Defeat of Napoleon
1807–1815

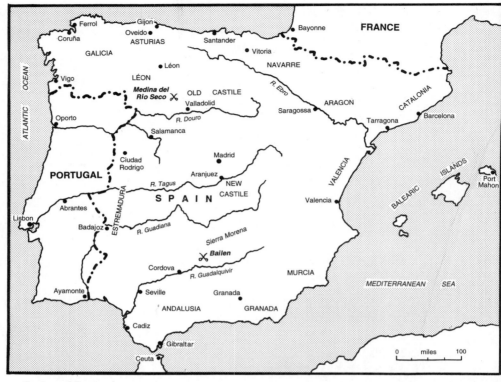

1   Spain and Portugal

BRITAIN
AND THE
DEFEAT OF NAPOLEON
1807–1815

Rory Muir

YALE UNIVERSITY PRESS
NEW HAVEN AND LONDON
1996

Set in Ehrhardt by Best-set Typesetter Ltd, Hong Kong
Printed in Great Britain by St Edmundsbury Press

Library of Congress Cataloging-in-Publication Data

Muir, Rory, 1962–
    Britain and the defeat of Napoleon, 1807–1815/Rory Muir.
    Includes bibliographical references and index.
    ISBN 0-300-06443-8 (cloth:alk. paper)
    1. Napoleonic Wars, 1800–1815 — Participation, British.   2. Peninsular War, 1807–1814 — Campaigns — Participation, British.   3. Waterloo, Battle of, 1815.
4. Great Britain — Foreign relations — 1800–1837.   5. Military art and science.
6. Wellington, Arthur Wellesley, Duke of, 1769–1852 — Military leadership.
I. Title.
DC232.M85   1996
940.2′7 — dc20   95-32097
                                                                            CIP

A catalogue record for this book is available from the British Library.

To my mother, Marcie Muir,

among whose collection of Australian children's books I found, at the age of ten, a copy of W. H. Fitchett's *Deeds that Won the Empire*; who gave me, a year later, A. G. Macdonell's *Napoleon and His Marshals*; and who has always set an example of scholarship, good sense and wit, which I can only hope to emulate.

with love

Contents

Maps

Illustrations

Maps

Illustrations

Preface

In the preface of his *The War in the Mediterranean, 1803–10*, Piers Mackesy wrote that 'the British conduct of the war against Napoleon still awaits the scholar'. His point was that while the campaigns of Nelson, Wellington and Sir John Moore have been admirably described, the role of the government in the central direction of the war has been largely ignored. This is important because 'Government alone could link together the diverse activities of generals, admirals, diplomatists and bankers, of strategy and politics and finance, and direct them towards a common goal'.

Since these words were written nearly forty years ago, Dr Mackesy's own *The Strategy of Overthrow* and *War Without Victory* have filled the gap for the War of the Second Coalition (1798–1801), while John Ehrman's superb *The Younger Pitt* has already covered the early years of the war, and promises to bring the story down to the beginning of 1806. In *Britain and the Defeat of Napoleon* I hope to complete the history of the long war from the dark days of early 1807 to the final overthrow of Napoleon and the Second Peace of Paris.

At first glance this period seems more familiar than the earlier years of the war. Napier's *History of the War in the Peninsula and the South of France* is a classic of English literature, while Sir Charles Oman's *A History of the Peninsular War*, which largely supersedes it, is both authoritative and attractively written. Sir John Fortescue's *A History of the British Army* complements Oman and covers aspects of the war beyond the Peninsula, while Sir Charles Webster's *The Foreign Policy of Castlereagh* has long been acclaimed. My debt to all these works is immense, and without them this book would have been much more difficult or impossible to write, but my perspective differs from theirs. Napier, Oman and Fortescue are mainly interested in the description of military operations: the wider aspects of the war are incidental to their purpose and, at least in the case of Napier and Fortescue, are the occasion for the expression of violent political prejudices (Napier was a Whig, Fortescue a Tory). Where the military historians are concerned primarily with military operations, Webster is most interested in

the detail of diplomatic negotiations; where they focus closely on Wellington or Moore, he concentrates on Castlereagh, even when Castlereagh's
view of events was not shared by the government in London. I hope to place
the campaigns and the negotiations in the context of the wider war, showing
how military, diplomatic, political and financial pressures all combined to
shape the policy of the British government.

The ministers in London faced an interlocking mosaic of problems in
managing Britain's war effort. In a single week, on a single day, they might
receive letters from Sicily, Sweden, India, Portugal and Canada all calling
for decisions, and each decision would have repercussions in the other
theatres. Obviously it would be unwise to adopt a strictly chronological
approach to such a range of questions, while it would be an equal distortion
to separate what are contemporaneous issues completely. I have therefore
blended the two approaches, describing separate topics in succession within
a broad narrative, and hope that this will keep any confusion to a minimum.

This book has evolved over many years. In 1984 I began working on a
doctoral thesis on 'the Campaigns of 1812 in the Peninsula', a topic which
I soon changed to 'the British Government and the Peninsular War, 1808 to
June 1811'. This thesis was successfully completed in 1988, and I began
research on what I then intended to be a sequel, bringing the war to its
conclusion. Thanks to a George Murray Post-doctoral Scholarship from
the University of Adelaide, I was able to spend much of 1990 and 1991 as
Visiting Fellow at the University of Southampton, doing further research
there on the Wellington and Palmerston Papers, at the Public Record Office
and the British Library in London, and at many other archives in Britain
and Ireland. On advice from friends and publishers I abandoned the idea of
writing two separate studies of the period 1807–15, in favour of the present
work. Chapters 2 to 8 of this book draw heavily on my thesis, but have been
largely rewritten and reduced by about half; and while I regret the loss of
many intrinsically interesting details, I suspect that most readers will find
the present volume sufficiently long, and I did not wish to obscure the view
of the forest by the study of too many trees, shrubs, leaves and flowers.

Over the course of the last ten years I have accumulated more obligations
than I can possibly acknowledge here, however some must be mentioned.
First, the University of Adelaide which provided financial and other support while I was writing my thesis, and subsequently the George Murray
Scholarship. I owe particular thanks to my supervisor Professor Austin
Gough for his encouragement and confidence in me as the thesis changed
shape, and to Professor Trevor Wilson and Dr Robin Prior who provided a
model of an enlightened and wide-ranging approach to military history.
Next I must thank the staff at the University of Southampton who facilitated my sojourn as Visiting Fellow, particularly Professor Paul Smith and
the secretary of the Department, Pam Rowland, for her practical help. Most
of my time at Southampton was spent working on the Wellington and
Palmerston Papers in the Archives Department of the University Library

where I benefited greatly from Dr Christopher Woolgar's knowledge, suggestions and friendship. Few manuscript collections can be looked after with such scrupulous care and attention, and Wellington's letters, which passed through many vicissitudes in their day (some being immersed in the Tagus *en route* back to England), have now found a secure and comfortable home. Future generations of scholars will benefit, as I have done, from the painstaking work of Dr Woolgar and his assistants: Karen Robson, Farah Wajid, Mary Cockerill, Laura Mitchell, Karen Sampson and Anne-Marie Steel.

In my research I have almost invariably found librarians and archivists helpful and obliging, often going far out of their way to assist me. At home, the Barr Smith Library of the University of Adelaide, and the State Library of South Australia have been my principal resources, and both are so familiar that I almost take them for granted, yet they have been indispensible. In Britain my thanks are due to the staff of the British Library, the Public Record Office, the West Yorkshire District Archives in Leeds, the Public Record Office of Northern Ireland in Belfast, the Department of Manuscripts at the University of Nottingham, and all the other archives I have worked at — a full list will be found in the bibliography. Small archives have fewer resources for visitors, and I owe special thanks to Mrs Jane Waley, archivist of the Harrowby Manuscripts at Sandon Hall, Staffordshire, for her hospitality and help during my visit in the summer of 1991. And also to Miss F. J. E. Moorhead, personal secretary to the Marquess of Normanby, who went to great trouble to answer at length my queries about the Mulgrave Papers in 1988.

I must thank all those who have given me permission to see and quote from copyright material: Crown copyright material in the Public Record Office, British Library and other institutions is reproduced by kind permission of Her Majesty the Queen; material from the Public Record Office of Northern Ireland is quoted with permission of the Deputy Keeper of the Records of Northern Ireland; the papers of Lord Harrowby and his brother Richard Ryder in the Harrowby Manuscripts Trust are quoted by kind permission of the Earl of Harrowby; the Manuscripts Department, University of Nottingham Library gave me permission to quote from the Portland Papers, including the correspondence of Lord William Bentinck; the Palmerston Papers are quoted by permission of the Trustees of the Broadlands Archives; while the University of Southampton has permitted me to quote from the Carver manuscripts. The illustrations were supplied by the Department of Prints and Drawings of the British Museum, who also granted permission for their reproduction. The Earl of Harewood not only allowed me to quote from the Canning Papers, but as long ago as 1986 greatly facilitated my research by giving permission for me to have many of these letters photocopied, thus enabling me to make the most of a brief visit to Leeds. Lord Raglan kindly arranged for me to have access to the revealing correspondence between Wellington and his brother William

Wellesley-Pole, and gave permission for me to quote from it. Finally I must thank David Holland Esq. not only for permission to quote from the Perceval Papers, but for his interest in my work, and for his enjoyable and stimulating letters.

Professors Norman Gash, Donald Horward and Paul Smith, and Drs Piers Mackesy and John Cookson all read my original thesis or a modified version of it, and I am most grateful for their comments and suggestions which helped in its further development and encouraged me to continue my research.

Dr Charles Esdaile has been a friend for almost ten years now, since I met him when we were both working on the Wellington Papers in Southampton — he as Wellington Fellow — in the summer of 1986. Since then we have corresponded regularly and his encouragement and advice, drawing generously on his unrivalled knowledge of the Spanish side of the Peninsular War and deep reading of British sources, has been both invaluable, and one of my great pleasures in writing this book.

Finally my debt to my parents is incalculable for their love, keen interest in my work, and many-faceted support. They brought me up among books and instilled in me a fascination with history little guessing the direction it would take.

Introduction

In February 1793 Britain went to war with Revolutionary France, little realizing that the conflict would last more than twenty years. Yet the government did not enter the war lightly. Pitt and his Foreign Secretary Lord Grenville had a sincere love of peace and had rejected Burke's impassioned calls for a crusade against the Revolution. They went to war for the most traditional of all reasons: the search for security in the face of French aggression in the Low Countries. It is true that the war soon acquired an ideological dimension, largely due to sympathy for the French cause among radical groups in Britain, but this was always secondary, and the war continued long after it had faded into insignificance. Equally, while most British ministers would have liked to see the Bourbons restored, with a constitution, this did not prevent them from discussing peace with successive French governments from as early as 1795.

At first the British government expected the war to be brief, for Britain was joining a coalition which was soon extended to include all the principal powers of Europe, while France was rent with divisions and upheaval. The immediate threat to the Low Countries was quickly defeated, and Britain supplied an auxiliary army of some 40,000 men (many of them German troops hired from their princes) to support the Austrians in Belgium. The Royal Navy asserted and maintained its command of the sea, while expeditions were dispatched to conquer French colonies. Victory appeared to be within sight when, in August 1793, the great naval base at Toulon declared against the Revolution and invited in British and allied forces.

But French desperation turned the tide of the war, and soon allied forces were in full retreat and the coalition was in tatters. Toulon fell before the end of 1793, Belgium and Holland were overrun in 1794–5, and in April 1795 the remains of the British auxiliary army were evacuated from Hanover after a harrowing retreat through a severe winter. Even the expedition to the West Indies had suffered inordinate losses from disease, so that the only consolation for the government was the success of the navy in the Battle of the Glorious First of June.

Peace overtures were opened with Paris, but they foundered on the instability of the French government and the ambition of its more radical members. The war was now carried on mainly in the Rhineland and northern Italy, for Austria was France's principal remaining enemy and Britain's only important ally. These theatres were too remote for British military intervention, but she gave the Austrians a substantial subsidy and naval cooperation in the Mediterranean. She also occupied the Dutch colonies at Ceylon and the Cape of Good Hope, and continued to make intermittent, expensive progress in the Caribbean.

During 1796–8 Britain was dealt a succession of heavy blows. General Bonaparte conquered northern Italy and advanced to within seventy miles of Vienna, forcing the Austrians to make a separate peace in April 1797. A serious financial crisis compelled the Bank of England to suspend cash payments and rely on paper currency from February 1797. This abandonment of the gold standard lasted the rest of the war and was generally beneficial to the economy, but at the time it naturally appeared extremely ominous in a country renowned for its financial stability. Another symbol of national pride was shaken in April and May 1797 when the Channel fleet mutinied at Spithead and the Nore. Fortunately the government responded with sense and moderation, promising to improve the appalling conditions which were the seamen's principal grievance, and after two months of intense anxiety the mutinies were overcome. Then, in May 1798, Ireland erupted in a full-scale but short-lived insurrection against British rule.

French attempts to exploit these difficulties were curiously ineffective. They could not mount a naval expedition quickly enough to take advantage of the naval mutinies, of which they had no advance warning. Their Irish contacts were much better, and in December 1796 they actually got an army safely to Bantry Bay, only for it to be dispersed by gales before the troops could land. A smaller force was sent to aid the rising in the summer of 1798, but it arrived too late and was easily defeated by the British forces. The appointment of Bonaparte to command the 'Army of England' in October 1797 appeared to promise decisive action, but after examining the available forces and the probable opposition, he decided against a direct attack and recommended instead an expedition to Egypt as a way of striking against Britain's Indian Empire. He succeeded in conquering Egypt, which the French held from July 1798 until September 1801, but Britain's command of the sea gave her a decisive superiority in operations outside Europe. Nelson defeated the French fleet at the Battle of the Nile (1 August 1798), isolating Bonaparte's army, which the British attacked and defeated at their leisure in 1801 — long after its commander had slipped back to France.

Meanwhile the British government had set about constructing a second coalition against France, including Austria and Russia. But it is misleading to imply that this or any of the other coalitions was primarily the result of British diplomacy or British gold. The other powers fought, as Britain did, for their own perceived interests. The expansion of French power and — earlier — the promulgation of revolutionary doctrines threatened them all, and that is why they went to war. Subsidies and diplomacy facilitated the formation of the coalition and helped to pay for the armies, but their importance was limited.

Although the Second Coalition gained some early victories, especially in Italy where all Bonaparte's conquests were retaken, the tide soon turned in favour of the French. A combined Anglo-Russian expedition to Holland became bogged down and was forced to reembark. Masséna won a great victory at Zurich and Russia withdrew from the war. Bonaparte returned from Egypt, seized power in the coup d'état of Brumaire, then led an army across the Alps to defeat the Austrians at Marengo. Six months later Moreau defeated the Austrian army of Germany at Hohenlinden, and Austria withdrew from the war, leaving Britain once more without allies.

At the same time the political situation in Britain was transformed. Pitt the Younger had been Prime Minister since 1784. His position was greatly strengthened in the early 1790s when the Whig party split over its attitude to the French Revolution and the war, and the Duke of Portland led the more conservative Whigs into a union with Pitt, leaving only the radical rump under Charles James Fox in opposition. Portland and his followers received important ministerial positions, but to a large extent the war was run by an inner cabinet consisting of Pitt, Grenville and Henry Dundas, the Secretary for War. Physical exhaustion, hard drinking and the strain of the the war took their toll, and the three sometimes quarrelled among themselves, and offended the King by failing to take sufficient account of his views. This tension came to a head when Pitt proposed a measure of Catholic Emancipation in the wake of the Union with Ireland. George III was implacably opposed to concessions to the Catholics, arguing that they would violate his coronation oath. As a result, Pitt and many of his ministers resigned in February 1801. But although Pitt resigned, he did not go into opposition, and assisted in the formation of a new government under Henry Addington, who had been the Speaker.

Addington was solid, conservative and uninspiring, but his very mediocrity, combined with his staunch opposition to the Catholic claims, appealed to the King and many members of the Commons. He recognized that the country was weary of war and opened negotiations with France. Bonaparte was equally eager to consolidate his recent conquests and his position in France, while he hoped that peace with Britain would enable him to revive France's naval power and colonial empire. The terms of the Peace of

Amiens (March 1802) were widely criticized in London, for Britain gave up all her colonial conquests except Trinidad and Ceylon, and promised to evacuate Malta, without ensuring the real independence of the Low Countries or the French satellite republics in northern Italy. But the interval of peace, though brief (it only lasted fourteen months), was most welcome, and it was not unreasonable to put Bonaparte's professions of peaceful intentions to the test.

Both sides, however, had unrealistic expectations of the benefits they would derive from the peace, and both were quickly disillusioned. The British press abused and lampooned Bonaparte, who responded by trying to bully, not cajole Britain. The breach came in May 1803 when Britain refused to evacuate Malta. It was just over ten years since the war had begun; France was now united and stronger than ever, and Britain was without Continental allies: the prospect was not encouraging, but the government was undaunted.

Addington remained in office for twelve months after the renewal of the war, primarily because Pitt was reluctant to move into open opposition. This and a number of other differences led to a split between Pitt and Grenville, who had made an unlikely but durable alliance with Fox and the Whigs. With the country threatened by invasion, there was a widespread hope of a broadly based government including Pitt, Fox and Grenville, but the King vetoed the inclusion of Fox, and Grenville would not take office without him. Pitt returned as Prime Minister in May 1804, but his government was little stronger than Addington's, from whom he was soon seeking Parliamentary support.

Meanwhile Britain remained on the defensive. Napoleon proclaimed himself Emperor and made extensive preparations for the invasion of England. He recruited, organized and trained the finest French army of the era and needed only to gain command of the Channel for a few days to make his attempt. But the French navy had deteriorated during the Revolution, being demoralized by a number of defeats at the hands of the British, and losing skills and experience as a result of the British blockade. Napoleon's plans for gaining temporary superiority in the Channel failed miserably, with Trafalgar being only the final blow after a series of less dramatic setbacks. Even if Napoleon had got his army to England, it is by no means certain that he would have succeeded — extensive preparations had been made to meet the French and there was no inclination to surrender.[1] Yet it was undoubtedly the best chance he ever had of securing the complete defeat of Britain. After 1805 his invasion preparations — the flotillas, harbours and so on — rapidly deteriorated, and while he continued to build warships he could not find experienced, capable crews. Equally important were the increasingly powerful British coastal defences, which would have made an invasion extremely difficult. Napoleon never seriously contemplated invading Britain after 1805 and had to rely on costly and inefficient indirect means to attempt to defeat her. Neither Britain nor France was capable of defeating the other without the extensive help of allies, except perhaps by a long-drawn-out war of attrition.

Thwarted in his hopes of conquering Britain, with some relief Napoleon turned east in August 1805 to confront the new coalition which was mobilizing against him. Prussia again remained neutral, but Austria and Russia had combined in a new attempt to reduce the power of France. Napoleon, however, understood war as his adversaries did not, and by rapid marching he surrounded the foremost Austrian army and forced it to surrender at Ulm before its men knew that they were in danger. He exploited his advantage by a rapid advance up the Danube valley and captured Vienna. Prussia became alarmed at Napoleon's success and considered entering the war, but before she could move, Napoleon had crushed the Austro-Russian army at Austerlitz and Austria was again forced to make peace.

The news of Austerlitz arrived in England as Pitt lay on his sick-bed. According to legend he pointed to a map of Europe and said, 'Roll up that map: it will not be wanted these ten years', then turned his face to the wall and died. His government could not survive without him, and the King had no choice but to lift his ban on Fox. Grenville became Prime Minister in a broad coalition, 'the Ministry of All the Talents', though this excluded the members of Pitt's last government. Fox became Foreign Secretary, Addington (now Lord Sidmouth) was a member of the cabinet, and William Windham, a great orator and friend of Burke, became Secretary for War and the Colonies.

Fox had always opposed the war, and in office he made a determined effort to make peace with Napoleon, offering greater concessions than ever before, and showing a willingness to accept a France more powerful than the most ambitious dreams of Louis XIV. But Napoleon was more interested in encouraging dissension between Britain and Russia than in making a final peace settlement. When d'Oubril, the Russian negotiator, granted further concessions to the French, the British cabinet reluctantly followed suit, only to see the whole peace process collapse when d'Oubril was disowned by his own government. Russia and France prepared for a renewal of active hostilities, and Fox and his colleagues accepted that the war must go on.

In later years Napoleon made several overtures to Britain for peace, proposing Russian mediation after Tilsit in 1807 and making a direct approach in April 1812. These proposals were mainly designed to justify the war to the French and wider European public, and for diplomatic purposes. In 1807 Russia had just become a French ally, so could hardly act as an impartial arbitrator, while in 1812 the crucial question of Spain was left ambiguous, and a request for clarification was ignored. In any case the British government was now resolved on carrying on the war, and would only have considered making peace if the French had offered substantial concessions. Napoleon's power was now too great for peace to be safe, and although there was no immediate prospect of victory, there was also no imminent danger of absolute defeat. In October 1807 Canning explained the government's reasons for rejecting Russian mediation:

> Could any peace settle Europe now, in a condition in which it could remain? Unquestionably not. But it would sanction and settle some dozen of green and tottering usurpations: and leave Bonaparte to begin anew. And that is why he is anxious for it. It is perfectly natural for him to like to sum up his accounts and strike his balance every now and then, and then to begin upon a new score. But that is not our interest. Our interest is that *till* there can be a final settlement that shall last, every thing should remain as unsettled as possible: that no usurper should feel sure of acknowledgement; no people confident of their new masters; no kingdom sure of its existence; no spoilator secure of his spoil; and even the plundered not acquiescent in their losses.[2]

Not everyone in Britain was convinced by these arguments: Whitbread and some other radicals continued to believe that Napoleon was a man of peace, forced against his will into endless wars by the inveterate hatred of his enemies. Only a few members of the Opposition went this far, but their deeply pessimistic leaders, freed from the responsibilities of office, sometimes toyed with the idea of a negotiated peace.[3] Among the wider public there appears to have been general support for the war, although peace petitions were occasionally raised in depressed manufacturing areas. Britain continued the war as she had begun, seeking a settlement of Europe which would contain French power and, preferably, remove the Low Countries from French domination and control.

After Austerlitz the war continued, although active military operations were largely confined to the Mediterranean. In January 1806 Lieutenant-General Craig withdrew from Naples in the face of a French invasion, but secured Sicily, which despite many vicissitudes retained a British garrison for the rest of the war. Craig returned home in April due to ill-health, and the command devolved onto Major-General Sir John Stuart, who led a British expedition to Calabria at the end of June, where he defeated a French army under Reynier at Maida (4 July 1806). The victory was psychologically important, showing that British troops could match the French in open battle, and it removed the French threat to Sicily for the rest of the year, but it did not open the road to Naples, and by the end of July Stuart and his men were back in Sicily. Here he was mortified to find that he had been superseded by Lieutenant-General Henry Fox, brother of the statesman, who had just arrived with extensive reinforcements from England. Stuart resigned in a huff and returned to England where he was given a hero's welcome.

Less than a fortnight after Stuart's account of Maida reached London, even more dramatic news arrived from South America. In 1805 Commodore Sir Home Popham and Lieutenant-General Sir David Baird had been sent by Pitt with an expedition to recapture the Cape of Good Hope, which they did in January 1806. After a few months in Cape Town the ever active and plausible Popham persuaded the usually sensible Baird to lend him a thousand troops for a wholly unauthorized attack on Buenos Aires. The expedition was remarkably successful at first, with the Spanish garrison making little resistance, and the great city falling to the British force before the end of June. Popham and Beresford, who commanded the troops, wrote home asking for instructions and reinforcements and included glowing accounts of the wealth and prosperity of their conquest. The news made a sensation in Britain and led to a speculative commercial boom. British merchants had long wanted access to the South American market and responded to Popham's news with frenzied expectations which sometimes bordered on the ridiculous. The government was swept up in the eager tide; success palliated Popham's insubordination; 4,000 reinforcements were hastily dispatched, and soon plans were afoot for completing the conquest of all Spanish America with a few small expeditions amounting to little more than 20,000 men. But then the news arrived that Beresford and his small army had been forced to capitulate. The expeditions to Chile and Mexico were abandoned, and Lieutenant-General Whitelocke was sent to take command with orders to recapture Buenos Aires and liberate Beresford and his men. Montevideo was taken by the first wave of reinforcements before Whitelocke arrived, but his attack on Buenos Aires (5 July 1807) was such a disaster that he was forced to agree to withdraw all his forces from the Rio de la Plata in return for an exchange of prisoners. On his return home Whitelocke was court-martialled and cashiered in disgrace, while Popham, the instigator of the whole adventure, suffered no more than a severe reprimand and was quickly re-employed.

Meanwhile the war in Europe revived in the autumn of 1806 with Prussia joining Russia against Napoleon. But the Prussians were no more efficient than the Austrians, and after barely a week of active operations Napoleon crushed their armies at the twin battles of Jena and Auerstädt on 14 October 1806. Prussian resistance collapsed and French forces overran almost the entire country, capturing countless fortresses and thousands of prisoners, and forcing the Prussian court to flee to Königsberg in the furthest corner of East Prussia. By the end of the year Napoleon was at Warsaw, but the slow-moving Russians had at last taken the field. There was a bloody, indecisive battle at Eylau in February, where Russians and French fought each other to a standstill, before the dreadful weather made further operations impossible, and both sides retired into winter quarters.

The Talents showed little ability or inclination to help their allies. Britain and Prussia were formally at war because of the Prussian annexation of Hanover at the beginning of the year. Grenville was growing despondent, disliked Prussia, and was disillusioned with Continental alliances, while the Whigs disliked making common cause with Russian and Prussian autocracy. The ambitious plans for South America, which were current in the autumn of 1806, absorbed most of the available troops in Britain, while Grenville was worried by the state of the nation's finances. As a result allied requests for subsidies and an expedition to northern Europe were coolly received. Lord Hutchinson was sent to Prussia in November with nothing more than authority to draw up to £200,000 in Treasury bills, if the Prussians were in dire need. A Russian request to raise a loan of £6 million in London was firmly rejected; and direct aid was limited to £500,000 owing from Pitt's last subsidy treaty. Nor would they do anything to encourage Austria to enter the war, even though this was the principal allied hope after the Prussian débâcle.[4]

The one theatre where the Talents were prepared and able to act was the Mediterranean, where their concern had been aroused by growing French influence at Constantinople. In November Admiral Duckworth was dispatched with a squadron under orders to compel the Turks to make peace with Russia and expel the French ambassador, by forcing the Dardanelles and threatening to bombard Constantinople. If they refused he was to capture or destroy their fleet. At the same time instructions were sent from London which led to the capture of Alexandria by 6,000 British troops from Sicily under Major-General Fraser. But neither of these expeditions prospered. Duckworth succeeded in forcing the Dardanelles only to be thwarted by contrary winds and Turkish procrastination, so that he was forced to make a humiliating and dangerous retreat back into the Aegean. And Fraser's attempt to besiege Rosetta led to a bloody defeat at El Hamed, where he lost nearly a thousand men, although he managed to maintain his position in Alexandria. These expeditions did nothing to help the allies in Poland, and even if they had been successful in forcing the Turks to make peace with Russia, it is unlikely that they would have done much to abate the Czar's growing resentment of Britain.

While the Talents squandered their resources in futile expeditions to South America and the eastern Mediterranean, Napoleon struck at the foundations of British power with his Berlin Decrees of 21 November 1806. There had been restrictions on trade between Britain and France since the outbreak of war in 1793, but the conquest of Prussia gave Napoleon control over the great commercial centres of north Germany, such as Hamburg, and led him to attempt to exclude British exports from the entire Continent. Napoleon hoped that his Continental System would drain Britain of specie and destroy the confidence on which her entire financial system depended. Although these hopes were never fully realized, the economic war posed a severe strain on Britain, and limited her ability to subsidize her allies. The British government retaliated with a series of Orders in Council declaring the whole Continent under blockade, and requiring that neutral vessels obtain a licence to trade with ports under Napoleon's control. This led to great resentment in the United States and was one of the principal causes of the War of 1812; but the economic hardship it caused in Europe helped to strengthen the underlying hostility to Napoleon's hegemony.

The Ministry of All the Talents did not long survive the winter of 1806–7. Fox had died on 13 September 1806 and his charm had animated and held together the unlikely coalition. Early in the new year the government achieved its one great triumph: the abolition of the slave trade, a reform which Pitt had personally supported but never managed to pass. Then the ministers addressed the question of Ireland and the Catholic claims, and proposed removing all remaining restrictions on the positions Catholic officers could hold in the armed forces. In the face of the King's resolute opposition Grenville at first seemed to give ground, raising hopes of a compromise, but then reverted to his original position. The King felt that the ministers had tried to trick him and not only refused his consent but demanded a pledge that the issue would never again be raised in his lifetime. This gave Grenville and the Whigs what many of them now most wanted: a great constitutional issue on which to take their stand. They resigned towards the end of March, and Pitt's supporters returned to power.[5]

The new government, with a few minor changes, was to conduct the war for the next two and a half years, while its members were to dominate British politics for the next two decades. The Prime Minister was the same Duke of Portland who had led his supporters to join Pitt in 1794. He had been Prime Minister before in 1783 (as a Whig) and had immense experience in many senior offices. But Portland was now sixty-nine years old, ill, lethargic and incapable of acting decisively or giving the real leadership his young ministers needed. He seldom spoke in the Lords and was often absent from cabinet. His influence on the government's policy was slight, while his procrastination in 1809 was to help to destroy the ministry.

Portland was no more than a figurehead, a nominal leader, yet his presence in the government was essential. The real strength of the government lay in a group of young efficient ministers none of whom stood out sufficiently to be generally acceptable as the leader. Portland's age and prestige, and the genuine respect he inspired, made him eminently suitable to preside over a cabinet of equals. The Portland ministry has often been described as a government of departments, one in which individual ministers pursued their own policies in their own departments with little coordination or coherence. This is a considerable exaggeration, at least in respect of the management of the war. Important decisions were usually made by the cabinet as a whole, not by individual ministers, and on a number of occasions, as we shall see, the relevant minister's own views were overruled. But the lack of a strong leader meant that disputes within the cabinet could drag on for months before being decided. Pitt had run the war with the assistance of Grenville, Dundas and one or two other ministers. Under Portland there was no such inner cabinet, and most or all of the eleven (later thirteen) cabinet ministers had to be consulted and convinced before a policy could be adopted. Yet on the whole the cabinet was reasonably efficient. Most of its members had served in previous cabinets, and there seems to have been a general willingness to cooperate and accept advice and suggestions.

The four most important ministers in the government were Canning, Castlereagh, Hawkesbury and Perceval. Canning, the new Foreign Secretary, was the most brilliant and colourful minister, and certainly the greatest orator in the government at a time when oratory was still politically important. He was a man of biting wit and invective, with immense confidence in his own ability, who often inspired either great friendship or deep dislike and distrust. He had played a leading role in the *Anti-Jacobin* and in 1809 was involved in the foundation of the *Quarterly Review* as an alternative to the Whig *Edinburgh Review*.* Canning collected round him a group of talented followers and friends including William Huskisson, George Rose, John Hookham Frere, Charles Ellis and Lord Granville Leveson Gower, many of whom held junior ministries or diplomatic posts. Much of the history of the Portland government can be attributed to the tension between Canning's energy, impatience and perfectionism, and the more staid conservative qualities of his colleagues in the cabinet.

Castlereagh was Secretary of State for War and the Colonies — a post he had already held for six months in Pitt's last government. He had far greater experience of high office than Canning but was not generally so well regarded. Partly this was because he was usually a poor speaker in Parliament, but he was unpopular for other reasons. His manner was cold and arrogant (which may well have sprung from a deep-seated shyness) and his reputation was still damaged by accusations of the corrupt means used to force the Act of Union through the Irish Parliament when he was Chief Secretary. The later assumption that he was Canning's rival in the Portland government appears to be an overstatement. Both were important ministers, but Canning was soon regarded as essential to the government's survival, while Castlereagh was not seen by his colleagues as contributing much to the strength of the ministry. No one considered making Castlereagh Prime Minister in the crisis of 1809, and only after he left office that autumn did his reputation begin to rise.

The Home Secretary was Lord Hawkesbury, who succeeded his father as Earl of Liverpool in December 1808. An ungainly, awkward man when young, Hawkesbury had great ability though little obvious brilliance. A Christ Church contemporary of Canning, the two men maintained a long

---

*   Some of Canning's occasional verse is still remembered, for example these lines from *New Morality*, first published in the *Anti-Jacobin*:

> A steady patriot of the world alone,
> The friend of every country but his own. [i.e. the Jacobin]

and

> Give me the avowed, erect and manly foe;
> Firm I can meet, perhaps return the blow;
> But of all plagues, good Heaven, thy wrath can send,
> Save me, oh, save me, from the candid friend.

friendship despite many vicissitudes and fits of jealousy. For many years Canning underestimated Hawkesbury's ability and was incensed when Addington made him Foreign Secretary in 1801 — where indeed he was not regarded as a success. In the Portland government the two men were friends, but neither rivals nor allies; and it is hard to detect any distinctive contribution Hawkesbury made to the conduct of the war.

Canning, Castlereagh and Hawkesbury were all born in either 1769 or 1770; Spencer Perceval was some seven years older. He had been a successful lawyer, and Attorney-General in Addington's government. In 1807 he hoped to return to this post and was only persuaded with difficulty to accept the office of Chancellor of the Exchequer and leader of the government in the Commons. He had no special expertise in finance and relied heavily on William Huskisson, the Secretary to the Treasury and an acknowledged authority on the government's finances. He was appointed leader of the House of Commons because he was a staunch opponent of Catholic Emancipation (unlike Canning and Castlereagh), because he came from an old English family, and because his ability was gradually being appreciated.[6] As leader he came into frequent contact with George III, who greatly liked his honesty and straightforwardness. Perceval was hardworking, devout and intelligent, if unimaginative. He was not a great orator, but a capable and courageous debater. His management of the Commons during the Portland government was open to criticism, but overall no one was to increase their reputation as much as he did over the next five years.

The six other cabinet ministers, all of whom were in the Lords, were less important. Mulgrave (First Lord of the Admiralty) and Chatham (Master-General of the Ordnance) were both able but lazy, and presided over the further ossification of departments badly in need of reform. Both were senior lieutenant-generals, although neither had seen much recent service. Nonetheless, Chatham's opinion in particular carried considerable weight on strategic questions, and he was promised an important command in 1808 and received one in 1809. Eldon, the reactionary Lord Chancellor, was a strong link with the King. He was an intelligent, energetic man, reputedly better at identifying weaknesses in proposals than in suggesting plans.[7] Lord Bathurst was later to prove an excellent Secretary of State for War and the Colonies (1812–27), but in the Portland cabinet he was only President of the Board of Trade, and apparently restricted himself in the main to the affairs of his office. Finally, John Fane, tenth Earl of Westmorland, as Lord Privy Seal, and Lord Camden, as President of the Council, contributed little if anything of value. Westmorland was said to be a boorish fool whose lack of manners appalled Lord Wellesley, while Canning called Camden 'Lord Chuckle' and found him intensely irritating.

The individual ability of these ministers was considerably more important than it would be today, because the administrative machinery supporting them was so much smaller. To take one example: the staff of the Foreign

Office in 1807 consisted of the Foreign Secretary (George Canning), two under-secretaries, a dozen clerks and a few miscellaneous officials such as a librarian; while Castlereagh's staff at the War Department was even smaller. This meant that the task of making policy was very largely confined to the ministers themselves, sometimes assisted by confidential advisers who might or might not hold a relevant office. Three such advisers are worth mentioning: Edward Cooke, one of the under-secretaries for War and the Colonies, was an old friend of Castlereagh and had worked with him in securing the passage of the Irish Act of Union. Cooke 'was not an adminis-trator . . . [but] "a shrewd, outspoken man"', intensely loyal to Castlereagh yet not afraid to disagree with him.[8] Colonel Charles Stewart, the other under-secretary in the department, was a hotheaded, indiscreet cavalry officer, who was to play many roles in the next few years thanks to the patronage of his half-brother Lord Castlereagh. Sir Arthur Wellesley was Chief Secretary for Ireland, but in addition acted as unofficial military adviser to Castlereagh and the cabinet on strategic questions, as he had previously done to Lord Grenville in 1806–7.

A much larger staff was of course needed to implement policy once it was made: the Foreign Office had its embassies, though their staffs were small, while two separate structures were responsible for administering the army. The Secretary *at* War was a junior minister (although he was sometimes a member of the cabinet) who was responsible for the army's finances and for all troop movements within Britain. He presided 'over that remarkable rabbit warren of red tape and civilian clerks which was the War Office',[9] and had well over one hundred staff to assist him. The office gave its holder no say whatever on strategy, although if he was a member of cabinet he would naturally take part in its discussions on all subjects. The other structure of military administration was the Horse Guards, at whose head stood the Duke of York, George III's second son, who had been made Commander-in-Chief of the army in 1795. This military bureaucracy was responsible for the internal workings of the army — training, discipline, promotion and so on. Inevitably there was sometimes friction between the Horse Guards and the War Office, and in 1810 the young Palmerston (Secretary at War) became involved in a violent controversy with the aging Sir David Dundas (York's replacement as Commander-in-Chief). The Commander-in-Chief had no right even to be consulted on strategic matters, but Castlereagh and the cabinet did frequently seek his advice, and on some occasions also that of other senior officers in the Horse Guards. In addition to the War Office and the Horse Guards, the Commissariat (which answered to the Chan-cellor of the Exchequer) and the Ordnance were involved in the administra-tive and logistical affairs of the army.

But the cabinet was only one arm of government and its power was much less in relation to both Crown and Parliament than it is today. In theory the King had the power to accept or reject his ministers' advice on any subject, but this power was weakened by their ability to resign if their advice was not taken. In practice the King's immense experience (he had been on the throne for well over forty years) and his businesslike habits ensured that when he chose to intervene he could have a real influence over the government's decisions. He took a keen interest in military matters, particularly the internal administration of the army, but also questions of strategy, on which he expressed strong views during the first year of the Portland government. His interventions became less frequent with the outbreak of the Peninsular War, although he continued to play an important part in the selection of officers for senior commands. His greatest role, however, was at times of ministerial crisis when he exercised his right to choose his servants, i.e. to nominate the Prime Minister, and to insist on the inclusion or exclusion of certain individuals. Obviously constraints affected this power, but political parties in this period (except to some extent the Whigs) were fragmented, and there remained a large number of M.P.s who would support the government of the day regardless of its composition. It is not true that a government with royal support could not be overturned — for Perceval was nearly defeated in 1810 despite George III's unequivocal support — but even a weak government might survive.

Parliament — or rather the Commons — was also more independent and fluid than today, due to the weakness of the parties. No government could survive if it lost the confidence of the Commons, although the ministers did not automatically resign if they lost one or two votes on questions of secondary importance. To gain the confidence of the Commons the ministry had to include a number of men of proven ability. To retain this confidence it had to perform reasonably well. Addington was forced from office because he had lost the confidence of Parliament; Pitt's colleagues would not continue without him because they knew that they did not possess it; and the Talents were driven from power by the King. The cabinet governed from day to day, but in 1807 neither Parliament nor the King was a rubber stamp.

Public opinion, both within the governing class and in the population at large, could also influence the government. Thus the ground swell of popular support for the Spanish cause in the summer of 1808 encouraged the government to promise more and more British support, while the subsequent reaction, particularly after Coruña, made it harder to renew those commitments. But in general the populace and the press were more interested in scandals than strategy, producing an excessive reaction to perceived failures, as in the furore over the Convention of Cintra, or allegations of corruption such as those made by Mary Anne Clarke against the Duke of York in 1809. Popular discontent over the economic effects of the war had more foundation, and when skilfully harnessed by Henry Brougham in 1811 and 1812, it ultimately forced the government to abandon the Orders in Council. But such occasions were rare, and in general the ministers were able to conduct the war without undue concern for popular opinion.

Despite her reputation as a maritime power, Britain's military forces were surprisingly powerful. The effective strength of her regular army was approximately 150,000 rank and file on 1 January 1804, and rose steadily throughout the war against Napoleon, reaching some 260,000 rank and file towards the end of 1813. Although part of this increase was provided by foreign troops (such as the excellent King's German Legion and the less impressive Chasseurs Britanniques), who grew from 17,000 men in 1804 to 54,000 in 1813, the majority were raised from Britain's own population of some 17 million (including 6 million Irish). The growth in the total size of the army is all the more remarkable as it suffered constant heavy losses, mainly due to disease. This 'wastage' rose from about 17,000 men per annum between 1803 and 1807 to more than 24,000 men in 1809, 1812 and 1813. In all, the army lost some 225,000 men (of whom 188,000 were British) in the eleven years 1803 to 1813 inclusive.[10]

In addition to the regular army there were several layers of home defence forces. The most efficient of these was the regular militia, a full-time, well-trained body of between 60–90,000 men. The militia could not be sent to serve overseas, or even, until 1811, to Ireland. Its purpose was solely the defence of Britain, and this limited role enabled it to be raised by conscription when voluntary recruiting fell short. To compensate for the obnoxious use of compulsion, some provision was made for the families of militiamen (unlike those of the regulars) and the balloted men were permitted to pay someone else to substitute for them. As the pay of both militia and regulars was much below that in the general community, such substitutes were in great demand and could charge a very high fee — £40 or more in some cases. This was, of course, more than most poor workmen could afford, but they grouped together in insurance clubs, so that of 26,000 men balloted for the militia in England in 1807–8 only 3,129 served in person, all the rest providing substitutes. This fierce demand for substitutes naturally reduced voluntary enlistment in both the militia and the regulars.[11]

Finally there were the Volunteers — an enormous mass of part-time soldiers who had been encouraged to join local units and receive military training from a mixture of patriotism when Napoleon threatened invasion, and a promise of exemption from the militia ballot. These units varied widely in quality, but some minimum standard was achieved by the appointment of regular officers to inspect them, while the Lord Lieutenants had the power to disband inefficient units. Windham disliked the Volunteers and withdrew the minimal government assistance they received, and abolished their exemption from the ballot, planning to replace them with a system of universal military training. But Castlereagh recognized that this was a chimera, and on taking office in 1807 he first revived the Volunteers, who had naturally wilted under Windham's neglect, and then transformed the bulk of them into a local or sedentary militia. This militia too was raised by ballot, but no substitutes were allowed. The men were liable to do training for twenty-eight days per year (later reduced to fourteen) and except in case of an invasion could only be asked to serve in their own or an adjacent county. Neither the Volunteers nor the local militia could have successfully resisted regular troops, let alone Napoleon's Grande Armée, in the open field, but in the event of an invasion they would have supplemented the garrisons of important towns and fortresses, protected their home districts against detached parties of the enemy, guarded French prisoners, and acted in large bodies in the enemy's rear. Nonetheless, it may be questioned if such a force — which ultimately rose to over 300,000 men — justified its cost in the years after 1807.

Much of the regular army was kept at home as well as the two types of militia. There was an obvious need for a strong army in Ireland and for substantial garrisons in the Channel Islands. Many second battalions of regiments were also stationed in Britain, being too weak or inefficient to take the field except in an emergency, but able to feed a steady stream of trained recruits into the first battalions overseas. These units could be used to help support the civil authorities in the event of riots or other public disorder, although the importance of this role should not be overstated. Britain's colonies and colonial conquests also required large garrisons. Thus on 1 June 1807 the East and West Indies each absorbed nearly 20,000 men; 4,000 were at the Cape of Good Hope and a similar force in Canada and Nova Scotia; while many smaller detachments were scattered across the globe, with even New South Wales requiring 490 men. Britain also kept a very substantial force in the Mediterranean, guarding Sicily, Malta and Gibraltar, but also, in part, available for offensive operations.[12] The combined demands of home and colonial garrisons meant that only a small part of the British regular army was ever available for operations on the Continent. Thus Wellington at Vitoria in June 1813 had only 52,000 British troops out of a total army of 255,000; while a few months later Napoleon was able to lead some 200,000 men at the Battle of Leipzig. But if the British army could never hope to match the numerical strength of the forces of the great powers of the Continent, there was at least the consolation that the British troops used for active operations were among her best — a fact which largely accounts for the high quality of Wellington's army.

When Castlereagh returned to the War Department in March 1807 he was dismayed at the state of the army. A substantial part of the disposable force of the country had been sent to South America, while most of Britain's colonial garrisons were under strength, as was the home establishment. The situation was made worse by the fact that most of the second battalions in Britain were excessively weak — averaging only about 250 men each — so that they could not even be relied upon for home defence. This led Castlereagh to argue against sending any substantial force to the Continent to aid the allies — although here he was overruled by the cabinet.[13]

To remedy this situation Castlereagh invited nearly 30,000 militiamen to volunteer into the regulars, and replaced them through a mixture of ordinary recruitment and the ballot. On the whole this scheme proved a great success, although it inevitably did great immediate damage to the efficiency of the militia. Castlereagh's successors at the War Department followed his precedent, and the army was saved any more of the disruptive restructuring which had marked the early years of the war against Napoleon.

But this shortage of men was not the only constraint on British operations. Mounting an expedition required large numbers of transport ships which were expensive to hire. Such ships could normally only carry a few hundred infantry, or fewer than a hundred horses per ship, so that a large expedition might require hundreds of vessels. The Walcheren Expedition in 1809, for example, needed more than 600 vessels of all kinds, including naval escorts, although this was an exceptionally large force. And even when the ships and the men had been found, there were still many problems to be overcome. These included the complex and inefficient organization of Britain's military, in which the artillery and engineers had a completely separate establishment from that of the army and were represented in cabinet by the Master-General of the Ordnance, while the Commissariat fell under the purview of the Treasury. Then there was the dependence of sailing ships upon the weather: adverse winds could keep an expedition in harbour for weeks or make it dangerous to linger off the coast. But perhaps the most crippling problem of all was the slowness and unreliability of communications. By the time that a request for orders reached London, was considered, and the reply reached its destination, the situation could have changed so dramatically that the new orders would be completely inappropriate. This left the government with little option but to issue discretionary orders to its generals. The man on the spot usually was in a better position to judge the wisdom of an attack, but the system was not without its dangers. Selfish generals sometimes abused their discretion to the detriment of the common cause, while most generals felt that it imposed upon them an unwanted responsibility which could be exploited by politicians in the event of failure. This feeling was not entirely unjustified, but the alternative of arbitrary orders to be obeyed no matter how inappropriate was obviously worse.

Naval affairs caused the new government less immediate concern. Britain's command of the sea was reasonably secure, although it required constant attention and the dedication of the squadrons who rode out the North Sea and Atlantic gales while maintaining the blockade of French, Dutch, Spanish and other enemy ports. Napoleon continued to build vessels in ports throughout his Empire, from Hamburg to Venice, and to talk of vast concerted operations which would drive the British from the seas. Some of this was pure fantasy: schemes requiring close cooperation of such traditional enemies as Russia and Turkey, Prussia and Sweden, were unlikely to prosper, especially when these powers had little interest in their success. There is even a suspicion that Napoleon's shipbuilding was primarily intended to alleviate unemployment and discontent in some of the areas which suffered most from the economic war. In the meantime the efficiency of the French navy steadily declined, owing to a lack of experience at sea. The few extended excursions of French squadrons after 1806 mostly ended in miserable failure.[14]

But even if secure, Britain's command of the sea was not absolute. It was always possible that a small French force might take advantage of bad weather and slip through the blockade and mount a raid on Ireland, or even the British mainland. French, and later American, privateers were a constant irritant, capturing British merchantmen within sight of the coast of Sussex and Kent. In the Indian Ocean a French squadron operated with great success from Mauritius until its base was captured in 1810. And in the Mediterranean the Toulon squadron posed particular difficulties, for the prevailing winds meant that it could not be securely blockaded.

There was another, more insidious, problem facing the Royal Navy. Britain had entered the war in 1793 with a relatively new fleet in excellent condition. By 1803 it was showing considerable signs of wear, which had grown worse by 1807. The new government embarked on a major programme of refitting older vessels and building new ones. This was naturally expensive, and expenditure on the navy continued to rise until it reached a peak of over £20 million in 1813.[15] As a result of this activity the battle fleet of the navy, although sometimes stretched by the many demands on it, was sufficient to maintain control of the seas. However, throughout the war there was a severe shortage of frigates and smaller vessels, which hindered operations of all kinds, including amphibious expeditions and naval cooperation with the allies.

There were few naval battles of any importance in the later years of the war, because Napoleon's squadrons seldom ventured out of port. In April 1809 Cochrane's daring attack on a French squadron in Basque Roads destroyed four French capital ships and damaged others. Two years later Captain Hoste, with four frigates, defeated a greatly superior force off Lissa in the Adriatic. In 1810, however, the British suffered a rare defeat at Grand Port, Mauritius, though they had their revenge when they captured the island a few months later. Neither these actions, nor the innumerable smaller encounters with French warships or privateers, had much effect on the general course of the war. After Trafalgar the great majority of British naval losses were due to the weather, not enemy action, and the real triumph of the navy lay in the constant, grinding, unglamorous work of the blockade, not in the few fleeting moments of glory. For it was the blockade which maintained Britain's command of the sea, and this in turn underpinned her role in the defeat of Napoleon. The presence of her fleets in the Baltic and the Mediterranean, as well as in the North Sea and the Atlantic, increased her influence with the Continental Powers, and enabled her to land an expedition almost anywhere from Copenhagen to the Dardanelles.

The command of the sea was equally important, of course, for operations beyond Europe. By 1807 Britain had already secured most of her colonial objectives, and her government, in general, sought to reduce her garrisons to the minimum safe level. Even so, some offensives were undertaken after 1807. In the West Indies, Martinique was captured early in 1809, and Guadeloupe a year later. This removed the last French possession of any importance in the region, and as Spain was now an ally, the government felt able to let its Caribbean garrisons dwindle away until they were barely sufficient to maintain order. On the other side of the world British forces from India captured Mauritius in 1810, and Java in 1811, thus removing the last enemy bases in the eastern seas. This ended a persistent and costly threat to Britain's Indian trade, and allowed ships to be withdrawn to take part in the war with the United States in 1812; while Java was in itself an immensely valuable prize. Nonetheless, as the government recognized, these colonial operations were peripheral to the main conflict, for Napoleon could only be defeated on the mainland of Europe.

PART ONE

Thrust and Counterthrust
1807–10

I

The First Year of the Portland
Government, 1807–8

When the Portland government took office at the end of March 1807, the new ministers did not know the extent of the problems which they had inherited. Over the next few months bad news poured into London from almost every quarter of the globe: from Egypt and the Dardanelles, from India (where there had been a sepoy mutiny at Vellore) and South America, and above all from the Baltic. In March 1807 the war in Poland was in a state of fitful hibernation after the bloody slaughter at Eylau, but with the coming of spring active operations would soon resume, and the new ministers had much to do if they were to influence events.

The tardiness and parsimony of the Talents had seriously offended Britain's allies, and there were many in the Emperor Alexander's entourage who favoured a negotiated peace.[1] Canning moved quickly to signal that the change of ministers was matched by a change of policy, authorizing Lord Hutchinson to pay the Prussians £100,000 to cover their immediate expenses until a formal subsidy agreement could be signed, and making similar arrangements for the Russians. Negotiations were delayed by the slowness of communications, but on 27 June Canning signed 'the simplest subsidy treaty of the entire war' with Prussia, by which Britain agreed to pay £1 million in three instalments over a year, in return for a Prussian promise to devote all her resources to the war against Napoleon.[2] Six weeks earlier Granville Leveson Gower, Britain's ambassador to Russia, had been instructed to offer the Russians even more generous aid, although the precise sum depended on whether some money should be reserved for Austria, if she could be induced to join the coalition. Not even King Gustavus IV Adolf of Sweden, who thus far had done the allies more harm than good with his quarrels, his eccentric schemes, and his constant demands for more funds, escaped Canning's bounty, with all the Swedish demands being granted, even though they set a dangerous precedent.[3]

As well as money, the allies wanted military cooperation, preferably a substantial expedition to Hanover landing around the mouths of the Elbe and Weser. This posed great problems for the new government, for when

Castlereagh arrived at the War Department he found that, thanks to the Talents' concern for economy, there were insufficient transports available to carry an expedition, while the army was seriously under strength. He at once set to work to improve matters, but even at the end of May he was arguing that it would be hazardous to dispatch an expedition to the Continent while Britain's home defences were so weak. But the cabinet decided that the importance of sustaining the war on the Continent justified the risk. The ministers would have liked to send their expedition to Hanover, which would have greatly simplified its logistical problems, but decided that this would be too rash unless Austria entered the war or Germany rose against the French. They therefore decided, on 1 June, to dispatch 8–10,000 men of the King's German Legion under Lord Cathcart to Stralsund in the Baltic, as the first division of an army which they hoped would eventually amount to 34,000 men. At Stralsund Cathcart's expedition would join Swedish and Prussian forces and threaten Napoleon's flank and rear, while if the allies advanced successfully, later divisions of the army could join him by landing in Hanover. The first troops sailed on 19 June, and began disembarking near Stralsund on 8 July: but already it was too late.[4]

During April and May the principal armies had remained in their cantonments in Poland, while attention concentrated on the siege of Danzig, which finally surrendered on 26 May. Operations were resumed in the first week of June with the Russians taking the initiative although they were outnumbered. They gained the advantage at Heilsberg on 10 June, but then were caught in disarray and decisively defeated by Napoleon at Friedland on the 14th, losing some 20,000 casualties and eighty cannon. Friedland destroyed the Emperor Alexander's willingness to continue the war, and he immediately sought a truce. This led to the famous meeting on the raft in the River Niemen at Tilsit on 25 June 1807 which converted the hostile emperors into friends and allies. Negotiations over the details of the peace settlement continued for more than a week. Russia emerged with slightly more Polish territory than before and permission to extend her conquests from the Turks in Moldavia and Wallachia. She would also offer to mediate between Britain and France, and if her offer was not accepted, she promised to close her ports to British trade and declare war. Sweden, Denmark and Portugal were to be invited, and if necessary compelled, to follow suit, and Napoleon encouraged Alexander to look to conquering Finland from Sweden. In return the Russian Emperor accepted Napoleon's settlement of Germany, and abandoned Prussia, which lost nearly half its territory, including its Polish provinces which became the 'Grand Duchy of Warsaw', nominally ruled by the King of Saxony, but in fact a French protectorate. With Prussia emasculated, Austria cowed and Russia transformed into an ally, Tilsit appeared to establish Napoleon's hegemony over western and central Europe beyond challenge.

News of Friedland reached London on 30 June and led Canning to fear that Russia would make peace, although he naturally did not anticipate the reversal of alliances. Over the next ten days this news was followed by a variety of reports of French preparations to invade Denmark, while by 12 July rumours were circulating in London that the Danish fleet intended to close the Sound, and might even be used by the French to invade Ireland.[5] Anglo–Danish relations had been difficult since late 1806. The Danes were intent on preserving their neutrality, but their concessions to Napoleon were viewed with suspicion in London, and in December Lord Howick (who had succeeded Fox at the Foreign Office) warned bluntly that the British government would not permit the Danish fleet to fall into French hands. Matters were not helped by intemperate Danish protests at the Orders in Council, and by several reports (which later proved false) that Danish coastal defences were being strengthened and that their fleet was being prepared for sea. By 9 June Canning believed that 'the disposition at Copenhagen is so unfriendly as to want nothing but the appearance of being able to insult us with impunity, to break out into open defiance'.[6]

It thus seemed likely that Denmark would succumb to French diplomatic pressure and join an alliance against Britain, or else would make little effective resistance to a French invasion. On 14 July Lord Mulgrave therefore proposed sending a powerful naval squadron, of twenty or twenty-two ships of the line, to Danish waters where they could both watch the Danish fleet and help the Danes resist a French invasion. The King highly approved this precautionary measure but expressed grave doubts when, three days later, Castlereagh proposed adding an army to the fleet on the grounds that if things came to extremities, Copenhagen would be more easily attacked from the land than the sea. The King argued against any act of unprovoked aggression which might make Russia hostile and lead to a revival of the League of Armed Neutrality.[7] The cabinet was concerned by the King's doubts and Portland went down to Windsor to explain their policy and the reasoning which lay behind it in more detail. The King listened and, though not convinced, let the government pursue its measures without further opposition.

On 22 July the government received further intelligence from the Continent, including what purported to be an account of the meeting between Napoleon and Alexander at Tilsit, in which the former proposed the formation of a maritime league against Britain, and Alexander neither accepted nor rejected the idea. The source of this intelligence has aroused a great deal of speculation, including the scarcely credible story that a British agent, Colin Mackenzie, attended the Emperors' meeting in disguise. More plausibly it has been suggested that a senior Russian figure, probably General Bennigsen, who was unhappy with Alexander's volte-face, gave this information to Mackenzie, who arrived in London on or about 21 July. Canning's steady refusal to disclose the government's sources of intelligence when pressed in Parliament has added to the air of mystery surrounding the whole affair, which is unlikely now ever to be fully explained.[8] But whatever the source, or the accuracy, of the news which arrived on the 22nd, its importance has been exaggerated. For while it no doubt strengthened the government's resolve, the decision to dispatch the expedition to Denmark had already been taken.

Admiral Gambier sailed with the fleet on 26 July with instructions to prevent the Danes reinforcing their garrison on Zealand, while acting with all possible civility and avoiding provocation. Castlereagh had already written to Cathcart appointing him to the command of the army and ordering him to withdraw his troops from Stralsund and join the expedition off Denmark. On 30 July transports carrying the remainder of the army, some 18,000 men, sailed from England — they reached Denmark on 7 August and were joined by Cathcart, sailing ahead of his troops on the 12th.

But although all these preparations had been made for an attack on Copenhagen, Canning at least still hoped to avoid violence.[9] With the fleet sailed Francis Jackson, an envoy to the Prince Regent of Denmark, who was to propose that the Danes join an alliance with Britain against France. Canning's hopes were not based on any belief in Danish affection for Britain, but rather on a calculation that by siding against Britain the Danes would lose their colonies and much of their trade, and perhaps even imperil their possession of Norway; against this, of course, war with Napoleon would mean the loss of Holstein and Jutland, and danger to Zealand and the other islands. Probably Canning's hopes were always too optimistic, for it is hard to see why the Danish Court would reverse its existing predilections and favour Britain over France on terms such as these, especially when the ultimatum came from Britain. But it appears that Jackson reduced whatever slim chance may have existed, by mishandling his mission and needlessly irritating the Danish Crown Prince and Count Bernstorff, his minister. In any case the Danes rejected the overture, and on 14 August Jackson joined the British fleet with news that his mission had failed.[10]

Early on the morning of 16 August the British troops began disembarking on Zealand and on the following day Copenhagen was invested. There was some natural and creditable distaste among the senior British officers for their mission, and the hope seems to have existed for some time that the Danes would make only a show of resistance before coming to terms. But although the Danish defence was neither very active nor very able, it was no mere pretence. On 24 August Cathcart tightened the investment of Copenhagen by occupying the suburbs and establishing new batteries in the shelter they provided. A few days later Sir Arthur Wellesley defeated an attempt to relieve the city, and on 31 August, with his batteries ready, Cathcart summoned the Danes to surrender. His summons was rejected and at 7 p.m. on 2 September the bombardment began, quickly setting fire to many parts of the town and causing heavy civilian casualties. The bombardment continued intermittently until the 5th, when the Danish commandant asked for an armistice in order to capitulate, thus sparing the city the further horrors of being stormed and sacked. A Convention was signed on 7 September by which the Danes surrendered their entire fleet plus all their naval stores to Britain, and the British commanders promised to withdraw from Zealand within six weeks.[11]

The expedition had been a complete success and the Danish navy had almost ceased to exist. Fifteen captured ships of the line and many smaller vessels were brought into British ports, while a number of other old or partly constructed ships were destroyed at Copenhagen. Four of the ships of the line and some of the frigates were incorporated into the British navy, and even returned to the Baltic under their new colours. The Danish fleet never recovered from the blow, and although the activity of its gunboats posed a menace to British merchantmen, it was never more than an irritant to the Royal Navy. The operation established British domination of the Baltic for the rest of the war, for both Russia and Sweden were anxious to avoid any serious hostility with Britain at sea.[12]

Despite, or even because of, its success, the morality of the attack on Copenhagen has been much debated, both at the time and ever since. The King continued to regard the expedition as 'a very immoral act', and made a point of not enquiring which of his ministers was its chief architect, though all the world knew that the principal share, whether of praise or blame, was due to Canning.[13] The Opposition strenuously attacked the government on it in Parliament, and were joined by Sidmouth and his followers, although Wilberforce, the conscience of the House, eventually came down on the side of the government, albeit with some reservations. But the most common reaction was relief and pleasure that the expedition had succeeded, mixed with pity for the Danes, and some unease over the whole question. Even Canning, writing privately to his wife, protested a little too much that the expedition was fully justified.[14]

News of the attack reverberated round Europe, providing wonderful material for Napoleon's propaganda, but making other neutrals uncomfortably aware that they could not rely on British forbearance. It strengthened underlying hostility to Britain in Russia, but led to an immediate if temporary softening of Russia's language. The Russians even urged the British government to maintain a British garrison on Zealand in order to protect Sweden from a French invasion.[15] The ministers in London had already been thinking along these lines, but were fortunately dissuaded by strong protests from Cathcart and Gambier. The Russian overtures were almost certainly due solely to fear of a British attack on their naval base at Cronstadt. The British government considered this operation but decided against it, not because they trusted Russia's assurances, although Canning still underestimated the sincerity of Alexander's commitment to the French alliance, but because they knew that the Tilsit policy was deeply unpopular in Russia, and they did not wish to create an obstacle to Alexander again reversing his alliances. The few Russian ships at Cronstadt posed little threat to the Royal Navy, as the following years were to prove, while the delay in hostilities with Russia enabled British merchants to secure most of their vast interests and cargoes in Russian ports. While some of the premises underlying British policy towards Russia in the second half of 1807 were over-optimistic, the policy itself could hardly have been bettered.[16]

British policy towards Sweden was more difficult, for faced with the combined hostility of Russia and France the Swedes had little hope of successful resistance. Britain therefore urged Sweden to make peace with her enemies even if this led to a nominal state of hostilities with Britain. But Gustavus would not listen and the British government found itself dragged reluctantly by a sense of loyalty into supporting Sweden in a war she could not win.[17] Early in February 1808 Britain agreed to pay Sweden a subsidy of £1.2 million per annum. A fortnight later Russia invaded Finland, while Denmark declared war at the end of March. A strong British naval squadron was dispatched to the Baltic as soon as the weather permitted, and its presence and activity foiled a French invasion from Denmark. However, the British ships could do little to help the Swedes in Finland, where the war was going badly. The Swedish minister in London pressed hard for the assistance of British troops and far exceeded his instructions in the assurances he gave the British government. With some misgivings the cabinet agreed to send Lieutenant-General Sir John Moore with 12,000 men, on the understanding that they would be used to relieve Swedish troops guarding against an invasion from Denmark. But when Moore arrived in May he found that Gustavus, who in turn had been misled by Edward Thornton, the British envoy to Stockholm, was full of wild and impractical schemes for invading Norway or Denmark. Heated quarrels resulted in the King ordering Moore's arrest and the general's hasty retreat to the ships from which his troops had never disembarked. The whole ridiculous affair led to much ill-feeling both between Britain and Sweden, and between Moore and the ministers.[18]

Gustavus continued the war with little success until March 1809, when he was overthrown in a palace coup. The new government made peace with France and Russia, accepting the loss of Finland, which remained a Grand Duchy of Russia until 1917. During the next few years the war shifted away from the Baltic, but each spring the British fleet returned and maintained a powerful presence, reminding Russians, Prussians, Danes and Swedes that if Napoleon was master of the land, Britain was mistress of the sea.

While the Baltic was the principal theatre for British activity during the first six months of the Portland government, the Mediterranean also figured quite largely owing to the confused legacy left by the Talents. Duckworth had made his unsuccessful attempt to coerce the Turkish government at the end of February, but the news of his failure did not reach London until April. Fraser did not capture Alexandria until March, and his subsequent travails caused a succession of problems for the new ministers, until British forces finally evacuated Egypt in September. These problems were compounded by the slow and uncertain passage of letters from the Mediterranean, by the perennial problem of Britain's difficult relations with the Neapolitan Court, now in exile at Palermo, and, at the end of May, by the arrival of news of a mutiny among foreign troops at Malta.

Duckworth's failure confirmed the desire of the new ministers to put an end to their unfortunate hostilities with Turkey, and in May Canning dispatched Sir Arthur Paget, an experienced and capable diplomat, to Constantinople to negotiate a peace. This did not reflect any lack of support for Russia, for the Russians themselves were now seeking an end, or at least a suspension, of their war with Turkey, and Paget was instructed to use his best endeavours to assist their emissary, the Corsican exile, Pozzo di Borgo.[19]

While not rejecting such diplomatic support, the Russians made it clear that what they really wanted was military activity, principally in northern Europe, but also, if possible, in the Mediterranean. In response to this pressure Castlereagh prepared instructions to General Fox, the British commander in Sicily, to prepare an expedition to the mainland, which, the minister calculated, might comprise 8,000 British and 12,000 Neapolitan troops. The King was highly sceptical, regarding the British force as inadequate and the Neapolitans as worthless, but as the instructions to Fox were discretionary, he let them pass having made his opinion clear.[20]

The King's doubts were vindicated, for the affairs of Sicily were far less promising than Castlereagh believed. The British commanders, General Fox and his energetic, opinioniated deputy Sir John Moore, had quarrelled with the Court and with William Drummond, the British envoy. The Neapolitan army had already attempted a landing in Calabria and had been forced to retreat in disorder, and was now at least as demoralized and worthless as George III believed. Finally the British force in Sicily had already been reduced, unknown to Castlereagh, by the need to dispatch 2,000 reinforcements to Fraser in May. The generals therefore used their discretion and aborted Castlereagh's plan when his instructions reached them at the end of June. As the war in the Baltic was already over, the expedition could have done no good even if it had achieved some immediate success — which was unlikely given the forces available. The incident does not reflect well on the government's strategic judgement, for an offensive in Italy that summer was probably never feasible.[21]

The news of Tilsit naturally put an end to all thoughts of offensive operations and created a number of delicate problems. A Russian fleet under Admiral Siniavin had been operating in the Mediterranean since the beginning of 1805, and Russian troops occupied Corfu, some of the other Ionian islands, and positions in Dalmatia. Neither the British government nor Admiral Collingwood, who commanded the British naval forces in the Mediterranean, knew how Tilsit might affect Siniavin's operations.

Collingwood took every precaution and watched the Russian fleet closely but he avoided provoking hostilities, as did Siniavin, who was personally hostile to the French and admired the British. Meanwhile Canning instructed Leveson Gower to inform the Russian government that while Britain wished for good relations, she could not permit the Russian fleet to return to the Baltic, or even to winter at Naples. Instead he hoped that they might winter at an English port, and the Russian ambassador to London even began making preparations for their reception. In November Siniavin passed the British squadron blockading Cadiz, and one of his frigates informed Admiral Purvis that they were heading for Portsmouth, although other sources indicate that in fact they were under orders for the Baltic.[22] But once in the Atlantic, the squadron was battered by storms and forced to take refuge in Lisbon, arriving at an extremely delicate moment, as the French army under General Junot was advancing through Portugal. There the Russian ships remained until the following autumn, arousing fears in Britain that they might take Junot's troops on board and make a descent on Ireland. Lisbon was promptly blockaded, but the Russians showed no signs of stirring. Meanwhile the Russian troops had handed over their positions in the Adriatic, including Corfu, to the French and had returned home through Austria.

The departure of the Russians from the Mediterranean simplified matters for Britain, but nonetheless the government's policy remained uncertain for much of the rest of the year. Sicily was the key to the Mediterranean, but it required a large garrison and relations with the Court were always difficult. Generals Fox and Moore wanted Britain to force reforms on the Court which they believed would be good for Sicily and would make her a more effective ally. Drummond, the British envoy, initially agreed but soon came to believe that the Sicilian opposition was incapable of governing the country, and that the best policy was cordial cooperation with the Court.[23] He and Moore quarrelled violently and their divisions would undermine any British policy. Canning was inclined to send out 'either a general or a minister of sufficient standing to control both the Court and his colleague and prevent bickering and insults. [Lord] Wellesley might be the man for the job — there is so much he could do in the Mediterranean and Sicily is the ideal base.' The offer was made, but Wellesley declined and the division between civil and military representatives continued, although less acrimoniously, until 1811.[24]

General Fox had been recalled in July, largely at Moore's instigation. Fraser's expedition was withdrawn from Egypt in September and returned to Sicily. This enabled the government to order Moore, with 8,000 men, to proceed to Gibraltar in case he was needed in Portugal, and from thence home and ultimately, as we have seen, to Sweden, late in the spring of 1808. But Moore's departure left British forces in Sicily under strength and without an adequate commander, while the French in Naples were threatening an invasion. Early in 1808 Castlereagh consulted Fox, Moore and Sir

John Stuart, all then in England, and as a result decided to send Stuart back to Sicily with some 6,000 reinforcements, bringing the total force in the island to 16,000 men. The choice of Stuart was to prove unfortunate, for while he faced great problems, he displayed little energy or enterprise in dealing with them.

Nonetheless, Britain maintained her position in the Mediterranean over the next few years. The Turks signed a formal peace in January 1809, while Collingwood continued to watch the French fleet, protect British trade, and harry the enemy in the Adriatic, until his health broke down entirely and he died at sea in March 1810. The Spanish uprising of 1808 diverted the government's attention from a theatre which, despite its underlying importance, was too remote to be convenient for offensive operations. It was not until 1811 that the cabinet was forced to reconsider some of the basic assumptions of its Mediterranean policy.

After Tilsit Napoleon was able to turn his attention to Portugal, Britain's last remaining ally on the mainland of Europe. He had extensive, though as yet ill-defined, plans for the future of the whole Iberian Peninsula, but for the moment he was happy to maintain the pretence of a warm alliance with Spain and gain her cooperation against Portugal. On 19 July he informed the Portuguese minister in Paris that Portugal must close her ports to Britain and seize all British goods in the country or risk his hostility. These demands were elaborated on 12 August when the French and Spanish ambassadors in Lisbon presented notes effectively threatening war if Portugal did not join them in an active alliance against Britain by the end of the month. A Portuguese offer to close their ports to British ships and sever diplomatic relations was rejected as inadequate, and on 30 September the two ambassadors left Lisbon, although without a declaration of war. Napoleon had begun assembling a small army at Bayonne before the end of July, and this force of some 25,000 men under General Junot crossed into Spain on 18 October to invade Portugal. Five days earlier Napoleon had proclaimed in the *Moniteur* that 'the house of Braganza has ceased to reign in Europe', and a fortnight later (27 October) he signed the Treaty of Fontainebleau with Spain, partitioning Portugal between them. It only remained to complete the conquest and, if possible, seize the Portuguese fleet, treasure and royal family, before the British could intervene. On 12 November Junot reached Salamanca and received orders to push forward with all haste.

But the British government was not taken unawares by the French threat to Portugal. The ministers learnt of Napoleon's demands in the last week of August and immediately ordered Cathcart to detach 10,000 men from his army at Copenhagen as soon as operations permitted. As they had already ordered Moore to bring 8,000 men to Gibraltar, they hoped to have sufficient forces available to intervene in Portugal, especially as their intelligence indicated that it would take the French at least three months to reach

Lisbon. At this stage their intention was to send a force to the Tagus 'to assist — i.e. in a certain sense to compel — the embarkation [of the Court] for the Brazils'.[25] Steps were also in hand to occupy Madeira, under a pledge to restore it when mainland Portugal regained its liberty. But then the British government received a full explanation from Lisbon of all the French demands and of their proffered concessions, together with an urgent appeal to Britain for understanding, and earnest assurances that if these concessions did not satisfy Napoleon, the Court would sail for Brazil rather than submit to the French. The frankness of this appeal from an old ally persuaded the cabinet, despite some hesitation, to stay their hand.[26] Preparations for intervention continued, but Britain refrained from precipitating the crisis. In fact, the Portuguese government was desperate to avoid conflict with either Britain or France, and vacillated between them, offering concessions to each in turn and sometimes to both simultaneously. At one moment it was promising Britain commercial concessions in Brazil and the peaceful occupation of Madeira; at the next it was strengthening the naval defences of Lisbon. In the end it was the remorseless advance of Junot's corps and Napoleon's implacability which decided the question, though not without a great deal of last-minute hesitation. It was only when the British fleet imposed a strict blockade of Lisbon, stopping grain ships carrying food for the city, and when news arrived of Junot's imminent approach, that Prince João (Regent for his mother, Maria I) at last consented to embark. It was none too soon, for the Portuguese fleet sailed on 29 November and on the following day leading elements of Junot's army entered Lisbon without a shot being fired.[27]

The emigration of the Portuguese royal family brought considerable benefits for Britain, by far the most important being the opening of the Brazilian market to British trade, which soon extended, through a flourishing contraband trade, to include much of Spanish America as well. This more than compensated for the loss of direct trade with Portugal, which even in 1806 had only been worth £1.7 million, or 4 per cent of total British exports.[28] The British trading community in Portugal had received ample warning of the impending crisis and had taken successful precautions to minimize its losses. Brazil was the jewel in the Portuguese colonial empire, but other colonies also attracted British attention. Strategically and commercially important, Madeira was occupied before the end of the year, and the British government also considered occupying Portuguese outposts on the coast of Africa, but decided they were not worth garrisoning. Even Macao was briefly occupied by a British force from India, but was soon given up in the face of strong Chinese opposition.[29]

The establishment of a friendly government in Rio de Janeiro naturally gave a new perspective to Britain's interest in South America. News of Whitelocke's capitulation had reached London on 11 September: Canning was not greatly dismayed, but Castlereagh seems to have been genuinely angry and disappointed.[30] Various possibilities presented themselves, of which the most obvious was to cut Britain's losses and concentrate on the war in Europe. Yet there were few obvious openings for action in Europe, and South America continued to exercise its lure. The dream of conquest on a grand scale was exploded, but the temptation for action on a smaller scale remained, and appealed to a surprisingly wide range of figures. Lord Liverpool, Hawkesbury's father, suggested that Britain should reconquer Montevideo and add it to the Portuguese Regent's Brazilian empire, while the Duke of York argued on the contrary that the emigration of the Portuguese court strengthened the case for Britain securing a South American port of her own.[31] Castlereagh seems to have agreed with this thinking, for on 21 December he proposed that a force of 8,000 men be sent to capture Montevideo, where it would protect British and Portuguese interests and create an entrepôt for British trade.[32] But the cabinet resisted the temptation and their restraint was rewarded, for the dispatch of another expedition to South America would have greatly impeded the government's response to the wonderful, and wholly unexpected, opportunity which was to arise in Europe in 1808.

2

From Bayonne to Cintra: The First Months of the Peninsular War

Britain lacked the military resources to create lasting strategic opportunities for herself on the Continent. Without allies she was powerless to take the war to Napoleon, and Tilsit appeared to establish his hegemony beyond challenge. Yet within a year Napoleon's blunder in Spain had rescued Britain from her isolation, and provided her with an alliance which was to last until the end of the war.

When Napoleon decided to intervene in the Peninsula, he had of course no way of guessing the results of his actions, and it is ironic that his decision arose as much from caution as from greed. Certainly he coveted Spain's treasure, fleet and colonies, but he also feared that she would betray him. This was no paranoid fear, for in October 1806 when Napoleon was at war with Prussia the Spanish government had made unmistakable preparations to change sides, and had only drawn back from the brink when it learnt of the Prussian defeat at Jena–Auerstädt.

Spain had been a French ally since 1796, but the war had taken a heavy toll, with her trade and colonies suffering from British attacks. The court favourite, Chief Minister and effective ruler of Spain, Manuel Godoy the 'Prince of the Peace', had recognized that Spain had nothing to gain from the war and tried to live up to his title. Thus he welcomed the Peace of Amiens and only re-entered the war in December 1804 when the British seizure of the Spanish treasure fleet left him no alternative. Godoy's dislike of the French alliance was increased when the renewed war led to the destruction of the pick of the Spanish fleet at Trafalgar (21 October 1805), hence his preparations to join the allies when he thought that Napoleon would have his hands full facing the combined resources of Prussia and Russia.

Following the Prussian débâcle, Godoy hastily sent renewed protestations of loyalty to Napoleon, who chose to accept them at face value as he was still busy confronting the Russian armies in Poland. But Napoleon was not deceived, nor did he forgive, he merely bided his time for a more convenient moment. The Spanish threat had caught him unawares, and while not directly dangerous it might have been extremely embarrassing to a ruler whose position was justified by his military prowess. There is little doubt that from this time Napoleon was determined to take control of Spain and Portugal and so secure their loyalty and — by modernizing their governments — their efficiency as allies.

Napoleon might have conquered the Peninsula in a few weeks with the *Grande Armée*, but even after Tilsit it was needed in Central Europe to support his hegemony. In any case he did not want a war, nor did he believe that one would be necessary to effect the transfer of power he desired in his servile ally. He therefore decided to achieve his ends through intrigue backed by a limited force consisting mainly of fresh conscripts.

Napoleon's first step in this slower, less direct, method of conquering an ally was to 'borrow' 15,000 Spanish troops under the Marquis de La Romana in March 1807 and use them to garrison towns in North Germany and Denmark. This had the double advantage of freeing some of his own troops and disrupting the Spanish army. He then arranged the conquest of Portugal, in which Spain took part as an ally, sending another 20,000 Spanish troops out of the way. Under the pretext of reinforcing Junot he introduced large French forces into northern Spain, from one end of the Pyrenees to the other. In February and March 1808 these troops seized control of the most important fortresses of northern Spain by a mixture of trickery and force, while another body of French troops advanced south towards Madrid.

These moves naturally alarmed the Spanish Court, where nerves had already been worn thin by a series of squalid domestic intrigues. In desperation Godoy planned to resist the French,[1] while at the same time retiring with the Royal Family towards Seville from where they could flee to Cadiz and even South America if the French triumphed. But Godoy was generally hated and distrusted by the populace and there were serious riots at Aranjuez, twenty-five miles south of Madrid, which halted the Royal progress and finally led the pathetic Carlos IV first to dismiss Godoy, and then to abdicate (17–19 March 1808). His popular son and heir took the throne as Ferdinand VII amid wild public rejoicing.

Ferdinand promptly returned to Madrid where Murat, 'The Emperor's Lieutenant in Spain', had arrived the previous day at the head of 20,000 troops. Ferdinand knew that he could not hope to rule Spain without Napoleon's acquiescence, so he was dismayed to find that neither Murat nor the French ambassador would acknowledge his claim to the throne. Yet the French did not reject him outright, and by half-promises and outright lies they lured him to Bayonne to meet the Emperor. There, on French soil, he was confronted with his outraged parents and ordered to abdicate. When he was faced with the alternative of martyrdom, his resistance soon collapsed, and on 6 May 1808 he resigned his claim to the throne.

Napoleon appeared to have succeeded completely and he chose as the new ruler of Spain his elder brother Joseph, who had had some success in introducing reforms to Naples. But already the trouble was brewing that was to deny Joseph the chance of proving his capacity as a moderate enlightened ruler. The influx of French troops, the political turmoil and the disappearance of the old royal family had led to discontent and restlessness throughout Spain. Minor incidents were contained until 2 May 1808, when there was a large bloody riot in Madrid (the Dos de Mayo), which Murat savagely repressed. A false calm followed which lasted for three weeks while the people in the provinces absorbed the news and some secret preparations for a rising were made. Then, in the last week of May and the first days of June, province by province the whole country rose against the French and the long bloody war began.

The Spanish risings were popular, conservative and local. Once the established authorities agreed to take the lead against the French the uprisings lost most of their revolutionary overtones. Given the French occupation of Madrid and central Spain, it is not surprising that political power fragmented and that the newly established provincial juntas behaved as almost independent governments. As such they were well placed to exploit the first wave of popular enthusiasm, but their lack of unity and their rivalry impeded the development of a sensible strategic plan. Most of the old, regular Spanish army was in the provinces of Andalusia and Galicia, whose Juntas were inclined to use it as much for regional as for national purposes.

Nonetheless, the French were in an uncomfortable position, although they did not immediately appreciate their danger and continued to overextend their forces. The French army in Spain was not large and included a high proportion of inexperienced conscripts. The lines of communication which ran from the Pyrenees to Madrid lacked protection and appeared vulnerable to a Spanish attack from Galicia. The Spaniards under Cuesta and Blake tried such an attack but were defeated by Bessières at Medina del Rio Seco on 14 July 1808. This victory should have secured the French position, but its impact was lost when a complete French army of 20,000 men under General Dupont surrendered at Bailen in southern Spain a week later. Bailen was a great defeat for the French and its impact was enormously increased when Joseph needlessly panicked on hearing the news and fled with his French troops all the way back to the Ebro. This foolish action, as much as Bailen itself, gave the Spanish uprising credibility and damaged Napoleon's prestige throughout Europe.

In the months before the uprising the British government had watched the increasing French presence in Spain with concern. The cabinet had various sources of intelligence. Lieutenant-General Sir Hew Dalrymple, the commander of the garrison at Gibraltar, was in communication with the Spanish General Castaños and sent home detailed reports of events in Spain, which were supplemented by the dispatches from British admirals off the coast. There were also three junior British diplomats in Spain, John

Hunter, Charles Vaughan and Andrew Archdekin, on a mission concerning British prisoners of war. Hunter and Vaughan were eventually imprisoned by the French, only to be released by the Spanish uprising. While sometimes helpful, their reports of events in Spain took so long to reach London that they were seriously out of date. The British government also tried to introduce at least two real spies into Spain, but these attempts seem to have failed, or at least produced little important information.[2]

Britain could not hope to check the spread of French power in Spain, so British policy in the first half of 1808 concentrated on attempts to reduce its impact. A small force of some 5,000 men under Major-General Brent Spencer was available for active operations, and in the middle of January Castlereagh ordered it to the Peninsula. Spencer was first to investigate the possibility of attacking a squadron of Russian warships which had taken refuge in Lisbon harbour. If, as Castlereagh suspected, this proved too difficult for Spencer's force, he was to proceed to Gibraltar and consider a coup de main against the Spanish fortress of Ceuta, while an attack on the Spanish squadron in Port Mahon, Minorca, was subsequently added to his objectives. But first Spencer was delayed by bad weather until late February, and then he found that both Lisbon and Ceuta were too strong for him to attack. Port Mahon might have been more practical, but by the time these instructions reached him the Spanish uprising had transformed the scene.[3]

Spencer's failure and the progress of events in Spain seriously alarmed the British ministers. They recognized that the events at Aranjuez had seen the installation of a puppet government completely subservient to Napoleon; and they feared that this would enable the French to gain control of Spain's vast American empire and turn it first against Brazil and then against Britain. They therefore decided to attempt to forestall the French by reviving their South American strategy in a different form. The object now would be to break Spain's colonial power by assisting the independence forces in her colonies. Britain would make no territorial claims and while recommending a monarchical government would not seek to impose it. She would provide auxiliary forces to aid in the struggle — Castlereagh mentioned some 13,200 men — but it was clear that the plan would only succeed if it aroused widespread local support in the Spanish colonies. The King gave his approval to this plan on 22 April 1808, although it was not to be put into execution until August, when the weather would be most suitable and the expeditionary forces would be fully prepared.[4]

But long before August, events had moved in a quite different direction, and the initial British response to the uprising depended on the initiative of the officers closest to Spain, notably Dalrymple at Gibraltar. Early in May Dalrymple had learnt that there was unrest in Cadiz following the arrival of news of the Dos de Mayo, and he had sent Spencer to join Admiral Purvis off the great Spanish port to take advantage of any opportunity which might arise. Spencer had some contact with the local authorities and issued a proclamation to the inhabitants, but his presence did little to encourage the Spanish patriots, who always distrusted British intentions towards Cadiz. Nonetheless, when Seville and Andalusia rose against the French in the last week of May they appealed to Gibraltar for British aid. Dalrymple responded with encouragement and what limited material aid he could afford, and passed on their requests to London. He also sent an able officer (Major Cox) to represent him at Seville, and another (Captain Whittingham) to the headquarters of General Castaños, who assumed command over all the Spanish forces in Andalusia on 30 May.[5]

The Spaniards suggested that Spencer's force should join Castaños's army, but the British generals judged that it was too weak to operate in the interior and would only offer to garrison Cadiz or another Spanish fortress, thus freeing its garrison to join the main army.[6] Not surprisingly this was rejected and some tension arose over Spencer's continued presence off Cadiz. Eventually a compromise was devised with the Spaniards accepting British naval help in capturing Rosilly's squadron. This was achieved on 14 June, and Spencer then felt able to accept suggestions that he might best further the common cause elsewhere. He sailed to Ayamonte on the Portuguese border where his presence led a small French column to withdraw back to Portugal. Then he joined Admiral Cotton off the Tagus but again decided that Junot's force was too strong for him to attack, estimating it this time at 20,500 men. He therefore returned to Cadiz, which he proposed to save if the French under General Dupont should defeat Castaños. Whatever the Spaniards thought of this prospect, they let Spencer disembark his men on the other side of the bay from Cadiz. Here the British troops remained for nearly three weeks until Dupont was defeated, and Spencer finally left to join Sir Arthur Wellesley's force in Portugal.[7]

While it is easy to laugh at Spencer's peregrinations, it is difficult to see how else he might prudently have used his force. To march into the interior of Spain with 5,000 men, no base, no transport, no lines of communication and no instructions, to join an allied army of which he knew almost nothing, would have been to invite disaster and risk court-martial even if he had been successful. In fact he was in the frustrating position of being in the right place at the right time but without any role to play. By contrast, Dalrymple played his part to perfection, showing considerable diplomatic ability and an understanding of the wider strategic position.

The government did not learn of these developments until it was too late to influence or control them. Through some unfortunate hitch in communications all Dalrymple's dispatches from late March to early May arrived together between 21 and 25 May. The cabinet's initial reaction was contained in a dispatch from Castlereagh to Dalrymple of 25 May 1808. This suspended Spencer's attack on Port Mahon, and approved Dalrymple's correspondence with Castaños. The government looked forward to open opposition to the French in southern Spain, and promised to send reinforcements to build Spencer's force up to the 10,000 men which they mistakenly thought Castaños had required. Until the reinforcements arrived Spencer was to keep his force united and not to commit it to the interior. Finally they hoped that Dalrymple would vigorously encourage the Spanish resistance while discreetly avoiding any pledge of his government's faith.[8]

On the same day Castlereagh wrote a private letter to Dalrymple in which he concentrated on the action that should be taken if the Spanish cause failed. South America and Cadiz were the most important objects for Britain. Castlereagh hoped that Cadiz would become the refuge and rallying-point for the Spanish patriots, and that Dalrymple would facilitate their passage to South America where they would secure the colonies against French influence.[9]

These two letters show that while the government leapt at the apparent opportunity in southern Spain — even promising to commit 10,000 men to a cause of which it knew little — it suspended rather than abandoned its previous plans. This was clearly the sensible approach: resistance to the French in Spain could do Britain no harm even if, as must have seemed probable, it quickly collapsed. Napoleon's reputation would suffer if he was forced to conquer an apparently loyal ally and it would increase Britain's chances of success in South America.

During the following fortnight the new policy was consolidated: on 2 June George III approved the arrangements that had been made for a force of 8,000 men assembling at Cork and intended for 'service on the coast of Spain or eventually in South America, should no favorable opening present itself in Europe for their exertions'. On 4 June Castlereagh was given authority over all military and naval units off the south-west coast of Spain in order to coordinate the government's policy.[10]

Then on 8 June 1808 British strategy was given another twist by the arrival in London of news of an uprising, not in Andalusia, but in Asturias — a small mountainous province in northern Spain. The messengers were a fully accredited deputation from the ancient provincial assembly which had happened to be in session when the rising took place. They had left Oviedo on 26 May, embarked at Gijon on the 30th, landed at Falmouth and arrived in London early on 8 June. They brought with them an appeal for assistance from the Asturian Junta and unconfirmed news of risings in the other provinces of northern Spain.[11]

The Asturian deputies received a rapturous welcome in London. Celebratory dinners were held in their honour, they were lionized by fashionable society, and when they went to the theatre the performance had to be suspended for an hour, such was the commotion. The Spanish rising was the first really good war news (except Copenhagen) for nearly a year and its appeal transcended normal social and political barriers. The popular poet Thomas Campbell thought he should die of joy if the Spanish cause succeeded and of misery if it failed, while almost all the royal dukes eagerly volunteered to lead British forces to the aid of Spain.[12]

The press encouraged the popular enthusiasm, with *The Times* immediately calling on the government to act 'with the utmost promptitude' and hoping that 'there will be no bartering about terms, no stipulation for retributive concessions or advantages to England . . . [and] no attempt to interfere in the internal administration of the country'. The Whig *Morning Chronicle* agreed, and claimed that 'At this moment, the English people would cordially acquiesce in any effort, however expensive, that could assist the cause of that brave and noble nation'. Even Cobbett, by now a radical and a trenchant critic of the war, believed that 'This is the *only* fair opportunity that has offered for checking the progress of Napoleon. It is the only cause to which the people of England have heartily wished success', and demanded action without hesitation or delay.[13]

London was caught in a Spanish fever which lasted until the end of the year. Each fresh piece of news — whether good or bad — was eagerly awaited and much discussed. The war in Spain was by far the most common topic of the satirical prints which were produced in the second half of the year. No less than eleven new prints on affairs in Spain were produced in July alone. These ranged from a relatively crude caricature of the events at Bayonne to a fine print by Gillray depicting the Spanish bull tossing Napoleon, much to the delight of the crowned heads of Europe who looked on (plates 1 and 2).[14]

The extraordinary response to the arrival of the Asturian deputies is not hard to explain. The idea of a popular rising against the French in Spain was new and exciting; it appealed to Whig ideology and Pittite pragmatism. Unlike the other powers of Europe, Spain had played only a small part in the Revolutionary and Napoleonic Wars, so there was little knowledge of her limitations as an ally and plenty of scope for wild hopes of her potential. That Asturias was only a small province in a second-rate power was conveniently forgotten, while the very lack of information enabled every group in Britain to believe that the Spanish patriots reflected their own particular ideological views.

On 15 June, a week after the deputies arrived in London, Sheridan raised the Spanish cause in Parliament. According to Wilberforce:

> Sheridan would, against the advice of all the opposition friends, electrify the country on the Spanish business. He came down to the House, but the opportunity being delayed, he going upstairs got so drunk, as to make him manifestly and disgracefully besotted. Yet he seemed to remember a fair speech, for the topics were good; only he was like a man catching through a thick medium at objects before him. Alas, a most humiliating spectacle; yet the papers state him to have made a brilliant speech etc.[15]

A letter from Whitbread to Grey confirms that Sheridan was 'so exceedingly drunk that he could hardly articulate', a fact which raises doubts of the validity of the speech printed in *Parliamentary Debates* — although it could have been provided by Sheridan subsequently. The opposition of Sheridan's friends sprang from the belief that he intended 'to create a Cry for himself as distinguished from all of us', not from any dislike of the Spanish cause.[16]

In fact most leading Whigs strongly supported the Spanish patriots at this time. Fox's nephew, Lord Holland, and Francis Horner both remained ardent advocates long after Spain became unpopular, but in June 1808 Lord Grey and even Whitbread were privately in favour of granting British aid to the Spaniards. The former declared that 'To assist the Spaniards is morally and politically one of the highest duties a nation ever had to perform', while the latter wrote that 'we ought and must give them every possible assistance'. Only a few croakers and mavericks like Lord Auckland and the Duke of Norfolk opposed aid to Spain and predicted disaster; and their views went unheeded.[17]

Although he had just come from a dinner for the Asturian deputies, Canning was evidently not drunk when he replied to Sheridan's incoherent speech. He declared that there was 'the strongest disposition on behalf of the British government to afford every practicable aid' to the Spaniards. 'We shall proceed upon the principle, that any nation of Europe that starts up with a determination to oppose . . . the common enemy of all nations . . . becomes instantly our essential ally.'[18] Canning's speech caught and expressed the ardent hopes and naive enthusiasm which the Spanish cause had provoked in Britain. It was a transient mood with disillusion following inevitably, but before it disappeared the strength and unanimity of public feeling led Britain to become deeply involved in the affairs of Spain and Portugal.

Behind the scenes there was rather more caution than Canning's speech implied. One minister, Lord Westmorland, is said to have opposed any aid to Spain, declaring that 'The Spaniards had got themselves into a d–d scrape, and if we did not look sharp they would drag us in too'.[19] Westmorland's views counted for little, but he was not the only member of cabinet to have reservations. Lord Eldon welcomed the Spanish rising, but mainly because it would facilitate the government's plans for ensuring that the Spanish fleet and colonies did not fall into the hands of the French. George III also urged caution and wished to delay a formal reply to the Asturian plea for assistance until fresh reports from southern Spain had arrived. But the cabinet as a whole disagreed, believing that 'the danger of delay in a moment so critical was of all things most material to be avoided', and on 11 June it presented the King with a reply to the Asturian deputies.[20] This declaration, signed by Canning, assured the Spaniards that

his Majesty is disposed to grant every kind of assistance to efforts so magnanimous and praiseworthy . . . [and] that no time shall be lost in embarking for the port of Gijon the succours that you require, as being the

1. Billingsgate at Bayonne or the Imperial Dinner!
[Rowlandson], 10 July 1808, B.M. Cat. no. 10,996

This engraving satirizes the quarrels of the Spanish Royal Family at Bayonne, with Queen Maria Luisa ('a dishevelled coarse-featured termagant', in Dorothy George's words) denouncing Prince Ferdinand and denying that he is the son of the King. The Prince replies in kind, while the King (playing a violin) and the younger members of the Royal Family want only to be left in peace. Godoy unavailingly seeks to silence the Queen from the far end of the table. Napoleon looks on and threatens to send them all to the Round House.

The squalid domestic intrigues in the Spanish Court reached their climax at Bayonne, and Rowlandson's view, though crude, is not greatly exaggerated.

most pressingly necessary; he will . . . [also] send a naval force capable of protecting the coast of Asturias against any attempt which the French may make.[21]

The declaration concluded with a promise that Britain would support any other province of Spain which rose against the French. The King 'entirely' approved the Note 'as it appears to him sufficiently cautious and entirely appropriate to [the] circumstances', and it was immediately published.[22]

The government moved swiftly to implement these promises. Orders were issued for shipments of arms, equipment and money to be prepared, and the first of these sailed before the end of the month. The Asturian and later all the Spanish prisoners of war were freed, and efforts were made to equip them to take the field. Naval squadrons were ordered to protect the

2. The Spanish Bull Fight or the Corsican Matador in Danger
Gillray, 11 July 1808, B.M. Cat. no. 10,997

The Spanish bull, having broken loose from its chain, tosses Napoleon into the air while trampling Joseph under foot. The assembled sovereigns of Europe watch on with delight.

An adapted version of this plate circulated in Spain, and Dorothy George speculates that the design may have been suggested by Canning.

Spanish coast and the first steps were taken to make contact with the Marquis de La Romana. Detailed information was still scarce and on 19 June a military mission of three officers, Lieutenant-Colonel Dyer, Major Roche and Captain Patrick, was sent to the Asturias. Their orders were to supervise the landing and distribution of the supplies they brought with them, to gather intelligence on the strength and quality of the Asturian troops, and to collect whatever information they could on the French forces and events in neighbouring provinces.[23]

The main emphasis in the Spanish requests for assistance was on arms, equipment and money, while their attitude to direct British military cooperation was, to say the least, ambiguous. Castaños had asked for British troops and the Junta of Andalusia repeated this request, although it never pressed the point. The Asturian Junta presented a request for 10,000 men to Mr Hunter, the acting British consul in Oviedo, on 18 June, but their representatives in London appear to have rejected a proposal to send British forces to their province. Finally the Galician representatives firmly opposed any idea of sending a British army to northern Spain when they reached London, and their Junta confirmed this when Sir Arthur Wellesley consulted them at Coruña on 20–21 July.[24]

There were several reasons for this reluctance to receive British troops. The bulk of the old Spanish regular army had been stationed in Galicia and Andalusia, so these provinces were not short of trained men. Revolutionary fervour had produced overconfidence which was heightened by the (often minor) Spanish victories. Then there was Spanish pride — a natural emotion in a nationalistic movement. There was also considerable suspicion of Britain's motives, while it must be remembered that the British army at this time lacked the reputation it gained in the Peninsular War, so that informed Spaniards almost certainly underestimated its worth.

Despite this lack of encouragement the British government was determined to send an army to the Peninsula. Ever since it had taken office the Portland Ministry had been searching for an opportunity for large-scale intervention on the Continent, but even if the cabinet had been reluctant, public enthusiasm for Spain was so great that it would have been difficult for them not to act. Thanks to Castlereagh's reforms of the army there was even a disposable force with transports available for action. Spencer's small corps was already off the coast of Spain, while a rather larger force was being prepared at Cork, and other units could be mobilized, although not so quickly. On 14 June Sir Arthur Wellesley was given command of the troops at Cork, and preparations to make them ready to sail were hastened.

Meanwhile the government hesitated over where to send Wellesley's expedition. The ministers' first impulse was to send it to northern Spain where the spirit of resistance appeared most vigorous, but the Asturian deputies checked this plan. Southern Spain and Cadiz provided the most obvious alternative, but the reports arriving in London towards the end of June were over a month old and had been written before the rising had broken out in Andalusia. There remained a third possibility: an attack on the French army in Portugal. Although the ministers remained uncertain, Castlereagh ordered Lieutenant-Colonel Browne to Oporto to gather intelligence on the state of the Portuguese insurrection and the strength of the French. Nonetheless, the cabinet did not finally commit itself to Portugal until 30 June, and as late as the 26th Castlereagh was still hoping that 'some more light may break upon us'. The arrival of the Galician deputies that same day decided the question, for they not only reassured the cabinet about the state of affairs in northern Spain and made it clear that they did not want any British troops, they specifically asked that the British army be sent to Portugal. Wellesley's instructions were settled and dispatched on 30 June.[25]

There were sound arguments for sending an army to Portugal: if Junot's army were eliminated it would remove a threat to the flank and rear of the Galicians and free some thousands of Spanish troops imprisoned by Junot. If the French were driven out of Portugal communications between the

Spanish patriots in northern and southern Spain would be secured. The capture of Lisbon would also be valuable from a purely British point of view. It would remove Siniavin's squadron of nine Russian warships from contention, and put an end to fears that they would combine with Junot's troops for a descent on Ireland. The Royal Navy would welcome access to Lisbon's fine harbour, and relief from having to blockade it, while the liberation of Portugal would no doubt please Prince João in far-off Brazil.

When the British ministers discussed Wellesley's instructions they lacked any fresh reliable intelligence from Portugal. At the end of February Spencer had claimed that Junot had 40,000 troops, but the risings in Spain and Portugal and the defection of the Spanish troops in Junot's army had clearly created a new and unpredictable situation. And although Lieutenant-Colonel Browne had been sent to Oporto to gather news, it would be some time before his first reports could be expected. The ministers therefore ordered Wellesley to proceed ahead of his expedition to Coruña to gather intelligence and assess the situation. If he felt that Junot was too strong for his force, combined with Spencer's, he was to wait at Vigo until he could be reinforced from home.[26]

But on the evening of 30 June — the day these instructions were sent — a dispatch was received from Admiral Cotton, who commanded the British squadron blockading Lisbon. Cotton declared that there were no more 'than 4,000 French Troops in Lisbon, from whom the Spaniards are now completely separated; and against whom the populace are highly incensed; so that ... five or six thousand British troops might effect a landing'. This was welcome news and even the King acknowledged it to be 'very satisfactory'. Wellesley's instructions were promptly altered so that he was ordered to send a confidential officer to Coruña rather than proceeding there himself, while he was to accompany the fleet to the Tagus 'with the least possible delay'.[27]

Sir Arthur Wellesley received his instructions at Dublin on 3 July and sailed with his expedition from Cork on 12 July after having been delayed for several days by adverse winds. He was thirty-nine years old and had already proved his ability as an independent commander in a series of fine campaigns in India. Although not a politician, Wellesley had excellent connections on both sides of politics and held an important post (Chief Secretary of Ireland) in the Portland government. Sir Arthur's eldest brother, the Marquess Wellesley, was a major political figure. A Pittite but an old, close friend of Lord Grenville, he had made his reputation as Governor-General of India. It was through his influence that Sir Arthur had been made an aide-de-camp to the Marquess of Buckingham (Grenville's eldest brother) in 1788, and later given the opportunity to prove himself in India. Nonetheless, by 1808 Sir Arthur Wellesley was beginning to emerge as a figure in his own right. He proved a competent and efficient Chief Secretary of Ireland; he advised Castlereagh on military matters, and he served with some credit, although in a subordinate capacity, in Cathcart's Baltic expedition. He had already impressed a number of cabinet ministers with his ability, and it was for this reason that he was given the command of the expedition to Portugal.

Wellesley's instructions granted him liberal discretionary powers, as he later told the Cintra Enquiry:

> The general object of the expedition was to aid the Spanish and Portuguese nations; the principal object was to attack the French in the Tagus. But I considered myself authorized by my instructions to pursue any other object, if I thought it more likely to conduce to the benefit of the Spanish and Portuguese nations.[28]

This broad discretion was unavoidable given the government's lack of information, and it is clear that it did not cause Wellesley any uneasiness. Indeed, he immediately exceeded it, by ignoring Castlereagh's second instructions and proceeding ahead of his force to Coruña.

Wellesley's force was only the advance guard of a substantial British army which the ministers hoped to employ in the Peninsula. In addition to his 11,000 men,[29] and Spencer's 5,000, there was Moore's force of approximately 10,000 men which was expected to return soon from Sweden, while another 10,000 men were being made ready in Britain. The total force might thus comprise some 35,000 men and be the largest British army to take the field for many years.

Neither the objective nor the command of this army had yet been finally decided. Edward Cooke, the Under-Secretary for War, and Colonel J. W. Gordon, the Commander-in-Chief's military secretary, both wrote memoranda urging the importance of concentrating Britain's efforts in northern Spain. This would certainly have had many advantages, but the government had first to secure Spanish cooperation and await the outcome of the campaign in Portugal.[30]

Meanwhile the question of the command of the combined army aroused considerable feeling and even some public controversy. Wellesley had only been promoted to lieutenant-general on 25 April 1808, and consequently lacked the seniority for so important a command. There is no doubt that the Duke of York would have liked to take the field again, despite the failure of his earlier campaigns. But there was widespread opposition among the public and in the press to the Duke's being given the command and a caricature even appeared entitled 'He *Cannot* Go to Spain, or Canning's Death Blow' in which an unrecognizable but heroic Canning declares, '70,000 Souls 6 Millions sterling — he shall not go — I will resign first . . . no — no — Death to *his* Hopes or *my* Countrymen' (plate 3).[31]

But in fact the ministers had already decided to give the command to Lord Chatham, the Master-General of the Ordnance and a member of cabinet. Chatham was a senior lieutenant-general, and had seen some active service, although none since 1799, but while plainly he did not owe his

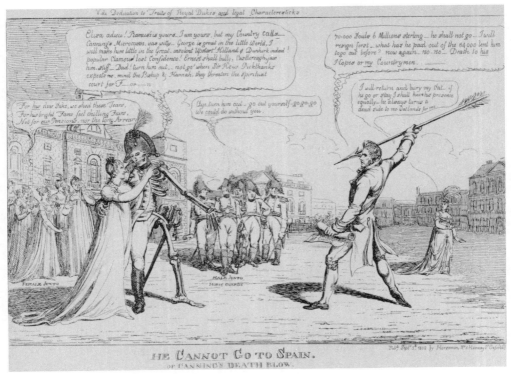

3. He *Cannot* go to Spain or Canning's Death Blow
[Williams], 5 Sept. 1808, B.M. Cat. no. 11,023

The Duke of York, half man, half skeleton, stands in front of the Horse Guards, bidding adieu to a woman, perhaps his sister Elizabeth, or possibly a mistress. (See Dorothy George's Catalogue entry for the reason for thinking it might be the Princess.) Behind her a 'Female Junto' weeps 'For *his* dear Sake . . . Not for *our* Pensions, nor the long Arrears'. On the far right the Duchess of York complains of his neglect.

Evidently the Duke's private life was already attracting adverse publicity. A few months later, in early 1809, allegations that he had been involved in the illicit sale of army commissions and promotions by his former mistress Mary Anne Clarke were to lead to a great scandal and eventually his resignation.

In the foreground of the print, dramatically posed with quill-like javelin in hand, stands a figure purporting to be Canning, though there is little or no resemblance. Canning is shown as determined to thwart the Duke's ambition to lead the British army to Spain, referring to the failure of his previous campaigns in 1793–4 and 1799.

While the Duke certainly hoped for the command there is no evidence, other than this print, that Canning led the opposition to his ambitions, or that Castlereagh supported York (as is implied in the Duke's speech). In fact it seems most unlikely that any of the ministers ever seriously considered entrusting another British army to the Duke, although many aspects of this complicated question remain obscure.

appointment purely to military ability, the whole affair remains obscure. There is a contemporary rumour that he owed the appointment to the intervention of the King, but this seems unlikely given the Duke of York's aspirations to the command. Alternatively, some of his colleagues may have looked to Chatham as ultimately replacing Portland at the head of the government — an idea which Canning briefly favoured in April 1809 —

and hoped that military success would enhance his prestige. But this is mere speculation. His lethargy in command of the Walcheren expedition in 1809 suggests that it was fortunate that he did not reach the Peninsula in 1808.[32]

These plans were disrupted by the arrival of Spencer's letter of 24 June, in which he estimated Junot's force at over 20,000 men, of whom nearly 13,000 were near Lisbon. This made the ministers doubt if Wellesley could succeed, especially as Spencer also announced his intention to attack the French force at Ayamonte, and so might not be able to rejoin Wellesley. The government responded by ordering the brigades of Acland and Anstruther to depart for Portugal as soon as possible — they sailed on 19 July. Fortunately Moore's corps was also available, having just arrived from Sweden, and it too was ordered to Portugal as soon as it had been revictualled.[33]

This sudden disruption of the government's plans reopened the whole question of the command of the army. The ministers would have liked to have left Wellesley in charge, at least until Junot had been defeated. But as Wellesley was junior to both Moore and Moore's second-in-command, Lieutenant-General Hope, these generals would have had to be landed in England while their troops were sent on to Portugal — a very public mark of disfavour, if not outright disgrace. The Duke of York and the King intervened to prevent this, indicating that the command required a senior officer.[34] Chatham seems to have been unwilling or unready to sail at such short notice, while Moore lacked the seniority required by the King and the Duke (he was 88th of 130 lieutenant-generals), and in any case he was disliked and distrusted by the ministers, who believed that he had mishandled affairs in Sweden. Faced with this dilemma the cabinet selected Sir Hew Dalrymple, the thirteenth most senior lieutenant-general and probably the best-informed senior officer on the affairs of Spain in the British army. The appointment was widely welcomed, although Dalrymple had seen little active service and had never commanded an army — but then, successful experience in the field was rare among the higher ranks of the British army.

Dalrymple was appointed only 'for the present' and the cabinet imagined that he would play more of a supervisory than an executive role. In explaining the decision to the King, Castlereagh wrote that 'it is probable that the force may act in two separate corps', one operating against Lisbon, the other protecting Cadiz. Castlereagh also hoped that Dalrymple's appointment, with Sir Harry Burrard as his deputy, would allow 'the most active and distinguished young officers being brought forward under them'.[35] In other words Dalrymple was only given the command temporarily, until the preliminary operations had been completed and Chatham was ready to assume his responsibilities; and while Dalrymple held the command, he was to give Wellesley every possible opportunity to enhance his reputation. Castlereagh made this last point clear in an extremely ill-judged letter to

Dalrymple in which he recommended Wellesley to Dalrymple's 'particular confidence' because of his close connections with the ministers, which made it 'desirable for you, on all accounts, to make the most prominent use [of Wellesley] which the rules of the service will permit'.[36] While obviously well intended, this letter was bound to do more harm than good and was typical of the shabby treatment Dalrymple received from the government.

Dalrymple was appointed because the Duke of York and the King insisted that the claims of seniority could not be ignored. Sir Harry Burrard may have been made Dalrymple's deputy for the same reason, or because the ministers did not want Moore to command the expedition if he arrived in Portugal before Dalrymple. Burrard had considerable experience in subordinate roles, was widely liked and had the support of the Duke of York; but he lacked ability. Cautious, conservative and amiable, he was an excellent deputy provided that he was never left in command himself.[37]

Sir John Moore visited London briefly and was incensed by the garbled version of these events he heard from his friends. Castlereagh badly mishandled several interviews with him, and there was an acrimonious exchange of letters which Moore believed was part of a deliberate attempt to provoke him into resigning.[38] This may be true, but it is surely more probable that the ministers were simply out of patience with (as they saw it) a vain and troublesome general.

The decisions which the government made during these few days in the middle of July dramatically shaped the campaign in Portugal, and led to the absurd situation of the British army having three different commanders in the space of twenty-four hours. And yet in general the ministers had acted with prudence and good sense. Once they received Spencer's news they had no choice but to reinforce Wellesley. They did their best to keep the command in his hands, and when they were forced to give way, the choice of Dalrymple was, in the circumstances, quite reasonable. Only their treatment of Dalrymple is really reprehensible, though their attempts to further Wellesley's interests after he was superseded were certainly misguided. The ministers must bear some responsibility for the confusion which their decisions created in Portugal, but no one could have anticipated or avoided the situation which arose or its consequences.

Blissfully unaware of these developments, Wellesley chose to ignore the change to his original orders, and sailed ahead of the fleet to Coruña where he arrived on 20 July. He was given a warm and enthusiastic reception by the people and by the Junta of Galicia, whose feelings of affection for Great Britain were enhanced by the independent arrival on the same day of a British diplomatic representative — Charles Stuart* — who brought with him £200,000 in aid.

---

* Later Lord Stuart de Rothesay; not to be confused with Castlereagh's half-brother Charles Stewart.

2   Central Portugal: Sir Arthur Wellesley's campaign, 1808

At Coruña Wellesley was given much encouraging but generally inaccurate news from all over the Peninsula. There were unfounded accounts of
victories over the French in Andalusia and Catalonia, and although the
Galicians admitted that their own army had been defeated at Medina del
Rio Seco a week before, they were not alarmed, and grossly exaggerated the
French losses in the battle. The Junta told Wellesley that there was a
flourishing insurrection in Portugal and urged him to proceed to liberate
that country from Junot's army, which they estimated at about 15,000 men.
The only disappointment was the lack of any news of Spencer's force.[39]

From Coruña Wellesley sailed south, reaching Oporto on 24 July. Here
he was given substantially the same account of affairs as he had received at
Coruña, while the Bishop of Oporto (who led the Portuguese insurrection)
promised the support of 5,000 men and some logistical aid. Again there was

no news of Spencer, but Wellesley hoped that he might be with Admiral Cotton off the Tagus.[40]

Wellesley ordered his transports to Mondego Bay, which he regarded as the most likely place for a landing, and sailed on to confer with Admiral Cotton. The next few days were to contain a succession of disappointments for Sir Arthur, the first being the discovery that Spencer and his troops had sailed back to southern Spain in the hope that they could play some role in defending Cadiz against Dupont. Wellesley promptly ordered Spencer to return to Portugal unless engaged in active operations of great importance. Three days later Wellesley learnt of Dupont's surrender at Bailen and correctly deduced that Spencer would hasten to join him.[41]

From Cotton Wellesley received Spencer's detailed estimate of the French forces in Portugal which had been compiled from the accounts of three Hanoverian deserters. This gave Junot a total of over 20,000 men, nearly 13,000 of them in the vicinity of Lisbon. These were substantially higher figures than Wellesley had been given at Oporto and Coruña, although in fact they were still a considerable underestimate. While Wellesley chose not to believe this intelligence, he did not completely disregard it.[42]

Wellesley rejoined his fleet at Mondego Bay on 30 July and there received his third and most unpleasant surprise: Castlereagh's letters of 15 July announcing his reinforcement and supersession. There is no doubt that he was bitterly disappointed, although he promised Castlereagh that 'I shall not hurry the operations, or commence them one moment sooner than they ought to be commenced, in order that I may acquire the credit of the success'.[43]

In fact it is debatable whether he should have commenced operations at all or whether he should have waited for the arrival of the reinforcements that would make success a certainty. He justified his decision to begin landing troops on the grounds that any further delay would discourage the Portuguese patriots. This is barely plausible, for the reinforcements would make the state of the Portuguese insurrection almost irrelevant. Castlereagh had instructed Wellesley to continue operations as quickly as circumstances permitted, but the final judgement was up to Wellesley, and only success could justify his decision.[44]

The landing — through heavy surf — was begun on 1 August and completed on the 5th — the very day on which the leading elements of Spencer's force arrived in the Bay. It was not until 9 August that the united British army of some 14,000 men was ready to advance from its beach-head. Wellesley used this time to try to put his woefully inadequate commissariat on a proper footing, and to meet the Portuguese General Bernardino Freire at Montemor Velho on the 7th to arrange plans for the advance. Their cooperation proved short-lived, for within a week a sharp dispute led to the separation of the two forces, Freire leaving approximately 2,000 Portuguese troops with Wellesley.

Junot heard quickly of the British landing and recalled General Loison, who had been on an expedition against the Portuguese insurgents in Alemtejo. To cover Loison's retreat, and if possible to slow the British advance, Junot sent General Delaborde forward with a small force of some 4,350 men. There was a brief skirmish on 15 August, but the two armies made their first real contact on the 17th at Roliça. In the morning Delaborde skilfully delayed the British advance, forcing Wellesley to deploy his army and then retiring to a second stronger position just when Wellesley's attempts to outflank him were becoming serious. He might well have repeated these tactics in the afternoon if the British troops in the centre had not attacked prematurely — before the outflanking columns were in position and before Wellesley gave the word. The result was some bloody fighting before the French withdrew, in which they lost 600 casualties and prisoners, and the British lost almost 500.[45]

Roliça was a hotly contested but strategically unimportant combat. The result was never in doubt as Wellesley had nearly four times as many troops (including the Portuguese) as Delaborde. Wellesley wrote a detailed and generally accurate account of the action, exaggerating only the numbers of the French engaged, 'at least 6,000 men', and their losses, '1,500 men'.[46] The news of the victory was greeted with more excitement than understanding in England and it helped to create unrealistic expectations of future success.

On the day after Roliça Wellesley was informed that Acland's brigade from England had arrived off Peniche and that Anstruther was close behind him. On 19 August the British army moved to Vimiero where it covered the disembarkation of Anstruther's brigade that evening and Acland's the following day.

Wellesley intended to resume his advance on 21 August but his plans were thwarted by the arrival late on the 20th of Sir Harry Burrard, who had sailed ahead of his convoy on the frigate H.M.S. *Brazen*. Wellesley joined Sir Harry on board just as the latter was about to land, and described the strategic position and his plans. Burrard was an experienced officer but in 1798, and again in 1799, he had taken part in expeditions which had failed when bad weather had disrupted communications between the fleet and the army that depended upon it. He was also concerned at the complete French superiority in cavalry and he correctly judged that Wellesley was underestimating Junot's numbers. He therefore forbade any further advance until Sir John Moore's force should arrive.[47]

Meanwhile Junot had collected his army together and was marching to attack the British with some 13,000 men: he had left 6,000 to maintain his hold on Lisbon — a blunder which cost him any chance of victory, for Acland and Anstruther had raised the Anglo-Portuguese army to at least 20,000 men.[48] The French attacked on the morning of the 21st and although Burrard had joined the army, he left its command in Wellesley's hands. The French attacks were scattered and poorly coordinated, reflecting little credit

on Junot's generalship although the troops fought well. By noon the last
French reserves of infantry had been defeated and Wellesley was on the
point of ordering a general advance which would have converted the French
retreat into a rout, when the unfortunate Burrard intervened to prohibit
again any advance. Sir Harry did not appreciate that the defeat of the
French army had transformed the strategic position and he maintained that
his arguments of the previous evening against any advance retained their
validity.[49] This was sheer nonsense and it is impossible to defend his
decision. Some risk is inescapable in war and the opportunity to disrupt
Junot's army completely and so reap the full fruits of victory was not one
which should have been missed.

Vimiero ought to have decided the campaign, for even without any
pursuit the French had been soundly defeated, losing about 2,000 men to
the British loss of 720. Wellesley's account of the battle was similar to that
of Roliça in being generally reliable except on French casualties, which he
put at 'not . . . far short of 3,000 men'. This was increased in a later letter to
4,000.[50]

On the morning after Vimiero Sir Hew Dalrymple arrived and took
command of the army. He was in the uncomfortable position of replacing a
successful general in whom the army had confidence, when the moment for
exploiting the victory had passed. He did not approve of the way Wellesley
had conducted the campaign and he was pessimistic about its outcome.[51]

Within a few hours of Dalrymple's arrival the French General
Kellermann entered the British camp under a flag of truce. With the reality
of his defeated army in front of him Junot had considered his options and
decided that a negotiated evacuation of Portugal on generous terms was the
best of the possibilities facing him, while even if the negotiations failed they
would gain time for his army to rally. The proposals which Kellermann
conveyed to the British were wide-ranging and audacious in their claims.
The French army was to be returned to France in British ships without
surrendering its arms, equipment, baggage and so on. Once landed it would
be free to resume the war immediately. The Russian naval squadron would
be free to sail from Lisbon unmolested. In return the British would gain
undisputed possession of all those places in Portugal held by the French,
including the frontier fortresses of Almeida and Elvas.

Amazingly all three British generals believed that these terms were
acceptable, although Wellesley objected to their being included in the Suspension of Arms (rather than the final convention) and to the language in
which they were couched. Admittedly they knew that provisions concerning the Russian squadron would probably be disallowed by Admiral Cotton,
and Wellesley at least appreciated the disadvantages of involving the French
at all on this point, but they all accepted the central point that the French
army should be returned to France.[52]

Had these terms been proposed before Vimiero they might have provided an honourable and satisfactory, if somewhat tame, end to the

campaign. But the defeat of the French army at Vimiero and the arrival of Sir John Moore's corps off the Portuguese coast had completely changed the balance of forces in Britain's favour. There was now no danger of the British army being defeated and a reasonable chance that if pressed the French would be too dispirited to make much further resistance. Of course there was a risk that Junot might make a protracted and bloody defence of Lisbon or that he might escape with his army into Spain, but Wellesley's whole campaign had involved much greater risks than these. The acceptance of these terms reflected an unwarrantably pessimistic outlook which can only be explained as lack of confidence on the parts of Dalrymple and Burrard, and Wellesley's chagrin at losing his command and contempt for his successors.[53]

At Kellermann's suggestion the Suspension of Arms which incorporated these terms was signed, not by Dalrymple, but by Wellesley. This has led to a controversy over their relative responsibilities for the document. At the Cintra Enquiry Wellesley admitted that

> It is perfectly true that I advised the principle of the arrangement, and that I assisted the Commander-in-Chief in discussing the different points with Gen. Kellermann, and that I gave him my opinion when he asked it, and when I thought it desirable to give it him.[54]

But Dalrymple was present throughout the negotiations; he accepted some but not all of Wellesley's advice; and if the principles of military responsibility mean anything, they mean that he, not Wellesley, was responsible.

The terms granted in the Suspension of Arms were confirmed with some relatively minor improvements (from the British point of view) in the definitive Convention of Cintra which was signed on 30 August 1808. The document had many objectionable features over and above the central concessions permitting the evacuation and free passage of the French army and Russian sailors.[55] It showed little consideration for the feelings of the Portuguese and granted political concessions which were quite outside the scope of a normal military convention. This insensitivity was surprising, for Dalrymple generally handled the delicate political situation in Portugal with great skill. He was, however, less effective in managing his army, which became demoralized, disorganized and faction-ridden. Wellesley's presence was an embarrassment and Dalrymple was glad to give him leave to return home following the death of his temporary replacement as Chief Secretary for Ireland.

Dalrymple had certainly been placed in an unenviable position. He had arrived in the middle of the campaign knowing little of his army or the strategic situation and was immediately confronted with the need to make important decisions. But heavy demands are inevitably made on the holders of high office, and the position might have been far worse — if, for example, Wellesley's army had been defeated. Both armistice and convention contained concessions which no British general should ever have been willing to grant, and which had nothing to do with the details of the military position. Dalrymple had proved his ability at Gibraltar, but in Portugal he blundered and while we can sympathize with him, his subsequent disgrace was not unmerited.

Ever since Wellesley had sailed with his army from Cork the British government and public had been eagerly waiting for news from the Peninsula. On 24 July the ministers were concerned to learn of the Spanish defeat of Rio Seco, but their fears turned to jubilation when, in the space of a few days (8–11 August), news arrived of Dupont's capitulation at Bailen, Bessières's retreat from León, and Joseph's flight from Madrid. Castlereagh's optimism did not stop at capturing Lisbon or even at driving the French from Spain: 'how glorious to England it would be, after recovering Portugal, by her Command of the Sea, to meet the Enemy at the Foot of the Pyrenees, and to forbid his return to France'. On the same day Castlereagh's under-secretary wrote with a little more caution: 'Dupont's Surrender has raised us to the Skies — we think Junot will *now* try to make himself a golden Bridge, but don't let him carry away his Plunder.' So even before news of Wellesley's safe arrival had reached London, the success of his campaign was being widely taken for granted.[56]

After an anxious fortnight without news, Captain Campbell, Wellesley's aide-de-camp, arrived with news of Roliça and Vimiero and a report that on the day he left the army (22 August) 'General Kellermann had arrived with a flag of truce to treat for a capitulation of the French army in Portugal'.[57] The country went wild with excitement; even Cobbett and the London radicals lauded the ministers, who were not slow to make the most of the victory. The Tower guns were fired and Roliça treated as a victory of equal stature with Vimiero even by those — like Castlereagh — who should have known better.[58]

To the public, and even perhaps to the ministers, the complete surrender of Junot's army appeared only a matter of time. But only a few days after Captain Campbell reached London, the Chevalier de Souza, the Portuguese envoy to London, protested to the government at the terms he alleged had been granted to the French in an armistice. The ministers and the King were horrified and agreed that no British officer, let alone Sir Arthur Wellesley, would agree to such terms. As Souza's information was unofficial, they concluded that there had been some mistake, and that if not totally spurious, the terms represented French proposals at the beginning of the negotiation, not its final outcome. Nonetheless, they were naturally uneasy, and more impatient than ever for news from Portugal.[59]

Unfortunately Dalrymple had neglected to write home until 3 September, and his dispatch did not reach London until the 15th, more than ten days after Souza's protest, by which time Canning, Portland, Chatham and Hawkesbury had left the capital. Faced with the confirmation of their worst fears, the remaining ministers endeavoured to make the best of the news, by treating it as a victory, in the hope that the public would follow their lead. But firing the Park and Tower guns only raised expectations even higher, increasing the shock and disillusionment when the real nature of the news became clear. A caricature by Williams called '(*Extraordinary* News)' expresses the mood well. In the first scene John Bull, at supper with his wife, reacts to the sound of the guns with surprised delight: 'The Tower Guns at this time of Night! *Extraordinary* News arrived! by Jupiter we've sent Juno [*sic*] to the Devil, and taken the Russian Fleet! — Illuminate the House call up the children and tap the gooseberry wine Mrs Bull, we'll drink to our noble commanders in Portugal.' The second scene shows a small crowd of well-dressed elderly men outside an office listening in stunned amazement to one of their number who reads details of the Convention aloud from the *Extraordinary Gazette*. One member of the crowd protests that the French should not be allowed to take away their ammunition: 'What! carry away sixty Pounds [*sic*] a Man! why that ought to have been in the pocketts of our brave fellows! D—n me if I ever believe the Tower Guns again!!' (plate 4).[60]

This sequence of initial jubilation almost immediately followed by dismay was not limited to London. The artist Joseph Farington was in Cheshire and recorded in his diary for 16 September: 'This night news was brought from Newcastle under Lyme of Surrender of Junot and His army, in Portugal. The Bells rung till midnight.' But on the following day,

> in the evening the London Post brought newspapers which contained an account of the disgraceful convention with Junot, which allowed Him and His Army to be transported to France with their arms and much of their plunder in British Vessels. This turned the joy which had been excited by the report of the day before into lamentation.[61]

The King was reported to be 'exceedingly angry', while Wilberforce confided, 'I have been deeply hurt. The stroke fell just when our feelings made the discord of such a note the most inharmonious.' Lady Bessborough wrote that 'the terms seem madness', while even after the initial shock Moira was still bitter: 'we have bungled . . . the most glorious opening that fortune could have presented'. Lord Auckland could not 'recollect any instance in which the feeling of all parties were so strong and so warm as they are with respect to the French convention'. The disappointment was felt by all classes as well as by all parties and it has been suggested that only the distraction of a fire at Covent Garden prevented serious rioting.[62]

The newspapers fanned the flames of the nation's fury. According to Farington, 'every newspaper contained expressions of the warmest kind condemning the act as most disgraceful to Great Britain, and unjust to Her Allies. — *The Sun, The Globe, The Pilot, The Traveller, The Star,* — papers of all parties concurred in execrating the measure.' Even before learning the details of the Convention, *The Times* had made its own position clear: 'We can hardly refrain from shedding tears . . . the common cause has suffered

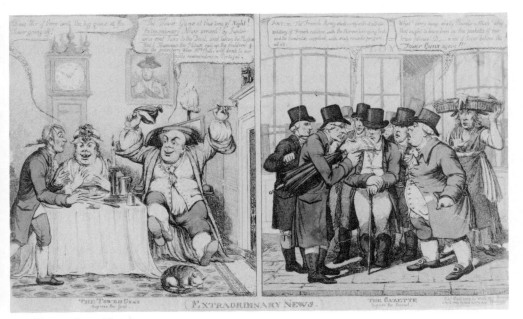

4. (*Extraordinary* News)
[Williams], Sept. 1808, B.M. Cat. no. 11,034

most grievously by this expedition to the Tagus; it has been cruelly detrimental to our affairs, and, above all, to our character.'[63]

But while the ministers in London shared the general dismay, they were already half prepared for the news by Souza's story. Accordingly Castlereagh advised the King, only two hours after the dispatches arrived, that although he and his colleagues felt 'deep disappointment . . . at the terms which have been conceded to the enemy, they . . . do not perceive that there is any sufficient ground upon which they could advise your Majesty to oppose any obstacles to the Conventions agreed to being carried into effect'.[64]

But one minister at least was unable to take the news calmly. Canning was outraged at the terms of the Convention, and wrote to Perceval:

a few hours reflection has shewn me all the disgrace and disaster of this transaction . . . I think that there is [not] the least chance or possibility of the transaction turning out to be such as we can approve. And if we do disapprove of it, I cannot foresee any circumstances which could reconcile me to our omitting to mark our disapprobation of it in the strongest manner. . . . This Convention must be distinctly *ours*, or *our Commanders*. We must judge *them*, or the Public will judge *us*. And I confess, unless there are circumstances to come out, of which I can form no conjecture, I shall not be prepared to consent to take an atom of responsibility for this work upon our own shoulders.

The mischiefs to result in it appear from every point of view, and in every quarter of the world.

Portugal . . . must hate us for the Article giving up their Plunder. Instead of hailing us as deliverers, they must consider us as having interfered only to sanction and secure French Robbery. By no other probable combination of circumstances could the French not only have kept what they had stolen, but have carried it out of the country unmolested. . . . It makes me sick with shame to think of it — and in what Country after this — in what part of Italy — of Spain, or the North, shall we be received with open arms as deliverers?[65]

Later that day, when he had seen the full text of the Convention in the *Extraordinary Gazette*, Canning wrote again to Perceval:

I confess it is even worse than my expectations. The Substance to be sure I could not expect to be different, but I did not think that I should find every *sore place* touched in the coarsest manner; and all the shameful parts of the transaction brought forward with such unsparing, such studious and laboured particularity.[66]

Over the next few days Canning's anger grew rather than abated, and he expressed it in a series of vivid, eloquent letters to friends and colleagues. Gradually his views crystallized, and he argued that the government should threaten to disown the Convention if it was not modified. He particularly disliked the 5th Article, which protected the 'property' of the French army, for he feared it would enable them to keep their plunder, and the 16th, 17th and 18th Articles, which touched on political questions.[67]

Other ministers also disliked the 5th Article, though Castlereagh told Canning, 'your suggestion however of *breaking the Convention*, rather than suffer any plunder to Escape . . . goes much further than any opinion stated in Cabinet'.[68] Nonetheless, they first modified, and then halted, their initial response to Dalrymple's dispatch in order to take account of Canning's views, and perhaps also to see if the popular fury would die away.

Wellesley's signature on the Suspension of Hostilities caused great dismay among the ministers and complicated their response. Canning felt that

It is indeed a grievous consideration that Wellesley's name is mixed in this transaction — He too I think must account for the armistice which he signed on the 22nd — and if he cannot do so satisfactorily he is available no longer for the high purposes for which he seemed destined.

If he can — why should not *local* rank make him equal to *any* command, without regard to the technicalities of army etiquette?[69]

Hawkesbury wrote that 'The treaty is moreover particularly painful as till explained it tarnishes the Reputation and glory of those whom we should most wish to uphold'. While Harrowby, who was near the cabinet though

5. The Convention of Cintra. A Portuguese Gambol for the Amusement of John Bull
Woodward, 3 Feb. 1809, B.M. Cat. no. 11,215

This is one of many satires modelled on the popular nursery rhyme 'The House that Jack Built'. The text reads as follows:

I   This is the City of Lisbon.

II   This is the Gold that lay in the City of Lisbon.

III   These are the French who took the Gold that lay in the City of Lisbon.

IV   This is Sir Arthur (whose Valour and skill, began so well and ended so ill) who beat the French who took the Gold that lay in the City of Lisbon.

V   This is the *Convention* that Nobody owns, that saved old Junot's Baggage and Bones, altho' Sir Arthur (whose Valour and skill) began so well and ended so ill, had beat the French who took the Gold that lay in the City of Lisbon.

VI   These are the Ships that carried the spoil that the French had plundered with so much toil, after the Convention which nobody owns, that saved old Junot's Baggage and Bones, altho' Sir Arthur (whose Valour and skill, began so well but ended so ill) had beaten the French who took the Gold, that lay in the City of Lisbon.

VII   This is John Bull in great dismay at the sight of the Ships which carried away, the gold and silver and all the spoil, the French had plundered with so much toil, after the convention which nobody owns which saved old Junot's Baggage and Bones altho' Sir Arthur (whose Valour and skill, began so well but ended so ill), had beaten the French who took the Gold, that lay in the City of Lisbon.

not then in it, told his wife, 'One great misery is, that Wellesley seems so deeply implicated . . . the very man to whom we most look'd up as a General.' Castlereagh argued that 'we ought well to weigh how we can best save, together with our own character and that of the country, *the instrument*, which of all others seems capable . . . of consoling us and the world for any faults which he himself or others have committed'.[70]

Essentially, then, Canning believed that Wellesley should account for his part in the Convention, while Castlereagh believed that even if Wellesley had been at fault, his talents were too valuable to be put in jeopardy. Yet in the end Canning was satisfied by Wellesley's private explanation of his support for the Convention, and the two Secretaries of State most concerned with the war both remained warm partisans of the young general. Indeed, Wellesley believed that he had the full support of all the cabinet except Lord Chatham, who, perhaps from pique, had disapproved of the conduct of the whole campaign.[71]

Dalrymple had no such support, and on 21 September he was recalled. The controversy did not die away, and the attempt by Wellesley's friends, in and out of office, to defend him had the effect of merely drawing attention to his role in the affair. When Lady Bessborough visited Dublin at the end of September she reported that

> The D. of Richmond shews about some letters of Sir A. Wellesley that make one's blood boil. The first is just after the battle, saying he hopes soon to have still better news to send, but that not a moment is to be lost; that he has tried already, and hopes still to persuade Sir H. Burrard to renew the attack. . . . The letter is written by bits, with ye utmost vexation, saying in one part 'that *Dowager Dalrymple* and *Betty Burrard* are Haggling with Kellermann on inadmissable terms, and losing a glorious opportunity of having the whole French army at our mercy.' . . . He next says he is call'd upon to sign the most disgraceful convention that ever was made, that he has resisted to everything short of Mutiny, and only submits to the command of his superior Genl.[72]

Yet she concluded by wondering, 'Why did he not throw up his commission? He might have been sure of being reinstated.' Her correspondent, Granville Leveson Gower, was even less impressed: 'This, in my opinion, does not exculpate Wellesley, who ought rather to have suffered his right hand to be cut off than put his signature to such disgraceful Terms.' And these were the reactions of people prejudiced in Wellesley's favour. The press campaign prompted a backlash from other papers, with *The Times* concluding: 'Sir Arthur is settled; and all that the injudicious zeal of his friends can now do, is heap obloquy upon those who have supplied the proofs of his guilt.'[73]

The government established a Board of Enquiry which began sittings on 17 November and published its report on 22 December. The Enquiry approved the armistice after Vimiero by six votes to one, and the terms of the Convention by four votes to three, while unanimously recommending no further proceedings. But the result of the enquiry had little importance. The military men who composed it had no interest in causing trouble. Only Lord Moira, a distinguished soldier and friend of the Prince of Wales, was prepared to argue the issues at any length, and his report still makes interesting reading.[74] But by the time the Enquiry had opened, the public's attention had moved from Portugal to the dramatic events unfolding in Spain. Most people had already made up their minds about Cintra and Sir Arthur Wellesley; a damning report could still have destroyed his career, but the Board's approval of the Convention had little influence.

And so the affair ended, as such affairs usually do, in the muffled whimper of an official enquiry. Sir Arthur Wellesley's reputation had been bruised and he had lost all the glory he had gained at Roliça and Vimiero. But the ministers' confidence in him was undiminished and he avoided involvement in Moore's campaign. The government also lost all the credit it would otherwise have gained from its prompt reaction to the Spanish uprising and from Wellesley's victories in Portugal. The Opposition tried to exploit Cintra in Parliament in 1809 but with little success; the issue, and the passions it generated, had grown cold and been supplanted by the collapse of the Spanish armies and Moore's retreat. Yet the dismay caused by Cintra had damaged the government's reputation; not all the blame was heaped on the generals, and any failure, whoever was to blame, lowered the standing of the ministry. More serious than this was the damage to the government's cohesion. Canning was deeply alienated. He considered resigning and later regretted that he had not done so.[75] This was the origin of his discontent which was to explode in April 1809, and which eventually brought down the government. Quite why he felt the blow so keenly is not at all clear, but he was a passionate, active, committed man who poured his energy into whatever he undertook. This was his strength and also his weakness. Some of his colleagues were more phlegmatic, others more controlled. None possessed his brilliance, his energy or his inspiration.

Finally Cintra destroyed the early unanimity of support for the war in the Peninsula. Popular enthusiasm declined sharply and the Opposition distanced itself from its early support. The initial euphoria had gone and could never be replaced. British participation in the war in Portugal and Spain had become and would remain a controversial political issue.

3

The Road to Coruña,
August 1808–January 1809

Napoleon was understandably furious when he learnt of Joseph's unnecessary retreat from Madrid to the line of the Ebro. The blow to his prestige and to that of French arms was even greater than that of Bailen, while Joseph lost whatever credibility he had as King of Spain. The only way to minimize this damage was to crush completely the Spanish rising and so reassert to the world the Emperor's primacy in the art of war. One may argue with hindsight that the Emperor ought to have abandoned the Peninsula south of the Ebro, but in August 1808 there was no reason for him to choose a course which was certainly humiliating and not without risks of its own. Nothing in the Spanish rising indicated that the war would be tenaciously fought long after the Spanish regular armies were defeated.

Napoleon was determined to conquer Spain and this time he intended to do the job properly, with no half-measures or undue haste. The French position on the Ebro was safe and he could afford to devote three months to the concentration of reinforcements and the shoring up of his position in central Europe. Already there were almost 100,000 French troops in Spain; between 5 and 17 August he ordered a further 130,000 men to the Peninsula.[1] Of these, three corps and four divisions of cavalry came from the Grande Armée in Germany; most of the rest were drawn from Napoleon's allies in Italy and the Confederation of the Rhine; and finally, last but not least, were the Imperial Guard. Unlike the conscripts who had surrendered with Dupont, these were veteran troops, well organized and well led.

But in strengthening his hand against Spain Napoleon inevitably weakened his hold over central Europe. With Russia his ally, and Prussia still prostrated by the débâcle of 1806 and the terms imposed on her at Tilsit, Napoleon's position should have been secure. But the Russian alliance had quickly cooled, German nationalism was beginning to waken, and Austria was becoming increasingly hostile. It was not a time in which Napoleon wished to be hundreds of miles from the cockpit of Europe immersed in a war in the heart of Spain.

Still, the war in Spain could neither be avoided nor deputed, and success there would do much to dampen the ferment in Germany and consolidate French hegemony. To hold the line until this could be achieved Napoleon played his Russian card by holding a spectacular summit with Alexander at Erfurt (27 September–14 October). The actual negotiations at Erfurt did not go particularly well for Napoleon: his position was much weaker than at Tilsit and he had to make more concessions than he gained. Nonetheless, he benefited from the conference enormously — the very public reaffirmation of the Franco-Russian alliance cooled the hotheads in Germany and Vienna, while his concessions to Russia slowed her drift into renewed antagonism.

It may thus have been with an easier mind that Napoleon left Erfurt on 14 October. He stopped only briefly in Paris before continuing his journey, entering Spain at Bayonne on 3 November, and taking command of his army on the 5th. Most of the reinforcements had now arrived, although Junot's corps — so conveniently returned by the British — had not yet fully recovered from its seasickness, and was lagging a little behind. Napoleon had already laid his plans and he wasted no time in launching an offensive which he was quite confident would destroy the Spanish armies and put an end to the miserable, unwanted, troublesome war.

The Spaniards reacted to Joseph's retreat from Madrid with a mixture of jubilation and relaxation. Their already excessively high confidence soared to new levels and they began to behave as if they had already won the war. The last French troops left Madrid on 1 August; the first Spanish troops did not enter the capital until the 13th, while Castaños with the leading elements of his victorious army did not arrive until 23 August. The French retreat had been so precipitate and the Spanish advance so lethargic that there was a clean break between the armies. It was several months before major operations were resumed.

In this lull the Spaniards set about creating a new government. There was some disagreement about the form this should take, and some reluctance on the part of a few provincial juntas to give up their power, but the need was so obvious that it overrode all objections. A Supreme Junta was formed comprising two deputies from each of the provincial juntas and one from the Canary Islands. There is no doubt that the Supreme Junta was neither very wise nor very efficient. British observers were frustrated by its concern for formalities and by its apparent failure to recognize the urgent military crisis facing Spain. Yet they did not fully understand all the Junta's problems. The concern for titles and ceremony was, in part, an attempt to bolster the Junta's authority, which rested on shaky legal foundations. The machinery of government through which the Junta had to rule had been completely disrupted by the French occupation and the popular uprising. Given these and other problems, it is not really surprising that the Junta achieved little.

The most serious British grievance against the Junta was its failure to appoint a commander-in-chief to coordinate the Spanish armies and to define the role which the British army could play in future operations. The arguments in favour of appointing a supreme commander were so obvious and so strong that the British could not comprehend why the new Spanish government failed to do so. In fact there were two powerful reasons: with some justification the government felt that it could not trust such power in the hands of any one general, and the government itself probably lacked the power to force the other generals to submit to the authority of a genera-lissimo.[2] The Spanish armies were firmly based on their provinces and if the commander of the Army of Galicia, for example, had objected to being subordinated to the commander of the Army of Andalusia, he might well have received support from his provincial junta. Neither central nor civilian government was firmly established in Spain in this turbulent time.

The comparatively easy victory of Bailen and Joseph's unexpected retreat from Madrid led to an unreasoning overconfidence and a relaxation of effort just at the time when Napoleon was concentrating his resources against Spain. For this the Supreme Junta cannot be blamed — they first met on 25 September, only six weeks before Napoleon began his great offensive. The chief responsibility must rest with the local authorities who failed to tap the great resources of the newly liberated provinces of Old Castile, New Castile and León, and who failed to maintain the early momentum in many other provinces. For example, Andalusia had only 50,000 men under arms at the beginning of November, although it had had 40,000 in July.[3]

Nonetheless, by November the Spaniards had more than 100,000 men in their front line on the Ebro and many more in reserve. The quality of these troops was not particularly high and they were badly led. The Spanish generals had devised a common plan on 5 September but they did not abide by it. In many ways this did not matter — their defeat by Napoleon was inevitable. Spain was a second-rate power which could not possibly defeat France without the assistance of at least one of the great powers of central Europe. The pattern of the war in the Peninsula with its succession of advances and retreats had already been established. So long as neither side could gain a complete victory a successful allied advance simply made the French retreat and concentrate their forces until they had regained the superiority. The French would then, in their turn, advance until their forces were overextended and the allies regained the initiative. This equilibrium was not really stable — it required an increasing British presence to sustain the allied cause — but it lasted until the collapse of Napoleon's Empire following the Russian campaign.

The British government gave support to the Spanish patriots in a variety of ways. The dispatch of Wellesley's army to Portugal was one form of assistance. More direct and possibly more useful was the generous material and financial aid which was sent to Spain. Accounts differ but it is clear that by the middle of November over 120,000 muskets, millions of cartridges, and vast quantities of other equipment had actually reached Spain.[4] Over £1 million in silver had been sent before November; a further £585,000 was sent at the end of that month and another £220,000 had been sent in the form of Treasury bills.[5] These sums virtually exhausted Britain's reserves of specie and so created a problem that was to haunt her war effort over the next few years. This did not restrict her ability to supply equipment and goods that were produced in England and could be paid for in paper currency — Britain was not generally short of money, simply of precious metals. In fact it seems that the revolution in Spain reduced the supply of, as well as increasing the demand for, Britain's bullion reserves, for 'It is only by a direct but secret Understanding with the late government of Spain, under the Connivance of France, that any Considerable Amount of Dollars has been collected in England'.[6] The revolution disrupted this secret arrangement and Britain could only hope to replenish her supplies if she was allowed to trade with Vera Cruz, i.e. exchange British merchandise for Mexican silver. But this raised the extremely prickly subject of British trade with Spanish America in general and it remained a delicate and troublesome issue in the relations between the allies.

A third form of British aid makes one of the great romantic stories of the Peninsular War. This was the rescue by British ships of Romana's Spanish corps from Denmark. Even before the Spanish rising the British government had considered whether it might be possible to win over Romana and his men, but two attempts to establish contact had ended in failure. News of the Spanish uprising led the cabinet to authorize another attempt. The agent was a Scottish monk, Brother James Robertson (an old acquaintance of the Duke of Richmond, Lord Lieutenant of Ireland), who had returned to Britain after some years on the Continent. Robertson received his instructions on 10 June and was taken to Heligoland, from whence he was landed on the Continent by a smuggler. His task was considerably complicated by the fact that the Spanish corps had been moved from Holstein and Hamburg to scattered quarters in Denmark — and he could not speak Danish. Still, by cool courage and considerable common sense he succeeded in reaching Romana and convincing him that his proposals were genuine. Romana accepted his offer and with some difficulty word was sent back to London. The actual escape did not go entirely according to plan, and only two-thirds of the 14,000 Spanish troops got away, but it was still one of the most remarkable feats of secret service performed during the Napoleonic Wars. The escape was on 7 August and by 11 October Romana's corps was concentrated at Santander in Spain.[7] As it was based on no single province (unlike the other Spanish armies), the British government agreed to pay its expenses until the Supreme Junta could do so. The glamour of the escape and their own role in it made the British ministers and public take a special, proprietary interest in the fortunes of Romana and his men. Romana himself landed in England and met members of the cabinet, who seem to have been most impressed by him.[8]

The British military missions to Spain might be regarded as another form of aid, although their role seems to have been primarily to gather intelligence and distribute material aid, rather than to help train and organize the new Spanish levies. This is confirmed by the fact that the missions each consisted of a handful of officers without the drill-masters and non-commissioned officers that a training mission would require. These missions collected a great quantity of information which they sent back to London, but the slowness of communications and the unreliability of the information undermined its value. The quality of the officers sent to Spain varied widely. Some were shrewd, perceptive and discreet; others were incompetent; while a few, such as Colonel Doyle, considerably embarrassed the British government by their interference in Spanish politics.

The most important mission was that of Lord William Bentinck, who was sent to Madrid by Sir Hew Dalrymple, to make arrangements with the Spanish government for the advance of the British army into Spain. Bentinck was deeply depressed by what he found: there was no Spanish commander-in-chief, and the Minister for War was a nonentity. Gross incompetence combined with blind confidence to hinder public affairs, and he could not even get reliable information on the quality of the roads leading from Portugal into Spain. He had some talks with General Castaños, but found that even Castaños knew little of the plans of the other Spanish generals. Yet these talks were the only indication that Britain could gain of Spanish plans and of the role the British army could play within them. If British strategic planning in 1808 was often faulty one must remember the dearth of useful information in which it occurred.[9]

The creation of the Supreme Junta allowed the British government to reopen diplomatic relations. The new envoy was John Hookham Frere, a close friend of Canning, who had already represented Britain in Madrid from 1802 to 1804. Frere was a witty, scholarly man, who had contributed to the *Anti-Jacobin* and who is chiefly remembered now 'as the inspirer of the style, stanza, and idiom of Byron's *Beppo* and *Don Juan*' and for his translations of Aristophanes.[10] But he was a poor man of business and his judgement of public affairs proved unreliable. He was an enthusiastic supporter of the Spanish rising and did not let the inefficiency of the Spanish government undermine his sympathy. He handled many delicate issues in Anglo-Spanish relations with tact and skill, and became popular with the Supreme Junta. Unfortunately this was at the cost of his detachment: he sympathized too much with the Junta's viewpoint and failed in his primary responsibility of effectively representing his own government. Most seriously, he failed to see through the Spanish accounts of the war, accepting their bombastic claims as true and — especially as seen in his correspondence with Moore — acting accordingly. Only Canning's strenuous defence and fierce partisanship saved him from being recalled in disgrace within six months of taking up his post.

The Anglo-Spanish alliance began with a welter of good will on both sides. The British were full of romantic ideas of noble Spanish grandees resisting the might of Napoleon, and freely gave vast quantities of aid without haggling or delay. The Spaniards in turn looked to Britain as an ally against France and — in some quarters — as a desirable model of a consti- tutional monarchy. But beneath this amicable surface there were consider- able tensions arising from such issues as British pressure to trade with South America, underlying Spanish suspicion of Britain stimulated by the memory of Gibraltar, and British frustration at what they saw as Spanish incompetence in waging the war. The fact was that the two countries were not natural allies, they shared little common history or culture, were largely ignorant of each other, and where not ignorant were inclined to antipathy. So long as the war went well these tensions generally remained submerged, but when the Spanish armies collapsed in November both sides became disillusioned. Yet their common hostility to Napoleon drew them back together after a few months, in an alliance which they both found irritating but essential.

During July and August, while Wellesley's army was sailing to Portugal and fighting the French, Castlereagh and his colleagues were trying to plan the next stage of the campaign. They had little institutional support or pro- fessional advice, and lacked reliable intelligence on the size and plans of the French and Spanish armies. This shortage of information even extended to such basic points as the nature and existence of roads running from the ports of northern Spain, where the British army might be disembarked, to the interior, where it would have to operate.[11] These problems were not unique to the war in the Peninsula, indeed they were characteristic of British warfare in the eighteenth and early nineteenth centuries, but they were worse than usual in the early months of the Peninsular War, as British armies had seen little service in Spain since Marlborough's day.

From the moment the Asturian deputies first arrived in London, there was strong interest in Britain in the fate of northern Spain. Edward Cooke and Col. J. W. Gordon both urged the government to concentrate its efforts there, and Sir Arthur Wellesley supported their arguments from Coruña. When news arrived in the middle of August of the French retreat to the Ebro, it was clear that the centre of the war was shifting to the north. Well before this, during July, Canning frequently argued that a small force (perhaps 3,000 men) should be sent to Asturias to establish a British pres- ence, and to provide some protection for the province. The Asturians had lost their initial reluctance to receive British forces and were now pressing for military assistance, especially cavalry and artillery.[12]

Castlereagh was equally convinced of the importance of northern Spain, but was hampered by logistical difficulties, especially the shortage of horse transports, while his initial plans had been disrupted by the need to reinforce Wellesley's army. On 10 August he proposed a new plan of campaign: a light corps of 8–10,000 infantry and all the British and Portuguese cavalry that could be spared would be detached from Portugal and sent to help the Spanish armies to drive the French from Madrid. The force of 10,000 men which was ready at home would be sent immediately to Asturias, where they would be joined by more troops from Portugal as soon as operations there were concluded. Castlereagh hoped that an active British presence in the Asturias could lead to risings in the more easterly of the northern provinces such as Biscay, which lay across the French lines of communication. He even dreamt that a British army — cooperating with the Armies of Asturias and Aragon and aided by risings in Biscay — could cut off Joseph's retreat to France and force him to surrender.[13]

But this plan immediately ran into problems. The Duke of York had already indicated his strong opposition to any division of the army and his lack of confidence in the Spanish forces. News of the French retreat from Madrid cast doubt on the role of the light corps, and the cabinet proved unable to come to a decision, with 'long and repeated Discussions and little done and similar Opposition to whatever is proposed'.[14] Finally, at the end of August, the cabinet agreed

> *not* to send the 10,000 men to the North of Spain, at present, as we know so little of the probability of their being supported from Portugal *but* to send orders to Dalrymple to hold 15 or 20,000 [men] in readiness to embark for the North of Spain whenever his Operations presented the opportunity, meaning on our part to send 10,000 Men, from hence as soon as we knew the 15 or 20,000 Men from Lisbon could be released. We decided at the same time, that the 10,000 should assemble at Plymouth in their transports ready to sail at a moment's warning & that Baird who commands 5,000 of the 10,000 should come from Cork to Plymouth — that they might all be together.
>
> . . . Lord Chatham objected to all the propositions but without bitterness.[15]

The idea of sending a 'light corps' into the interior of Spain was thus abandoned, and the cautious advocates of concentration even managed to prevent Baird's force being sent to northern Spain in advance of the troops from Portugal. Still, the basis of a plan of campaign is clear: the bulk of Dalrymple's army was to sail to one of the northern Spanish ports — no choice had yet been made between Coruña, Gijon and Santander — where it was to be joined by Baird's 10,000 men from home, and also by Romana's 10,000 regulars. Their operations would depend on the circumstances at the time and the plans of the Spanish generals. The choice of a northern port as the base of operations rather than Lisbon provided shorter lines of communication and supply, a more secure link with the fleet, and — as Castlereagh curiously put it — 'it will render their return etc overland more easy when the proposed service shall have been effected'. Evidently Castlereagh thought of the British army returning after a short but triumphant campaign. Certainly he was feeling optimistic, for he went on to tell the King that the ministers 'cannot but flatter themselves' that the accession of 40,000 regular troops to the Spanish cause 'must not only accelerate his [the French] expulsion from Spain, but may also contribute, if his retreat shall be delay'd, to the destruction of a considerable proportion of his army'.[16]

Yet despite the rhetoric, the plan was surprisingly cautious. The abandonment of the idea of sending a light corps into Spain could be justified on the grounds that the continued French retreat made it unnecessary, but why take the decision to send troops to northern Spain long before it could be implemented? Two factors seem to have been present: one was that the government did not know how the campaign in Portugal was progressing (news of Roliça and Vimiero arrived at midnight that night), which inclined the cabinet to caution; the other was the news that the Biscay provinces had risen, which inclined them to action.

The decision of 31 August therefore seems to have been a compromise between the bolder members of the cabinet — who certainly included Castlereagh and Canning — and their more cautious colleagues. It did not provide a detailed plan of campaign but it confirmed that 'the north of Spain' would be the theatre for British operations, and this enabled Castlereagh to tell Dalrymple that he could proceed there with the army without further orders from home if there was an emergency.[17] Castlereagh's proposed strategy of attacking the French flank and rear through Biscay and other provinces to the east of the Asturias was not mentioned and although it was not explicitly excluded, it may already have been abandoned. In any case it became impossible when it was decided to base the British army at Coruña rather than Gijon or Santander further east. As Castlereagh explained to Lord William Bentinck, Santander was felt by all military men, and especially Romana, to be too far forward and hence too exposed to the danger of a French attack before the British army could be fully concentrated and equipped for service.[18] This was undoubtedly true, and Castlereagh's plan — reasonable in early August — would have led to disaster in October.

The decision to base the British army at Coruña led almost inevitably to the adoption of a strategy which was first expressed in an unsigned memorandum from the Horse Guards dated 23 September.[19] This argued that the French were now stronger than the Spaniards and that there was a large gap in the centre of the Spanish line. This was on the plains — good cavalry country — and lack of cavalry was the greatest Spanish weakness. Britain had no shortage of cavalry, although finding horse transports was a problem. Given the probable strength of the French forces, a weak British army would be quite useless: she should concentrate every man she could in a strong army that would be able to defend itself if necessary without relying on Spanish cooperation. The memorandum concluded with a detailed if optimistic statement showing how 60,000 men could be found for service in Spain.

On the same day that this memorandum was written the cabinet took the disagreeable but necessary decision to appoint Sir John Moore to command the army. The ministers still did not like or trust him, but they had little real choice. Chatham's strategic views were now at odds with those of his colleagues, and in any case his appointment would be too blatantly political in the aftermath of Cintra (the furore was then at its height). There was no obvious general in England who could be appointed over Moore's head, and the failure of Dalrymple and Burrard made the cabinet unwilling to experiment. Canning accepted this decision with the greatest reluctance and many forebodings. Nor was the King pleased — he would still have liked the command to go to a more senior officer — but he accepted the argument that the staff of the army in Portugal should be spared any further disruption if possible.[20]

Moore's instructions, issued on 25 September, drew heavily on the ideas in the anonymous Horse Guards memorandum of the 23rd, although his army is put at only 30,000 infantry and 5,000 cavalry. Of these, 10,000 men under Sir David Baird would sail from Falmouth to Coruña, while the rest would be drawn from the army in Portugal, and Moore was given the choice of taking them by land or sea. The army would assemble either in Galicia or on the borders of León, and it was to cooperate with the Spaniards in the expulsion of the French from Spain. A more detailed plan would depend on the intentions of the Spanish commanders, with whom Moore was ordered to consult.[21]

These instructions were considerably less detailed and precise than many of the plans which the cabinet had considered earlier. Unlike Castlereagh's proposals in August, they did not contain any clear conception of the role which the British army was to play — the orders simply specified a point of assembly (Galicia or the borders of León) and a general objective (the expulsion of the French from Spain). This vagueness was quite appropriate, for it was intended that the British army would cooperate closely with the Spanish armies and its movements would necessarily be shaped by theirs. The opportunity for turning the French flank — if it had ever existed — had long since passed, and the British government was surely correct in determining to use its army to strengthen the Spanish line at its most vulnerable point.

The lack of precision in the orders gave Moore a broad discretion — possibly broader than was desirable, given the lack of trust between him and the British cabinet — but this was unavoidable as the ministers could not hope to foresee even the general shape of operations. The greatest flaw in the British plan was that it was simply too late. For the British army to play

3   Portugal and North-West Spain: Sir John Moore's campaign, 1808–9

its intended role in the campaign it would have had to have been concentrated in León in September — a time when its orders were only just being issued and the army itself was still in Portugal and England. This delay arose first from the initial Spanish refusal to allow the British army to land in northern Spain, and secondly from the concentration of excessively large forces for the Portuguese campaign (although the reasons for this were sound at the time). Put another way, the British could not keep pace with the rapidly changing course of events because of slow communications and the logistical restraints of amphibious operations. The ministers were well aware of the need for haste, but there was little they could do to overcome these problems.

Sir Hew Dalrymple left Lisbon on 2 October and a few days later Castlereagh's letters appointing Moore to the command arrived. Moore was both pleased and surprised: 'There has been no such command since Marlborough for a British officer. How they came to pitch upon me I cannot say, for they have given sufficient proof of not being partial to me.'[22] Castlereagh had sent a conciliatory private letter with the instructions and Moore replied in a friendly manner, thus patching over the ill-feeling left by their earlier, acrimonious exchange.

Although Castlereagh had given Moore the choice of moving his army by land or sea, it is clear that he expected that the general would ship at least his artillery and some of his infantry to Coruña. But Moore decided to march his whole army overland, arguing that another sea passage would disrupt the army's organization, and that Baird's force alone would strain the already depleted resources of Galicia. He soon found, however, that marching overland had its own disadvantages: the roads of northern Portugal were said to be dreadful and the autumn rains were approaching. With great reluctance Moore decided that he must send his artillery along the Lisbon-Badajoz-Madrid highway, although this involved a lengthy detour and further divided his army.[23]

The consequence of Moore's decision was that his army would not be fully united until it approached the front line — perhaps at Valladolid or even Burgos — whereas Castlereagh had instructed him to concentrate the army in Galicia or on the borders of León, more than a hundred miles to the rear. At the time this seemed to matter little, for both the ministers and the general were envisaging an offensive campaign to drive the French out of Spain. Yet it does make a nonsense of Moore's complaint, when things began to go wrong, that ministers had ventured the army too far forward, and that Baird's force should have landed at Cadiz, and the whole army united in safety at Seville. For, of course, if Moore had obeyed his instructions, the army would have united in safety, albeit in Galicia not Andalusia.[24]

The preparations to march were hampered by many problems, including a shortage of specie and the inexperience of the British officers — particularly the commissaries — in moving a large body of troops far from the coast. Nonetheless, the bulk of Moore's army was on the move by 18 October, and the advanced guard crossed the Spanish frontier at Ciudad Rodrigo on 11 November. Further north, Sir David Baird was having problems. His force arrived at Coruña on 13 October, but the local authorities refused to allow him to land without express permission from the Supreme Junta. This wasted nearly ten days, and when Baird's force began to disembark, he too faced great difficulty collecting transport and supplies.

By the middle of November the British army was still widely dispersed, and far from ready to go into action. But Napoleon had taken command on 5 November, and in a series of crushing victories, had routed the Spanish armies of the left and centre in less than a week. The Spanish right under Castaños and Palafox survived for almost a fortnight, but only because Napoleon was trying to surround them. The attempt failed, but they were badly beaten at Tudela on 23 November: Castaños's men fled in disarray, while Palafox's Aragonese retired within Saragossa to endure another appalling siege. With the disintegration of all the regular Spanish armies, Napoleon felt free to advance on Madrid. He brutally forced his way through an attempt to block his path at Somosierra and arrived outside Madrid on 2 December. The city was indefensible, and although the inhabitants were briefly inclined to die heroically, they peacefully surrendered on 4 December and the French reoccupied the Spanish capital.[25]

News of the Spanish defeats reached the British generals spasmodically as they advanced into Spain. Baird heard the first reports even before he left Coruña, and by the time he reached Astorga on 22 November he was so alarmed that he decided that it would be too risky to continue his advance until his force was united and ready for action. Moore learnt of the collapse of the Spanish centre and the French occupation of Burgos when he reached Salamanca on 13 November. He halted to allow the main body of his army to arrive from Portugal, and on the 15th he was told that the French had advanced to Valladolid, only a few marches away. He prepared to retreat, and was greatly relieved when further intelligence revealed that there was no more than a brigade of French cavalry at Valladolid.

Moore stayed at Salamanca for more than three weeks while his army grew closer together. At first he was very gloomy, complaining of lack of news, Spanish cooperation and money. He was irritated to receive cheerful letters from Castlereagh, and replied in the most pessimistic terms, emphasizing the Spanish defeats and even hinting that Portugal was indefensible. He also complained to Frere of lack of Spanish cooperation and warned that if things did not improve, 'it will become my duty to consider alone the safety of the British army, and to take steps to withdraw it from a situation, where, without the possibility of doing good, it is exposed to certain defeat'.[26]

But as the days passed without the French advancing against him, Moore's confidence slowly grew. He looked forward to uniting the British army, and decided that rather than tamely withdrawing into Portugal, he would throw caution to the winds and advance to support Castaños and the remaining Spanish armies. It was a dangerous plan and Moore sought to implicate Frere in his decision by asking his advice. Frere warmly supported the bolder course, but before he could even send his reply, he was disgusted to learn that Moore had again resolved on retreat, and privately concluded that the talk of an offensive was no more than a sham.[27]

Moore's fragile confidence had been turned to despair by the news of Tudela, and for the next week he only waited for Hope's column to join him to begin his retreat. Then, on 5 December, he received an emotive appeal from the governors of Madrid begging that he would march to the relief of their city, which they claimed was determined to resist the French. Later that day Colonel Charmilly — an adventurer whom Moore had already met and distrusted — arrived with dispatches from Frere and a graphic eyewitness account of the popular determination to defend Madrid.[28] Moore was sceptical of these reports, but could not bring himself to ignore them, and again decided to take the offensive. He knew the risks involved and told Baird to continue preparations for an eventual retreat along the road to Coruña, explaining: 'I mean to proceed bridle in hand; for if the bubble bursts, and Madrid falls, we shall have a run for it.'[29]

On this same day Colonel Charmilly, unaware of Moore's change of plan, produced a second letter from Frere in which the diplomat demanded that Charmilly's evidence be examined by a council of war. Moore dismissed this foolish attempt to subvert his authority with the contempt it deserved and sent Charmilly packing without giving a hint of his real plans.

Moore had no intention of marching on Madrid, for his army was far too small to confront Napoleon's main force directly. Rather he planned to strike at the French lines of communication near Burgos, in the hope that by creating a major diversion in Napoleon's rear he would give the Spanish armies time to rally. On 9 December he learnt that Madrid had fallen but he continued to advance, changing direction on the 14th when an intercepted French dispatch revealed that Marshal Soult's corps was isolated near Saldana. The soldiers were delighted at the prospect of action, while Moore too was probably happier to be running great risks by advancing than to be safely retreating. Certainly it took the sting out of an extremely offensive and foolish letter which Moore received from Frere, who was still under the impression that the British army was in retreat.[30]

The first contact between British and French troops occurred on 12 December when the British cavalry surprised a small French detachment at Rueda. This and subsequent skirmishes alarmed General Franchesi (commander of the division of French cavalry in the region) and Marshal Soult, who began to prepare for action. On 21 December Lord Paget surprised and defeated Debelle's brigade of cavalry at Sahagun in what Oman calls 'perhaps the most brilliant exploit of the British cavalry during the whole six years of the war'.[31] Sahagun brought no immediate strategic benefit — although it gravely alarmed Soult — but it reinforced the already high self-confidence in the British army.

Late on 23 December, as the army was beginning the final stage of its advance against Soult, Moore received word from Romana that Napoleon was moving against them. There was no choice but immediately to abandon the offensive and hastily begin to retreat. The soldiers grumbled unhappily but Moore knew that he could not afford to delay. Already there was a danger that Napoleon might reach the Galician passes before the British and cut off their escape. And so the epic retreat to Coruña began.

Napoleon had in fact been slow to understand the location and intentions of the British army. He had clung to his belief that Moore was retreating on Lisbon after he had definite evidence to the contrary, and even when he abandoned this idea he replaced it with one misconception after another. But once Napoleon understood that the British were hundreds of miles from their base and still advancing, he made an enormous effort to concentrate resources against them. The bulk of the French army left Madrid on 21 December and hastened north-west through the Guadarrama with Napoleon marching at their head in a famous blizzard.

The two armies rapidly converged on Benavente but the British won the race and their line of retreat was assured. When the leading French troops arrived at Benavente on 27 December they were repulsed by a British rearguard in a celebrated skirmish. On the last day of 1808 Moore reached Astorga and decided to continue his retreat to the coast. Supplies were short and winter was rapidly closing in. Even if Moore had managed to repulse the French at Astorga, or at some later point during his retreat, little would have been gained. The British army would not benefit from a winter spent in the Galician mountains and it would be tempting fate to dally in front of Napoleon.

After Astorga Moore's principal problems were the weather, lack of supplies, and the gradual breakdown of discipline in his army, not the French pursuit. Napoleon abandoned the chase on New Year's Day 1809. The British had eluded his grasp and would make their escape safely back to their ships. Meanwhile trouble was brewing at home in Paris, and Austria was growing restless. It was not a time to go on a wild goose chase through the barren wastes of Galicia. Soult with a strengthened corps could shepherd the British back to the sea, while the rest of the army which Napoleon had assembled for the pursuit was dispersed in every direction.[32]

The retreat to Coruña was full of horrors as semi-starvation, drunkenness and winter combined to play havoc. Only the rearguard and a few other regiments maintained their discipline, and straggling became rife. On 9 January the army reached the sea at Betanzos, and the worst was over. Moore let the troops rest on the 10th, and late on the next day the army reached Coruña where ample supplies were waiting for the weary soldiers. Here Moore made the unpleasant discovery that the transports which were to evacuate the army had been sent to Vigo by mistake, and had yet to return. There was no choice but to wait patiently and re-equip the army from the stockpiles of weapons which had accumulated at Coruña.

The French arrived a couple of days after the British. Soult was not eager to attack, for his men had suffered almost as much advancing through Galicia as the British had in their retreat, and the French found no supplies of food and weapons waiting for them. Soult's army was only a shade larger than the British,[33] but after such a long pursuit neither honour nor the Emperor would be satisfied if he passively watched his enemy escape. Soult therefore gave his men a couple of days' rest and attacked on 16 January 1809.

Moore had drawn his army up in a generally strong position some two miles from Coruña. The rough broken nature of the country made the powerful French cavalry largely ineffective, thus negating Soult's greatest advantage. The weak point in the British line was on the right flank beyond the village of Elvina. Soult perceived this and concentrated his efforts on trying to turn the British flank while pinning that end of the line with frontal attacks. A strong battery of French artillery on high ground opposite Elvina supported the attacks of the French infantry and inflicted many casualties, including Sir David Baird, whose wound cost him his left arm. The bloodiest fighting of the day was in and around Elvina, which changed hands several times as each side brought up fresh troops. Moore had anticipated Soult's plan of attack, and had strong reserves protecting his far right and supporting his front line near Elvina. Judiciously introducing these reserves, he had little trouble in repulsing the French attacks. Towards the close of the day Moore himself was mortally wounded, although he lived to see his army victorious. While Moore was an inspiring trainer and leader of men, his brief campaign does not provide a fair test of his abilities as a general. He aroused devoted loyalty in many, including William Napier, the future historian, and this as much as anything ensured that he would be well remembered, while his heroic death and Charles Wolfe's popular verses describing his burial ('Not a drum was heard, not a funeral note . . .') clothed his memory in an aura of romance. The command of the British army devolved onto Lieutenant-General Hope, who prudently dismissed the temptation to counter-attack Soult and concentrated on embarking the army safely.[34]

And so the campaign, which had begun with such high hopes, ended in a profitless victory and embarkation. Once again the British army had ventured onto the Continent only to be driven off in disorder. Neither Sir John Moore nor the British government were to blame for this. The British army could not stand by itself against the full force of Napoleon's army, so the collapse of the Spanish forces made the British retreat inevitable. It is to Moore's credit that he managed to extricate his army safely, and at the same time disrupt Napoleon's plans for conquering Portugal and southern Spain. Indeed, it is hard to see how the British army could have been used more effectively. There was no way in which it could have stopped the tide of French conquest, and if it had been in the front line on the Ebro in November, it would certainly have been overwhelmed. Moore's achievement was considerable, but this was not immediately obvious in Britain, where the gruelling retreat and battered condition of the army were more apparent than the disruption to Napoleon's plans.

In England the ministers and public had watched the unfolding of Moore's campaign with great interest and growing apprehension. At first hopes were high, and although early reports of French victories caused some anxiety, only the habitual pessimists despaired. Then, around 10 December, Castlereagh received no less than five gloomy letters from Moore, written in the first shock of the Spanish defeats. Moore warned that 'Reverses must be expected'.[35] The British army is certainly too much adventured, and risks to be brought into action before it is united, and before its stores, ammunition etc are brought forward to enable it to act . . . I see nothing that has a chance of resisting the force that is now brought against this country. There seems neither to be an army, generals, nor a government . . . the ruin of the Spanish cause . . . [seems] to me so inevitable, that it [will] very soon become my duty to consider alone the safety of the British army, and withdraw it from a contest which risked its destruction, without the prospect of doing the least good. . . . your lordship must be prepared to hear that we have failed; for situated as we are, success cannot be commanded by any effort we can make. . . .[36]

The only consolation he could offer was that the British army had stood up well to the rigours of the campaign. In the last of these letters Moore did mention his scheme to abandon his communications and march to the aid of Madrid, but the ministers did not realize that he was serious.

The ministers were shocked by these letters, but the official response from Castlereagh was everything that Moore could have wished. The government approved the decision to retreat while regretting the necessity for it. There was no hint of blame directed at Moore and they accepted his assessment that León and Castile would fall, but hoped that both the south of Spain and the more remote provinces in the north would continue to resist. This was combined with a strong letter from Canning to Frere telling him that the British army was retiring into Portugal so that it could unite, that it had no intention of giving up the struggle, but that it was the only British army and it could not be endangered for an inadequate object. Canning added that the army would not again advance into Spain until the Spaniards had a coherent plan and had established better communications with the British generals.[37]

But in private Canning in particular felt considerable disquiet. He hated the idea of disembarking the reinforcements in order to send empty transports to Lisbon as Moore had requested, fearing that this would encourage 'a shameful retreat', whereas the reinforcements might lead Moore into the successful defence of Portugal. He thought that Moore was exaggerating the dangers of his position, and on 11 December wrote privately to Castlereagh: 'I cannot help doubting upon reflection whether we have not been somewhat too despairing in our instructions to Moore, and taken too hastily the colour of our General's representations'. He was particularly disturbed by Moore's letter of 25 November in which Sir John had described the Portuguese frontier as indefensible, and implied that if the French advanced against him he must evacuate his army. Canning suspected that Moore simply wanted to bring his army home as quickly as possible, and it was in order to avert this military, political and diplomatic disaster that the government raised the idea that if Moore was forced to embark his army from Lisbon, he should proceed with it to Cadiz, rather than bringing it home.[38]

In the event these concerns proved premature if not altogether ill-founded. Moore gained his second wind and abandoned the idea of a precipitate retreat into Portugal. On 5 December he announced that his junction with Hope was secure and — later that day — that he would not retreat until he saw what had happened at Madrid. These letters arrived on 16 December and were much more to the taste of the ministers, so that even Canning's suspicion of Moore subsided into uncertainty.

But then, on 30 December, Canning received copies of the correspondence between Frere and Moore, and foolishly believed Frere's rosy picture of affairs. He wrote to Castlereagh that 'The Cause of Spain is safe, if Moore does not ruin it. And if he does, I hope we are prepared to throw the responsibility where it ought to rest.' On the same day he told the Prime Minister that if Moore 'persisted in *running away* . . . I have no hesitation in maintaining, as an individual opinion, that he ought to be recalled to answer for his conduct'. 'I confess my blood boils when I think of what has been lost, for want of a little enterprize, of a little *heart*.' 'I do not deny Genl. Sir J. Moore's military Skill. — I do not doubt his personal gallantry. — I do not question his disposition to act faithfully by his Country in any cause. — But I do most intimately and conscientiously believe, that under the present circumstances, acting under the present government, the cause of Spain is not safe in his hands.' On the following day he wrote again to Portland to urge that Lord Moira be appointed to the command of the British forces in the Peninsula.[39]

If it is hard to believe that the hotheaded, passionate and impetuous Canning could seriously propose replacing Moore in the middle of the campaign only a few months after Cintra, it *is* impossible to understand how the aged, experienced and usually phlegmatic Duke of Portland could actually agree to the proposal, but that is what he did.

Portland replied to Canning's first letter on 31 December before he received the second. He agreed that an attempt should be made to remove Moore if they thought it could succeed, but he foresaw considerable opposition to the attempt. Portland believed that the only man capable of doing the job was Sir Arthur Wellesley, but his appointment would arouse great hostility among his superiors, who would feel cheated, and it might lead to a shortage of good subordinates. He was not keen on the alternatives to Wellesley:

> Can we who remove Moore for Political Reasons, look with more Confidence to Ld. Moira? and what Alternative have we! None I fear but the D. of York himself and a moment's Reflection ought to convince me of the Absurdity of such an Idea and the absolute impossibility of its being listened to. . . .[40]

Canning's second letter, evidently written before he received Portland's reply, impressed the old Duke with its strongly put argument in favour of Moira. Such an appointment would certainly lessen the problems of sacking Moore, he acknowledged in his reply on New Year's Day, and Moira was certainly no more hostile politically to the government. Could they discuss the matter further as soon as possible before broaching it to the cabinet?[41]

There the evidence ends, with no record of any discussion or of whether the idea was ever put to cabinet — although it seems unlikely, for if cabinet had discussed it, it is probable that more evidence would have survived. One would like to say that there was no chance of the cabinet ever agreeing to such a foolish scheme, but the fact that the government's ablest minister (Canning) and its most experienced one (Portland) could agree to it destroys any easy confidence on the subject. We can hope that a revival of good sense led to the abandonment of the idea, but it seems more likely that it was news of the rapidly changing situation in Spain that decided the question.

By 9 January news of Moore's retreat as far as Astorga had reached London, and Moore's good friend Colonel Gordon expressed the anxiety of many when he wrote: 'It appears to me *now* that your situation is most perilous, as I cannot but suppose that Buonaparte will push rapidly on, and press You to the utmost: — if he does this in force it seems to me that the re-embarkation of all Your Army is not to be effected.' Sir Arthur Wellesley agreed, as he later admitted: 'You see the account of the Action at Corunna. I was certain that nothing could save the Army but an attack by the French; & it is only to be lamented that we have lost two such valuable men as Sir John Moore and Sir David Baird. The latter I conclude cannot live.'[42]

As news of the army's retreat slowly trickled in, Canning urged his colleagues to throw the whole blame for the failure of the campaign on Moore — where he genuinely believed it belonged. But that general's heroic death changed the political equation completely, and Castlereagh led the way with a generous eulogy and by proposing a monument in St Paul's. This took the wind out of the Opposition's sails, and it was some time before they found, in the Charmilly episode and Frere's role in the campaign, the right angle from which to attack the government. Canning privately admitted that Frere had blundered, and in April decided that the only way to save his friend's career was to move him to another embassy.

The political storm over Moore's campaign exacerbated the damage that had been done by Cintra. It completed the popular disenchantment with the Peninsula, so that in the first half of 1809 the public's attention in Britain was concentrated on domestic scandals — notably the affair of the Duke of York and Mary Anne Clarke — and the revival of reform. The Opposition reflected and encouraged this change of mood with only a few individual exceptions, such as Lord and Lady Holland (who were then travelling in Spain) and Francis Horner, continuing publicly to support Britain's involvement in the Peninsula. Canning was further alienated from his colleagues and grew more impatient and frustrated than ever. As Wendy Hinde has remarked, Canning 'never learnt to make the best of a disappointment'.[43] As the months passed he grew increasingly unhappy and regretted his failure to resign over Cintra. He disapproved of the government's tactics in defending the Duke of York and chafed over the deterioration in the political strength of the ministry. Yet it was Canning who recognized that the war must be continued and who first perceived the opportunity that existed in Portugal.

4

In Search of a Strategy, December 1808–April 1809

The months following the defeat of the Spanish armies were crucial to the continuation of Britain's involvement in the Peninsular War, as the ministers struggled to salvage a suitable role for her army from the ruins of their high hopes. Gone for ever was the prospect of an easy victory, of quickly expelling the French from the Peninsula and perhaps even invading the south of France. At first the cabinet thought simply of transferring Moore's army to Cadiz, and there continuing the struggle at least to preserve Andalusia from the French. But unforeseen difficulties arose which forced the government to reconsider completely its relations with Spain and which led eventually to the choice of Portugal as the focus for Britain's efforts in the Peninsula. At the same time overtures were received from Austria which promised a renewal of the war on the Continent, and which suggested that Britain's efforts might have more effect if they were concentrated in north Germany or the Low Countries, rather than in the Peninsula.

The British government turned its attention to Cadiz as early as 9 December 1808, issuing instructions to Moore and Frere which emphasized the importance of preserving Cadiz from the French, and agreeing to any Spanish request for a British force to make up part of its garrison. But it was not until the middle of January that the ministers, belatedly realizing that Moore's army would have to be evacuated from Coruña, returned to the question. They now saw Cadiz as the ideal base for British operations in southern Spain: its possession would ensure the secure evacuation of the army even in the event of defeat, while the gesture of trust shown by the Spaniards in admitting a British garrison would allay the resentment caused by the lack of effective cooperation with Moore and his army. At the same time 4,000 men under Major-General Sherbrooke were sent out to protect Cadiz against any sudden French attack.[1]

But these plans went awry: Sherbrooke's convoy was dispersed by a gale that forced it back into port and delayed it for several weeks, while Moore's army was so battered by the campaign that it had to come home to recover.

On the other hand, the pursuit of Moore had disrupted all Napoleon's plans for completing the conquest of the Peninsula and carried much of his army to the remote north-west of Spain. The remaining French forces near Madrid were far too weak to take the offensive, let alone to conquer Andalusia and threaten Cadiz. Frere realized this and knew that Cadiz was a sensitive subject likely to arouse Spanish jealousy. He therefore only raised the question briefly, and did not press it, being sure that in an emergency he could persuade the Spaniards to admit a British garrison.[2]

All might yet have gone well had it not been for Sir George Smith, the British military agent at Cadiz. Smith's instructions were simply to convey any urgent Spanish request for British troops to Sir John Cradock, the commander of the British forces at Lisbon. But Smith was concerned at the poor state of the defences of Cadiz, and worried that a sudden French attack might threaten the fortress before British help could arrive. With the best of intentions, though little judgement, he wrote to Cradock on 19 January asking him to send any troops he could spare, so that they would be on the spot if an emergency arose. This letter presented Cradock with a dilemma: his own force was not large and Smith made it clear that there was no emergency, but he knew the importance of Cadiz and that he would be blamed for its loss if he rejected Smith's appeal. Afraid of this responsibility he weakly agreed, and dispatched 4,000 under Major-General Mackenzie at the beginning of February.[3]

Mackenzie arrived off Cadiz late on 5 February. The Spanish authorities had received no prior warning and were naturally suspicious, as there were no French troops within 300 miles. They refused to let the British troops into the town and referred the matter to the Supreme Junta. The Spanish government was equally suspicious: Spaniards had already been betrayed by one long-standing ally (France), and by many of their own number; now it looked suspiciously as if their new ally was intent on betraying them as well, and was engaged in a de facto partition of their country with Napoleon.

Frere did his best to allay these suspicions, though he had been caught off guard by Smith's action. He felt that it was important to avoid a public rebuff of the British force, a feeling which was strengthened when, a few days later, he received dispatches from London showing the government's increasing concern for Cadiz. He therefore tried to find a compromise so that at least some of Mackenzie's force could be admitted to Cadiz. Protracted negotiations followed which led to mutual exasperation but no solution, until Cradock unexpectedly cut the Gordian knot by recalling Mackenzie to help defend Portugal against Soult. The British force sailed on 6 March and arrived back in Lisbon on the 12th, together with Sherbrooke's force, which it had met en route.

The events at Cadiz had far-reaching effects on the course of the war. The British government was forced to reconsider its whole involvement in the Peninsula at a time when Anglo-Spanish relations were at their nadir. The British public had lost their enthusiasm for Spain. They were shocked at the deplorable condition of Moore's army when it returned, and at the numerous tales of Spanish indifference and callousness which the soldiers told. Even the ministers felt that the Spaniards had failed to support Moore, and on 25 January Canning warned Frere that if the Spanish government refused to admit a British garrison into Cadiz,

> there is an end of the War in Spain — of the British Operations there I mean — for after the reception which the British Army has met in the north, and after the loss of Ferrol with all its shipping, it is hopeless to expect that the system of sacrifice . . . can be carried further with the consent of Parliament or of the Country.[4]

There were also a number of other irritations weakening the alliance: the extravagance of the Spanish requests for aid; their refusal to grant British merchants access to their American colonies; their failure — despite British warnings — to keep their naval squadron at Ferrol out of French hands; the disappointing performance of their armies; their internal divisions and their unbusinesslike habits. Britain had welcomed Spain as an ally with unprecedented generosity and wildly inflated hopes; now her disillusionment was almost equally exaggerated.

The British ministers were able to find some consolation for the deterioration in their alliance with Spain in an improvement in relations with Austria. The Austrian government had never been reconciled to its defeat in 1805, but it had felt too weak to join Prussia and Russia against France in 1806–7. By 1808 the war party in Vienna was gaining confidence, much encouraged by Napoleon's difficulties in Spain and at home, which were rather overstated in Metternich's dispatches from Paris. Tentative overtures were made to Prussia and Russia but received little encouragement, while the Archduke Charles, the commander-in-chief, argued that the army was not ready for war. The campaigning season of 1808 passed with Austria remaining at peace, but as autumn slipped into winter the momentum for war grew, and even the Archduke Charles gave his approval. By Christmas the decision had been made.[5]

Britain had not forgotten Austria, even in the midst of her excitement over Spain. During August 1808 London was full of rumours of war between France and Austria, including one report of a battle in Poland in which the French were said to have lost 12,000 men killed.[6] While these stories were groundless, the British government had made discreet diplomatic overtures to the Court of Vienna, which were warmly received by Count Stadion, the leading Austrian minister. Contact was quietly maintained between the two governments during the autumn, but communications were very slow as messages had to be conveyed by Hanoverian or Sicilian diplomats through the Mediterranean, rather than by the far more direct route through northern Germany.[7]

At the beginning of December a detailed proposition from the Austrian government reached London. The Austrians explained that while they regarded war as inevitable, they hoped to delay it till the spring to give their forces more time to prepare. They had no shortage of men, for they could put 400,000 effectives into the field, but they needed all possible financial assistance. On the basis of Britain's offers in 1805 they asked for a subsidy of £2.5 million to help cover the initial cost of mobilizing their forces, followed by £5 million per annum once the war began.

The scale of this audacious request seems to have stunned the British government. Not only was it more than Britain had ever given to a Continental Power before: it was more than she had ever considered giving to all the Continental Powers together. Further, Britain's reserves of specie had been drained by the war in Spain, and the Continental System prevented the use of bills of exchange for large sums. Canning therefore replied on 24 December that while Britain welcomed the fact that Austria recognized the dangers which were facing it, she could not promise aid on anything like this scale. Austria must look to her own people for financial as well as military resources — indeed, her only chance of success was if there was a universal determination to prosecute the war. Britain was already helping Austria by assisting the Spaniards to distract Napoleon, and if Austria did go to war, Britain would send all the financial aid she could afford at the time.[8]

This cautious response was dictated partly by financial constraints, but also by doubts about Austria's sincerity. Late in November Canning had told Chatham: 'If Austria would act now, She might be of great use. But I confess I have my suspicions that this show of alacrity is only occasioned by her apprehensions of our making Peace.' And a month later J. M. Johnston, a confidential British agent in Vienna, reported home his doubts that the war party would prevail in Austrian counsels.[9] Even if Austria did act, the experience of many previous campaigns gave British ministers little reason to expect that she would succeed. Nonetheless, the government obviously had to take into account the possibility of a new war in central Europe when making their own strategic plans for the coming season. The news was encouraging, but also unsettling, and this uncertainty helps to explain the hesitation and procrastination which marked British policy in the first months of 1809.

In the wake of the rebuff at Cadiz, it was by no means clear where in or beyond the Peninsula Britain would concentrate her military effort. The likelihood of an Austrian war gave north-western Europe or the Mediterranean increased appeal, while there were obvious arguments for some kind of reconciliation with Spain. Meanwhile there remained a British presence in Portugal left over from Wellesley's and Moore's campaigns, which for a time had been neglected, if not quite forgotten.

In the confident early days of Moore's advance, when the expulsion of the French from Spain still appeared possible, Portugal had naturally been a low priority. It was not until the middle of November that the British government had appointed Lieutenant-General Sir John Cradock to command the British forces left in Lisbon, and Mr John Villiers as minister plenipotentiary to the Portuguese Regency. Cradock was an experienced officer of good standing, whose appointment was unexceptionable. But, according to the diplomat Francis Jackson, the choice of Villiers provoked 'no small surprise and merriment even amongst the friends of the new minister . . . Villiers is a man turned of fifty who has all his life been doing nothing: a mere courtier, famous for telling interminably long stories'.[10] While Jackson's view is tinged with jealousy and spleen, the selection of Villiers does reflect the chronic shortage of skilled diplomats from which Britain suffered throughout this period.

Villiers faced no easy task in Lisbon, for Portuguese politics were exceptionally tangled and confused. When the Court had fled to Brazil in 1807 Prince João had left behind a Regency Council, but some of its members had actively cooperated with the French. Dalrymple had reconstituted the council, purging members who had compromised themselves; but the legality of the new regime was disputed, among others by Souza, the Portuguese minister to London. Even once this problem was resolved relations with the Portuguese government were not easy. The Regency Council lacked the power to act decisively, and too many decisions had to be referred to Brazil, which caused immense delays even when the Portuguese Court did not vacillate or procrastinate.

Villiers's immediate tasks were to send home reliable information on the state of Portugal; to use his influence, if necessary, to strengthen the Regency Council; and to offer it aid in raising an army. This aid was subject to stiff conditions: Villiers was to exercise considerable control over the money spent, and the troops raised with it were liable to serve the common cause anywhere in the world. The Portuguese government did not finally agree to these conditions — which appear unnecessarily onerous — until March 1809.[11]

Cradock faced even greater problems than Villiers. He arrived on 13 December to face the immediate prospect of Moore retreating with his army into Portugal, and perhaps even back to the ships. This prospect faded as Moore took the initiative, and Cradock did all he could to support him, by selflessly pushing forward every available man to Moore's army. But soon Moore had passed over the horizon, and Cradock knew that he intended to retreat on Galicia not Portugal. This left Cradock with the ragtag ends of an army, of whom about 5,000 men could take the field. It was far too few to defend Portugal, as Cradock well knew, and there was little help to be looked for from the Portuguese army, which was in a state of utter chaos. Cradock concentrated his army just outside Lisbon and waited for the French advance which would force him to embark his troops and sail home. Unfortunately his intentions were all too obvious, and aroused great popular resentment among the Portuguese who, having no wish to see Junot return, cursed the British and even murdered a few soldiers. Meanwhile

Cradock's army gradually grew in strength as invalids recovered, stragglers from Moore's army found their way to Lisbon, and reinforcements arrived from home. At the end of January, as we have seen, he was able to detach Mackenzie with 4,000 men to Cadiz, but Cradock remained despondent, and showed little hope of being able to defend Portugal when the long-delayed French advance should finally come.[12]

Late in December the Portuguese government took the initiative and asked Britain for the loan of a general to reform and command their army. According to Villiers the request was unprompted and arose from the difficulties which Forjaz, the Minister for War, was having in reforming the army. No officer was named officially, but in private Villiers was told that the choice of Sir Arthur Wellesley would be welcomed. Villiers endorsed this suggestion, commenting that Wellesley was venerated in Portugal, but he privately doubted that Wellesley would accept the command.[13]

Canning replied privately on 14 January that the government was considering the request and that he hoped it would soon be accepted. The Duke of York had agreed that a number of junior British officers be allowed to serve in the Portuguese Army and that these officers be given one step of promotion as an incentive. A fortnight later Canning wrote again and explained that 'Sir Arthur Wellesley is thought too good for the Portuguese. — Will Doyle do?'[14]

Lieutenant-General Sir John Doyle's name was probably suggested by the Duke of York, who believed that he was 'the only British Officer who would undertake or be pleased with the Situation [?] of Commander in Chief of the Portuguese Army'. Doyle, who was then serving in Guernsey, was senior to Wellesley though junior to Cradock, and if he had accepted the command of the Portuguese army, it would have made it almost impossible to appoint Wellesley over his head only a few weeks later. But he was not appointed, apparently because the letter offering him the command went astray.[15]

As the weeks passed without anything being decided, Canning grew more and more impatient, circularizing his colleagues on 10 February to urge that some action be taken to save Portugal before it was too late. Canning wanted a clear commitment that Britain would make a serious attempt to defend Portugal. But Castlereagh was unenthusiastic, and it was he, Wellesley's old friend and patron, who opposed Wellesley's appointment to Portugal, despite the fact that Sir Arthur was willing to accept it.[16] The old myth that Castlereagh deserves the credit for Britain's commitment to Portugal is completely fallacious, being based on his constant friendship with Wellesley. Ironically it was Canning, whom Fortescue so disliked, who had the 'desperate struggle to prevail with the Cabinet', not Castlereagh, his hero among politicians.[17]

Canning did not gain the commitment he sought at the cabinet meeting, nor did he get Wellesley appointed, but he did not completely fail, for on 15 February Major-General William Carr Beresford was appointed to command the Portuguese army. Beresford was then forty years old, a tall man with unprepossessing manners and a glass eye. He had experience dealing with the Portuguese, having commanded the British expedition to Madeira and for a time acted as liaison officer with the Portuguese authorities after Cintra. He had some knowledge of the language, although he did not write it well, and his earlier career had been undistinguished apart from his command of the first, unauthorized and inglorious expedition to Buenos Aires. It has been suggested that he owed his selection to Wellesley's recommendation, or to the fact that as a major-general he was junior to Wellesley. However, the government had been willing to appoint Doyle, who was senior to Wellesley, while few other British officers would have accepted the appointment. Events proved that Beresford was an excellent choice. His reforms to the Portuguese army were immensely successful and laid the foundation for all Wellington's successes from 1810 onwards; but at the time the Portuguese government may well have felt disappointed at the selection of a man whose talents were as yet unproven.[18]

Canning was not satisfied by Beresford's appointment and continued to press for an increased British presence in Portugal. On 24 February he sent another circular round the cabinet arguing that the Spanish refusal to admit British troops into Cadiz made the defence of Portugal the most suitable strategic objective for Britain in the Peninsula. 'If we think the trial worth making at all, we ought surely to make it in the most advantageous manner, with the best instruments we can.' This in his view meant that the British army should be increased to some 15,000 men, that more should be done to mobilize Portuguese resources, and that Sir Arthur Wellesley should be sent to Portugal to command both armies.[19]

But the cabinet remained unconvinced, and Canning expressed his frustration to Villiers: 'It is no want of urgency on my part, or of willingness on Sir A. Wellesley's — but, but, no matter what the impediments are, I shall get over them if I can. . . .' And again: 'I am persuaded, as sincerely and as strongly as you could wish me to be, that Sir A. Wellesley at the head of a large combined force in Portugal, is the first necessary element of success to the Spanish cause.'[20] He had consulted Wellesley, who believed that 5,000 reinforcements and the return of Mackenzie and Sherbrooke (which would bring the army in Portugal up to around 20,000 men) would be sufficient — indeed it would have to be, for there was no prospect of finding more men for Portugal for a long while.

Despite his frustration, Canning was gradually winning the battle. On 27 February Castlereagh had issued orders for Sherbrooke and Mackenzie to return to Lisbon and expressed the government's intention 'to use every exertion to strengthen the defences of Portugal', and to maintain a British presence there 'for as long as possible'. While hardly a rousing call to arms, this was a distinct improvement on his instructions of a month before which had assumed that evacuation was inevitable.[21]

This pessimism is hard to explain. It is true that Sir John Moore had expressed doubts whether the Portuguese frontier was defensible; but

Moore's remarks were made in a very different context, and his judgement was not highly regarded by the ministers. Moreover, the government had received a detailed and considered opinion to the contrary. This came from Colonel Rufane Donkin, an intelligent officer on Cradock's staff who had toured the frontier, and who argued that the line of the Ponsul and Coa Rivers was very strong, though it needed an army of 30,000 men with forty or fifty cannon to hold it against a major French attack. While this was more men than Britain could spare, the general tenor of Donkin's report was most encouraging.[22]

On 7 March Sir Arthur Wellesley contributed his highly valued opinion to the argument in a famous memorandum. In this Wellesley proposed a comprehensive scheme, not merely for the immediate defence of Portugal, but for her transformation into a powerful ally who could assist Britain in turning the tide of the war in the Peninsula. These ideas were not new — Wellesley had outlined some of them in August 1808 before he even landed in Portugal, and Villiers and Canning had advocated them throughout 1809. In essence the argument was that if Britain would defend Portugal for a time and provide the resources to rebuild her army, she would gain a subsidiary force strong enough to make the combined Anglo-Portuguese army a major player in the struggle in the Peninsula.[23]

But even Wellesley's memorandum did not carry the day, and a fortnight later, on 21 March, Canning was near despair, telling the Prime Minister that 'Portugal is a source of constant, daily, and nightly uneasiness to me'. And then suddenly, on 26 March, the battle was over, and Castlereagh wrote to the King conveying the cabinet's recommendation that Sir Arthur Wellesley be appointed to command the army in Portugal, which should be reinforced by a further three regiments of cavalry. The following day the King acquiesced, while expressing his reservations at 'so young a Lieut-General holding so distinguished a command while his seniors remain unemployed' and insisting that if the army was subsequently increased the claims of these senior officers be considered.[24]

The reason for this abrupt success is obscure — for it does not appear to have been due to fresh intelligence from the Peninsula or Austria. Possibly the cabinet had only just realized that with the return of Mackenzie and Sherbrooke to Lisbon, and the arrival of Hill's reinforcements, they would have a substantial army in Portugal which ought to be commanded by a general whom they implicitly trusted. Possibly Canning's insistence finally wore down his opponents, or perhaps his success was due to the end of the Parliamentary crisis over the Duke of York which permitted the ministers to concentrate their attention on the war for the first time in months.

Yet even Wellesley's appointment did not signal the complete adoption of his ideas by the cabinet. His instructions were cautious and defensive. The ministers, including Canning, remained disillusioned with Spain, and were unwilling to look beyond the immediate defence of Portugal. And so the foundation of Britain's future strategy throughout the war was laid, not as the keystone of a master plan, but as an ad hoc decision to try to preserve an existing asset. The advantages of Lisbon as the base for the British army were not obvious compared with those of Cadiz. It was not a natural fortress, the focus for Spanish resistance, or the centre of trade with Spanish America; rather it was strategically marginal, and the capital of a nation whose military and financial resources were feeble. Yet as Wellesley had already perceived, the very weakness of Portugal, which made her totally dependent on Britain, could be turned to advantage. It was this weakness which enabled the British to force through the painful but essential reforms that were to make the Portuguese troops an integral part of Wellington's army. Britain could never have coerced Spain as she coerced Portugal; nor, without outside help, would the Portuguese have continued the struggle with the obstinacy and determination which the Spaniards consistently displayed. More by good luck than good judgement the ministers had hit upon the best possible strategy for the British to pursue in the Peninsula, although it took a considerable time for them to appreciate the fact.

The long tussle over Portugal had by no means preoccupied the ministers during the first three months of 1809: indeed, one explanation for the delay in reaching a final decision is that the government's attention was absorbed by other issues, most notably the scandal over allegations by the Duke of York's former mistress, Mary Anne Clarke, that the Duke had accepted bribes in return for promotion and other advantages to army officers. The allegations were disproved, but the Duke's conduct was widely regarded as indiscreet and he reluctantly resigned on 18 March. The King promptly, and without consulting his ministers, appointed the ageing Sir David Dundas to the command, on the understanding that Dundas would retire as soon as it was politically convenient for the Duke to return to the Horse Guards.[25]

Meanwhile intermittent contact continued with Austria. On 13 February the government learnt that Napoleon had returned to Paris, and that 'war with Austria is considered as certain'. On the same day Canning recommended to the King that Benjamin Bathurst be sent to Malta with instructions to proceed to Vienna to represent Britain, if and when war broke out, or if he was invited by the Austrian government. The choice of Bathurst was careful: though a diplomat, he was sufficiently obscure for his departure not to be noticed.[26]

The Austrians had already dispatched a representative to London: Count Wallmoden, a Hanoverian officer and descendant of George II by one of his mistresses (and father-in-law of Count Stein, the recently dismissed Prussian minister). Wallmoden reached London on 28 March 1809, bringing with him confirmation that Austria was about to go to war, and an appeal for British financial and military assistance. Their proposals were still very ambitious: an initial subsidy of £2 million followed by £400,000 per month, and a request that the British mount diversions in Italy, the Peninsula and northern Germany.[27]

The evident resolve of the Austrian government made Britain more sympathetic than in December, but the constraints on British aid remained real. Canning promised to dispatch £250,000 to the Mediterranean at once, and to do his best to build up a war chest of up to £1 million at Malta for Austria's use in the event of war. Even to raise this much bullion Canning had to appeal to the Spanish government, which had recently received large shipments from South America, to provide silver in exchange for British bills of exchange. To raise further funds for Austria the British government proposed a novel scheme to sell between £3 million and £4 million of British 5 per cent exchequer bills in Vienna, the interest to be paid twice yearly in Vienna by Britain, and the capital raised going directly into the Austrian exchequer. It was a generous offer, but the Austrian treasury rejected it as impractical. In the event, the temporary collapse of the Continental System when Napoleon concentrated his forces led to a surge in British exports, enabling the government to raise money through the more traditional means of bills of exchange. In less than three months, from early April to early July, Britain provided Austria with almost £1.2 million in subsidies. It was less than Austria had asked for, and far less than she needed, but given Britain's other commitments, and the effect of the Continental System on her balance of trade, it was not discreditable. As we shall see, the money was sorely missed in other theatres.[28]

Military cooperation proved even more difficult. The government would not undertake a major new commitment in the Mediterranean: it was too remote, the necessary men and money were not available, and the ministers were sceptical of the advantages of extended operations in Italy. In any case, with the Austrians about to begin the war, there was no time to organize a campaign from London. But the ministers had no objection to the British commanders in the Mediterranean taking the initiative with their existing forces and acting to support the Austrians; and to some extent this is what happened. Admiral Collingwood organized naval cooperation in the Adriatic, and Sir John Stuart mounted a diversionary attack in the Bay of Naples. With more energy and better judgement Stuart might, perhaps, have achieved more; but as the Austrians began the campaign behind the Isonzo, and were soon in full retreat, there was little which Britain could do to assist them in the southern theatre of operations.[29]

The Austrian plea for British exertion in the Peninsula had been partially answered already with the appointment of Wellesley to Portugal, and it may have had some influence when the ministers reluctantly agreed to extend his operations into Spain (see below, p. 92). This left the Austrian request for a diversion in north Germany between the Ems and the Elbe. There were good arguments for such an operation, and the Austrians were not the only party proposing it. The government had already received pressing solicitations from Ludwig von Kleist, who claimed to represent a secret insurrectionary organization in Prussia and the small states of Germany. The British treated Kleist's claims with caution, especially as he was wanting money and lacked the support of his government. Yet Kleist's credentials appeared genuine as far as they went, and even if his claims were exaggerated, his evidence suggested that a British army would receive significant local support, while there was the chance that its arrival would spark a series of patriotic risings across Germany. An expedition to northern Germany would have a far more direct influence on the Austrian war than operations in Italy or the Peninsula, and if the Austrian cause prospered, such an expedition might help to bring Prussia into the war.[30]

These arguments certainly had an appeal: but they were not unfamiliar to the ministers who had been persuaded by them in 1805, and had dispatched a large expedition, which had arrived at Bremen just in time to hear the news of Austerlitz. As this had shown, a British expedition to northern Germany was totally dependent on the success of its Continental allies. If they failed, Napoleon could concentrate his forces against the British, and they would have no alternative but a hasty and ignominious evacuation, having achieved nothing. This was one argument against such an expedition. Another was that to be effective the force sent to northern Germany had to be a substantial army capable of extended operations, while the troops available in Britain were a heterogeneous collection, some good regiments still suffering from the effects of the retreat to Coruña, others being second battalions of poor quality, and the whole lacking cohesion. Finally, an extended campaign would require large amounts of specie, which was simply not available.

There was an alternative operation, long contemplated, which minimized these disadvantages: this was to strike at Napoleon's great naval base at Antwerp and at his squadron in the River Scheldt. A coup de main such as this, with limited objectives, would not require allied cooperation or extensive campaigning from the army, and would cost far less. If successful it would achieve an important British objective — French forces in the Scheldt had given the Admiralty nightmares for years — while at the same time creating a diversion for Austria. The cabinet had favoured such an operation in March, before Wallmoden reached England, but there had not been enough troops available. The plan was revived in May and Castlereagh, consulting no one but Portland, offered the command to Chatham, who accepted it after characteristic delay and hesitation. It was to prove a singularly inappropriate choice for an expedition whose success would always depend on its speed and boldness.[31]

The government was still not finally committed to the expedition. During the last days of May Castlereagh sought advice from the Commander-in-Chief and other leading officers at the Horse Guards. Sir David Dundas replied that while 'the object to be obtained is a most important and desirable one', the 'service is one of very great risk, . . . in which the safe return of the army so employed may be very precarious', and the other officers were almost equally discouraging. Despite this response Castlereagh did not give up the plan. Reports from the Scheldt described the defences as being in poor condition and the garrisons much depleted by the needs of the Austrian war.[32] Early in June he consulted Sir Home Popham, a daring naval officer with special expertise in combined operations and some knowledge of the Low Countries. Popham was much more encouraging than the officers at the Horse Guards, but he stressed the need for haste, stating that the expedition must sail by the end of June or risk disruption from adverse weather. On 5 June the government received an unenthusiastic report from General von der Decken, who had been sent to reconnoitre the situation in northern Germany, which led the cabinet finally to decide against that plan, at least for the moment. Three days later news reached London of an Austrian victory over Napoleon at Aspern-Essling. If Britain was to take advantage of Napoleon's preoccupation with affairs on the Danube and strike a blow in favour of Austria, she should delay no longer. On 15 June the cabinet therefore gave preliminary approval to the Antwerp plan, subject to further information on one point of detail. This was resolved within a week and on 21 June the ministers formally recommended that the operation proceed. The blind old King had seen many expeditions sail from Britain in his long reign, and evidently he had doubts about this one, for he acquiesced in the decision with reluctance, expressing his regret that 'the information upon which the practicability has been finally decided had . . . been so imperfect'. Events were to prove that his doubts were not misplaced.[33]

5

The Military Campaigns of 1809, April–September

By far the most important campaign for Britain in 1809 was fought on the Danube hundreds of miles from the nearest British troops. If the Austrians had defeated Napoleon, or even held their own and protracted the war into 1810, the whole balance of forces in Europe would have shifted.

The Austrian army began the campaign on 9 April by invading Bavaria without a declaration of war. Although Napoleon was expecting war, the sudden commencement of hostilities caught the French forces in some disarray. But the Archduke Charles was intimidated by Napoleon and lacked the confidence to exploit his advantage, while the French troops, though inferior to the *Grande Armée* of 1805–7, were still better than the Austrians. A few days of hard marching and fighting, culminating in the confused Battle of Eckmühl (22 April 1809), restored the French position, and the Austrians retreated to the north bank of the Danube. Napoleon did not directly pursue them but advanced down the Danube valley to Vienna, which he captured on 13 May.

The rapid French advance destroyed Austrian hopes of gaining the initiative and encouraging widespread risings in Germany and Italy. There were a few small outbreaks, most famously that of Major Schill, but the only serious problem for the French and their allies was a courageous and patriotic uprising against the Bavarians in the Tyrol. Prussia remained quiet, while the Russians occupied some Austrian territory in Poland — much to the annoyance of the pro-French Poles. But these were secondary operations and incidental to the course of the war.

From Vienna Napoleon had to cross the Danube to advance against the Archduke Charles, and all the bridges had been broken. On 18 May the French established an advanced position on the island of Lobau a few miles downstream from Vienna, and on the 20th their leading troops crossed to the north bank and occupied the villages of Aspern and Essling. But the Archduke Charles was closer than Napoleon had realized, and on the afternoon of 21 May he attacked the 24,000 French who had crossed the river with an army of 95,000 men. The Battle of Aspern-Essling lasted until the early hours of 23 May. As the French struggled desperately to hold their position, the single bridge which was their lifeline was repeatedly broken and repaired. Finally Napoleon ordered his forces to withdraw back to Lobau on the night of 22 May. Each army had lost in excess of 20,000 casualties, including the intrepid Marshal Lannes, who was mortally wounded. Aspern-Essling was the greatest defeat Napoleon had ever suffered, and it reverberated around Europe. But his army was still intact and occupying Vienna, and his secret enemies, including the Prussians, would not venture into open hostilities without a clearer sign of his demise.

After the battle both generals concentrated their efforts on collecting as many troops as possible for the next, decisive encounter. The Austrians recalled their army under the Archduke John from Italy, but it had to march by a circuitous route to avoid Napoleon, and arrived too late. Napoleon was more successful, gathering troops from far and wide, including his Italian army, under his stepson Eugène Beauharnais. When he again crossed the Danube he had an army of almost 190,000 men, over 30,000 more than the Austrians.

Napoleon had made meticulous preparations for his second attempt, reconnoitring the ground and paying particular attention to the vital bridges. The crossing began on the night of 4/5 July, still from Lobau but at a point slightly further downstream. The Battle of Wagram lasted two days (5–6 July), with many changes of fortune. On the whole, Napoleon found the opposition tougher than he had previously encountered, while the large numbers of troops and their lower quality inhibited his tactical finesse. In the end the Austrians were soundly defeated, though not completely broken. Both armies lost nearly 40,000 casualties and prisoners.

The French army slowly advanced after the Austrians but there was no vigorous pursuit. A few days later there was a combat at Znaim (10–11 July) which was followed by an armistice (12 July) and peace negotiations which dragged on until October. By the Treaty of Schönbrunn (14 October 1809) the Austrians ceded Illyria to the French Empire, Salzburg to Bavaria, and western Galicia to the Duchy of Warsaw, and agreed to pay a large indemnity and join the Continental System. It had taken Napoleon barely three months to crush Austria, despite his entanglement in Spain.

The Austrian war had little immediate effect on the balance of forces in the Peninsula. Napoleon had ordered the Imperial Guard to follow him when he left Spain in late January, and in April he briefly withdrew Mortier's corps from active operations in case it was needed in Germany — though this did not prevent it playing an important part in French operations in July. Otherwise French units received fewer drafts and reinforcements, and the French marshals fewer instructions, but there was no great reduction in French strength in Spain.

Before Napoleon had returned to France he had dictated a wildly overoptimistic plan to complete the conquest of the Peninsula. Soult was ordered to push south from Coruña into Portugal, occupying Oporto and Lisbon by the middle of February. He was then to lend one of his divisions to Victor, who would invade Andalusia by an unexpected route beginning at Badajoz, thus securing surprise. The last Spanish provinces on the east coast were to be secured by the two corps commanded by Mortier and Junot when they had captured Saragossa. Bad roads, winter weather and fierce local opposition delayed Soult so that his invasion of Portugal did not begin until 9 March and he did not reach Oporto until the 29th. There he halted, resting his army and attempting to cultivate Portuguese support for French rule. The French forces in central Spain were too weak to launch a large-scale offensive, but they held their own fairly easily, defeating Spanish counter-attacks at Ucles in January and Ciudad Real and Medellin at the end of March. News of these last defeats caused great concern when it reached London, just as Sir Arthur Wellesley was about to sail for Portugal.

Wellesley's initial instructions, issued on 2 April, stated that although 'The defence of Portugal . . . [was] the first and immediate object' of his command, he could use his discretion in determining how best he could cooperate with the Spaniards as well as the Portuguese. But on the following day these orders were amended, to prohibit Wellesley from embarking on any campaign in Spain without 'the express authority of your government'.[1] This was explicitly done as retaliation for the Spanish refusal to admit British troops into Cadiz, and Wellesley was instructed that if Frere announced that the Spanish government had changed their mind on this point, he should immediately detach an adequate force for its defence. This was an awkward provision for Wellesley, who might thus suddenly be required to remove several thousand men from his army, and it shows the continuing importance which the ministers placed on Cadiz.

Wellesley sailed on 15 April and arrived in Lisbon a week later, where he was relieved to find that neither Soult nor Victor was advancing against him. He quickly decided to seize the initiative and go onto the attack, choosing Soult as his first target, because an attack on Victor would need Spanish cooperation and take longer to prepare. The British reached the Douro opposite Oporto on 12 May, but the French had broken the bridge and were hoping to hold the line of the river for a few days while they organized a leisurely retreat into Spain. Their guard was slack, however, and the British found four old wine barges, which they used to carry small parties of troops across the river, who then occupied the Bishop's seminary — a strong isolated building whose approaches could be covered by artillery fire from the British bank. By the time the French noticed what was happening the British were well established in the seminary and beat off some hastily organized attacks. Error was compounded when, in order to make another attack on the British position, the French withdrew their garrison from the town. Many of the Portuguese inhabitants promptly crossed the river in their small boats, and returned carrying British soldiers. Soult's army fled in great confusion, pursued for a week by Wellesley until the French abandoned all their artillery and equipment and took to goat tracks to escape. The operation was brilliantly conceived and executed, and reveals a bold, opportunistic streak in Wellesley which has often been forgotten. He was justly proud of his triumph, although his boast to Villiers that Soult '[is] so crippled that he can do no harm, and he may be destroyed by Romana', proved over-optimistic.[2]

The reaction in England to the news of Oporto shows how far attitudes to the Peninsula had become partisan in the wake of Moore's retreat. Supporters of the government naturally rejoiced, and though Castlereagh did his best to keep expectations within reason, even his own father believed that the news presaged the liberation of the whole Peninsula. The Opposition for their part were equally wrong-headed in their despondency and determination to minimize the victory, with Grey, for example, writing that 'Wellesley's success . . . appears to have been nothing more than an affair of a rear-guard, and is ridiculously magnified'.[3]

The news of the victory arrived most opportunely, just as the ministers were considering a letter from Wellesley, written only a fortnight after he arrived in Portugal, asking that his instructions be altered so that he could conduct operations against the French, and in particular Victor's corps, well beyond the Portuguese frontier. The request received indirect support from Frere, who wrote urging that the British army play a greater role in Spain, notwithstanding the continuing Spanish refusal to make any concessions over Cadiz.[4] But there was strong opposition to the idea in London, both from the cabinet and the King. Only a month before, Canning had told Frere that 'there is a fixed determination not to hazard a British Army (*the* British Army) again in Spain on anything like the same terms as before'.[5] The ministers did not trust the Spaniards, and had no wish to venture their army in the perils of an extended campaign where the support of an unreliable ally would be essential. On the other hand they trusted Wellesley as they trusted no other general. His ability was widely recognized in the cabinet, not least by Canning, who wrote to Frere that 'In Wellesley . . . you will find everything that you can wish — frankness — temper — honesty quickness — comprehensiveness — and military Ability — not only eminent beyond any other military Commander that could be chosen — but perhaps possessed by him alone, of all our Commanders, in a degree that qualifies for great undertakings.'[6] But it was not just Canning who approved of Wellesley — within the cabinet he was a general favourite as well as a favourite general.

Nonetheless, reluctance breathes through every word of the cabinet's permission, which allowed Wellesley 'to extend your operations in Spain beyond the provinces immediately adjacent to the Portuguese frontier, provided you shall be of opinion that your doing so is material in a military point of view, to the success of your operations, and not inconsistent with the safety of Portugal'.[7] This made it perfectly clear that if Wellesley chose to launch an extended campaign in Spain, the decision and the responsibility were his — they merely granted him, at his request, the discretion to do so if he thought it best.

But although the cabinet gave their consent reluctantly they did not hesitate to support Wellesley with as many men as they could. Already the elite Light Brigade had been ordered to Portugal, although it was detained for many weeks, first by the effects of the Coruña Campaign, and then by contrary winds. At the same time as they gave Wellesley permission to extend his operations into Spain the ministers also ordered that a further 5,000 men be sent out to him. This reinforcement would, they hoped, secure him against any sudden disaster, and so permit the return of some of the large and expensive fleet of transports in the Tagus — ships that were needed for the Walcheren expedition.[8]

The government also did its best to find specie to send to Portugal, but it was only with a great effort that they could gather £230,000 in 'dollars, doubloons and Portugal gold' and dispatch it in early June.[9] This arrived in Lisbon on 15 June and did not reach the army, which was waiting for it at Abrantes, until 25 June. By this time Wellesley was almost frantic with impatience. As early as 5 May he had written to Huskisson (the Secretary to the Treasury) explaining the dire financial position of the army and requesting that £100,000 in specie be sent immediately. As time passed the problem grew worse and Wellesley was forced to 'request' a loan of £10,000 from the merchants of Oporto. The army could not be paid and the troops began plundering the countryside. After his pursuit of Soult Wellesley brought the army down to Abrantes but he did not dare begin his advance into Spain until at least some money arrived and discipline was restored.

Wellesley's temper was not improved by the wait at Abrantes, and he complained frequently, bitterly and unreasonably of want of support from home, for example telling Villiers, 'We are terribly distressed for money. . . . I suspect the Ministers in England are very indifferent to our operations in this country.' This preposterous statement was not an isolated outburst and shows one of the least attractive sides of Wellesley's complex character. Whenever his plans were frustrated he lashed out without considering that those he was attacking might be just as concerned to overcome the obstacle as he was himself. He seldom showed much appreciation for the problems of others, particularly when they involved money. Thus on 11 June he seriously wrote to Castlereagh that the government should send £200,000 in specie to Portugal *each month* for some months. This was far beyond the government's means, but it was Wellesley, not the ministers, who had urged the advance into Spain for which the money was needed. Faced with this barrage of complaints, Castlereagh and his successors responded with the utmost tact, redoubling their efforts to secure specie, and soothing their troublesome general with reassurances and flattery.[10]

Despite his grumbles, Wellesley had high hopes for the coming campaign. Although there were large French forces in Spain they were poorly distributed, with too many men in the remote north-western provinces, and too few in central Spain. Wellesley hoped that by combining his own army with that of Cuesta and gaining the cooperation of General Venegas in La Mancha, he could force King Joseph either to evacuate Madrid or fight at a disadvantage. In either case he was confident of driving the French back to the line of the Ebro, and possibly beyond, although the ultimate success of the campaign would depend on events in Germany.[11]

Wellesley's plan needed the cooperation of the Spanish armies, and this inevitably involved him in Spanish politics — about which at this time he knew little. The Supreme Junta was riven with factions. Many of its members distrusted the British, but there was also great distrust of the political ambitions of some of the Spanish generals, notably Cuesta. Those who distrusted Cuesta welcomed the return of the British army to Spain, hoping that it would act as a counterweight, and were dismayed when Wellesley argued, on purely military grounds, that Cuesta's army should be reinforced. Cuesta himself was suspicious of the British, while Frere was deeply involved in Spanish politics, and generally sympathized with Cuesta's opponents. None of this boded well for easy cooperation.

Wellesley left Abrantes on 27 June, and the advanced guard crossed into Spain on 3 July, reaching Plasencia on the 8th. During the march the British general received reports that Soult's corps had withdrawn from Galicia and that Mortier's was at Valladolid. He asked Cuesta to occupy the Puerto de Baños and the Puerto de Perales — the passes which lay on the left flank of the British advance — but was not greatly concerned, believing that Soult merely intended to push into northern Portugal and ravage the countryside.[12]

On 11 July Wellesley and Cuesta met at the Spanish headquarters. There had already been some differences over their plans, but they now agreed to advance together against Victor, while Venegas kept Sebastiani's French corps busy in La Mancha. After the meeting Wellesley wrote to Frere, 'The general sentiment of the army . . . appears to be contempt of the Junta and of the present form of government; great confidence in Cuesta, and a belief that he is too powerful for the Junta, and that he will overturn that government.' Frere communicated this to Martin de Garay, the sympathetic Secretary of the Junta, and an opponent of Cuesta. Garay replied — perhaps with a touch of bravado — that Cuesta was unfit to command his army, and offered to replace him if Wellesley would make a formal complaint. But then, in another interview, Garay asked what the British army would do if Cuesta attempted to mount a coup, and Frere could only reply that he 'could not imagine that any case could occur in which Sir A. Wellesley would think it right or I for him to shed a single drop of Spanish blood in any of their civil disputes'. And there, for the moment, the matter was allowed to rest.[13]

But it was not long before another issue arose which threatened allied cooperation. The British had advanced into Spain expecting to hire trans-

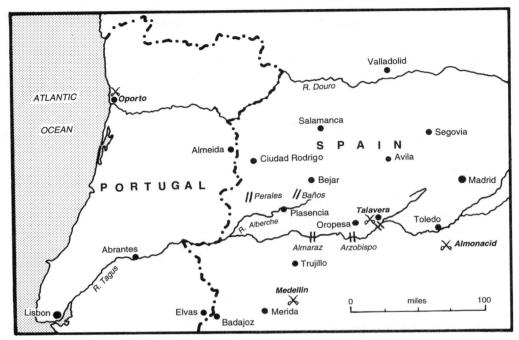

4   The Talavera campaign, 1809

port locally and to find plentiful supplies. But Estremadura was a poor province which had been stripped bare by the passage of French and Spanish armies, while the British commissaries were still very inexperienced. The problem was a serious one, but Wellesley's reaction was extraordinary. He accused the Spaniards of deliberately withholding supplies and threatened to withdraw from the campaign if he was not provided with transport. Frere made strong representations to the Spanish government, who promised to solve the problem, although in reality there was little that it could do.[14]

These promises satisfied Wellesley for the moment, and the advance continued. On the afternoon of 22 July the allies came up with Victor's army which was occupying a strong position near Talavera and Wellesley proposed a dawn attack on the 23rd, to which Cuesta reluctantly consented, only later to change his mind and refuse. He was probably right, for the ground was difficult and broken, the enemy active and alert, and the Spanish troops not the best: a night march was likely to lead to chaos and confusion, if not an outright defeat. The allies would have done far better to have attacked on the 23rd, but instead they spent the day wrangling, and Victor, who realized that he was heavily outnumbered, slipped away that night.

Wellesley now announced that he would advance no further. He had fulfilled his obligations, Victor was in full retreat, and the army had not been provided with the transport and supplies it needed. The British troops had received no food for the last two days, although it 'is ridiculous to pretend that the country cannot supply our wants'. He told Frere that the English people would never allow another of their armies to be sent to Spain when they heard how he had been received, although when writing to Castlereagh he was optimistic that the problem would be resolved.[15]

At first sight this looks like a crude attempt to extort supplies which Wellesley genuinely, if mistakenly, believed were being withheld; but there is another possible interpretation. Cuesta would certainly pursue Victor with or without the British, and Wellesley had no doubt that he would 'get himself into a scrape'. 'If the enemy discover that we are not with him, he will be beaten, or must retire', but 'any movement by me to his assistance is quite out of the question'. This remarkable statement is made all the more sinister by another letter from Wellesley to Frere on the same day:

> I find Gen. Cuesta more and more impractical every day. It is impossible to do business with him, and very uncertain that any operation will succeed in which he has any concern. . . . He has quarrelled with some of his principal officers; and I understand that all are dissatisfied with him. . . .
>
> Upon the whole, I understand that there is a material change in the sentiments of the army respecting him; and I am told (although I cannot say that I know it to be true) that if the government were now to deprive him of the command, the army would allow that their order should be carried into execution. However, I think that the government, before they take this step, ought to have some cause for removing him, the justice of which would be obvious to everybody, or they ought to be more certain that their order would not be resisted by the army than I have it in my power to make them.[16]

Reading this letter it is hard to avoid the conclusion that Wellesley was deliberately abandoning Cuesta in the expectation that he would be defeated, and then removed from his command. The logistical problems facing Wellesley were certainly serious, but halting his army in the exhausted country around Talavera would only make them worse. His whole conduct in the affair was extraordinary. To withdraw his army in the middle of a promising campaign was bad enough, but at the same time to attempt to subvert the position of his Spanish counterpart is scarcely credible. It is interesting to consider Wellesley's reaction if Cuesta had suddenly withdrawn his army while at the same time conspiring with the Whigs in London to have Wellesley sacked. That Wellesley was a military genius and Cuesta a bumbling fool is true, but is this in itself a sufficient excuse?

Compared with Wellesley in the matter, Cuesta appears a champion of harmony and good will between the allies rather than the surly, suspicious old man that he was.

As Wellesley expected, Cuesta had no hesitation in pursuing the French, but Victor was now joined by King Joseph, with a large part of his small reserve, and Sebastiani, who had given Venegas the slip. The combined French army had some 46,000 men compared with Cuesta's 33,000; but the old Spaniard quickly realized the danger and was able to fall back to Talavera without disaster. The allied armies reunited and occupied a strong position which Wellesley had chosen running north from the town to a steep hill, the Cerro de Medellin, some three kilometres away. The Spaniards occupied the right of the line, where the ground was broken by many enclosures, while the centre and the Cerro de Medellin were held by the 20,000 men of Wellesley's army.

The French advanced guard arrived opposite the allied position on the evening of 27 July, and Victor launched an immediate partial attack on the Cerro de Medellin which was repulsed with heavy loss after some hard and confused fighting. The battle was renewed at 5 a.m. on the next day, with another, more carefully prepared attack on the crucial hill: this too was defeated, although a British counter-attack got out of hand and suffered heavily. A long lull followed which lasted the rest of the morning and into the afternoon. Soldiers of both sides mingled freely as they got water from the Portina brook and recovered their wounded comrades. Apart from the hotheaded Victor, the French commanders had no wish to renew the battle, for they knew, as Wellesley and Cuesta did not, that Soult, with 50,000 men of his own, Ney's and Mortier's corps, was advancing through the Puerto de Baños onto Wellesley's lines of communication with Portugal. If Joseph and his generals could hold their position for a few days, the allies would be trapped between the two French armies. But then news arrived that Venegas had advanced to Toledo and was threatening Madrid. Unless troops were promptly dispatched against him the capital would fall, and all Castile would probably burst into furious rebellion. Yet it would be dangerous to make any significant detachment, as the allies already outnumbered Joseph's army. It was an awkward dilemma and led the French to decide to try a third, much bigger, attack on the allied army, which, if successful, would resolve their problems.

The new French attack stretched along the whole British line and beyond, with an attempt to turn the allied left flank. The Spaniards on the allied right were barely engaged, but Cuesta detached two divisions (one of infantry and one of cavalry) and a battery of heavy field artillery (12-pounders) which gave the British good support. The crucial fighting in this phase of the battle occurred in the centre of the allied line, not on the hill. Sherbrooke's division, including the Guards and two brigades of the King's German Legion, repulsed the first French attack, but pursued too far and became disordered. A second French attack swept them back, and

Wellesley had only Mackenzie's brigade and the 48th Foot to hold the line. It proved just sufficient: the French attack was halted and finally driven back, as were their other attacks on the rest of the line. For a time the battle had hung in the balance, but in the end the French were completely defeated and demoralized, though not routed.

Talavera was the largest and bitterest battle the British army had fought in sixteen years of war. It suffered 5,400 casualties (one in four of those present), of whom 800 were killed. The French lost over 7,000 men, including 761 dead, while the Spanish losses were light.[17] On the night after the battle the French withdrew behind the Alberche and were not pursued.

After the battle events moved rapidly. At first the allies hoped to capture Madrid, but then they learnt of Soult's advance, although not the size of his army, which they put at only about 20,000 men. The British had received valuable reinforcements just after the battle (the famous Light Brigade) and the army was full of confidence. Wellesley therefore proposed that he should march back and defeat Soult while the Spaniards held Talavera: with Soult out of the way the allies could still advance against Madrid. Cuesta agreed to this plan, but soon received a captured letter which revealed Soult's true strength. He therefore followed Wellesley with his army, hoping that together they could defeat Soult and continue the campaign. Wellesley at first refused to believe that Soult had such a powerful army, and when he was convinced, he insisted on immediately retreating to the south bank of the Tagus and giving up the campaign. This disgusted Cuesta, but then it was not the Spanish army which had borne the brunt of the fighting at Talavera. One consequence of the sudden change of plan was that Victor reoccupied Talavera on 5 August, capturing hundreds of British wounded, who felt that they had been abandoned by Cuesta.[18]

This was not quite the end of the campaign. On the 8th Soult forced the Tagus, mauling Cuesta's rearguard in the process, and on the 11th Venegas was defeated, in a battle he should never have fought, at Almonacid. The French had the opportunity to extend their operations, but for various reasons — including the excessive heat — chose not to. Both sides fell back on the congenial occupation of mutual recrimination. Cuesta was good at this, but did not enjoy it for long — on 12 August he was partially paralysed by a stroke and he resigned his command on the following day.

So ended the Talavera Campaign, which had promised so much and delivered so little. The glorious and hard-fought victory was barren, for despite it the French were in a better strategic position in August than they had been in June, and Anglo-Spanish relations were certainly no better. Wellesley had had his campaign in Spain and it was a costly failure. Yet it would be unfair to criticize the general plan of campaign too harshly. The strategic opening which Wellesley sought to exploit really existed, and if the campaign had succeeded it would have dealt an enormous blow to the reputation of French armies in the Peninsula and throughout Europe. It only failed because, quite fortuitously, the French evacuated their forces from Galicia after Ney and Soult had quarrelled, and because Soult recognized the opportunity to strike at the British lines of communication. In the actual conduct of the campaign there is much both to admire and criticize. On the one hand the military skills shown in the advance, and the handling of the army at Talavera; on the other the behaviour towards Cuesta and the tantrum over supplies which threatened to derail the whole campaign.

The reaction in England to the campaign had little to do with such considerations. Despite Oporto, expectations were generally low: the public remained disillusioned with Spain, and were preoccupied with the Austrian war and the expedition to the Scheldt. The ministers were a little anxious, although their faith in Wellesley remained undiminished. Castlereagh responded to some criticism of the general by telling his brother, '*Every step Wellesley has taken since he landed appears to me to have been full of Judgement, and he has fulfill'd every wish I could have formed*'; a fortnight later he added that far from being too cautious, Wellesley was, if anything, too bold. The government welcomed news of Talavera with relief, Canning telling a friend, 'I never received so welcome news. The plot to run down Arthur Wellesley was thickening — But God be praised, this defeats it entirely.'[19] There were the customary celebrations, and Wellesley was created 'Baron Douro of Wellesley in the county of Somerset, and Viscount Wellington of Talavera, and of Wellington in the same county'. But the casualty lists brought much grief, and George III was not the only one who 'deeply laments that success, however glorious, has been so dearly bought'.[20]

News of the subsequent allied retreat, and particularly stories of Cuesta's 'abandonment' of the British wounded, fuelled the reaction and further soured the popular mood towards Spain. The radical Whigs bitterly criticized Wellesley's peerage and the handsome pension which went with it, alleging that he had only fought for a title. The Common Council of the City of London called for a rigid, impartial and general enquiry into the campaign, while even so gallant a soldier as Thomas Graham was hostile: 'The honor bestowed on Sir A. W. for the worst campaign ever made is too ludicrous and evinces a partiality the most disgraceful.'[21] This reaction became lost in the political crisis which was engulfing the Portland Ministry in the aftermath of the Walcheren Expedition, but nonetheless it helped to confirm the Opposition's hostility to the Peninsular commitment in general, and criticism of Wellington in particular. There was no political consensus on the strategy Britain should adopt in 1810.

On 28 July 1809, the same day as the Battle of Talavera, and more than three weeks after the Battle of Wagram, the British expedition to the Scheldt finally set sail. It was 'incomparably the greatest armament that [had] ever left the shores of England': nearly 40,000 troops in over 600 vessels, including thirty-five ships of the line.[22] Castlereagh had assembled such a large force in order to give it every chance of success, but the preparations had taken time, and already the best of the season was gone. News of Wagram and the Austrian armistice reached London before the armament sailed, but the ministers still hoped that Austria might resume the war and that the expedition might encourage her.

The expedition to the Scheldt was an immensely complicated operation, or rather series of operations, all subject to the vagaries of wind, weather, current and shoals in one of the trickiest waterways in Europe. Bad weather posed problems from the outset, forcing the British constantly to amend their plans. Nonetheless, two of the three initial landings, those on the islands of Walcheren and South Beveland, were successful and the troops pushed forward with great energy. Flushing, the main port on Walcheren, was besieged on 1 August, and the small fort of Batz at the far end of South Beveland was occupied without resistance on the following day, so that the leading British forces were within fifteen miles of Antwerp. But the third attack, on Cadsand, was first postponed because of confused orders and the weather, and then abandoned altogether as the French received substantial reinforcements. This failure jeopardized the success of the entire expedition, for without possession of Cadsand British vessels could not push up the West Scheldt until Flushing had fallen, and without the troops and heavy guns carried by these vessels there could be no advance beyond Batz.

Flushing was a well-fortified town, with a garrison of 5,000 men, and could only be taken by a regular siege. The British began constructing batteries on 3 August, but it took them nearly a week to drag the heavy siege guns across Walcheren island in the rain and mud. Meanwhile the garrison of Flushing had been increased to nearly 8,000 men as the weather prevented the Royal Navy stopping French troops slipping across the channel from Cadsand. On 7 August the garrison made a sortie but were beaten back, while the sea-dykes were cut in an attempt to flood the British trenches. But the siege continued, and on the afternoon of 13 August the bombardment began; the town was set on fire, but held out until early on the 16th when it surrendered. The British took nearly 6,000 prisoners, while another 1,800 'enemy' troops deserted (many of them Prussians and Spaniards who had failed to escape with Romana in 1808).

The time lost in the siege of Flushing could not be regained. Since the first appearance of the expedition the French had been hurrying troops to Antwerp and other points under threat. The defences of Antwerp had been strengthened and the naval squadron was now upstream beyond the town. There were nearly 50,000 French and Dutch troops facing the British by the time Flushing fell: they were not of the best quality and were not well organized, but more were arriving every day. Even if everything had gone according to plan it is doubtful if Chatham's army could have taken Antwerp; the failure at Cadsand and delay at Flushing made it virtually impossible.

After the fall of Flushing the expedition slowly moved forward to Batz, with bad roads and adverse winds delaying both men and ships. According to contemporary critics Chatham was personally dilatory and failed to inspire any sense of urgency or purpose, while his relations with Strachan, the naval commander, were increasingly strained. It was not until 23 August that the expedition was concentrated at Batz, and then another couple of days were spent reconnoitring French positions and preparing plans for a further advance. The leisurely pace of these movements suggests that Chatham had already given up hope of taking Antwerp. On 26 August he discussed the prospect for operations with Strachan and senior naval and military officers, and they concluded that there was little chance of success. A council of war on the following day endorsed this opinion, and with their support Chatham decided to abandon the expedition. Now that the decision was made, Strachan objected, possibly in an attempt to throw all the blame for failure onto the army, and open dissension between the commanders was added to the expedition's other problems.

The withdrawal proved almost as slow as the advance. The last British troops did not leave South Beveland until 6 September, and it was not until the 14th that Chatham sailed for England, leaving behind a garrison of 19,000 men on Walcheren which the government still hoped to retain. These delays were costly, for fever had appeared among the troops on South Beveland early in August and had quickly spread to Walcheren. By 28 August there were 4,000 men sick on South Beveland alone, a figure which had doubled by 3 September. A few days later the total for the whole army was 11,000 men sick, or more than a quarter of the entire force. The troops left on Walcheren suffered dreadfully: by 1 October 9,000 were sick and another thousand had died. Altogether nearly 4,000 British soldiers died of 'Walcheren fever', compared with only 106 who were killed in action during the whole expedition. Many of those who survived were permanently weakened and had recurrent attacks of fever, so that as late as March 1812 Wellington was complaining of the unhealthiness of troops who had served in the expedition. There were still 11,000 men on the sick list on 1 February 1810, and their slow recovery hindered the government's efforts to reinforce the army in Portugal.[23]

The severity of the fever should have led to the rapid evacuation of Walcheren, but the decision was delayed for months by the collapse of the Portland government, and by hopes that Austria would resume the war. It was not until 4 November that orders were issued for the destruction of the island's defences, and the last British troops did not embark until 9 December. But the lesson had been learnt, and when Liverpool replaced Castlereagh as Secretary for War he insisted that in future British efforts should be concentrated in the Peninsula.[24]

When the attack on Antwerp was abandoned, 1809 was still far from over, but the strategic opportunity created by the Austrian War had gone, and the

British government had completely failed to exploit it. The sole achievement of lasting significance to come from the campaigns of 1809 was the consolidation of the British hold on Portugal — an achievement that was to be put to the test in 1810. Not only had the government failed to exploit the opportunity, it had not even systematically tried to do so. The decision to defend Portugal was made in isolation, not as part of a wider strategic plan. The ministers had then allowed themselves to be bullied into a campaign in Spain which they did not want and could not afford. The commitment to Portugal and Spain precluded the alternative of a campaign in north Germany, while they allocated far more resources to the Walcheren expedition than it was ever likely to justify. In short, the ministers lacked a coherent vision or an overall plan. The cabinet was deeply divided and in desperate need of strong leadership. But the limitations of the British government were not the cause of the allied failure in 1809. Napoleon's Empire was simply too strong for the combination of Austria, Spain and Britain. Better management might have achieved greater immediate success — for example, the capture of Antwerp or Madrid — but nothing short of a crushing French defeat on the Danube could have brought the allies victory in 1809.

6

Old Wine in New Bottles:
The Perceval Government,
September 1809–June 1810

In the autumn of 1809 the Portland government collapsed. Its fall was due to Canning's restless impatience and the weak leadership of Portland himself. Canning's discontent stretched back to the government's handling of the Convention of Cintra, and the subsequent appointment of Moore to the command of the army. Many later issues had exacerbated it, of which the most important were probably the long delay in sending Wellesley back to Portugal, and the mismanagement of the government's forces in the Commons, exemplified by the enquiry into the Duke of York's conduct and the feeble defence of Frere. At the end of March 1809 Canning therefore wrote to Portland and announced his intention to resign. Portland was dismayed, for Canning was acknowledged to be one of the government's most successful ministers, and perhaps the best orator in the Commons. It was doubtful if the government could continue without him. Portland invited Canning to Bulstrode, where they discussed the problem between 4 and 8 April. There is no detailed record of these talks, but it appears that Canning explained that he felt the government lacked leadership, and Portland offered to resign. According to one of Canning's closest friends they discussed various schemes, including one by which Chatham would become the new Prime Minister, Portland would remain in the cabinet, Lord Wellesley would replace Castlereagh at the War Department, and Mulgrave would move from the Admiralty to the Ordnance.[1]

But these changes were never implemented. The King refused to accept Portland's resignation and Canning was persuaded to remain in office with only the removal of Castlereagh and his replacement by Lord Wellesley. Yet even this was not done: one pretext after another was produced to delay the implementation of the promise, and weeks and then months passed. Gradually almost all the members of the cabinet except the unfortunate Castlereagh were told of what was intended and sworn to secrecy. None of them liked it, and most privately blamed Canning, although they accepted that he was far more important to the government than Castlereagh. Canning himself was made impatient and suspicious by the delay, and protested at the secrecy; he again attempted to resign, but he was assured by the King and by Portland that he would not be disappointed.

Then, on 11 August, Portland suffered a paralytic stroke. Although he recovered quickly it was clear that he could not remain Prime Minister for long: a few days later George III told Bathurst and Liverpool to begin looking for a new leader. On 28 August Perceval wrote to Canning suggesting that they consult together and select a suitable peer to replace Portland as the figurehead of the government. Canning could not agree to this: he was convinced that the government needed effective leadership — a view which must have been reinforced both by Portland's indecisive procrastination over the previous four months, and by signs that the government was about to face a major financial crisis (see below). He therefore told Perceval that he could not accept a compromise peer — the times demanded a strong Prime Minister in the Commons and only one of them could fill that role — and that he would not serve under Perceval. Poor Perceval was genuinely distressed by this: he acknowledged the desirability of a new Pitt, but believed that any attempt to give pre-eminence to Canning or himself would tear the government apart.[2]

Soon after this exchange of letters the ministry fell apart: Portland resigned on 6 September rather than remove Castlereagh, Canning resigned on the following day, and Castlereagh, who only now learnt of the long intrigue against him, on the 8th. For ten days Castlereagh brooded over his injury. He was angry with all his colleagues, for they had known and agreed to his removal without giving him any chance to defend himself. Naturally his particular grievance was against Canning, and on 19 September he challenged him to a duel in terms which left no room for explanation. As Castlereagh was an excellent marksman and Canning had never fired a pistol before in his life, this was neither very brave nor very honourable.[3] The two men met at 6 a.m. on 21 September on Putney Heath. At the first exchange both fired and missed. Castlereagh then demanded a second opportunity to murder his colleague and the seconds reluctantly agreed. This time Canning was hit in the thigh and Castlereagh felt that his honour was satisfied.

'The wound, as it happens, is a very good wound, as wounds go,' one of Canning's friends told another, 'but an inch more to the right [and] it would have killed him.' It healed well, and within three weeks Canning was sufficiently recovered to resign the seals of the Foreign Office personally to the King, and to give the curious monarch a full account of the encounter and of his wound. The King hated duelling, but was very kind to Canning, and certainly did not blame him for an affair which he could not avoid. Most people criticized Castlereagh for the challenge, but Canning's intrigues were also widely condemned, and in the long run the duel helped to begin a revival of Castlereagh's reputation. Despite wide publicity there were no legal proceedings, and it did not pose an obstacle to either man taking office then or later.[4]

Meanwhile the remaining ministers chose Perceval as their leader and considered their future. They knew that the loss of Canning and Castlereagh, the retreat from Talavera, and the failure at Walcheren would weaken them in Parliament, but at first they hoped to carry on unaided. A revolt of junior ministers — Huskisson, Rose, Long and Bourne, who all knew the temper of the Commons, had ties to Canning and were worried by the state of the budget — forced the cabinet to reconsider. On 18 September the ministers recommended to the King that he authorize an overture to the Opposition for the formation of a coalition government. The King was most reluctant, but finally agreed on 22 September, while making it plain that he hoped that the negotiations would fail.[5] And so they did: Grey rejected the approach out of hand, and though Grenville was less abrupt, he would not break with Grey on the question. The Opposition leaders saw no reason to join a coalition with ministers they despised, when they were convinced that Perceval's government could not last more than a few months and that its fall would open the way for them to gain unfettered control of the government.

Although unsuccessful in its primary aim, the overture helped Perceval by rallying wavering Pittites to his side, and by showing the Commons that he had tried to include the talented men of the Opposition in his ministry. Nonetheless, he faced a formidable task in constructing a cabinet which would appear to the Commons to be capable of running the country. Many of those he approached rejected his offers outright, while others promised support but declined office or imposed unacceptable conditions. An attempt to acquire Lord Sidmouth's supporters without their chief failed miserably; yet including Sidmouth would have offended many old Pittites, including Lord Melville, whose influence over Scottish members was still immense. As it was, Melville gave only guarded support, permitting his son, Robert Saunders Dundas, to take the Board of Control and a seat in cabinet, but not the War Department. After several other refusals, Liverpool agreed to leave the Home Office and take the War Department, while Perceval's amiable but ineffectual friend Richard Ryder, brother of Lord Harrowby, reluctantly took the Home Office, knowing that it was beyond him. The Duke of Portland returned to the cabinet without portfolio, but he died on 30 October 1809 after an operation. Among the junior ministers the young Lord Palmerston became Secretary at War, but was not to make his reputation for many years, and Wellington's brother William Wellesley-Pole replaced Robert Dundas as Chief Secretary for Ireland.

With Liverpool's arrival at the War Department came two new under-secretaries: Cecil Jenkinson, his half-brother, whom he brought with him from the Home Office, and, from June 1810, Colonel Henry Bunbury. Jenkinson resigned in June 1810, when about to marry an heiress, and was replaced by the young Robert Peel, who was just beginning his long political career: neither he nor Jenkinson aspired to have any real influence over the government's military policy. Bunbury, on the other hand, was an experienced staff officer who had served in Holland under the Duke of York in 1799, and in the Mediterranean in 1806–9. He had strong views of his own on strategy, favouring greater efforts in the Mediterranean and diversionary attacks on the coast of Spain, but although Liverpool sometimes mentioned these ideas to Wellington, they made little impression.

None of these changes appreciably strengthened the government, and Perceval desperately needed a prominent recruit of high standing, preferably one who had remained largely detached from the Portland government without being hostile to it. The obvious candidate was Marquess Wellesley, Wellington's eldest brother, who had made a great reputation as Governor-General of India (1797–1805), where he had displayed ability, energy and aggression. Wellesley had wide political contacts: his oldest friend was Lord Grenville, he had been an admirer and follower of Pitt, a friend of Sidmouth since their days at Oxford, and more recently he had formed an informal alliance with Canning. He had been offered high office in both the Ministry of All the Talents and in the Portland government, but had declined until allegations of misconduct in India had been fully dealt with in Parliament. With these out of the way he had accepted Canning's offer, in the spring of 1809, to go on a diplomatic mission to Spain, but had kept postponing his departure with the result that he did not arrive until after Talavera had been fought. He treated the Spanish government with haughty disdain, and quickly tired of diplomatic negotiations which were obviously unlikely to make any progress. Yet he retained a very high opinion of the potential of Spain, although he believed that British money and leadership were needed to realize it.

Perceval offered him the Foreign Office and he accepted without hesitation, arriving in England at the end of November. Wellesley was not a modest man, and he returned home believing, with some justice, that he was saving the government. In return he expected to be the real power in the cabinet. Perceval might manage the Commons, the finances, clerical patronage and the like, but Wellesley expected his colleagues to defer to him on foreign policy and the war. After all, 'None of them had acquired much fame either as war ministers or diplomatists, and Lord Wellesley flattered himself that he would have little real difficulty in persuading them to adopt *his opinions* regarding the best mode of maintaining the contest with Buonaparte.'[6] Here were the seeds of future dissension; more immediately Wellesley created problems by demanding the Garter vacated by Portland's death, even though it had been promised elsewhere.

Even with Wellesley's acceptance of office, few people expected the new government to last for long. Lord Eldon reported that 'Bets here go twenty to one that we never face [Parliament]', but he added with spirit, 'odds are sometimes lost'.[7] Despite an embarrassing defeat at the election of the Chancellor of Oxford University, the ministry survived and presented itself to Parliament on 23 January 1810. The first test of support in the Commons was the debate and vote on the Address from the Throne outlining the government's policy, which included a pledge to maintain the war in the Peninsula as long as there was any prospect of success. The Opposition misjudged their strength and moved a strong amendment which drove Canning, Castlereagh, Sidmouth, their supporters and many independent members into voting with the government, giving it a comfortable majority of 263 votes to 167. This was encouraging, but not decisive, and on 26 January a motion for an enquiry into the Walcheren Expedition was passed, despite determined opposition from Perceval and Canning, by 195 votes to 186, Castlereagh voting for the enquiry. Two days later the ministry was again defeated, this time in elections to the finance committee. Another Prime Minister might well have resigned, but Perceval was a doughty fighter who had always known that the task would not be easy, and who was determined not to resign unless he was defeated in a vote of confidence.

Attention now shifted to the enquiry into Walcheren, which was conducted by a committee of the whole House of Commons during February and March. At first things went well for the ministers, with Castlereagh astonishing the House with an excellent speech. But then the Opposition discovered that Chatham had breached constitutional convention by submitting an account of the expedition directly to the King. For nearly a fortnight the government teetered on the brink of irrecoverable defeat. On 6 March the ministers were beaten by 221 votes to 188 and it was obvious that only Chatham's resignation could save the administration; even so it required a long cabinet meeting and a violent harangue by Lord Wellesley before the noble Earl, procrastinating to the last, finally gave way. The sacrifice of Chatham (who, with Castlereagh, was chiefly blamed for the failure of the expedition) satisfied the House, and the government sailed through the remaining votes with comfortable, though not large, majorities. When it came to the point, a majority of the Commons preferred to go on with Perceval and his weak ministry rather than to force the King to accept Grey and Grenville, or seek salvation in some alternative arrangement of Pittites.

Canning was not the only aspirant who may have been privately disappointed by this result. Lord Wellesley had stood aloof from his colleagues throughout the Walcheren debates, pointedly remarking that he had never approved of the expedition. Had the ministry fallen he was in a good position to rally all shades of Pittites in defence of the King, but his ambition was rather too obvious, and his colleagues cannot be blamed for finding it unendearing.[8] Perceval's standing was greatly enhanced by his fighting defence of the government during the enquiry, and he had the full support of all his ministers save Wellesley, who continued to regard him almost with contempt. The two men were personally incompatible: Perceval was a modest, prudent evangelical, who concealed and regulated his ambition, but who was inflexible in his principles; Wellesley was a profligate and a libertine with a touch of genuine grandeur, but who also combined indolence with immense pride and vanity, and who was as extravagant in his ideas as with his fortune. The conflict between them was to dominate the cabinet for the next two years.

Among the junior ministers who resigned with Canning, none was more missed than William Huskisson, the financial expert who, as Secretary to the Treasury, had done much of the work in shaping Perceval's budgets. Huskisson was a loyal supporter of Canning, but he had concerns of his own about the financial management of the country which had led him to threaten resignation as early as 18 August. On that day he sent a 7,000-word memorandum to both Perceval and Canning, ranging widely over the government's conduct of the war but concentrating particularly on financial problems, and declaring that the government must have an effective head if the country was to survive. This view tied in well with Canning's claims, and may have been concerted with him, but there is no doubt that the financial problems facing the Treasury, and Huskisson's concern at them, were both real.[9]

The most immediate problem worrying Huskisson was the shortage of specie which had so affected British operations during the spring and summer. He had borne the brunt of the complaints from Wellington and Chatham, and he knew that the shortage had been temporarily overcome rather than truly solved. He calculated that an army of 40,000 men in Portugal would cost £2.5 million a year, of which half would be extraordinary expense. In addition to this, £1.5 million would have to be found for the Portuguese army and aid to Spain, while another £1.7 million would be needed for Sicily, of which approximately £1 million was extraordinary. Thus the government would need to find nearly £6 million per year, although some of this could be paid in goods or bills of exchange. Huskisson bluntly warned:

> I wish to be understood as entertaining strong doubts whether it will be practical to provide the remittances for these two Services for any length of time, unless we can obtain very great facilities for procuring Bullion in [Spanish] America, and those facilities can only be given, upon any permanent or productive scale by opening to us the Trade of that Continent.

But serious as this problem was, it was overshadowed by Huskisson's anxiety about the budget. From the beginning of the war in 1793 the British treasury had borrowed heavily to cover the greatly increased spending which the war required. As a result, Britain's funded debt rose from £232 million in 1793 to £509 million in 1802.[10] After a severe crisis in 1797–8 Pitt had increased taxation heavily, but even so the government still had to borrow each year to cover its expenditure. The interest on these loans, and a contribution to the sinking fund for their eventual repayment, together amounted to about 6 per cent of the loan, and this money had to be secured by an increase in taxation. This security was essential, for it underpinned the confidence in the British financial system on which the government's ability to raise money depended. But by 1809 the system was beginning to break down, owing to the difficulty of raising new taxes and a considerable increase in spending under the Portland government. Already in 1806 the Ministry of All the Talents had failed in its plans to impose taxes on pig iron and private brewing, and had had to resort to a much criticized and ultimately abandoned 'New Plan of Finance'. During the Portland government the cost of the war had risen sharply from an average of £37 million in 1805–7 to £42 million in 1808, and £44 million in 1809.[11] While some of this increase could be attributed to the outbreak of the Spanish war, Huskisson had no doubt that the more fundamental cause was the failure of the Duke of Portland to bring to his office of First Lord of the Treasury 'the Character and Efficiency which ought to belong to it as a check upon the general Expenditure of the Empire'.[12] And, sounding a very modern note, he said that the main departments of state would always want to spend more money, and that restraints had to be placed on them from elsewhere within the government. It was notorious that this had not been so under the Duke of Portland, with one outside observer commenting that he had been surprised

> that the Treasury exercised so little control over the other departments in matters of expenditure. Indeed in the manner in which the business has of late years been transacted there, you might almost have at once transferred it over to the Bank of England, upon which all the great offices should draw at pleasure; this sounds absurd, but the practice was not far short of it.[13]

Moving from the general to the specific, Huskisson pointed out that the current budget required £22.5 million to be raised by loans, which would require new taxes producing £1,350,000 per annum to secure the interest and the contribution to the sinking fund.

> Can we find new Taxes to this Amount, and for how many years?
> Is the present Government sufficiently strong to carry thro' such Taxes in Parliament?
> Would not the effect of their increased pressure speedily create in the Country a Clamour for Peace, and give strength to that which already prevails for reform?

His conclusion was that a large reduction should be made in the government's expenditure, unless the ministers were convinced that they would be able to make peace on good terms within a very few years. He did not advocate the withdrawal of the British army from the Peninsula, but some of his proposed reductions — particularly of troopships — would certainly have impeded its operations and possibly even threatened its safety.

As most of the government's expenditure was devoted to servicing the national debt, which could not be tampered with, and to the armed forces, the latter naturally attracted Huskisson's attention. We need not follow his arguments in detail, but he hoped to make wide-ranging cuts: £1.5 million

from the Navy, £2 million from the transports, £1 million from the Ordnance, and £2 million from the army. This last saving was to come from

> the Reduction of some second and third Battalions; of several of the local and
> provincial Corps; by a Recasting of the Garrison and Veteran Battalions; by
> a close Inspection into the recruiting Establishments of the Regiments; by a
> Reduction in the Waggon Train and several other Arrangements a very
> considerable diminution of Expense may be effected, without any dimin-
> ution of real efficiency.

Other proposals included dismounting one-fifth or one-quarter of the
cavalry, and reductions in the staff of the army at home. Beyond the
regulars, he urged the abolition of the Volunteers, and a drastic reduction in
the local militia, whose organization he, like many other observers, strongly
attacked.

Even if all these savings were made, the government would still have to
borrow large sums and raise taxes to cover the interest charges, but
Huskisson argued that if the government made these economies it would
have much less trouble getting its new taxes through Parliament. Finally he
added that far from peace solving these problems, it would make them
worse unless the war taxes were retained and military establishments radi-
cally reduced.

Huskisson's gloomy view of the country's fortunes was fully endorsed by
George Rose, another Pittite with long experience of financial questions. If
anything, Rose was even more emphatic, declaring that 'It follows therefore
of *absolute necessity* that unless our Expenses can be very greatly reduced, we
cannot continue to exist long as an independent Nation'. Perceval was much
impressed by Huskisson's arguments, and in the dying days of the Portland
government circulated a paper to the cabinet urging that drastic economies
were essential and accepting 'the necessity of limiting the scale of operations, and of endeavouring as far as possible to confine the War to a War of
Defence'.[14]

As soon as the new government was formed Perceval, who now combined
the offices of First Lord of the Treasury and Chancellor of the Exchequer,
just as Pitt had done, sent copies of his paper to both Lord Wellesley and
the King. George III replied that he had 'long seen with concern the
encreased [*sic*] expenses of the War and had felt the necessity of reducing
them', while Wellesley declared himself 'fully impressed with the necessity
of founding all our Plans of Military Operation on the basis of our Financial
means'.[15]

But it was easier to urge the necessity of economy than to find savings,
and by January 1810 Perceval had almost despaired. After studying the
question closely he had reluctantly come to the conclusion that 'We cannot
without absolute reduction of Army, or Navy, make any [great] saving . . . a
most terrible truth, but, at least as far as this year's expense is concerned I
believe it to be an indisputable one'.[16] He was even inclined to drop any

reference to economies in the King's Speech lest it raise false expectation, but was persuaded to keep it by Harrowby, who argued that such a public commitment would help keep a rein on fresh outlays. The cabinet had already approved an increase in Wellington's army and in the subsidy to Portugal, and the arguments of economy counted heavily against any further increase in this commitment. This tension mirrored and exacerbated the personal tension between Wellesley and Perceval.

Although the government failed to make the economies Huskisson and Rose had prescribed, it did not face bankruptcy. The economy in 1809–10 was more buoyant than the pessimists realized, with the result that revenue from existing taxes exceeded expectations. The boom did not last, however, and about the middle of 1810 the British economy went into a severe recession which was made much worse by the rigid application of Napoleon's Continental Blockade in 1810 and 1811. This placed great pressure on the British financial system, but it proved unexpectedly flexible and resilient. New markets were found for British exports in the Mediterranean and southern Europe, although some industries suffered and there was considerable unemployment and unrest. The full effects of the recession were not felt on the British budget until the summer of 1812, and by then Napoleon's Russian campaign had weakened his enforcement of the Continental System, while Wellington's victories inspired confidence in London. Nonetheless, the strain was considerable and if Napoleon had succeeded in Russia, or even if he had delayed his campaign for another year or two, Britain's ability to sustain the war would have been severely tested. With hindsight Huskisson's criticisms can appear unduly pessimistic, but in the autumn of 1809, with Austria just defeated and Russia still an ally of Napoleon, victory seemed a long way off, and it was only prudent to manage the war on the assumption that it might last another ten, fifteen or even twenty years.

The British army in the Peninsula saw little action between the end of August 1809 and the end of June 1810. After Talavera and the unwelcome appearance of Soult on his lines of communication, Wellington had withdrawn south of the Tagus and taken up a defensive position, but the French halted their advance and went into cantonments. The British suffered greatly from lack of provisions in their new quarters, so at the end of August Wellington fell back to the valley of the Guadiana near Badajoz. Supplies were more plentiful but the location was unhealthy and the number of sick greatly increased. Even so, Wellington remained there until December, partly at least owing to Spanish pressure. This delay greatly added to the discontent in the army that had arisen from the privations of the campaign and the retreat after Talavera. The confidence, at all levels of the army, in Wellington's ability had been badly shaken, and when news arrived that Austria had made peace many officers expected that the army would soon embark for home.[17]

But the British government had no intention of withdrawing from the conflict — indeed, before the end of August the cabinet asked Wellington if it would be possible to combine the defence of southern Spain with that of Portugal. Wellington was thoroughly jaundiced with all things Spanish and must have winced at the thought of another campaign requiring close cooperation with the Spanish forces, but he gave the question careful and fair consideration, and outlined the arguments on both sides in his reply to the government. He was convinced that it would not be possible to defend both Portugal and Andalusia against the forces which Napoleon could now send to Spain, no matter how much cooperation the Spaniards provided. But he admitted that he would 'not be surprised if the advantage of the possession of the fleets of Spain, and the certainty that the army could be embarked at Cadiz, which is not, in the Tagus, quite clear, should induce our government to prefer the operation in the south of Spain to that in Portugal'. If this was the case, he recommended that extensive guarantees of cooperation be demanded from the Spanish government, including both the presence of a British garrison in Cadiz and the subordination of the Spanish general to the British commander. But the government in London was already firmly committed to the defence of Portugal, and neither the Portland nor the Perceval cabinet gave any serious thought to abandoning their old ally in order to undertake the defence of Andalusia. Spain had proved too difficult and unreliable an ally to be the sole focus for Britain's efforts in the Peninsula.[18]

The Spanish government had also been considering the implications of Austria's defeat. Wellington had urged them to remain on the defensive and conserve their forces against the storm which was to come, but the Supreme Junta's hold on power was weak, and it decided to launch a full-scale attack on the French before their reinforcements arrived, in the hope of gaining victories which would inspire the patriots to resist the inevitable French onslaught. Wellington regarded this as rank folly and refused Spanish pleas to cooperate, which led to much ill-feeling on both sides. His military assessment proved correct, for despite some early success the Spanish campaign proved a disastrous failure. Their northern army under the Duque del Parque defeated a small French force at Tamames on 18 October and captured Salamanca; when the French were reinforced del Parque prudently withdrew, but he was caught at a disadvantage at Alba de Tormes on 28 November, and though not badly beaten in the battle, his inexperienced army disintegrated in the retreat. The southern offensive by the 50,000-strong Army of La Mancha under General Areizaga was even less successful. Their initial advance caught the French off-guard, but Areizaga dithered and the advantage was lost. On 19 November a French army of a little over 30,000 men brought Areizaga to battle at Ocaña, and despite being heavily outnumbered, inflicted the worst single Spanish defeat of the war. The Spanish lost 4,000 casualties and 14,000 prisoners, and the remainder of their army was totally broken and demoralized.

The victory at Ocaña opened the war for the French invasion of Andalusia, but they did not immediately take the road south. When King Joseph had concentrated his forces for the campaign he had lost effective control over much of Castile, and he wanted to reassert his authority before embarking on a vast new enterprise. There was also his terrible brother to consider and he wrote repeatedly seeking approval, but Napoleon remained silent. And so it was not until January 1810 that the French armies swept forward into Andalusia. They met with little resistance, for few of Areizaga's men had returned to the colours. Seville fell on 31 January, but Cadiz, the greatest prize of all, was saved. The Duque de Albuquerque hurried with his small army direct from Estremadura and reached the great port on 3 February — only two days before the French. His march saved the city, which had been left without an adequate garrison, and the French were forced to begin a siege which was to continue, without any real hope of success, for the next two years.

The conquest of Andalusia changed the entire balance of the war. Its loss crippled the regular Spanish resistance: never again were they able to bring 100,000 men into the field for a single campaign as they had in the autumn. Henceforth Wellington's Anglo-Portuguese army was to be the principal allied force in the Peninsula, though the guerrillas and the remaining Spanish regular forces ensured that the great majority of the French troops in Spain were needed to hold 'conquered' provinces in submission. Andalusia was itself a prime example of this, for it required an army of 70,000 men to maintain French control, and whenever Soult reduced his garrisons to collect a field army for active operations, the countryside would burst into revolt. Joseph, and by implication Napoleon, have often been criticized for directing their efforts against Andalusia before attacking the British in Portugal. In part, this is being wise after the event, but the French must also have considered that so long as Andalusia remained unconquered, a successful attack on Portugal would simply lead the British to move their army round to Cadiz. A large force would be needed to garrison Portugal, and nothing would have been gained except the destruction of the Portuguese army, which had yet to prove that it would fight.

The fall of Andalusia and the threat to Cadiz led the Spanish authorities finally to admit a British garrison. The first British troops arrived on 7 February from Gibraltar — too late to have saved the fortress. They were joined a few days later by three battalions of infantry from Wellington's army, which were soon followed by two Portuguese battalions. This force was later substantially increased when the British government sent out troops direct until it reached almost 10,000 men under the command of Major-General Thomas Graham. Wellington complained at such a large force being devoted to the defence of Cadiz, which he did not believe was in any real danger, and the British government responded by giving him authority to draw on the garrison as he saw fit, provided that some British presence was maintained.

On 28 February 1810 the new British minister to Spain arrived at Cadiz. This was Henry Wellesley, the youngest of the Wellesley brothers, who was to remain in Spain until 1821. By the time he arrived the Supreme Junta had abdicated and had been replaced by a Regency Council which, with frequently changing membership, was to provide the executive government of Spain for the rest of the war. Preparations had also begun for the summoning of the Cortes, which eventually met in September. Relations between Britain and Spain remained difficult during 1810. The Spaniards complained that Britain gave them little direct military and financial aid, while Talavera, Ocaña and the loss of Andalusia had reduced Spain's reputation in Britain to its nadir. Yet the alliance was maintained, and the scars of 1809 slowly faded as both sides contributed to the common war effort without the need for close cooperation.

British strategy in 1810 concentrated on the defence of Portugal. On 15 December 1809 Liverpool had spelt out the terms of the government's commitment. The subsidy to Portugal would be increased to nearly £1 million per annum, and Wellington's army would be reinforced by 5,000 infantry and a regiment of cavalry. Owing to the financial problems facing the government there could be no further increase in the subsidy, and it was 'absolutely necessary' that the Portuguese government adopt 'vigorous and effective measures' to make up any shortfall.[19] And Liverpool went on to warn that 'The expenditure of this country has become enormous, and if the war is to continue, we must look to economy'. Huskisson's warnings were having their effect and the ministers were 'anxious to know, with some certainty, that we have our money's worth for our money'.[20] Finally, on 2 January 1810, Wellington's instructions were formally amended to prohibit him from advancing beyond the Spanish frontier unless he was satisfied that he would receive effective Spanish cooperation and logistical support.[21]

The rapid fall of Andalusia shook Wellington's confidence and he wrote home asking what he should do if the Spanish resistance collapsed completely enabling the French to concentrate overwhelming forces against Portugal. Should he 'defend this country to the last' or make an orderly evacuation, taking with him as many Portuguese as possible who would leave before the moment of crisis arrived? Such doubts were most uncharacteristic and they did not last long: just over a week later he told the government that although the defence of Portugal might perhaps become unprofitable, he should be allowed to judge if and when the army should be evacuated on purely military grounds.[22]

The cabinet agreed, and Liverpool wrote to Wellington that although the safety of the British army was the first concern, 'His Majesty would be unwilling that His Army should evacuate Portugal before circumstances should render it absolutely necessary'.[23] But in private the ministers were anxious about the safety of their army. Wellington had not explained, and never did explain, how he planned to defend Portugal, and the consensus of military opinion, both at home and in letters from the army, was that it was indefensible and that the army would have to be withdrawn as soon as the French advanced in force. Nor were Wellington's own letters always encouraging. For example, on 24 January he told Liverpool that the discipline of the army had improved, but he still feared that the troops 'will slip through my fingers, as they did through Sir J. Moore's, when I shall be involved in any nice operation with a powerful enemy in my front'. Liverpool therefore wrote privately to Wellington on 13 March indicating that he 'would rather be excused for bringing away the army a little too soon than, by remaining in Portugal a little too long, exposing it to those risks from which no military operations can be wholly exempt'.[24] This was no doubt intended as nothing more than a gentle hint to err on the side of prudence, but Wellington reacted with fury. He told Charles Stuart, who had recently replaced Villiers as British envoy in Lisbon, that he would not accept 'private hints and opinions from ministers, which, if attended to, would lead to an act directly contrary to the spirit, and even to the letter, of the public instructions'. And he was even more forthright to his brother William Wellesley-Pole: 'I won't have publick Instructions which authorize a fair manly line, & private hints which direct one which would disgrace us for ever.' To Liverpool he was a little less blunt: if the government lacked confidence in his judgement, it should issue him with detailed instructions which he would follow to the letter; but otherwise, 'All I beg is that if I am to be responsible, I may be left to the exercise of my own Judgement; and I ask for the fair Confidence of Government upon the measures which I am to adopt.' Liverpool responded to this by reassuring Wellington that 'the fullest confidence is placed in your discretion in the important and delicate service in which you are engaged'.[25] And for the rest of the year and beyond, the government gave Wellington a free hand in the planning and conduct of his operations, Liverpool occasionally making suggestions for Wellington to consider, but making it clear that the final decision rested with the general. This does not mean, of course, that the ministers' doubts and anxieties about the campaign had been dispelled, but they were willing to trust their commander and hope that their confidence was not misplaced.

Unfortunately this correspondence was not Wellington's only grievance with the ministers, and with Liverpool in particular. He bitterly resented Liverpool's warnings on the need for economy and believed they reflected a lack of commitment to the cause of the Peninsula. And, according to a letter from Charles Stewart to Castlereagh, he complained that the business of the War Department 'is not done half so well as when you were there, that Lord Liverpool seems to decide on nothing', while equipment, supplies and so on 'are not forwarded with near the diligence they were in your time, and there is a great and evident laxity in the business of the office'. Stewart was, of course, a jaundiced witness, but as Adjutant-General he was well placed to judge.[26]

Wellington's temper was not improved by a recurrence of the specie shortage — just as Huskisson had predicted. This first made itself felt in

December 1809 and lasted until the middle of 1810 when the supply improved. During these months Wellington constantly badgered the government, demanding that they send him shiploads of bullion. 'You cannot conceive how much the want of Money distresses us . . .'; without £80,000 for the Portuguese government 'their army must disband'; 'If you cannot supply us with money, you ought to withdraw us. We are reduced to the greatest distress', and so on.[27] Admittedly the ministers had neglected the issue during the political turmoil of the autumn, but as soon as Wellington's first complaints reached them they did all they could to purchase more specie. They had some success, but the only real solution to the shortage lay in raising more funds in the Peninsula itself through the sale of bills of exchange on England. Thus in 1809 £466,000 was sent from Britain to the Peninsula in specie, while £2,174,000 was raised locally. In 1810 the respective figures were £679,000 and £5,382,000.[28] Merchants in the Peninsula bought these bills of exchange with specie in order to pay for British and colonial imports from London; the specie raised was paid into Wellington's military chest, from where it was used to pay the soldiers or the Portuguese government, ultimately returning to the merchants. But the system was not perfectly circular and shipments of specie were needed from London in order to maintain British credit. Even so, the price of bullion compared with British securities steadily rose throughout the war, and this was not the last specie shortage to trouble Wellington's relations with the ministers.

Wellington's other great complaint about the government in the first half of 1810 was the weakness of the ministry. He described the collapse of the Portland government as 'a most extraordinary history of the effects of inordinate personal ambition, gross want of Judgement, vanity & folly'.[29] And he expressed his support for the new ministry: 'for my part my wishes are in favour of Perceval & the Cabinet, and as far as I shall take any part in politicks I shall belong to them. But I don't conceive that I ought to embark in politicks to such an extent as to preclude my serving the Country under any administration that may employ me.' What Wellington really wanted was a strong united government which would vigorously support the war and yet give him a free hand.[30]

His assessment of the prospects for the new ministry was consistently pessimistic. On 1 March he told Liverpool, 'I am convinced that the Govt. cannot last', and a month later wrote to a subordinate: 'The government are terribly weak, and I think it probable will be beaten upon the Walcheren question.' Even when he heard that they had survived, he grumbled to William Wellesley-Pole, 'I think that Govt and Country are going to the Devil as fast as possible'.[31]

The weakness of the government mattered to Wellington in several ways. He knew that the Opposition and particularly the radicals opposed his campaign, and he feared that if he was defeated, the government would be too weak to protect him from their outcry: although exonerated by the enquiry into the Convention of Cintra, he had been severely scarred. He also felt that the ministers should show more leadership and 'take pains to inform the public and guide their opinion, and not allow every newswriter to run away with the public mind upon points essential to the interests of the country'. He believed that their political problems made the ministers more cautious: 'The government are terribly afraid that I shall get them, and myself, into a scrape.' 'The state of opinion in England is very unfavorable to the Peninsula. The ministers are as much alarmed as the public.'[32] These complaints were not wholly unfounded, but it is striking that Wellington shows little or no sympathy for the difficulties of the ministers. Indeed, the weakness of the government appears to have encouraged him to take a high and peremptory tone in his correspondence, which contrasts unfavourably with the constant courtesy and consideration he received from the ministers.

There was more support in Parliament for the defence of Portugal than Wellington realized. During February and March while the fate of the government was still uncertain, the Commons expressed its view in three separate votes. On 1 February a Vote of Thanks to Wellington for Talavera was carried without a division, although it was opposed by some of the more radical Whigs. There was naturally rather more opposition to Wellington's pension, especially as there were many who regarded the Wellesley family as overeager for honours, places and rewards of all kinds. Nonetheless, it was passed on 16 February by 213 votes to 106 despite great efforts by the Opposition to collect support. Finally, on 9 March, the Commons considered the Portuguese subsidy. Those speaking against it included the influential independent Henry Bankes and General Ferguson, who had served with distinction in the Vimiero campaign, while the argument for the subsidy, after Perceval had introduced it, was left to obscure and inept speakers. Yet when the House divided around 2 a.m. the Opposition's amendment was defeated by 204 votes to 142.

These votes show that the government's support for Wellington and the defence of Portugal certainly did not cost it votes. Only three days before the debate on the Portuguese subsidy the ministry had been heavily defeated on the censure of Lord Chatham. The floating Pittite factions led by Canning, Castlereagh and Sidmouth all supported the war, as did Wilberforce and many obscure independent members. But what must remain uncertain is how this support would have reacted to a serious defeat, or the evacuation of Wellington's army. The fall of Portugal, even without heavy military loss, would confirm the predictions of the Opposition, and do much to discredit Perceval's government. Yet even if the government fell, it might well be replaced by another Pittite ministry, led by Canning or Lord Wellesley, rather than by the Whigs.

Lord Wellesley would not have wished to gain the Premiership at such a price, but his ambitions were unsatisfied, and he was discontented with the cabinet whose members inexplicably failed to recognize his transcendent merit. However, thwarted ambition was not the only cause of disharmony between Wellesley and his colleagues: there were also important disagreements on questions of policy. In April and May 1810, after the end of the Walcheren debates, the government turned its attention to the war in the Peninsula. Wellesley argued that Britain's efforts 'were *just too short*: that an addition of no very great magnitude would enable Lord Wellington to do something towards expelling the French from Spain, and perhaps strike a blow that would revive the spirit of the nations of the North'. A little later, when news reached London that Masséna had entered Spain with a large body of French troops, Wellesley changed tack and claimed that the 'immediate safety' of Wellington's army now 'required a reinforcement to counterbalance the increased strength of the French army'.[33]

But Wellesley's ideas went far beyond the dispatch of more troops to his brother. With all the authority of his recent experiences in Spain, he argued for a much closer alliance with the Spanish patriots:

> That no permanent advantage could be expected unless the military and financial resources of Spain could be rendered available in nearly the same proportion with those of Portugal. That no real improvement could be looked for in the government of Spain without the active interference of the British government. That the British government was entitled to interfere directly in the management of the resources of Spain by the sacrifice of so much of her own blood and treasure in the Spanish cause. But that to render the interference of the British minister palatable and effectual, it would be necessary to give some pecuniary aid to the Spaniards.[34]

Wellesley probably intended sweeping reforms of the Spanish army and the introduction of British officers at all levels, including the overall command of the Spanish army. Later, however, he considered the alternative — if the Spanish government could not be made more efficient — of taking 30,000 Spanish troops into the British army in foreign regiments, again under British command and with British officers and equipment. He estimated the cost of this scheme at £3 million per annum.[35]

The scale of these plans is breathtaking. While other ministers doubted if Lisbon and Cadiz could be saved from the French, Wellesley dreamt of the salvation of the whole Peninsula. Proper training and equipment, good officers and above all regular pay and discipline would certainly have worked wonders with the Spanish army — as the excellent performance of Beresford's Portuguese was to show in the coming campaign. But would Wellesley's proposals have worked? The six years of the Peninsular War provide very few examples of amicable Anglo-Spanish cooperation, compared with innumerable cases of friction and irritation. Wellington's experience as Commander-in-Chief of the Spanish armies from late 1812 was most unhappy, and the few limited attempts which were made to imitate Beresford's success on a small scale had very disappointing results. Of course ministers did not know this in April 1810, but the bitter recrimi-

nations which followed the Talavera campaign, and Wellesley's own
fulminations against the inefficiency of the Spanish government, were
hardly encouraging.

An equally serious objection was, naturally, the cost. After all, this was
only a few months since even Wellesley, faced with Huskisson's dire warnings, had agreed on the need for economy. Now he disingenuously urged
'the *economy* of endeavouring to shorten the duration of the war, and the
wisdom of making our efforts before the Spaniards should become languid'.
The fact was that Wellesley was extravagant by nature; his imagination
might have been fired if Perceval had demanded dramatic, sweeping cuts,
but cautious, prudent accounting, and trimming of minor expenses, left
him cold. When pressed in cabinet he simply asserted that 'he could not
believe that the resources of England were reduced so low as to be unequal
to such an effort'.[36]

The other ministers regarded most of Wellesley's proposals as wildly
unrealistic and extravagant. As Liverpool told Wellington a few months
later:

> we must make our option between a steady and continued Exertion upon a
> moderate Scale, and a great and Extraordinary Effort for a limited Time,
> which neither our means Military nor Financial will enable us to maintain
> permanently.
>
> If it could be hoped that the latter would bring the contest to a speedy and
> Successful Conclusion, it would certainly be the wisest course; but unfortu-
> nately the Experience of the last fifteen Years is not encouraging in this
> respect.[37]

Yet they did not reject Wellesley's proposals out of hand, and Perceval
was even willing to consider a substantial loan to Spain if it could be used
to open the way for British trade to the Spanish colonies. Trade with South
America would revive manufacturing areas hard hit by Napoleon's Continental System, thus increasing revenue from existing taxes, and at the same
time would bring large fresh supplies of specie into Britain, relieving
pressure on the exchanges and enabling the government to keep Wellington
properly supplied. The 1810 budget included a £3 million Vote of Credit to
cover unforeseen contingencies, and Perceval was willing to lend £1.5
million, or even £2 million, of this money to Spain — though he warned
Wellesley that a loan of £2 million would leave the government very short
for other services, including Wellington's army in Portugal.[38] But the Foreign Secretary was most reluctant to link the loan to the trade with Spain's
colonies. He wanted the loan to generate good will and knew that any
concessions on this trade would be bitterly resented in Cadiz (now the seat
of the Spanish government), whose prosperity was based on the trade with
America. The question became embittered when Henry Wellesley
advanced £400,000 to the Spanish government on his own authority
without conditions, and Perceval sought to censure him against Lord
Wellesley's opposition.[39] The Spanish government would not budge on the

question of trade, and the British government refused any additional financial aid, although over the course of the year they sent nearly £300,000 of Ordnance supplies to Spain.[40] At the end of the year the prospect of Anglo-Spanish cooperation, except on the limited objective of securing Cadiz, was as remote as ever. But Lord Wellesley and Henry Wellesley — although not Wellington — continued to favour a much greater British role in Spanish affairs and the question was postponed rather than finally resolved.

Other aspects of the war also led to disagreements in the cabinet between Wellesley and his colleagues. The Foreign Secretary favoured a more conciliatory policy towards America, arguing that while the Orders in Council were justified in principle, they had become inexpedient. On the other hand he wished to adopt a peremptory tone in relations with Sicily and demand that the Court at Palermo grant concessions in order to allay popular discontent in the island. Perceval opposed his policies on both these questions and had little difficulty in carrying the cabinet with him:

> At length Lord Wellesley came to the conclusion that the narrow view which Mr Perceval took of foreign politics (which he ascribed to his having taken up the trade at a late period of life) was an incurable evil; and that it was the source of all the opposition he met with; and that the subjection of the Cabinet to Mr Perceval's opinions had become habitually so strong that argument and persuasion on his part was only waste of time and labour.[41]

By the time Parliament rose in June, Wellesley had decided that he would resign before it resumed sittings in November.

There were other grievances: Lord Wellesley prided himself on his literary style and resented the alterations made by the cabinet to his dispatches. More seriously, he hated the weakness of the government and repeatedly urged Perceval to seek recruits. But Perceval knew that there was little hope of gaining strength until the government's fate had been decided in the Walcheren debates. Once it had survived that test, he agreed to simultaneous offers to Canning, Castlereagh and Sidmouth, though he doubted whether they would be willing to act together. Surprisingly, six months in opposition had sunk Canning's pride to the point where he was willing to serve under Perceval and alongside his old foe Sidmouth. But neither Castlereagh nor Sidmouth would agree to serve with Canning. Wellesley, who had been reconciled with Canning, refused to see him thus ostracized, and none of the other ministers were willing to have Canning by himself, as Bathurst explained:

> I think as highly as you and anyone can of the value of that accession — not in the House of Commons only — but in this room — we should feel the value of it every day that we met. But my doubt is this — whether Canning's accession *alone* to the present Government would not lead to a change of the basis of the Government itself.[42]

With this stalemate preventing any substantial addition to the government, Perceval moved Mulgrave from the Admiralty to replace Chatham at the Ordnance, and brought in Charles Yorke to the Admiralty. Yorke appears to have been a competent if not distinguished minister, but he was unpopular in the Commons and his accession did little to strengthen the government. At Wellesley's insistence Perceval made another overture to Canning and Castlereagh in August, but Castlereagh remained obdurate and the approach quickly foundered. Its failure confirmed Wellesley in his decision to resign.

In many ways Wellesley's colleagues would have welcomed his intention had they known of it, for they were deeply disenchanted with him. This was not primarily due to the disagreements in cabinet, to which they were accustomed and which they took in good part. It was not so much even his suspected disloyalty and overly obvious ambition, although naturally these had an effect. What chiefly surprised and offended them was his inefficiency. As early as March 1810 William Wellesley-Pole told Wellington, 'I understand that he hardly does any business at his Office, that nobody can procure access to him, and that his whole time is passed with Moll [Raffles — a well-known courtesan, at this time Wellesley's mistress — who] . . . is rapidly ruining W——.' The Persian ambassador, who arrived in London in December 1809, was at first full of praise: 'Never before in England, indeed in the whole world, has there been a well-born minister of such tact and authority, such a paragon of perfection.' But as the months dragged by without any progress being made, the poor Persian became disillusioned and angry. Nor was it only foreign diplomats who suffered: even Henry Wellesley was kept waiting for seven weeks for instructions for his mission to Spain. Francis Jackson, the British minister in Washington, complained that his official dispatches went unanswered, and that without private letters from friends he would have no idea how his own government felt about the developments in the difficult relations with the United States. Stratford Canning, minister to the Ottoman Porte, later recalled that when Wellesley was Foreign Secretary he received no instructions at all for two years, and a total of only sixteen dispatches, of which seven were routine acknowledgements, while another was 'a request to use thicker envelopes when writing'. But the most serious of all Lord Wellesley's delays and omissions was his failure to keep Charles Stuart, Britain's envoy in Lisbon, informed and supplied with instructions during the critical months of late 1810.[43]

This inefficiency cannot be blamed entirely on his unhappiness with the government, for signs of it appear almost as soon as he took office. Yet obviously his enthusiasm for work was dampened by his defeats in cabinet. His lethargy damaged, but did not destroy, his public reputation and produced the greatest irritation among his colleagues and friends. Even Wellington, who was certainly no prude, was annoyed: 'I wish that Wellesley was *castrated*; or that he would like other people attend to his business and perform too. It is lamentable to see Talents & character & advantages such as he possesses thrown away upon Whoring.'[44]

Nonetheless, Wellesley remained a major figure in the government, and his loss would have been a great, possibly even a fatal, blow to its public standing. On the other hand Wellesley's departure would have opened the way for the inclusion of Castlereagh and Sidmouth without Canning: a change which would have made the government both more conservative and more coherent, if less popular. But it was not to be, for before Parliament returned in the autumn the ministry had lost its most important supporter and the country was plunged into a political crisis, just as the campaign in Portugal reached its critical point.

7

The French Invasion of Portugal, July–December 1810

Napoleon began preparations to finish the war in the Peninsula even before he signed the Peace of Schönbrunn (14 October 1809). On 7 October he ordered General Clarke, his Minister of War, to prepare nearly 100,000 reinforcements for the army in Spain — a figure which ultimately rose to almost 140,000 men. At first Napoleon intended to lead these fresh armies in person, but he gave up the idea when he divorced Josephine in December 1809 and married the Archduchess Marie Louise in April 1810. He hoped that by this dynastic tie he would establish an alliance with Austria which would further consolidate his position in central Europe and, by providing him with an heir, end damaging speculation within the Empire over the succession. Neither of these objectives was to be completely fulfilled, but at the time the marriage was felt as a heavy blow by all Napoleon's enemies.

He did not appoint a commander-in-chief for his armies in Spain. He may have been reluctant to trust such a large force (over 300,000 men) to any of his subordinates, but in any case the appalling communications in the Peninsula meant that effective command had to be devolved onto local commanders. The war in Catalonia or Andalusia could not be run from Madrid or Portugal, and broad strategic decisions allocating resources to regions could be made as well in Paris as anywhere else. Napoleon's continued general supervision of the war was thus quite reasonable — at least while he was in France — but when he was tempted to interfere in operational details his orders were so outdated that they were counterproductive or irrelevant.

With the regular Spanish resistance crippled by the occupation of Andalusia, Napoleon turned his attention to the expulsion of the British. On 16 April 1810 he appointed Marshal André Masséna, one of the most experienced and able of the marshals, to command the Army of Portugal. This force consisted of some 130,000 men, of whom only 86,000 were available for active operations. Napoleon believed that this was an ample force to conquer Portugal. He assured Masséna that 'the army of General Wellington is composed of no more than 24,000 British and Germans, and that his Portuguese are only 25,000 strong'. These last were 'poor troops' of no great importance. Napoleon was so confident that he told Masséna to take his time. 'I do not wish to enter Lisbon at this moment, because I could not feed the city, whose immense population is accustomed to live on sea-borne food. . . . spend the summer months in taking Ciudad Rodrigo, and then Almeida . . . [do] not hurry, but . . . go methodically to work.'[1]

This confidence, which virtually doomed the campaign before it began, was not unreasonable given the incomplete and inaccurate information available to Napoleon. He knew nothing of Wellington's preparations to meet an invading army, nor did he know of the progress which had been made in retraining the Portuguese army. Wellington's failure to assist the Spaniards, either in the Ocaña campaign or when Andalusia was invaded, appeared an admission of weakness. Napoleon had no reason to think highly of Britain's military capacity or resolve, and his low opinion was reinforced by intelligence gathered from English newspapers, which underestimated the size of Wellington's army and were pessimistic about its prospects. Altogether it seemed likely that the British would embark as soon as a sizable French army advanced against them.

In fact, of course, Wellington had no intention of embarking unless it was absolutely necessary. He had been preparing to meet a French invasion since late 1809 and was pleasantly surprised that the first half of 1810 slipped by before the French made their move. Each passing month enabled a further improvement in his defences, which were a skilful combination of traditional Portuguese methods with bold innovations based on a clear understanding of the possible lines of attack open to the French.

There were three main elements in Wellington's plan for the defence of Portugal: the Anglo-Portuguese army, the Lines of Torres Vedras and other fortifications, and the devastation of the countryside in the path of an invader. The army was the most obvious of these, and the only one of which Napoleon had even an inkling. But Napoleon regarded only the British troops as worthy of consideration and he underestimated their numbers. Wellington actually had 33,000 British and German rank and file in June 1810, which rose to 41,000 in October, and the quality of these troops was constantly improving as they gained experience.[2] Nonetheless, the British army by itself could have done nothing — it was only the re-creation of the Portuguese regular army which made the defence of Portugal possible. The long, tedious, exasperating work of Beresford and his subordinates bore fruit in 1810, when the Portuguese army which they had retrained and reorganized took the field and performed most creditably. Although lacking the experience and confidence which they later acquired, the Portuguese regulars doubled the size of Wellington's army without seriously diluting its quality.

In addition to the Portuguese regular army there was the partially trained militia and the untrained Ordenanza or levée en masse. The militia provided the bulk of the garrisons for the important Portuguese fortresses of Almeida, Elvas and Abrantes, and it was they who manned the Lines of Torres Vedras. They also operated in large units protecting northern Portugal from French incursions and harassing the flanks of the French army. The Ordenanza operated in much the same way as the guerrillas in Spain, ambushing small parties, killing stragglers and couriers, harassing foraging parties and so on. Such tactics helped to undermine the morale of the French army as well as increasing its losses through attrition.

The second element in the defence of Portugal consisted of three independent layers of fortifications. The outermost layer comprised the four frontier fortresses, two Spanish and two Portuguese. Badajoz and Elvas — both strong places with substantial garrisons — guarded the more southerly route into Portugal. Wellington always feared that the French would launch a subsidiary attack from this direction while advancing with their main army from the north. Such an attack would have forced him to retire hastily as far as Torres Vedras to prevent the southern French corps cutting off his retreat.[3] But Masséna lacked the men to make any substantial detachments and this southern theatre did not become active until early 1811. On the more northerly route lay Spanish Ciudad Rodrigo and Portuguese Almeida. These were less strong than their southern counterparts but they were still substantial fortresses which could not be taken without a regular siege. Wellington could not hope to halt a serious French invasion at the frontier fortresses, but he did expect them to delay the French advance, and make them use valuable rations before they could advance further.

Wellington's second layer of fortifications consisted of field works across several of the possible routes along which the French might advance through northern Portugal. The most important of these was at Ponte de Murcella, where he had constructed a series of redoubts behind the River Alva just above its junction with the Mondego. This created an extremely strong position in which Wellington could fight if he chose and which the French must pass if they were to continue their invasion by that route. The redoubts at Ponte de Murcella lay across the most probable line of French advance, but other routes had also been blocked, while Wellington's engineers had even destroyed one road completely, at the same time improving the roads which the Allies used for lateral communications. Wellington did not rely on these defences for halting the French invasion — a subsidiary French attack in the south would compel him to abandon them without a fight, and even if he defended them they might be forced. But if the French army was not overwhelmingly strong they provided a good opportunity for checking its advance, while the barren nature of the countryside meant that if the French could not continue moving forward, lack of supplies would soon force them to retire.

The most important series of fortifications were the Lines of Torres Vedras. These were actually a number of self-contained, mutually supporting forts, enhanced by engineering works such as the flooding of rivers and the creation of cliffs and escarpments. The Lines ran the whole twenty-nine miles from the Tagus to the sea so that neither flank could be turned, and they presented a formidable obstacle. And yet they were not impenetrable: by concentrating his army Masséna might perhaps have passed through them, though with fearful losses. But the beauty of the Lines was that they were manned, not by Wellington's army, but by the Portuguese militia supplemented by some regular gunners. The field army was held back ready to pounce on the French wherever they managed to fight their way through the Lines. Given the losses and demoralization which the French would suffer in penetrating the Lines, the result of such a battle would not have been in doubt.

In addition to the two main lines of forts running from the Tagus to the sea, Wellington had fortified the Heights of Almada on the southern bank of the Tagus. This was the final destination for any subsidiary French advance on the southern route from Spain, and if the French gained possession of these heights they could distantly bombard the ships in Lisbon harbour, making their position unpleasant if not untenable. The very last layer of defence was a short line of fortifications at St Julians which were intended in the last resort to cover the embarkation of the Anglo-Portuguese army.

The third element in Wellington's plan was the traditional Portuguese practice of stripping the countryside in the path of an invading force. Wellington hoped that starvation would force the French to retreat, possibly even before they reached the Lines. This was much the hardest element to implement, and if it had not been for the evil reputation the French had acquired during their earlier incursions into Portugal under Junot and Soult, it is unlikely that Wellington could have enforced it. Yet it was vital if Lisbon was not to become another Cadiz — unconquerable but contained. It was also the only element in Wellington's plan which used Masséna's own strength against him, for the larger his army the quicker it would starve. In the end the devastation of the countryside, especially in the crucial provinces near Lisbon, was far less thorough than Wellington had hoped.[4] But it was sufficient, and though the French held out for months, they were at last forced to retreat owing to the terrible losses they had suffered from lack of food and disease.

With hindsight we can see that these preparations were more than adequate to check any invasion that Masséna's army could mount. Napoleon had made the mistake of assuming that his enemy would remain inactive while he prepared his attack. To have had any real chance of success the French should have struck much harder, much sooner. But at the time Napoleon could not see the need for haste, and Wellington could not be sure that his preparations would be effective. Napoleon was foolishly confident and Wellington was anxious and tetchy.

Wellington's two greatest concerns were over the size and direction of the French attack, and whether the Portuguese troops would behave well in action. He could not know that the French would advance into Portugal with an army of only 70,000 men, and without the support of a subsidiary attack from Andalusia. He could not even be certain that Napoleon would not, after all, cross the Pyrenees with further reinforcements and lead his army in person.[5] At the beginning of May he even told General Graham that

> I do not think the service in this country is likely to hold out a prospect of any thing very brilliant: I must maintain myself on the Peninsula till it is necessary to withdraw from it; and when it is necessary to withdraw, I must carry off the army without disgrace, and without loss, if possible.[6]

In general he was more confident than this, and his confidence grew as the months passed, but despite his immense preparations, he was far from certain of success.

The ministers in London naturally shared Wellington's uncertainty, especially as private letters from senior officers in the army, including Charles Stewart, the Adjutant-General, and Sir Brent Spencer, Wellington's second-in-command, remained deeply pessimistic.[7] Nonetheless, the ministers continued to give Wellington their full support and complete discretion, demanding neither details of his plans nor assurances of success. But even so, Wellington remained discontented. He continued to believe that the ministers, and Liverpool in particular, were lukewarm in their support for the campaign, and starved it of resources. As the supply of specie had improved, his complaints moved on to the supply of troops.

On 14 November 1809 Wellington had asked for a force of 35,000 rank and file with which to defend Portugal. Allowing for sick and a garrison for Lisbon castle, he calculated that this would give him an effective field army of 30,000 British rank and file, plus the Portuguese.[8] The government had agreed to this figure and had dispatched reinforcements to bring Wellington up to strength. The protracted effects of Walcheren fever and the sudden need to find a garrison for Cadiz placed great strain on the British army — so much so that in June the Commander-in-Chief warned the cabinet that there was not a single line regiment in Britain that was fit to take the field.[9] But by sending drafts to regiments already in Portugal and drawing on other garrisons the government was able steadily to increase Wellington's army throughout the year. In January 1810 the total rank and file (including artillery and so on) was almost 32,000 men. By March this had risen to nearly 35,000 men, dropped to under 33,000 in June, but then rose steadily: 35,500 in August, 38,700 in September, 41,000 in October and nearly 43,000 rank and file in November.[10]

The ministers thus felt that they had done more than they had undertaken, but instead of praise they received bitter complaints from Wellington that the effective strength of his army remained below 30,000 men. This was true, at least until November, but it was due to the extraordinary rate of sick in Wellington's army, not any fault of the government. In November 1809 Wellington had calculated on around 3,000 sick, or ten per cent of his army. But the actual figure never dropped below 4,000 rank and file sick and the average was much higher. During the campaign it rose from just over 5,000 in July and August to 7,000 in September, to an incredible 9,405 on 25 October 1810 — or 23 per cent of Wellington's rank and file.[11]

While Wellington complained that 'Government have behaved with their usual weakness and folly about reinforcements', the cabinet became alarmed by the extent and cost of their commitment to the Peninsula.[12] By November 1810 Britain had no less than 49,000 rank and file in Lisbon and Cadiz: 40 per cent more than the 35,000 which the cabinet had agreed to a year before. This concern led Liverpool to warn Wellington, as early as 10 September, that the reinforcements then en route were for the immediate campaign only, and that when it had been decided the government would have to reconsider the scale of its commitment. 'I should deceive you if I held out the expectation that either the military or financial resources of this country would enable government to keep up an army to this amount in Portugal for any considerable length of time, in addition to all the other necessary drains upon the service.'[13] This warning naturally inflamed Wellington's distrust of the government.

Wellington had made meticulous preparations for the campaign, but the initiative at the outset inevitably lay with the French. Marshal Masséna arrived at Salamanca on 15 May 1810. Although only fifty-two years old, he was tired of war and had undertaken the new campaign with the greatest reluctance. But he had a superb record in the field, was one among the ablest, if not the ablest, of Napoleon's marshals and had taken a leading part in the Austrian campaign of 1809. While his lack of enthusiasm disappointed his subordinates, Wellington regarded him as a formidable adversary.

In accordance with Napoleon's instructions, Masséna went slowly and methodically to work, and by the end of May the French were firmly established in front of Ciudad Rodrigo. Wellington doubted that the Spanish governor, General Herrasti, would make a protracted defence, and sought to encourage him by promising to take any opportunity which arose to relieve the fortress.[14] But the French were too strong and too well managed, and although Wellington concentrated his army and brought it up to the front, he could do nothing to save Ciudad Rodrigo, which led to Spanish accusations of betrayal and considerable discontent in the British army. Despite Wellington's doubts Herrasti made a valiant defence and did not capitulate until 10 July, when a large breach made the fortress indefensible and the garrison's rations were greatly depleted.

Masséna moved slowly forward to undertake the siege of Almeida, investing it on 24 July after a bloody combat with the allied Light Division, whose commander, Brigadier Robert Craufurd, had delayed his retreat too long. The French proceeded at a leisurely pace, not breaking ground until 15 August. They were facing immense logistical difficulties, but their failure to live up to their reputation for rapid aggressive movements raised morale in the allied army. On 26 August Masséna had his first (and last) piece of luck of the whole campaign: by chance a shell fired into the town detonated the main magazine, causing a massive explosion which killed some 800 Portuguese soldiers and destroyed most of the town. Surrender was inevitable, but the precipitate behaviour of some Portuguese officers prevented the governor, Colonel Cox, from gaining favourable terms, and added to the widespread doubt among British officers about how the Portuguese would behave in action.[15]

Wellington was naturally disappointed by the rapid conclusion of the siege of Almeida, but the two sieges had gained him three months to improve the defences of Portugal. However, the fall of the fortress and the prospect of a French advance into the interior of the country led to a crisis in relations with the government in Lisbon. Many Portuguese, including some members of the Regency Council, feared that the British would embark and leave them to the mercy of the French. Attempts were made to force Wellington to stand and fight in northern Portugal, and to replace some of Beresford's appointees with other officers, while there was even some talk of replacing Beresford himself with the Duke of Brunswick.[16] These intrigues caused Wellington some anxiety, but they were more of an irritant and a nuisance than a real threat. Even the most disruptive members of the Portuguese Regency were firmly committed to the cause and in the last resort were therefore in Wellington's power. On 7 September he cracked the whip, threatening to withdraw his army from Portugal if the Regency attempted to interfere in operations or undermine Beresford's authority.[17] While this threat failed to endear him to his critics it was effective — at least for a time — and justified by the circumstances.

Masséna advanced with 65,000 men from Almeida on 15 September 1810. Hearing of Wellington's position at Ponte de Murcella, and being misled by wildly inaccurate maps, he turned aside from the main road after a few days and advanced along an abominable country track until he reached the Serra do Bussaco on 25 September. Wellington had followed the French movements with keen interest and transferred his army from Ponte de Murcella across the Mondego to Bussaco. Here he resolved to give battle in the hope of halting the French invasion, for the country was so barren that if the French could not advance, shortage of supplies would soon force them to retreat.[18]

The Serra do Bussaco was a formidable obstacle. It was a steep rocky ridge some nine miles long and reaching 1,800 feet above sea level, with its southern end resting on the River Mondego. It lay right across the line of the French advance, with precipitous broken slopes and deep gullies hindering any attempt to climb it. The terrain made cavalry useless, while the height of the ridge greatly disadvantaged the French artillery. Despite this, Masséna was confident of victory and did not attempt to turn the position. Wellington's only problems in holding the ridge were that it was too long to

5 Portugal and Western Spain: the French invasion of Portugal and the campaigns of 1811

be fully occupied by his army of 52,000 men (a track along the top of the ridge made this less serious), and that the broken ground would hinder a counter-attack. He could not have wished for a stronger position in which to give his Portuguese troops their baptism of fire.

The French plan of attack was crude and ill-prepared. Reynier's corps was to march on the right-centre (which the French believed to be the extreme right) of the allied position and, gaining the summit, to turn north and roll up the allied line, while Ney would simultaneously assail it from the front.[19] The attacks were made early in the day without proper reconnaissance or any sustained attempt to soften the enemy troops by skirmishing. Each attack followed a similar pattern: the French columns, screened by skirmishers, would advance up the hill under heavy fire, growing increasingly disordered and winded. As they approached the summit or just before, they would suddenly be counterattacked by fresh well-disciplined troops, and sent reeling back down the slope. The details vary from attack to attack, but this pattern essentially applies to them all. By early afternoon Ney and Reynier's corps had both been repulsed in disorder without making any impression on the allied position; Masséna prudently declined to commit Junot's corps to a new attack when there seemed no prospect of success.

Wellington was delighted with the result, particularly the performance of the Portuguese who, he told Liverpool, had 'proved that the trouble which has been taken with them has not been thrown away, and that they are worthy of contending in the same ranks as British troops'. Junior British officers writing privately were equally generous in their praise: 'The Portuguese astonished us by their coolness and bravery'; 'it has afforded proof that the Portuguese infantry are to be depended upon'; and 'They behaved in a most gallant manner, and full as well as the British'.[20] It was significant that exactly half the allied casualties were Portuguese, and their steadiness relieved Wellington of one of his greatest worries.

In all, the allied army lost 1,252 casualties, including 200 killed and 51 missing.[21] Many of these casualties were suffered in desultory fighting which continued long after the main attacks had been repulsed. Wellington claimed that the French loss was 'enormous' and that 'The enemy left 2,000 killed upon the field of battle', which led his supporters at home to put the total French loss at 10,000 casualties. But in fact only 515 French soldiers had been killed and their total loss, including over 300 prisoners, was less than 4,500.[22]

Masséna had been checked and his army defeated, but he had no intention of abandoning the invasion if he could find a way forward. On the day after the battle he ordered reconnaissances to see if the Bussaco position could be turned, and soon discovered a country road running through Boialvo and Sardão which outflanked it. Wellington was well aware of this road and on 19 September had ordered Colonel Trant to occupy it with his brigade of Portuguese militia. But a few thousand militia could not detain the French army unless they were defending a regular fortress, and two days later Wellington was still looking for another way of blocking the road.[23] He rejected the idea of detaching part of his field army to block the pass and was unable to devise any other solution. When he observed the French army move off towards Sardão he therefore abandoned his attempt to halt the invasion in northern Portugal and began his retreat to the Lines of Torres Vedras.

By his prompt withdrawal Wellington gained a lead of several marches over the French, so that his retreat was orderly and unhurried, with only a little skirmishing between his rearguard and the most advanced French troops. As the allies retreated they passed streams of Portuguese refugees fleeing with all their portable possessions from the horrors of war. Even before Bussaco there are accounts of the Portuguese peasants turning against the British when they retreated, while during the retreat to Torres Vedras there were outbreaks of soldiers looting, despite all Wellington's attempts to maintain discipline.[24]

On 7 October the rains began and a few days later the allied army retired within the Lines. Wellington was feeling confident and had already written to Charles Stuart that 'I am quite certain the French will not get Portugal this winter, unless they receive a very large reinforcement indeed'. To his brother Henry he simply wrote, 'I entertain very little doubt of our success', while he told Liverpool that

> as I conceive that I have reason to hope for success, I propose to bring matters to extremities, and to contend for the possession and independence of Portugal in one of the strong positions in this part of the country.[25]

As this implies, Wellington, and indeed the whole of his army, expected Masséna to attack as soon as his army reached the Lines. The men were as confident as their commander: 'Fear nothing — Masséna and his followers will be driven from Portugal — the sooner he attacks the better', and 'the fate of Portugal seems to be drawing to a crisis and the British army are in high spirits as to the result' were typical of the messages being sent home.[26]

But Masséna was far too wily to be caught twice in the same way. His army had already suffered heavily in the campaign, particularly when a large hospital he had established at Coimbra was captured by Trant's militia, and was now reduced to little over 50,000 effectives. Wellington's army on the other hand had been reinforced and had been joined by some 8,000 Spanish troops under Romana. By the time Masséna reached the Lines on 14 October his army was outnumbered. He probed the defences in a small combat at Sobral, but it was obvious that they were far too strong to be stormed by his depleted army. He remained confident that he could defeat Wellington in an open battle, so he dallied for a time in front of the Lines inviting Wellington to attack him. But Wellington was unwilling to take unnecessary risks, and after a month shortage of supplies forced Masséna to fall back some thirty or forty miles to Santarem on the Tagus, which he fortified.

Masséna had done all that was in his power, and he referred the problem back to Napoleon. It was for the Emperor to decide if the capture of Lisbon was worth sending another army to reinforce Masséna or ordering Soult to abandon the siege of Cadiz and invade Portugal south of the Tagus. In the meantime Masséna maintained his position, containing the allied army and keeping Napoleon's options open.

In Lisbon the remorseless French advance as far as Torres Vedras had caused great unease and even some panic as the city filled with refugees. Hare-brained schemes were circulated to prevent the British embarking and force them to fight, while much plate, jewels and other valuables were placed on board ships in the Tagus. Although there was no hint of a French party in the city, the government made a large number of political arrests, for which it was criticized not only by liberals in Britain, but even by Wellington. Yet the discount rate on British bills did not go beyond 34 per cent — which was less bad than might have been expected with the French army less than thirty miles from the capital. Almost as soon as the French advance was halted, the people of Lisbon began to regain confidence, but Wellington's scorched earth policy and the depredations of the French meant that it was years before life returned to normal for many poor Portuguese.[27]

The ministers and their supporters were generally anxious but hopeful about the campaign in Portugal, while most of the Opposition relished gloomy prophecies of defeat and disaster. The slowness of Masséna's initial advance and Wellington's growing confidence encouraged official opinion in London to such an extent that on 11 September Liverpool could tell the British commander in Canada that 'the Events of this Campaign have exceeded our most sanguine Expectations and certainly afford no very unreasonable Expectation that the Contest in the Peninsula may finally prove successful'. But the sudden fall of Almeida and rumours that it had been caused by treachery confirmed the Opposition in their views, and Lord Auckland was not the only patriot who would have gladly settled for the safe withdrawal of the British army.[28]

Anxious days and weeks followed until the news of Bussaco reached England on Saturday 13 October. Lady Holland was delighted with 'the brilliant repulse of the French', but few other members of the Opposition had any good to say of it. Lord Grey felt that it 'resembles in too many points the battle of Talavera. A vigorous repulse of the Enemy, a Post unoccupied which exposed our flank & rear, & the necessity of an immediate retreat. . . .' Tom Grenville thought that the French had gained the advantage, while Lord Auckland believed that Masséna had 'out-generaled us, and turned our position, and forced our strong post and fastness, and forced us to retreat over the Mondego'. He also questioned Wellington's 'truth as a writer of despatches' — a claim for which Wellington's fourfold vision of French dead at Bussaco provided some justification.[29]

The ministers, however, were delighted. The pro-government *Courier* claimed that 'we gained a glorious victory, and established our invincible superiority, . . . the French army was cut down like ridges of grass by the scythes of our mowers'. Liverpool conveyed the government's thanks to Wellington and told him that 'I never saw the King more entirely satisfied than he has been in the late operations of the army', although he was preoccupied with the illness of the Princess Amelia. The performance of the Portuguese drew special praise. General Charles Craufurd told his brother Robert in Portugal, 'As the Portuguese troops conduct themselves so well . . . I think one may be justified in being sanguine as to the result of the campaign', while the government marked it by conferring the Order of the Bath on Beresford.[30]

Expectations now ran wild, fuelled by a widespread miscalculation of the force of the two armies. Wellington's exaggerated figure for the French dead at Bussaco was commonly taken up and amplified. Palmerston had no doubt that 'The loss of the French was immense; ours trifling. The French left 2,000 dead on the field of battle & the private accounts State their wounded to be 8,000. Some make their whole loss amount to 16 or 17,000.'[31] By 18 October *The Times* took for granted that the French had lost 10,000 men at Bussaco and concluded that this left Masséna with less than 60,000 men, while Wellington had 81,000 Anglo-Portuguese. 'But now observe what towering hopes open to us, which the country may indulge, we may say, with the most perfect confidence.' 'Masséna appears to us, upon the present face of things, to have been infinitely too ardent, and to have involved himself in inextricable ruin . . . we do not see how it is possible for him to escape.'[32]

The next couple of weeks were tense with anxiety. Everyone expected the decisive battle to be fought in the last days of October. As *The Times* said, 'The Armies seemed all but engaged when we quitted them, and the stakes for which they were to fight were the fate of a Kingdom and their own safety'.[33] Slowly the excitement ebbed and people felt let down by the anticlimax. Lord Harrowby told his wife,

> The long delay of news gives me the sickness of hope deferred; and, tho' without the least reason, makes me grow less sanguine than I was. I shall not be at all surprised, if the account when it comes, brings nothing decisive: as I do not see why Masséna should not strengthen himself in his present position, & wait for the arrival of reinforcements before he ventures to attack.

Two days later Harrowby was consoling himself that 'The delay of Masséna clearly shows that he is afraid of attacking us at present', but this was no substitute for the expected triumph.[34]

The absence of victory confirmed the Opposition leaders in their views, even though their own prophecies of defeat also remained unfulfilled. On 1 November Grenville wrote to Grey:

> We are still without news from Portugal. . . . My own opinion remains unaltered, nor shall I shrink from avowing it whatever be the result of this battle. I think the project desperate and wicked; it puts to hazard our safety, failure may involve us in ruin, the utmost success cannot, I am confident, insure to us the least permanent advantage. In the meantime the internal state of this country and of Ireland is such as will speedily leave it no longer a matter of dispute whether we *can* maintain a war against France on the Continent of Europe.[35]

Grey replied on 9 November:

> I think I entirely agree with you on the subject of Portugal; all the probabilities were, and in my opinion still are, against eventual success there. I

have no faith even in the promised victory. . . . I could not deny that such a success would be worth the sacrifices we had made for it. But a doubtful or indecisive victory, and protracted operations, I should think little less ruinous (I am not sure they would not be more so) than an immediate defeat.[36]

The opinions of the leaders of the Opposition had suddenly assumed great importance, for towards the end of October George III had fallen seriously ill. All his life he was subject to attacks of porphyria, a then unrecognized physical disorder whose symptoms closely resemble madness. As the choice of the ministers rested with the monarch, and as the Prince of Wales had long been associated with the Opposition, the illness of the King produced a political crisis, just as it had in 1788 when the King had had his most serious previous attack. If the King died the Prince of Wales would assume the throne; and if the King lived but remained incapacitated, the Prince of Wales would be appointed Regent. In either case it was reasonable to assume that the Prince would appoint ministers in whom he had confidence, that is, his old friends the Whigs. Perceval's government was weak and not obviously successful, while the other Pittite factions were divided by bitter personal hostility. Many members of Parliament would support the King's or the Regent's right to choose his ministers, so that a new government would probably have commanded a substantial majority in the Commons; and if not, an election could be held which would certainly strengthen the position of the government of the day.

The King's condition fluctuated greatly during November and December 1810. Early in November the attack was so severe that his life was in danger, but thanks to his strong constitution he survived and steadily improved until late in the month, when there was a relapse which lasted into the second week of December. At times he was lucid and able to understand the political consequences of his illness, but at others he raved and was violent, and had to be constrained by a straitjacket. The doctors were unable to help him, and the treatment of those who specialized in madness was barbarous and probably counter-productive. But as he had recovered, despite the doctors, from previous attacks in 1788, 1801 and 1804, there was reason to hope for his recovery in 1810.[37]

Perceval accordingly delayed proceedings for as long as possible, just as Pitt had done in 1788. Parliament met on 1 November, but agreed to three successive adjournments, each of a fortnight, despite increasing opposition. Finally on 13 December Perceval agreed to establish a select committee to examine the King's doctors. Their evidence was generally encouraging, for they were confident that the King would recover, although they would not say how long this would take. In the last days of the year, two months after the King first fell ill, Perceval brought into Parliament proposals to establish a Regency.

While the ministers had procrastinated chiefly in the hope that the King would recover, they must also have hoped that news would arrive from

Lisbon of a great victory or of the French retreat, which would both secure Wellington's position and vindicate their policies. But the only news of importance from Portugal was of Masséna's retreat to Santarem, and this was open to a wide variety of interpretations, as Countess Spencer found:

> At Mrs Howe's it was explained to her as very good, and a proof of Ld Wellington's good Generalship making Masséna retreat, and Mr Long had *betted* (for the pleasure of betting with an Arch Bishop) (of York) that Masséna without a battle would be forc'd to retreat into Spain before February. On her return home she met with Ld Carlisle, who assur'd her Masséna had not retreated, but taken a better position, and plac'd us in a worse; that Ld. W. was no general at all, and fell from one blunder to another, and the most we had to hope was his being able to embark quietly and bring his troops in safety back to England, which he thought very doubtful.[38]

At the end of the year the Opposition remained convinced of the folly of Wellington's campaign and were full of forebodings for the New Year. Nor was their pessimism altogether unreasonable. Wellington had confidently told the government that the French would be unable to maintain their position for more than a few weeks before hunger would force them to abandon the invasion and retreat back into Spain, but after two months Masséna was still within a hundred miles of Lisbon and showed no sign of retiring. It was clear that Masséna could not take Lisbon with his present force, but Napoleon might well send, or even lead, another vast army into Spain in the spring, or order Soult to abandon the siege of Cadiz and attack Lisbon from the south-east. There was even the danger that the Portuguese might lose heart at the devastation of their country by opposing armies and seek terms from Masséna or betray the British. In London there were equal grounds for uncertainty. The King might or might not recover; a new government might or might not be formed, which might or might not maintain Britain's commitment to the war in the Peninsula. As the last days of 1810 ebbed away, it was thus far from clear whether the New Year would bring the first steps along the road to glorious victory and triumphant peace, or the humiliating loss of Portugal, and perhaps even a negotiated peace which would acknowledge Napoleon's hegemony.

PART TWO

The Widening War, 1810–12

8

The Turn of the Tide:
Britain and the Peninsula, 1811

New Year 1811 saw Britain immersed in the midst of a political crisis. Parliament spent all of January debating the terms of the Regency and the restrictions to be imposed on the Regent's powers. Much to the surprise of cynical observers, Perceval closely followed the precedent of 1788, making no effort to conciliate the Prince. His one concession to the fact that the Prince was no longer an impetuous youth of twenty-six, but a middle-aged, if not sober, man of forty-eight who had been behaving with great propriety since the crisis began, was to limit the restrictions to one year rather than three. The Prince was understandably outraged at this public humiliation and while he replied with careful dignity, he also encouraged his brothers to issue a solemn, and very unpopular, protest. The Opposition, urged on by the Prince, vigorously contested the restrictions, but except on one minor issue Perceval carried the day with remarkably few defections.

The restrictions did not hinder the Prince's ability to change the government, and Perceval and his colleagues expected to be dismissed as soon as the Regent was sworn into office. The Prince's attachment to the Whigs stretched back almost to his childhood and was founded on his close friendship with Fox and Sheridan, among others, and on their battles over many questions of common interest such as the Regency crisis of 1788. But after Fox's death in 1806 these ties had loosened. Grey and Grenville did not go out of their way to conciliate the Prince and pointedly neglected Sheridan. The Prince was growing older and took less delight in teasing his father, while his new mistress, Lady Hertford, was no friend to the Whigs. By the end of 1810 the Prince was still allied to the Whigs, but the warmth had gone out of the relationship, which was now based principally on the claims of political consistency, habit and old memories.

Nonetheless, if George III had died in 1810 the Prince would have asked the Opposition to form a government. But the King's incapacity made the question more complicated, for there was plainly no point in dismissing the ministers if the King was on the point of recovery, while there was the additional fear that news of a change of government might so agitate

the King as to impede his recovery. On the other hand, it was consti-
tutionally improper for the Prince to retain ministers in whom he had no
confidence.

Early in January the Prince consulted Lord Grenville, who advised him
to change the government unless the King seemed well on the road to
recovery. The Prince agreed and the Opposition leaders began planning a
ministry. After their experiences in 1806–7 the Whigs were determined not
to join a broad coalition and firmly rejected the suggestion, which had the
support of both the Prince and Lord Grenville, of including Canning to
strengthen the new government in the Commons. Inconclusive overtures
were made, however, to Huskisson, whose financial expertise was appreciated by all sections of the Opposition. The Prince's friends and supporters
were to be rewarded with some important positions (for example Moira was
to be Lord Lieutenant of Ireland), but none was to be in the cabinet. The
division of offices caused some ill-feeling, with both the more conservative
of the Grenvillites and the more radical Whigs feeling aggrieved. At one
point Lord Grenville's refusal to give up his valuable sinecure as an Auditor
of the Exchequer threatened to scuttle the whole ministry, but after some
unseemly squabbling a compromise was devised.

By the end of January the Opposition was ready to take office. Their
proposed cabinet, including Whitbread, possibly at the Admiralty, was not
devoid of ability or experience and was certainly not obviously inferior to
Perceval's weak ministry. The wisdom of its policies, however, is another
question. Grenville and Grey both remained extremely pessimistic about
the war in Portugal, as did almost all their colleagues. Lord Holland, the
great Whig champion of the Peninsula, wrote in his Memoirs:

> I had some scruples about the Spanish war. Lord Grenville, from economy,
> Lord Grey, from a propensity to criticise military movements, were disposed
> to contemplate it with less hope, and possibly less zeal, than myself. But as
> they agreed on the immediate necessity of supplying Lord Wellington's
> army with reinforcements and vigorously supporting the plans in which he
> was engaged, I saw no reason . . . for exacting a previous concurrence of
> opinion in certain contingencies which had not yet occurred. I was willing to
> take my chance of the zeal which the conduct and management of the war
> would inevitably have inspired in such ardent and sanguine minds as Lord
> Grey's and Mr Whitbread's.[1]

Unfortunately it is hard to give full credit to this account. Lady Holland's
Journal confirms that her husband did discuss the Peninsula with Grenville,
but no mention is made of reinforcements, or indeed of any conclusion
being reached.[2] It is impossible to know how a new government might have
handled the Peninsular commitment. Policies formed in Opposition are
frequently abandoned in government, and the military situation would have
dramatically improved before the new ministers could have implemented
their policies. Possibly a taste of military success would have converted

Grey and even Whitbread, while a return to office might have revived Grenville's ardour. And possibly not. All that can be safely said is that a change of government would have placed Britain's Peninsular commitment in question for some months at least, alarming her allies and placing a great additional strain on Wellington, who must have reacted by becoming more cautious in his operations. (For a hostile satirist's view, see plate 6.)

But there was to be no change of government. Throughout January the King's condition steadily improved and by the end of the month his doctors were convinced that he was certainly getting better, though they would not predict how long it would take before he could resume his royal functions. The Prince hesitated, but finally decided to retain the ministers, at least for the moment.

The Opposition leaders took the news philosophically, recognizing the difficulty of the Prince's position. But not all their supporters were so restrained, and among the angry, disappointed Whig rank and file rumours abounded of backstairs intrigue and betrayal. But as the King continued to improve during February it was generally recognized that the Prince had acted wisely.

The Prince informed Perceval of his decision on 4 February in an extraordinary letter in which he declared that

> the irresistible impulse of filial duty & affection to his beloved & afflicted father . . . alone dictates the decision now communicated to Mr Perceval.
>
> The motive for the continuance of the present servants of the Crown must of course cease upon an alteration of the circumstances which, in the contemplation of the Prince have demanded from him this present determination.[3]

In other words the ministers were retained on sufferance, and if the King died or his condition deteriorated they could expect to be dismissed. These were dangerous constitutional waters, for the letter clearly implied a lack of confidence in the ministers which, officially at least, the Regent could not feel; and if Perceval had chosen to take umbrage over the issue and had resigned, the Prince would have been in a very awkward position. But Perceval was too good a politician and too disciplined a man to take offence foolishly, and he even remarked that the letter was 'not more dry than could be expected'.[4]

Perceval and his colleagues thus survived another crisis and were confirmed in office, but nothing had been resolved, and the future of the government depended on the fluctuations of the King's condition, and the whim and will of one of the most irresolute princes in Christendom.

During the long political crisis the government's policy towards the Peninsula remained uncertain, and affected as much by financial as by political or military concerns. Britain had made an unprecedented effort in 1810 to stem the tide of French conquest at Lisbon and Cadiz. The

6.   Sketch for a Prime Minister, or how to purchase a Peace
[De Wilde], 1 Feb. 1811, B.M. Cat. no. 11,710

Lord and Lady Holland — she wearing the breeches — attempt to storm the Treasury, which is stoutly defended by Perceval. Lady Holland shelters Napoleon, who offers a bag of gold as a peace offering while holding a dagger in his other hand. She holds a document headed 'Lord Wellington's Recall'.

The Hollands' admiration for Napoleon was well known, but it is ironical that they should be accused of seeking Wellington's recall when they were some of the few members of the Opposition at this time who supported the Peninsular War.

Lady Holland was renowned for her forceful personality and keen interest in politics. Her husband — the nephew of Charles James Fox — championed liberal causes and, by his geniality and charm, helped soothe the resentment aroused by his wife's autocratic behaviour. At one point during the Regency crisis the Opposition considered making Lord Holland Prime Minister, though the real leadership would have remained with Lord Grenville.

ministers had trusted Wellington and braved the sceptics, and their judgement had been proved correct. Lisbon had been saved and Wellington
assured them that hunger would soon force Masséna to retreat. How would
the British government respond? Would it reduce its efforts in the Peninsula in order to conserve the nation's resources, or seek to seize the advantage? In theory the cabinet had already decided that Britain could not
sustain the existing level of operations in the Peninsula. As early as
September 1810 Liverpool had firmly told Wellington that the reinforcements he was being sent were only for the duration of Masséna's invasion,
and that 'the British army must be reduced as soon as the *present exigency*
will admit of it'. Wellington had appeared to accept this principle when he
asked for the loan of some more troops at the end of 1810, and in
mid-January Liverpool had clearly reiterated it.[5]

This determination briefly wavered in February, when Henry Wellesley
put forward a scheme for greater Anglo-Spanish cooperation (see below, p.
153). But new figures on the cost of the war killed this plan and gravely
alarmed Liverpool, who wrote to Wellington complaining that the cost of
the war in Portugal had risen from less than £3 million in 1809 to over £9
million in 1810 and that as most of this expense had been incurred in the last
few months of the year, it would rise still higher in 1811 unless steps were
taken to reduce it. He went on to express

> the unanimous opinion of every member of the government and of every
> person acquainted with the finances and resources of the country, that it is
> absolutely impossible to continue our exertion upon the present scale in the
> Peninsula for any considerable length of time.

Liverpool warned Wellington that this meant that the government faced the
choice of either reducing 'the scale of our exertion [in Portugal] or . . .
withdrawing our army altogether'. Plans for greater involvement in Spain
were out of the question, though Wellington might accept the command of
Spanish forces in provinces adjoining the frontier, provided this entailed no
extra expense and no commitment to operations in the interior of Spain.[6]

Fortunately the first flurry of this alarm soon passed, for when the
ministers came to consider the Portuguese subsidy a couple of weeks later,
they were much more liberal. On 26 January 1811 Wellington had written
to the Foreign Secretary describing the intolerable problems in relations
with Portugal which were caused by lack of funds. He had urged that
Britain should either take over the government of Portugal completely
or at least 'increase the subsidy to the real expense of 30,000 men'. The
ministers knew that although they had granted Portugal a subsidy of
£980,000 in 1810, the Portuguese government had only received about
£700,000 after the loss on the exchange and the cost of British officers
serving in the Portuguese army had been deducted. Lord Wellesley
evidently threw his full weight behind Wellington's plea and, according to
a contemporary rumour, he succeeded in squeezing an increase in the

Portuguese subsidy to £2 million per annum from Perceval 'as if it was so much of his blood'.[7]

Wellington must have been surprised as well as pleased at this decision, for only two days after writing to London he told Charles Stuart, 'I should deceive myself if I believed we should get anything'.[8] It probably helped improve his relations with the government, which had reached their nadir early in January with an angry outburst to William Wellesley-Pole:

> I think you are mistaken in your conjectures respecting the confidence reposed in me by the Cabinet, & the desire to reinforce this Army. I can't say what the sentiments & objects of the Cabinet are; but I think I can prove from the letters & the conduct of the Minister of the War Department that his sentiments & objects are entirely different from those you suppose. He has been dabbling in a Game separate from that to be played in this Country ever since he came into Office; & he has never acted with me upon any broad or liberal system of confidence.[9]

Pole was shocked at the violence of this criticism and did his best to reassure his brother:

> I am perfectly satisfied that you are mistaken in supposing that you do not possess the confidence of ministers. If there is anything like truth in man, there was never more implicit confidence felt in any General Officer, than is felt by Perceval, Lord Liverpool, and I firmly believe by all the other members of the Cabinet in You.[10]

Wellington's anger with the ministers was compounded by their political weakness, for he had no wish to see them replaced by the Whigs. As always, he took a desponding view of British politics, writing to Beresford: 'I think that when the Regent is appointed the ministers will resign, because it will be apparent that they do not possess his confidence.'[11] But he would not imitate them, telling his brother Henry:

> In the event of a change of government in England, I don't think it is likely that you will be allowed to continue in your office at Cadiz; but I recommend you to remain in it till you will be recalled, on the principle that it is a professional and not a political employment. If you should find that the business does not go on to your satisfaction, it will always be time enough to resign.
>
> I shall follow the same course; and indeed, adverting to the attacks of the Opposition upon me at different times, and the inconvenience which will be felt by any change, I am not certain that I shall not offer any new government which might be formed to stay as long as they might think proper.[12]

While certainly not apolitical, Wellington was dedicated to his profession and was convinced that he could not serve his country better than by commanding the largest army possible in Portugal. He could be irritable, petulant, thin-skinned and foolish, but that was when he was dealing with friends. To a new government he would explain the advantages of Britain's presence in Portugal, beg and plead for resources, threaten dire consequences of any change of policy, and ignore all slights and insults until he was either utterly defeated or got his own way. Then, and only then, would he deal with his new masters with the curtness he had adopted towards Liverpool (if he had been successful), or, if vanquished, turn against them the full force of his personality and his practised skill at exaggerated diatribe.

The winter of 1810–11 was cold and hard in England, with ice covering the west side of the Thames and nearly blocking the arches of Westminster Bridge. It was much pleasanter to be in sunny Portugal if you were well fed and had adequate shelter. The young officers in Wellington's army do not seem to have suffered, if Cocks's account can be trusted:

> We live very well, having plenty of mutton, beef, fowls, turkey, coffee, butter, bread, potatoes, and figs. My cellar — alias pigskins — is stocked with sherry, Collares, an excellent wine of this country like claret but not so strong, and some draught wine.[13]

The middle-class Portuguese soon recovered their courage after the French retreat to Santarem, and pleasure parties used to visit the Lines of Torres Vedras out of curiosity. But life was much harsher for the tens of thousands of Portuguese refugees who had streamed into Lisbon. Some precautions had been taken, but because the emergency lasted far longer than had been anticipated they proved inadequate, and there was hunger, disease and thousands of deaths among the civilians behind the Lines that winter.

Even so, the refugees were far better off than their compatriots who stayed behind and fell into the hands of the French, or indeed than the French themselves. Despite Wellington's orders the countryside had not been thoroughly devastated, and large stocks of food had been hidden rather than destroyed. As the weeks passed and hunger sharpened their ingenuity the French gradually uncovered these hidden stores, and so they continued to occupy their ground months after Wellington had thought that starvation would compel their retreat. But they suffered terribly, especially the inexperienced conscripts of Junot's corps. On New Year's Day 1811 Junot had over 8,000 sick from a total of fewer than 23,000 men. In the army as a whole there were nearly 19,000 sick and fewer than 47,000 men under arms.[14] In the following weeks the number of sick diminished — but only because the number of deaths increased. The veteran troops of Reynier's and Ney's corps suffered less: they were tougher, their experience stood them in good stead, and Ney's men had better ground to forage in. But even the survivors were terribly deprived, lacking not only food and shelter, but clothing, equipment and ammunition. And yet, if Wellington is to be believed, there was an illicit trade in luxury goods from Lisbon to the

French army, so that some officers at least did not go without coffee, sugar and so on.[15]

Masséna subjected his army to this appalling suffering because he had no real alternative. A winter retreat through barren Portugal, infested with militia and Ordenanza, with Wellington hot on his heels, was a recipe for disaster and possibly even for the complete disintegration of his army. In any case, it was his duty to remain for as long as possible to contain Wellington's army and to give Napoleon every opportunity to devise means to complete the conquest of Portugal. But even Masséna's iron will could not have maintained his position if his army had not received a substantial reinforcement under Drouet at the end of 1810. These men were not enough to enable him to take the offensive, but they reduced the risk of a successful allied attack, while of course adding to the number of mouths to be fed.

Both Wellington and Masséna conserved their strength during the winter, and the only active operations of any importance were further south where Soult collected a field army by stripping his garrisons to the bone, and advanced into Estremadura. He left Seville on 31 December 1810 with 20,000 men, including a high proportion of cavalry and a strong siege-train. His object was to destroy the Spanish Army of Estremadura and capture Badajoz and several lesser frontier fortresses. His force was not large enough to invade Portugal but his offensive would stage a diversion which might help Masséna.

Soult's campaign was immensely successful. On 22 January, after a short siege, he captured the antiquated fortress of Olivenza and 4,000 prisoners for the loss of fewer than sixty casualties. On 26 January he invested Badajoz, the strongest of the four fortresses on the Spanish-Portuguese border. On 19 February Mendizabal, who now commanded the Spanish army of Estremadura, foolishly offered battle at Gebora, just outside the fortress, and was routed with heavy losses. Despite this victory the siege dragged on into March, and Soult grew anxious, for he knew that Wellington had detached Beresford with a strong force to relieve Badajoz, and disquietening rumours were arriving from Andalusia. Finally, however, by 10 March, the French artillery had battered a practicable breach in the fortress walls and Soult demanded its surrender. General Imaz, the Governor, agreed to terms, and Badajoz surrendered on the following day. (Wellington was highly critical of Imaz's capitulation, which was certainly not very heroic, but as Beresford's relief column was at least a week away and the fortress had already held out for six weeks after Wellington predicted its speedy fall, the severity of his criticism appears unwarranted.)[16]

As soon as he had secured the fortress, Soult hurried back to Seville, leaving Mortier with 11,000 men to maintain the French position in Estremadura. He had taken over 20,000 prisoners in a brief campaign, in a hostile country, in the depths of winter, and it was no fault of his that his operations had failed to aid Masséna.

While he had been away, his enemies in Andalusia had been active. Ballasteros with 4,000 men marched within twenty miles of Seville and defeated several French detachments, but then fell back without venturing to attack the great city, unaware that its weak garrison consisted mainly of invalids and troops of doubtful loyalty. Further south, the allied forces in Cadiz made an attempt to break the siege. An army of 10,000 Spanish and 5,000 British troops, under the overall command of General La Peña, was detached and landed some miles down the coast so that it could threaten the French positions from the rear. Unfortunately the campaign did not go well. The marches were badly arranged and the British soon lost confidence in La Peña. On 5 March at Barrosa, as the army was approaching Cadiz, the French suddenly attacked. It was a confused battle in which the British did almost all the fighting, defeating a much superior force, but losing a quarter of their number as casualties. Naturally angry at La Peña's refusal to aid him in the fight, Graham withdrew his victorious but battered army into Cadiz, leaving the Spaniards with no option but to follow. With better leadership and more allied cooperation Barrosa would have led to the raising of the siege of Cadiz, and probably the temporary liberation of all southern Andalusia and even Seville. Yet Graham's decision seems wise, for operations were unlikely to prosper under La Peña's command. The campaign caused outrage in Britain, fuelled the conviction that Spanish generals were incompetent, and added greatly to the acrimony in Anglo-Spanish relations.

A few days before Barrosa, on 3 March 1811, Masséna at last gave the order to retreat. His army had suffered terribly, losing nearly 25,000 men in the invasion of Portugal. Of these, 8,000 were prisoners and almost all the remainder had perished: 2,000 or so in action, and the rest from the combination of malnutrition and disease. The campaign had failed because the French at all levels had underestimated Wellington's preparations — Masséna's army was simply too small for the task.[17]

At first Masséna hoped to halt his retreat in a new position in Portugal, but once his army began to move, its weakness became obvious. The troops still fought well, and there were a number of hotly contested rearguard actions with the pursuing British, but the army as a whole had lost confidence in its commander. On 22 March Masséna was forced to dismiss Marshal Ney for insubordination, when the latter refused to obey orders for an ill-judged attempt to resume the offensive. Ney left, but Masséna's plan soon foundered and he was forced to resume his retreat. An attempt to hold the line of the Coa was defeated at Sabugal on 3 April, and Masséna fell back to Salamanca. Here his army found the numerous reinforcements and the fresh supplies it so badly needed, and before the end of April it was again fit to take the field.

Wellington pursued the French to the frontier and then blockaded the Portuguese fortress of Almeida, in which Masséna had left a garrison but few supplies. At the end of April Masséna gathered his still weary troops together and, borrowing 2,000 cavalry from the Army of the North, advanced to relieve Almeida with a force of 48,000 men. Wellington's army had suffered from its rapid advance through Portugal and he had detached nearly 20,000 men under Beresford, so he could put fewer than 40,000 men in the field to bar Masséna's advance, but unlike the French, his troops were full of confidence. Wellington chose a fairly strong position a few miles in advance of Almeida at Fuentes d'Oñoro.

Masséna made a partial attack on 3 May, and there was heavy fighting in the village of Fuentes d'Oñoro itself, which changed hands several times during the day. By nightfall each side had suffered several hundred casualties, and the French had achieved nothing, other than to discover that the allied line was strongly held. Masséna spent the next day reconnoitring the terrain and laying plans to turn the allied right flank on the following day. Wellington also recognized the vulnerability of this flank and detached the newly formed Seventh Division to guard against the danger. However, when Masséna attacked early on the 5th, Wellington's decision proved one of the few serious tactical mistakes he ever made. The Seventh Division had been detached too far and was exposed to the full weight of Masséna's turning movement. It retreated with difficulty in a scrambling fight in which the strong French cavalry left no room for further mistakes. But after some anxious moments the allied line was re-established and the French attacks repulsed. The result was probably the least convincing of all Wellington's victories. In the two days of fighting, the French lost nearly 3,000 casualties, about 1,000 more than the allies, and they failed to relieve Almeida.[18]

On 8 May Masséna's army fell back, and on the night of the 10/11 May the French garrison blew up the fortress and escaped through allied lines. Wellington was furious and — not unfairly — blamed his subordinates, telling his brother, 'there is nothing on earth so stupid as a gallant officer'.[19] Nonetheless, the allies had regained Almeida and although it had been severely damaged, it was not beyond repair and subsequently proved a valuable base for operations against Ciudad Rodrigo. With its capture, the last French troops had been driven from Portugal.

Before he had recovered from his anger at the escape of the garrison of Almeida, Wellington received much worse news from Estremadura. As soon as Masséna had retreated from Santarem, Wellington had detached Beresford with 20,000 Anglo-Portuguese troops to relieve Badajoz. Beresford's advance had been delayed by the lack of a pontoon-train and other logistical difficulties, and hearing that Badajoz had fallen, he foolishly allowed himself to be distracted by some preliminary operations, so he did not invest the fortress until the first week of May. The French used this time to repair the fortress and establish in it a strong garrison, then their covering force retired before Beresford's advance in the hope that Soult could bring a relief force up from Andalusia.

Beresford's siege did not prosper. His siege-train was woefully inadequate and the British engineers were inexperienced, while the French defence was enterprising and determined. After barely a week, which had cost his army over 700 casualties and done nothing to dent Badajoz's defences, he was forced to give up the siege by news that Soult was rapidly approaching. Beresford sent his heavy guns and ammunition back to the Portuguese fortress of Elvas, collected his army, and advanced to meet Soult. He was joined by Blake and Castaños with 15,000 Spanish troops who had recently arrived from Cadiz. When the allies took up their positions at Albuera they outnumbered the French by almost three to two (10,000 British, plus 10,000 Portuguese and 15,000 Spanish, making a total of 35,000 allies, compared with 24,000 French). Nonetheless, Soult had no hesitation in attacking on 16 May and succeeded in turning the allied flank. Beresford was no Wellington, and although accounts are confused, it appears that he lost his nerve in the strain of battle; but his subordinates carried on, and in the end the day was saved by the tenacity of the British infantry who sustained terrible losses without breaking, and who eventually drove the French back in confusion. Both armies suffered greatly: the French lost 6,000 casualties, or a quarter of their force. Of the allies, the British alone lost 4,000 casualties, or 40 per cent of their men. Colbourne's brigade lost two-thirds of its strength when it was caught in the flank by Soult's Polish lancers, and six other regiments in the British army lost more than half their strength. The total allied loss equalled the French, and neither army was fit to renew the engagement. Both generals were stunned by the action, and it was a few days before the French were able to begin to limp back to Andalusia.

Wellington was aghast when he heard the news of the carnage. He told William Wellesley-Pole:

> The battle of Albuera was a strange concern. They were never determined to fight it; they did not occupy the ground as they ought; they were ready to run away at every moment from the time it commenced till the French retired; and if it had not been for me, who am now suffering from the loss and disorganization occasioned by that battle, they would have written a whining report upon it, which would have driven the people in England mad. However, I prevented that.[20]

After Albuera the allies painfully resumed the siege of Badajoz, beginning again from scratch, as the French garrison had used the interlude to level all the earlier works. Wellington hurried south and supervised the operations, but progress continued to be slow. The improvised siege-train collected from Elvas remained hopelessly inadequate, and Wellington complained of the lack of trained sappers and miners. Yet the British government had long since sent Wellington a good modern siege-train which lay on board ship in Lisbon harbour — presumably Wellington felt that the siege would be decided one way or another before the slow-moving heavy guns could reach the front.[21]

The French responded quickly to the renewed allied siege of Badajoz. When Soult had fallen back after Albuera he had found substantial reinforcements waiting for him in Andalusia. Even more important was the fact that Masséna had been replaced in command of the Army of Portugal by Marshal Marmont — young and energetic, a brilliant organizer and able strategist, with a reputation still to make, but boundless confidence in his own ability. Marmont quickly revived his army, dismissing senior officers, promoting juniors and inspiring everyone with his energy and enthusiasm. When Soult appealed for aid in relieving Badajoz, Marmont marched his whole army south and met Soult at Merida on 18 June. Together the two marshals had over 60,000 men, and although Wellington had brought some of his own troops down from the north, he could only put about 54,000 men into the field. He therefore abandoned the second British siege of Badajoz (which had cost nearly 500 casualties) and retired to a strong position on the River Caya. The French entered Badajoz in triumph on 20 June and closely inspected Wellington's position before sensibly declining to attack it. The marshals had achieved their objective: Badajoz had been relieved and revictualled, and remained in French hands for the rest of the year, and Wellington's offensive had been checked. The balance of forces had already swung so far that the French commanders now felt content to contain Wellington: they no longer expected to drive him back in disarray. After a few days posturing on the Caya the French withdrew: Marmont went north to Salamanca, Soult south to Andalusia, and all the armies suspended operations during the midsummer heat.

The British government greeted the news of Masséna's retreat with delight, but it did not immediately abandon its intention of reducing the size of its own army in Portugal. On 11 April Liverpool asked Wellington whether an army of 30,000 effective rank and file, supported by a reserve of 10–15,000 men kept ready to sail in Britain, would be sufficient to defend Portugal if the French attempted another invasion. He indicated that the cabinet had yet to decide whether or not to reduce Wellington's army, but suggested that he send home eight weak battalions, which might or might not be replaced. At the same time, however, he announced the dispatch of a regiment of light cavalry to help in the pursuit of Masséna.[22]

But behind this cautious approach lay a rising confidence. The ministers were encouraged by the growing prospect of war in northern Europe (see chapter 10 below) which promised that, at the very least, Napoleon would be diverted from the Peninsula for some time. Liverpool assured Wellington that 'You know our Means both Military and Financial are limited; but such as they are, We are determined not to be diverted from the Peninsula to other objects. If we can strike a Blow, we will strike it there.'[23]

The success of the British advance through Portugal and Wellington's victory at Fuentes d'Oñoro enhanced this new confidence. In the last days of May the cabinet took several crucial decisions for the future of the war in the Peninsula. The ministers gave up all idea of reducing Wellington's army and instead told him that more than 6,000 infantry would soon sail to join his army to make up for recent losses and to replace some of his most depleted units. In addition, a fresh regiment of light cavalry and the horses of another would be sent out, while a regiment of heavy cavalry was available if Wellington wanted it. He was also reminded that he had already been given authority to withdraw troops from the garrison of Cadiz to enlarge his army.[24] And, most important of all, the government issued Wellington with new instructions to supersede those issued at the beginning of 1810. Two versions of these new instructions survive. One, which is almost certainly the draft, cautiously gives him permission to engage in operations in the interior of Spain, provided that adequate arrangements had been made to ensure Spanish cooperation. The other version was much shorter and simpler, effectively giving Wellington complete discretion in the conduct of his operations.[25]

This decision marked a significant shift of policy by the Perceval government. For the first time since the government was formed it agreed to go beyond a strictly limited commitment to the defence of Portugal and to undertake an active role in the war in the Peninsula as a whole. It was a triumph not for the views of Lord Wellesley or his brother Henry, but for the quite different policy advocated by Wellington. Some Spanish troops might continue to serve with Wellington and under his command, but they were never to be as important to British strategy as the Portuguese. The primary thrust of Wellington's policy was the creation of a single powerful army completely under his control. It was the success of this policy which finally made Britain a significant military power in 1813, for the first time in the Revolutionary and Napoleonic Wars. Not that the ministers thought of this in May 1811. Their ideas were much less grandiose and they concentrated their attention on more immediate objectives. The escalation of British forces was undertaken cautiously, step by step, so that if any one step proved too much for Britain's resources it could be annulled. But the decisions made in May 1811 mark the beginning of this process and the adoption by the ministers of a new, more aggressive and optimistic attitude to the war.

Wellington's personal relations with the government improved greatly during the last nine months of the year. He was relieved by the result of the Regency crisis, but Liverpool's letter of 20 February complaining of the ballooning cost of the war did nothing to endear the government to him or remove his suspicions of the minister in particular. He replied by contesting Liverpool's figures in detail and pointed out that the comparison between the cost of the war in 1809 and 1810 was invalid because much of the army only arrived in April 1809. He urged it as a general principle that 'it was in the interest of Great Britain to employ in Portugal the largest army that could be spared from other Services', and recommended that if reductions had to be made, they should be achieved by reducing the number of British troops at Cadiz and in other garrisons.[26]

Gradually this distrust faded as the government's policy became more positive. In particular, the strong support Wellington received from the ministers over Albuera, when he had expected to be much abused, helped to establish trust. By July he was telling Wellesley-Pole that 'Lord Liverpool was quite right not to move thanks for the battle at Fuentes', while a month later he reacted to a shortage of specie with quite uncharacteristic mildness.[27] From the spring onwards he explained his plans to the ministers in much greater detail, which both reflected and encouraged greater confidence. At the end of the year relations were cordial, if not perfectly harmonious, although some traces of Wellington's prejudice against Liverpool persisted well into 1812.

Wellington's growing faith in the government must certainly have been helped by the steady stream of reinforcements which he received during the year. In January 1811 he commanded just over 42,000 British rank and file. This rose to 48,000 in April, and 52,000 in July, before reaching a peak of 57,000 in October. But, as in 1810, the benefits of these reinforcements were undermined by the high level of sickness in Wellington's army — the number of sick never fell below 10,000 after April and reached a maximum of over 17,000 in October. With other detachments this meant that Wellington's army seldom rose much above 35,000 effective British rank and file, despite the best efforts of the government.[28]

These British troops were supplemented by the Portuguese army, which continued to perform well during the campaigns of 1811. But while military cooperation prospered, other aspects of the alliance were beset with problems. Large parts of Portugal had been devastated by Masséna's invasion, the economy was crippled, Lisbon was filled with thousands of refugees, inflation soared and tax revenues fell. Public subscriptions in Britain and among the officers of Wellington's army provided some support for the refugees, and the increase in the British subsidy helped the government. But though the help was generous, it was insufficient, and the financial problems of the Portuguese government had a direct effect on its army. In May Wellington told Liverpool: 'The Portuguese troops with this part of the army don't produce in the field half of their effective strength, because the soldiers have been ill fed and taken care of; and vast numbers of them are in hospitals.' He added that the British commissariat was having to feed most of the Portuguese army, and that it was also dependent on British hospitals and supplies of ammunition.[29]

Wellington's relations with the Portuguese Regency Council were often difficult both in 1811 and later, although he increasingly left disputes to be handled by Charles Stuart. The British complained of Portuguese inefficiency and factionalism, and pressed for sweeping reforms of the

Portuguese government and taxation system. They had some successes, but many important decisions were referred to Brazil, which wasted months before a frequently unsatisfactory reply could be received. Problems, especially financial problems, remained in the alliance throughout the war, with their seriousness varying from season to season. But Portugal was making an immense military and financial effort for a nation of her size and comparative poverty, and the British subsidy covered only a small part of the cost of the war. Portuguese troops comprised a third or more of Wellington's army and, except for their cavalry, were almost equal to the British in quality, while Lisbon provided a secure and convenient base until the closing months of the war. In 1812 and 1813 as Wellington carried the war into Spain, relations with Portugal became less prominent, but they remained the essential foundation of all his operations.

Anglo–Spanish relations were even more troubled. Henry Wellesley was dissatisfied with the performance of the Spanish armies and understood that no real improvement could be expected without a complete change of system. In January he revived Lord Wellesley's earlier scheme, arguing that Britain should take over the Spanish armies as she had those of Portugal, with British officers to retrain the men, and with Wellington given sweeping authority as Commander-in-Chief. Britain would pay for the reforms by a loan to Spain of £8 to £10 million.[30]

Henry Wellesley knew that his plan would encounter powerful opposition from many leading Spaniards in Cadiz. Earlier, more modest attempts to retrain Spanish units with British officers had been thwarted, even when they had gained formal approval. But Wellesley had convinced himself (quite wrongly) that there was strong support for his schemes in the Cortes. Wellington was more sceptical. He told Lord Wellesley that 'The Spaniards would not, I believe, allow of that active interference by us in their affairs which might effect an amelioration of their circumstances'. Wellington instead proposed that he be allowed to subsidize the Spanish armies that operated near him, entirely at his own discretion, so that he could force them to cooperate with him. He was also most unenthusiastic about the idea of his being made Commander-in-Chief of the Spanish armies, unless Britain could ensure that they were regularly paid.[31]

In London, Liverpool was initially inclined to support Henry Wellesley's proposal, but abandoned it in the face of the need for economy.[32] Nor did the ambassador's preliminary overtures prosper in Cadiz. When he heard of Masséna's retreat, he seized the moment and proposed that Wellington be given command of the Spanish forces in the provinces adjoining Portugal, but the support he had so confidently anticipated in the Cortes failed to materialize. He therefore let the matter rest even when, in April, Lord Wellesley conveyed the government's approval for a modified version of his original proposal. This was that Wellington be given command of all the military and civil authorities in Galicia, Asturias, Estremadura and other provinces bordering Portugal, with the power to introduce British officers into the Spanish forces in those provinces. But while Britain offered to provide equipment and officers to the Spanish armies, it did not offer to pay them, let alone produce the massive loan which Henry Wellesley had suggested.[33]

Despite the failure of these sweeping proposals, 1811 saw more effective military cooperation between British and Spanish forces than any previous year of the war. Such cooperation led to much friction, with British generals seldom concealing their irritation at the inefficiency and lack of realism of their Spanish counterparts, while each side accused the other of pride and arrogance. But although the Spaniards had disgraced themselves at Gebora and Barrosa, they had fought courageously at Albuera, and still occupied the attention of the vast majority of the French forces in the Peninsula.

Outside the narrow confines of military cooperation, relations continued to be filled with acrimonious disputes on a wide range of issues. Spanish requests for enormous subsidies caused offence, as did continuing British pressure to trade with Spain's American colonies. These colonies were now full of discontent and in some cases in open revolt, adding a poisonous new element to relations between the allies. For revolt in the colonies dramatically reduced revenue remitted to Spain, adding to calls for a large subsidy from Britain, while the British were incensed by Spanish plans to suppress these revolts by sending out troops from the Peninsula. Altogether there was little love lost between the allies, and only their implacable hostility to the French united them.

There were no great victories to smooth relations between the allies during the second half of 1811. Wellington, having twice been foiled at Badajoz, turned his attention to Ciudad Rodrigo, and attempted to starve the garrison into submission. But Marmont borrowed troops from the Army of the North and advanced with such a large force that Wellington gave way with no more than a skirmish. Rowland Hill, who had replaced Beresford in command of the allied troops in Estremadura, added some lustre to the closing months of the year when he surprised General Girard's division at Arroyo dos Molinos and took nearly 1,300 prisoners for the loss of barely 100 casualties. Otherwise the forces in the western half of the Peninsula remained evenly balanced, with the allies holding the initiative, but being too weak to exploit it.

In eastern Spain, however, the French remained dominant. On 2 January 1811 Suchet had captured Tortosa, an important fortress guarding communications between Catalonia and Valencia. On 28 June he took the port of Tarragona, crippling the resistance in Catalonia. And on 25 October he defeated a large Spanish army at Saguntum, opening the way for the conquest of Valencia. Wellington feared that the loss of Valencia — a rich and fertile province — might seriously undermine the Spanish resolve to continue the contest and even open the way for peace negotiations.[34] But in fact it merely made the French armies more overextended and vulnerable. Napoleon ordered Marmont to detach troops to assist Suchet in the conquest of Valencia, believing that Wellington was too timid and slow to take advantage of a brief opportunity in the middle of winter. The year 1812 was to prove him wrong.

Masséna's retreat and the success of British arms during the spring of 1811 led to a dramatic change in the Opposition's position on the war in the Peninsula. On 18 March, before news of the French retreat reached London, they vigorously opposed the proposal to increase the subsidy to Portugal. Ponsonby, the Whig leader in the Commons, sarcastically remarked that 'our success consists in having lost almost the whole of Portugal, and that our army is now confined or hemmed in between Lisbon and Cartaxo'. And he went on to ask, 'How long can this country support this expense?' In the Lords a few days later, Lord Grenville attacked the government's whole strategy in the Peninsula, where 'three campaigns had more and more shewn its impolicy'.[35]

Unofficial reports of Masséna's retreat reached London by 26 March, although Wellington's dispatches did not arrive until 6 and 8 April. A few weeks later, on 26 April, Lord Grey seconded a motion by Lord Liverpool proposing a Vote of Thanks to Wellington and his army. Grey admitted that this marked a complete reversal of his earlier attitude and that he had expected a very different end to the campaign. His praise for Wellington was generous: 'by the most patient perseverance under unfavourable circumstances, and at the moment of action by the most skilful combination of force and the most determined courage, a great success had been achieved'. His previous views were only reflected towards the end of his speech when he warned the Lords that the victory might be followed by an even greater effort by Napoleon, and confessed that he still did not believe that an ultimate victory would be possible unless the Spaniards took a greater part in the war.[36]

Grey's lead was followed in the Commons where some of the most vociferous critics of the war admitted that they had been wrong, and by 1 May even Whitbread was enthusiastically endorsing the Vote of Thanks. Only Lord Grenville refused to join the new chorus, and his objections had always been based primarily on financial grounds. Yet the Opposition's conversion was less complete than it appeared. They refrained from public criticism and even supported the Vote of Thanks for Albuera, although they knew from officers in the army that the official account of the battle had been sanitized. But in private they remained extremely pessimistic throughout the year. In June, for example, Grey told Grenville that

the French are on the point of making a great effort in Portugal . . . which Lord Wellington . . . will find himself unable to resist. But even if such an effort could not take place or should not succeed, I am convinced the period when we shall be obliged to give up the contest from an absolute inability to support the expense, is fast approaching.

To which Grenville replied by doubting whether Grey was 'quite as strongly impressed as myself with the desperate and hopeless character' of waging war on the Continent.[37]

Wellington's success and the Opposition's volte-face on the Peninsular War greatly strengthened the government's position in Parliament during 1811. But in any case the heat went out of the Parliamentary struggle as all parties recognized that, for the moment at least, it was of less importance than the state of the King's health and the Regent's sympathies. The longest and most tedious debate of the session was on the recommendations of the committee of enquiry into the shortage of bullion which had been established against Perceval's wishes early in the session of 1810. The committee had been dominated by Huskisson and other concerned economists, and its findings urged the necessity of a resumption of cash payments within two years. Perceval vigorously opposed the recommendations, stating both publicly and privately that their adoption would be 'tantamount to a Parliamentary declaration that we must submit to any terms of peace rather than continue the war, which . . . would be found utterly impossible'. Faced with this official hostility and receiving only tepid support from the bulk of the Opposition, the committee had its findings decisively rejected by the House, which was bored to distraction by the whole debate.[38]

Despite the dire predictions of Huskisson and others, the nation's finances appeared to be relatively healthy in the spring of 1811 when Perceval delivered his budget. The revenue received in 1810 had actually exceeded estimates, and Perceval was able to finance the year's borrowing with little difficulty by increases in the duty on spirits, foreign timber, potash and foreign linen. But although it took some time to show in the government's finances, the economy was already moving deep into recession. The speculative boom of 1809–10 had collapsed, bankruptcies were soaring (from 1,089 in 1809 to 2,000 in 1811) and many parts of the Midlands suffered high unemployment.[39]

With the distress came social unrest. Petitions to Parliament were organized calling for assistance and, in some cases, for peace. The government flew in the face of conventional views of economics and issued Exchequer bills to aid hard-pressed manufacturers, but this had little effect. With unemployment came the usual disturbances, local riots and the like; but soon they took a new form with the first appearance of Luddites, who forcibly protested against the introduction of new machinery and new work-practices. Luddite activity lasted for a little over a year, varying in intensity over time and between regions. The local authorities, who had no means of countering it, were alarmed, and spread wild tales of secret drilling and subversive French agents. But the government in London remained calm. It deployed a few thousand troops to restore order in troubled areas and attempted to intimidate the Luddites by making frame-breaking a capital offence. Whatever the importance of these disturbances for the development of working-class consciousness and the radical tradition in

Britain, their impact on the government and on the conduct of the war was slight. The troops used against them came from the normal home garrison, although on at least one occasion the Duke of York cited the troubled state of the country in opposing the dispatch of another regiment of dragoons to the Peninsula.[40] Nor could even the interest of Byron's maiden speech make it an important issue in party politics.

The government's stronger performance in Parliament was matched by easier relations in the cabinet. Lord Wellesley remained the odd man out and continued to infuriate his colleagues with his inefficiency; but Wellesley himself was much less discontented. He was placated by the government's adoption of a more positive strategy in the Peninsula and was excited by promising developments in northern Europe. Unlike the other ministers, he went out of his way to cultivate the Prince Regent and encouraged the Prince's budding enthusiasm for the war. The two men had much in common: a scandalous private life, wild extravagance leading to colossal debts, a taste for gross flattery, and a marked dislike for hard work.

Perceval and the Prince, on the other hand, had many tussles over matters of patronage, while the Prime Minister refused to adjust the government's policies to suit the Prince's known views. On one issue, however, the Prince and the ministers were in complete agreement: the reappointment of the Duke of York to replace Sir David Dundas as Commander-in-Chief. The Prince had raised the question with Grenville in January, but the Opposition leader had been forced to admit that the hostility of the radical Whigs would prevent him proposing the measure. When the government announced its decision in May, most of the Opposition either supported it or remained silent, but some of the younger Whigs forced a debate and division on the issue. They were soundly beaten (296 votes to 47), but were warmly praised by the City radicals. The whole affair helped in the gradual alienation of the Prince from the Opposition.

The reappointment of the Duke is said to have been generally welcomed in the army. Before his resignation in 1809 there had been hints of ill-feeling between him and Sir Arthur Wellesley, but now William Wellesley-Pole could tell his brother that 'the Duke of York is most favourable to you, and most desirous to increase your Army'. Even before he received this letter Wellington greeted the news with warm approbation,[41] though the months and years ahead were to furnish many examples of heated disputes between the two men. The Duke was an able, though insufficiently flexible, administrator, who had played a great role in improving the quality of the army since his original appointment in 1795. He also provided the army with a strong voice in discussions with the government.

The Prince did not learn to love his ministers during the spring of 1811, although his sympathy for their opponents waned. He found his position uncomfortable and his duties onerous. Nearly thirty years of dissipation and self-indulgence proved poor training for the daily grind of official business, and he never acquired his father's prompt efficient habits. By the end of

February he was ill and out of spirits, and would have welcomed his father's recovery and with it his own liberation.

At that time, the prospect seemed likely, almost inevitable, for the King's health steadily improved during February and early March. When the Prince was indisposed for a few days at the end of February, one wag even suggested that the King be appointed sub-Regent to act for him.[42] In the middle of March George III had a setback which lasted for a week or so, but by the end of the month he had recovered the lost ground, and he continued to improve throughout April and early May, without ever quite satisfying his doctors that the recovery was complete. But in the middle of May he had a serious relapse, and reports of 20 May speak of his life as being in danger. He survived this crisis thanks to his tough constitution but his condition had deteriorated, and on 1 June the Queen reluctantly placed him in the care of Robert Willis, one of the doctors who specialized in the care of the mentally ill. The King was seriously ill throughout June and was much worse during July. By 15 July his life was plainly in danger and remained so until August, when he slowly recovered his physical strength. His mind, however, had gone beyond all hope of recovery. He lingered on, to all intents and purposes mad (for all that the cause was porphyria), abused by his doctors and largely forgotten by the world until 1820 when death finally released him.[43]

Throughout the summer of 1811 the British political world had followed the King's illness with rapt attention. When he appeared to be dying, the Whig *Morning Chronicle* had advised the ministers to meet the event with 'resignation'. On 20 July Lord Wellesley had sought an urgent interview with the Regent, 'before matters shall come to the last extremity at Windsor', at which he may have intended to stake his own claims to the Premiership. A week later Wellesley was advising Perceval not to prorogue Parliament until they knew if the King would survive the crisis. On 6 August Charles Arbuthnot, one of the Secretaries of the Treasury, told a friend that he had been hard at work, clearing arrears, in case the King died. 'Not that I have been expecting to be turned out, but as the chance of it must always exist I have been desirous of having no work upon my hands in case I should be called upon to render my accounts.'[44]

The crisis in the King's health passed, but as there was now no hope of his ultimate recovery the Regent's pretext for retaining his father's ministers had evaporated. Had he dismissed the government and brought in the Opposition, no one could have blamed him, for he would have acted consistently with the principles of his entire public life, after having shown every consideration for his father's feelings. But the Prince did nothing. He was lazy, indecisive and a moral coward. He shrank from action: from either dismissing Perceval or dashing the hopes of the Opposition. Nothing forced him to decide immediately, so he let matters drift on until the expiration of the restrictions on his powers in February 1812. There was no practical significance in the lifting of the restrictions, but they provided an excuse for delaying his decision, which the Prince eagerly seized. With hindsight we can see that the Prince's failure to dismiss his father's ministers in August 1811 was itself decisive. If his residual feelings of loyalty, affection and political consistency did not compel him to act then, they never would.

What would the Prince have done if George III had died in July 1811? The question is tantalizing, but unanswerable. He himself almost certainly did not know. During the six months of the Regency he had been slowly growing further away from the Opposition and closer to the ministers. In May the Prince's old friend Lord Moira had warned Grey that 'the Prince was daily accustoming himself more and more to these Ministers, . . . that finding himself in possession of the power of the Government, which went on without any trouble or difficulty to him, his natural dislike of exertion increased his indisposition to change; and that these feelings were very much assisted by the constant endeavours of the Duke of Cumberland and Lord Yarmouth to encourage and confirm them'.[45]

On 1 July the Regent held a dinner for the Opposition leaders at Carlton House, but over the next few weeks he also dined with various ministers — something he had sworn never to do. Thomas Creevey, the radical Whig and frequent guest of the Regent, was outraged, fiercely condemning the 'folly and villainy of this Prinny'.[46] Yet Creevey's anger did not stop him from dining at the Brighton Pavilion, though he proved his integrity by privately abusing his host.

In August Charles Arbuthnot was confident: 'it certainly is my decided opinion that shd the King die there wd be no change'. He understood that the Prince had come to support the government's conduct of the war, and thought that the Prince would hesitate to dismiss a government which Arbuthnot believed was popular and replace it with a generally unpopular Opposition. Yet Arbuthnot recognized that there was little sympathy between the scrupulous, evangelical Perceval and the extravagant, indulgent Regent, and he feared that the government might be broken on quarrels over patronage or the composition of the ministry. There is no doubt that the Regent's political allegiances were shifting, but it is impossible to say when they shifted decisively to the government.[47]

Parliament rose on 24 July and did not meet again until 7 January 1812. The intervening months were filled with intense political speculation. The Opposition did not yet give up hope, although its leaders were characteristically beginning to suspect that the grapes were sour. The long autumn months in the country encouraged political gossip and incessant letter-writing. Rumours flew around the country based on reports of the Prince's smile or frown, while almost every conceivable combination of politicians was suggested as the next government.

As the year drew towards its close, the Prince's behaviour became more erratic as the strain of the impending decision increased. In November he badly twisted his ankle while trying to show Princess Charlotte how to dance the Highland Fling. For several weeks he lay on a couch consuming vast quantities of laudanum and writing lachrymose letters to his mistress Lady Hertford.[48] Christmas came and the Prince had still to make up his mind. And so Britain ended the year as she had begun, with a looming political crisis hanging over the government.

9

Sicily and the Mediterranean, 1810–12

Domestic politics and the war in the Peninsula were the main focus of British attention during 1810 and 1811, but important developments were occurring in the Mediterranean, central and eastern Europe, and in Britain's relations with the United States which were to help shape the war in the years to come.

Throughout the long war the Mediterranean had the potential to become an immensely important theatre of operations. In 1793 the allied occupation of Toulon had seemed — briefly — to open the back door of France, but more commonly the allies were on the defensive. Napoleon's conquest of northern Italy in 1796–7 had led to the French occupation of Rome and Naples; and when, in 1797, he divided Venice and her territories with Austria, he retained possession of the Ionian Islands, including Corfu. The French were soon driven out of the Ionian Islands, but regained them by the Treaty of Tilsit, and Corfu remained in French hands until after Napoleon's abdication in 1814.

Napoleon was always convinced of the importance of establishing and maintaining a strong French presence in the western Balkans. When he defeated Austria in 1805 he demanded the cession of Dalmatia (i.e. the former Venetian territories on the eastern coast of the Adriatic); and after again defeating Austria in 1809 he obtained the Illyrian provinces, thus linking Dalmatia to the Kingdom of Italy and cutting Austria off from the Adriatic. Napoleon derived three main advantages from holding these territories: they were strategically useful in any future war with Austria, forcing her to divert troops from more important theatres; their possession, especially that of the great port of Trieste, blocked a major hole in the Continental System; and, perhaps most importantly, they provided him with a base for operations if the Ottoman Empire in Europe collapsed.

The decline of the Ottoman Empire had been one of the great questions of European diplomacy throughout the eighteenth century, as it was to remain until the First World War. The fate of Constantinople in particular aroused much speculation, with many powers, including France, anxious to ensure that it did not fall into the hands of Russia. Napoleon and Alexander amicably discussed the partition of the Turkish Empire at Tilsit, but as the warmth of the personal meeting faded, the French Emperor became reluctant even to approve existing Russian conquests in Moldavia and Wallachia. Napoleon's attitude to the Ottoman Empire was ambivalent: it was a useful ally in a war with Russia, but it was also a decaying power ripe for conquest. Essentially, he was anxious to preserve it until he could ensure that France received her proper share of the spoils in any division; and his ideas on the size of that proper share rapidly grew.

Britain opposed both French and Russian ambitions in the Near East. As early as 1791, in the Ochakov Crisis, Pitt had risked war in an unsuccessful attempt to make Russia disgorge recent conquests on the Black Sea. But the war with France led to alliances with Russia, which in turn sometimes led to a half-hearted war with the Turkish Empire. Hence Duckworth's abortive attack on Constantinople and Fraser's occupation of Alexandria in 1807. Peace was formally re-established with the Sublime Porte (as the Ottoman government was known) early in 1809, and for some years Britain and France competed for influence while the Turks continued their war against Russia.

Britain constantly endeavoured to check French advances in the Mediterranean. When Napoleon had invaded Egypt in 1798, Nelson had destroyed the French fleet at the Battle of the Nile, and in 1801 — long after Napoleon had returned to France — a British force under Abercromby had defeated the French army and forced it to capitulate. In 1809 Admiral Collingwood responded to the news of the Austrian defeat at Wagram and reports of French intrigues in Greece by arranging for the British occupation of all the Ionian Islands except Corfu, which was too strongly fortified for the available forces.[1] At the same time, on the mainland, Britain endeavoured to secure an alliance with the semi-independent Albanian warlord Ali Pasha of Jannina, without offending the Sublime Porte.

Despite this longstanding interest in the fate of Turkey, Britain's interests at Constantinople were neglected in 1811, there being no ambassador in residence. Fortunately Stratford Canning, the young acting minister, was a man of great energy and self-confidence who, acting virtually without instructions, did much to thwart French influence and maintain British prestige. Robert Liston had been chosen as the new ambassador in 1811, but he did not finally sail until March 1812. He was instructed to facilitate a peace between Turkey and Russia and to check French attempts to forge an alliance with the Porte. By the time he arrived in Constantinople in June these objects had been achieved, and Stratford Canning was claiming the credit. Canning became a great, forceful ambassador to Turkey over many decades, but he probably exaggerated his role in the events of 1812. While he may well have smoothed the path of the negotiations which led to the Treaty of Bucharest (28 May 1812), peace was only made possible by the belated Russian willingness to moderate their demands in the face of the imminent French invasion. The Turks were well aware of the insincerity of Napoleon's professions of friendship and shrewdly extracted the maximum advantage from their position.

Britain's interests in the Mediterranean extended beyond the preservation of the Ottoman Empire. The Mediterranean and southern Europe had always been an important market for British exports, and it became even more important as the threat posed by the Continental System grew. Between 1800 and 1805 British exports and re-exports to southern Europe averaged (on official values) £4 million per year, or 12 per cent of total exports. Between 1807 and 1812 this had risen to over £9 million per year, or 33 per cent, with the rise especially significant in 1811 and 1812, years when many of Britain's other markets were closed to her.[2]

The prosperity of this trade depended on Britain maintaining her command of the sea in the Mediterranean. In this she was greatly assisted by the Spanish rising of 1808, which removed the Cadiz and Carthagena squadrons from the ranks of her enemies, and which led directly to the capture of Rosilly's French squadron in Cadiz. The Spanish forces were too preoccupied with the land war to provide active naval cooperation, but the use of their harbours — especially Port Mahon, Minorca — and some logistical support was most helpful. In return the Royal Navy provided frequent support for the Spanish patriots, harassing French troop movements near the coast, landing British supplies for the guerrillas, and maintaining communications with besieged coastal fortresses such as Rosas. Lord Cochrane's operations on the Catalan coast in 1808 and Sir Home Popham's campaign in the Bay of Biscay in 1812 are only the highlights in a constant pattern of activity.

Napoleon ordered the construction of warships at suitable ports throughout his empire. In the Mediterranean theatre these included Venice, Naples, Genoa and — by far the most important — the great naval base at Toulon. It was from Toulon that Villeneuve had sailed at the beginning of 1805 on the cruise that was to end many months later at Trafalgar. This disaster left the Toulon fleet weak for several years, but by the beginning of 1808 it had been re-established through new building and the arrival of the Rochefort squadron. By the end of the war the Toulon fleet had grown to twenty-four ships of the line, including six 130-gun ships with more under construction.[3]

The French Mediterranean fleet posed special problems for the British, for unlike the Channel Ports, it proved impossible to maintain a close blockade of Toulon. This meant that the French ships were able to exercise at sea, and to establish a level of seamanship and discipline much superior to that of other French squadrons. Nonetheless, the Toulon fleet posed little direct threat to British command of the sea. While the French crews and captains were individually brave and not unskilled, they had little experience of manoeuvring as a fleet or sailing in rough weather. Weaknesses such as these had led to French defeats in every major naval battle of the war, and this in turn had led to a crushing sense of inferiority. Mere numbers were not enough to ensure a triumph, as Trafalgar had shown, and the French had little else in their favour. Even in isolated ship-to-ship contests, where French disadvantages counted for far less, they were almost invariably defeated.

The great worry for the British was not that the Toulon fleet would sail forth challenging the British to open battle, but rather that it would slip out under cover of bad weather, evade the blockade and strike a blow at allied positions before it could be caught. This was what happened in 1798 when Brueys's fleet escorted Napoleon's army to Egypt, capturing Malta en route, before Nelson could find it. Ten years later Ganteaume emerged from Toulon, made a rendezvous with the Rochefort squadron and — despite being scattered by gales — succeeded in conveying some supplies to Corfu before, uniquely, returning safely to Toulon.

The British admirals were haunted by the spectre of a repetition of this cruise, with some more serious object than the mere ferrying of supplies to Corfu. There was no shortage of vulnerable spots at which the French could strike. In the eastern Mediterranean they might again land an army in Egypt, or in southern Greece, or even in Crete. Further west they could attack Malta, Sardinia, Cadiz, Gibraltar or even, conceivably, Lisbon. The Balearics were a likely target and the weakness of their defences caused Admiral Fremantle, who was based there in 1811, such concern that he sought to borrow British troops from Cadiz and Gibraltar to strengthen their garrison. This was disallowed by higher authority, but the British government was well aware of the problem and it made repeated, though largely ineffectual, representations to the Spanish authorities to take greater precautions.[4]

However, the most likely object, and the most valuable prize for the French, was not the Balearics but Sicily, Britain's principal base in the Mediterranean. The original plan for Ganteaume's cruise in 1808 had been for him to collect 9,000 troops from Naples and land them near Messina while protecting the passage of a similar force in small boats from Calabria. This had only been abandoned in favour of the resupply of Corfu when a deterioration of Franco-Russian relations had led Napoleon to fear that Alexander might precipitate the breakup of the Ottoman Empire. It proved an opportunity wasted, but the British commanders in Sicily always had to be aware that the Royal Navy could not guarantee that the Toulon fleet might not suddenly sail, escape the blockade and land an army on the Sicilian coast, although it could ensure that such a project would be full of risks.[5]

Sicily was the lynchpin of British strategy in the Mediterranean, providing a convenient base for the navy and acting as an entrepôt for British trade. From Sicily British forces could threaten French possessions from Corfu to Catalonia, and in particular take advantage of any opportunity for intervention in Italy. Yet the cost was high: as well as paying a subsidy,

Britain promised to provide an army of no fewer than 10,000 men for the defence of the island. This proved inadequate, and with rare exceptions the British garrison amounted to between 15,000 and 20,000 men — which was a very considerable drain on her limited disposable forces. This army could be used for offensive operations in Italy, though even then the British generals were constantly aware of the dangers posed by the Toulon fleet, but only a relatively small part of it could be safely detached for operations further afield.

Britain's primary object in her relations with the government of Sicily was to ensure that the island did not fall either directly or indirectly into the hands of France. Unfortunately the Court and the government were bitterly unpopular with the people, while the Sicilian nobility resented their exclusion from office and the high place given to Neapolitan nobles and French émigrés. The King was weak, devious and passionately devoted to hunting, so that most official business fell into the hands of Queen Maria Carolina. She was voluble, erratic and tactless, greatly exacerbating the tensions in the island by her intense hatreds, love of intrigue, and almost total absence of common sense. She disliked and distrusted the British — feelings which they fully reciprocated — and at different times had endeavoured to obtain Austrian or Russian troops to replace them. Her great object was to regain Naples, on almost any terms, and she resented the fact that while the British government regarded this as desirable, it would not make it a sine qua non of peace with France.[6]

Early in 1807 the Ministry of All the Talents took such a serious view of the festering discontent in Sicily that it decided on full-scale intervention. The ministers were willing to suspend the subsidy and to adopt even more drastic measures to ensure the safety of the island. They believed that this could only be achieved if the Sicilian army was placed under the command of a British general who was given sufficient power to carry through sweeping reforms, including a substantial reduction in the size of the army. They also wished to impose a more truly Sicilian government in place of the existing administration, which was trusted only by the Court at Palermo. But the Talents fell before they could implement their policy, and the Portland government was much more cautious. This approach was supported by the British envoy to Sicily, William Drummond, who after initially favouring drastic action had become convinced that the Sicilian opposition was too fractious and divided to provide a real alternative to the Court.[7] For the next few years Britain avoided any great entanglement in the internal politics of Sicily, although the presence of her troops and the payment of the subsidy added to stability and so indirectly assisted the Court to maintain its grip on power.

The outbreak of the Peninsular War shifted the focus of British strategy away from the Mediterranean, and by 1810 Perceval's government was chiefly interested in finding a way to reduce Britain's military commitment to Sicily without endangering the security of the island. Orders were sent to

Sir John Stuart, the British commander in Sicily, to detach four strong battalions to join Wellington in Portugal. But the French under Marshal Murat, whom Napoleon had made King of Naples, were threatening an invasion from Calabria, and the Court at Palermo refused repeated demands to place its troops under British command. In the circumstances, Stuart was probably justified in retaining the troops, although there is some evidence that the threatened invasion of Sicily was seen by Napoleon primarily as a diversion.[8]

The events of 1810 forced the British government to reconsider its policy towards Sicily. Wellington had been deprived, at a crucial stage of his campaign, of four battalions on which he had calculated. The Sicilian government had behaved with extraordinary lethargy in the face of Murat's threatened invasion, and rumours abounded that the Queen was engaged in treacherous correspondence, and had even agreed to let the French into Sicily in exchange for the promised restitution of her beloved Naples. And finally, the state of domestic Sicilian politics had sharply deteriorated, with serious conflict between the local barons and the Court over questions of taxation and political power.[9]

British diplomats and soldiers had long advocated direct intervention in the internal affairs of Sicily, arguing that the government was so corrupt and unpopular that if Britain continued to support it, the local population would overcome their abhorrence of the French, and the defence of the island would become impossible. These views had been given currency in Britain by Francis Leckie — an able publicist who had lived in Sicily — and had been supported in a broader context by Captain Pasley in his influential work on the military policy of the British Empire. In Parliament the Opposition had strongly criticized the government's conciliatory policy in a series of debates on the Sicilian subsidy, so there was a climate of opinion in Britain which favoured intervention.

But the government had never been convinced by these arguments. Perceval believed that an active British policy risked exacerbating divisions within Sicily, and might even precipitate a revolution, while after intervention it would be difficult to ensure that a new Sicilian government would be stable or efficient. He was not convinced that the island could not be defended without wholesale reforms to its government, pointing out that British officers had been making similar claims for years, but that Sicily remained defended. As for the Queen, Perceval remarked that it was hardly surprising that she should be suspicious of Britain, when for years senior British figures in Sicily had been openly advocating drastic measures against her. Unless actual treachery could be proved, and Perceval was convinced that it could not, he felt that it would be 'an outrageous breach of faith' to intervene in the domestic politics of Sicily against the interests of the Court.[10]

By the end of 1810 both Lord Amherst, the British envoy, and Sir John Stuart had resigned, weary of the constant hostility of the Court. The

British government decided to appoint Lord William Bentinck to both positions in the hope of maximizing his influence and preventing the Court exploiting differences between civil and military representatives as it had in the past. Though only thirty-six, Bentinck was a major-general, with wide military and quasi-diplomatic experience, including acting as a liaison officer with the Austrian armies in northern Italy in 1799–1801 and, more recently, attempting to concert plans with the Spanish Junta in 1808. He was the second son of the late Duke of Portland, which had certainly helped his career, but the ministers had a genuinely high opinion of his ability. Perceval had offered him the position of Secretary at War in late 1809, and in 1810 he had been approached to go out to Portugal as Wellington's second-in-command, but he had declined both appointments. He was an able man of liberal inclinations, very cool in battle, and not at all afraid of responsibility, but not ideally suited to be a diplomat, as he lacked social graces and flexibility, being obstinate, intensely shy, and rather inclined to lecture.[11] However, the choice was limited, for throughout the closing years of the Napoleonic Wars, with the obvious exception of Wellington, Britain was extremely short of able diplomats, and of soldiers fit to be trusted with an independent command, let alone someone who could combine both roles.

Unfortunately Bentinck's first response after reading the correspondence from Sicily was to advocate forceful British intervention, which remained unacceptable to the Prime Minister; but after a short battle of wills Bentinck gave way and agreed to adopt the government's conciliatory policy.[12] The new envoy arrived in Sicily in July to find that the political situation was far worse than he expected. The Court had divided the Opposition and arrested five leading Sicilian barons, imprisoning them in harsh conditions on small islands off the coast. Nonetheless, he faithfully followed his instructions, assuring the Sicilian government that Britain had no intention of interfering in their domestic affairs. This delighted the Court, but when Bentinck then urged concessions to the Opposition, simply as friendly advice, it fell on deaf ears. After a fruitless month and with no prospect of success by perseverance, Bentinck boldly decided to return to England to convince the government to change its approach.

Bentinck's return so soon after leaving for Sicily created a sensation in official circles in London. Perceval's policy of conciliation had been tried and had failed utterly. After some, reportedly heated, tussles in cabinet, the Prime Minister gave way and agreed that the Foreign Secretary's stronger medicine should be tried. Fresh instructions were prepared for Bentinck, giving him control over the British subsidy, which was to be suspended until he was satisfied that effective steps were in train to improve the Sicilian army. He was also authorized to demand the release of the imprisoned barons, the introduction of more Sicilians into the government, and that he be given the command of the Sicilian army. If the Court rejected these demands and refused to cooperate, the British government stated their intention of withdrawing their army from Sicily. The cabinet remained unconvinced by continuing reports of the Queen's correspondence with the enemy, and without unequivocal proof of treachery it would not approve the use of force against an allied court.[13] The ministers were encouraged to adopt this principled stand by a report reassuring them that the safety of their army would not be seriously threatened even if the French were able to land, and by an underlying confidence that their bluff would not be called.[14] The Court of Palermo was totally dependent on Britain to defend it against France. It had spurned the hand of friendship and would now be made to feel its dependence. The Queen's jealous suspicion of Britain precipitated the very crisis she dreaded. One can pity her, but it was her refusal to compromise that forced the British government, much against its real wishes, to intervene decisively in Sicily's internal affairs.

Throughout 1811 Bentinck was closely involved in another strand of Britain's Mediterranean policy. This related to the widespread discontent which was reported from the great arc of mountain country that stretched from Grisons in the west, through the Tyrol and down into Dalmatia, and which also included much of northern and central Italy. During 1810 the British government had been approached by several groups of patriots from these lands with plans for raising an insurrection against the French, and requests for British money and support. But Britain remained extremely wary: the broad strategic position in Europe was unfavourable, so that such an insurrection was most unlikely to succeed; the ministers felt a deep-seated distaste for the idea of inciting any insurrection; and they had too many experiences in the past of confident patriots requesting British gold for schemes that came to nothing.[15]

At the end of 1810 a new proposal came before the ministers from a much more credible source. Count Nugent was a young Austrian officer of Irish origin who had visited Britain and mixed in society before. He represented Archduke Francis d'Este, the nephew and brother-in-law of the Emperor Francis of Austria. The Archduke's plan, which did not have the approval of the Austrian government, was that he be given sovereignty over the Ionian Islands where, with a little financial help from Britain, he would establish a small army including many patriotic officers whom Napoleon had forced the Austrian government to dismiss. This force would be used in the first instance to hold the Ionian Islands and to capture Corfu, while if Sicily were attacked it could rapidly move to assist the British garrison. But it would also have a wider role as the focus for all the discontent against French rule in Dalmatia, Illyria and Italy; and it would provide a solid nucleus of regular troops when the time came to give the signal for a rising. Nugent even went on to argue that the presence of such a force 'protecting' her southern flank would encourage Austria to break with France and to support Russia in a renewed Continental war, so that it provided the most effectual means available for Britain to aid Russia.[16]

Bentinck, who had known Nugent in Italy at the turn of the century, enthusiastically supported the plan, while shifting its emphasis from Illyria to Italy, which he believed was ripe for revolt. He told Wellesley that the Archduke appeared well suited to lead an Italian rising which, if well conducted, would be 'more mighty than that of Spain itself'.[17] But the British government was more cautious. It recognized that an insurrection in Illyria would place Austria in an extremely difficult position, and that she might ultimately be forced to aid the French in suppressing any rising. Even limited British support for the Archduke risked causing offence in Vienna. The ministers therefore asked Nugent to return to Vienna in the hope of persuading Metternich to give at least tacit support for parts of the Archduke's plan. Meanwhile Bentinck was instructed to gather information on the state of Italy.

A few months later, hopes for Italy were given fresh impetus when William Hill, the British minister in Cagliari, reported that he had been approached by one Alessandro Turri, who claimed to represent a large clandestine group of Italian patriots who were planning an insurrection against the French. Hill was at first naturally suspicious, but a personal meeting soon convinced him of Turri's sincerity. (We now know that Turri was a genuine patriot, but that he exaggerated his own importance, and that the real reason for his leaving Italy had been his elopement with a young baroness whom he passed off as his wife.)[18] Although Turri's plan differed significantly from that of the Archduke, it was clear that they could be reconciled.

Bentinck, who was back in England when news of Turri reached London, was fired with enthusiasm. The liberation of Italy appealed to him far more than the conduct of relations with the Court of Palermo, which he disliked and despised, and he strongly urged the British government to encourage the Italians. But still the ministers held back. The Peninsula remained their priority, and the resources they could spare for Italy were limited. Nonetheless, they gave general support and encouragement to the Archduke's plan, and specifically agreed to assist him to form an Italian corps in Sardinia. Bentinck was authorized to spend up to £100,000 on this corps, and the British government released a number of Italian prisoners of war and deserters so that they could join it. But the ministers refused to take any action to incite or precipitate an insurrection, and while they hoped that the Archduke was generally accepted as leader of the Italian patriots, they warned that they would do nothing to impose him. They still hoped for Austrian support, but would no longer refuse to support the patriots out of deference to the 'ambiguous and pusillanimous policy' of Vienna. There was a strong hint that the summer of 1812, when the government expected war in northern Europe, would be a good time for a rising, but it was accompanied by an equally strong warning that Britain had no wish to become involved in 'any partial, rash, or premature project'.[19] Essentially therefore the British government required the Italians to make the first move: if they rose up in revolt, then Britain would help them, and in order to be able to assist them effectively it would immediately support the creation of an Italian corps under the Archduke. Compared with Nugent's original proposals it was a cautious, narrow policy; but it was also careful and sensible, and reflected the vast and generally unfortunate experience of such proposals the British government had had over the previous twenty years.

British policy towards the Mediterranean in 1811 had been in a state of flux. In general the ministers regarded it as a subsidiary theatre and wished to reduce their commitment in order to free resources to support Wellington. But the recalcitrant attitude of the Court of Palermo and the temptation offered by the plans of the Archduke Francis led the government, almost against its will, to adopt a more active policy. Yet the overall view of the ministers had not changed: they continued to give priority to their operations in the Peninsula, and to regard northern Europe as the most promising theatre for a renewed Continental war. They shared little of Bentinck's enthusiasm for reform in Sicily or action in Italy, and this conflict, which had been present from the first, was to become more serious in 1812.

Bentinck returned to Palermo on 7 December 1811. He quickly exercised his new authority by presenting the startled Court with demands for a unified military command, the release of Opposition leaders and political liberalization; and when the demands were refused he enforced his will by suspending the subsidy and moving British troops into Palermo. His hand was greatly strengthened by the interception, in March 1812, of letters directly implicating the Queen in treasonable correspondence with the enemy. Although Bentinck did not himself take these letters very seriously, he used them to disarm his critics in London and gain further freedom of action. Nonetheless, the Court continued to conduct a vigorous rearguard action, and although the King officially made a form of temporary abdication, handing over the conduct of business to his son, the Hereditary Prince, he and the Queen continued to intrigue in private against the reforms.

Of all the issues facing the new Sicilian government, none caused more dissension than the framing of a new constitution for the island. The ministers in London had little taste for 'constitution making' with its quasi-revolutionary connotations; but Bentinck supported the idea enthusiastically, believing that the example of a constitution and good government in Sicily would rally progressive opinion throughout Italy against the French. Unfortunately the members of the new Sicilian government could not agree on the form a constitution should take, while the Court vehemently opposed the whole idea. After protracted discussions and argument, some-one suggested adopting 'the English constitution', and the idea quickly gathered support. Even the Court was willing to agree, partly from an exaggerated idea of the power of the British monarch, and partly because the proposal had become linked with an expedition to Naples. Bentinck, however, was appalled. He knew that the idea would be ridiculed in London (which it was) and felt that conditions in Sicily were so different from those in Britain that the proposal was wildly inappropriate. But faced with Sicil-ian agreement, he had little choice but to give way. The decision certainly damaged his reputation at home, even though the constitution which was finally adopted was far from being a slavish copy of English institutions.[20]

The new Parliament met on 18 June 1812, and Bentinck hoped that he would be able to reduce his role in Sicilian politics and concentrate his attention on military matters, while still acting as the ultimate guarantor of the new system. But Sicilian politics lurched from one crisis to another, and although Bentinck never gave up hope that in a few weeks he would be able to join the army, his attention was constantly dragged back to intrigues at Palermo. This gave the ministers in London the unfortunate, but not entirely erroneous, impression that Bentinck was giving a higher priority to Sicilian politics than to the war against Napoleon.

Bentinck's real passion, however, remained the liberation of Italy, and he saw the reform of Sicily principally as a means to this end. On returning to Palermo in December 1811 he was disappointed at reports of the state of Italy, and wrote home that if no better opportunity arose during the spring he would detach an expedition of some 10,000 men to mount a diversionary attack on Catalonia during the summer. Both the ministers and Wellington were delighted by this proposal. In reply, Liverpool warmly encouraged the Catalan plan, giving a broad hint that the government was growing ever more sceptical of talk of an Italian insurrection, while Wellington sent advice on how an expedition to eastern Spain could do most good, and arranged Spanish cooperation.[21]

But by the time these letters reached Sicily, Bentinck was regretting his proposal. The continuing instability of Sicilian politics meant that he dared not detach more than 6,000 men to Spain, which he believed was too small a force to serve any useful purpose, while fresh reports from Italy were far more encouraging. Early in June he decided to redirect the expedition to Italy, but three weeks later, and before any troops had sailed, he reverted to the original plan, though with palpable reluctance:

I cannot but regret the Detachment of so considerable a portion of this army upon an object which in mine & the general opinion promises no real Aid to Spain; but the Effect of which however terminating, will be to interfere very materially with the efficiency of this Army and almost disqualify it to take any decisive advantage of a favourable opportunity if it offered in Italy.[22]

Bentinck's hesitation probably did not seriously delay the expedition, but it further undermined the confidence which the cabinet felt in his judgement. Wellington was naturally furious, telling his brother Henry that 'Lord W. Bentinck's decision is fatal to the campaign, at least at present. If he should land *any where* in Italy, he will, as usual, be obliged to re-embark; and we shall have lost a golden opportunity here.' The ministers in London sympathized with Wellington, with Mulgrave, for example, telling Bathurst, 'I confess I foresee nothing but delays and disappointments . . . I am very much vexed at the course this business has taken.' And though Bathurst used soft words in writing to his young friend, he made it quite clear that the government believed that Bentinck had blundered, and that in future the Peninsula must take priority over nebulous insurrectionary schemes.[23]

After all the drama before the expedition even sailed, it proved a great disappointment once it reached Spain. Bentinck's instructions to Lieutenant-General Maitland were excessively cautious and pessimistic, while Maitland lacked the confidence and energy needed for an independent command. The British force arrived off the Spanish coast at the end of July 1812, having collected Whittingham's Spanish division at Port Mahon, which brought it up to a total strength of about 10,000 men. Maitland considered Wellington's plan for an attack on the French at Tarragona, but decided against it on learning that the garrison had been reinforced and that the navy would not guarantee his re-embarkation in the event of defeat. He then learnt that the Spanish Army of Valencia had been defeated at Castalla on 21 July, and hurried south to protect the port of Alicante against a French advance which never came. (Suchet had been alarmed by news of Marmont's defeat at Salamanca and fell back to Valencia, where he was joined by King Joseph and the refugees from Madrid on 25 August.)

The British army remained at Alicante engaged in ineffectual minor operations for the rest of the year.[24] As soon as Bentinck received Bathurst's reproof he set about collecting reinforcements for the expedition and was able to dispatch some 4,500 men by the middle of November. He hoped to command them himself but was detained in Sicily by yet another political crisis, and in his absence the army at Alicante passed through a succession of four different commanders in less than three months, following Maitland's resignation due to ill-health. Finally the British government appointed Lieutenant-General Sir John Murray to the command (a choice of which Wellington approved), but he did not reach Alicante until early in 1813.

Bentinck had originally intended the expedition to eastern Spain to be no more than a brief diversion, but Wellington wanted it to remain, and the government supported him and transferred the force from Bentinck's overall command to Wellington's, although the way was left open for Bentinck to assume personal command of the force if he could get away from Sicily, and he could still recall it if Sicily was faced with an imminent threat of invasion. Thus Bentinck lost control of that part of his army which was available for active operations and he would have lacked the resources to intervene effectively in Italy if his longed-for opportunity had finally arisen.[25]

Bentinck's conduct in 1812 has been severely censured. Fortescue, who disliked his liberal views, believed he displayed 'extreme gullibility', 'sluggish intelligence' and 'the characteristic selfishness of the enthusiast', and he concluded sweepingly that 'There is no more fatal obstacle to human progress than the crude aspirations of ambitious mediocrity'. Even Sir Charles Webster regarded him as 'a brilliant but unbalanced egoist, all the more dangerous because he was imbued with a species of liberalism', though Webster seems to have been writing chiefly with the events of 1813 and 1814 in mind.[26] But both Webster and Fortescue were writing before John Rosselli published his careful explanation of Bentinck's motives and conduct, and much which to them seemed perverse is now readily understood. Bentinck's reforms in Sicily, although certainly informed by liberal ideas, were not the product of a Whig-mad ideologue; and the principal motives underlying them were the desire to make Sicily a more useful and reliable ally, and an inspiration to the patriots of Italy. Bentinck certainly underestimated the obstacles which lay in his path and expected results much too quickly. But no one knew in 1811 or 1812 that the war would soon be over, and if it had lasted another five or ten years, as well it could have, Sicily might have become as useful an ally in her way as Portugal. This does not mean that Bentinck did not make mistakes, and it is quite clear that at times, particularly in 1813 and 1814, but also in 1812, he allowed his enthusiasm for Italy to take priority over the execution of British policy; but he was certainly no fool, and he had warned the government before he was first appointed that he was not suited to diplomacy.

10

Britain and the Continental Powers, 1810–11

Britain could not hope to defeat Napoleon, either by herself or with the aid of her Spanish, Portuguese and Sicilian allies. The war in the Peninsula and Mediterranean was a powerful diversion which absorbed Napoleon's resources and, like the economic war, made his rule unpopular, but it could not bring victory. If the Continent was to be redeemed it must be on the battlefields of central Europe, where Napoleon had established his domination in his great campaigns of 1805, 1806 and 1807. But Britain's power in central Europe was negligible, and the great powers of the Continent had been weakened by their defeat. In 1807 Napoleon set the seals on his victories by forming an alliance with Russia at Tilsit, and it had seemed that his power would be beyond challenge as long as this alliance lasted. But the Spanish fiasco upset the equilibrium, and when Napoleon withdrew many of his best units from Germany to send them to Spain in late 1808, Austria decided to strike. The result was the War of 1809, which revealed the hollowness of the Russian alliance, Britain's inability to help her Continental allies and, once again, Napoleon's genius for improvisation. Austria was defeated, but not quite destroyed; and it was abundantly clear that despite the war in Spain, Napoleon still controlled the destiny of Europe.

The defeat of 1809 chastened the Austrian government. The Emperor Francis and his ministers knew that Napoleon had toyed with the idea of dismembering their empire and deposing the Hapsburgs; and they accepted that another mistake would be fatal. Metternich had been an ardent advocate of war in 1809 when he was Austrian ambassador to Paris. But after the defeat, when he became foreign minister, he was the chief proponent of the new policy of conciliation and appeasement. Austria had lost Trieste, Illyria, Salzburg and some of her Polish territories through the war, and had to pay a huge indemnity. Compared with what Napoleon might have done, and with what he had done to Prussia in 1807, the terms were not unduly severe, but they left the Austrian government with crippling debts and severe domestic problems, which brought her close to national bankruptcy in early 1811. Austria was in no position to go to war in 1810 or 1811, and her leaders had no stomach for a renewed fight.

Prussia's position was rather different. She had been humiliated in 1806 and only survived the Tilsit settlement when Alexander pleaded on her behalf. Even so, Napoleon had attempted to reduce her to the status of a second-rank power such as Spain or Holland by depriving her of half her territory, reducing her population to less than six million, and subsequently imposing a limit of 42,000 men on the size of her army. This catastrophe opened the way for a group of zealous reformers to gain power, including Stein, Scharnhorst and Gneisenau, many of whose measures were liberal, and whose intention was to prepare the country for another war with Napoleon. But in 1808 Napoleon forced the dismissal and exile of Stein, and the reformers never completely controlled the government or won the confidence of the King. In 1809 they urgently pressed for Prussia to join Austria, but Frederick William was either too wise or too timid. He looked to Russia, not Austria, for support, and Alexander strongly warned him against war: the Tilsit alliance was cooling, but it was not yet cold. Without Russian support and encouragement Prussia would not go to war, unless Napoleon gave her no choice. The consequences of defeat were too serious and its likelihood too obvious.

Britain had little influence in either Berlin or Vienna. She could not offer either of the powers effective military cooperation or even large subsidies. Her principal efforts were concentrated in the Peninsula, while her financial resources were depleted by the effects of the Continental System. In any case the British ministers had become convinced that it was a mistake to seek to persuade other powers to enter the war. Many failed coalitions had taught them that the Continental Powers could only hope to prevail if they knew that they were fighting in their own interest and to the utmost of their power.

Nonetheless, the British government maintained unofficial communications with both the Prussian and Austrian governments. In Vienna Britain was particularly well represented. Count Hardenberg (the cousin of the Prussian Chancellor) was a tactful and experienced Hanoverian minister, who continued to represent Hanover (and thus, indirectly, Britain) after Napoleon had occupied it in 1806. Hardenberg's discretion won him the confidence of Metternich, and his reports to the Prince Regent, through Count Münster (the Hanoverian minister in London), provided the British government with some of its best information on Metternich's policies and the affairs of the Continent.

Hardenberg's efforts were helped, or more often hindered, by several minor British diplomats who quietly resided at Vienna despite the formal state of war between Britain and Austria. The best of these was probably J. M. Johnson, a young man who had been sent as a confidential but unaccredited agent to Austria in 1807, and who proved a generally discreet and reliable collector of information. Far different was Alexander Horn, whose scandalous career reads like a picaresque novel. Horn's indiscretion was only exceeded by his self-importance and his dislike for Metternich, and his expulsion by the Austrian foreign minister in early 1811 was not unmerited. But the most senior of the British (as opposed to the Hanoverian) agents was John Harcourt King, who had lived in Vienna for some years as a private individual. In the late summer of 1810 he returned to England and offered his services to Lord Wellesley, urging the Foreign Secretary to send him back to the Continent as a confidential but official agent to foster Anglo-Austrian relations. Wellesley agreed in principle, but dawdled so long that winter closed the Baltic route before King's instructions were even issued. As a result he had to proceed via Cadiz (where the Spanish government delayed him for three months), the Mediterranean and Turkey, so that he did not finally reach Vienna until late August 1811. Although King's journey was exceptionally prolonged, confidential dispatches and other missions sometimes took months to get from Britain to the Continent or back, so that even accurate reports could be hopelessly out of date by the time they reached London.[1]

Although Metternich was determined not to offend Napoleon, he went out of his way to attempt to conciliate the British, treating Hardenberg and Johnson well, and making other small friendly gestures, such as helping the escape of a number of British prisoners of war through Austria to Constantinople. His attitude to the Peninsular War varied: in July 1810 he believed that its demands were helping to moderate Napoleon's policy towards Austria and Russia, but early in 1811 he told Francis I that even the complete expulsion of the French from Spain would only be 'a partial diversion, scarcely affecting the main course of affairs'. Nonetheless, it is clear that he welcomed the war and had no wish to see the French triumph or the British reduce their effort.[2]

The British themselves did not think highly of Metternich or of Austria. The defeat of 1809, the French alliance, and especially the marriage of Marie Louise, were regarded with a mixture of pity and contempt. There was a strong and not unreasonable prejudice against Metternich personally, which the generally sympathetic reports of Hardenberg and Johnson could not overcome. Horn's description of Metternich might have aroused a fellow feeling with Lord Wellesley, but would not have appealed to the other ministers:

A Gamester, a *bon vivant* an *aimable Roué* by Profession he is always out of Pocket, and has repeatedly figured among the fashionable Bankrupts. . . . While he was at Paris, the Messengers from Vienna were obliged to look for him in Bagnio's and Coffee-houses . . . and his evenings were spent in the Company of the *soidisant* Queen of Naples.[3]

This distrust of Metternich lasted until 1814 and Castlereagh's mission to the Continent. In 1811 and 1812 Britain generally hoped for little from Austria, but even so her expectations were sometimes over optimistic.

There was far more underlying sympathy for Prussia than for Austria in Britain, but the British were not nearly as well represented in Berlin as in Vienna. Their principal representative was George Galway Mills, an ex-M.P. whose life had displayed such a liberal mixture of debts and indiscretions that this was not the only occasion on which he had to leave Britain to avoid debtors' prison. (He ultimately committed suicide in Australia in 1828, leaving a reputation, in a society whose standards were not the most demanding, of being 'a man of profligate character and dissolute habits'.) He had good connections in England, but the Foreign Office was aware of his failings, and he received strict instructions that his role was purely that of a conduit of communications.[4] In addition to Mills, there was only the occasional work of various Hanoverians who had good informal links with the Prussian reformers and with the Chancellor, Karl August von Hardenberg, who himself had been born in Hanover. The Hanoverian connection was immensely valuable to Britain in these years of isolation, complementing in diplomacy the excellent performance of the King's German Legion in the Peninsula.

The Prussian Chancellor may not have trusted Mills completely, and given Mills's indiscretion it would have been foolish if he had, but he saw him confidentially on a number of occasions and took the opportunity to put his policies in the best possible light for a British audience. Like Metternich, he was eager to conciliate Britain as far as possible without offending Napoleon. Hardenberg's own political position was vulnerable, balanced precariously between the conservatives and the reformers, with only the equivocal support of Frederick William to sustain him. His underlying hostility to Napoleon is much less open to question than Metternich's real motives, but he faced many of the same problems and had to pick his path even more warily. He sometimes deceived or at least misled Mills, but the British government retained a considerable fund of good will towards him and towards Prussia.

Beyond the Baltic lay Sweden, a small country whose power had greatly declined since the days of Gustavus Adolphus and Charles XII. In 1808-9 she had been defeated by Russia in a war which had cost her Finland. In 1810 French pressure had forced her reluctantly to declare war on Britain and join the Continental System. These measures, however, proved almost purely nominal. Britain had a powerful fleet in the Baltic which could have crippled the Swedish economy, but both sides refrained from active hostilities, and Sweden became a route through which many British goods were smuggled into Europe. The election of Marshal Bernadotte as Crown Prince of Sweden in August 1810 aroused British suspicions, which were not allayed by his protestations that his only loyalty now lay with Sweden, and that her interests alone would determine his policy. Yet the Baltic largely protected Sweden from Napoleon's armies, giving her an independence and importance greater than her size. Russia, Britain and France could all hope to influence Swedish policy, which as a result appeared either uncertain or inscrutable throughout 1810 and 1811.

Contact between the British and the Swedish governments was maintained through George Foy, an Englishman long resident in Sweden, and Baron Rehausen, the former Swedish ambassador to Britain who remained in London after diplomatic relations were formally suspended. More important than either was Admiral Sir James Saumarez, commander of Britain's Baltic fleet and chief advocate of the policy of forbearance towards Sweden. He displayed great tact and skill in handling his difficult duties, which were as much diplomatic as naval. Throughout 1810 and 1811 his fleet continued to use Swedish anchorages and purchased supplies from Sweden, while discreetly avoiding Swedish garrisons and maintaining an unofficial truce with Swedish vessels; all of which made an ultimate reconciliation between the two powers very much easier. Yet the results of Saumarez's good work were nearly lost when, early in 1811, the Swedish government seized large quantities of British goods which were being shipped under flags of convenience. The affair of the Carlshamm cargoes, as it became known, intensified British suspicions of Bernadotte and might have led to active hostilities if Saumarez had lost his customary coolness. Swedish motives remain uncertain, but probably combined the effect of French pressure with a crude need for financial gain. The affair was ultimately resolved by protracted negotiations, but it cast a shadow over Anglo–Swedish relations during the first half of 1811.[5]

But by far the most important of the European powers, other than France, was Russia. The Tilsit alliance almost guaranteed Napoleon's power, and after Austria's defeat in 1809 it seemed unlikely that Napoleon could ever be defeated without Russia taking a leading part. But despite Russia's obvious importance, Britain was virtually unrepresented at St Petersburg. Instead of clandestine but secretly acknowledged diplomats talking directly to senior ministers, as in Vienna and Berlin, in Russia Britain had to rely on stale public news and gossip picked up and conveyed by commercial correspondents. This lack of representation seems to have been partly a matter of chance, and partly a result of genuine hostility to Britain among many leading Russians, including the Chancellor Rumiantsev, who resented British domination of Russia's foreign trade.[6] Consequently the British government was ill-informed about Russian policy in these years and had no hope of directly influencing it, though of course the Peninsular War and the Orders in Council helped to mould the context in which Russia acted.

Fortunately for Britain, the Tilsit alliance was decaying because of its own internal contradictions. Indeed, it had been in decline almost from the outset, as the warmth of the meeting between the two emperors slowly cooled. At Erfurt in 1808 Alexander had renewed the alliance, but on more equal terms than at Tilsit and with more reservations. When Austria attacked Napoleon in 1809 Russia had, as promised, supported the French, but her military cooperation had been almost farcical and very obviously concerned to ensure that as much as possible of Austrian-occupied Poland should go to Russia rather than to the Duchy of Warsaw. Poland was one of the cankers eating at the heart of the alliance, for Napoleon's patronage of the Duchy of Warsaw (recreated from Prussia's gains in the partitions of Poland) carried with it the implicit threat of restoring the old Kingdom of Poland, which would involve depriving Russia and Austria of their shares of the spoil. Other issues also undermined the alliance, which had never been genuinely popular in Russian society. Alexander resented Napoleon's harsh treatment and continued occupation of Prussia, and felt that Napoleon had dishonoured his promises to support Russia's ambitions in the Balkans.

After the Austrian war Napoleon determined to divorce Josephine and marry again in order to secure an heir. At first he thought of one of Alexander's sisters, the Grand Duchess Anna, as his bride. But she was very young and her mother and sister were violently hostile to the match, while Alexander was unenthusiastic. A temporizing answer was sent, raising difficulties of age and religion, but not definitely refusing. Napoleon, perceiving the Russian coolness, was already looking elsewhere. There were a number of princesses available, including the daughter of the King of Saxony, the most loyal of Napoleon's German allies, but Napoleon was more ambitious: if he could not marry a Romanov, he would marry a Hapsburg. For Metternich, the chance to marry one of the Emperor Francis's daughters to Austria's most implacable foe was a heaven-sent opportunity. The Emperor Francis may have regarded it with rather less enthusiasm, but he too recognized its advantages. As for the poor Archduchess Marie Louise, she accepted her fate with resignation and in the event found it surprisingly agreeable.

Metternich was disappointed in his hope that Napoleon, mellowed by his marriage, would waive the more onerous terms he had imposed on Austria after her defeat. Nonetheless, the marriage did encourage the gradual realignment of forces in Europe which had already begun. Russia was no longer the one favoured friend of France. Austria was accepted as an ally and the Russians inevitably, if illogically, resented it. (Their attitude was not helped by the speed and manner with which Napoleon abandoned his courtship of the Grand Duchess Anna.) Other issues including renewed discussions about Poland continued to undermine the relationship, and by late 1810 the alliance existed in little more than name.[7]

In the last few weeks of 1810 both Napoleon and Alexander, acting independently, made relations much worse and even raised the prospect of war. In each case the issue related to the Continental System. On 13 December 1810 Napoleon annexed Holland, Hamburg, the old Hanseatic Towns, and the whole of the north German coast including the Duchy of Oldenburg. His intention was to reduce the smuggling, which was rife on this coast, and so make the Continental System more effective. The Russian government could not welcome this expansion of French power, especially as it brought Napoleon's empire to the shores of the Baltic for the first time, but Alexander had a more particular reason for objecting to the annexation of Oldenburg. His favourite sister, the Grand Duchess Catherine, was married to the heir of the Duchy, and the territory of Oldenburg had been guaranteed at Tilsit. To make matters worse, Napoleon had neither consulted nor warned Alexander. Clearly Napoleon was no longer prepared to conciliate Russia.

Before the news of the annexations reached St Petersburg, the Russian government had demonstrated that it too was willing to offend. By a famous *ukase* of 31 December 1810 Alexander dramatically increased duties on imports arriving by land, while reducing those coming by sea. In part this was a response to Napoleon's reorganization of the Continental System through the Trianon and Fontainebleau Decrees, but it breached the Tilsit agreements and was plainly directed in large part at imports from France. The restraints on trade had always been one of the most unpopular aspects of the French alliance in Russia, and the measure had domestic political as well as economic advantages. It was not followed by any opening of trade with Britain — which would have precipitated a break with Napoleon.

The conjunction of these two events brought Russia and France to the brink of war. Alexander reacted badly to the news of the annexation of Oldenburg, and in January 1811 he immersed himself in military plans and preparations. He estimated (over-optimistically) that there were only 46,000 French troops in Germany, who would be supported in the event of war by about 14,000 reserves from Holland and France, and 95,000 men of the Confederation of the Rhine, making an army of 155,000 men. Against this he claimed to have an army of 100,000 men ready to take the field at once, with a second army of equal size being prepared. He hoped to win Polish support by proclaiming the restoration of the Kingdom of Poland, linked indissolubly to the Russian crown, but with a liberal constitution. If the Polish army supported him it would add 50,000 men to his own forces and deprive Napoleon of the same number. Moreover, it would enable the Russian armies to sweep quickly forward, catching Napoleon by surprise, inspiring risings against him in Germany, and enabling the Prussians and the Danes to join the Russian forces. Alexander calculated that he would have some 230,000 men in the front line, supported by a second Russian army of 100,000 against Napoleon's force of 155,000 men.

But to have any hope of succeeding, even on his own sanguine assumptions, Alexander had to secure the support of the Poles, without antagonizing the Austrians, who still held some Polish provinces. To overcome this problem, in February 1811 he offered to swap Austria's Polish territories for Russia's recent conquests from the Turks in Moldavia and Wallachia — conquests which had seriously alarmed the Austrian government. If Austria joined his crusade, Alexander calculated on a gain of 200,000 men (certainly too many for the Austrian army at this time, though he may have assumed that her accession would be followed by Bavaria and the other small states of southern Germany). But active Austrian support was not essential to Alexander's plans: her neutrality combined with Polish and Prussian support would be enough.

Overtures were made to Vienna and Berlin early in 1811, and Alexander wrote privately in great secrecy to his old friend and former foreign minister, the Polish patriot Prince Adam Czartoryski, outlining his plans and asking if he could count on Polish support. The response was disappointing. The Court of Vienna declined the territorial exchange and discouraged any new war. The Prussians were non-committal and Czartoryski indicated that there was widespread distrust of Russia and loyalty to Napoleon in the Duchy of Warsaw. The hopeful assumptions on which Alexander had made his plans dissolved as soon as he put them to the test, and with the coming of spring he abandoned the idea of an offensive campaign.[8]

Some historians doubt if Alexander ever seriously considered war in early 1811, arguing that his preparations were so obvious that they were more likely to have been a diplomatic bluff than made in earnest.[9] While this is possible, Alexander was always prone to sudden enthusiasms and it is not unlikely that the sharp deterioration of relations with France should have precipitated him into thoughts of war, especially as Napoleon's forces were heavily committed to the war in the Peninsula at this time. With Masséna at Santarem, he may even have felt that if he did not strike soon, resistance in the Peninsula might be overwhelmed before he could take advantage of the diversion.

Whatever Alexander's intentions, his military preparations had widespread effects. There was a war scare in Paris and the price of stocks fell sharply. Napoleon appears to have been taken aback by Russia's hostility and realized that he was not well placed for an immediate war. He hastily took military precautions and endeavoured to placate the Russians. In Prussia the patriots were delighted at the prospect of Russia taking up arms and were eager to join in the cause. Franco-Prussian relations were very strained at this time: the Prussians were naturally appalled at the annexation of Holland and the Hanseatic Towns, while there were rumours that Napoleon was considering partitioning Prussia. French officials in northern Germany, probably overreacting, warned Napoleon in January 1811 that the Prussian army was being placed on a war footing. But the reformers did not control the Prussian government. Hardenberg was sympathetic but more cautious, and the King was even less inclined to risk his throne in another war. On 4 April 1811, Frederick William wrote to Hardenberg: 'All this reminds me of 1805 and 1806, when the Emperor's Court was seized with the same excitement. I am much afraid that the final result will again be an ill-combined war, bringing misfortune to the friends of Russia instead of delivering them from the yoke which oppresses them.'[10]

The war scare of January 1811 slowly faded away over the next few months. By March or April the immediate threat of war had disappeared: Alexander had tried the water and found it unpleasantly cold. With no prospect of Austrian or Polish support, and conflicting messages from Prussia, he gave up his plans for an advance into Germany and decided to stay on the defensive. He may well have been encouraged by news of the successful British defence of Portugal against Masséna, for in May he wrote: 'I intend to follow the system which has made Wellington victorious in Spain and exhausted the French armies — avoid pitched battles and organize long lines of communication for retreat, leading to entrenched camps.'[11] In the meantime he met Napoleon's conciliatory messages with fair phrases, and did not publicly query their sincerity. But whatever words the two emperors mouthed, the Tilsit alliance was dead and buried. War was not really inevitable, for Napoleon could still have avoided it, but it had become highly likely.

Britain was no more than an observer of the war scare, and a belated and ill-informed observer at that. The British government had been aware of Russia's growing discontent with the French alliance since at least November 1810; but the closure of the Baltic in winter hampered communications, so that in the first months of 1811 most of the reports reaching London came from Prussia, and this sometimes gave a rather strange impression of events. Thus while Mills reported that Hardenberg was convinced that Alexander was only waiting for a suitable opportunity to strike, he also conveyed the Chancellor's warning that Prussia could not join Russia without active Austrian support. But a few weeks later Hanoverian sources supplied the Foreign Office with details of Prussian military plans which were based on a presumption of an alliance with Russia.[12]

Early in April 1811 the prospect of a renewed war in northern Europe encouraged the British government to adopt a more aggressive strategy in the Peninsula, and Liverpool wrote to Wellington to assure him that the government would not allow its effort to be diverted from the Peninsula. Reports reaching London from St Petersburg at this time still spoke of the increasing likelihood of war, but the Foreign Office already doubted Alexander's resolve: 'though His Imperial Majesty begins to see the tendency of Bonaparte's ambitious designs, he does not yet appear to be fully aware of the vigorous line he ought to adopt'. Nonetheless, the British government was greatly impressed by accounts of the Russian army, which it believed had immensely improved since 1807.[13]

In the middle of May Lord Wellesley set down his views on the state of Europe in a long memorandum for a junior diplomat and friend who was about to embark on a mission to Spain. Wellesley accepted that the immediate prospect of war in northern Europe had faded, but he still believed that the Peninsula created a diversion which absorbed French energy and resources, relieving pressure on the other Continental Powers and creating the opportunity for them to strike against Napoleon when the time was ripe.[14]

Wellesley looked to Russia as the power most likely to challenge French hegemony, and was encouraged by her break from the Continental System and her military preparations. However, he argued against overtures to Russia aimed at inciting her to oppose Napoleon. He believed that the example of Austria had proved that 'the continental powers of Europe required a curb and not a spur', and that 'Russia would either suspect our advances, or be encouraged by them to make demands of money and armies which we could not satisfy; and in either case the final result would be to excite jealousy or dissatisfaction'. Britain's policy must be shaped by her resources, which were heavily committed to the Peninsula, so that she must be scrupulous to avoid arousing the expectations of potential allies. 'In the event of a rupture between Russia and France, it is certain that we can give Russia no money, and it is probable that it will not be in our power to give her military assistance. Aid may perhaps be afforded by maritime operations, and by supplies of arms and stores.'

In surveying the rest of Europe, Wellesley was equally cautious. He recognized the intense hostility to France in the Prussian army, but nonetheless felt that Prussia was in such a weak state that she would have to support France in a war between France and Russia. However, 'Prussia would rise against France in any favourable crisis'. He did not believe that Austria was happy in her alliance with France, or that the marriage of Marie Louise to Napoleon had strengthened relations. He hoped that Austria would remain neutral if war broke out between France and Russia; indeed, he believed that her government was so weak and her finances in such a deplorable state as to give her little alternative. Again he felt that the underlying sentiment was good: Austria 'cannot wish well to France, nor can she wish for the subjugation of Russia'; but there was distinctly less sympathy in London for Austria than for Russia.

Not surprisingly, Wellesley suspected Bernadotte, the new Crown Prince of Sweden, even more than Metternich. 'Bernadotte says that as he is now a true Swede, he naturally adopts all the true feelings and interests of his country, and is therefore hostile to the ambitious projects of Buonaparte. But his affectation is so gross and absurd that Lord Wellesley cannot persuade himself to give credit to Bernadotte's protestations.' Wellesley, however, did believe that Sweden was open to pressure from Britain and Russia, and he did not expect her active hostility.

Overall, Lord Wellesley was confident of ultimate victory in the war, foreseeing a time when 'the state of Europe, and of the world, will be more advantageous to England than it has ever been since the House of Bourbon was unfortunately placed on the throne of Spain'. Even Wellington, who was so much more cautious and realistic than his brother, was optimistic:

> If there is war in the north this year I think we shall make Boney's situation in Spain this year not *a bed of roses*; if there is not a war in the north this year, it is impossible that his fraudulent & disgusting tyranny can be endured much longer; & if Great Britain can only hold out I think we shall yet bring the affairs of the Peninsula to a satisfactory termination.[15]

Wellesley's cabinet colleagues shared his, and Wellington's, faith in ultimate victory, but by the middle of the year they had grown more cautious
in their views of the immediate prospects for the Continent. For example,
Charles Yorke, the First Lord of the Admiralty, wrote to Admiral
Saumarez:

> I am very sceptical on the subject of the various reports from Russia and
> Prussia. Matters are hardly ripe as yet for any decisive alterations, and the
> French have too strong a hold on Germany and Poland. Nothing effective
> can be done till the Germans and Italians decide on imitating the Portuguese
> and Spaniards by making a *national* war on the French determined to *conquer*
> or perish *altogether*.[16]

During the summer, communications with the Continent improved and
the number of clandestine contacts between the British government and the
Continental Powers increased. At the end of July Prince Lubomirski, an
aide-de-camp of the Czar, arrived in London on a confidential mission. Few
papers concerning Lubomirski's visit have survived, but it appears that his
primary purpose was to try to sell the Admiralty some timber from his
Black Sea estates (which it declined). However, as he was granted an
audience with the Prince Regent and presented the Foreign Office with a
lengthy memorandum on the state of the Russian army, his mission may not
have been as insubstantial as it appears.[17]

There were some other tentative gestures of conciliation between Britain
and Russia at this time: the British government sent home all 374 Russian
prisoners of war it held, and in return the Russians assisted the departure of
a number of British citizens who had been trapped in Russia by the war. On
the other hand, a Russian attempt to purchase a large quantity of saltpetre
or gunpowder failed miserably. After tortuous negotiations the British
government agreed to the export provided it was carried in British vessels.
But the convoy attracted unwelcome publicity, and when it reached Russia
it was not permitted to enter harbour or land its cargo, presumably to avoid
provoking the French. As this incident implies, there was no general
resumption of Anglo-Russian trade in 1811, although there was a significant
increase in trade in 'neutral' vessels, which led the British government to
impose stricter conditions on the licences it granted to import Baltic com-
modities. Altogether 1811 saw an uneven thawing in Anglo-Russian
relations, with both sides showing a mixture of good will and suspicion
towards the other. Unfortunately there continued to be no reliable channel
for confidential communication between the two governments: British
hopes that Spanish and Portuguese diplomats might provide such a link
were soon disappointed.[18]

Hopes for war revived in the second half of August, when news reached
London that Napoleon had furiously denounced Russian policy at a diplomatic reception on his birthday (15 August). Such public scenes had pre-
ceded other wars, notably the break with Britain in 1803, and the British

government quickly sought more detailed intelligence. Colonel Dörnberg, one of the invaluable Hanoverians, was sent to test the mood of the patriots in Prussia and northern Germany, but was warned to be careful not to raise hopes of British subsidies. And Count Nugent set off to return to Vienna where — as well as discussing Italian schemes — he was to assess Austrian policy and see if a reported rift between Metternich and the Emperor Francis could be exploited. Nugent carried with him a personal letter from the Prince Regent to the Emperor Francis which, while devoid of much substance, was intended to raise the level of communication and the amount of good will between the two powers.[19]

Relations between Britain and Austria were still uncertain and tentative. Johnson had reported from Vienna that the dire financial plight of the Austrian government would prevent it taking any part (on either side) in a war that year, and that the country appeared to be 'falling rapidly [in]to decay from internal Decrepitude'. Society and the army were both hostile to the French, and news of Wellington's victories was greeted with joy, but this feeling would count for little if, as seemed quite possible, the whole empire dissolved in chaos. The British government, though unsure of Austrian policy, was inclined to think that she would remain neutral in the event of war, possibly intervening against France if the allies gained some initial successes. Meanwhile the insurrectionary schemes promoted by Nugent and the Archduke Francis, and others observed by British agents in Vienna, alarmed Metternich and made him more eager to conciliate Britain in order to prevent her sponsoring these conspiracies.[20]

But Prussia, not Austria or Russia, was the object of most British interest in the late summer of 1811, and this was due to developments on the Continent in which Britain, at first, had no part. In May 1811 the Prussian government had secretly proposed an alliance with France which would guarantee Prussia's territory. This flatly contradicted some of Hardenberg's earlier assurances to Mills, and the Prussian minister later claimed that he made the proposal knowing that it would be rejected. This is simply incredible, and while some historians claim that Hardenberg was always interested in exploring the possibility of an alliance against France, as well as with her, it seems more likely that with the prospect of a forward Russian campaign rapidly fading, an alliance with France offered the best prospect of preserving Prussia intact, distasteful as it undoubtedly was to Hardenberg.[21]

Whatever Hardenberg's motives, the proposal was made; and received no answer. Perhaps Napoleon feared that a Prussian alliance would offend Russia prematurely; or perhaps he was reluctant to guarantee Prussia's existing territory, thinking that he might wish to use some of it to reward other allies, possibly compensating Prussia with new territories further to the east. His prolonged silence deeply alarmed the Prussian government, and led it to take military precautions and make overtures to Vienna and St Petersburg. In August an anxious Hardenberg renewed his overture, and Napoleon responded by demanding the removal of General Blücher (whose hatred of the French was well known), the cessation of preparations for war, and that Prussia either sign an unconditional offensive-defensive alliance with France or join the Confederation of the Rhine, neither of which, given the fate of Oldenburg, appeared to give much guarantee for Prussia's existing territories.[22]

These demands precipitated a full-blown crisis. The reformers naturally advocated war, and though Hardenberg was sceptical of some of their claims, he favoured resistance if support could be obtained from Russia and Britain. The King, however, was much more doubtful. He had no faith in the reformers' plans for popular uprisings, writing on one memorandum from Gneisenau, 'Nobody would come!' and 'Good — as poetry!' The death of Queen Louise in 1810 had made him more irresolute than ever, while his faith in Czar Alexander was at a low ebb. He was most reluctant to go to war, but given Napoleon's evident hostility, he agreed to send Scharnhorst to Russia to appeal for support, and also to approach Austria and Britain.[23]

The British government knew nothing of the trouble brewing in Prussia until the beginning of autumn. The reports received from Mills during the summer had described deep popular hostility to the French, especially in the army, but had generally played down the likelihood of immediate conflict. But during September both Mills and Hanoverian sources reported active military preparations on all sides. On 8 September the Foreign Office issued orders for the secret dispatch of 10,000 stand of arms with accoutrements and 3,000 barrels of gunpowder to be shipped to the Baltic with as little delay as possible.[24]

A few days later Admiral Saumarez was instructed that in the event of war he should provide 'every practicable assistance, . . . [consistent] with the safety of His Majesty's ships'. He was to do nothing, however, until the actual commencement of hostilities — probably in order to avoid the risk that indiscreet British actions might precipitate a war which the Prussian government could still hope to avoid. The cautious Admiralty appended a characteristic warning that Saumarez should not keep his fleet in the Baltic too late in the season, or give the Prussians so many supplies as to reduce his effectiveness in protecting British trade. The Foreign Office also began preparations to send a mission to Sweden in the hope of securing her active support for Prussia, though various problems delayed its departure for a few weeks.[25]

On 5 October fresh reports reached London, including two letters from Gneisenau stating that Prussia was determined on war and had made plans for vigorous resistance; that she had no need for troops, but was short of arms and ammunition; and that 'Our object is to gain time, to prolong the war, to become victorious . . . [by] imitating the fabian system; and if we are to fall, that we will only submit after a long and glorious defence.'[26] These letters were brought by Col. Christian Ompteda, a Hanoverian officer whose brother Louis had been in close contact with Hardenberg throughout the spring and summer. Ompteda had left Prussia in the middle of September after an interview with Gneisenau and personally testified to Prussia's determination to resist the French. Gneisenau had told Ompteda that the Prussian army had between 100,000 and 130,000 men, but admitted that he had no knowledge of Russia's intentions, though he hoped that she would cooperate in the defence of Silesia.[27]

The British government responded promptly to all this news. It had already given orders for large quantities of arms and ammunition to be shipped to the Baltic: 25,000 stand of arms on 27 September and, on 1 October, twenty-five siege guns for the defence of fortresses and five batteries of field artillery. The Admiralty warmly approved the steps which Saumarez had taken to help Prussia (as hostilities had yet to break out, these consisted chiefly of letting corn and other supplies into Colberg through the British blockade) and authorized him to leave two or three gun brigs (later considerably increased) to aid in the defence of Colberg during the winter, when he was forced to withdraw the rest of his fleet. On 8 October the government doubled the quantity of arms ordered for Prussia, giving instructions that a further 25,000 muskets, twenty-five siege guns and five field batteries be prepared. These were very large quantities of arms, and it is greatly to the credit of the much abused Ordnance that the first consignment of these weapons was shipped and ready to sail by 22 October, and that the last were all ready by the end of the month.[28]

On 5 October Charles Yorke explained the government's view of the state of northern Europe to Saumarez. The mission to Sweden was now almost ready to sail and Yorke hoped that

> if Prussia is actually obliged to have recourse to hostilities, Russia will not and cannot suffer her to be crushed without making every possible effort to relieve her. This may afford a favourable opportunity both for Sweden and Denmark to break the French yoke; and one may justifiably entertain the opinion that a cordial union of the four powers for that purpose may be successful considering how matters stand in the peninsula.[29]

On the same day that Yorke wrote this letter, Lord Wellesley had an interview with Edward Thornton, the diplomat he was sending to Sweden. Thornton was a reasonably competent career diplomat who had represented Britain before, not altogether happily, in Sweden in 1808. In the interview, and in the instructions which were prepared a few days later, Wellesley explained that the mission was an attempt to make Sweden commit herself: 'Great Britain cannot permit the present state of relations between the two countries to subsist, because it is deeply injurious to the interests not only of Great Britain, but of every Power excepting that of Bonaparte.' The threat implicit in the instructions, which was never spelt out, was that if Sweden did not join actively with the allies, Britain would transform the nominal state of war between the two countries into active hostilities. This was one of the rare occasions in these years on which the

British government abandoned its principle of not seeking to pressure or induce another country into war with Napoleon, against the judgement of its rulers. And even on this occasion Britain neither sweetened the carrot nor flourished the stick. Just as Thornton's instructions made no explicit threats, they also contained no inducements, although Wellesley knew that Bernadotte was eager to secure Norway, and possibly a West Indian island, for his adopted country in order to console it for the loss of Finland and so secure his own position. This restraint arose in part from genuine distaste for Bernadotte's naked greed, for Sweden had no legitimate claim on Norway, which had been part of the Kingdom of Denmark for centuries; and partly from distrust, for Wellesley feared that Bernadotte's protestations of independence and interest in Norway might be no more than a ruse, and believed that French control of the Norwegian ports would pose a serious threat to Britain and Ireland. Whatever the motives, Wellesley's restraint reduced the mission's chances of success, for Bernadotte was always reluctant to commit himself and would not risk breaking with France unless the situation on the Continent clearly favoured the putative allies.[30]

Unfortunately for Thornton, the tide was beginning to run the other way even before he left England. By 13 October the British ministers had learnt that Napoleon had returned to Paris, which they regarded as a strong indication that war was not imminent. A few days later a batch of letters from Mills arrived, the last of which was dated 19 September. The British agent reported that affairs had taken a pacific turn, with both sides making conciliatory gestures, though military preparations continued in secret. Finally, on 22 October, Count Münster received dispatches from Louis Ompteda in Berlin and a letter from Gneisenau of 24 September. According to Ompteda, Hardenberg had confronted the French ambassador to Berlin and warned him that Prussia would resist any attack. The ambassador had replied on 24 September that Napoleon was well disposed towards Prussia, and eager to conclude an alliance with her, but that the Prussian government must halt all preparations for war, or the ambassador would withdraw from Berlin and the French would occupy the country. Hardenberg had gone on to explain to Ompteda that as Prussia had not received any assurances of support from Russia, she had no choice but to enter into negotiations for an alliance in order to gain time, but 'Ompteda might *firmly rely upon this, that the proposed alliance would not be concluded*', and preparations for war would secretly continue. Hardenberg's frankness in giving this full explanation was partly explained when he added that the French had insisted that news of the negotiations be sent to St Petersburg and be published in the Berlin *Gazette*. Gneisenau's letter, while generally confirming Hardenberg's account of events, made it clear that he had opposed negotiations with the French and favoured increased preparations for war, but that his advice had been ignored.[31]

Although Münster found the news 'very alarming', Wellesley was not displeased, believing that 'it is certainly desirable that more time should be

given for the preparation of the Northern Powers against France'. This
view was probably influenced by reports from John Harcourt King in
Vienna, which stated that while Metternich had refused Prussian appeals
for assistance and was strongly opposed to an immediate war, he hoped to
have an army of 300,000 men to assert Austria's independence and cooperate with the other powers against France as soon as the Austrian government's finances had been stabilized.[32]

Unfortunately it is clear that King had been deceived, possibly in order
to discourage his evident interest in the insurrectionary schemes.
Metternich still had no thought of joining in a war against France. He
expected that the new year would bring war between France and Russia,
and was convinced that Napoleon would win. Austria might be able to stand
aloof and preserve her neutrality, but if she did so the new settlement of
Europe would be made with no consideration of her interests whether in
Poland or in the Balkans. The Austrians had no wish to see Napoleon's
power increased, but believing that Russia had little hope of victory, they
felt it simply made sense to support the French. By early December the
Emperor Francis and Metternich had decided to make a formal military
alliance with France, although the decision was not made public, nor the
treaty signed, until 1812.[33]

The Russian government viewed events in central Europe almost equally
cautiously. Alexander had responded to Prussia's appeals for help with
some limited promises of assistance, but the enthusiasm of early 1811 had
died; he no longer wanted to precipitate war or carry it into Germany; and
he gave the Prussian patriots little encouragement. The opportunity for an
offensive war had long since passed, if it ever really existed; and in a
defensive war, in which the French would be forced to invade Russia,
Prussian support would be more an embarrassing complication than a real
help. The Russian government was turning inwards and made no response
to British overtures.

By the time Edward Thornton arrived in Sweden in the middle of
October 1811, it was clear that immediate war was growing ever less likely.
The Swedes listened to his arguments and did their best to conciliate
Britain without yielding anything of substance, but once all the issues had
been discussed they asked him to go home.[34] It was too late in the season for
Britain to act against Sweden, Russian policy remained inscrutable, and it
was not a moment to offend the French. Bernadotte clung precariously to
his seat on top of the fence and watched the way the winds blew.

At the end of 1811 Britain thus remained formally at war with all the
Continental Powers. The stresses and strains of the year had shown that
Napoleon's hegemony was widely resented, but that despite the diversion in
the Peninsula, his hold on central Europe was too strong for any of the
powers to risk trying to break it. Britain lacked the leverage to influence
significantly the policy of any of the great Continental Powers. Continental
statesmen knew that whenever they chose, or were forced, to break with

Napoleon, they could rely on British support; but they also knew that direct British aid would count for little in the crucial battles which would decide their fate. Given the limited resources and influence available, the broad lines of British policy in 1811 appear to have been well judged, although some of the details, such as Thornton's mission to Sweden, were clearly mistaken. Frustrating as it was for Wellesley and his colleagues, they could do little more than observe and encourage, and wait for what the new year would bring.

11

The Triumphs and Tribulations of 1812

At the beginning of 1812 the future of the British government hung in the balance. On 17 February the Regency restrictions would expire and the Prince would have to make his choice. Would he retain his father's ministers whom he had so often derided, or call to power his old friends the Whigs, or seek some third way? Throughout 1811 he had drifted steadily away from the Whigs. He disapproved of their agitation of the Catholic Question and was offended by their opposition to the reappointment of the Duke of York as Commander-in-Chief. He did not personally like either Grey or Grenville, while Sheridan, Erskine and Moira, his closest political allies, had little influence in the Opposition.

There is no doubt that the war, and particularly Wellington's successes in the Peninsula, played a part in the slow shift of the Prince's sympathies towards the ministers. The Opposition's credit had been badly damaged by their frequently made and frequently disproved predictions of disaster, while the Prince's love of pageantry and thwarted military ambitions were gratified by the receipt of captured flags and trophies, and the tidings of victories. But other influences were also at work. The Prince's mistress Lady Hertford was a strong supporter of the government, as were the Dukes of York and Cumberland, who saw a good deal of the Prince at this time. The Prince's original commitment to the Whigs had owed more to Fox's geniality and a desire to irritate his father than to political principles, and personal factors now played an equally important part in its gradual dissolution.

But if the Prince was unlikely to turn to the Opposition to form a government, it did not necessarily mean that he would leave the administration as he found it. He might seek a broader ministry including Canning, Castlereagh and the Prince's own band of followers, under a new leader more personally compatible than Perceval. Wellesley had been hoping and planning for this result for much of 1811. He had sedulously courted the Prince, discussing the state of northern Europe with him, encouraging his budding enthusiasm for the war and for Wellington's triumphs, and gently hinting that Perceval was not the man to steer the country through the difficult but exciting times that lay ahead. When the cabinet had discussed the budget for the Regent's establishment, Wellesley had argued strongly for a more generous allowance, and made sure that his views were made known at Carlton House — conduct which had naturally disgusted his colleagues.[1]

By the end of 1811 Wellesley was fairly confident of the Prince's partiality; but his great fear was that the Prince's natural indolence and political cowardice would overcome his wish for a change. Wellesley was not willing to continue to serve under Perceval, and he made this quite clear by submitting his resignation on 16 January 1812. This was a calculated attempt to break up the government, but it failed miserably. While recognizing the political danger, most of Wellesley's colleagues were delighted at his impending departure, and none offered to resign with him. Perceval was eager to seek fresh support at once, and some preliminary approaches were made, but the Prince persuaded Wellesley to remain in office for a few more weeks.

On 13 February 1812 the Prince wrote to his brother the Duke of York announcing his intention of retaining the ministers in office and expressing his hope that some of his 'old friends' in the Opposition would join with them for the good of the country.[2] The overture was an empty gesture designed to save some shreds of political consistency for the Prince. Perceval was unhappy with the letter, fearing that it would lead to a maze of negotiations, but as the Prince surely anticipated, Grey and Grenville rejected it outright. The Prince then, on 15 February, confirmed Perceval in office.

On the following day Wellesley, having heard only a garbled account of these transactions and not knowing that the Prince had already committed himself to Perceval, had a long interview with the Prince in which he urged the need for a broadly based government including himself, Canning and Castlereagh, and suggested Lord Moira as its head. It was extraordinary and grossly improper that the Prince thus allowed Wellesley to outline all his plans when the decision had already been made; and he then compounded his bad behaviour by informing Perceval and Eldon of Wellesley's proposals. The cabinet immediately met and threatened to resign if Wellesley's resignation was not immediately accepted.[3] The Foreign Secretary thus departed at last, betrayed by his own ambition and by the Prince, whose strange handling of this affair simply added to the considerable distrust with which he was regarded by all political factions.

Perceval emerged from the crisis with his prestige enormously enhanced. All the world knew how little he had done to court the Prince, and yet he had been unequivocally confirmed in office. With Wellesley gone and several other ministers eager to retire, he set about reshaping his cabinet. Castlereagh accepted the Foreign Office, where he was to remain for the rest of his life. His reputation had steadily risen since he left office in 1809, though he was still dogged by the memory of Walcheren. He had greatly improved his debating skills, and while he would never be able to dominate the House with his oratory, he provided useful support for Perceval. Charles Yorke retired from the Admiralty and was replaced by Lord Melville (Robert Saunders Dundas, son of Pitt's close colleague who had died in 1811), who proved a competent but uninspiring administrator. Perceval also made room, against the Prince's wishes, for Sidmouth and his group of stolid Tories, who were given three unimportant posts in cabinet. William Wellesley-Pole was also promised a seat in cabinet (as Treasurer of the Navy) at the end of the Parliamentary session. The net effect of all these changes was to make the government marginally more competent and decidedly more conservative.

All the members of the cabinet viewed Lord Wellesley's departure with pleasure and relief, but outside the ministry there was some regret. Wellington and Henry Wellesley naturally deplored the loss of a brother in cabinet who had always advocated open-handed support for the war in the Peninsula. More surprisingly Count Münster, who had worked closely with Wellesley in 1811 and must have had ample experience of his tardiness and inefficiency, still expressed his 'deep concern' at Wellesley's departure from 'a branch of the administration, of vital interest to all Europe, and which can never be filled again in an equal manner'. Lord William Bentinck wrote in a similar vein from Palermo when he heard the news. Bentinck of course had received far more sympathy and support from Wellesley than from the other ministers when he put forward his plans for Sicily and Italy; but his 'extreme regret' was for the loss which he believed the whole country suffered by Wellesley's retirement. Given Wellesley's undeniable inefficiency, such reactions seem strange, but he was recognized as a man of enlarged views who championed the vigorous prosecution of the war against all obstacles. The assessment of Lord Holland — long a political opponent — is perhaps overgenerous, but it explains why throughout 1812 there were many who believed that Wellesley was the best man to lead the country through the war. 'He had more genius than prudence, more spirit than principle, and manifestly despised his colleagues as much as they dreaded him. . . . [He was] rather a statesman than a man of business, and more capable of doing extraordinary things well than conducting ordinary transactions with safety or propriety.'[4]

Wellesley and Canning now combined in declared opposition, but on 19 March Wellesley damaged his reputation by losing his nerve and failing to make a much heralded attack on the government, and the initiative passed back to the old Opposition. The Whigs had reacted with great bitterness to the Regent's 'betrayal' and did all they could to offend him, including attacking his mistress, Lady Hertford, and championing the cause of his hated wife. But their principal efforts were devoted to a great debate on the Catholic Question (23 to 25 April) and the popular campaign for the repeal of the Orders in Council. This was skilfully led by Henry Brougham, who

organized a flood of petitions from depressed manufacturing areas throughout the country. Perceval at first tried to resist any concessions, despite the
disquiet of some of his colleagues, including Lord Sidmouth, who favoured
modifications to the Orders in Council to conciliate the Americans (for
more on this aspect of the problem, see chapter 13 below). But Brougham's
campaign was too successful to be ignored, and on 28 April the Prime
Minister reluctantly agreed to an enquiry, although he remained opposed to
any substantial change.

Then, on 11 May 1812, Perceval was assassinated in the lobby of the
House of Commons. His death produced some immediate panic, with fears
of a revolutionary conspiracy to overthrow the government. But it was soon
found that his murderer was an unbalanced bankrupt named Bellingham,
who blamed the government for his losses and his ill-treatment in Russia.
Despite his obvious insanity, Bellingham was quickly tried, condemned and
executed, provoking an outcry from liberal lawyers and from a section of the
populace who regarded him as a hero.

Perceval's death precipitated a long political crisis. Liverpool was chosen
by his colleagues as the new Prime Minister, and he made overtures to
Canning and Wellesley, but they were rejected. The attempt to carry on the
government without recruits was defeated on 21 May, when the Commons
narrowly passed a motion calling on the Prince Regent to form a strong and
efficient administration. Liverpool then resigned and the Prince asked
Wellesley to see if he could form a ministry. But Wellesley had bitterly
offended the ministers by an untimely posthumous attack on Perceval in
The Times, and despite heavy pressure from the Prince, they refused to have
anything to do with him. He turned to the Whigs, but they were reluctant
to enter a coalition or agree to Wellesley's plan to increase spending on the
Peninsula.[5] After more than a week of fruitless negotiation, the Regent
revoked Wellesley's authority and asked his old friend Lord Moira to
attempt to form a government. Moira succeeded in patching together a
weak ministry, which was heavily dependent on Canning and his friends,
but which had assurances from Liverpool and others that they would join in
a few months.[6] At the last minute, however, the Duke of Norfolk and Lord
Erskine — two of the Carlton House party destined for high office —
withdrew, and as a result Moira resigned his commission. A new government was now urgently needed for official business. The Regent appointed
Lord Liverpool Prime Minister; presented Parliament with much the same
ministry as had been defeated three weeks before. A similar motion of no
confidence was again moved, but on 11 June 1812 it was defeated by over a
hundred votes.

The result of the crisis left the Opposition feeling cheated, and many
Whigs believed that the negotiations had been skilfully orchestrated by the
Regent to keep them out of office. This view of events greatly flatters the
Prince's political ability and cunning. The Opposition had deliberately
offended him, so naturally he endeavoured to avoid calling on their leaders

to form a government; but if the Commons had really wanted the Oppo- sition, he would have had to accept them, just as his father had in 1783 and 1806. However, the Commons was far from enthusiastic about Grenville and Grey; it wanted a strong, vigorous administration, and was most inclined to see it in a junction between Perceval's ministers on the one hand, and Wellesley and Canning on the other. The lengthy negotiations proved this to be impossible, and the Commons then accepted Liverpool's admin- istration by a handsome majority rather than force the Prince to turn to the Opposition.

Nonetheless, for the next few weeks the government appeared vulnerable and its prospects most uncertain. On 1 July it came within a single vote of defeat in the Lords on the Catholic Question, while in the Commons Castlereagh managed affairs so badly that Arbuthnot (the Secretary to the Treasury) insisted that without Canning the government could not survive another session. Liverpool made a determined effort to bring Canning, who was an old friend, into the cabinet. Castlereagh was willing to give up the Foreign Office but insisted on retaining the lead in the Commons. At this, Canning's pride baulked, and in 'the most disastrous political miscalcul- ation of his whole career' he refused the offer, much to the regret of both the Prime Minister and the Prince Regent.[7]

So the existing ministers remained in office without any new recruits of substance to make up for the loss of Perceval. Liverpool of course became Prime Minister and appointed Nicholas Vansittart as his Chancellor of the Exchequer. Richard Ryder retired and Sidmouth moved to the Home Office. Most of the other ministers remained where they were, including Castlereagh at the Foreign Office and Melville at the Admiralty. Liverpool offered the vacant War Department to William Wellesley-Pole, but he declined it and joined Lord Wellesley in opposition: a decision which enraged Wellington (see below, p. 208). Lord Bathurst took the War De- partment and did his best to soothe Wellington, whom he greatly admired. Bathurst was a genial, pleasant man inclined to leave well alone, but a competent and sensible minister, who managed his department well and was frequently a peacemaker in cabinet. With Liverpool and Castlereagh he was one of the inner group of ministers who were responsible for the day- to-day management of the war.

In the midst of all the confusion and uncertainty the normal business of government had to continue, and on 17 June Vansittart introduced Perceval's last, posthumous budget. Total budgeted expenditure increased by nearly £4 million (£58,188,000 in 1812, compared with £54,308,000 in 1811), with most of the increase being spent on the army and managing the debt. There were fresh taxes designed to raise nearly £2 million on leather, glass, tobacco, horses and male servants; but this was not enough to satisfy Huskisson, who strongly warned the Commons of the dangers of the country's increasing burden of debt, which had already led to rising interest rates and which threatened to throw doubt on the government's credit.

Contemporary critics other than Huskisson were muted out of respect for Perceval's memory, but even Denis Gray, Perceval's biographer, admits that it was the least successful of his budgets. Expenditure exceeded the estimates, the revenue was flat, and consequently borrowings soared. Trade was already beginning to pick up as Napoleon's attention was diverted from the Continental System to the war with Russia, but it took time for this improvement to flow through to the revenue. In the meantime, Britain's finances showed the strain of the extra exertions she was making in the Peninsula. If the situation had not improved in 1813, the ministers would have been hard pressed to maintain, let alone increase, their efforts in Spain.[8]

A few weeks before Perceval's death, in the middle of April, the British government had received one of those token overtures of peace from Napoleon which he often sent before engaging in a new war on the Continent. On this occasion he offered to make peace, with each side retaining its conquests: the House of Braganza being confirmed as rulers of Portugal, the King of Sicily confirmed in that island, but Murat recognized as King of Naples. The integrity and independence of Spain was to be guaranteed, and it was to be ruled by the Cortes under 'the existing dynasty' — a carefully ambiguous phrase. The British ministers were convinced of Napoleon's insincerity and believed that the approach was a blatant attempt to sow dissension between Britain and her allies, and to allay discontent in France. Castlereagh promptly replied, enquiring simply what was meant by the phrase 'the existing dynasty'. If Napoleon meant Ferdinand VII, Britain would be happy to negotiate; but if he meant his brother Joseph, the proposal was totally inadmissible. Napoleon never responded to this letter, although he drafted an uncompromising response which he intended to send from Moscow or St Petersburg.[9]

The incident is interesting, for it suggests that Britain might have been willing to make peace with a far stronger France than had existed in 1802–3 or even 1806. Of course, Spain under a restored Ferdinand VII would be unlikely to return to the French alliance, but this did not offset the emasculation of Prussia in 1806–7, and the defeat and subordination of Austria in 1809. In fact such an end to the Peninsular War would have done much to consolidate Napoleon's power, even though it would have been a great blow to his prestige in the short term. But it is not safe to conclude too much from Castlereagh's reply, which was intended primarily to test Napoleon's sincerity. The British government did not need to reconsider its war aims unless Napoleon proved that he really was willing to release and restore Ferdinand and withdraw all his troops from Spain. In the meantime, the British reply demonstrated good faith to its allies (though it brought little comfort to the Court of Palermo), while similar French overtures to Cadiz also made no progress.

During 1812 the French completely lost the strategic initiative in the Peninsula. In part this was due to Napoleon's preparations for his invasion of

Russia: in January 1812 he ordered the withdrawal of 27,000 men from Spain, and they were some of his best troops, the Imperial Guard and the Polish regiments. There was also a great reduction in the number of drafts and recruits sent to the regiments which remained in Spain, so that their constant small losses were not replaced. As a result the total strength of Napoleon's forces in the Peninsula fell from 354,000 in July 1811 to 262,000 in October 1812.[10] Yet with more skill and greater coordination the French forces might have maintained the rough equilibrium that had been established in the second half of 1811. They failed to do so partly because of the mistakes of their generals, partly because of Napoleon's interference, and largely because of Wellington's careful preparations and brilliant opportunism which displayed generalship of the very highest quality.

Throughout the year the British government gave the war in the Peninsula the highest priority. It fully endorsed Wellington's bold strategic plans, gave him a free hand in the conduct of his operations, and concentrated all the available resources in support of his campaign. Naturally there were some problems, most obviously a serious recurrence of the shortage of specie in the first half of the year. But despite the disappointments of the second half of 1811, there was no wavering in the ministers' faith in Wellington, and as triumph followed triumph from January to August, their most optimistic forecasts seemed about to be realized. Disappointment followed, but their confidence was unshaken, and their hopes were deferred, not abandoned.

The year began with a great British success. Wellington had learnt the lessons of his unsuccessful attempts to take Badajoz and Ciudad Rodrigo in 1811. He knew that he must be able to strike quickly and hard against each fortress if he was to take it before the French concentrated an overwhelming army for its relief. And he had also learnt that he could not rely on an improvised siege-train such as he had collected from Elvas the previous year. During December 1811 he put all these lessons to good effect, making meticulous preparations for the siege of Ciudad Rodrigo. He secretly collected large quantities of siege materials in northern Portugal and brought a good modern siege-train up from the coast to Almeida, only a few miles from Ciudad Rodrigo, by the end of the year, without the French discovering any clue to his intentions. Wellington was much encouraged when Marmont, convinced that the British were incapable of taking the offensive in the middle of winter, obeyed Napoleon's orders and detached a substantial part of his army to assist Suchet in the conquest of Valencia. This unexpected piece of good fortune sealed the fate of Ciudad Rodrigo, but Wellington's plans would probably have succeeded without it.

On New Year's Day 1812 Wellington issued orders for the investment and siege of Ciudad Rodrigo. The harsh winter conditions created many problems and caused some delays, but they also ensured that the French were taken by surprise. The fortress was invested on 8 January and that night some outworks were taken by storm. The batteries opened fire on 14 January, and by the 19th they had battered two practicable breaches in the walls: Wellington ordered the storm for that night. It was a fine evening though bitterly cold. Wellington had planned the assault with care, but there was confusion in the dark and some of the attacks were mistimed, increasing the allied losses. Nonetheless, the fortress was carried, where-upon the storming troops lost all discipline, and looted and pillaged the town until well into the following day. The allies lost nearly 500 casualties in the storm, of whom just over 100 were killed, including General Craufurd, the commander of the Light Division.[11]

Neither Marmont nor Dorsenne, the commander of the French Army of the North, knew that Wellington had moved against Ciudad Rodrigo until 15 January, when it was far too late. Marmont immediately gave orders to concentrate his army, but he could not hope to relieve the fortress until the beginning of February. Wellington had time to spare, and perhaps should have spent a few more days battering Ciudad Rodrigo in order to make the storm easier and less costly, but after the disappointments of 1811 it was not surprising that he should be in a hurry. Far to the south in mild Seville, Soult learnt of the siege and its result at the same time, on 31 January: if it did not send a cold shiver down his spine it should have, for Badajoz would plainly be next.

Wellington issued orders for preparations for the siege of Badajoz as early as 28 January, but heavy rain delayed the movement of troops and supplies and also hindered the repairs to Ciudad Rodrigo. The army began moving south in the middle of February, but Wellington remained in the north until 6 March to mislead the French. Sixteen heavy howitzers were brought down by road from Ciudad Rodrigo, but the remaining artillery for the siege of Badajoz was brought up from the coast: some cannon sent out especially from England, others borrowed from the fleet.[12] Wellington arrived at Elvas on 11 March and Badajoz was invested on the 17th.

Badajoz was a much more powerful fortress than Ciudad Rodrigo, with a garrison of 5,000 men and an active and enterprising commander, General Phillipon, who had withstood the British sieges in 1811. There seemed no reason to believe that Soult and Marmont could not combine and march to its relief as they had done in the previous year, but Wellington was confi-dent, and on 14 March he told his brother Henry that 'I hope to be strong enough for a stiff affair with [Marmont] and Soult, and to take the place too. I shall not give the thing up without good cause.'[13] He had earlier hoped to prevent, or at least delay, the junction between the two French marshals by getting Hill to destroy the bridge at Almaraz on Marmont's shortest route south, but the heavy rains had forced the postponement of this operation. In the end it hardly mattered, for Napoleon chose to intervene and ordered Marmont not to march south to the relief of Badajoz, but to invade northern Portugal instead, arguing that this would force Wellington to abandon the siege and hurry north. Whatever the theoretical merits of this plan, it was foolish to impose it on a general who was convinced that it was pointless. With more vigour and daring it is just possible that Marmont might have taken either Ciudad Rodrigo or Almeida by a coup de main, for both their defences were in poor condition. But he simply marched into northern Portugal, virtually ignored the fortresses, dispersed some Portuguese militia, devastated some already desolate countryside, and retired into Spain having accomplished nothing.[14]

Thanks to Napoleon, therefore, Wellington had only to face Soult in Estremadura, and Soult could not hope to collect enough men by himself to relieve Badajoz. This proved fortunate, for progress was slow, hampered by more heavy rain and the activity of the garrison. The batteries did not open fire until 25 March, and it was not until 5 April that there was a practicable breach. Wellington was inclined to order the storm that night, but his engineers successfully begged for another day's battering. The assault was set for 10 p.m. on 6 April. All three breaches were to be stormed, while there were to be diversionary attacks on other parts of the fortress. What followed was the most dreadful night of the Peninsular War. The French garrison had made elaborate and deadly preparations to meet the assault. Their numbers, fire and morale were all undiminished, and they were well led. The main assault on the breaches failed with horrific losses, but several of the diversionary attacks succeeded as the bulk of the garrison had been concentrated in defence of the breaches. Once the British troops were in the fortress they were able to attack the French in the rear, and resistance crumbled. At 6 a.m. on 7 April Phillipon surrendered.

The storm of Badajoz cost Wellington's army 3,713 casualties, of whom over 800 were killed; to this must be added another 957 casualties suffered in the siege before the storm, making a total loss of 4,670 men (1,035 killed). Only at Talavera and Albuera had the allied army suffered such losses. Moreover, the heaviest losses were borne by a few regiments which had been exposed to the heaviest fire at the breaches. Three battalions of the Light Division (1/43rd, 1/52nd and 1/95th) alone suffered 855 casualties in the storm, including 165 men killed.[15]

The appalling siege was followed by equally appalling scenes of rapine, pillage, murder and looting. All troops run wild when they take a town by storm, but the sack of Badajoz went far beyond the normal limits of disorder into drunken savagery comparable with the worst excesses of the Thirty Years War. It mattered not at all to the soldiery that it was a Spanish town, an allied town, for they were far beyond such restraints. Authorities differ as to whether the sack of Badajoz lasted twenty-nine hours or 'three full days',[16] but whatever its duration, it is deplorable that Wellington did not take more effectual steps to minimize the disorder. The sack of Ciudad Rodrigo had given clear warning of what would happen, and while some pillaging was inevitable, order ought to have been restored on the morning of 7 April.

Whether Wellington's conduct of the siege, and in particular his decision to order the storm on 6 April, is equally open to criticism is a moot point. Badajoz was always going to be difficult and costly to take; and although a few days' more battering would have made the breaches easier, they would also have given the French more time to prepare interior defences. There was little Wellington could do to subdue the garrison before the storm, and Phillipon was far too good an opponent not to take full advantage of every opportunity. Nonetheless, the immensely heavy casualty list leaves the impression that the siege might have been conducted more skilfully.

In less than four months, in the worst season of the year, Wellington had seized the keys to Spain. He held the initiative, and the campaigning season was only just beginning. It remained to be seen how he used his advantage.

Wellington's first step was to improve his own lateral (that is, north-south) communications by restoring the bridge at Alcantara, and to damage those of the French by destroying the bridge at Almaraz. He entrusted this latter operation to Rowland Hill, who accomplished it on 19 May with the loss of fewer than 200 casualties. It was a well-planned, well-executed operation, similar to Hill's earlier triumph at Arroyo dos Molinos (28 October 1811). Wellington now had the chance of striking north against Marmont, or south against Soult. Originally he had favoured the invasion of Andalusia, but circumstances had changed. Marmont would soon receive a new siege-train with which he could seriously threaten Ciudad Rodrigo and Almeida if Wellington disappeared into Andalusia. Alternatively, Marmont might follow Wellington south and combine with Soult, for the season was now sufficiently advanced to allow him to collect supplies on the way. On the other hand, neither Caffarelli (the new commander of the Army of the North, replacing Dorsenne) nor Soult could spare many men to aid Marmont, if he should be the target of Wellington's operations. The choice was clear, and at the beginning of June Wellington began to concentrate his army.[17]

On 13 June Wellington crossed the Agueda with an army of nearly 50,000 men (approximately 28,000 British, 15,000 Portuguese and 4,000 Spanish; he had left Hill with nearly 20,000 Anglo-Portuguese troops in Estremadura to protect his flank). On 17 June the allied army occupied Salamanca and invested three fortified convents held by the French. These minor works held out for ten days, seriously disrupting the allied advance and inflicting some 350 casualties. Marmont concentrated his army as quickly as he could, but it was widely dispersed and on 20 June only five of his eight divisions (some 25,000 men) had joined him. Nonetheless, he advanced on Salamanca, and his appearance forced Wellington temporarily to suspend his operations against the convents. On the night of the 20th Marmont was joined by two further divisions, bringing his strength up to 35,000 men. Wellington, despite his numerical superiority, occupied an extremely strong position outside Salamanca and invited the French to attack him, but Marmont was too wily. Instead he dawdled at the foot of the allied position, and invited them to attack *him*. It was a rash offer, but Marmont was arrogant and seems to have believed that the allied troops were incapable of manoeuvre and that Wellington was a timid tactician.

Wellington resisted the temptation, and after some slight skirmishing the French retired on 22 June, leaving the convents to their fate. Marmont's overconfidence was enhanced, and he would retain his illusions for another month exactly.

During the rest of June and the first three weeks of July, the two commanders watched each other closely. After the fall of the convents Marmont fell back to behind the Douro at Tordesillas. He was joined on 1 July by General Bonnet with the last of his eight divisions, but Caffarelli was unable to honour his promise to send Marmont reinforcements. The Army of the North was kept fully occupied: the Spanish VI Army had advanced from Galicia to besiege Astorga, while Sir Home Popham, with a small squadron and two battalions of marines, was staging a series of diversionary raids on the Biscay coast in conjunction with the local guerrillas. Napoleon had made King Joseph commander-in-chief of his armies in Spain in March, and Joseph ordered Soult, Suchet and Caffarelli to reinforce Marmont. Intercepted copies of these letters alarmed Wellington, but the French generals calmly ignored them. On 9 July Joseph decided to evacuate most of New Castile and march to Marmont's aid with all the troops he could collect without abandoning Madrid: about 14,000 men. Unfortunately for the French, all the dispatches announcing this important news fell into the hands of the guerrillas, who passed them on to Wellington, so that Marmont was unaware that reinforcements were on their way. Marmont was meanwhile worried, quite unnecessarily, that Wellington might be joined by part or all of Hill's force from Estremadura, and he therefore decided to take the offensive.

Active operations resumed on 16 July after a fortnight's lull. Marmont brilliantly out-manoeuvred Wellington, crossed the Douro at Tordesillas, and forced the allied army to retreat. On 18 July there was a confused skirmish in which Wellington and Beresford were nearly captured with their staff. The two armies marched in parallel within half a mile of each other, but with no more than some petty combats. This dangerous, demanding manoeuvring continued for a few days. It placed great strain on both generals, for at such close quarters the slightest mistake could be fatal. The French continued to have the better of it, forcing the allies to fall back. On 21 July Wellington was again near Salamanca, occupying the ground he had held a month before, but Marmont out-flanked him, and he wrote to Lord Bathurst that he would have to fall back towards the Portuguese frontier.[18]

Early on the 22nd Wellington prepared to retreat and sent his heavy baggage to the rear, but he still hoped that the French might attack him or that a favourable opportunity for a battle might arise. The allies had approximately 50,000 men in the field, mostly deployed behind some gentle hills, about two miles south of Salamanca. The French were no more than a mile further south, with rather fewer men but stronger artillery. Marmont was convinced that the British would continue their retreat and during the

22nd he grew rather careless, perhaps because of the strain of the previous week. About midday Wellington was sorely tempted to attack, when he saw that several French divisions had strayed too far apart to support each other, but he restrained himself, apparently on Beresford's advice. Marmont had also seen the danger, and the failure of the allies to attack confirmed his overconfidence. As the afternoon progressed he badly overextended his left flank in an effort to turn Wellington's position. As a result his army was spread much too thinly and became vulnerable.

The Battle of Salamanca began with some artillery exchanges and skirmishing near the village of Arapiles in the early afternoon. Between three and four o'clock Marmont was severely wounded by a British shell, and soon afterwards General Bonnet, his second-in-command, was also disabled, so that for much of the battle the French army was left leaderless. It probably mattered little, for the fatal mistake had already been made, and the divisional commanders fought as well as they could when taken at such a disadvantage.

About the same time that Marmont was wounded, Wellington issued the orders for a general attack. The British Third Division, supported by a magnificent charge by the heavy cavalry, caught the French left wing in disarray and rolled it up with little trouble. In the centre there was some fierce fighting, and the initial attack by Cole's Fourth Division and Pack's Portuguese was repulsed and the French counter-attacked. But Wellington had ample reserves and soon drove the French back in confusion. Ferey's division covered their retreat for a time before it too was broken, late in the evening, in some of the bloodiest fighting of the day. Only Foy's division on the far right of the French army escaped in good order.

Salamanca proved conclusively that Wellington and his Anglo-Portuguese army could manoeuvre and attack just as ably as they could defend a strong position. The French army was routed with very heavy losses, probably in the order of 14,000 casualties, including 7,000 prisoners, many of them wounded. As well as Marmont, four of his eight divisional commanders were wounded, two of them mortally; and his army lost two eagles and twenty cannon. The allied army suffered some 5,000 casualties, including 900 killed. Four senior British officers were wounded (Beresford, Cotton, Leith and Cole) and one killed (Le Marchant). Wellington was struck by a spent musket ball at the close of the battle, but was unhurt.[19]

The allied pursuit miscarried as the Spanish General Carlos de España had evacuated the castle at Alba de Tormes without informing Wellington or breaking the bridge. This allowed the French army to escape, though there was some contact on 23 July when a brigade of the King's German Legion cavalry broke the French rearguard at Garcia Hernandez in a famous exploit. On 25 July Wellington called off the pursuit at Flores de Avila: the remnants of Marmont's army had escaped, and his own troops badly needed a brief respite after their exertions.

Having abandoned his pursuit of Marmont's army, Wellington was uncertain how he should act. The principal remaining French armies in Spain — Caffarelli in the North, Suchet in the east, and Soult in the south — were all far distant. If they combined they would vastly outnumber the allied army and would force Wellington to retreat, but the allies had the central position, and the French could only unite by long circuitous marches, and by abandoning either Andalusia or their communications with France. On the other hand, if Wellington concentrated all his forces against just one of these armies, he would leave his flank and rear exposed to attack from the others. It was a knotty problem, which Wellington never satisfactorily solved. Salamanca had been a decisive victory which had temporarily eliminated Marmont's army from calculation; but even without Marmont's army, the French still had a predominance of force in the Peninsula, if they were willing to abandon some of their conquests and concentrate their scattered garrisons.

Faced with this uncertainty, Wellington decided to occupy Madrid and bring up Hill's force from Estremadura. This forced King Joseph to flee eastwards with his small army and an enormous train of French officials and Spanish supporters, who found refuge with Suchet in Valencia. Wellington entered Madrid on 12 August amid scenes of wild rejoicing. The Spanish capital had little purely military significance, although large supplies of arms and equipment were captured with it. But the symbolic importance of the liberation of Madrid was immense. It gave the Spanish patriots reason to hope after four bitter years of war, suffering and defeat, and it encouraged Napoleon's enemies throughout Europe. But it remained to be seen if Wellington could maintain his position.

The British government was delighted with Wellington's victories, and the ministers greatly appreciated his willingness to explain his plans for future operations. In return they sent him praise, encouragement and a steady stream of reinforcements. In the twelve months from the beginning of December 1811, almost 20,000 rank and file (approximately 22,500 all ranks) sailed out from Britain, while Wellington was joined by a further 4,700 men from the garrison of Cadiz.[20] The Duke of York was so concerned by the level of these reinforcements that he protested that the government was leaving the country undefended, but the ministers were unmoved by his warning. Unfortunately this massive commitment was not reflected in any significant increase in the effective strength of Wellington's army. The hard fighting at Badajoz, Salamanca and later at Burgos cost the army dearly, while the long gruelling campaign swelled the already high number of sick. According to one return found among Wellington's papers, 10,207 British soldiers of Wellington's army died during 1812, while a further 1,720 had to be discharged and 1,092 deserted. Thus the army lost over 13,000 men during 1812. In addition, the number of sick rose from an already high figure of 13,400 in January to over 20,000 in August, when it comprised almost 40 per cent of the British rank and file. As a result the effective strength of Wellington's British rank and file, which began the year at 36,000, never reached 40,000.[21]

The British government was less successful in supplying Wellington with specie than with men, particularly in the first half of the year. Liverpool had pinned his hopes on the importation of large quantities of specie from the East Indies, but when the ships arrived in March he was 'cruelly disappointed'. He then considered Wellington's idea of issuing Exchequer bills in the Peninsula, but after much discussion the plan was rejected, probably wisely, as it would simply have competed with other forms of British security traded on the Lisbon and Cadiz markets. Wellington was now feeling the shortage acutely, and frequently brought it to the attention of the ministers, although his complaints were noticeably less shrill than in 1809. When Bathurst took over the War Department in the middle of the year, Wellington told him simply, 'Our principal and great want is money, with which I am afraid you cannot supply us sufficiently. But we are really in terrible distress; I am afraid, in greater distress than any British army has ever felt.'[22]

There was a worldwide shortage of specie in 1812 caused by a number of unconnected factors. The revolt of the Spanish American colonies severely disrupted the supply, while both the war with the United States and Napoleon's invasion of Russia increased the demand. As a result the market price for gold rose sharply from an average in 1811 of £4 15s 6½d per ounce for gold bars to £5 1s 3d in 1812, while foreign gold coin climbed to £5 11s 0d at one point.[23]

Bathurst tackled the problem with speed and decision. He knew that the government could not supply Wellington through purchases on the open market as this would simply drive the price higher, so he sought less obvious alternatives. He began by demanding that the Bank of England release some of their reserves of foreign gold coin and gold bars. He met with some resistance, but by the end of August he could tell Wellington that they had released £76,424 while less than a fortnight later continuing pressure had produced another £100,000. With the support of Liverpool and Vansittart, Bathurst then demanded a further £100,000, and by the middle of October the Bank had reluctantly agreed to provide £100,000 a month for four months.[24] These sums far exceeded the Bank's reserves of foreign coin, but Bathurst had discovered an old legal loophole permitting the export of guineas to pay British troops abroad. This justified his demands on the Bank, but he then deliberately risked impeachment by instructing Wellington to use the guineas for all necessary purposes, and not just to pay the army. It was not altogether in jest that Bathurst told Harrowby, 'For this I shall have my Head off, if we should not succeed'. But Harrowby, like the other ministers, approved, reassuring his friend, 'I hope you will not lose your head for your dealings with the Bank. You and all of us should deserve to lose it, if we refrained from using a vigour beyond the law to enable Lord W. to pursue his successes and it is fortunate that you have a decent legal cloak for so good a deed.'[25]

The first guineas reached Lisbon in the middle of November and the result certainly vindicates Bathurst's policy, yet it is worth remarking that the government's heavy demands on the Bank placed a considerable strain on Britain's financial system, which was already under pressure. This risk would of course have been increased if the war had gone badly, for example if the Russians had capitulated to Napoleon. It is tempting to contrast Bathurst's energy and daring with Liverpool's inaction in the first half of the year; but Liverpool played a major role in the negotiations with the Bank of England, while as Secretary for War he may well have been hampered by Perceval's cautious conservatism on financial questions.

Another irritant in relations between Wellington and the ministers was friction with the Admiralty. After years of complaining about Admiral Berkeley, Wellington now objected to his routine transfer to another station and was only partly mollified when Liverpool gave him a choice of Berkeley's successor. He also feared, with some reason, that the navy were not taking sufficient precautions against American privateers acting in the Channel and Bay of Biscay, and certainly his concerns did not deserve the brusque rejection which they received from Lord Melville.[26] Yet 1812 also saw probably the best example of naval cooperation of the whole war in the Peninsula: Popham's campaign on the north coast of Spain, which did so much to distract Caffarelli from Wellington's operations. But even this led to tension. Wellington generously acknowledged Popham's help, and objected to the Admiralty's attempt to withdraw the squadron when the season advanced and autumn gales became a threat to the ships on the exposed Biscay coast. Wellington had his way, and Popham remained until well after the allies had begun their retreat from Burgos (see below, p. 215), but even so he grumbled.[27]

Underlying all these issues was a more serious cause of tension: the succession of political crises in London and Wellington's desire for a strong stable government. The ministers did all they could to conciliate Wellington, and he responded honourably, though at times ungraciously.

Perceval and Liverpool were most anxious how Wellington and Henry Wellesley would react to the resignation of Lord Wellesley at the beginning of the year. They wrote to both men in the most flattering terms, described events from their own point of view (which naturally did not reflect well on Lord Wellesley), and expressed their determination to pursue the war in the Peninsula with vigour.[28] As soon as the Regency restrictions expired Perceval recommended, and the Regent gladly approved, Wellington's elevation to an Earldom with a pension of £2,000 a year. This one act began the unrestricted Regency with a fine flourish which appealed to the Prince, signalled the government's continuing commitment to the war, and consoled Wellington for the loss of a brother in cabinet. A few weeks later, on

10 March, Henry Wellesley received his reward, being made a Knight of the Bath.

Wellington appreciated his honour, but he was still not altogether happy with the government. He wrote sympathetically to Lord Wellesley that 'the republic of a cabinet is but little suited to any man of taste or high views', and complained 'that the government are not aware of the difficulties in which I am constantly involved from defects and deficiencies of all descriptions', concluding that the war was not being funded adequately. Not all his doubts about Liverpool seemed to have been allayed, for he greatly regretted that Castlereagh went to the Foreign Office, rather than returning to the War Department, and interpreted it as a sign of the government's weakness.[29]

Nonetheless, Wellington continued to give tacit support to Perceval's administration. His brother William Wellesley-Pole remained Chief Secretary of Ireland, and Perceval planned to bring him into the cabinet at the end of the Parliamentary session. Pole's letters to Wellington at this time were highly critical of Lord Wellesley and supportive of the government, even though he was unhappy that Perceval was only offering him the treasurership of the navy, rather than a more senior office.[30]

Wellington was naturally shocked by news of Perceval's assassination, even though his obituary of the Prime Minister was no eulogy: 'Mr Perceval was a very honest Man, whose views were rather limited by professional habits & those acquired by long practise in His House; and I think he did not take a sufficiently enlarged view of our situation here; nor does Ld. Liverpool.'[31] Yet he wished Liverpool well in his attempt to form a government, though he doubted that he could succeed without at least the support of Canning. Like most of the Commons, he probably hoped to see a junction of the old ministers with Wellesley and Canning: certainly he did not wish the Opposition in office, and he did not believe that Wellesley could succeed in forming a government independent of 'the two great parties'.[32]

Wellesley-Pole, however, took a different line, declaring that Perceval's assassination made Catholic emancipation an imperative necessity, and acting in concert with Lord Wellesley. Liverpool twice offered him the War Department but he refused, much to the annoyance of Wellington, who regarded him as ideal for the post. Over the following months Pole bitterly repented his decision and pestered Wellington to put pressure on the ministers to admit him to the cabinet. Wellington did make his regret at Pole's exclusion from office well known, but there was no vacancy and no inclination to make one.[33] Pole had seriously offended the ministers and damaged his reputation by his abandonment of the government in its darkest hour and by his sudden change of heart on the Catholic Question which — while it may have been sincere — seemed to most observers to be nothing more than naked opportunism.

With Pole excluding himself from office, Wellington gave Bathurst a courteous, if not enthusiastic, welcome to the War Department. Privately he condemned the vanity and jealousies that had crippled the attempt to form a broader government, but he did not particularly blame Liverpool or his colleagues. Indeed, he seems to have wished the ministry well, though he continued to doubt if it could survive for long in the Commons without substantial reinforcements. When Pole reproached him for not doing more to secure an office for him, Wellington replied that it was not for him to tell the Prince whom to choose for his ministers, that he was not willing to take an active part in domestic politics, and that he fully understood and sympathized with the ministers' objections to Lord Wellesley.[34]

Henry Wellesley, however, was less well disposed to the government, telling Charles Arbuthnot, 'I cannot think the Ministers justifiable in their conduct to Lord Wellesley, nor should anything induce me to remain here after the treatment he has met with at their hands, were I not apprehensive that my sudden resignation might be attended with inconvenience both to the public service & to Lord Wellington personally.'[35] As Anglo-Spanish relations were about to enter a particularly delicate phase, it is certainly fortunate that Wellesley did not resign as — with all his faults — he was well established at Cadiz, and it is unlikely that his successor would have been an improvement.

Wellington's relations with the ministers during the remainder of 1812 were reasonably cordial, though not intimate. Lord Wellesley's supporters criticized Wellington for being cold and ungrateful in not lending support to his brother's politics, and were incensed at the use the government made of Wellington's name in defending itself against Parliamentary attack. But Wellington did not believe that the failure at Burgos was due to any lack of support from home, and regarded Wellesley's and Canning's criticisms of the administration as ill-informed.[36] In general he continued to try to avoid becoming embroiled in domestic politics, but early in 1813 he defended the government in letters that were clearly intended for wide circulation.[37] This naturally exacerbated the frequently difficult relations between Wellington and his eldest brother. According to his son's diary, Lord Wellesley reacted without joy to the news of Salamanca and became consumed by jealousy. In June 1813, Richard Wellesley recorded a long conversation with his father, who was evidently in his cups:

> He described Well[ington] as having become a *Govt. runner*; He should not spare him in Parlt. Well[ington] had done him every possible injury — owed him gratitude; *He* owed nothing to Well[ington]; Would have recalled him if he had been employed by L[ord] W[ellesley] for the *Burg*[os failure]. *desired Well[ington's] failure.*[38]

But by this time Lord Wellesley's political star was rapidly waning, while the glory of his younger brother, which had already far surpassed his own fame, was soon to grow even brighter with the triumphs of the Vitoria campaign.

The liberation of Madrid by Wellington and his Anglo-Portuguese army marked a dramatic shift in the balance of power between the allies in the Peninsula. In 1811, when Wellington was unable to advance far beyond the Portuguese frontier, Spaniards could continue to believe that they were leading the struggle against the French, and that they had nothing to learn from the British. Natural pride was fed by the bombastic claims of generals, and fanned by the absurdly unrealistic press in Cadiz, which reported defeats as victories, skirmishes as battles, and Albuera as a Spanish triumph in which the British played little or no part. Wellington's triumphs dented these illusions for a little while at least. The Spanish government bestowed titles and honours on him to mark his victories, and he responded by entering Madrid flanked by Spanish commanders and by proclaiming the new constitution wherever he went. But nothing could conceal the fact that it was the Anglo-Portuguese, not the Spanish, army which recaptured Madrid after four years of war, or that the Spanish forces played an insignificant role directly in Wellington's successes. Of course, the whole war continued to depend on the Spanish resistance, both the guerrillas and the regular forces, which carried on absorbing the attention of most of the French forces in Spain, but by August 1812 it had become clear even to the Spanish government that the best hope of driving the French back beyond the Pyrenees now lay with Wellington and his army.

The British government had long been weary of the incompetence and unreasonableness of its Spanish ally. Innumerable issues, some serious, some petty, clouded relations, ranging from the intrigues of the Princess of Brazils, through Spanish neglect of the garrison at Ceuta, to unrealistic Spanish expectations of financial aid, which in turn was linked to that great bugbear, the state of Spain's American colonies and Britain's desire to trade with them. By the middle of 1811 the British government appears to have been chiefly concerned to avoid any closer entanglement in the details of Spanish affairs. Even the controversial attempt to mediate between Spain and her colonies was undertaken more in an ill-judged effort to avoid alienating either party than with any real hope of success.[39]

But Henry Wellesley was deeply involved in the politics and intrigues of Cadiz. He received little guidance or instruction from his brother at the Foreign Office, and worked at furthering Britain's interests, as he saw them, with more activity than most of the cabinet in London would probably have approved. Throughout much of 1811 he combined with sympathetic Spanish politicians, notably Andrés Angel de la Vega, to bring down the Blake Regency and to replace it with a more friendly and efficient administration. At the same time he continued to advocate much more extensive British aid to Spain, provided that the Spanish government allowed extensive British involvement in their affairs. For example, at the end of October

1811 he recommended to London that Britain clothe, feed and arm at least 100,000 Spanish soldiers, on condition that they be placed under Wellington's command.[40]

In the middle of December Henry Wellesley sent the secretary of his embassy, Charles Vaughan, home to argue the case for greater aid to Spain. Vaughan's departure alarmed the Spanish politicians, and the need to conciliate the British helped bring down the Blake Regency in January 1812. Henry Wellesley played a substantial part in the formation of the new Spanish government, which proved much more friendly, though only marginally more effective. Thus one half of his policy largely succeeded: the other failed utterly.

Vaughan arrived in London at the end of the year, to find Wellesley alienated from his colleagues and on the point of resigning in the hope of being asked to form a government of his own. But the question was discussed and decided by the cabinet before Wellesley committed himself. His pen certainly softened the blow — as well it might, for at least by his silence he had badly misled his brother — but implicit in the reply was not only a rejection of Henry Wellesley's proposals, but also a condemnation of his policy and activity. The ambassador was told that the British government did not believe that changes in the composition of the Spanish Regency would make any significant difference, so long as it remained at Cadiz, and that the government was not willing to demand any such changes. He was instructed not to raise the issue of the command of the Spanish armies again until Wellington was satisfied that sufficient improvements had been made in their forces, and their logistical support, to make the command worth accepting. The cabinet firmly rejected Henry Wellesley's proposal to threaten to withdraw the British garrison from Cadiz and to suspend the subsidy if British demands were not accepted: clearly Spain was less dependent than Sicily, and had to be treated with more respect. These instructions were softened by formal approval of Henry Wellesley's conduct of a number of issues, and he was authorized to take an active role to ensure that British aid got to front-line Spanish troops, and to protest at the dispatch of Spanish forces to America, but the underlying message was clear: the British government did not wish to become more deeply enmeshed in the internal affairs of Spain. Britain lacked the resources to finance the reorganization and retraining of the Spanish army, and the ministers accepted Wellington's advice that without proper financial backing the command of the Spanish armies was useless.[41]

On the whole, Wellington approved of the government's policy, and on several occasions advised Henry Wellesley not to interfere too much in Spanish politics. But Wellington also had some ideas of his own. Early in May 1812 he suggested that he be given complete control over all British aid to Spain, so that he could direct it solely to Spanish commanders who cooperated with his operations. He argued that this would give him far more real control over the Spanish armies than the nominal command, and would get the best value from the limited funds available. The British government welcomed this proposal and instructed Henry Wellesley to follow Wellington's advice for funds already en route, and informed him that future funds would be directed to Lisbon for Wellington to distribute. But Henry Wellesley was naturally horrified at an arrangement that would strip him of much of his influence in Cadiz, and wrote to Wellington in some distress offering to resign. Wellington in turn was upset by his brother's reaction, and immediately dropped the proposal. Control of the subsidy remained in Henry Wellesley's hands, though he paid more attention than ever to Wellington's wishes.[42]

Despite this setback, Wellington gained considerable influence over Spanish military affairs during the early campaigns of 1812. The local commanders cooperated readily with him, and the Spanish government consulted him before transferring troops from one province to another. Wellington remained justifiably irritated at the personal extravagance of commanders such as Castaños, and at the inefficiency of the government which, for example, failed to maintain an adequate garrison for Ciudad Rodrigo once it had been retaken, but in general there was a greater willingness to cooperate than had been evident in recent years.

Wellington's victories in the spring and summer of 1812, and especially the liberation of Madrid, made him a genuinely popular figure in Spain for the first time, while his prompt proclamation of the Constitution wherever he went disarmed the suspicions of the liberales. Despite the sack of Ciudad Rodrigo and Badajoz, many Spaniards began at last to believe that their alliance with the infuriating, arrogant and repulsive British might possibly prove worthwhile.

In September there was another crisis in Spanish politics, with the liberales again seeking to change the composition of the Regency, which had grown increasingly conservative. Henry Wellesley was approached to lend his support to the move, and agreed on condition that a new government appoint a commander-in-chief and make a number of other reforms. Vega, who had just been elected President of the Cortes, was personally eager to appoint Wellington, and managed to persuade his fellow liberales to agree, using a mixture of political and military arguments. On 22 September the Cortes secretly voted to offer Wellington the command of the Spanish armies. The precise terms of the offer were clouded in ambiguity and rhetoric, but it was probably intended to limit Wellington's authority to operational matters. Vega, however, assured Henry Wellesley that Wellington would be given whatever powers the ambassador thought necessary.[43]

The offer took Wellington and the British government completely by surprise. Neither was enthusiastic, but both recognized that it would be impossible to refuse unless the terms of the offer were manifestly inadequate. Wellington played for time by referring the matter home, while the British government gave its approval in principle, but added the condition that Wellington had to be satisfied that his powers were sufficient. Wellington formally accepted the command on 22 November and visited Cadiz at the end of the year, where, in a series of sometimes difficult meetings with the Spanish government, he managed to get his way on most of the questions which were at issue.

Long before this, on 11 October, the Spanish Minister for War had instructed his generals to obey Wellington's orders. A fortnight later, General Ballesteros publicly denounced Wellington's appointment, and suspended his operations, which Wellington was hoping would divert Soult from his advance on Madrid. Ballesteros issued a flamboyant nationalist proclamation and evidently hoped that the army and people would rally around him, but his appeal failed, and within a week he was arrested without difficulty. Wellington laid considerable stress on the incident when explaining the failure of his operations in the last months of 1812, but it seems most unlikely that even the most active cooperation from Ballesteros would have done anything to alter the result of the campaign.[44] But as Wellington's army retreated, Ballesteros's popularity rose, and soon there were many in Cadiz who regarded him as a noble patriot.

Military cooperation between British and Spanish forces, and specifically the issue of the command of the Spanish armies, had been a source of contention throughout the war. Wellington's appointment to the position did nothing to resolve these problems. Indeed, by bringing him into closer contact with the Spanish government, it substantially added to the amount of friction in the alliance. With insufficient funds and limited authority, he was unable to reform the Spanish army, although he did achieve some modest improvements. Despite Ballesteros, his new position did ensure smoother cooperation between the armies in the field, and as the campaign of 1813 brought them much closer together this was undoubtedly important. So, overall, the command probably aided the allied cause, even though it exacerbated the tensions in relations between Britain and Spain. But in this respect as in others, the high hopes aroused by the liberation of Madrid were disappointed.

When Wellington entered Madrid on 12 August 1812 he dominated central Spain, but had large French armies to the north, east and south of him. He had about 40,000 men with him, while Hill with 18,000 men was still in Estremadura. The French still had over 260,000 men in the Peninsula, but many of these were fully committed protecting their lines of communication in northern Spain, holding down Aragon, Navarre, Catalonia and other areas from which they could not be withdrawn. Indeed, Wellington's position could only be challenged if Soult abandoned Andalusia, or Suchet gave up Valencia, which would isolate Soult. Clearly the overall interests of the French demanded that Soult evacuate southern Spain, thus freeing his army of 55,000 men for active operations. On 2 August King Joseph instructed Soult to do so, but the French marshals, and Soult in particular, had so often ignored royal orders that no one could guess how Soult would react. Seville is a beautiful city and the French had become well established there, while Soult had enjoyed the fruits of his viceroyalty, building up an excellent private art collection among other pursuits. His first reaction to Joseph's order was to suggest that the King take refuge at Seville, if necessary abandoning communications with France until Napoleon could send reinforcements. But after a short struggle, military discipline and his own sound strategic sense prevailed, and he agreed to abandon Andalusia and march to join the King and Suchet at Valencia. The siege of Cadiz was raised on 24 August, more than thirty months after it began. Two days later Soult set out from Seville with an immense train of baggage and reached Valencia at the beginning of October.[45]

At Madrid Wellington faced the choice of remaining inactive and letting the French combine against him at their leisure, or taking the initiative, in the hope of forestalling them. He preferred the latter and decided to ignore Suchet and Soult in the hope that if he left them alone they might remain in their provinces, where they had many problems with the local Spanish forces (both regulars and guerrillas), the garrison of Cadiz, and the Anglo-Sicilian force at Alicante. Wellington ordered Hill's force to Madrid from Estremadura and left many of his own troops there, including the tried and tested Third and Light Divisions. This whole force of nearly 35,000 men (including Carlos de España's Spanish division) was placed under Hill's command, and given the task of defending Madrid and protecting Wellington's flank and rear from Suchet and Soult.

Wellington marched north with nearly 30,000 men on 1 September 1812. His object was to push back the remnants of the defeated French Army of Portugal which Clausel had managed to restore to some sort of order. Wellington planned a limited operation, not a sustained offensive, to secure his northern flank before returning to Madrid to face the more serious threat which might come from Soult and Suchet. But he made the uncharacteristic mistake of underestimating his opponent, leaving behind his best troops and not ordering up a siege-train.

Wellington reached Valladolid on 4 September and advanced against Clausel, who prudently retired. On 16 September Castaños joined Wellington with 11,000 men of the Spanish VI Army, but the allies were unable to bring the French to battle, Clausel continuing to fall back slowly, while the allied advance was unaccountably torpid and unenterprising.[46] On 18 September Clausel retreated beyond Burgos, leaving a garrison of 2,000 men in the castle. Although the ancient defences of Burgos had been greatly strengthened by the French, it was not a modern regular fortress like Badajoz and Ciudad Rodrigo, and it could not have held out for long against a well-prepared siege. But Wellington had only an improvised and grossly inadequate siege-train of three heavy guns and five howitzers. With more forethought additional guns might have been brought up — indeed, two ship guns were carried, with immense labour, over the mountains from Popham's squadron on the coast — but Wellington never took the siege seriously enough. He relied on mining the defences and partial attacks which proved both costly and unsuccessful. He finally abandoned the siege on 22 October, having wasted a month and suffered over 2,000 casualties for nothing. Certainly the army was stale, and the besieging troops lacked the daring and dash of the Third and Light Divisions, but even so staunch a defender of Wellington as Sir John Fortescue acknowledges that 'this abortive siege of Burgos was the most unsatisfactory operation on Wellington's part during the whole of the Peninsular War'.[47]

While Wellington had been checked at Burgos, the French had been gathering their forces. Clausel had been superseded by Souham, who brought some 7,000 reinforcements to the Army of Portugal. Caffarelli had brought up 12,000 men of the Army of the North — all that could be spared of its 43,000 men, the rest being tied down as garrisons or being harassed by the guerrillas and Popham's squadron. Altogether the French had some 50,000 men facing Wellington in the north, while he had only 24,000 Anglo–Portuguese and 11,000 Spaniards. Nor was the situation any better further south, where Soult and King Joseph, having combined in Valencia, had begun to advance on Madrid. Suchet did not join them, but as they had over 60,000 men he was not needed. Hill had about 38,000 men, including just over 4,000 under Colonel Skerrett who had joined him from the garrison of Cadiz. Given the imbalance of forces on both fronts, the allies had no choice but to withdraw, at least until their army was united. On 31 October Hill's rearguard abandoned Madrid, less than twelve weeks after it had been liberated.

On 8 November the allied army was reunited behind the Tormes, but the retreat continued. The French followed, continuing to outnumber Wellington, although Caffarelli returned to the north while other detachments had to be made for garrisons. Nonetheless, when the French armies combined, King Joseph had some 80,000 men under his nominal command. Despite this strength Wellington offered battle near Salamanca, but remembering Talavera, Bussaco and Fuentes, the French refused to attack him in a position of his choice, and by turning his flank forced him to continue to retreat. The abandonment of Salamanca completed the collapse of the logistics and morale of the allied army, and the remainder of the retreat to the Portuguese frontier was almost as chaotic and ill-disciplined as Moore's retreat to Coruña. During the next few days the allied army lost over 3,000 men owing to straggling, desertion, privation and the bitter weather. The French pursued, taking many prisoners, but not risking a general engagement. On 28 November Wellington issued a scathing circular blaming all the ill-discipline of the army on its subordinate officers.[48] While not totally unjustified, this indiscriminate condemnation caused great resentment, which still smouldered half a century later. The fact was that the entire army, including its commander, was disappointed at the miserable end of the campaign, and exhausted after the most strenuous year of the entire war.

And so despite all the earlier triumphs, the allies ended the year back on the Portuguese frontier. Yet much had been achieved: Ciudad Rodrigo and Badajoz remained securely in allied hands, the siege of Cadiz had been raised, and the French had completely abandoned Andalusia. No cold calculation of the balance of forces at the beginning of the campaign could have hoped for more; but the great victory of Salamanca and the liberation of Madrid had raised expectations to a pitch which could only have been satisfied by driving the French back to the Ebro. The sense of disappointment affected all the allies, in the army, in London, in Cadiz and in Lisbon, and it did not help interallied relations.

The campaign of 1812 shook French power in Spain to the core. The shaky authority of Joseph's regime was shattered and was never restored. But it is worth remembering that if Napoleon had been victorious in Russia, the spring of 1813 would probably have seen French reinforcements pour over the Pyrenees, just as they had done in the spring of 1810 after the defeat of Austria. These reinforcements could have restored French power in Spain, kept Wellington behind the Portuguese frontier, and even reconquered Andalusia, while the fillip which the Spanish patriots had received in 1812 would have turned to despair. The war in the Peninsula was just one part of the wider struggle, and Spain could only be liberated if Napoleon's power as a whole was broken, or if the war became so costly that he decided to cut his losses.

Throughout the first nine months of the year the papers in England were filled with good news of Wellington's campaigns, for as well as the great triumphs of Ciudad Rodrigo, Badajoz, Salamanca and the entry into Madrid, there were many smaller affairs such as Cotton's success at Villa Garcia (11 April) and Hill's at Almaraz (19 May) which sustained the air of rejoicing. These victories reflected well on the government and strengthened its position both in Parliament and in the country as a whole.

The Opposition generally refrained from public criticism of Wellington's campaigns in 1812. Thus when Perceval moved a Vote of Thanks for the capture of Ciudad Rodrigo on 10 February, there was no dissent and General Tarleton, who had in the past frequently derided Wellington, now praised him with almost equal lack of restraint. Even Wellington's promotion in the peerage and accompanying pension was opposed only by the radical Sir Francis Burdett, who argued that Wellington, with an army of 200,000 men [sic], should not have taken so much time and trouble to defeat Masséna, who had only 60,000 [sic].[49]

Privately, however, the Opposition remained very pessimistic about the war as a whole, and about Wellington's campaigns in particular, constantly finding fault and making gloomy predictions. Even the news of Salamanca could not sweeten Lord Auckland's day: 'Marmont's unaccountable folly has given a fortunate brilliancy to Lord Wellington's campaign, which was leading to a lame and impotent conclusion.' But Grey acknowledged that 'it must have been quite decisive, and it certainly does open a prospect of more favourable consequences both in Spain and in the North than could a few months ago have been reasonably looked for. I suppose there is no bounds to the exultation of the Prince and his Ministers. The former, I have no doubt, has by this time nearly convinced himself that he won the battle in person.' Lady Bessborough wistfully expressed what many Whigs must have been feeling: 'the only reason I wish to have friends in office is that I might once in my life be allowed to rejoice at our successes, and not always be damp'd by doubts and buts and ifs etc'.[50]

As Grey supposed, the ministers and their supporters enjoyed their triumph. The cabinet marked Salamanca by making Wellington a marquess, and granting him £100,000 to sustain the honour — with the only objection coming from Mulgrave, who thought it should have been £150,000. At the Regent's command the Archbishop of Canterbury prepared a special prayer of thanks for the victories which was read in every church in the three kingdoms. The ministers ordered that the *Extraordinary Gazette* containing the news of the victory be translated into French and German, and distributed as widely as possible on the Continent through smugglers and other unofficial channels. London was illuminated for three nights and, according to one junior minister,

> Lord Wellesley did not think it undignified to drive about the streets in his chariot and receive the applause of the mob, who with their fickleness were greatly delighted with the good news and broke some of Burdett's windows forgetting that two years ago they had broken the windows of half the houses in town in order to do honour to the said Baronet's unworthy escape.[51]

Liverpool was elated by the news of the capture of Madrid and told Peel that 'the prospect in the Peninsula was never so brilliant, and I trust the campaign will not close without the French being driven at least across the Ebro'. Lady Bessborough now declared herself an open and enthusiastic admirer of Wellington: 'Every officer of whatever rank, whom I have hitherto spoken with seems to have such reliance on his unerring judgement, such confidence in the impossibility of defeat when he commands, that his name alone must be equivalent to half an army.' Gossip reported that when the eagles captured at Salamanca were presented to Lady Wellington, 'she kiss'd them, said "They are mine," and fainted away'.[52]

Britain's prospects in the late summer of 1812 seemed bright. Not only was the war in Spain prospering, but the harvest was good, the Luddite disturbances were dying down and the economy was gradually improving. Even Ireland was in a state of 'extraordinary tranquillity' according to Peel, which he attributed to the good news from Spain.[53] And though accounts

7. Effects of the Arrival of French Eagles in England
[Brooke], 1 Oct. 1812, B.M. Cat. no. 11,905

The trophies of Salamanca reached London on 16 August and were greeted with much rejoicing. London was illuminated and windows not lit up were broken by the mob. The first frame shows the crowd stoning Sir Francis Burdett's darkened house while cheering his neighbour. A funeral procession marks the death of the hopes of the Whig party. The two almost nude figures in the foreground represent discord and faction who are dismayed by the news.

In the second frame four men representing England, Ireland, Wales and Scotland celebrate Wellington's victory, while the British lion beside them tramples on French eagles and standards.

from Russia were more uncertain, there was at least no sign of another Tilsit.

Liverpool was much too experienced and wily a politician to let such an opportunity pass, and in September 1812 he called an election. There was never any doubt that his government would be returned, for governments in those days did not lose elections, but the poll gave a shake to the composition of the Commons, and many individual contests were hard fought. Canning gained a triumph in the relatively open seat of Liverpool, though a number of his supporters lost their seats. This was partly redressed by gains by Lord Wellesley's followers, so that the third force had about twenty committed supporters in the new Parliament.[54] The Opposition also suffered, losing a number of seats and many of their best speakers: Romilly, Brougham, Creevey, Tierney, Horner and William Lamb were all defeated, though seats were eventually found for them. Some government supporters felt that the triumph should have been greater, but Liverpool was satisfied with the result.

The new Parliament was opened by the Prince Regent in person on 30 November 1812, and as Liverpool anticipated, the main threat to the government was an onslaught from Canning and Wellesley. The failure of

Wellington's siege of Burgos and his miserable retreat to the Portuguese frontier gave them the issue they needed. They attacked the government with great vigour for not supporting Wellington adequately or reinforcing him soon enough. They argued that responsibility for the failure rested solely with the ministers and implied that only a government under their leadership would provide Wellington with the means of victory. Behind these attacks lay a struggle as to who should be recognized as the true heirs of Pitt: Canning and Wellesley, or Liverpool and his colleagues. Moreover, Canning at least wanted to take over the existing government rather than destroy it utterly, and to keep some of the existing ministers in a new administration. Wellesley was less sure and there are indications that he was already drifting away from Canning towards his old friend Lord Grenville, who was being notably courteous to him in debate.[55]

The attack on the government was, for a time, fast and furious. Many uncommitted members were inclined to sympathize with Canning and Wellesley, regretting that men of such obvious ability were out of office, and feeling keenly the disappointment of Wellington's retreat. But the government stood firm. Castlereagh, who led the battle in the Commons, 'made a very good speech indeed on the thanks to Lord Wellington', and generally raised his reputation in the House enormously.[56] After a few weeks the attack began to flag from want of ammunition. Canning and Wellesley could not produce any decisive evidence that Wellington was unhappy with the government; indeed, the ministers constantly claimed the contrary and quoted Wellington's letters to prove it. Meanwhile the news from Russia was good and the disappointment over Wellington's retreat was gradually eclipsed by the dawning realization of the extent of Napoleon's losses. By early in the new year it was plain that the attempt to escalade the government's fortress had failed, and Canning and Wellesley were a spent force. For the first time since 1809, a new year began without the British government facing a political crisis; nor did it do so at any point during that long, difficult, but immensely rewarding year.

Britain and Napoleon's Invasion of Russia

One of the most evocative dates of the nineteenth century is the year 1812. But for most people it is not Perceval's assassination, Wellington's triumphs or the war with America that it conjures up; rather it is Tchaikovsky's music, the loves of Natasha Rostova, and the destruction of Napoleon's army amid the snowy wastes of Russia. The story of Napoleon's invasion of Russia, the burning of Moscow and the disastrous French retreat has become a modern legend, and as with most legends the ending appears inevitable. Overweening ambition will meet its nemesis despite all the plans and guile of man. But Napoleon's defeat was not inevitable, and to understand the events of the year properly one must make a conscious effort to put aside one's knowledge of the outcome and try to examine events as contemporaries saw them, in all their perplexity and confusion.

Britain played only a peripheral role in the events of 1812 in northern Europe. But as her ministers were well aware, the result of Napoleon's campaign would critically affect the balance of forces throughout Europe; and they did what little they could to thwart his plans, without abandoning their underlying strategy of concentrating their military efforts in the Peninsula. Their approach remained, at least in principle, simple: they would not seek to induce or pressure any power to go to war, but they would give support and encouragement to any ally who did appear. In practice there was more ambiguity, especially in the already ambiguous relations with Sweden, while the demands of the Peninsula and the financial problems facing the government severely constrained the amount of aid Britain could offer. This ensured that Britain's role was small, and although generally honourable, it never quite reached the heights of Galahadian purity which the Opposition demanded.

When the prospect of war in northern Europe in 1811 had finally faded away, the British government was not disheartened. Wellesley and his colleagues had been encouraged by the breadth and strength of opposition to Napoleon, but they had believed that the northern powers would benefit from a few more months of peace in which to prepare for war.[1] But the winter had cooled the hotheads in Berlin, and Napoleon had used the time well. Frederick William and Hardenberg had always seen greater security, if little pleasure, in an alliance with Napoleon, provided one could be arranged on reasonable terms. Napoleon's unremitting hostility had driven them to consider the prospect of war in 1811, but neither Austria nor Russia had promised effective support, while a relaxation in Napoleon's attitude had eased tensions. Early in 1812 Napoleon had tightened the screw again, moving troops up to the Prussian border and demanding that Prussia immediately agree to a treaty of alliance or face extinction. Scharnhorst and some of the patriots urged resistance, but the cynical, disillusioned King, who had experienced the humiliation of defeat more poignantly than any of his subjects, refused to listen and agreed to the French terms. The treaty, which was signed in February and ratified early in March, provided for the occupation of most of Prussia by French troops, pledged Prussia to provide huge quantities of food, horses and other supplies, and a contingent of 20,000 men to aid in a war against Russia. The reformers were outraged, and a few Prussian officers resigned from the army in disgust, but it is difficult to see that Frederick William had a real choice. Yet the alliance left Prussia in an invidious position, for she had much to fear and little reason to hope, whoever won the war. Frederick William did his best to avert lasting Russian resentment by writing secretly to Emperor Alexander to explain that, although 20,000 Prussian troops were about to invade Russia, this in no way indicated any diminution of his warm friendship. Alexander understood the situation perfectly, but only his triumphant victory at the end of the year enabled him to forgive completely.[2]

The Austrian government was in a stronger position and obtained commensurately better terms. Her contingent of 30,000 men was only half the number Napoleon had requested, and he had also had to agree that it would serve as a single unit under an Austrian general who would take orders only from him, and not from his subordinates. More significantly, Napoleon had guaranteed Austrian territory in Galicia (southern Poland), which at least ensured that Vienna would receive substantial compensation if the Kingdom of Poland was restored. Like Frederick William, the Emperor Francis wrote to St Petersburg pleading necessity for taking part in the invasion, but Alexander knew that Austria had more room to manoeuvre and his relations with Vienna remained cool until well into 1813.

France and Russia now prepared for the inevitable conflict. Napoleon was far from underestimating his task and not only collected an enormous army but paid detailed attention to its logistical needs. Almost all the Russian generals agreed on the need for a defensive campaign, with initial retreats to wear down and weaken the advancing French, and there was much talk of imitating Wellington's successful defence of Portugal. But they had no idea of the strength of Napoleon's army, imagining that it would not amount to more than 200,000 or 250,000 men at most — less than half the real figure. This miscalculation rendered all their plans and preparations invalid, and threw the Russian campaign into confusion from the outset.[3]

The Russians were somewhat more successful in their diplomatic preparations. They courted Sweden assiduously, and with some success, and in May belatedly made peace with Turkey, thus freeing their Army of the Danube to take part in the war against Napoleon. However, they made no overture to Britain in the first half of 1812, other than a renewed and ultimately successful application to purchase a large quantity of saltpetre. Presumably the Russian government felt that Britain could give little direct assistance and was unwilling to risk precipitating the conflict with Napoleon. But it is also true that Britain was unpopular in some circles in St Petersburg, including that of the Chancellor Rumiantsev, while Alexander himself was ambivalent.

British opinion of the Russian Emperor was unflattering. Early in April, Liverpool told Wellington of the likelihood of war in the north:

> If the Emperor of Russia was really determined upon a *guerre à mort* & to sacrifice either Petersburg or Moscow for a Time, rather than conclude a dishonourable Peace, I should feel great confidence in the result — but the weakness and unsteadiness of that Monarch's Character, & his inconceivable folly & obstinacy in continuing the War with the Turks under present circumstances, preclude the possibility of relying upon His Intentions. — Whatever may be the issue of the Contest it will at least have the effect of directing the Exertions of Buonaparte for the present to the North East of Europe, it opens therefore a prospect to the Allies in the Peninsula, of which every practicable Advantage ought to be taken.[4]

Liverpool and his colleagues expected that Sweden would actively support Russia in the coming war. Napoleon had caused great offence in Stockholm by forcibly occupying Swedish Pomerania early in the year, and Bernadotte had made approaches to London and St Petersburg. At the end of March the British government decided to send Edward Thornton back to Sweden. Castlereagh, who had replaced Wellesley as Foreign Secretary, instructed Thornton to conclude promptly a simple treaty of peace with the Swedes: if he met any reluctance or procrastination, he was to return home at once. Nonetheless, Britain disclaimed any intention of pushing Sweden into war with Napoleon: 'If Sweden thinks She can avoid a war with France consistently with Her Own Security and Independence, it is no part of the Policy of Great Britain to precipitate Her into such a Contest.' But if war did come, Britain offered the cooperation of her Baltic fleet to protect the Swedish coast. On other issues the British government was far from forthcoming: offering some material aid, but firmly stating that the demands of the Peninsula prevented her from offering any subsidy at all. Thornton was told that Britain might consider Bernadotte's desire for a West Indian island, under certain conditions, but that he was to discourage discussion of the question of Norway, and that Britain certainly could not guarantee

Swedish possession of territory which she had yet to acquire. This reserve was to be explained, frankly and ingenuously, as the result of considerable residual distrust of Bernadotte in London. It was a novel form of wooing, but one hardly suited to a Gascon.[5]

Thornton received a warm and flattering reception in Sweden and was easily led, contrary to his instructions, into discussions of the terms of an alliance, while the peace remained unsigned. The Swedes did not raise serious objections to Thornton's proposals — though they pressed for British 'concurrence' in the conquest of Norway — while a personal interview with Bernadotte left him convinced of the Crown Prince's hostility to Napoleon. But though full of fair words, the Swedes constantly procrastinated and refused to commit themselves. This was natural enough: Sweden was a small country, and although war between France and Russia appeared increasingly probable, a sudden reconciliation, or even a second Tilsit, would leave her exposed and vulnerable.

As the weeks passed, Thornton's negotiations became more complicated rather than simpler. The Swedes agreed to make peace, but only if a triple alliance with Russia and Britain was signed at the same time. Thornton had already had talks with the Russian envoy General van Suchtelen, who had responded to assurances of good will by suggesting that if Britain really wished to help Russia, she might like to take over an old Russian debt of £4 million owed to Dutch bankers. This was, of course, totally unacceptable, and may have been intended only to delay matters, which it did. The British government had hopes that Russia could be helped by forging a northern alliance between Sweden and Denmark, which would threaten Napoleon's flank and rear in the event of war. But Bernadotte continued to press his claims to Norway, arguing that he needed its conquest to justify the war to the Swedish people and console them for the loss of Finland. As Norway had been part of the Danish Kingdom for centuries, this ambition made an alliance between Sweden and Denmark impossible. Meanwhile the Spaniards managed to complicate affairs further by promising Russia a subsidy, and then expecting Britain to find the cash.[6]

Matters thus dragged on until the middle of July, when news of Napoleon's invasion of Russia brought immediate progress. Within a fortnight both Sweden and Russia had signed a peace with Britain. The British government promised Sweden £500,000 in material aid, but would not give her a subsidy while the conquest of Norway remained the first Swedish priority. However, if the Swedes would direct their attention to an immediate expedition to northern Germany, Castlereagh indicated that a subsidy might be forthcoming. Bernadotte was very disappointed with this response: the Swedish army was wretchedly ill-equipped and needed money to take the field, but his own political position in Sweden was not secure, and he dared not make too heavy demands on the country, which was not wealthy, at the commencement of the war. Bernadotte was an avaricious, posturing liar, but in this instance his concerns appear to have been well founded. Certainly he convinced Thornton that without a British subsidy there could be no military cooperation in 1812, and early in August Thornton took the highly irregular step of embarking to return to London to plead Sweden's cause.[7]

Napoleon's armies crossed the Russian frontier on the night of 24 June 1812 without a declaration of war. Alexander was at the headquarters of his forces at Vilna and remained with the army for the first stage of the campaign, but his presence only added to the disorder caused by rivalry between the Russian generals and a confused chain of command. At first the Russians fell back in accordance with their plans to a fortified camp at Drissa, where they intended to stand and fight. They reached Drissa on 9 July, but soon realized that Napoleon's forces were too strong for them to resist, and after extended talks they abandoned the camp and continued their retreat. On 17 July Alexander was finally persuaded to leave the army and went to Moscow to rally the population and raise recruits and money for the war. Despite the Emperor's departure, however, the Russian high command remained divided and quarrelsome.

Barclay de Tolly, the Minister of War and commander of the principal Russian army, continued the retreat. On 27 July near Vitebsk he offered battle, but fell back when Napoleon concentrated his forces. By the beginning of August the Russians had reached Smolensk and united Barclay's army with that of Bagration. The long retreat had caused great discontent in the army and in the country as a whole. At Smolensk Barclay reluctantly consented to assume the offensive, but did so without spirit or confidence, and after a few days which only further alienated his subordinates he fell back to Smolensk. Napoleon advanced on Smolensk hoping for a decisive battle. The advance had greatly weakened his army, more from the need to make detachments to garrison conquered provinces and from straggling, heat, exhaustion and illness, than from losses in action; but he still had a decisive superiority. The Russians defended Smolensk stubbornly on 17 August, but that night Barclay gave the order to continue the retreat.

Historians have sometimes argued that Napoleon should have halted at Smolensk, but Moscow was only 230 miles away and he felt sure that the Russians would not abandon their ancient capital without offering battle, thus giving him another chance to gain the crushing victory which would decide the campaign. The Russians fell back to within seventy miles of Moscow but then, near a village called Borodino, they turned to fight, just as Napoleon hoped. Barclay was no longer in overall command. Even before news reached St Petersburg that Smolensk had been abandoned, the Emperor Alexander had given way to pressure and appointed Kutusov, whom he heartily disliked, to the supreme command.

The Battle of Borodino, fought on 7 September 1812, was one of the most appalling of the Napoleonic Wars. The French had a slight numerical advantage (about 130,000 men compared with about 120,000 Russians), but the Russian position had been strengthened by a number of earthworks. There was a heavy concentration of artillery on both sides, and the battle-field was relatively small, leading to bloody fighting and little tactical finesse. The French are said to have lost over 30,000 casualties; the Russians over 40,000. Both sides were utterly exhausted, and on the following day the Russians wearily retired towards Moscow: they had been defeated, but certainly not routed, and Napoleon had failed to achieve the crushing victory he wanted.

Less than a week later the Russian generals held a council of war in which they decided to abandon Moscow without further resistance. The French occupied the city on 14 September and halted their advance a little beyond. The impetus which had carried Napoleon's army hundreds of miles for-ward was spent, and any further advance would simply weaken his forces without bringing victory any closer. He could only hope that Alexander's will to resist would crumble in the face of Russia's devastating losses, and that he would sue for peace.

News of the progress of the war was naturally followed with keen interest in Britain. The Opposition, with their unhappy knack of completely mis-judging military matters, were certain that Russia would be defeated and demanded assurances in Parliament that Britain had done nothing to en-courage the Russians to embark on hostilities. In reply, Castlereagh told them that 'the language of this government to Russia was always that of caution, and not of excitement. It was always signified to her, that if she were to determine upon war, she must look only to her own resources, and not to this country.'[8]

Despite the reserve implied by this answer, the ministers and their advisers had hopes of Russian success. On 21 July Wellington told Bathurst that 'If the Emperor of Russia has any resources, and is prudent, and his Russians will really fight, Buonaparte will not succeed.' A month later Liverpool was less guarded:

> The accounts from the north of Europe are by no means unsatisfactory. Bonaparte has not been able to conceal his difficulties even in his bulletins. The Russians appear to be acting with great prudence, and if they will but persevere in their defensive system, and avoid a general action till the French armies are exhausted, and their spirit broken, by the different wants which must in that case soon assail them, the result of the campaign may answer the most sanguine expectations which could have been formed of it. In the different partial actions which have taken place the Russians have dis-tinguished themselves, and have proved that, if well led, they are not unequal to the contest.[9]

As Castlereagh had made clear, there was little that Britain could do to assist the Russians, but some steps were taken. Before the end of August orders were given for 50,000 muskets to be sent to Russia, and a further 50,000 were ordered after news of the fall of Moscow reached London —

though this second shipment did not reach Riga until the summer of 1813, owing to the closure of the Baltic in winter. Sir Francis d'Ivernois, a noted Swiss banker, was sent to St Petersburg to advise the Russian government on financial questions. He was warmly received and seems to have done good work, though he failed to convince the Russians that Britain was facing severe financial problems of her own. Finally, the Royal Navy cooperated with the Russians in the Baltic, playing an important role in the successful defence of Riga. Other than these, admittedly slight, forms of assistance, the British government could only hope to help Russia by encouraging the Swedes to mount an expedition to northern Germany, which the ministers believed would threaten Napoleon's flank and rear, and act as a powerful diversion in favour of the Russians.[10]

On 24 July 1812 the British government appointed an ambassador to Russia. The Russians had indicated through Thornton in May that they would like to receive a British minister of high rank who would display energy and force of character, and who possessed the entire confidence of the British government. They even mentioned Lord Wellesley's name — an intriguing suggestion which reveals little knowledge of Wellesley himself (who had high rank and force of character, but not energy) or of British politics.[11] Wellesley of course was ineligible. The British government was emphatic in its lack of confidence in him; and he would not have served, as he still hoped to become Prime Minister within months.

Instead the government appointed Lord Cathcart, who had been promoted to full general on 1 January 1812 (and was thus considerably senior to Wellington). Cathcart was fifty-six years old, and had had a long and successful military career, having served in the American War of Independence, the Low Countries in 1794–5, commanded a large expedition to north Germany in 1805, and the Copenhagen Expedition in 1807. George III had liked and respected him, and he was trusted by the ministers, perhaps by Castlereagh in particular.[12] His blood was blue — he was tenth Baron Cathcart in the peerage of Scotland — and he had spent two years in Russia in his youth when his father was ambassador to St Petersburg.

As ambassador, Cathcart had only two drawbacks: he had commanded the Copenhagen Expedition, which had aroused strong Russian disapproval; and he lacked ability. Sir Charles Webster describes him as 'a rather stupid man who lacked both insight and energy and never grasped the problems with which he was confronted'. This may be unduly harsh — though it is certain that he neither electrified nor dominated the scene — but even Webster acknowledges that 'his military profession and decorous exterior made him a favourite of the Tsar and he could sometimes get concessions from Alexander when no one else could approach him'.[13] Cathcart was reasonably competent at the normal business of his office, but did little by the force of his personality to increase British influence with the Russian government.

Cathcart was instructed to meet Thornton in Sweden and conclude a simple peace with Russia. If the Russians refused or demanded a subsidy he was to return home at once, but Castlereagh regarded this as most unlikely, and in fact Thornton had already signed a peace treaty. The British government had no objection in principle to giving Russia a subsidy, but its means were so limited that Cathcart was only authorized to provide £500,000 before February 1813. This figure was so small and unlikely to satisfy Russian needs that Castlereagh advised Cathcart to discourage all applications and to bring the money forward only in the event of pressing need.

But Cathcart was not simply ambassador to Russia; he was also Britain's chief representative in northern and eastern Europe and he was instructed to lose no opportunity of persuading the courts of Berlin and Vienna to give 'a better direction to their counsels'. He was also to press the Swedes to adopt a plan of campaign and begin operations as soon as possible. The British government now accepted that Bernadotte was determined to strike a blow at Denmark before landing in Germany, and they dispatched a squadron of gunboats and a siege-train to help the Swedes attack Zealand, in the hope that if the operation began quickly, it might be completed in time to allow Bernadotte to land in Germany before winter.[14]

Cathcart sailed from Yarmouth before the end of July, and on 8 August met Thornton on his way home to plead for more aid for Sweden. Thornton sensibly returned with Cathcart to his proper post, and on 11 August Cathcart was presented to the Swedish court. After a few days in Sweden Cathcart was convinced that Bernadotte was eager to act, but that the Swedish army was in poor condition and that it would be too weak to act on the Continent without a leavening of Russian troops, and, if possible, more British financial aid.[15]

Towards the end of August Cathcart and Thornton accompanied Bernadotte to meet the Russian Emperor at Åbo in Finland. The proceedings at Åbo were steeped in unreality and bore a distinct resemblance to Tilsit, except that on this occasion it was Alexander who played the part of the magnanimous and generous host. Napoleon had taken Smolensk and was advancing on Moscow, but the Czar calmly discussed the size of the auxiliary army he would lend to the Crown Prince of Sweden for the conquest of Norway, and increased it from 15,000 to 35,000 men. Nor did the talk stop there. Each man flattered the other's not inconsiderable vanity and talked of how best to settle Europe after Napoleon's overthrow, Alexander making it clear that he thought Bernadotte would rule France excellently — far better than either Napoleon or the contemptible Bourbons. It was surely not the first time that this idea had occurred to Bernadotte, who was never noted for excessive modesty, but to hear it said by the Emperor of all the Russias was pleasant indeed. This idea, planted in such fertile soil at Åbo, was to become a troublesome weed in 1814.

Nonetheless, the meeting did produce a few practical results. It dispelled any lingering Russian fears that Bernadotte might suddenly break his alliance with them and invade Finland and threaten St Petersburg. It enabled them to withdraw 15,000 men from the garrison of Finland to aid in the defence of Riga and operations further south. (Officially these troops were temporarily diverted from the auxiliary corps that was to aid Bernadotte's operations, but Alexander privately recognized that the Swedes were unlikely to take the field in 1812, and was glad of a way to free them for more pressing tasks.) The personal warmth between Alexander and Bernadotte was not feigned, and the meeting bolstered the Czar's confidence and ego — which was not unimportant, as he was soon to face the news of Borodino and the fall of Moscow.

Cathcart's role at Åbo remained that of an observer, and not one privy to the innermost talks. But the Emperor Alexander treated him kindly and Rumiantsev praised Britain's campaigns in the Peninsula, and her efforts to encourage Sweden to take an active part in the war. There was no talk of a subsidy or a formal alliance, and Rumiantsev firmly postponed any discussion of commercial questions. For his part, Cathcart neatly sidestepped an invitation to endorse the provisions agreed at Åbo, which included the disposition of hypothetical conquests, at least one of which (Swedish retention of Zealand as well as Norway) was highly obnoxious to Britain.[16]

Cathcart accompanied the Emperor back to St Petersburg, where he was very well received and where he remained for the rest of the year. The Russians did not request financial assistance, and he did not draw on the £500,000 which Castlereagh had put at his disposal. There was little that Cathcart could do, other than appear cheerful and confident — which he did with some effect, pointedly leasing his official residence for three years, even though government departments were making preparations to evacuate the capital.[17] He did his best to keep London informed of the course of the campaign, but this was not easy: Borodino was officially announced as a great Russian victory, and news of the fall of Moscow was suppressed for more than a week. There was a handful of British military attachés with the Russian armies, but most proved of dubious value, while one, Sir Robert Wilson, was a self-important and dangerous intriguer, devoid of veracity and common sense. For their part the Russians remained well disposed both to Cathcart personally and to Britain, and at the end of September, in a spontaneous gesture of good faith, the Emperor offered to send the Russian fleet to winter in British ports lest the French capture it when it was immobilized by the winter ice. Cathcart naturally welcomed the proposal, and by early November the fleet had sailed. While it proved an unnecessary precaution, this gesture made a great impression on the British ministers, and went a long way to removing their remaining distrust of Alexander's sincerity and perseverance.[18]

With the fall of Moscow, the fate of the campaign hinged on the Czar's determination to fight on. Cathcart did his best to encourage confidence, telling Alexander that, in his opinion, 'it seemed impossible to conceive that the invading army could escape destruction'. But, strangely, Alexander, who was normally the most irresolute of men, did not hesitate in this great crisis. He would not hear of peace: the war must go on at least until the invaders were driven back beyond the Russian frontier. In this decision he appears to have accurately judged the mood of the army and the people, for when a French emissary arrived at Kutusov's headquarters, he was sent back with the reply, 'That the Man who dared propose peace, would be considered by the Sovereign, by the Army, and by the King, a Traitor'.[19]

Meanwhile Napoleon's position was growing more and more difficult. The great fires which had swept through Moscow soon after the French occupation destroyed much of what had been left when the population abandoned the city. Unlike Vienna, Berlin and even Madrid, the French had captured only the husk of a great city. Napoleon's immensely long lines of communications were already being harassed by bands of peasants and Cossacks much like the guerrillas of Spain, while the Russians were assembling new armies to the north, south and east. Napoleon considered advancing on St Petersburg but recognized that his army was already too weak to do so. He could not remain for the winter, for even if the army were stronger and supplies were more plentiful, he would be cut off for months from Paris, and already there had been intrigues. In the middle of October Napoleon began his retreat from Moscow.

The next two months saw the complete disintegration and almost total destruction of Napoleon's vast army. This was as much due to the demoralization and disorganization of the army as to the severity of the weather or the activity of the Cossacks. The Russians claimed to have taken prisoner 6,000 officers and 130,000 men; to have cremated 308,000 French and allied corpses; and to have captured 900 cannon, 100,000 muskets and 25,000 vehicles. The true figures will never be known, but modern estimates put Napoleon's losses even higher, at between 500,000 and 570,000 men (including prisoners), approximately 200,000 horses, and 1,000 cannon. The Russians too lost very heavily: perhaps 150,000 of their soldiers died, while even more were disabled by frostbite and wounds, not to mention the countless civilians who lost their lives or their homes.[20] The horror and the suffering represented by such figures cannot be imagined, though it can be glimpsed through the memoirs of the survivors. Most of the remaining troops were broken by their experiences: some staggered out of Russia only to die of exhaustion in Poland, while others deserted the colours and returned home, where the tales they told did little to increase Napoleon's popularity. The invasion of Russia was over and Napoleon had failed catastrophically.

Throughout the autumn the ministers in London remained confident that Russia would triumph if only her government remained resolute. On 7 October Colonel Bunbury told Bathurst that 'The French account of the

Vat as usual shall Ve say in
 de Bulletin?

By Gar he is almost lost!!!

Say!!!! why Say We have got into Comfortable Winter Quarters, and the Weather is
very fine & will last 8 days longer. say we have got plenty of Soup meagre plenty
of Minced meat — grilld Bears fine Eating — driving Cut us off to the Devil
Say we shall be at home at X mas to dinner — give my love to darling — dont let
John Bull know that I have been too poxed — tell a good lie about the Cossacks
D — e it tell any thing but the Truth

Boney Hatching a Bulletin   or   Snug Winter Quarters!!!

8.   Boney Hatching a Bulletin or Snug Winter Quarters!!!
George Cruikshank, Dec. 1812, B.M. Cat. no. 11,920

One of the many caricatures on Napoleon's retreat from Moscow, this also satirizes his famously inaccurate army bulletins. The 27th Bulletin (27 Oct.) included the passage, 'It is beautiful weather, the roads are excellent; it is the end of autumn; this weather will last eight days longer, and at that period we shall have arrived in our new position.'

battle of Moskwra [Borodino] is far from making me despondent. A few more such victories and Napoleon is undone.' Liverpool told Peel that Cathcart's account of the battle was 'very satisfactory' and that:

> There exists, as all our letters confirm, the best possible spirit in Russia and if the Government will persevere for a month or six weeks longer, Bonaparte will be under difficulties which he has not yet experienced. It is a comfort to reflect that he is now nearly eight hundred miles from the Russian frontier.

If Liverpool wrote with the judicious propriety becoming in a Prime Minister, the young Fred Robinson could, as a junior minister, adopt a more colloquial air:

> I think the Russians will get Buonaparte into a tremendous scrape, if they will but fight it out. I hold this opinion in spite of the prognostications of Croker, who goes about saying they will get licked, for no other reason but because everybody else hopes for another result.

The Opposition had, of course, constantly predicted a Russian defeat, and Croker was not quite the only pessimist on the government's side.[21]

Other British observers were considering the implications for the Peninsula of the war in Russia. On 16 September Colonel Torrens, the Duke of York's military secretary, wrote to a fellow officer: 'May the Russian War continue long enough to allow Lord W[ellingon] to finish his noble work! And when the French are once out of Spain — if the Spaniards do not keep them out they deserve to be a conquered Nation.' The government had already authorized Wellington, after Salamanca, to conclude a convention with the French for their evacuation of Spain. With the news of Napoleon's difficulties in Russia the ministers began to consider where Wellington's army could best be employed: in the Pyrenees, or further afield in Italy, Holland or northern Germany. These hopes proved premature, but the discussions were useful as they led to a better understanding between Wellington and the ministers on the course of future operations.[22]

It took some time before the public in Britain realized the extent of the disaster which was overwhelming Napoleon's army. As late as 1 November Lord Grey could tell Grenville that accounts from Russia led him to conclude, 'as you probably have done, that no reasonable hope of success is to be entertained in that quarter'. And the Opposition in general was slow and reluctant to admit the Russian success — partly, at least, because their increasingly liberal views made them hostile to Russian autocracy.[23] The ministers were less inhibited in welcoming the triumph of an ally, and as fresh accounts came in during November and December they rejoiced whole-heartedly. Only the escape of Napoleon himself, when some accounts had raised hopes of his capture, led to some disappointment. Public excitement rose through December to reach a climax at the end of the year. One diarist wrote on 19 December: 'People in the City, as elsewhere, seem to be going crazy, in their expectations of the consequences of the Russian successes. . . . One would suppose they saw now, not only the Continent but — according to the French phrase — Heaven opening before them.' Yet this same diarist more than a month before had been almost equally unrestrained in his hopes when he learnt of Napoleon's evacuation of Moscow:

> [It] raises ones hopes very high; for if the tide of success thus begins to roll steadily from him, in the double war he now has on his hands, we may sooner than we expected see the end of Mr. Boney. The prestige of his name — that spell which has so often struck terror into the heart of the soldier, and, one may say fearlessly, into the hearts of some Generals also, and paralyzed the best efforts of even the most able of Russian and Prussian commanders — once gone, and the invincible conqueror defeated in two or three great battles, everything may be looked for; Europe may again be free. Doubtless there will be a desperate struggle and much blood will yet be spilt before the desired end comes; but I venture to think it is coming.[24]

He was right.

13

A Foolish and Unnecessary War: Britain and the United States, 1811–13

In the midst of all the hopes and fears which abounded in the summer of 1812, Britain's relations with the United States presented the British government with a most unwelcome distraction. Anglo-American relations had been troubled for many years, principally because of tensions arising out of the war with France. The extension of the economic war following the Berlin and Milan decrees and the Orders in Council led to a further deterioration in relations. The Americans argued that the Orders in Council — which prohibited neutral trade with Napoleonic Europe except under licence — were both illegal and self-interested, and aimed at smothering competition to British trade. Their other great grievance was the question of impressment. This was the British practice of halting merchant ships at sea (British vessels — not American — suffered the most) and forcibly removing British-born sailors, compelling them to join the Royal Navy. Odious in itself, it was made all the more objectionable by the British refusal to recognize American citizenship, so that naturalized citizens of the United States were being compelled to serve in a foreign navy. The British responded that American citizenship was readily — and false papers even more readily — obtainable; that they had no intention of seizing sailors born in the United States; and that when such men were seized by mistake, they were released as soon as they could be traced. Like the wider use of impressment, the practice was indefensible in principle; it was founded on the attitudes of an era already passed, and maintained purely for pragmatic reasons.

Both issues raised questions of national sovereignty and independence on which the adolescent United States was particularly sensitive. The feelings aroused by these long-term problems were heightened by British intransigence and the haughty attitude of some of her statesmen and envoys, especially Francis Jackson (envoy to Washington, 1809–10). Relations were brought to the brink of war in 1807 when H.M.S. *Leopard* stopped and insisted on searching the U.S. frigate *Chesapeake* for British seamen; and, when this was refused, enforced her demand with a ten-minute cannonade against the unprepared American vessel. This incident clearly violated British policy — Britain never claimed the right to search U.S. Navy vessels — and in due course the British government made a grudging apology, and even paid some compensation. This averted war for the time being, though the American government imposed its own restrictions on trade (first the embargo act, later the non-intercourse act) in an attempt to apply economic pressure to both Britain and France. (Napoleon's officials frequently seized those American ships and cargoes which had travelled under British licence or touched at British ports, because in doing so they had violated the Continental System. This even led some American advocates of war to propose fighting France as well as Britain.)[1] In March 1811 the Madison administration, despite ample evidence to the contrary, accepted French assurances that the Continental System had been relaxed and officially permitted trade with France, while renewing the prohibition on trade with Britain. This blatant example of partisan special pleading convinced many in Britain that Madison was little better than a French agent and that the United States was an undeclared enemy.

Yet the British government must take a substantial share of the responsibility for the souring of relations, for its response to American complaints had been foolishly harsh and unyielding. The last thing Britain wanted was war, or even a serious dispute, with the United States, at a time when the war with Napoleon was absorbing all her energy and resources. Even if the British government felt that it could not give way on the fundamental issues of impressment and the Orders in Council, there was ample room for conciliatory gestures and concessions on details which would make the measures less repugnant, and show a willingness to take America seriously. Unfortunately, however, years of dealing with Napoleon had taught the British ministers that any concessions would be seen as a sign of weakness and would simply open the way for further demands. It must also be admitted that many within the British government felt a distinct dislike of America and its ways, both its democracy and its lack of polish. But more important than this was British preoccupation with other matters, combined with a conviction that imperfect though the American system of government was, it would not be so foolish as to begin a war which would certainly bring it much harm, and from which it could not hope to benefit.

For while the war between Britain and France had placed the United States in an awkward situation which had led to many petty, and a few major, indignities, it had also brought great material benefits, and could have brought more had it not been for the self-defeating policies of embargo and non-intercourse. The American merchant marine had grown from 558,000 tons in 1802 to 981,000 in 1810, while the value of American trade had leapt from less than $60 million before 1793 to nearly $250 million in 1807.[2] These figures help to explain why the maritime states of New England, which were the principal sufferers from both the Orders in Council and impressment, consistently opposed the war.

Why then did the American Congress take the initiative and vote for war in June 1812? Certainly it was not due to popular pressure, for though the war had some vocal supporters, it was generally unpopular throughout most of the country.[3] In part, the pressure came from ambitious young politicians, who had beaten the patriotic drum as an easy way of making a name for themselves, and who had gone too far to draw back. In part, it was the mistaken idea that war would lead to the easy conquest of Canada and Florida. Economic depression and a belief that Britain had stirred up trouble with the Indian tribes also had an influence. And yes, there was also genuine patriotism, irritated beyond endurance by the real grievances against Britain. The relative importance of these ingredients, however, remains a matter for debate.

Whatever the motives, the decision was one of stark folly, for the United States was totally unprepared for war. Presidents Jefferson and Madison had deliberately allowed the small but effective army and navy, created by Washington and Adams, to decline, even while they adopted a policy of confrontation with both Britain and France. In January 1812 Congress voted to increase the army from 10,000 to 35,000 men, but did not provide the funds needed for the expansion, or take any effectual steps to maintain or improve the quality, or the logistical support, for the regular forces. When war broke out, the United States army had some 11,700 men, of whom 5,000 were new recruits.[4] The navy was better prepared, although the scores of gunboats which had been built on Jefferson's orders proved virtually useless. Even so, seven frigates — far larger and better armed than their British equivalents — and a similar number of sloops made a respectable force, though not one, of course, which could hope to challenge the might of the Royal Navy in open battle. But the most extraordinary decision of the Congress was to refuse to make any financial provision for the war they were about to embark upon. War taxes were proposed and voted, but they would only come into effect once war was declared, and as they were chiefly customs duties and other taxes on trade, they would obviously suffer severely from the inevitable British blockade. As a result the American government was virtually bankrupt by the end of 1813. Such policies help to explain why the British government did not take the United States more seriously. But despite this manifest lack of readiness for war, the House of Representatives voted by 79 to 49 for war on 4 June; the Senate followed (19 votes to 13) on the 17th, and on the next day, 18 June 1812, President Madison signed the bill declaring war.

The decision to go to war over such longstanding issues took the British government by surprise, especially as it had already adopted a much more conciliatory policy towards the United States. From the beginning of the year the naval squadron based at Halifax had withdrawn its patrols fifteen leagues or more from the American coast, while in May the Admiralty had issued orders to its commanders to exercise 'all possible forbearance towards the Citizens of the United States'.[5] More significantly, the Orders in Council had finally been repealed in June, Perceval's death having removed their greatest defender. Their revocation owed more to domestic political factors (Brougham's campaign and the disasters in the manufacturing districts) than to any desire to conciliate the United States, but as it removed one of the principal American grievances, it is not surprising that the British expected a speedy settlement of the war as soon as the news reached Washington.

In the meantime Bathurst resisted considerable pressure to reinforce the British garrison in Canada.[6] When the war broke out, this consisted of some 4,000 British regulars — four line battalions, a Royal Veteran battalion, and some artillery — plus about 3,000 locally raised regulars, and many thousands of largely untrained and unarmed militia of doubtful loyalty. The only reinforcements en route, or which were likely to reach Canada before winter closed the St Lawrence, were two battalions of regular infantry which, it had been intended, would replace two battalions of the existing garrison, but which would now simply augment it. The naval squadron at Halifax comprised one ship of the line, eight frigates and many smaller vessels at the outbreak of war; but by January 1813 this had been increased to eight ships of the line and fifteen frigates.[7]

Lieutenant-General Sir George Prevost, the Governor-in-Chief of British North America, shared his superiors' hopes of an early settlement of the war, and on receiving the news of the repeal of the Orders in Council, he proposed an armistice which was accepted by Major-General Dearborn in August, only to be denounced on Madison's orders a month later. Prevost was a good administrator and a sound strategist, who, since his appointment in October 1811, had made great and largely successful efforts to gain the support of French Canadians. Recognizing the weakness of the force under his command, Prevost decided to remain on the defensive, believing that so long as the British remained passive, the Americans would be paralysed by disunion.

This strategy worked well in 1812. Madison ordered Dearborn to attack Montreal, but the Governors of the New England states refused to call out their militia, as neither their states nor the Republic as a whole were under attack.[8] Consequently it was not until November that a force of 6–8,000 men could be collected for Dearborn's offensive, which then petered out amid logistical problems and quarrels before it reached the border. A small party of Americans did manage to cross the frontier on the night of 19 November, but soon withdrew having suffered a few casualties, mostly self-inflicted, when the troops became separated and confused and fired upon each other. On 23 November Dearborn's army retreated into winter quarters.

Although Dearborn's advance was intended to be the principal American offensive of the year, there was much more serious fighting in Upper Canada. Here Major-General Isaac Brock's inspiring leadership overcame serious problems to defeat American attacks, and maintain and improve the

British position. Brock had only about 1,700 British and Canadian regulars under his command, most of whom were committed to defend the narrow front between Lakes Erie and Ontario, around Niagara. But the first important action occurred further west, at the other end of Lake Erie, when Brigadier-General William Hull invaded Canada with 2,500 men. Hull soon lost his nerve, however, and retreated back to Detroit. Brock followed with about 300 regulars, 400 militia and 600 Indians, and so intimidated Hull that he capitulated with his entire force on 16 August, after scarcely any effort at resistance.

The Americans performed rather better a few months later when the long-awaited offensive at Niagara was finally launched. On the night of 12–13 October and the following morning, about 1,000 American troops crossed the river and established themselves in Queenston. Brock hurried to the scene and led the counter-attack in person, but he was killed by an American shot and the counter-attack failed. Had the Americans been able to bring a steady stream of reinforcements across the river, they might well have established themselves on Canadian territory; but the militia refused orders to embark, and by the end of the day all the Americans who had crossed had been driven back or forced to surrender.

Thus the first six months of the war brought nothing but defeat and humiliation to the American forces on land; at sea, however, the situation was reversed. U.S. Navy frigates won a series of single-ship encounters against their lighter British counterparts, beginning with the defeat of H.M.S. *Guerrière* by the *Constitution* on 19 August. Smaller American ships — sloops and brigs — were equally successful, gaining the advantage in seven out of eight encounters with equivalent British vessels during the course of the war. These successes helped bolster American morale and caused outrage in Britain, where the triumphs of the navy had come to be taken for granted. By the end of the year there were bitter reproaches not only from the Opposition, but from members of the government. For example, Robert Peel, Chief Secretary for Ireland, told his friend Henry Goulburn, under-secretary for War and the Colonies, 'If the report of the loss of another frigate captured by the Yankees be true, I hope the Admiralty will be impeached.'[9] The fact was, as Mulgrave had admitted years before when he was First Lord, that the Admiralty had concentrated its efforts and resources on its main battlefleet in order to ensure its superiority over the French, and the frigates and smaller vessels had suffered accordingly.[10] Once reports of the early defeats reached London, the Admiralty greatly strengthened its forces off America and issued orders for its frigates to cruise in pairs or small squadrons and avoid single-ship encounters. This greatly reduced the problem, and on 1 June 1813 the Royal Navy salvaged some of its pride, when Captain Broke of H.M.S. *Shannon* defied orders and engaged in a duel with the *Chesapeake*, capturing the American frigate.

Embarrassing as the naval defeats undoubtedly were, they caused less material damage than the attack on British trade by American warships and privateers. These extended far and wide, with the *Essex*, a 32-gun frigate, even making a famous cruise in the South Pacific in which she is said to have taken almost £600,000 worth of prizes. Gradually most of the U.S. Navy ships were captured or blockaded in port, but the privateers flourished, increasing throughout the war, with many taking their prizes into French-held ports. It has been estimated that they took some 1,300 prizes, but at least one-third of these were recaptured. Such depredations naturally led to further complaints being directed at the Admiralty; but trade protection had always been a sore point, and while marine insurance rose sharply on some routes, it appears that the general rate was no higher in 1812, 1813 or 1814 than in 1810 or 1811.[11]

But neither successful commerce raiding nor the occasional defeat of a frigate threatened Britain's command of the oceans, and Napoleon made no attempt to exploit the diversion by sending any of his squadrons to sea. Similarly, American attacks on British trade were more of an irritant than a threat, with both imports and exports much higher in 1812 and 1814 (there are no figures for 1813) than in 1811. On the other hand, the war crippled American trade, with U.S. exports falling from $45 million in 1811 to $25 million in 1813 and only $7 million in 1814.[12]

These export figures would have fallen much more quickly if the British government had not issued licences for American ships to take flour to Spain and Portugal to feed Wellington's army. The scale of this trade is staggering, rising from 220,000 barrels of flour in 1810, to 830,000 in 1811, 940,000 in 1812 and 970,000 in 1813. Then, when the opening of northern Europe made the supply unnecessary, the British simply stopped issuing licences and the trade collapsed: fewer than 5,000 barrels of American flour were exported to Spain and Portugal in 1814. Of course the Americans knew that the food they exported went to feed their enemy's army, but even ex-President Jefferson defended the trade: 'If we could by starving the British armies, oblige [t]hem to withdraw from the peninsular [*sic*], it would be to send them here; and I think we had better feed them there for pay, than feed and fight them here for nothing.' It is hard to assess the importance of this trade for Britain's war effort. Wellington was certainly concerned at the prospect of war with America, and took care to seek out alternative sources of supply in north Africa and the Mediterranean. It therefore seems probable that if the Americans had stopped their exports in 1812, it would have caused the British inconvenience and perhaps additional expense, but without seriously jeopardizing Wellington's operations. This, however, remains speculation.[13]

Britain gradually extended her blockade of the American coast: at the end of 1812 the exits of the Delaware and the Chesapeake were blockaded; in May 1813 this was extended from Long Island to Mississippi, and a year later the entire American coast was placed under blockade. The blockade and the activities of Canadian privateers were very effective not only in stopping America's foreign trade, but in disrupting the local coasting trade. As land transport was prohibitively expensive over long distances, the blockade produced great economic dislocation, with severe shortages and gluts of the same goods in different parts of the country.

At the end of 1812 the British government recognized that there would be no quick end to the war, and took steps to reinforce Prevost's small army. Three line battalions were dispatched to Bermuda to proceed to Canada as soon as the St Lawrence was open, and further troops followed, so that over the course of 1813 Prevost's command increased from about 7,700 British and Canadian rank and file (including the Veteran battalion) to about 13,700.[14] This was still not a large army, and much of it consisted of locally raised forces and battalions of inferior quality which would not have been sent to join Wellington. Nonetheless, the war probably cost Wellington three or four — possibly more — battalions of good infantry in 1813, including the two (the 41st and 49th Foot) which Bathurst had intended to replace in Canada in 1812. He also lost the cooperation of two battalions of marines which had operated so usefully on the north coast of Spain in 1812, which were withdrawn and sent to join the fleet off America. But while these men, both infantry and marines, would have been useful in 1813, they amount to only a small fraction of the reinforcements actually sent to the Peninsula in 1812 and 1813.

Despite these additional troops the British remained largely on the defensive on the Canadian frontier in 1813, while the Americans mounted a series of attacks, some of which showed considerably more care and endeavour than those of 1812, but all of which were ultimately unsuccessful. The first important encounter of the year was the result of an American winter offensive in the north-west, which was defeated with heavy losses at Raisin River, near Detroit, on 23 January. This appeared to leave the Americans exposed to a sustained counter-attack in this theatre by the British and their Indian allies, but although Colonel Proctor, the British commander, made several advances in the middle of the year, he was forced to fall back on each occasion. On 10 September the Americans gained control of Lake Erie after an important and hard-fought naval engagement, and Proctor retreated further into Canada, only to be defeated at the Battle of Thames. But the Americans could not exploit their advantage and soon fell back to the frontier, occupying no more than a few positions on the Canadian side of the border. They thus recovered the territory they had lost in 1812 and early 1813, and checked the Indian threat to their western settlements, but they did not make any significant gains of their own.

Further east the Americans made a successful attack on the Niagara front at the end of May, but attempts to advance further were checked by defeats at Stoney Creek and Beaver Dams in June. Six months later the British counter-attacked, driving the Americans back across the border, capturing Fort Niagara on the American bank of the river, and devastating American towns and settlements on the frontier. This was, in part, in retaliation for the destruction of York (Toronto) in April — one episode in a war of raids and naval actions on Lake Ontario in which the Americans gradually gained the upper hand. The burning of the Parliament buildings at York incensed the British, and partly explains — though it does not justify — the deliberate destruction of Washington in 1814.

But the crucial theatre of operations lay not on the Lakes, at Niagara or Detroit, but along the St Lawrence, Canada's vital artery. The Americans could end the war in Canada at a stroke if they could capture Quebec, but they never felt strong enough even to make the attempt. Late in the autumn of 1813 they prepared to advance on Montreal, as the next best objective, but the campaign was crippled from the outset by the lateness of he season, poor and divided leadership, and, more fundamentally, the lack of adequate logistical and administrative support. The separate American columns suffered defeats at Chateauguay (25–26 October) and Chrysler's Farm (11 November) before the campaign was abandoned and the American army fell back into winter quarters.

By the end of 1813 the United States had little to show for eighteen months of war. Most of its navy, despite its early victories, had now been driven to take refuge in port; its foreign trade was conducted only under British licence, and that tolerance was now being withdrawn; and its army had failed to pose any serious threat to Canada, despite the long, exposed frontier. Worse still, the fundamental assumption on which the war was based — that Britain would continue to be preoccupied by the war in Europe — appeared increasingly open to doubt. There was no rational ground for believing that the country could gain anything — whether territory in Canada, concessions on impressment, or national 'honour' — by prolonging the war; but it was still some months before the American government opened direct negotiations with Britain, and the fighting continued throughout 1814 and into 1815.

The British government had not sought war with the United States, and when war came it frequently professed its desire to reach a negotiated settlement. But the American attack, coming as it did at the height of the war against Napoleon, aroused considerable British resentment, which was increased by the humiliation of the defeats at sea and the burning of York. Wellington confessed that an American defeat would give him intense satisfaction, while J. W. Ward, a man of wit and liberal views on many questions, was even more explicit: 'we seem to be leading the Yankees a sad life upon their coasts. I am glad of it with all my heart. When they declared war they thought it was pretty near over with us, and that their weight cast into the scale would decide our ruin. Luckily they were mistaken, and are likely to pay dear for their error.'[15] When the war began, Britain had no object other than its speedy end, but as it continued and the balance of forces gradually shifted in Britain's favour and resentment in Britain grew, the ministers began to consider demanding modifications to the U.S.-Canadian border, measures to prevent the U.S. maintaining a naval force on the Lakes, and a satisfactory settlement for Britain's Indian allies. The press demanded far harsher terms, with *The Times*, among others, calling for the overthrow of President Madison, or even the dissolution of the Union.[16] But the government remained, as ever, preoccupied with the affairs of Europe; it resented the cost of the war and hoped for an early settlement with some concessions, both desirable in themselves and to appease opinion at home. The events of 1814, however, can best be considered in chapter 18, where they can be seen in their proper context.

The war with America was a tiresome, pointless distraction for Britain; a nuisance, but not a serious threat. This was due more to the lack of preparation for war under Jefferson and Madison than to intrinsic weakness, for the United States had the potential to be an extremely awkward opponent for Britain at a time when her resources were concentrated on the war in Europe. As it was, the war against Napoleon continued to take priority, and British interests in America did not suffer significantly. However, if the war in Europe had taken a different turn, if Napoleon had triumphed in Russia and been able to enforce the Continental System with even greater thoroughness, the American war would have become more seriously inconvenient. It was not the straw to break the British back, but it was an additional burden which would have significantly reduced her margin of safety. No wonder the British found it hard to forgive their American cousins.

PART THREE

The Defeat of Napoleon, 1813–15

14

From Tauroggen to the Armistice: Britain and the Continental Powers, December 1812–June 1813

The last French troops staggered out of Russia on 14 December 1812. There were scarcely 7,000 men under arms in the main body of the army, though the corps guarding each flank had suffered rather less, and there were many thousands of stragglers. Napoleon had already left the army on 5 December, giving the command to Marshal Murat, while he hurried back to Paris to create a new army to prop up his tottering Empire. Murat continued the retreat, reaching Königsberg on 19 December and Posen on 16 January, where he handed over the responsibility to Eugène Beauharnais (Napoleon's stepson) and thankfully set off for sunny Naples. Eugène had only about 12,000 men immediately under his command (most of them were second-line troops and reserves, not veterans of the Russian campaign), but reinforcements were hastening towards him, and by the middle of February he could expect to command a substantial army. His task was to maintain as bold a front as possible without risking a further defeat. The loyalty of Napoleon's allies, particularly Prussia and Austria, was now open to question, and it remained to be seen whether Russia would carry the war into central Europe or open peace negotiations.

The British ministers were as anxious as Eugène to know Russia's intentions. Napoleon's defeat provided the best opportunity for a decade to reduce the power of France, and they could not help feeling that if this chance were missed, it might not recur in their lifetime. Castlereagh was to define Britain's war aims more precisely later in the year, but at the outset the British government simply hoped that the Continental Powers would assert and maintain their independence and break Napoleon's hegemony in central Europe, while Wellington broke it in Spain. Britain's own efforts would continue to be concentrated in the Peninsula, but she would do what she could to help Russia — both directly, by sending arms and later money, and indirectly by encouraging Sweden to mount a diversion in the French rear.

The slowness of winter communications with northern Europe hampered Britain's efforts and Castlereagh gave Cathcart broad discretion:

Whatever scheme of policy can most immediately combine the greatest number of powers and the greatest military force against France, so as to produce the utmost effect against her, before she can recruit her armies and recover her ascendency, is that which we must desire to promote. . . . whatever plan can be devised for ensuring success in this main point will not meet with opposition here.[1]

But for some time Cathcart was in no better position to influence events than Castlereagh, for when Alexander left St Petersberg to join the army in December he prohibited any of the diplomatic corps from accompanying him. It was not until the middle of February that Cathcart received permission to follow, and he did not reach headquarters until early March. In the meantime the only British agent with access to the Czar was Sir Robert Wilson — that 'dangerous Coxcomb', as Castlereagh called him[2] — who had spent most of the campaign imitating the Cossacks and intriguing against Kutusov. Luckily Alexander knew Wilson too well to take him seriously, and gently warned him off when his indiscretions became really troublesome.

Fortunately Alexander needed no British encouragement to carry the war beyond his own frontiers. He rejected the advice of Kutusov and others that the war was over when the French had been driven beyond the Niemen, or that he should limit his ambitions to the conquest of a few provinces in East Prussia and Poland. Territorial expansion for its own sake never had much appeal for Alexander, and he was now committed to a crusade against Napoleon whose objects he probably did not closely define even to himself. But whatever the ultimate goal, the direction of Russian policy rested solely with the Emperor. The Chancellor, Rumiantsev, remained in St Petersberg to conduct routine business, while the young Count Nesselrode accompanied the Czar in the field, but more as a diplomatic secretary than as an adviser. Kutusov, though ailing, remained in command of the army until his death in April, but neither he nor any of the other generals had influence over the broad direction of the war; indeed, they could not even prevent Alexander meddling in operational details. In the middle of January the Russian armies resumed their advance, and when Cathcart finally reached headquarters it was at Kalisch, more than a hundred miles west of Warsaw.

If direct British influence on the Russian government in the first weeks of 1813 was minimal but unnecessary, it was rather greater and much more needed in Sweden. The British ministers had been disappointed by Bernadotte's failure to take any effective part in the campaign of 1812, but they still believed that he was sincere and made allowances for the practical problems he faced. They were particularly pleased when, in November 1812, Sweden formally recognized the Spanish government at Cadiz, despite Bernadotte's family connection with Joseph Bonaparte (they had married sisters), and when the French chargé d'affaires was finally expelled from Sweden in December. In January 1813 Castlereagh sent Major-General Alexander Hope to Sweden to help Thornton and the Swedes plan an expedition to the Continent. Hope was authorized to offer a subsidy of £1 million for Sweden, and a further £1 million to pay the German Legion which Russia had formed, and which she was now happy to transfer to Bernadotte's command. Britain also agreed to support Sweden's claim to Norway and to indulge Bernadotte by granting Sweden the wealthy Caribbean island of Guadeloupe. These terms were extremely generous — far more generous, given the relatively small size of the Swedish army, than Britain was able to give any of the other Continental Powers in 1813, but the British government believed that the affairs of Europe were delicately poised, and that prompt Swedish intervention could help tilt the balance against Napoleon.

Despite this generosity the negotiations went on for three weeks before a treaty of alliance was signed on 3 March. As ever, Bernadotte argued for more money: partly from natural cupidity but not entirely, for Sweden was a poor country and the British subsidy would only cover part of the cost of the campaign. More seriously, he still wished to direct his operations against Denmark and Norway in the first instance, and the French only later if at all. Hope and Thornton made concessions on both issues, advancing £215,000 immediately to help cover the cost of mobilizing the Swedish army, while the remainder of the subsidy, far from lasting a full year, would extend only until October, when a new agreement would be made. They insisted that Bernadotte's army operate on the mainland of Europe, but accepted that its first campaign might be against the Danes in Jutland, not the French in Germany. Bernadotte recognized that he would not get better terms than these, especially as Prussia had just joined the allies, and Russia was showing increasing signs of impatience and disillusionment with Sweden.[3]

Unfortunately the signature of the treaty was not followed by the rapid and effective Swedish intervention on the Continent that Britain wanted. The first Swedish troops did not land at Stralsund until the middle of March, and it took another two months to bring their numbers up to 15,000 men and for Bernadotte to join them. While this delay was largely due to practical problems and Swedish poverty, it also reflected a sharp deterioration in relations between Sweden and Russia. The Russians had made diplomatic overtures to Denmark, promising extensive compensation for the loss of Norway, and perhaps even a way of avoiding that loss, if Denmark joined the allies. When the mission failed, the Russian government claimed that their emissary Prince Dolgorouki had exceeded his instructions, but Bernadotte's suspicions had been aroused and were not easily allayed. A further bone of contention was his demand that, as promised at Åbo, he be given command of a Russian corps to aid him in his campaign

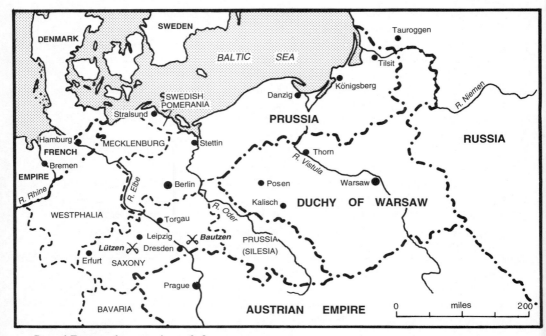

Central Europe: the campaigns of 1813

against Denmark. As Alexander was advancing through Poland into Germany intent upon Napoleon's destruction and needed every man he could get, it is not surprising that this request was coolly received, though Alexander did assure Bernadotte that when his army reached the front a Russian corps would be placed under his command.

Bernadotte's grievances were therefore not entirely groundless, nor were the logistical and financial problems he faced insignificant; but by the end of May his army had achieved nothing for the allied cause, and when news arrived of the armistice he was devastated, realizing that if peace were made, he had not earned, and would probably not receive, any favours from the allies. Indeed, rather than gain Norway, or even regain Stralsund and Swedish Pomerania, Sweden might actually lose territory if a new peace resembled Tilsit.

While Britain was thus concentrating her efforts on Sweden with disappointing results, the allied cause on the Continent was prospering as the

Russian armies advanced and Prussia changed sides. The Prussian volte-face began on 30 December 1812 when General Yorck, commander of the Prussian contingent in the *Grande Armée*, signed the famous Convention of Tauroggen with the Russians, declaring his corps neutral and withdrawing it from the war. While Yorck's move delighted many Prussian patriots who loathed the alliance with Napoleon, it horrified Hardenberg and the King. Only four days earlier Hardenberg had written: 'It is of the utmost importance to show for the present the greatest devotion to Napoleon's system and alliances, and to give to all our measures the appearance that they are being taken to support France.'[4] This did not mean that either Hardenberg or Frederick William really favoured the French cause, but they regarded the defection as premature, exposing the country to appalling risks if Alexander came to terms with Napoleon, or if the Russian advance was defeated. Frederick William also resented the insubordination of Yorck's action and never forgave the general, although he continued to hold high commands throughout the Wars of Liberation.

It is thus not altogether surprising that the Prussian government immediately disowned the Convention and ordered the arrest, imprisonment and court-martial of Yorck. Before this news reached him, Yorck had already compounded his offence by abandoning his neutrality and giving active cooperation to the Russians. He ignored the orders from Berlin when he received them, arguing that the King was constrained by the French presence and secretly approved of Yorck's actions. He successfully appealed first to the garrison of Königsberg and then to the provincial assembly of East Prussia to support him. So the Russians entered East Prussia as allies not enemies, and the province mobilized its resources in their support while the King protested impotently from Berlin.[5]

Hardenberg still hoped to find an alternative to total dependence on Russia, and appealed to Vienna either to join Prussia in an alliance with the Russians, or to form a combination of the two central European powers in an armed neutrality designed to force France and Russia into peace negotiations. This latter policy mirrored many of Metternich's objectives, and its associated conditions favoured Austria greatly; but though tempted, Metternich rejected the Prussian overture, preferring to keep his freedom of action. The Prussian emissary returned with nothing other than vague expressions of good will, and the Prussian government, encouraged by the rapid retreat of the French and advance of the Russians, committed itself to a close alliance with Russia.[6]

The sword having been drawn, there was no point in half-measures, for if the war were lost Prussia would be doomed. On 9 February universal conscription was instituted, and at the end of the month Prussia signed the Treaty of Kalisch formalizing the alliance with Russia. Both powers pledged themselves not to make a separate peace, and to wage the war with an army of no fewer than 150,000 men for Russia and 80,000 for Prussia (supplemented by a national militia). Prussia was to be restored to her size and power in 1806 but not necessarily to her precise frontiers, and while East Prussia would remain with the Hohenzollerns, there was an implicit understanding that Prussia would lose most of the Polish territory which she had held until 1806 (which had then become the core of the Duchy of Warsaw) and receive compensation in Saxony. This was the origin of the Polish-Saxon problem which bedevilled allied relations for the next two years. The treaty reflected the unequal position of the two powers and for the rest of the war Prussia usually acted as a faithful but subordinate ally of Russia.

Britain played no significant role in the evolution of Prussian policy: she was too distant, and winter communications were too slow and unreliable. Gneisenau had taken refuge in London in August 1812, and in January 1813 persuaded the cabinet to support an attempt to win over the garrison of Colberg, but events overtook the plan before it could ever be implemented. In February Hardenberg informed Louis Ompteda of the negotiations under way with Russia, and asked him to let London know that when Prussia formally broke with France she would be requesting money and munitions from Britain. The British government anticipated this request and 54 cannon, together with arms, ammunition and stores for 23,000 men, were soon dispatched to the Baltic to be shared between the Prussians and Russians. In the middle of March, even before news reached England of the formal declaration of war between Prussia and France, the cabinet decided to reopen diplomatic relations, and Castlereagh began drawing up instructions for the new envoy which would include the offer of a substantial subsidy.[7]

Castlereagh selected his half-brother Sir Charles Stewart for the post. It was a strange, almost bizarre, choice which caused much surprise. Colonel Torrens at the Horse Guards was not alone in feeling that 'Stewart is a good hearted excellent fellow and I wish him every success; but I greatly fear that he is not calculated to be an ambassador'. Years later Wellington told Croker, 'Castlereagh had a real respect for Charles's understanding, and a high opinion of his good sense and discretion. This appears incomprehensible to us who knew the two men.'[8] Stewart was the epitome of a dashing *beau sabreur*: brave to a fault, wildly indiscreet, hot-tempered and also fond of intrigue. His military ambitions had been checked by Wellington, who would not entrust him with the command of a division of cavalry, while he wanted active employment to help recover from the death of his wife. Castlereagh may have originally intended that Stewart act primarily as military commissioner with the allied armies, but Stewart insisted on full equality with Cathcart and he was appointed Britain's principal diplomatic representative to Prussia. Nonetheless, he chafed in negotiations, and was never happier than when touring the outposts, or charging a battery, sword in hand. His courage, élan and honesty won him some friends, especially among military men, but he was not a good diplomat and — as he sometimes recognized — he was out of his depth dealing with Hardenberg and Humboldt, Metternich and the Czar. Brotherly affection is a fine virtue, but in this instance Castlereagh carried it to excess.

The British government's welcome for the accession of Prussia was much increased by the contrast with Austria's more cautious policy. In December 1812, only a week before Tauroggen, Liverpool had told Wellington:

> I wish we could see any prospect of a wiser policy being adopted by Austria and Prussia, and particularly by the former; for I have no doubt that the latter would act, if she could rely upon the support of Austria. If these two powers would really take advantage of the Russian successes, we might have hopes of effecting the deliverance of the Continent; but nothing can be more abject than the councils of Vienna at this time, and I fear that neutrality is all that can be expected from them. We are doing our best, however, to rouse them. . . .[9]

This contempt for Austrian policy was encouraged by the generally critical reports received from British agents in Vienna in late 1812 and early 1813. In October 1812 Cathcart had sent Lord Walpole, one of his staff, to try to persuade the Austrians to change sides. Walpole arrived in Vienna in the middle of December and stayed for over a month, having several private interviews with Metternich. But his mission was a complete failure and he wrote home in irritation that 'Metternich's ignorance upon most subjects is extreme, but his vanity not less'. A few weeks later John Harcourt King declared that Metternich 'has only one object in view, which is a general peace, and, provided he attains that end, he is not anxious what the conditions may be. His only ambition is to be pointed out as the pacificator of Europe, for no other reason than to satisfy his vanity, and not from any direct desire to restore the ancient splendour of the house of Austria, or of striking a blow at the power of France.'[10]

Although these views were coloured by some personal feeling, they reflect a fundamental difference in perspective between Britain and Austria. British views of the Continent were shaped by twenty years of war with France. For Britain, France was unequivocally the enemy, and disputes between the other Continental Powers were dangerous distractions which had enabled France to divide and conquer successive coalitions. Castlereagh and his colleagues did not dismiss Austria's fear of Russia as of no account, but they did regard it as secondary to the struggle to break Napoleon's hegemony — a struggle which they knew would require the full cooperation of the three main Continental Powers.

Things were more complex for the Continental Powers, each of which had at times been Napoleon's ally, as well as his enemy. Russia was now committed to war with France, though the example of Tilsit prevented the other powers from relying on her constancy in the event of defeat. Prussia had been forced by circumstance to throw in her lot with Russia, but Austria was more distant from the theatre of operations, and Metternich was determined to preserve his room to manoeuvre for as long as possible.

The news of the French disaster in Russia had come as a complete surprise to Metternich. He had expected the campaign to produce another triumph for Napoleon and had believed that the fall of Moscow signalled the Russian defeat. He even offered his services to help negotiate the peace on Napoleon's terms, so he was naturally somewhat taken aback by the actual result of the campaign.[11] On the whole he welcomed the reduction in Napoleon's overwhelming power, but it posed a number of problems for him. His position in the Austrian government was by no means invulnerable, and he was very closely associated with the French alliance. If that policy proved a failure, Metternich's reputation and position would be in danger. Given his genuine fears of Russian ambitions — not only on the Danube and in Poland, but (in terms of influence not territory) in Germany, western Europe and the Mediterranean — the prospect of a successful Russian advance through central Europe was deeply disturbing. Even if the Russian advance was not successful, further warfare would only hurt the already crippled Austrian economy, while there was great danger that Austria would be dragged in on one side or the other. Yet the most obvious alternative — a settlement between Alexander and Napoleon from which Austria and Prussia were excluded — posed equal risks, for if Napoleon was forced to make concessions, they would be in areas of prime concern to Austria, such as Poland and the Danube.

Faced with this array of dangers, Metternich sought peace and stability — though King exaggerated in saying that he was not concerned with the terms of a settlement. The first requirement was that Austria should play a leading role in the peace negotiations, not simply, or even principally, to gratify Metternich's considerable vanity, but to protect her interests when they were at their most vulnerable. The next was to ensure that French concessions went as much to strengthening Austria and Prussia as to Russia, for Metternich's ultimate objective was to restore the central European powers to the strength and independence they had had in 1805, and to minimize both French and Russian influence in the affairs of Germany. On the other hand, Metternich had no sympathy for Britain's determination to remove Napoleon's forces from Spain and Holland, which he regarded both as an insuperable obstacle to peace negotiations, and as intrinsically undesirable, weakening France too much and so reducing her value as a counterpoise to Russia.[12]

In pursuit of this policy Metternich moved Austria out of the French alliance and into a position of neutrality. On 30 January — a month after Tauroggen — Schwarzenberg signed a convention with the Russians at Zeyes, and retired with the remains of his corps (the Austrian contingent in Napoleon's army) into Austrian territory. Count Bubna was dispatched to Paris, and Baron Lebzeltern to Alexander's headquarters at Kalisch, with carefully tailored peace proposals. Both were given a courteous hearing, but made no progress, for neither Alexander nor Napoleon was ready for peace.

At the same time (early February) Baron de Wessenberg was sent to London with similar proposals. He did not arrive until the end of March and was met with a chilly rebuff, which proved typical of relations between the two powers during that spring. This was not surprising, nor based on any misunderstanding, though it was compounded by miscomprehension and mutual suspicion. Britain and Austria were pursuing fundamentally different and opposing policies. Britain sought to mobilize the Continent to break Napoleon's hegemony, while Austria sought a general pacification. Metternich complained that the British wanted eternal war on the Continent while they enriched themselves, and the British accused Metternich of cowardice. A 'premature' peace such as Metternich proposed would have been a disaster for Britain, and British statesmen could not understand why any Austrian minister should have been so anxious to preserve the predominance of France, especially under a ruler such as Napoleon. But Metternich seems to have had little anxiety to recover lost Austrian territory, except perhaps Illyria, and in many ways he was happier dealing with Napoleon than with Alexander. So long as this remained Austria's policy, there was little or no hope of an improvement in relations.

In the seven weeks it took Wessenberg to travel from Vienna to London the military situation in Europe had changed substantially. Russian armies had advanced on a broad front across northern Germany from the Vistula to the Elbe. Their reserves trailed far behind, while large forces had to be detached to besiege French-held fortresses in Poland, but they still amounted to about 100,000 men. The Prussian regular army and its reserves were being mobilized, and acted in support of the Russians, even before the formal declaration of war on 16 March. The Prussian army was constantly expanded during 1813 and ultimately numbered almost 300,000 men, but in the early spring there were fewer than 60,000 men ready to take the field.[13] Further north, the Swedish advanced guard reached Stralsund before the end of March, but reinforcements were slow to arrive and it took no significant part in the spring campaign. Some of the smaller states were toying with the idea of neutrality: Denmark was still listening to allied overtures and refusing to commit itself, while the Saxon General Thielmann held Torgau against French and allies alike. Metternich was actively courting the German Princes, encouraging them to follow Austria's lead: Bavaria and Saxony were both tempted by these proposals, and the King of Saxony actually signed an alliance with Austria at Prague on 20 April after allied forces had overrun his Kingdom, but both returned to their French allegiance when Napoleon took the field.[14] Meanwhile Napoleon was busy in Paris creating a new army, and criticizing the movements of Eugène Beauharnais, who remained in overall command of the French forces in Germany.

Eugène's task was far from easy, for although the forces under his command were quite substantial — he now had up to 80,000 men in the field — they were scattered, poorly organized and demoralized. Too many troops had been left in eastern fortresses, including 30,000 men in Danzig (though a third of these were sick). Cossacks and 'Free Corps' roamed far in advance of the main Russian armies, and reliable news was scarcer than ever. On 18 February Eugène retreated behind the Oder, and a few days later he abandoned Berlin and retired with his main force to Wittenberg on the Elbe. The allies followed, but their forces were seriously overextended and there was little serious fighting in the first three months of the year, with both sides suffering far more from illness and the weather than from enemy action.

On 12 March the French commander in Hamburg, fearing a popular insurrection and inaccurate reports of the approach of large enemy forces, abandoned the city. Six days later General Tettenborn, a German in the Russian service, occupied the great port with a flying column of a few thousand men. The fall of Hamburg was of great importance, for it was the key to north-west Germany and a major commercial and financial centre. Its loss was the final death blow to the Continental System and would greatly assist the allies to raise funds. Napoleon had recognized its immense importance and had annexed it to the Empire in 1810, so its loss was also a great symbolic blow: the allies had invaded the Empire. Finally, allied possession of Hamburg interrupted communications between France and Denmark, and made it far less likely that the Danes would enter the war against the allies. For all these reasons Napoleon was furious at the loss of the city, and ordered Marshal Davout with a large force to recapture it. The French began to press in on Hamburg at the end of April when the main allied armies were preoccupied with events further south. Tettenborn had received a few reinforcements — including two Swedish battalions — and cooperated with newly created Hanoverian forces nearby. Together they managed to delay the French advance for a month, but eventually the pressure proved too much; Tettenborn and his garrison slipped away on 30 May, and the city capitulated to Davout, who held it for the Emperor for the rest of the war.

One of the great advantages which Hamburg gave the allies was quick and easy communications with Britain, thereby avoiding the long detour through the Baltic. Sir Charles Stewart arrived there on 18 April only five days after leaving Yarmouth, and stayed for a couple of days equipping his party and gathering news, which he sent home in a long and optimistic letter, concentrating on the prospects for the coming campaign.[15] He reached Berlin on 22 April and had discussions with officials there, who assured him that Denmark was about to join the allies, and suggested that Britain might like to provide funds to bribe French commanders to surrender their fortresses in eastern Prussia and Poland. Sir Charles declined this proposition, and hastened on to allied headquarters at Dresden, spurred on by reports that Napoleon had left Paris to join his army.

Stewart reached Dresden on the evening of 25 April and over the next few days he and Cathcart presented their government's proposals to Prussia and Russia. As the senior representative, Cathcart took the lead, actually letting the Czar read Castlereagh's dispatch of 9 April which outlined the British position at considerable length. Castlereagh explained that Britain's resources were already under considerable strain from her immense efforts in the Peninsula and the commitment of £2 million to Sweden (including the money for the German Legion). However, the collapse of the Continental System following the advance of the allied armies offered the prospect that the British government could raise more funds both at home and abroad, and this enabled the British government to offer its allies an additional £2 million for the remainder of the year, to be divided between Russia and Prussia. Britain suggested, but did not insist, that Russia take two-thirds and Prussia one-third of the subsidy, and asked that as much as possible be taken in military stores and goods rather than money, as the exchange was still very adverse. In return Britain wanted an undertaking that Russia would employ an army of 200,000 men in the field exclusive of garrisons, and Prussia half that number. This provision caused some difficulty, for Alexander felt unable to commit himself to more than 160,000 men. Cathcart agreed to this and the Prussian figure was reduced to 80,000, although they would have happily promised more in return for a larger share of the subsidy. The result was unfair, for in the autumn campaign the Prussians had more men in the field than the Russians, yet received only one-third of the subsidy; but the Russians were operating far from their bases and had suffered much more in 1812, so perhaps deserved special treatment. Britain also offered and required an official commitment that none of the allies (including Britain) would make a separate peace. This was a standard provision in any alliance and was agreed to without demur.

In addition to the direct subsidy of £2 million, Britain agreed to pay the costs — estimated at £500,000 — of the Russian fleet which had wintered in Britain. As this money was spent in Britain it did not add to the burden on the exchange, which was the principal, though not the only, constraint on British largesse. More importantly, Britain was willing to support, albeit with misgivings, a Russian proposal to issue a paper security on the Continent in order to raise ready money for the war. Castlereagh proposed that the issue be limited to £5 million, and that it yield 5 per cent interest and be redeemable six months after a definitive peace or on 1 July 1815, whichever was sooner. Britain was to be responsible for half the capital and interest, Russia one-third and Prussia one-sixth, while the proceeds were to be divided two to one between Russia and Prussia, and spent solely on the armies in the field. Negotiations over the issue of this 'Federative Paper', as it was known, dragged on for months, becoming ever more complicated. In the end, Britain reluctantly accepted an allied proposal which halved the issue to £2.5 million, with Britain responsible for the whole. A treaty to this effect was signed on 30 September 1813, but it was followed by further delays and in the end no securities were actually issued, Britain discharging her obligation by paying Russia and Prussia directly, and in full, in 1814 and 1815.[16]

The subsidy question dominated negotiations, but some other issues were discussed. Cathcart again raised the issue of British trade with Russia but without immediate results, while Stewart had an even more delicate topic to discuss with the Prussians. Count Münster and other Hanoverians were alarmed at the Convention of Breslau, in which Russia and Prussia appeared to take to themselves the right to settle the affairs of Germany. Castlereagh was not much concerned, for the integrity of Hanover was guaranteed, but he agreed to ask Prussia to cede Hanover three small enclaves of Prussian territory within Hanover: the bishopric of Hildesheim, the County of Ravensburg and the Principality of Minden. Cathcart had indicated that there would be little problem with the transfer: Prussia had lost the territories at Tilsit, Russia supported the idea, and Hardenberg did not object to it. But when Stewart raised the matter formally he met strong Prussian resistance, and had to drop the claim to Ravensburg and Minden to gain the cession of Hildesheim, which was the territory of most concern to Münster.[17]

These negotiations were scarcely begun when they were interrupted by a new phase in the campaign, for the report which Stewart had heard in Berlin was correct: Napoleon had taken the field. Never had the Emperor's genius for improvisation been so tested as when he returned from Russia with only a few months to create a vast new army. But he did not have to start completely from scratch. He had already, in the autumn of 1812, summoned conscripts of the class of 1813 to the colours and this produced 137,000 men who were already partly trained. He supplemented this by incorporating 80,000 men of the National Guard into the regular army, and made further demands on the population, including calling up conscripts of the class of 1814. Some of these later measures did not produce results until the middle of the year, and as time went on discontent grew in the Empire and more and more men evaded the draft. Napoleon also took large numbers of men from the navy to strengthen his artillery, and in July Cathcart noted with satisfaction that these units had suffered heavily in the spring campaign, and would take a long time to recover.[18] To stiffen the raw recruits raised by conscription, Napoleon withdrew some 20,000 men — picked veterans, non-commissioned officers and officers rather than whole units — from his armies in Spain. Given the scale of his disaster in Russia, this was an extraordinarily modest withdrawal, but Napoleon had decided that it was better to try to maintain his position in Spain rather than reveal his weakness to all the wavering states of Europe by withdrawing to the Ebro or the Pyrenees. After all, what loyalty could he expect from the

German Princes if he publicly abandoned his own brother? Yet cutting loose from the Spanish imbroglio would not only have freed many thousands of additional troops to act in the decisive theatre, it would also have reduced a significant cause of discontent within the Empire and the army.

By these means Napoleon had an army of more than 200,000 men ready to take the field in April 1813, but mere numbers were not enough, and the new army had many serious defects. The men were young, ill-trained and did not know their officers, so that their units lacked cohesion. The cavalry was extremely weak, for Napoleon had been unable to replace the tens of thousands of horses he had lost in Russia, and this weakness also had some effect on the artillery. The support services of the army suffered even more, and exacerbated the inexperience of the troops, who were unskilled in foraging for themselves, and highly susceptible to disease and fatigue. It was probably the worst army Napoleon ever commanded, yet the troops were brave and imbued with confidence in their commander.

Napoleon left St Cloud on 15 April and spent a week at Mainz, completing the organization of the army before advancing to Erfurt on 25 April. The allied armies were overextended and their command divided. Kutusov died on 28 April, and Alexander appointed Wittgenstein in his place — which produced such strong protests from Miloradovich and Tormassov that a compromise had to be devised. Just as in 1805 and 1812, Alexander's presence with the army and his constant interference destroyed the authority of his general. The allies were also heavily outnumbered in the immediate area of operations, while both sides suffered greatly from poor intelligence. As Napoleon advanced on Leipzig, clashes between the two armies became more common, although neither side knew the precise location of the other's main force. On 1 May there was more heavy skirmishing, and Marshal Bessières, one of Napoleon's most loyal subordinates ever since the Italian campaign of 1796–7, was killed by a cannon ball.

On the following day the allies advanced and attacked Ney's corps on Napoleon's flank, near the town of Lützen. At first the allies had a numerical advantage and the French were driven slowly back, but Ney was less isolated than he appeared, and French reinforcements arrived steadily, threatening both allied flanks. Eventually Napoleon had more than 100,000 men compared with about 73,000 Russians and Prussians, and Wittgenstein was forced to retreat. The allies had lost the first battle of the campaign, but their army was not broken, partly at least because the French cavalry was too weak to pursue them effectively. Among the casualties was Scharnhorst, the great Prussian reformer, who was mortally wounded.

After the battle the allies retreated across the Elbe, and Napoleon occupied Leipzig and Dresden. There was some dissension among the allied generals, for the Prussians were naturally anxious to cover Berlin, while the Russian lines of communication ran further south through Poland. 'God in Heaven, does this then mean I must go back to Memel after all?' asked the

King of Prussia, with memories of the despair of 1806–7, but the allied generals agreed to make a stand in a strong position at Bautzen, a few miles beyond Dresden.[19] Meanwhile Austria increased its efforts to organize an armistice and peace talks, but without success, for both sides still hoped to decide the campaign with a single victory. The King of Saxony, faced with a peremptory ultimatum from Napoleon, even abandoned his new-found neutrality and hastened back to his old patron.

The armies met in the two-day Battle of Bautzen (20–21 May 1813). The allies had the advantage of the ground, but were somewhat outnumbered from the beginning (96,000 men compared with 115,000). The French frontal attacks made costly progress throughout the first day, driving the allies from their positions behind the River Spree. On the second day Marshal Ney, with a further 80,000 men, arrived from the north, threatening the allied right flank and rear, while Napoleon prepared a massive attack against the weakest point in the allied line: the hinge between their old front and their new front against Ney. It was a plan which had brought Napoleon victory in many previous battles, and the allied army ought to have been destroyed; but they fought with great courage and determination, only grudgingly yielding ground, while some of the French attacks, especially Ney's, lacked dash and vigour. Again the allies were defeated, but again they withdrew in reasonable order in the face of an ineffective French pursuit.

Bautzen left both armies with serious problems. The allies were discouraged by two successive defeats, and Wittgenstein resigned the command to take responsibility, although in fact Alexander had been effectively in command of the army throughout the battle. On 31 May Alexander appointed Barclay de Tolly to the overall command, but he continued to interfere, overruling Barclay who wished to retreat into Poland to reorganize the army. Things were almost equally bad in the French army. It had actually lost more heavily than the allies at Lützen and Bautzen — about 40,000 casualties in all — while the hospitals were overflowing with the sick, 90,000 according to one account.[20] Its rear was infested with Cossacks, supplies of ammunition were dangerously low, and after two fruitless victories even Napoleon's confidence was shaken. In these circumstances both sides agreed to an armistice, hoping to use the interval to reorganize and strengthen their forces, and to conciliate Austria. Events proved that this was a mistake on Napoleon's part and that he would have done better to carry on the campaign in the hope that a third allied defeat would break up the coalition, but he felt that his young troops would suffer more than the allies from attrition in a long campaign, while the weakness of his cavalry would magnify a defeat just as it had minimized his victories. Hostilities were suspended on 2 June and two days later both sides signed the Armistice of Pleiswitz, extending the truce until 20 July.

Neither of the British representatives at allied headquarters was consulted about the armistice. Characteristically Cathcart did not complain at this neglect and accepted Alexander's assurances that Russia would not make peace except on terms which fully protected Britain's interests, and that a show of negotiations was necessary to bring Austria into the war. But Stewart was seriously alarmed, writing privately to Castlereagh: 'I fear political treachery and the machinations that are in the wind more than any evils from Bonaparte's myrmidons. We must keep a sharp look-out, especially since our refusal of Austrian mediation. We are not considered (from all I see going on) in the Cabinet.'[21] This concern appeared justified when the British diplomats were again excluded while Austria discussed with Prussia and Russia the terms which she would present to Napoleon. Since the end of 1812 the British government had dreaded the possibility that the allies might make a premature and unsatisfactory peace, leaving Britain either to continue the war almost alone, or accept a disappointing and disadvantageous settlement. The armistice and the peace negotiations brought that prospect much closer.[22]

There was, of course, nothing the British government could do to prevent her allies making peace on any terms which they could get, but Britain's views could have been more forcefully and effectively represented. Cathcart was too phlegmatic, too lazy and too ready to accept Russian assurances, while Stewart lacked experience, authority and skill in diplomacy. Nor did they agree with each other. Although Cathcart displayed his usual patience, and Stewart attempted, at least at first, to be tactful, they differed too much, in character and opinions, to work well together. Less than two months after joining the headquarters Stewart wrote home that 'Lord C[athcart] takes two days to consider a despatch, and two to write one, and he never begins to think till other people have done. . . . [He] will be more of a Russian than an Englishman soon, he is so bigoted to his Emperor.' Not surprisingly, Cathcart did not express himself quite so freely in writing home to Stewart's half-brother the Foreign Secretary, but he exercised his seniority, and warned Stewart to be more cautious in what he said to the Prussians, pointing out that in the end they would follow Russia's lead — a sound argument, but not one likely to appeal to a man of Stewart's vanity.[23]

The halt in operations allowed negotiations on the subsidy treaties to be completed. Alexander told Cathcart that he would quite understand if the British representatives did not wish to sign because of the armistice, but Cathcart very sensibly went ahead, and the treaty with Prussia was signed on 14 June, and that with Russia on the following day.[24] This at least imposed a formal, if unenforceable, obligation on the allies not to make peace without Britain, while the prospect of subsidies provided some slight inducement to maintain the alliance. Payments under the treaty, however, were suspended for the duration of the armistice (though Stewart advanced the Prussians £100,000 to cover their immediate needs), and as the allies had so far received little direct aid from Britain, they were under little real obligation to her. Despite the treaties, if Russia and Prussia believed that it was in their best interest to make peace with Napoleon they would do so, and Britain would be left lamenting.

Not everyone shared the government's view of Britain's national interest. As early as 30 November 1812 Whitbread had moved his annual motion calling on the ministers to open peace negotiations with Napoleon. This received almost no support, with Ponsonby, leader of the Opposition in the Commons, speaking against it. But as the extent of Napoleon's losses in Russia became clear and allied prospects brightened in the spring of 1813, the Whigs increasingly inclined towards peace. On 29 June 1813 Holland and Lauderdale entered a formal protest in the proceedings of the Lords when an amendment they had moved, calling for negotiations, was defeated. Looking back, they strongly criticized the government for not making a determined effort to make peace as soon as Napoleon returned from Russia:

> It would then have been easy to devise, and honourable to propose such conditions of peace as, without humiliating the pride, or interfering in the internal government of France, would, if acceded to, have secured the independence of all powers directly or indirectly allied with his Majesty, and would, if rejected, have exposed to the indignation of Europe the unjust pretensions of the enemy. . . . The omission of all public overtures for peace, and of all distinct declarations of the object of the war, has obviously enabled our enemy to recruit his armies, to animate his people, and to retrieve his affairs.[25]

When the ministers pointed out that on his return from Russia Napoleon had publicly proclaimed that he was unwilling to treat for peace unless Joseph Bonaparte was acknowledged as King of Spain, the Whig lords replied that he had only taken such a hard line because he knew that the British government was intransigent. On the following day in the Commons Whitbread repeated these arguments and criticized Sweden's claims to Norway, and Russia for her share in the partition of Poland. In reply Castlereagh praised Whitbread's integrity, but asked why he never called on the French government to disgorge any of its conquests (plate 9).[26]

The Opposition did not believe that peace negotiations would necessarily succeed, but they believed that they should be pursued with earnest sincerity, and their notion of acceptable terms was certainly much less demanding than that of the government. Grey took a gloomy view of the prospect of the allies on the Continent, and even when his fears had been repeatedly disproved, he urged a quick peace on moderate terms lest the coalition break up under the strains of the war. Grenville, on the other hand, became increasingly bellicose as he began to see at long last a chance of the victory for which he had striven throughout the 1790s. Unlike Grey, he favoured subsidies to the allies and believed that it was Britain's best — and last — chance to break Napoleon's power.[27]

9.   The Working of the Prophecies of Samuel the Prophet, or The Brewer Suffocated in his own Work Tub

[W. Heath], 12 Nov. 1813, B.M. Cat. no. 12,099

A satire on Whitbread's frequent gloomy predictions about the war, and their failure to come true. Whitbread (whose fortune came from the brewery and who was commonly referred to as 'the brewer') is in the cask. John Bull advises him to desist from prophecies.

Yet the views of the two wings of the Opposition were reversed when it came to the Peninsula, for Grenville continued to regard Wellington's campaigns as a waste of men and money — though he did not say so publicly. But Grey, Holland and the great bulk of the Whigs now favoured the war in Spain, which produced some odd paradoxes as Lady Bessborough found: 'We din'd at Holland House yesterday; it was very pleasant, except for every now and then that tone of incredulity or indifference to our successes — not in Spain, for I cannot make out the consistency of their views; they would defeat Buonaparte in Spain, and let him defeat the allies in Germany.'[28] Evidently the connection between the two contests was either not understood or, more probably, was wilfully disregarded. The Hollands and many other liberals continued to regard Napoleon as a great man who had made a terrible mistake in invading Spain, but who was otherwise benign, and whose rule was infinitely preferable to the tyrannical despotisms of Russia, Prussia and Austria.

The principal focus of the Opposition's attack on the government's foreign and military policy was the treaty with Sweden which was debated only a few days after news of the armistice reached London. The ministers themselves disliked Bernadotte's claim to Norway and had agreed to support it only out of expediency. Yet Bernadotte had given the allies no effective help in the three months since the treaty had been signed. This gave the Opposition and Canning a wonderful opportunity to attack the government, as even Castlereagh admitted: 'I never recollect impressions so adverse. The transfer of Norway — the supposed loss of Danish concert — the Armistice — the fall of Hamburgh — the Swedish army inactive.' 'Half our friends came down to the House determined either to vote against us or go away.'[29] But the Opposition failed to consult Canning and totally mismanaged their case, while Castlereagh made 'the best and most dexterous speech I ever heard him make; and Canning, angry, dispirited, and embarrassed, was as much below as his adversary had been above himself'. This was the verdict, not of a sycophantic government backbencher, but of J. W. Ward, one of Canning's own supporters, and he concluded: 'So the Government gained its greatest victory upon its worst case, and, for anything that I see, may last as long as Liverpool and Castlereagh live.'[30]

Soon after this debate Canning dissolved his connection with Lord Wellesley and released his followers from their ties to him, so that they would be free to accept any offers of places from the government. He bitterly regretted his folly of 1812 in refusing 'the management of the mightiest scheme of politics which this country ever engaged in, or the world ever witnessed, from a miserable point of etiquette, one absolutely unintelligible . . . at a distance of more than six miles from Palace Yard.'[31] He recognized that there was now no hope of storming the Treasury benches, and early in 1814 he resolved to travel abroad, partly with the legitimate hope of restoring the health of his invalid son, and partly for a change of scene.

The session of 1813 also saw considerable criticism of the government's financial policies. On 3 March Vansittart, the Chancellor of the Exchequer, had introduced his immensely complicated 'New Plan of Finance', which was designed to reduce greatly the demands of the sinking fund. Tierney, Huskisson and Henry Thornton all attacked it vigorously in a series of debates, but could not inspire the Commons to oppose proposals which offered the prospect of increased spending on the war with little need for new taxes after the first year. The budget presented on 31 March showed a very large increase in estimated spending: from £58.2 million in 1812 to £72.1 million in 1813. The greatest increases were in the extraordinary expenses of the army (which increased by £4.5 million, so that total spending on the army approached £30 million), and in the vote of credit which doubled to £6.2 million: this uncommitted money was used to provide subsidies to allies, in addition to the Portuguese and Sicilian subsidies which were entered separately in the budget. There was also a modest increase in spending on the navy, which no doubt reflected the demands of the American war.[32]

This increase in expenditure was financed partly by additional taxation (chiefly a 25 per cent increase in customs duties which was expected to yield nearly £1 million per annum); partly by increased revenue from existing taxes due to a recovery of trade; but principally by more borrowing. Net receipts from loans rose dramatically: £16.6 million in 1811; £25.4 million in 1812; £38.4 million in 1813.[33] Such increases could not be sustained indefinitely, but the financial market was cheered by the progress of the war and not alarmed by Vansittart's financial innovations. The loan was therefore raised without undue difficulty, although the Bank of England was forced to buy more government paper than it really desired. But if the allies were defeated, or if they made a compromise peace which left Britain with the necessity of maintaining a large army and navy, this confidence might quickly evaporate and place the whole financial system in jeopardy. The ministers knew that heavy borrowing increased this danger, but felt, in this as in other respects, that they had been presented with a unique opportunity to defeat Napoleon, and should seize it despite the risk.

Neither Canning nor the Opposition posed any serious threat to the government in 1813. The ministers, led by Castlereagh and Vansittart, remained weak in the Commons, but they had benefited from the election, and the events of 1812 had clearly shown the difficulty of forming an alternative administration. Parliament rose on 22 July and did not resume until 4 November. By then the Whigs were more inclined to peace than ever, but Grenville was able to silence them — except Whitbread — by pointing out that the public mood was so strongly against them that talk of a moderate, quick peace would be suicidally unpopular. Even so, the known attitude of the Whigs probably had some effect in softening the policy of the government, and in making it more willing to enter into peace negotiations throughout the second half of 1813 and the early months of 1814.

15

Wellington Victorious: The Liberation of Spain, January–October 1813

When Wellington retreated to the Portuguese frontier at the end of 1812, the French were left with only a precarious hold over central and northern Spain. Andalusia had been abandoned and there could be no thought of reconquest without massive reinforcements, while many of the provinces which the French still nominally held were in full revolt. Then came the news of Napoleon's disaster in Russia and the recall of some 20,000 experienced troops from the Peninsula. Joseph moved his capital from Madrid to Valladolid, but left a French garrison in Madrid and spread his forces widely throughout Castile. Much to the King's delight, Soult was recalled to serve in Germany, leaving Joseph, assisted by his chief of staff Marshal Jourdan, in command of some 95,000 men in central Spain, and with a vaguer suzerainty over the 40,000 men of the Army of the North, and the 60,000 in Aragon, Valencia and Catalonia under Suchet and Decaen.

The greatest problem facing the French in Spain in the spring of 1813 was the continued insurrection in the northern provinces of Navarre, Biscay and so on. Clausel, who replaced Caffarelli in command of the Army of the North at the beginning of the year, was unable to crush the revolt and dispatches were taking a month or more to travel from Paris to Valladolid. On Napoleon's orders the great bulk of the Army of Portugal was sent to aid Clausel, and with its help he began to make some slow progress against Mina and the other guerrillas. But the season was advancing, and Joseph became alarmed in case Wellington attacked before these troops returned, for he had now only the Army of the South and his central reserve (together less than 60,000 men) under his immediate command. But Napoleon scoffed at these views, declaring that Wellington could not put 50,000 men into the field.[1] Clausel thus received contradictory orders from two masters, and naturally gave priority to his own operations.

During the autumn and winter of 1812–13 the British government had discussed its plans with Wellington and considered the implications of the news from Russia. Liverpool, Bathurst and Wellington all agreed that Britain's first concern should be to drive the French from Spain, and that when this was achieved the army should cross the Pyrenees and continue its advance into southern France. They wisely rejected the suggestion put forward by Colonel Bunbury (under-secretary at the War Department) that once Spain was freed the bulk of the army should be moved to Italy or northern Germany. As Wellington pointed out, the army would take six months to recover from such a move, while it was by no means certain that the line of the Pyrenees would be safe, or indeed that the Portuguese government would continue its cooperation. Within this broad line of policy, the ministers, as was their custom, gave Wellington complete discretion in the conduct of his operations.[2] The possibility of transferring the bulk of the army to Germany once the liberation of Spain was completed was discussed again in the middle of the year, but was again quickly rejected.[3]

The Anglo-Portuguese army had been utterly exhausted by the exertions of 1812 and Wellington allowed it many months' rest to recover its strength. He planned to open his campaign at the beginning of May, and divided his time in the winter between routine business, improving the Spanish army, and hunting three times a week with a pack of English foxhounds kept at headquarters. Many of the senior officers returned to England on leave, and Wellington was able to ensure that some of the least competent did not return. Others, wounded in 1812, were welcomed back to the army.

Wellington's advance began in the middle of May, having been delayed for a couple of weeks by the slow-moving pontoon-train and a particularly dry spring, which retarded the new season's grass and corn that he needed for forage. He sent a large part of the army north, across the Douro, while still in Portugal, and the rest of the troops followed early in the campaign, so that the allied advance constantly turned the French right (i.e. northern) flank. This left Joseph and Jourdan with little choice but to fall back hurriedly, while sending urgent messages to Clausel imploring him to return the Army of Portugal.

By 9 June the French had retired as far as Burgos without offering any serious resistance. The fortress, which had so thwarted Wellington in 1812, was in a poor state of repair and lacked supplies for a long siege. Deciding that it was untenable, the French destroyed it on 12 June and continued their retreat. Wellington and the whole army were delighted, while Bathurst wrote:

> There is a very general satisfaction felt at the success of your movements, which have exceeded the most sanguine expectations. The blowing up of Burgos has been particularly gratifying, as we had made up our minds to the loss of time and men in the capture of the place; and this having been accomplished without any loss, made the friends of the officers on service look very happy at the Regent's ball on the night the news arrived.[4]

The French retreat was impeded by vast convoys containing the plunder of five years' ruthless occupation, and thousands of Spanish refugees who had compromised themselves by cooperating with the enemy. But every time that the army halted in a strong position in the hope of delaying or stopping the British advance, it would find that its right flank had already been turned and that it must hurry back to secure its retreat. Even the line of the Ebro was turned in this way: Wellington marched his army on mountain tracks across the headwaters of the river while the French waited far downstream on the main road. Hard marching not hard fighting was what Wellington demanded of his troops at this stage of the campaign, and they answered superbly.

Joseph and Jourdan were still unable to get into reliable communication with Clausel, but as they retired into his theatre of operations they collected two of the divisions of the Army of Portugal, and began to hope that he would soon join them with much of the Army of the North, as well as the remainder of the Army of Portugal. On 19 June at Vitoria they faced a difficult decision. They now knew that when Clausel came it would be from the south-east, from Logroño on the Ebro; but their natural line of retreat was north along the main highway to San Sebastian and France. If they continued to withdraw they must either abandon the highway (the only practical route for the convoys they were escorting), or give up the chance of a junction with Clausel who, they thought, was now only one or two days' march away. Unwilling to quit Spain without a show of resistance, they decided to halt and offer battle, hoping that Clausel would join them before Wellington attacked, or even that Wellington would continue to manoeuvre against them rather than risk a general engagement.[5]

The French position was not particularly strong, and their army was heavily outnumbered (approximately 57,000 French combatants, compared with 75,000 allies), for Clausel did not arrive in time. Never had Wellington fought at such an advantage, and he made elaborate and ambitious plans for the battle, hoping to turn both French flanks and cut off their retreat. The Battle of Vitoria was fought on 21 June 1813 and the French army was completely routed. Yet Wellington's plans were not altogether successful: the allied left wing under Sir Thomas Graham cut the highway to France, but did not attack the opposing French with much vigour, apparently because of a misunderstanding of Wellington's orders — which were far from clear. Lord Dalhousie's division lost time in a difficult preliminary march through the mountains, thus delaying the attack in the allied centre. This meant that Hill's attack on the right faced more serious resistance than was expected. The attack still succeeded, but Hill's men could not advance quickly enough to cut the road to Salvatierra and Pamplona, and it was along this (easterly) road that the French retreated. They lost some 8,000 casualties, including 2,000 prisoners and all but two of their cannon, but no eagles — only a single battalion standard of a unit which had been disbanded. The allies lost about 5,000 men, for there had been some heavy fighting on both the right and in the centre. The two Spanish units engaged; Morillo's division under Hill's orders and Longa's division (formerly guerrillas, now incorporated into the regular army) under Graham behaved particularly well.

Vitoria was a great victory which effectively liberated all of northern Spain apart from Catalonia. The campaign had been brilliantly conceived and executed; that the battle did not quite meet Wellington's expectations was due in part to the difficulty of coordinating the attacks of four separate columns in mountainous country where lateral communications were extremely difficult, and perhaps also in part to Wellington's habit of strenuously discouraging initiative in his subordinates, especially his cavalry officers.[6]

The French fled in disorder and abandoned the great convoys they had been protecting. Among the loot was five million francs which had just arrived to pay the army: Wellington hoped to secure this to pay his own troops, but scarcely any of it reached the military chest. As well as this official treasure there was the private baggage of officers and generals who had been serving in Spain for years and who had pillaged wherever they had gone. Now the looters were looted, as thousands of allied soldiers — and some officers — of all nationalities made up for years of hard beds, poor food and little pay. Soldiers staggered away with more silver than they could really carry, with one sergeant in the 95th Rifles (Edward Costello) later claiming to have got nearly £1,000. Those who were themselves too squeamish to plunder bought fine horses and mules remarkably cheaply over the next few days. Wellington fumed and denounced the army's lack of discipline in excoriating letters home, but it is difficult not to feel some sympathy for the soldiers' view that they had earned their windfall. Among the treasure was the fine collection of great pictures taken by Joseph from royal palaces throughout Spain. Wellington sent them home to England till their fate could be decided, and in due course King Ferdinand VII officially gave them to the victor of Vitoria. They can still be seen in Apsley House in London.

Wellington also sent home Marshal Jourdan's baton, a trophy which so delighted the Prince Regent that he replied by making Wellington a field marshal in the British army. The ministers had urged this promotion after Salamanca but the Duke of York had successfully resisted it then, arguing that it would only encourage resentment and jealousy among senior officers left unemployed at home. Yet Wellington's promotion actually enabled those unemployed officers to serve under him for the first time — the Duke of Richmond and Sir John Hope both immediately offered their services, and the latter's offer was accepted, much to Wellington's satisfaction.[7]

This was not Wellington's only honour or reward in 1813. At the beginning of the year he had been made Colonel of the Royal Regiment of Horse Guards (the Blues) — a post both honourable and lucrative. In March he became a Knight of the Garter on the death of the Marquess of Buckingham, whose aide-de-camp he had been at Dublin Castle in 1788–9. The Portuguese made him Duque da Victoria in April, while Parliament thanked him and his army for Vitoria without dissent — Lord Holland giving a panegyric on his skill.[8]

After Vitoria Wellington could have advanced straight up the main highway into France, capturing or driving back the Biscay garrisons, and investing San Sebastian and Bayonne before they were prepared for a siege. He had enough men to leave a strong force at Vitoria to protect his flank and rear from Clausel, and to detach a light force to harry Joseph's retreat; the threat to Bayonne would bring Joseph and Clausel hurrying to its defence, for it was their principal arsenal, and if the allies succeeded in besieging it, they would be forced to draw their supplies of equipment, artillery and ammunition from as far afield as Toulouse and Bordeaux.

But Wellington was not so bold. Instead he pursued first Joseph and then Clausel, but with little hope of trapping either, for there had been no vigorous pursuit on the evening of the battle, and the French had made a clean break. Joseph's army passed Pamplona on 24 June and hurried on to the Pyrenean passes, with only a few skirmishes between its rearguard and Wellington's leading troops. For a brief time Clausel appeared to be in more danger, for he did not hear of the battle until the 22nd and his outriders actually appeared on the hills above Vitoria before he learnt of his mistake; he beat a hasty retreat down the valley of the Ebro to Saragossa, and from there to France by a roundabout route, easily eluding Wellington's attempts to intercept him. The allied armies then drove the French from the mountain passes, but made no attempt to enter France, instead besieging San Sebastian and Pamplona. The lines of communication from Lisbon were now inordinately long, but Wellington had foreseen the problem and had given orders to move his base of operations to Santander and the small but excellent port of Passages only a few miles behind the army. It was a striking example of the advantages of sea power, though the Biscay coast was dangerous for shipping in autumn and winter.

Napoleon was furious at the news of Vitoria, which he attributed entirely to the folly of Joseph and Jourdan, both of whom were stripped of their offices and severely disgraced — although soon partially rehabilitated. Soult was sent from Dresden to take command with sweeping powers to reorganize the army, and told to take the offensive and relieve the besieged fortresses. Even now Napoleon deceived himself, greatly underestimating the strength and effectiveness of Wellington's army.

Soult arrived on 11 July and soon instilled a new sense of confidence in the army by flattering the troops and blaming their defeat on the incompetence of his predecessors. He had nearly 120,000 men under his command (including Clausel), but only about 85,000 of these were available for active operations. There was no hope of cooperation from Suchet, who had abandoned Aragon and was about to withdraw from Valencia. The artillery lost at Vitoria had been replaced from the magazines of Bayonne, but the army was so short of transport that the troops began the new campaign with only a few days' food and little hope of getting more.

10. Boney receiving an account of the Battle of Vittoria . . .
George Cruikshank, 8 July 1813, B.M. Cat. no. 12,069

Napoleon greets the news of Vitoria with anger and despair. In the background the Emperor Alexander says, 'Now is the time', and Frederick William adds, 'Now or Never! will you not join us?', both speaking to Emperor Francis of Austria.

British sources naturally tended to exaggerate the influence the news of Vitoria had on the negotiations in Germany.

Wellington's quiescence had allowed the French to rally; he occupied the passes from Roncesvalles to the sea and pursued the siege of San Sebastian with vigour, while blockading Pamplona. On 25 July an attempt to storm San Sebastian failed with the loss of nearly 600 casualties. On that same day Soult launched his offensive, not, as Wellington expected, across the Bidassoa near the coast, but through the inland passes of Roncesvalles and Maya. The result was nine days of heavy, confused fighting collectively known as the Battles of the Pyrenees. The initial French attacks were beaten back with heavy loss, but Wellington's subordinates disregarded his orders and fell back that night abandoning the passes. Soult's advance was finally checked in two bloody battles at Sorauren (28 and 30 July 1813) within sight of Pamplona. Instead of retreating directly back to the passes, Soult then struck out at an angle, imperilling his whole army, but finally making his escape. The short campaign had cost him some 13,000 casualties, and left the army thoroughly demoralized and disorganized. Wellington had lost about 7,000 men: his troops, including the Spanish, had fought extremely well, but the campaign showed further signs of poor staff work and complete lack of strategic judgement on the part of some of his subordinates.[9]

Napoleon was delighted with news of Soult's initial success which reached him on 1 August. As usual he made the most of it, instructing his foreign minister to

> circulate the news that in consequence of Marshal Soult's victory over the English on July 25, the siege of San Sebastian has been raised, and 30 siege guns and 200 waggons taken. The blockade of Pamplona was raised on the 27th: General Hill, who was in command at that siege, could not carry off his wounded, and was obliged to burn part of his baggage. Twelve siege guns (24 pounders) were captured there. Send this to Prague, Leipzig, and Frankfort.[10]

Wellington could have exposed this tissue of lies to ridicule if he had followed the defeat of Soult by the immediate invasion of France, but for the third time he declined the opportunity. After Vitoria he could have swept up the highway and invested Bayonne while Joseph's men were still trudging through the mountains, or he could have followed Joseph and Clausel and attacked the French again before they had rallied from their defeat. In either case success was almost certain, for the French had been too thoroughly defeated to offer serious resistance. News that Wellington had successfully invaded France would have had an incalculable effect on the peace negotiations in Germany. Russia, Prussia and Sweden would be immensely encouraged, Britain's prestige and influence enormously enhanced, and Napoleon might even have been forced to make concessions. Certainly it would have spread despondency in the French army and dealt a massive blow to Napoleon's reputation both at home and abroad. Austria's reaction is less easy to imagine, and the result may possibly have been an immediate peace on terms less favourable than those ultimately obtained in 1814, but whatever the eventual result, it seems clear that a wonderful opportunity was allowed to pass.

Why? Not because of the sieges of San Sebastian and Pamplona: for they could have been securely masked by Spanish troops, and their relatively small garrisons (4,000 at Pamplona, 3,000 at San Sebastian) would pose little threat to Wellington's rear. (Later, however, when Soult's army had rallied again after San Marcial the blockade of Pamplona did delay Wellington's advance, for he dared not bring Hill's corps down from Roncesvalles to the Nivelle to take part in the offensive until Pamplona had fallen.[11] But when the French had just been broken — whether after Vitoria, the Battles of the Pyrenees or, later, immediately after San Marcial — this did not apply.)

The principal explanation seems to be Wellington's very pessimistic view of the armistice and peace negotiations. As early as 17 June he had told his brother Henry that 'I don't think that the Russians and Prussians can agree to the armistice without submitting entirely'. Two months later he was equally gloomy: 'I confess that I am not satisfied with the state of affairs in the north of Germany. . . . It appears to me that Buonaparte has the allies, including Austria, exactly in the state in which he would wish to have them.'[12] He feared that he would advance into France only to be met by news of a Continental peace, and be forced to retreat in the face of the large reinforcements which Napoleon would then be able to send Soult. Rather than risk this, he preferred to occupy strongly the Pyrenean passes and remain on the defensive until he learnt the result of the peace negotiations.[13]

Two objections can be made to this reasoning. First, as Soult's offensive showed, the Pyrenees were far from perfect as a defensive line. The allied army had to cover a very long front with poor lateral communications, enabling the French to concentrate an overwhelming force at one point. Wellington could not be everywhere, and on 25 July Soult had managed to force the line with an inferior army. Liverpool suggested fortifying the passes with field works such as those used at Torres Vedras, but Wellington rejected this as impractical, and in any case the line could always be turned by an advance through Roussillon and Catalonia.[14] In other words, if a Continental peace were made, and if Napoleon chose to attack the allied army in Spain with a greatly superior force, Wellington would probably be forced to retreat, possibly as far as the Portuguese frontier. But would Napoleon choose to begin the war in Spain all over again? Certainly he would find it much easier not to, if southern France had not been violated by an allied invasion. But this is speculation, and there is no hint of this line of thought in Wellington's correspondence.

The second objection, which is much simpler, is that Wellington totally ignored the effect of his advance on the peace negotiations. He believed that the allies were disheartened and Austria cowed, but did not see the inspiration they would derive from a successful British invasion of southern France.

However, there was another strand to Wellington's reluctance to advance: he feared that his army — particularly the Spanish troops — would so plunder and loot and wreak their revenge in France that they would raise a popular insurrection against them as bad as the guerrilla war in Spain.[15] When he did finally advance into France he took elaborate precautions to improve the discipline and supply of the army, and when some Spanish units misbehaved he sent the bulk of their army home, keeping only those he could supply through the British commissary.[16] This was one aspect of a wider fear, that invading France might unleash a new wave of popular patriotism or even another Revolution, filling Napoleon's armies and dooming the Continent to another twenty years of war.

Yet even when all this is taken into account, Wellington still appears strangely timid and reluctant to advance across the frontier. As late as 19 September he told Bathurst that,

I see that, as usual, the newspapers on all sides are raising the public expectation, and that the Allies are very anxious that we should enter France, and that our government have promised that we should, *as soon as the enemy should be finally expelled from Spain;* and I think I ought, and will bend a little to the views of the Allies, if it can be done with safety to the army, notwithstanding that I acknowledge I should prefer to turn my attention to Catalonia, as soon as I shall have secured this frontier.[17]

Of course there were dangers in moving forward and logistical problems to be overcome, but all war involves risks and the allied army was now immensely superior to the French in every respect. Contrary to the old myth, Wellington was not normally an overly cautious or defensive general, but this seems to have been an exception. Certainly it is difficult to imagine Nelson or Napoleon being so intimidated by a political frontier.

The allied army remained on the Bidassoa until October, and then advanced slowly in the face of strong resistance and the inconveniences of winter in the mountains, not reaching the Adour until February 1814. The siege of San Sebastian continued, and despite the defeat of the first attempt to storm it, the engineers persisted in their false line of attack. The defence was resolute, ingenious and very able: the Governor, General Rey, matched Phillipon's superb defence of Badajoz. After some delay Wellington was able to bring an overwhelming siege-train to bear, which silenced almost every cannon in the fortress and battered down a 300-yard breach in the walls. But Rey had prepared formidable interior defences, so that when the second assault was made on 31 August, the storming troops mounted the breach to be faced with a sheer drop of twenty feet and heavy enemy musket fire. For two deadly hours the stormers made little progress, but finally a way was found, the fortress was carried, and Rey and part of his garrison retired to the castle where they continued to resist until 8 September. Inevitably the town was thoroughly sacked, though not with quite the brutality of Badajoz; but the inhabitants may have suffered even more, for high winds spread fires throughout the town. The storm cost almost 2,400 casualties, of whom 856 were killed, some leading units losing more than half their men and three in four of their officers.

Soult made another determined effort to relieve the fortress on the day of the storm, but was completely defeated at San Marcial, losing some 4,000 casualties. The allies lost 2,500 casualties, mostly Spaniards, who again performed very well. By now the French had suffered three major defeats in less than three months and had lost confidence in themselves and their general. Soult expected to be attacked following his defeat and could not have offered much resistance, but again Wellington remained on the defensive, allowing his opponent more than a month to rally his army and throw up field works along the line of the Bidassoa. It was not until 7 October that Wellington made even a limited advance, while Pamplona was not finally starved into submission until the last day of the month.

Wellington's campaigns had a tendency to end with an anticlimax: Cintra, the retreat from Talavera, the battle which never happened at the lines of Torres Vedras, the barren second half of 1811, and the heartbreaking retreat from Burgos and Madrid in 1812. One Whig wiseacre predicted a similar retreat in 1813: he was wrong in fact, but right in spirit, for the five months (July to November) in the Pyrenees were a tame sequel to the splendid five weeks which led to Vitoria.[18]

While Wellington was conducting the main campaign at the western end of the the Pyrenees, there were still large armies in eastern Spain. At the beginning of the year Suchet was occupying Aragon and Valencia with 35,000 men, while Decaen was trying to hold down Catalonia with 25,000 troops. They were opposed by three regular Spanish armies (Copons in Catalonia, 10,000; Elio near Alicante, 15,000; and Del Parque to the rear in Murcia, 13,000), plus numerous guerrilla bands and the Anglo-Sicilian army at Alicante (some 18,000 men, including Whittingham's Spanish division).[19] Both sides faced serious problems. The bulk of the French forces were tied down in garrisons, so that it was with difficulty that Suchet could put 15,000 men into the field, or Decaen 8,000. The Spanish troops were of mixed but generally inferior quality: Del Parque's army was decidedly bad, but Copons's troops were experienced and well led. The Alicante army was a heterogeneous collection of units of many nationalities: some regiments were certainly reliable, others were more doubtful, while the whole army was terribly short of transport.

At the end of February Sir John Murray assumed command of the Alicante force and soon opened a cautious offensive. But before this could make much progress he received orders from Bentinck in Sicily to send two of his best battalions to Palermo. The King of Sicily had attempted to resume power, Bentinck had brought troops into Palermo and wanted reinforcements in case the situation deteriorated. In the event he did not need the battalions from Spain: by the end of March the King had given way, restoring the regency (or 'Vicarate') of his son, and agreeing to the exile of the Queen. The British government formally approved Bentinck's use of coercion, but Castlereagh privately hinted that he had gone too far.[20]

In Spain, Murray's aborted offensive had led to a counterstroke from Suchet who attacked the Alicante army at Castalla on 13 April with only 13,000 men compared to Murray's 18,000. The French were severely rebuffed, losing about 1,000 casualties, but there was no pursuit, and for the next six weeks the armies sank back into inactivity.

Wellington had devised an elaborate and well-constructed plan for the armies on the east coast. Murray and his men, with a powerful siege-train, were to go by sea to besiege Tarragona, the important fortress on the coast road between Barcelona and Valencia. When Suchet marched to relieve the fortress, Elio and Del Parque were to advance through Valencia, driving back the remaining French. The only objection that can be made to this plan is that Murray had no confidence in its success; and that lack of confidence virtually doomed it from the outset. Wellington had made Napoleon's mistake of trying to conduct war at a distance through unwilling subordinates. Murray's force embarked at the end of May, and landed safely near Tarragona on 2 June. The fortress was in a poor state of repair, but the attack was mismanaged and progress was slow. Copons joined Murray with 7,000 men of the Army of Catalonia, so that the allies had 23,000 men to conduct and cover the siege. But Murray was distraught with anxiety, imagining the worst possible circumstances and then turning his fears into certainties. He quickly convinced himself that Suchet and Decaen were descending on him from opposite directions with vastly superior forces, and on 12 June he ordered that the siege be abandoned, most of the siege guns spiked and left behind, and the troops embarked with all haste. His panic was equally unnecessary and disgraceful: he outnumbered the approaching French, and his flight exposed Copons to considerable danger. It was a rare example of such blatant cowardice in an officer of his rank. He was court-martialled in 1814, but only convicted of lesser charges.[21]

Fortunately Bentinck arrived a few days later, relieved Murray of the command, and returned with the army to Alicante. He would have liked to assume the offensive in Valencia, but many of the troopships had been dispersed in a storm, and the army was desperately short of mules, horses and other land transport. While the Anglo-Sicilian army had been at Tarragona the Spanish armies had advanced into Valencia, but Suchet had withdrawn fewer men than Wellington had anticipated, and Del Parque was defeated at Carcagente on 13 June, losing 1,500 casualties and prisoners. Affairs on the east coast thus returned to their position of the spring, for Suchet made no attempt to take the offensive.

This equilibrium might have been maintained indefinitely if it had not been for the news of Vitoria, which reached Suchet early in July. With Wellington victorious at the foot of the Pyrenees, the French position in Aragon and Valencia was untenable and Suchet was forced to evacuate rapidly the provinces which he had conquered and subdued with such labour in 1810–12. His withdrawal was neat and efficient, though he has been criticized for leaving substantial garrisons in a number of fortresses.[22] Yet he knew how difficult it had been to capture these strongholds, and hoped that a turn in the tide of the war would see the French return to Valencia.

Bentinck believed that Suchet was in full retreat to France, or at least northern Catalonia, so that his disposable force could be sent to reinforce Soult or the Emperor. This was a reasonable assumption, but in fact both Suchet and Clarke, the Minister of War in Paris, were convinced of the need to defend Catalonia and prevent the allies from threatening Roussillon, and Napoleon did not contradict them.[23] Bentinck was misled by this assumption and twice advanced overconfidently into Catalonia, only to be forced to retreat — the second time after his leading troops were surprised and routed with heavy loss in a night attack at Ordal (13 September 1813). This was the last action of any consequence on the east coast in 1813. Soon afterwards, Bentinck was forced to return to Palermo and left the army under Major-General William Clinton — who was so lacking in confidence that he immediately begged Wellington to supersede him. But Wellington could not spare a senior officer, and correctly judged that Clinton's modesty would prevent him doing anything rash. So operations on the east coast ended tamely, but they had achieved their purpose, for without the (largely illusory) threat which the Anglo-Sicilian and Spanish armies posed to France, Suchet would surely have been ordered to detach heavy reinforcements either to Soult or to Napoleon in Germany.

Bentinck returned to Sicily to face yet another political crisis which threatened to destroy his reforms. This time the problem was not with the Court, but with Parliament and within the government itself. Recent elections had introduced a number of radicals into Parliament, and they cooperated with the conservatives to block the budget. Lord Montgomerie, who was acting in Bentinck's place, was a weak man in poor health, quite unable to control events. The Sicilian ministers quarrelled among themselves, the British were growing increasingly unpopular with the people, and there were serious food riots. Bentinck reached Palermo on 4 October and tried to persuade the radicals to pass the budget. When these negotiations failed he persuaded the Prince to dissolve Parliament and form a new government, though this violated the constitution. For the next few months Bentinck was the effective ruler of Sicily, even throwing into prison two nobles who dared to criticize his actions. In November and December he toured the island and was struck again by its potential richness and squalid misgovernment. He wrote to the Prince — not as a practical proposal but a mere 'Philosopher's dream' — that the island would be far happier annexed to the British Crown with compensation for the royal family. It was an extraordinarily naive and foolish letter. The Prince and the King were both naturally much alarmed and protested to the British government over Bentinck's head. The ministers in London quickly and truthfully disavowed any ambition to occupy Sicily permanently, and privately cursed Bentinck's ineptness — for the very suggestion was capable of arousing similar fears in Spain and Portugal, and antagonizing Austria and Russia. Fortunately the affair did not become public until March 1814, when it was too late to do much harm, except to Bentinck's own reputation. This had already suffered from his obvious lack of enthusiasm for the war in Spain, and repeated efforts during 1813 to persuade Wellington and the British government to approve an expedition to Italy. But as the long-promised Italian insurrection failed to appear, scepticism in London hardened into a determination not to be distracted from the main war. These growing doubts of Bentinck's judgement were to be confirmed by the events of 1814.[24]

Relations between Britain and Spain were paradoxical in 1813. On the one hand military cooperation had never been better. Wellington's great advance to Vitoria was underpinned by the northern insurrection, which in turn had been encouraged by British successes in 1812 and by supplies received from the Royal Navy on the Biscay coast. Spanish units played a valiant part at Vitoria and in the Battles of the Pyrenees, and were particularly prominent at San Marcial, while other Spanish troops were responsible for the blockades of Pamplona and Santoña. Their operations on the east coast were less successful, but they never betrayed their ally as Murray did Copons. For the most part Wellington's relations with his Spanish subordinates were good, though a heated exchange of words with Henry O'Donnell, Conde de Abisbal, led to the Spaniard's resignation.

Yet at the same time, Wellington's relations with the Spanish government were marked by an incessant stream of acrimonious disputes, beginning slowly in the spring and building up to a climax in the late summer and autumn. Wellington was so infuriated that in August he submitted his resignation in the hope that the threat would break the impasse; but instead the Spaniards procrastinated, shuffling the question from one organ of government to another, and not finally requesting Wellington to retain the command until the end of November. The issues in dispute are too complex to detail here: often they concerned the extent of Wellington's authority as commander-in-chief, and the government's undermining of his influence by promoting officers he had sent to the rear in disgrace, while neglecting those he recommended for promotion. Then there was the Spanish government's inability or reluctance to raise resources to feed, pay and clothe its troops. Wellington was never able to use half the Spanish troops who were available, simply because they could not be paid and fed in the Pyrenees. The British also believed that the incompetence and, sometimes, the active hostility of local Spanish officials was encouraged by the Spanish government. Wider issues also caused tension. The British normally had no love of the Catholic Church, but they believed that it had been one of the mainstays of popular resistance in Spain, and were horrified when the *liberales* in Cadiz launched a concerted attack on its power, privileges and influence. The libels of the press in Cadiz added a constant irritant to relations, for not all were as laughable as the story that Castaños had offered the crown of Spain to Wellington, on condition that he became a Catholic. The sack of San Sebastian produced a tremendous outcry — much of which was perfectly justified, but not the suggestion that Wellington had connived at the town's destruction for commercial reasons.

Wellington reacted to all this with alternate anger and cold cynicism. He was disgusted by the impracticality and bombast of the *liberales* and felt no sympathy for their reform programme. He sometimes wrote foolishly of striking at the democrats or threatening to withdraw the army from Spain, but when Bathurst suggested that Wellington use force to overthrow the *liberales,* he sensibly replied that such interference would only make things worse.[25]

By the end of 1813 Britain and Spain were heartily sick of each other, for the long alliance had built up a great accumulation of grievances and dislike. But neither side had entered the alliance from altruism or love of the other's *beaux yeux,* and the fundamental conjunction of interests remained in place. Thus when news of the armistice and peace negotiations reached Cadiz, Sir Henry Wellesley was delighted and rather surprised by the resolute Spanish refusal to contemplate any terms short of the complete and immediate withdrawal of all French troops from the Peninsula, and the unconditional release of King Ferdinand. So long as these demands remained unfulfilled it was in the interests of both governments to concentrate their hostility on the French.[26]

Relations with Portugal were much simpler and easier, though not without problems. Portuguese troops remained a vital component of Wellington's army and their performance won much praise. General Picton wrote home that at Vitoria, 'There was no difference between the British and Portuguese, they were all equal in their exertions, and are deserving of an equal portion of the laurels', while Wellington described them as 'the fighting cocks of the army'.[27] The Portuguese government, however, did not feel that its army had received the credit it deserved for its part in Wellington's victories, and even suggested that the Portuguese troops be concentrated in a single corps under a Portuguese general. Wellington was able to block this dangerous proposal, and took good care to emphasize Portuguese achievements in his public as well as his private letters home. The British government created the difficulty on another question, when Castlereagh ruled that contrary to previous practice the value of all arms, clothing and equipment be deducted from the Portuguese subsidy (previously 30,000 troops had been treated separately). As Portugal's finances had been in a dire state in 1812 the implications of this decision appeared serious, but in the event Portuguese revenue flourished in 1813 (it increased by 20 per cent partly because of the sale of some Crown lands), while the actual value of the British subsidy increased from £2.3 million in 1812 to £2.5 million in 1813.[28] Recruitment for the army also posed problems, with a serious shortfall in the middle of the year. This was overcome by extending the age bracket for recruits and reducing exemptions, though by the end of the year the government was proving reluctant to send recruits forward to join the army. This reflected a gradual cooling of enthusiasm for the war as the French were driven further and further from Portugal. Ministers like Dom Miguel Pereira Forjaz began to consider that when the war was over Britain would no longer be a dominant influence in Portuguese politics, and that they should strengthen their position by improving their ties with other factions and distancing themselves from the British. Suspicion of Spain also revived, together with the realization that

Britain would do little to help Portugal regain Olivenza and the other slips of territory she had lost in the brief war of 1801. But these were straws in the wind: ominous for the future, but little affecting the strength of the alliance in 1813.[29]

Essential as the Spanish and Portuguese troops were to Wellington's campaign, the backbone of his army remained British. The government in London had made an enormous effort to reinforce Wellington in 1812, and at the beginning of 1813 he received two fresh, strong brigades of cavalry, but this exhausted the supply, and for the rest of the year it could do no more than make up his losses. Nonetheless, Wellington's army was far stronger in 1813 than in 1812. The troops were seasoned, and so less likely to fall ill, while for the first time the army was issued with tents and camped under canvas. As a result no more than 20–25 per cent of the army were sick at any one time, compared with up to 40 per cent in 1812. This meant that Wellington had an average of 42,700 effective British rank and file in 1813, compared with 34,700 on average over the whole of 1812. The strength of the army was remarkably stable over the course of the year, though it naturally reached a peak in April and May before the campaign began and dipped to a trough with Vitoria and the Battles of the Pyrenees. In round terms, Wellington had almost 60,000 British rank and file (42,700 effective on average), plus 30,000 Portuguese (about 20,000 effective) and perhaps 25,000 Spanish troops acting with the army — to which must be added the troops on the east coast. Including officers and detached men, the Anglo-Portuguese army alone amounted to almost 100,000 men.[30]

Wellington had only one serious quarrel with London over manpower in 1813: the Duke of York tried to insist that veteran units be sent home to recruit when they became greatly reduced in size, while Wellington — who regarded a single acclimatized, experienced soldier as worth two or three newcomers — wished to combine them into provisional battalions. There is no doubt that the Duke of York was correct in theory, but given the state of affairs in 1813 he should have been more flexible. Wellington appealed to the ministers, who were reluctant to interfere but devised a compromise: Wellington lost the remains of four cavalry regiments (the horses were drafted into other units and the men sent home), but only two of the eight battalions of infantry the Duke had sought to recall.[31]

Specie, that other great bone of contention, was also relatively quiet in 1813. Large supplies had been obtained from India, while the collapse of the Continental System gave Britain access to European bankers — though there was fierce demand from the Continental Powers. Nonetheless, the government was able to ship more than £1.7 million in gold and silver to the Peninsula over the year. Of course the army continued to rely primarily on credit and specie raised locally, but the generous supply from England eased all problems, so that for much of 1813 Wellington's letters home on the subject were pleasant, cordial and even appreciative. A temporary shortage did develop in the last weeks of the year, but this was relieved by very large shipments in January 1814.[32]

Wellington did, however, have problems with both the Ordnance Department and the Admiralty. He loudly complained of delays in receiving additional equipment for the second siege of San Sebastian, and on 22 July Bathurst admitted that 'unaccountable confusion between the Transport Board and the Ordnance' meant that the convoy was not yet ready to sail, although the guns had been at Portsmouth for two months and the transports had been ordered three weeks before. Colonel Torrens, at the Horse Guards, had no doubt where the blame lay, telling Wellington that 'nothing connected with the executive government of the country requires reform more than this Ordnance Department. It is, as now constituted, the greatest clog about the State. It is a mélange of jealousy, intrigue, and stupid prejudice; and to nothing but the neglect of the Board is the failure in your supplies to be attributed.' Torrens was in a good position to judge, and the Ordnance may well have been to blame in this instance, but in general its performance in 1813 was superb, supplying vast quantities of arms, ammunition and equipment to every corner of Europe.[33]

Wellington's dispute with the Admiralty continued the angry exchanges of 1812. He had two main grievances: the failure of the navy to protect his lines of communication from the depredations of American privateers, and its failure to blockade San Sebastian closely during the siege. The first was a serious concern, for a number of merchantmen and at least one troopship were captured off the coast of Portugal early in the year. (The transport contained forty men and sixty horses of the 18th Hussars — but they were released for a ransom of £3,000.)[34] The admiral in Lisbon seems to have been at fault, sending his frigates on distant cruises in search of rich prizes.[35] The question of San Sebastian is more difficult to judge, for the Admiralty had a deep-seated distrust of the Biscay coast and were very short of small vessels. It was probably impossible to cut off completely coastal traffic between Bayonne and the besieged fortress, but the ease and frequency with which French vessels ran the blockade, taking in reinforcements and supplies, and bringing out the wounded, suggests that the navy could have done much more.

With a little good will and moderation on both sides, these difficulties might have been amicably resolved, but for once Wellington encountered an official — J. W. Croker, the Secretary to the Admiralty and reviewer in the *Quarterly* — who shared his taste for intemperate language. After years of almost obsequious deference from the ministers Wellington was equally astonished and outraged at Croker's letters. Bathurst attempted to soothe the incensed Field Marshal:

You must not read Croker's compositions as you would those of any other official person. He has a talent for writing sharply and with great facility. When this is coupled together, it is a great misfortune in an official person.

His style is often what it should not be, when he addresses himself to Departments. At least *I* have often found it so, but I have not taken any notice of it, for I know he does not mean anything by it — And as for you, you are the God of his Idolatry.[36]

But Wellington was not appeased, complaining to his brother William that 'I have heard nothing more . . . about the Admiralty; excepting that Lord Bathurst has told me that Mr Croker is in the habit of writing Impertinent letters and that I ought not to mind them!!'[37]

Indeed, Wellington was somewhat out of humour with the ministers in general in the second half of 1813. In August he told Pole: 'There are two of the Govt. who I think must go: I mean Lord Melville [First Lord of the Admiralty] and Lord Mulgrave [Master-General of the Ordnance]. Both have neglected us here most shamefully.' In September he was complaining of Croker's 'blackguard abuse', while by December he confided that he was 'a little inclined to believe that they think I have done them as much good as I am likely to do them; and that they don't feel any great desire to put themselves out of their way to gratify any wish of mine'. By the New Year this 'little inclination' had hardened into certainty: 'I am quite certain that the Govt are tired of me and my operations; and wish both to the Devil.'[38]

It should be unnecessary to point out how foolish, ungrateful and totally groundless were these complaints, or to rehearse again the limp excuse that Wellington was merely 'letting off steam'; but it is worth pausing to note two issues which, while they clouded Wellington's relations with the government, probably also led him to exaggerate his discontent when writing to his brother William. The first was that Wellington had asked for, but failed to receive, preferment for his clerical brother Gerald. Liverpool was scrupulous in his use of Church patronage, and conflict over Gerald Wellesley was to recur far more seriously in 1826–7; but even in 1813 the refusal irked Wellington considerably.[39] The second problem concerned William Wellesley-Pole himself. Ever since the autumn of 1812 Pole had been chafing at his exclusion from office and repenting his refusal of the offer of the War Department. His impatience was the catalyst for the breakup of the Canning-Wellesley third party, and he was intensely disappointed when this was not followed by the offer of a cabinet post — the honour of organizing a fête for the Prince Regent to celebrate Vitoria proving small consolation. Wellington had already, in 1812, made clear to Liverpool his regret that Pole was out of office, and he repeated this in 1813. But the ministers generally had a poor opinion of Pole, regarding him as a turncoat with little influence in the Commons, and Liverpool could not even make room in cabinet for Canning — whose terms were now reasonable, and whom the Prime Minister still greatly admired. Wellington was probably too realistic to be much hurt by this rebuff, but when writing to Pole he had every reason to magnify his discontent with the ministers — both to show his fraternal feelings and to avoid further importunities.

Whether or not this was his intention, the effect was the same, for at the beginning of February 1814 we find Pole humbly apologizing for having troubled Wellington earlier, and urging him not to worry about his (Pole's) political prospects.[40]

Outside Wellington's correspondence with Pole, and the irritation over the Ordnance and the Admiralty, there is little sign of any serious problems in relations between Wellington and the government in 1813. The old worries of manpower, specie and the political stability of the ministry had all been resolved, and surely not even Wellington could sincerely doubt the government's commitment to the war in the Peninsula? Yet while the letters to Pole can be discounted, they cannot be completely dismissed, and it does seem that as the year drew towards its close and the war in Germany reached its climax, Wellington felt that his achievements were being put into the shade.

16

From the Armistice to Frankfort: Britain and the Continental Powers, June–November 1813

News of the Armistice of Pleiswitz caused much concern in London, with even some of the ministers fearing that the Continental Powers were about to make peace. This would present Britain with a terrible dilemma: to continue the war almost alone with virtually no prospect of victory, or to join with the allies in making an unsatisfactory peace in the hope that the wartime coalition could be recreated at the first sign of renewed French aggression. At one point in June Bathurst was so depressed by the lack of Spanish cooperation and flagging enthusiasm in Portugal that he wondered if Britain would be justified in continuing the war simply to drive the French from the Ebro to the Pyrenees. This was never a serious proposal. The British government would not abandon its ally, and Wellington was implacably opposed to any partition of Spain: 'I would prefer to have Joseph as King of Spain, without any cession to France . . . than to have Ferdinand with the Ebro as the frontier.' Yet it is significant that the thought even crossed Bathurst's mind.[1]

Wellington's victory at Vitoria effectively solved the Spanish question. Napoleon could no longer maintain Joseph's claim to any part of Spain, and Britain could take part in peace negotiations if she wished. The danger remained that Russia and Prussia might make peace on terms which were unacceptable to Britain, but it had been greatly reduced, while the obstacle which had threatened to break up the coalition at the outset of negotiations had been removed. Britain still had particular obligations to her allies, but they were unlikely to cause major problems. Portugal and Spain had been liberated and Sicily was secure. Britain was pledged to attempt to regain Naples for the King of Sicily, but this was not a sine qua non of peace. Sweden's claim to Norway might prove more troublesome, but a compromise was possible, and it was not an issue of great importance to France.

Nonetheless, it is clear that the British ministers hoped that the Continental Powers would continue the war. They believed that Napoleon was still far too powerful for peace to be safe or lasting, and some objects of particular concern to them were either still debatable (Hanover, the fate of the north of Italy and of Hamburg), or clearly out of reach (the complete independence of the Low Countries from France). But they judged that it was more prudent to join with the allies in peace negotiations than to remain aloof and so open a fissure in the coalition for Napoleon to exploit. On 5 July, three days after the news of Vitoria reached London, Castlereagh therefore wrote to Cathcart outlining, in three categories, Britain's aims in any negotiations. In the first category, without which Britain would not be party to any peace, were the claims of Spain, Portugal, Sicily and Sweden. In the second, which the government regarded as almost equally essential, were the strengthening of Austria and Prussia so that they could form 'some counterpart in the centre of Europe to the power of France'. The interpretation of this deliberately vague instruction would depend on the views of the Continental Powers themselves. Also in this category was 'the complete and absolute restoration' of Hanover, and it is hard to imagine the British government accepting any compromise on this demand. The independence of Holland was a more ambitious claim, and though one dear to British hearts, it was the point most likely to be sacrificed in negotiations, for the French were still in complete control of the country, and none of the Continental Powers gave it such a high priority. The third category consisted of points which Britain regarded as of general importance, but on which she would follow the lead of her allies. This comprised the settlement of Germany, Switzerland and Italy, in such a way as to reduce French influence and protect the allied powers.[2]

While this dispatch naturally left many points open for negotiation, it represented the most coherent statement of Britain's war aims for many years. Britain was willing to make peace with Napoleon, but she wished to restrict his power as much as possible, while strengthening the Continental Powers to resist any new French expansion. It does not quite contain a complete list of Britain's objectives, for it mentions only the independence of Holland, and the British government was almost equally concerned with the fate of Belgium, in particular the great naval base of Antwerp, and the creation of some permanent barrier protecting the Low Countries against France. But this was clearly unobtainable in July 1813, and raising it would only risk Britain being blamed for the breakdown of the peace talks. Castlereagh explained to Cathcart, 'The risk of treating with France is great, but the risk of losing our Continental Allies and the confidence of our nation is greater.' And,

we must contend for as much as the Allies can be brought to stand to with firmness and spirit. But it is vain to suppose that we can inspire the determination, if it does not exist. We may animate by our counsels as well as by our example, but we must avoid the appearance of idly pressing them against the grain. Such a line might weaken our influence, and would incur the responsibility of whatever disunion or failure followed.[3]

While the British government thus prepared to make peace if necessary, the ministers anxiously scanned dispatches from Germany for signs that the allies would resume the contest. They went to great lengths to send news of Vitoria to allied headquarters as quickly as possible, hoping that it would be an inspiration, and fearing lest Napoleon would gain some diplomatic advantage from his prior knowledge of the battle. They recognized the importance of Austria, but they did not despair of victory even if she remained neutral, provided Russia, Prussia and Sweden remained united. Early in July, Liverpool told Wellington, 'If Austria would now declare, we might really hope to put an end to the tyranny which has been so long oppressing the world; but on this event no reliance can, I fear, be placed. The dispositions of Russia and Prussia are good, and Bernadotte is using every endeavour to persuade them not to make peace. . . .' Towards the end of the month, Bathurst wrote that accounts from Germany were more promising, before adding, 'As for Austria, I cannot have much confidence in her. But it will be a grand crash, if they all fight.'[4]

Although the cabinet was anxious to improve its links with Russia and Prussia, it suspended payment of the subsidies for the duration of the armistice, while warmly approving Cathcart's decision to sign the treaties, and even Stewart's advance of £100,000 to the Prussians. A major British arms depot was established at Stralsund, complete with a small British garrison, in anticipation of an autumn campaign, and £100,000 in specie and bar silver was shipped to the Baltic for the use of the allies as soon as active operations were resumed. More broadly, Cathcart's failure to obtain any commercial concessions from Russia caused regret, and a Russian offer of mediation in the war with the United States was firmly rejected, while Cathcart was instructed not even to discuss the question of maritime rights at a general congress. On the other hand, the government did announce that it was willing to return many of its colonial conquests in return for concessions on the Continent, although Dutch colonies would only be returned if the complete independence of Holland was secured. These instructions hint at the half-submerged tensions within the coalition which helped make the British government fear the lurking dangers of a peace conference more than the fortunes of war. Castlereagh repeatedly told his envoys to stress to the allies the scale of Britain's pecuniary and military efforts, but he knew that there was a thread of jealousy and dislike of Britain in many Continental Courts.[5]

Metternich certainly showed no great love of Britain at this time, continuing to regard her as an obstacle to his plans for peace. He had no interest in Britain's particular objectives and wished to keep allied demands low in order to increase the chance that Napoleon would accept them, and to ensure that France would remain strong enough to act as a counterweight to Russia. He therefore insisted on excluding Cathcart and Stewart when he discussed peace terms with the allies in the middle of June. These discussions resulted in the Treaty of Reichenbach (27 June 1813), in which

Austria pledged herself to join the allies in war with Napoleon, if he did not agree to Austria's minimum terms for peace. The four principal demands were: the dissolution of the Duchy of Warsaw, the enlargement of Prussia, the return of Illyria to Austria, and independence for Hamburg and Lübeck. In addition to these points, Austria would endeavour to obtain the abolition of the Confederation of the Rhine, and full restoration to Prussia of all the territory she had lost since 1805; but she was not committed to war if these could not be obtained. If, however, peace proved impossible, and Austria did go to war, she pledged to continue the struggle until all these objects were achieved, and even accepted a wider allied programme including the independence of Holland and the expulsion of the French from Italy — although the status of this commitment was ambiguous.[6]

Britain's interests were pointedly ignored in this agreement, with Spain not being mentioned in even the final, broadest, category of claims (the news of Vitoria had yet to arrive). This neglect, combined with the exclusion of Britain's envoys from the talks, had an ugly look, and Stewart's alarm at the peace negotiations and his suspicions of Russia steadily grew. But Alexander seems to have kept Cathcart reasonably well informed of what was going on, and the Reichenbach treaty did not commit Russia or Prussia to make peace even if Napoleon agreed to all Austria's demands. Cathcart reported home that the negotiations were a necessary preliminary to bringing Austria into the war on the side of the allies. But if Napoleon accepted the overture and peace negotiations began in earnest, Britain would be at a disadvantage and would struggle to gain concessions on points which she regarded as being of the greatest importance.[7]

Metternich proceeded to Dresden, where he had a famous interview with Napoleon on 26 June which lasted for hours but proved indecisive. The Austrian proposals, which appeared excessively moderate to the allies, seemed outrageous to Napoleon: why should he yield territory when he had won two battles in succession? But Napoleon wanted more time to reorganize and strengthen his army, and Metternich, while desperately wanting the negotiations to proceed, also knew that the Austrian army needed time to prepare to take the field. They therefore reached a compromise, extending the armistice from 20 July to 10 August, while Napoleon promised to send a delegation to the peace conference at Prague. The allies were furious when they heard that Metternich had agreed to extend the armistice, but the need to conciliate Austria meant that there was little they could do except complain and agree.

The Prague Congress was supposed to begin on 5 July, but Caulaincourt, the chief French representative, did not arrive until the 28th, and then lacked full authority, so that the Congress never formally met. Plainly Napoleon shared the British government's preference for open hostilities rather than the less tangible dangers of protracted negotiations. All his life he had risked his fortune and gambled for high stakes, and the situation in 1813 was not so different from that in 1805 or 1806. Of course, hindsight suggests that he should have moderated his ambitions and accepted an Empire broadly defined by France's 'natural frontiers' of the Rhine, Alps and Pyrenees. Many in France, including Talleyrand, Caulaincourt and some of Napoleon's generals, wanted such a peace, but it would have been wholly out of character if Napoleon had accepted it. One might even say that had he been the man to accept such a peace, he would never have made the great conquests he had; and the road to Damascus does not run between Dresden and Prague.

Even if Napoleon had accepted Austria's terms, peace was far from certain. There is no evidence that Alexander ever seriously considered making peace in the middle of 1813, and more than ever before he controlled Russia's foreign policy absolutely. He signalled his intentions by sending Baron Johann von Anstett, an Alsatian émigré who was virulently hostile to Napoleon, to the Prague Congress. Frederick William of Prussia was more willing to consider a negotiated settlement, but his principal advisers, Hardenberg and Humboldt, together with almost all the Prussian generals, strongly favoured war, and they carried the debate, Humboldt representing Prussia at Prague. Yet if Austria was satisfied, would the allies have risked carrying on the war without her? The question remains open, but it suggests another: could Austria remain out of a war which would decide the fate of Europe and which, if she did not participate, would leave either France or Russia the predominant power in central Europe?

In the event these questions remained unanswered, for Napoleon's refusal to enter into serious negotiations left Austria with no alternative but to declare war on 12 August. Active operations did not immediately resume, and even in these last days Metternich made some final, despairing attempts to salvage the peace talks, but in vain.[8] Both sides had agreed to the armistice for military reasons, and in order not to offend Austria. Neither was ready for peace, except on favourable terms, and not all Metternich's skill could conjure an agreement out of thin air. But why did Metternich want peace so badly? Was it simply that he feared that victory would make Russia too powerful, or that the war might release revolutionary forces in Germany? Possibly; but Metternich was fascinated and intimidated by Napoleon, and it seems equally likely that he feared that war would lead to new French triumphs and another dictated peace even harsher than that of 1809.

The British government was delighted at the resumption of the war, and Castlereagh admitted to Cathcart that 'However sanguine you had taught us to be on the issue, we were nevertheless, deeply anxious'. The accession of Austria was greeted with particular pleasure tinged with surprise. The longstanding distrust of Metternich naturally did not evaporate overnight, and the Prince Regent is said to have delighted in repeating malicious gossip about him to all and sundry.[9] Castlereagh seems to have been less hostile, and was certainly more diplomatic. He had already instructed Cathcart to open direct communication with the Austrian government and to inform it that if Austria joined the allies she could expect £500,000 in aid immediately. Yet even this encouragement was accompanied by the now familiar disclaimer, 'It is not for Great Britain to goad other powers into exertions which they deem inconsistent with their own safety'.[10] This was at the end of June, and a fortnight later Britain formally accepted Austrian mediation in conjunction with the allies. A fortnight after that, at the end of July, Castlereagh appointed an ambassador to Austria, and chose for this onerous position George Hamilton Gordon, fourth Earl of Aberdeen.

Even when every allowance has been made for the need to send a man of rank, and for the spirit of the age, it was an extraordinary choice. Aberdeen was only twenty-nine years old, had never held public office, and his chief qualification, other than his title, was that Pitt and Dundas had been his guardians. This patronage evidently singled him out for a brilliant career and he had already declined a number of diplomatic posts offered by Wellesley and Castlereagh. He accepted the Austrian embassy with some hesitation, soon regretted his decision, and within weeks of arriving on the Continent was seeking to return home. Britain desperately needed a powerful voice to represent her interests in the allied councils, someone with the full confidence of the cabinet, whose eminence gave him a natural and unobjectionable predominance over Cathcart and Stewart. The ideal choice, as events were to show, would have been Castlereagh himself, but it was probably too soon to think of sending the Foreign Secretary, who was also leader of the Commons and one of the government's few capable ministers in the Lower House, out of the country when there was no prospect of the end of the war in sight. If not Castlereagh, then one of the other ministers or a senior politician close to them should have been sent. Of the cabinet, Harrowby was the most suitable, if his health permitted, for he was a former foreign secretary who had gone on a similar special mission to Prussia in 1805. William Wellesley-Pole lacked the stature and experience for the task, while Canning, who had both, was ruled out by his quarrel with Castlereagh. Many of Castlereagh's diplomatic appointments seem ill-judged — possibly Cathcart, certainly Stewart — but none was as extraordinarily inappropriate as that of Aberdeen.[11]

The new ambassador left London for Yarmouth on 6 August, but because of the loss of Hamburg he had to travel via Sweden and the Baltic and did not reach allied headquarters until early September, when the campaign was well under way. The allies had taken advantage of the armistice to develop a coherent plan of campaign for all their armies. The sovereigns and their generals had met at Trachenberg from 9 to 12 July. Cathcart and Thornton were admitted to some of these discussions, which Stewart only missed because he was absent inspecting the Swedish army. One of the main objects of the Trachenberg meeting was to conciliate Bernadotte, whose mortification and disaffection had reached the point of threatening to withdraw from the war. For once, flattery alone, though helpful, was not enough to satisfy the Gascon. Gritting their teeth, the

Russian and Prussian generals had to agree that Bernadotte be given command of a great allied army in the north with no fewer than 22,000 Russians and 40,000 Prussians to add to his 30,000 Swedes and 10,000 Germans. In return Bernadotte agreed to concentrate his operations against the French, and leave Denmark until the main campaign was decided. Bernadotte also claimed credit for the plan of campaign devised at Trachenberg, although he has many rivals for this honour. In essence the plan was that the allied forces be divided into three armies: that of the North under Bernadotte (approximately 100,000 men), the Army of Silesia under Blücher (some 90,000 men), and the large, mainly Austrian, Army of Bohemia under Schwarzenberg (perhaps 230,000 men). These armies were to press in on the French, attacking detached forces, but falling back whenever they were faced by Napoleon and his main army, until the French were exhausted and the allies were close enough to come together to deliver a single massive coup de grâce. The plan was not without risks — retiring in the face of an enemy such as Napoleon was always dangerous — but at least the allies had learnt enough from all their defeats no longer to expect a quick, easy victory.[12]

On the last day of the Trachenberg conference news of Vitoria arrived, providing an encouraging portent for the future. Alexander ordered that a Te Deum be sung to celebrate the victory (for the first time ever for a triumph not won by Russian arms). The British representatives were ecstatic with pleasure and wildly exaggerated the influence of the news, claiming that it inspired Austria and the allies with the courage to risk war rather than make peace. While this is fanciful, the victory did give Britain, and hence her representatives, greater importance in the eyes of the allies, and after the news they were treated with more consideration. There was even some talk of offering Wellington the overall command of the allied armies, although this was more a graceful compliment than a serious proposal, and in any case Wellington had already indicated that he would not accept such a position.[13]

For some time the question of the command remained open. Bernadotte would have liked it, but he was unacceptable to everyone else. Early in August an agreement was reached that the diplomatic Schwarzenberg should be made commander-in-chief, but no sooner had operations begun than Alexander demanded that he be given the position. Metternich vehemently opposed this, and finally carried the day by threatening to withdraw Austria from the war rather than consent. This brought the always prickly personal relations between the two men to a new low, while relations between Russian and Austrian commanders at all levels were marked by constant bickering, quarrels and jealousy throughout the autumn campaign.[14] The supreme command itself did Schwarzenberg little good: his authority over Blücher and Bernadotte was almost purely nominal, and he was unable to prevent Alexander, and even Frederick William, from constantly interfering in his operations. But the position would have been infinitely worse if Alexander had had the formal authority to override

Schwarzenberg's plans on the advice of the favourite of the moment. Schwarzenberg may not have been a great general, but he fully earned Blücher's toast to 'the Commander-in-Chief who had three monarchs at his headquarters and still managed to beat the enemy!'[15]

Both sides had used the armistice to collect enormous armies. Napoleon probably had about 450,000 men in Germany, with a further 250,000 still forming or in reserve. The allies certainly had more: perhaps 500,000 men in the field, and another 350,000 coming up, including troops detached to blockade French-held fortresses in Poland and eastern Germany, and a new Russian army of some 60,000 men under Bennigsen which was still being organized in Poland. All these figures are mere approximations, but never before had such large armies raged across central Europe.[16] The autumn campaign lasted only a couple of months, but the demands of so many men and horses devastated the countryside. Napoleon had built up enormous magazines in Dresden, but shortage of horses made his transport service inadequate, and his young troops suffered severely from hunger in the last weeks of the campaign. The allies probably suffered less, for they had wider tracts of less ravaged country to draw on, yet even Barclay de Tolly complained to his wife: 'the Tsar and myself do not get forage — the Austrians want everything for themselves'.[17] These problems were compounded by an exceptionally wet autumn: many battles were fought in the rain, rivers flooded, mud was everywhere, and the poorly fed troops on both sides succumbed to illness and disease.

Such conditions did not favour Napoleon's rapid, decisive manoeuvres, and his army still suffered from weak cavalry and an excessive proportion of raw troops. Nonetheless, he almost won a decisive victory in the first fortnight of the campaign, when the Army of Bohemia attacked Dresden on 26 August. Dresden was Napoleon's centre of operations and vital to his campaign; its defences were strong and it had a substantial garrison under one of his most capable subordinates, Marshal St Cyr. Nor was Napoleon, with his main field army, as distant as the allies imagined. He had the opportunity of cutting off the allied retreat and attacking them in the rear, while their attention was concentrated on their attacks on Dresden. Such a victory might have destroyed the Army of Bohemia, decisively shifted the balance of forces in the campaign, and perhaps even have driven Austria from the war. But it was not to be: Napoleon received alarming reports that Dresden would fall within twenty-four hours if not reinforced, and so took the bulk of his army to aid in the defence of the city, sending only Vandamme with a single corps to threaten the allied retreat. This decision cost Napoleon the best opportunity he was to have in the whole campaign.[18] Even so, the resulting Battle of Dresden (26–27 August 1813) was a substantial French victory: the allies lost heavily and were forced to retreat into the Bohemian mountains in considerable disorder. But the French pursuit was not very effective, and Vandamme's corps was — more by chance than design — cut off and almost destroyed at Kulm on 30 August. This defeat, with others suffered by Oudinot at Gross-Beeren (23 August) and Macdonald at Katzbach (26 August), offset the advantage gained at Dresden.

The next six weeks of the campaign did not maintain this early pace, and the Trachenberg plan worked well, with Napoleon unable to get to grips with any of his opponents, while his subordinates continued to suffer defeats, such as Ney's defeat by Bernadotte at Dennewitz (6 September). The allies kept Napoleon constantly off-balance, while his plans were unusually hesitant and indecisive, and his troops were exhausted by constant marching and countermarching. Time was on the side of the allies, and Napoleon's failure to win a decisive victory dimmed his prestige within his own army and among the German Princes. On 8 October patient diplomacy by Metternich bore fruit when Bavaria defected to the allies by the Treaty of Ried, bringing with her an army of 36,000 men, well placed to threaten French communications. Napoleon had already attempted to shorten his line of operations by retiring to the left bank of the Elbe and moving his base from Dresden to Leipzig, some sixty miles west. He launched another offensive against Blücher and Bernadotte, but they continued to elude him and he was forced to return south hastily as Schwarzenberg attacked Leipzig.

The allies were now ready to try their fortune in another grand set-piece battle, so Schwarzenberg did not retreat but maintained his attack even when Napoleon returned, while Blücher and Bernadotte followed hard on the Emperor's heels. The result was the Battle of Leipzig (16–19 October), the greatest battle of all the Napoleonic Wars. Napoleon had nearly 200,000 men with 700 cannon in the field, compared with the allied forces which rose from 250,000 to over 350,000 men with, in the end, 1,500 cannon. The enormous forces involved and their generally poor quality encouraged a bloody battle of attrition, with little room for the tactical brilliance which Napoleon displayed in his greatest victories. The French generally fought well, but could not resist the pressure brought against them. As the tide of battle turned against Napoleon, the small Saxon contingent (about 4,500 men) defected to the allies on 18 October — possibly against the wishes of its King. The French began to give ground and were soon in full retreat. The premature destruction of a bridge over the River Elster trapped some 20,000 men of the French rearguard: most surrendered, but some tried to escape, including the Polish Marshal Poniatowski, who drowned in the attempt.

The decisive battle of the campaign had been fought, and Napoleon had been defeated. His army lost some 73,000 casualties in the battle, and many more in the subsequent retreat to the Rhine through illness and desertion. His remaining German allies quickly abandoned his cause and made terms with the allies, although a Bavarian attempt to block the French retreat was brushed aside after a savage battle at Hanau (30 October). When Napoleon reached the Rhine at the beginning of November he had about 70,000 men left with the colours and another 40,000 stragglers; but even this remnant of his army would be further reduced by the ravages of typhus. He left behind 100,000 men in garrisons across Germany and Poland, but they could not hold out for ever. Danzig capitulated on 29 November after a siege lasting most of the year. Stettin and Modlin followed soon after, while St Cyr and the large garrison of Dresden surrendered as early as 11 November. And each of these capitulations freed a large allied force to join their main army.[19]

Leipzig is often called the 'Battle of the Nations', and Napoleon's defeat is ascribed to an upsurge of national patriotic sentiment across the Continent rebelling against French hegemony. But in fact such feelings seem to have been mostly restricted to a fairly small intellectual minority who had little real influence on events. The 'people's wars' in Spain and Russia were largely conservative, local, xenophobic reactions to violent foreign intrusion. The great bulk of even the Prussian army was made up of reluctant peasant conscripts whose loyalty was first to their region, second to Prussia, and not at all to Germany as a whole. The smaller German states proved remarkably loyal to Napoleon and only abandoned his cause when his defeat appeared inevitable. There was widespread popular hostility to the French, bred of years of petty oppression and the appropriations of war, but this did not lead to mass volunteering for the army, guerrilla activities against the French, or even popularity for the 'liberating' armies. Of course there were exceptions: thousands of students and other idle young men joined fashionable regiments (volunteer jäger battalions in particular), believing that they were taking part in a great patriotic struggle; and it was they, not the peasant conscripts from Brandenberg, who wrote memoirs and histories of the war. Indeed, it could be argued that the greatest importance of the 'Wars of Liberation' (1813–15) in the creation of modern nationalism was in providing material for patriotic legends and the sense of a shared national past which developed during the nineteenth century. This may overstate the case, for the actual experience of serving in Blücher's army may have broadened the loyalty of many of the reluctant conscripts. But it is not clear how this relates to the troops from the smaller German states and from most of Italy, who fought for, not against, the French until the last months of the war. How did a retired hussar from Baden, who had fought against Austria in 1809 and Prussia in 1813, and whose brother had died in Russia, look back on the long war?[20]

The generals and statesmen who controlled the armies in 1813 mostly had an ambivalent or hostile attitude to popular nationalism. The enthusiasm of Gneisenau and Stein was checked by the caution of Hardenberg, Frederick William and the Czar, and overwhelmed by the intense antipathy of Metternich. Yet the campaign of 1813 *was* fundamentally different from those of earlier years — except 1812. The allies mobilized their resources on an unprecedented scale and showed more toughness and resolution in the face of adversity. Their armies were not better than in previous campaigns, indeed in some ways they were worse, but neither the Prussians nor the Austrians showed the fragility which they had displayed in earlier campaigns: they took heavy losses but retreated in good order and continued fighting. They had learnt some lessons from experience and no longer underestimated Napoleon as they had done in previous years. Still, many of the faults of past coalitions remained and were even exacerbated. The allies quarrelled among themselves as much as or more than ever before, Alexander continued to interfere outrageously in operational concerns, and the allies found no general comparable with Napoleon — or even equal to the Archduke Charles.

Why, then, was Napoleon defeated? First and foremost because the losses sustained in Russia, combined with the debilitating effects of the war in the Peninsula, undermined the strength of the Empire and its allies, and left it vulnerable. Losses not just of men's lives, but of veteran cadres, trained horses, artillery and equipment, popularity and prestige: the Russian disaster afflicted Napoleon in many ways, and meant that his new army lacked the quality of its predecessors. The war in Spain not only helped to undermine Napoleon's Empire, it also absorbed 200,000 good troops in 1813 who were vitally needed in Germany. Despite these losses, Napoleon was able to hold his own in the spring campaign against Russia and Prussia, but when Austria joined the coalition after the armistice the odds shifted heavily against him. This was the first time since 1795 that the great Continental Powers had combined against France, and it was the first time ever that they had combined in such a whole-hearted effort. Napoleon's defeat was still not inevitable, and his strategical and tactical brilliance had found triumphant victory hidden amongst almost equal perils previously. In 1813 he failed to overcome the odds: the allies were more wary, his army was less good, the weather was bad, his subordinates were weary, and, it must be said, some of the old brilliance was lacking.

During the campaign, allied diplomacy had continued among the horrors and discomforts of war. Aberdeen felt these severely and his letters home abound in accounts of crudely amputated limbs outside field hospitals, followed closely by complaints at his wretched quarters and poor provisions. He had reached allied headquarters early in September, thus missing Dresden and Kulm, and was most graciously received by Metternich, who was now anxious to improve his relations with Britain, and who recognized that Aberdeen was not a man to resist flattery. Soon, very soon, Aberdeen was writing home to tell Castlereagh that Metternich was a much misunderstood man, a sincere friend of Britain, stalwart in the struggle against Napoleon, earnest in his desire for a peace which would satisfy all just claims, and not at all devious or duplicitous, or even very clever. Barely a week after arriving Aberdeen was 'well contented' with Metternich, and the following day he was conveying, with evident approval, Metternich's urgent appeal for an increased subsidy, while ten days later he solemnly told

Castlereagh that 'Metternich continues as cordial and confidential as possible. I think this man must be honest; yet it may be, after all, that he is only a most consummate actor. I will be sufficiently cautious, but I will also retain the favourable opinion I have of him until I see some good ground to change it.'[21] Poor Aberdeen! The last faint glimmer of doubt flickered and went out; he staked his pride and his vanity on Metternich's goodness and soon was lecturing Castlereagh:

> Do not think Metternich such a formidable personage; depend on it, I have most substantial reasons for knowing that he is heart and soul with us; but, my dear Castlereagh, with all your wisdom, judgment and experience, which are as great as possible, and which I respect sincerely, I think you have so much of the Englishman as not quite to be aware of the real value of foreign modes of acting. . . .[22]

Metternich had gained this ardent advocate through fair words alone, for he had made no substantial concession on any of the outstanding issues between the two countries. When Aberdeen raised the question of access to Austrian markets for British commerce, Metternich was encouraging, only to report later that Emperor Francis had strong views on the subject which made progress difficult.[23] A more important question was the fate of Murat, Napoleon's brother-in-law and King of Naples. The British government was willing to make peace with Murat if he gave up Naples in return for compensations elsewhere in Italy, so that Naples could be returned to Britain's ally the King of Sicily. However, if it was absolutely necessary, Britain would reluctantly agree to leave Murat in Naples and look for compensation for the King of Sicily. Metternich, on the other hand, had engaged in negotiations with Murat since early in 1813 and evidently wished to keep him in Naples. Aberdeen had been at allied headquarters for less than a fortnight before he had revealed to Metternich that in the last resort his government would agree to leaving Murat in Naples. This destroyed any hope the King of Sicily had of regaining his beloved mainland kingdom, while even his compensation was soon in doubt, despite the fact that Murat, though still communicating with Metternich, continued to lead Napoleon's cavalry throughout the autumn campaign.[24]

Aberdeen's arrival thus did nothing to strengthen Britain's voice in allied councils: indeed, his quarrels with Cathcart and Stewart probably weakened it further. A striking example of Britain's lack of influence occurred soon after he arrived, when Austria, Prussia and Russia signed the Teplitz treaties of alliance, on 9 September. The most notable thing about these treaties from a British point of view is that their definition of allied war aims ignored almost every issue of particular concern to Britain. There was no mention of Spain, Portugal, Sicily, Holland or Norway — only Hanover was included together with the restoration of Austria and Prussia to their strength in 1805, and the dissolution of the Duchy of Warsaw and the Confederation of the Rhine. It would not have cost the allies anything to include Spain, Portugal and Sicily, for they were already secured; and it might be argued that Norway was a separate matter not directly related to the objects of the war against France; but this still left Holland, a point of immense importance to Britain, and moreover one which should have been established as an allied war aim by the Reichenbach treaty. The most likely interpretation of this omission, and of other ambiguities in the treaty, is that Metternich sought to make room to manoeuvre in future peace negotiations with Napoleon.[25]

Britain continued to subsidize the allies, even while her interests were thus being neglected. By September the Prussians had received more than 100,000 muskets complete with powder and flints, while the Russian armies had received 100,000 muskets, 116 pieces of field artillery, and 1,200 tons of ammunition. In all, more than £1 million worth of military stores was sent to the Baltic in 1813. Britain also shipped £300,000 in specie to the Continent for Prussia and Russia during the year, despite the general shortage caused by the war. In October the British government extended the Swedish subsidy for twelve months (or until the end of the war) at the reduced, but still generous, rate of £100,000 per month. It also continued to maintain the German Legion in Bernadotte's army, and sent cadres of the King's German Legion to help in the reconstruction of the Hanoverian army. There was even a handful of British troops fighting with the allies in the autumn campaign, for a British rocket brigade (i.e. a battery of horse artillery armed with the new, and only partially successful, Congreve Rockets) had been attached to Bernadotte's bodyguard. This brigade took an active part in the Battle of Leipzig, while Sir Charles Stewart joyfully abandoned the pitfalls of diplomacy to lead the Brandenberg Hussars in a very gallant charge.[26]

The network of subsidy agreements was completed on 3 October when Aberdeen and Metternich signed an Anglo-Austrian treaty of alliance. This was very similar to the existing treaties with Prussia and Russia. Both parties agreed not to make peace independently, and Austria promised to maintain an army of 150,000 men in the field in return for a subsidy of £1 million. Cathcart had already paid the Austrians £500,000; the remainder was to be issued £100,000 per month, and a new agreement negotiated in April 1814 if the war still continued. The Austrians were to receive no equivalent of 'Federative Paper', and Metternich failed in a determined effort to have arms and military stores regarded as additional to, not part of, the subsidy. Austria thus received less aid than Prussia or even Sweden — but this was a natural consequence, as the British saw it, of her entering the war so belatedly.[27]

The Austrian treaty was satisfactory to the British government as far as it went, but it did little to ensure allied adoption of British war aims. Castlereagh and his colleagues had been unpleasantly jolted by the armistice and the subsequent peace negotiations. The result had vindicated Russian good faith, but the ministers now looked for a means of securing the alliance more firmly, not only to ensure that British objectives were part of any future allied peace proposal, but, equally important, to perpetuate the alliance against France even after peace was made. For the cabinet had come to believe that this was Britain's only hope of a lasting peace with Napoleon in the long term, and it was even ready to sacrifice some immediate British objectives in order to strengthen the alliance. On 18 September Castlereagh sent Cathcart a draft treaty which he hoped Britain, the Continental Powers and Sweden would sign, and to which Spain, Portugal and Sicily could then be invited to accede. An accompanying letter of explanation defined the objects of the war on a generous scale, including Britain's particular concerns: the independence of Holland 'with an adequate barrier' against France; the transfer of Norway to Sweden; the restoration of Naples to the King of Sicily or adequate compensation; as well as the end of French influence in Germany and Italy. Castlereagh regarded these aims as unobjectionable, but he would probably have been willing to make concessions on individual points in order to gain allied agreement. Much more novel was the fourth clause of the proposed treaty:

> That after peace shall be concluded by common consent, there shall continue between the said High Contracting Parties a perpetual defensive Alliance for the maintenance of such peace, and for the mutual protection of their respective States.[28]

Thus all the allies would be bound in a permanent defensive alliance against France, providing security for Europe against the French aggression which had not only kept Europe at war for the last twenty years, but which had caused the wars that had dominated the century before that. It was a peculiarly British vision: France was the disturber of the European equilibrium, and if France was restrained, everyone else would be happy. European statesmen saw things rather differently. For them France was but one player in a much more complex game, and they had alternated between enmity and alliance with her as their perceived national interests had dictated. It was only six years since Alexander had embraced Napoleon at Tilsit, and he might yet wish to do so again once the Corsican was sufficiently humbled, while Metternich always hoped to preserve a strong France as a counter to Russian predominance. Castlereagh's vision did not even appeal to the Prussian generals, who wanted not to contain Napoleon, but to destroy him. And yet, after all, one cannot help but wonder if the narrow British view was not the wisest: whether, two or three years after making peace with Napoleon, Austria, Prussia or Holland might not have been wishing for a defensive treaty uniting the rest of Europe which it could invoke in the face of French pressure. The effectiveness of such a treaty is, of course, another question, but it may well have had a deterrent effect, and can hardly have been worse than no treaty at all.

Castlereagh hoped that his proposals would be accepted with little hesitation or delay, and expected Russia's support in encouraging the other powers to agree. But his dispatches were delayed by contrary winds and did not arrive until the middle of the Battle of Leipzig, at which point military operations gave little time to discuss the idea for some weeks. When Cathcart at last caught Alexander's attention he found him far from encouraging, although Russia's objections were never clearly spelt out. In fact, Alexander's main worry was probably that the proposal might force him to specify Russia's claims, in Poland and elsewhere, which could lead to a crisis in the coalition and open confrontation with Metternich, before he was ready. Throughout the year he had maintained a careful silence on the subject in the face of Metternich's subtle probing.[29]

Stewart and Aberdeen had also been sent copies of the plan and met with less resistance, Stewart reporting on 24 November that the Prussians had no objection and would be happy to sign. Metternich was also superficially encouraging, but his evasiveness and proposed alterations suggest that he was almost as opposed to the idea as Alexander.[30] Negotiations dragged on till the end of the year without making any significant progress. Castlereagh was puzzled and dismayed by the fate of his proposal; he had already been outraged at the neglect of British interests in the Teplitz treaties, and this new rebuff added to his suspicions and helped to persuade him that Britain needed better representation on the Continent.

The need for such a general alliance was soon made even more evident. After the final breakdown of the armistice Metternich had ignored several tentative diplomatic approaches from Napoleon, recognizing that negotiating during the campaign would risk breeding disastrous distrust within the coalition. But Leipzig changed everything and Metternich hoped that Napoleon would be so chastened by defeat that he would accept allied terms. Greater difficulty lay in persuading the allies to agree to talks. Fortunately for Metternich, Nesselrode (who was acting as Russian foreign minister) privately agreed with him in wanting a peace on the basis of France's 'natural frontiers'. Alexander, however, still showed no inclination to make peace or even to define his ultimate objectives, and he, not Nesselrode, controlled Russian foreign policy. But following Leipzig, the Czar was preoccupied with military matters and the ceremonial entrance to Frankfort, and he appears to have given his consent to an overture, believing that it would be rejected, and that this rejection could be used to justify publicly the invasion of France.[31] Given Russian support, Metternich did not worry unduly about Prussia. He claimed that Frederick William knew of and approved the contact, but Humboldt recorded the King's disapproval in his diary, and of the three, Metternich's veracity is the least dependable.[32] If he had felt the need to do so, he would also have proceeded without British approval, but Aberdeen's easy complaisance made this unnecessary. Where Castlereagh was willing to make peace to satisfy the allies, Aberdeen was positively eager: he was genuinely horrified by war, and he wanted to go home with all the éclat of having negotiated a peace settlement. He even let pass with only a protest a reference to

Britain's maritime rights — a sacrosanct issue for the British government, which would have created a storm at home, and ensured that Britain began any peace negotiations founded on the overture at a disadvantage, having to fight to have this obnoxious item removed from the discussion.

Metternich's overture took a strange unofficial form, due to the lack of any real allied support for it. A captured French diplomat, Baron St Aignan, joined Metternich and Nesselrode in a discussion over the terms the allies wanted for peace. Aberdeen joined them as if by chance, and added his comments. St Aignan drew up a memorandum of the discussion which was read over by the three ministers on the following day and approved by them. The terms were essentially France's 'natural frontiers' of Pyrenees, Alps and Rhine — and though the absolute independence of Holland was stipulated, its frontier was not. These terms were remarkably — excessively — generous, by far the best Napoleon could expect in the wake of Leipzig, though they would require him to yield some territory he still held, in Hamburg, Holland and northern Italy. But they were not official and may not have proved definitive. In fact it must remain an open question whether Metternich could have persuaded Russia and Prussia to make peace on these terms if Napoleon had accepted them immediately.

But the French did not accept immediately: the overture was too vague and suspicious, and so, to test the water, they proposed a peace conference at Mannheim without preconditions. This was unacceptable to the allies, but Metternich succeeded in including an official restatement of the terms proposed to St Aignan in their response. This reply reached Paris on 2 December, and Caulaincourt, the new and pacific French Foreign Minister, immediately accepted it. It is not clear whether Napoleon sincerely intended to make peace, or whether he was merely trying to encourage discord in the coalition, for the allies now backed away from their offer, stating that no peace conference was possible until a British plenipotentiary with full powers arrived, and that military operations would continue in the meantime. This appears a clear example of bad faith, but circumstances had changed in the month since the initial allied offer, for news had arrived that Holland had risen in revolt against the French, and there were reports that Belgium was ready to follow. Nonetheless, the St Aignan overture remains highly suspect. Did Metternich really believe that he could manoeuvre, threaten or cajole his allies into a peace they did not want, or was it all a propaganda gesture which went wrong?[33]

Napoleon's acceptance of the allied proposals did not fatally split the coalition, but it did add to the animosity between Alexander and Metternich, while the whole business set the British representatives at loggerheads with one another. Even the patient Cathcart resented Aberdeen's transparent attempt to garner all the glory of peace for himself, while Stewart, incandescent with fury, ranted at Hardenberg — who was himself angry at the overture. The allies sent Pozzo di Borgo to London to request that a senior British diplomat be sent out with full powers to make peace,

Metternich apparently suggesting that Lord Wellesley or Canning be chosen. This was, of course, unacceptable, and Castlereagh first suggested Harrowby; but after a lengthy cabinet meeting on 20 December the Foreign Secretary was persuaded to go himself. It was probably the most important and sensible decision of Castlereagh's career; and while it seems obvious in retrospect, it was a great novelty and innovation for a serving Secretary of State to leave the country for an extended period, not accompanying his sovereign, on official business.[34]

The year 1813 was the most successful Britain and her allies had enjoyed in twenty years of war. It was a situation of great promise: many dangers had been transformed, and victory, which only two years before had seemed a visionary goal which might not be achieved for a generation, was within sight if not yet within grasp. But it must be admitted that British diplomacy — though not British arms or British gold — played little part in this happy transformation. Russia continued the war and was joined by Sweden, Prussia, Austria, Bavaria and the other German states, all for their own good reasons. This was natural enough: Britain was not fighting from altruism, and it is hard to believe that any government would be justified in fighting a war that was not in its national interests. What is more striking is Britain's lack of influence within the coalition, displayed time and again throughout the year, though fortunately without doing lasting harm. One explanation is obvious: the poor quality and lack of coordination of the British representatives with the allied armies, and for this Castlereagh, who personally selected them, must bear a large measure of the blame. But other, more deep-seated factors were also at work. The allied rulers acknowledged the contribution to victory of Wellington and the war in the Peninsula, but only perfunctorily. It was a distant, remote struggle, which they had read about in papers for years, but which meant little to them personally. The diversion of 200,000 French troops in Spain lacked the immediacy and impact of the defeat of 20,000 French under their eyes at Kulm. So careless were they, that they signed capitulations which released French garrisons on conditions which did not prevent them fighting in Spain.[35] This neglect was possible because they knew that they could take Britain for granted. It was inconceivable that Britain, Spain and Portugal would make a separate peace with Napoleon, freeing his armies in the Pyrenees to turn the scales in Germany; yet Wellington's operations were constantly constrained by the fear of a Continental peace. There was nothing the British government could do about this. They made some limited use of their supply of money and arms to gain concessions on a few points of particular importance, but the ministers recognized that it would be counterproductive to press this too far. Otherwise they simply had to hope that the common interests they shared with the allies would lead to mutual cooperation and a peace which would satisfy Britain and her allies.

Attitudes to Britain among Continental statesmen varied from day to day and issue to issue. Gratitude for subsidies, regret that they were not larger,

11. Political Chess Players, or Boney Bewilder'd — John Bull supporting the Table
Design by G. Humphrey, executed by Williams, 4 March 1814, B.M. Cat. no. 12,193

John Bull supports the world on his back, disregarding the money which spills from his pockets. (But many other caricatures of this period show great resentment at the cost of the war, and particularly subsidies to the allies — sometimes shown as John Bull being bled dry by quack doctors.)

Europe is a chessboard. Napoleon has lost most of his pieces and is at a loss. The prominent allied figure, left foreground, is Bernadotte; on the right is a handsome Wellington who remarks, 'I shall move soon and I hope play Well in turn.' Most of the other allies are represented: Alexander moves a knight, beside him is Francis of Austria, and behind is Frederick William of Prussia. Behind Wellington is an unidentified figure (possibly representing Holland), while on the extreme right Ferdinand of Spain, just released, hurries to join the allies.

and good fellowship in the alliance predominated. After all, Britain's own territorial claims on the Continent were slight, scarcely extending beyond Hanover, and most of her claims on behalf of her allies were intrinsically inoffensive (though the Austrians greatly disliked Bernadotte's claim to Norway). But there was a streak of jealousy which emerged from time to time, although never with the force of the rivalry between Austria and Russia and the personal antipathy between Metternich and Alexander. Britain had prospered while the Continent suffered: she had swept the oceans clear and now controlled almost every desirable colony in the world, save those of Spain and Portugal. She posed no threat to any of the Continental Powers, but her domination of trade and her success were resented, particularly by some Russians. Russia's view of the question of maritime rights did not coincide with Britain's, and the Armed Neutralities of 1780 and 1800 had not been forgotten. There was a hint of this in the Russian offer to mediate between Britain and the United States, and when Castlereagh proposed his general alliance, the Russians suggested that all the allies have a say in the final allocation of the colonies Britain had conquered. The words of a modern historian capture and express this resentment perfectly:

> With a certain obtuseness born of being shielded by the Channel from the grossest facts of international life, Castlereagh thought his country entitled to a major voice in continental affairs while refusing others a corresponding voice in non European matters. On the continent, balance of power; on the high seas, British hegemony.[36]

Such feelings were natural, but they were not justified. The gross facts of international life were that £7.5 million in subsidies, and an army of 100,000 men in the Pyrenees, gave Britain a voice in Continental affairs, while none of the Continental Powers had the means of supporting any pretensions on the high seas without Britain's good will. Twenty years of war had shown that Britain could survive without her allies, while they would probably have been ruined without her. Whether judged on principle, justice or crude power, Britain's claims were reasonable. Castlereagh's task when he reached the Continent would be to ensure that Britain gained the voice she deserved in European affairs, while soothing the resentment of her allies.

17

The Invasion of France,
November 1813–April 1814

The first allied troops to invade France crossed, not the Rhine, but the Bidassoa, a fortnight before Leipzig was fought and won. After his defeat at San Marcial (31 August), Soult had gone onto the defensive and constructed a series of field works protecting the French frontier along the Bidassoa on a twenty-three-mile front. But this stretched his army too thinly and on 7 October 1813 Wellington suddenly attacked, turning Soult's right flank by advancing across the broad tidal estuary of the Bidassoa — 1,000 yards of mud and sand banks with a shallow river in the middle — on paths pointed out by local fishermen. The French were taken completely by surprise and fell back in disorder while an allied attack in the centre carried some of the field works. The passage of the Bidassoa was brilliantly conceived and executed, but Wellington failed to take full advantage of his victory. He could easily have occupied St Jean de Luz, five or six miles in the rear, that day, while the French were in confused retreat, and so turned the line of the Nivelle, the next river, but he made no attempt to pursue and allowed Soult to rally his army unhindered.

For five weeks the armies faced each other, the French throwing up more field works, while Wellington waited for Pamplona to fall and completed his preparations for his next advance. Pamplona capitulated on 31 October, and on 10 November Wellington attacked. The Battle of Nivelle was considerably more costly and less elegant than the passage of the Bidassoa (about 3,300 allied casualties compared with 1,600 at the Bidassoa), but the result was broadly similar: the French were forced to retreat, but there was little or no pursuit.

Another month passed before Wellington continued his advance, crossing the River Nive and approaching Bayonne. Soult had greatly strengthened the fortifications of Bayonne, but on this occasion he did not rely on passive defence. Instead he waited until Wellington's army was divided in half by the river, then hurled his army first at one half, then at the other. The result was a series of hard-fought, often confused actions known as the Battles of the Nive (9–13 December) in which the allies were often hard-pressed, but ultimately succeeded in maintaining their position and repulsing the French attacks with heavy losses. Over the five days of fighting the French lost some 6,000 casualties, about 1,000 more than the allies. Again there was no pursuit, and Wellington soon put his army into winter quarters.

Three battles in two months had brought Wellington barely twenty miles into France. Soult's troops had fought well, but not that well, for if the allies had advanced briskly after crossing the Bidassoa, pressing their advantage and not giving the French time to rally, they could have reached the Adour and invested Bayonne by the middle of October with far fewer casualties than they actually sustained. But Wellington was curiously hesitant and uncertain, arguing at various times that the weather, the need to know what was happening in Germany, and the risk of provoking a French popular insurrection deterred him from advancing further. Yet none of these reasons really explains his slow, fitful advance towards Bayonne, and it is hard to avoid the conclusion that Wellington's heart was not in the invasion of France at this time. He had no confidence in the plans of the allied powers to invade France across the Rhine — which he regarded as rash — and he rather hoped that negotiations would lead to a moderate peace.[1] In the meantime he was more intent on obtaining a secure and comfortable position for the winter than in driving Soult as far back as possible.

Relations with Spain were another factor contributing to Wellington's caution. On 27 November he told the British government that in the event of a serious defeat, 'I think I should experience great difficulty in retiring through Spain into Portugal, the Spanish people being hostile'. And he urged the ministers to present Spain with an ultimatum threatening to withdraw the army if conditions were not met.[2] This crisis soon blew over, with the Spanish government confirming Wellington's position as commander-in-chief of their armies and generally adopting a much more conciliatory line. But immediately another potential crisis emerged: the Treaty of Valençay. After his defeat at Leipzig Napoleon decided to try to put an end to the war with Spain in the hope that this would force the British to withdraw their army and so release the 160,000 veteran troops he still had on his southern front. He therefore sent his former ambassador to Madrid to meet Ferdinand VII, who was being held in comfortable detention at Valençay, and on 10 December they signed a treaty which, once it was ratified by the Cortes, would put an end to the war. Napoleon was evidently misled by the constant friction between Britain and Spain, and really believed that the treaty would be implemented, but Ferdinand saw in it nothing more than a passport to freedom. Napoleon would not, however, let his captive go until the treaty was ratified, and the Cortes unanimously rejected it, arguing that Ferdinand was not a free agent.[3]

Wellington was rather surprised and very pleased with this response, telling his brother Henry, 'It appears to me that the Spanish government have managed this matter remarkably well, and I should not be surprised if

Ferdinand were sent back to Spain.'[4] He did not, however, approve of the resolution of the Cortes that Ferdinand be required to swear allegiance to the constitution before resuming his royal position, asking the obvious question: 'I don't know what is to be done if he will not swear to the constitution on the frontier. Is he then to be sent back?'[5] Fortunately it was clear that if Ferdinand were released it would be through Suchet's army in Catalonia, so Wellington would not be confronted with this embarrassing dilemma.

After this, Wellington's relations with the Spanish government remained reasonably cordial for the rest of the war, although Henry Wellesley was disappointed that the *serviles* were unable to replace the *liberales* when the Cortes moved to Madrid at the beginning of 1814. Wellington had rather more trouble with Spanish subordinates, who resented the exemplary punishments he imposed for pillaging and his decision to leave the bulk of the Spanish army in Spain. Eventually, in March 1814, he did bring two more Spanish divisions forward, and gave them a prominent part in the Battle of Toulouse where, although their attack was repulsed, they showed commendable spirit and suffered very heavy losses.

Napoleon did not wait to see if the Spanish government would honour the Treaty of Valençay before ordering large drafts of troops from Soult and Suchet. By the end of January Soult had sent off 3,000 cavalry, 11,000 infantry and three batteries of artillery to join the Emperor's army, while Suchet's much smaller but less threatened army produced 8,000 infantry, 2,000 cavalry and two batteries. Thus Napoleon was able to gain 25,000 fully equipped veterans to help in his defence of France, and when these troops took the field against the allies they naturally provoked some discontent and pointed questions about Wellington's inactivity, which all Castlereagh's talk of bad roads could not allay — as he recognized.[6] But with Paris and the heart of the Empire threatened, it was inevitable that Napoleon would draw on his armies on the periphery for reinforcements; indeed it is surprising that he did not draw on them more heavily. These were not the only men Soult and Suchet lost, however: during the Battle of Nivelle three battalions of German infantry in Soult's army deserted en masse to Wellington and were shipped home, while a fourth battalion and 2,400 German troops in Suchet's army had to be disbanded and sent to the rear. Soult had already lost an Italian brigade — sent to join Eugène in the defence of Italy — and a Spanish brigade, which had to be disbanded. Suchet had 800 picked men withdrawn to join the Imperial Guard, and both marshals lost many men, as veteran cadres were withdrawn to form the backbone of newly raised units, few of which ever saw any action. All this was in addition to normal losses through sickness and enemy action — Soult's army lost 16,000 casualties in the Battles of the Bidassoa, Nivelle and Nive, though many of the lightly wounded would soon have returned to the ranks. As there was little to replace these losses save a few thousand unwilling conscripts, both French armies shrank substantially in size.

Unfortunately there are few reliable figures, but it would seem that the total force under Soult's command fell from nearly 110,000 men (including sick and garrisons: only about 70,000 were in his field army) in the autumn of 1813 to about 75,000 (43,000 effective troops in the field army, and 15,000 men besieged in Bayonne) in the following spring. Over the same period, Suchet's army declined from about 50,000 to a little over half that number, much of it in the fortresses of eastern Spain.[7]

Wellington had no problems to compare with these, though this did not stop him grumbling that the British government was diverting reinforcements from his army to other theatres. There was a fragment of truth in the complaint, but the government was very short of men, and the latest attempt to gain recruits for the regulars from the militia had fallen far short of expectations. Nonetheless, the gross strength of the British component of Wellington's army remained fairly constant (at just over 60,000 rank and file including sick), with enough drafts and reinforcements arriving from home to make up losses. The army also remained healthy despite the winter weather, and its morale was excellent.[8]

During December and January Wellington suffered a severe, temporary shortage of specie, but thereafter money flowed in freely — with even a leading banker in Bayonne supplying specie in exchange for Bills on the British Treasury (this at a time when Bayonne was still occupied by the French army!). With easy communication open with the Continent, the British government now had little difficulty raising large sums in specie, especially as it now had Nathan Rothschild purchasing on its behalf — reportedly even if Paris.[9]

Despite promises to the contrary, it was not until the middle of February that Wellington resumed active operations, more than a month after he learnt that the allies had crossed the Rhine. He advanced across the Adour and completed the investment of Bayonne in which Soult had left a very large garrison. Soult fell back until, on 27 February, he gave battle in a strong position at Orthez. There was some mismanagement in the early stages of the battle, but nonetheless the allies stormed the French position and forced Soult to give way. The French lost nearly 4,000 casualties, and many more men deserted after the battle. The allies suffered about 2,200 casualties including Wellington, who was slightly wounded — not badly enough for him to have to relinquish the command, even for a moment, but it made riding painful for a week or more.

Yet again there was no effective pursuit, although Wellington now had an overwhelming superiority of cavalry. Soult retreated, not north towards Bordeaux but east towards Toulouse, partly for logistical reasons and partly in the hope of drawing Wellington after him. But Wellington was now strong enough to pursue two objects at once, and on 8 March he detached Beresford with 12,000 men to occupy Bordeaux, while he slowly followed Soult with the bulk of his army.

7 Northern Spain and France, 1814

The expedition to Bordeaux was undertaken for political not military reasons. As the fourth largest city in France with a population of over 90,000,[10] it was important in itself, but Wellington hoped that its occupation might be the catalyst for the rising in favour of the Bourbons which he had been half expecting since he entered France. Officially neither Wellington nor the British government would encourage the royalists, for it was still possible that the allies and Britain might make peace with Napoleon, and the ministers in London refused to sponsor an uprising if they might then be forced to abandon it to Napoleon's mercy. Wellington did not agree with this decision: 'I cannot discover the policy of not hitting one's enemy as hard as one can, and in the most vulnerable place. I am certain that he would not so act by us, if he had the opportunity. He would certainly overturn the British authority in Ireland if it was in his power.'[11] He believed that the

French would follow the allied lead, favouring the Bourbons in private, but being unwilling to risk public declarations while the allies continued negotiating with Napoleon. Nonetheless, Wellington obeyed his instructions, ordering Beresford to give the royalists tacit encouragement while making it quite clear that Britain could give them no guarantee of protection. This perfectly reflected the policy of the government, which had allowed the Duc d'Angoulême to join Wellington's headquarters incognito, provided his behaviour was reasonably discreet.[12]

Beresford occupied Bordeaux on 12 March without difficulty — there were very few French troops in the area and they had retired across the Garonne. The British were received with great ceremony and rejoicing. Count Lynch, the Mayor of Bordeaux, had been a Girondist in the Revolution and a faithful servant of the Empire, but a trip to Paris at the end of 1813 had convinced him that the writing was on the wall, and when he returned to Bordeaux he had actively supported and encouraged the royalist party. He greeted Beresford before the assembled dignitaries of the town and a large, enthusiastic crowd, denounced Napoleon, and proclaimed his allegiance to Louis XVIII. Beresford responded cautiously that he occupied the town under orders from Wellington. A few hours later the Duc d'Angoulême arrived posthaste to a rapturous reception, but his and Lynch's attempts to implicate Wellington publicly in their cause were sharply snubbed. Possibly because of this, the fervour of the royalist restoration in Bordeaux quickly faded, its leaders became anxious and despondent, and proved totally unable to raise any troops to support their cause; but this ultimately mattered little, while the news that Bordeaux had declared for the Bourbons made a great sensation in London, Paris, and at allied headquarters (see below, p. 322).[13]

On 18 March Wellington resumed his leisurely advance on Toulouse, with Soult falling back before him. The French army reached the city on the 24 and was re-equipped from its great arsenals. On 3 April Beresford, with nearly 20,000 men, crossed the Garonne on a pontoon bridge which then broke. For four days Wellington's army was divided in two by an impassable river, but Beresford's position was strong and Soult was probably wise not to attack. On Easter Sunday, 10 April 1814, Wellington attacked the outer defences of Toulouse, which were strongly held by Soult's army. The assault did not go according to plan and the army suffered more than 4,500 casualties (compared with 3,200 French casualties) before it ultimately carried the position. There was no fighting on the 11th: Wellington's men were exhausted and Soult was preparing to retreat, for he did not want to risk being besieged in Toulouse with his entire army. That night the French slipped away and made a clean break, and on the following morning the municipal officials and townspeople of Toulouse, all wearing white cockades for the Bourbons, gave Wellington a rapturous welcome. Reports arrived later that day (the 12th) of the end of the war, and although Soult did not formally accept the news until the 17th there was no further fighting between the main armies. Yet even Toulouse was not the end of the killing. On 14 April the garrison of Bayonne made a savage but pointless sortie in which it suffered over 900 casualties and inflicted almost as many, including the British commander Sir John Hope, who was wounded and captured. Two days later, in the last action of the Peninsular War, the garrison of Barcelona made a similar if less costly sortie, with the loss of a few hundred casualties.

It is ironical that events on the east coast should thus come to prominence in the dying gasp of the war, for there had been no other fighting of significance in Catalonia in late 1813 or 1814 — the largest action being a skirmish at Molins de Rey on 16 January. When Suchet was ordered to send 11,000 men to join the Emperor in January, he reluctantly left a large garrison (7,500 men) in Barcelona and fell back with the remainder of his army to Gerona. In the middle of February the Spaniards captured the fortresses of Lerida, Mequinenza and Monzon — but not Tortosa, Rosas or Barcelona — by a treacherous *ruse de guerre*, thus neatly completing the circle begun by the French seizure of the border fortresses in 1808. On 7 March Suchet dispatched another infantry division (9,661 rank and file) to join Napoleon. They were diverted to retake Bordeaux but the war ended before they could arrive. Suchet retained his position in Catalonia until the end of the war, when he made his submission to the new government and was given the command of Soult's army — much to the latter's annoyance.

The events of 1813 and 1814 clearly demonstrate the subordinate nature of the war in the Peninsula and southern France; for it was not here, but in Germany and northern France that Napoleon's fate was decided. Or so it seems. But consider for a moment what would have happened if the Treaty of Valençay had worked as Napoleon had hoped. Spain and probably Portugal would have made peace, and Wellington's army, deprived of its base of operations, would have been forced to embark and return to Britain, whence it would have been redeployed in Holland weeks, or rather months, later. Even at the very end of the war there were at least 80,000 French troops on the southern front: in Soult's army, Suchet's army, Bayonne, Barcelona and the other fortresses still in French hands, not to mention all those which had already fallen to the allies. With an additional 80,000 veterans under Napoleon's direct command, the campaign of 1814 would have been very different — whether or not the ultimate result was the same. In truth there was but one war against Napoleon, and though victory or defeat on one front might not immediately or directly affect the other, they were indissolubly linked.

Events in Sicily and Italy had much less impact on the war as a whole in 1814 than those in Spain and the south of France. On 11 January Austria signed a peace treaty with Murat confirming his possession of Naples and even offering the prospect of territorial gains in the Papal States in return for his active cooperation against Napoleon. Bentinck was disgusted with this treaty. He had an intense dislike of Murat, probably dating from the stories he heard of the Dos de Mayo when he was in Madrid in 1808, and he correctly judged that Murat was not to be trusted and might well betray the allies if the fortunes of war swung back in Napoleon's favour. While he signed an armistice with Murat on 3 February, he refused to recognize his claim to Naples and encouraged the Court of Palermo in its natural revulsion. This was contrary to British policy, but it was not long before Castlereagh was applauding Bentinck's prescience.

But Bentinck's other use of his discretion won less favour in London. He continued to promote the idea of a permanent British protectorate in Sicily and flouted British policy towards Italy. At the end of February he sailed with a small expeditionary force and landed, on 9 March, at Livorno (Leghorn). In theory he was cooperating with Murat and the Austrians in their campaign against Eugène, Napoleon's Viceroy of Italy; but in practice he was hoping to realize his dream of a free and independent Italian Kingdom. On 14 March he issued a proclamation offering Italy British help in overthrowing Napoleon so that she could 'resume her ancient splendour among the independent Nations'; but it produced no response and once again hopes of an Italian insurrection proved to be groundless. Bentinck was rude to the Austrians and quarrelled furiously with Murat. On 18 April he occupied Genoa and a week later proclaimed the restoration of its ancient republic, having modified its constitution. This breach of his instructions was to cause trouble, for the British government had already agreed that Genoa should be incorporated into the Kingdom of Piedmont and Sardinia, to strengthen that kingdom as a buffer to French expansion in Italy. Castlereagh's patience was all but exhausted, and he told Liverpool that Bentinck's 'mismanagement [has] at least doubled all the natural dangers of Murat's rascality'. But at least for the moment Bentinck was past caring what London, or Vienna, thought; as his biographer has noted, he 'was neither the first nor the last proconsul to kick over the traces when, after having in effect ruled a satellite country, he was suddenly told to obey instructions which he disliked'. But Bentinck lacked the power to implement his dream in Italy, and on 8 June he returned to Sicily having completely lost the support of the British government and aroused the dangerous antipathy of Metternich.[14]

Holland was of far more direct and immediate concern to the British government than Italy, and throughout 1813 the ministers had kept a close eye on the Low Countries. In the spring of 1813 when the allies had swept across Germany and occupied Hamburg there had been brief hopes of a Dutch rising, but Napoleon's recovery soon showed that it would have been premature. At the end of May Bathurst ordered Major-General Dunlop to occupy the island of Borkum off the mouth of the Ems with a small force (three weak battalions). He was to do nothing to excite a Dutch revolt, but was to be ready to give assistance when the moment arrived. British interest in Holland had been stimulated by Prince Dolgorouki's disastrous mission to Copenhagen (see above, p. 245), where he was reported to have offered the Danes compensation in Holland for the loss of Norway. This idea was equally unacceptable to the British government and the Prince of Orange, who hastened to London, arriving on 25 April 1813. Relations between London and the exiled Stadtholder had never been good, and some members of the British cabinet, including Bathurst, were inclined to pass over the Prince in favour of his son the Hereditary Prince, a young man who was serving as one of Wellington's aides-de-camp, and who, they understood, was much more popular in Holland. But as the Prince now sought to conciliate the British government and Wellington reported that the son was young and inexperienced, this idea gradually faded into the background. On 18 May Castlereagh assured the Prince that the British government was convinced of the importance of Holland, but that it believed that it was too soon for an immediate uprising to succeed. Another five months were to pass before Napoleon's defeat at Leipzig opened the way for the liberation of Holland.[15]

On 15 November 1813 the French garrison left Amsterdam. Two days later a small patriotic uprising at the Hague called for independence under the House of Orange. At three o'clock in the afternoon of 20 November the semaphore station at Yarmouth transmitted the message, 'Complete revolt in Holland. Dutch Baron on his way to the Prince of Orange. Texel fleet in mutiny.' The news created a sensation in London. Wilberforce recorded in his diary the Battle of Leipzig, Wellington's victory at Nivelle, and 'the glorious news from Holland, better than all the rest', while even that resolute pessimist Lord Auckland was moved to joy, regarding it as 'the best and most important event of this most eventful year'.[16] Lady Bessborough reported the arrival of the Dutch emissaries:

> The Chaise arriv'd cover'd with Orange Ribbons, and threw the Foreign Office into commotion by enquiring for the Stadt holder, and saying that they must go to him first as their Prince. . . . The Poor Stiff P. of Orange cried on their saluting him as Stadt Holder, and delivering to him the invitation from the people of Holland.[17]

The Prince of Orange, accompanied by Lord Clancarty, the newly appointed British ambassador, arrived in Holland on 30 November. Two days later 20,000 muskets were unloaded, and on 6 December they were followed by 1,500 British troops — detachments of the Foot Guards. More than twenty years before, the war had begun with just such a detachment of Guards being hastily sent to aid in the defence of Holland. On 14 December Clancarty called for the urgent dispatch of more troops as the French were in disarray, and the great fortresses of Antwerp and Bergen-op-Zoom appeared vulnerable to sudden attack. The troops were already on their way. As early as 21 November Bathurst had approached Sir Thomas Graham,

12.   A Long Pull, A Strong Pull and a Pull Altogether
[Rowlandson], 25 Nov. 1813, B.M. Cat. no.12,102

An early reaction to the news of the Dutch revolt. A group of allies with John Bull in the foreground, beside him a Spaniard and behind them a Russian, a Prussian, an Austrian and one other, pull over the Dutch fleet, much to Napoleon's fury. In the background are ships representing the allied fleets, and the 'Sunset of tyranny'. Behind Napoleon his brother Joseph laments, 'Oh Brother Nap Brother Nap we shant be left with half a Crown apiece.'
    News of the revolt of Holland produced great excitement in Britain, but the French fleet in Antwerp was not easily captured.

home from the Peninsula on sick leave, begging him to accept the command of a scratch force destined for Holland. Graham was extremely reluctant, for he saw little hope of glory and considerable risk of disgrace in an expedition whose purpose was as much political as military, but after some persuasion he accepted. He had about 8,000 men, but they were an odd assortment of units which for one reason or another had been deemed not good enough to send out to Wellington. It was, quite simply, a very bad army.

    Bathurst explained the objects of the expedition to Wellington a few weeks later: in the first place it was very desirable that Britain be seen to be taking an active part in the liberation of Holland; and then there was the great French naval base at Antwerp. 'Our great object is Antwerp. We cannot make a secure peace if that place be left in the hands of France.' 'In this the Allies feel no common interest with us. Some, absurdly jealous of our maritime power, may even wish Antwerp to remain with France.'[18] This was not an isolated comment: a month before, Castlereagh had written to Cathcart, 'I must beg you never to lose sight of Antwerp and its noxious contents', and in the middle of January Harrowby considered, 'Antwerp and Flushing out of the hands of France are worth twenty Martiniques in our own hands'. Napoleon agreed, for even at the end of March, with defeat staring him in the face, he would not give up his claim to Antwerp.[19]

Graham's force reached Holland on 17 December, having been delayed by contrary winds. By the time it was disembarked and equipped for the field, the French had rallied and the fleeting chance of seizing Antwerp had gone. Nonetheless, in January and early February Graham made two attacks on Antwerp in concert with General Bülow, the commander of the Prussian forces in the Low Countries. The second attack included an attempt to destroy the French fleet by long-range bombardment but this, like the first attack, failed completely. Bülow was then ordered south to support Blücher's attack on Napoleon, and at the end of February Bathurst decided to recall some of the British troops. Before they left, Graham attempted a surprise attack on Bergen-op-Zoom on the night of 8 March. At first all went well, the British gaining a secure foothold on the walls and advancing into the town, but as the night went on, the fighting became more and more confused and the French garrison gradually gained the upper hand, eventually capturing or driving out all the British troops. Graham was greatly mortified by this defeat, which closed his distinguished career on a sour note, but the Prince Regent, the ministers and the whole army acquitted him of blame and went out of their way to praise him.

The expedition to Holland thus failed to achieve its specific purposes and the two fortresses remained in French hands until the end of the war. But this does not necessarily make it a mistake: Antwerp was too important for the government to miss any chance of seizing it, while the presence of the British force in Holland gave greater weight to Castlereagh's arguments about the final settlement of the Low Countries.

The events in Holland had one unexpected side-effect: they helped complete British disillusionment with Bernadotte. Considerable doubts had been created by the failure of the Crown Prince to contribute to the spring campaign in 1813 or to save Hamburg from Davout, but they were largely allayed by his prominent role in the autumn campaign culminating at Leipzig. But then, instead of pushing forward to liberate the Low Countries as the British government begged him, Bernadotte turned aside to attack Denmark. In a way this was quite fair: he had already twice postponed the accomplishment of Swedish objects until the French had been defeated, and he did not trust the allies to fulfil their bargain once the war was won, for he knew that Austria opposed the transfer of Norway, and Russia's support was fickle. The conquest of Denmark proved simple and easy, though it was protracted by Austrian attempts to mediate. On 7 January the Danes sued for peace, accepting the loss of Norway in return for Swedish

Pomerania and other compensation. (Ultimately they exchanged Pomerania for Lauenberg, which Hanover had ceded to Prussia.) Edward Thornton signed a peace treaty with the Danes in which he promised the return of her colonies (but not Heligoland), and a subsidy of £400,000 for 10,000 men. The subsidy rather annoyed the British government, for not only was there little prospect of Danish troops ever taking the field against Napoleon, but the subsidy granted was above the standard rate and Thornton had acted without authority. Nonetheless, after some grumbling from Castlereagh, the ministers ratified the treaty and paid the subsidy.[20]

By itself, the Danish diversion would not have completely cost Bernadotte the sympathy of the British ministers, but they could not forgive his open reluctance to go to Holland and destroy what he had helped to create as a soldier of the French Revolution. As the allies closed on France Bernadotte became more restless and unstable than ever, at one moment trying to preserve France from the horrors of an allied invasion, and at the next dreaming of replacing Napoleon. At a human level nothing could be more natural, but such conflicting passions did not encourage confidence among the allies. As early as 31 December Bathurst had noted that the 'Prince Royal is certainly too French to wish Antwerp to be wrested from France', and Castlereagh felt the greatest unease at the thought of Bernadotte commanding all the allied forces in the Low Countries. Nonetheless, later in 1814 Britain honoured her pledge, and the Royal Navy was used to blockade Norway and help coerce the Norwegians into accepting the union with Sweden. It was an unsavoury business, and none of the British ministers liked it, but they would not break their word, despite the considerable political embarrassment it caused at home.[21]

While Britain's military effort in 1814 was concentrated in the south of France, with subsidiary operations in Catalonia, Italy and Holland, the main focus of British policy was on relations with the allies — particularly Russia, Austria and Prussia — and the vexed question of whether, and on what terms, to make peace with Napoleon. On 20 December 1813 the cabinet had decided to send Castlereagh to the Continent. The primary purpose of his mission was to represent Britain at the peace conference which was to be assembled following Napoleon's acceptance of the Frankfort proposals, and the ministers spent some days discussing Castlereagh's instructions. Great emphasis was placed on the need to ensure the independence of Holland, with a defensible frontier including Antwerp. The fate of Belgium was more uncertain: the British government was anxious to separate it from France, and thought of uniting it with Holland if the Emperor Francis did not wish to establish one of his brothers there; for a completely independent Belgium was regarded as dangerously vulnerable to French pressure. Britain was willing to return many of her colonial conquests to obtain these objectives, but not those of strategic importance such as Malta, Mauritius and the Cape of Good Hope. The underlying assumption was that peace would be made with Napoleon as the ruler of France, and Castlereagh still hoped to provide for future security by perpetuating the coalition beyond the conclusion of a peace treaty. He placed great importance on maintaining harmony within the Coalition and on avoiding the suspicion that Britain was an obstacle to peace, though he believed it was essential to continue military operations during the negotiations.[22]

Castlereagh left London on 28 December in bitter winter weather and was forced to wait at Harwich until New Year's Day before his ship, H.M.S. *Erebus*, was able to sail. Soon after he left London the government received letters from Wellington conveying reports of strong support for the Bourbons in southern France and the suggestion that the presence of a Bourbon Prince might lead to a royalist uprising.[23] This produced a flurry of activity as messengers hurried between London and Harwich. Liverpool had two meetings with the Comte d'Artois, brother of the putative Louis XVIII, and made it clear that the British government could give no open support to the royalist cause except in concert with its allies, unless a general rising already existed in France. He strongly discouraged plans for Artois to sail directly to Bordeaux while the Ducs de Berri and Angoulême (Artois's sons) left for Wellington's army, saying that although the British government would not forcibly prevent their departure, it would not give them passports or passages in naval ships, and Wellington would be ordered not to receive them at headquarters. This warning checked the first flurry of Bourbon enthusiasm, and when the Duc d'Angoulême joined Wellington at the beginning of February he did so incognito and behaved discreetly until the rising at Bordeaux. Artois also left England, not for Bordeaux, but for Switzerland where he hoped to influence the allies, while the Duc de Berri went to Jersey. Before he left, Artois had an interview with the Prince Regent, who showed none of the government's caution, warmly endorsing the Bourbon cause, and an account of this interview quickly appeared in the press.[24]

None of the cabinet agreed with the Regent's open support for the Bourbons, but there was some divergence of opinion among the ministers. Bathurst would have liked to make a gesture in favour of the Bourbons, suggesting a proclamation that the restoration of the Bourbons would lead to an immediate armistice, while Harrowby believed that Castlereagh should press the allies to take up the royalist cause. Mulgrave, on the other hand, was very sceptical of the claims of support for the Bourbons in France and believed that open support for them would simply enable Napoleon to rally French opinion behind him. Castlereagh did not go quite this far, but he strongly urged caution, fearing that the allies would regard any British patronage of the Bourbons as an attempt to scuttle the peace negotiations. Britain was committed to negotiations with Napoleon, and it would be time enough to consider the royalist cause if and when those negotiations failed, although he did promise to raise the question with Metternich when he reached allied headquarters.[25]

Beneath these shades of opinion, all the ministers believed that the restoration of the Bourbons offered the best hope of lasting peace and security for Britain, while a negotiated settlement with Napoleon would be full of risks and uncertainty. But they also believed that they could not impose the Bourbons on France by force — the Spanish uprising providing a graphic and obvious example of the dangers of such a policy. They differed over tactics, but not over the ultimate objects of the war. For the moment, Castlereagh's view carried the day, but over the following weeks as news of allied advances streamed into London, the ministers at home grew increasingly uneasy at his caution.

Castlereagh and his small party arrived at The Hague on 7 January to an enthusiastic welcome. He had discussions with the Prince of Orange about the latter's desire to add as much as possible of Belgium to Holland, and about the projected marriage of the Hereditary Prince to Princess Charlotte, the only child of the Prince Regent and heir presumptive to the British Crown. Both governments approved the match which would seal their alliance, though both agreed to ensure separate lines of succession: Britain and Holland would never be united under the same monarch. Even so, the Russians appear to have disliked news of the engagement, possibly because they had hoped that a revival of Dutch maritime power might help reduce Britain's domination of the seas.[26]

On 8 January Castlereagh pressed on with all speed, travelling on wretched roads through one of the worst winters for decades. The Rhine and the Thames both froze — the latter so solidly that hundreds of people crossed it on foot between London and Blackfriars bridges, and among other festivities cards were printed and an ox roasted on the ice.[27] Despite the severity of the weather and the many French-held fortresses blockaded in their rear, the allied armies pressed forward. Schwarzenberg invaded Switzerland — as much for political as military reasons — and crossed the Rhine before the end of the year, advancing towards the Langres plateau. He still commanded much the largest allied army, composed predominantly of Austrians and troops from the smaller German states, but also including a corps of elite Russian Guards. Blücher, with his much smaller army, crossed the middle Rhine on New Year's Day, while there were other allied forces in the Low Countries. Some calculations give the allies, including reserve troops, nearly 900,000 men, but only a fraction — perhaps a quarter — of these ever reached the front. Even so, the allies had an overwhelming superiority of men, for Napoleon does not seem to have been able to put more than 60,000 men into the field at the beginning of the campaign, though recruits and the reinforcements from Spain brought this up to about 80,000 men at one time. One reason the allies advanced through the winter was to deny Napoleon the time he needed to create a new army. No wonder they were surprised at Wellington's two months of inactivity, and unimpressed with the suggestion that heavy rain had made the roads of southern France impassable.[28]

On 18 January Castlereagh arrived at Basle. where he found most of the allied sovereigns and ministers, though the Emperor Alexander had been unable to contain his impatience and had hurried forward to join the armies at Langres. By far the most important of Castlereagh's meetings — indeed one of the turning-points of his life — was the series of interviews he had with Metternich. Although Aberdeen's enthusiasm may have softened the feeling, both men had years of hostility and distrust to overcome, but they were pleasantly surprised with each other and soon established a rapport which was to be one of the central features of European diplomacy for most of the next decade. Only three days after they first met, Metternich told Schwarzenberg that 'Lord Castlereagh is here and I am very pleased with him. He has everything: grace, discretion, and moderation.'[29] Both ministers were eager to establish good relations, Castlereagh to maintain harmony within the Coalition, and Metternich to gain British support in checking Russian ambitions. Metternich smoothed the path to agreement by making substantial concessions, accepting that the Frankfort proposals had to be modified, and specifically that Holland should gain territory in Belgium, to give her a good military frontier including Antwerp. He also accepted Prussian claims to large tracts of territory on both banks of the Rhine north of the Mosel — a proposal which Castlereagh strongly supported in the hope that Prussia's presence would help to contain France and reduce her influence in Germany.[30]

For his part, Metternich was very pleased with the British government's restraint in not openly championing the Bourbon cause and in supporting peace negotiations with Napoleon. Castlereagh suggested that there were four possible forms which the government of France might take: '1st Buonaparte. 2nd A French general, suppose Bernadotte. 3rd A Regency. 4th The Bourbons.' Britain objected to the second and third possibilities as being unstable and giving excessive influence to one or other of the powers: Russia, if Alexander's protégé Bernadotte replaced Napoleon; Austria, if the Empress Marie Louise became Regent. Metternich readily waived Austrian support for a regency in return for British help in countering the nightmare of Bernadotte as ruler of France. He said that while he would personally like to see the Bourbons restored, he believed that the allies should make every effort to negotiate a peace with Napoleon, and that the government of France should ultimately be left to the French to decide. Castlereagh was happy to accept this response.[31]

Some differences remained between the two men: Castlereagh still seriously underestimated the depth of the tension between Metternich and Alexander, and naively believed that most of the disputes between the allies could be resolved by a little good will and a frank and open discussion. He wanted to exclude France from the settlement of Europe beyond her

frontiers, while Metternich was still anxious to maintain French involvement to help counter Russia. Nonetheless, their outlook was remarkably
close, largely because allied successes had greatly reduced the differences
between British and Austrian objectives, but also because they worked well
together.

The diplomacy of 1813-15 was intense and highly personal, and the
individual ability, character and compatibility of the statesmen significantly
influenced the course of events. Castlereagh may not always have shone in
the House of Commons, but he quickly established a distinctive and formidable presence in allied councils. Thus Wilhelm von Humboldt, the
Prussian diplomat, 'admired his intelligence and calm *aménité:* "He con-
ducts himself with moderation and firmness, and from the first moment was
a conciliating influence here." '[32] Even the Czar, with whom he had many
disagreements, respected Castlereagh's judgement and temper, and never
felt the same personal hostility towards him which he felt for Metternich.
Part of this success may have been due to the fact that he was a new face,
dealing with men who were weary of each other's company and foibles; but
more was due to Castlereagh's own qualities. Frederick Robinson, the
friend and junior colleague who accompanied Castlereagh on the mission,
described him with some pardonable exaggeration:

> The suavity and dignity of his manners, his habitual patience and self-
> command, his considerate tolerance of difference of opinion in others, all
> fitted him for such a task; whilst his firmness, when he knew he was right, in
> no degree detracted from the influence of his conciliatory demeanour.[33]

But Robinson tactfully understates what almost everyone else saw as
Castlereagh's leading characteristic: as one young admirer put it, 'he is
impenetrably cold', or, more charitably, 'His placidity of course never
ruffles'.[34] One wonders how much of the nineteenth-century Continental
stereotype of the English gentleman — cold and collected, austere and
reserved, intellectual and heartless — derives from Castlereagh, who soon
became the best-known British statesman of his generation in Europe. Was
he perhaps the ultimate model for Phileas Fogg?

After a few days at Basle, Castlereagh, Metternich and all the allied
headquarters moved forward to join Alexander with Schwarzenberg's army
at Langres. They found that the Czar had no interest in negotiating with
Napoleon, but wished to push the campaign forward by marching on Paris.
When Castlereagh tackled him directly on his reported support for
Bernadotte, he said that it was for the French to choose their government,
but he could not conceal his dislike for the Bourbons. Castlereagh argued
that it would be better for Europe if France were ruled by the pacific
Bourbons, and expressed the fear that while a march on Paris might bring
Napoleon to terms, 'it might also give birth to a Jacobin explosion, or to an
effort in favour of some other military chief, against which the Allies could

have no remedy'. He admitted privately to Liverpool that he shared Austrian doubts of Alexander's perseverance if his march on Paris was defeated or seriously checked — might he not then withdraw from the war or accept very inferior peace terms?[35] Castlereagh's arguments could not have carried the day by themselves, but Metternich threatened to withdraw Austria from the war if the peace negotiations did not continue, and this enabled Castlereagh to act as mediator, forcing concessions from Alexander, who found that he had little support even among his own generals and diplomats. In the end, the allies all agreed to carry on the campaign and negotiations simultaneously. Schwarzenberg was given a free hand in the conduct of operations, while Napoleon would be offered peace on the basis of the ancient frontiers of France, i.e. those in 1792, with possibly some slight augmentation of territory. Metternich would have preferred more generous terms, Alexander no terms at all, but Castlereagh could feel well pleased.[36]

Castlereagh, however, failed completely on a subsidiary issue. He wanted the allies to issue a broad statement of their plans for the settlement of Europe, hoping to reduce the scope for future disagreements. But Alexander refused to detail Russia's claims, for he had no wish to precipitate a crisis with Austria over the extent of Russian ambitions in Poland while he still needed her cooperation in France. This disagreement and the other arguments at Langres strengthened Castlereagh's growing distrust of Alexander and completed the move whereby Austria displaced Russia as Britain's most favoured ally. Given the strength of hostility towards Austria and Metternich which had grown up in Britain since the marriage of Marie Louise to Napoleon, and which had been heightened by Austrian policy throughout the first half of 1813, it was a remarkably rapid and complete transformation, especially as the events of 1812 and 1813 had made Alexander a great hero in Britain.

While the allies were arguing at Langres, Napoleon had taken the field and was advancing against Blücher. On 29 January, the day the allied ministers reached a formal agreement, the French Emperor gained the advantage at the Battle of Brienne. But three days later Blücher had his revenge at the Battle of La Rothière, bringing greatly superior forces to bear in a confused action fought amid heavy snow falls. Neither battle was decisive, though La Rothière was a damaging blow to Napoleon and forced him to fall back to rally his forces.

On 5 February 1814 the long-promised peace conference opened at Châtillon. Austria was represented by Count Stadion, Prussia by Humboldt, Russia by Razumovsky. Castlereagh had expected to represent Britain in person, but as none of the other ministers was doing so, he appointed Cathcart, Aberdeen and Stewart to represent Britain jointly. Stewart and Cathcart bitterly complained at being recalled from their armies, but Castlereagh told them that 'You have both had fighting enough to satisfy reasonable appetites'.[37] Although he would not admit it, he was unwilling to trust Aberdeen to act alone. Their performance won few plaudits, though in his memoirs Caulaincourt compliments them on being 'forthright, frankly on the side of their own interest, but straight-forward men', in contrast with 'the rest of the plenipotentiaries [who] were passion, bitterness, and vengefulness personified'.[38] Caulaincourt came to Châtillon earnestly hoping for peace, and on 9 February he wrote privately to Metternich offering to accept the ancient frontiers as the basis of negotiation in return for an immediate armistice. The Russians, however, would not agree, and Razumovsky, who had already done all he could to delay and thwart the negotiations, was recalled by the Czar. At the same time Metternich, who was with Alexander and the army at Troyes only ninety miles east of Paris, urgently summoned Castlereagh, who had been watching the negotiations at Châtillon, for the Coalition was on the point of dissolution.

The meetings and arguments at Troyes resembled those at Langres. Alexander announced his intention of marching on Paris and summoning an assembly of notables to choose a new French government, which he hinted would be dominated by Bernadotte, or possibly one of the younger Bourbons: the Duc de Berri or the Duc d'Orléans. (This reflected both his genuine contempt for Louis XVIII and his desire to ensure that any new French regime owed its existence first and foremost to him.) Metternich again threatened to withdraw from the war, but after La Rothière, Alexander felt that he could defeat Napoleon and capture Paris without Austrian help. Castlereagh had two long interviews with the Czar, urging that the allies were not willing to insist on the fall of Napoleon as a prerequisite of peace, for if they did so, Napoleon might continue the war, even if Paris fell. But Alexander would not compromise, and attempted to undermine Castlereagh's authority by circulating a letter from Count Lieven, the Russian ambassador in London, which showed that neither the Prince Regent nor Lord Liverpool was happy at the idea of making peace with Napoleon.[39]

The Coalition was saved, not by Castlereagh, nor by Metternich, but by Napoleon. After La Rothière he had withdrawn and rallied his army, receiving the invaluable reinforcement of the veteran divisions which he had recalled from Soult, and then returned to the attack. Between 10 and 14 February he inflicted three stinging defeats on Blücher's army at Champaubert, Montmirial and Vauchamps, sending it reeling back in a disorderly retreat. He then swung south and attacked the already retreating Schwarzenberg on 18 February, gaining his fourth victory in nine days. News of these defeats brought Alexander's dreams of a triumphant promenade crashing to the ground, as the allied headquarters had to fall back hastily, some fifty miles to Chaumont. The campaign was still far from lost, but memories of past defeats came flooding back and for a few days almost everyone at allied headquarters was thoroughly unnerved, with

Schwarzenberg pressing for an armistice, and Alexander confirming doubts of his resolution by urging the advantages of an early peace. Despite reassurances from Metternich and Hardenberg, Castlereagh was seriously alarmed, fearing that the allies might reduce their terms and offer Napoleon a more generous peace.[40] Gradually the danger passed as the allies recovered some confidence. They agreed to continue negotiating at Châtillon on the same terms as before: if Napoleon accepted, they would make peace and his position would be secure — unless the French themselves overthrew him. If not, the war would continue, but there must be no more talk of unilateral marches on Paris. Caulaincourt had offered to accept the ancient frontiers in return for an armistice: now he was offered both, and a preliminary peace treaty as well. But the brilliant victories had inspired Napoleon as much as they had depressed his enemies, and he now declared that he could never accept any terms which fell short of the Frankfort proposals. Caulaincourt implored him to reconsider, and the allies gave him until 10 March to give a final answer. In the meantime the war went on.

Even before the crisis had passed, Castlereagh wrote home demanding an explanation and refutation of Lieven's letter, for he knew that he could not hope to represent Britain effectively unless he was known to have the full confidence of the British government. Liverpool replied, expressing 'the greatest grief and concern' at the affair, and assuring Castlereagh that he had the cabinet's full support. He admitted that he had told Lieven 'that it would be a great blessing that we should have to conclude peace with any other person at the head of the French Government other than Buonaparte', and that the Regent had probably expressed his well-known support for the Bourbons, but he was surprised and distressed that Lieven should so misinterpret the British constitution as to believe that the private views of the sovereign and the Prime Minister would have any influence on Britain's foreign policy. Plainly Liverpool had been uncharacteristically, and the Regent characteristically, indiscreet, though it also seems likely that Alexander deliberately misinterpreted Lieven's letter to strengthen his hand in his dispute with Castlereagh.[41]

Even so, Alexander was quite correct in stating that public opinion in Britain was strongly opposed to peace with Napoleon. Castlereagh was well aware of this, for ever since he had sailed from Harwich he had been followed by a stream of letters from friends and colleagues, describing the growing bellicosity of the public mood. As early as 5 January Edward Cooke wrote that 'the general, I may say universal, principle is — no peace with Bonaparte!' A week later Liverpool confirmed that 'the disposition in this country for *any* peace with Buonaparte becomes more unfavourable every day. I hear it from all quarters and from all classes of people.' The following month he told Castlereagh, 'You can scarcely have an idea how *insane* people in this country are on the subject of any peace with Buonaparte', while William Hamilton, Cooke's colleague as under-secretary at the Foreign Office, put it more colloquially: 'The cry of No Bourbon! no peace! is become as popular, since you went away, as No song, no supper, ever was in more quiet times.'[42] The public believed that victory was in sight and were in no mood to be cheated of its fruits. J. W. Ward expressed the common feeling when he wrote:

> I suppose we shall have peace, and I shall be glad of it, and yet I own I have a pleasure in seeing this confounded people that have tormented all mankind ever since I can remember anything, and made us pay ten per cent upon our incomes, to say nothing of other taxes, plundered and insulted by a parcel of square-faced barbarians from the Wolga.[43]

Castlereagh might haughtily inform the Czar that 'acting here in discharge of a responsible trust, I must be guided by the dictates of my own judgment, and not suffer myself to be biased by any supposed wishes formed in England, in ignorance of the real circumstances upon which we were now called upon to decide', but it was clear that any peace he made with Napoleon would be bitterly unpopular in Britain.[44] Fortunately the Whigs' inclination to peace and dislike of the Bourbons were too well known for them to exploit the popular mood or, Liverpool thought, news of a treaty might bring down the government. As it was, there were signs that the Prince Regent was distancing himself from his ministers, and even rumours that he might send for Lord Wellesley.[45]

Nonetheless, the ministers continued to support Castlereagh, although it is clear that they wished that he was rather less wedded to a negotiated settlement. As early as 6 January Liverpool had warned that while the government still hoped to obtain peace with Napoleon, Castlereagh must not allow the negotiations to be indefinitely protracted.[46] Five weeks later, after describing the intensity of public feeling in Britain, he commented, 'This ought not to make any substantial difference in the course of our policy — but it renders it necessary that we should not *lower* our terms.' He then added a long and important postscript:

> The only material point on which we differ with you is as to the *overthrowing* of Buonaparte. We incline to the opinion that this event is desirable whatever might be the *immediate result* of it. No individual in France is capable of succeeding him, and if the ancient dynasty was not restored in the first instance, it would be the ultimate consequence.
>
> No Government, be it what it may, could be so bad for Europe as Buonaparte; the very hatred which is borne to him by the people of other countries, and which he knows to exist, is for the same reason an obstacle to the continuance of peace, which would not be applicable to any other Government, however implacable in other respects. I admit, however, that if France continues to support Buonaparte, we must make peace with him, and that we ought not to look to his destruction by any means which, in progress, will tend to separate the allies.[47]

This letter did not reach Castlereagh before his clash with Alexander, but he had received Liverpool's earlier warning that 'we ought at the same time not conceal from ourselves or our Allies that any peace with Buonaparte will only be a state of preparation for renewed hostilities'.[48] This suspicion was not unjustified. After the victories at Montmirial and Montereau, Napoleon wrote to his brother Joseph, 'Had I, before the last operations, concluded a peace with the old frontiers, I would have taken up arms in two years' time and have told the nation that it was not a peace, but a capitulation.' While more than a month later he told the peace-loving Caulaincourt, 'The peace they tried to force on you at Châtillon could have been nothing but a truce, for no one ever subscribes to his own disgrace: nor would I have been willing to do so.'[49]

Any attempt to overthrow Napoleon brought with it the risks of a protracted civil war, or a Jacobin revolution, or Russian domination of western Europe, but the attempt to negotiate with Napoleon and restrain him in future by a perpetual alliance surely involved at least equal dangers. Castlereagh may have been better advised to use some of his undoubted powers of persuasion to encourage the Austrians to look to a Bourbon, not a Napoleonic, France as their counterweight to Russia, while still attempting to thwart Alexander's patronage of Bernadotte, and temper the extremes of both his optimism and his pessimism. For so long as the allies continued to negotiate at Châtillon they effectively discouraged any open expression of opposition to Napoleon within France.

Castlereagh might well have adopted such a policy if he had detected any real support for the Bourbons as he travelled through eastern France. However, he found 'the people quiet everywhere, and good-humoured. . . . They spoke freely against Buonaparte to me on the journey; but I traced little disposition to an effort, and no apparent interest about the old family.'[50] Other reports confirm the weakness of Royalist sentiment in the region, but the population did not remain quiet for long. The allied forces lacked the discipline, finances and logistical services of Wellington's army; many of their soldiers had old scores to settle, while others were habituated to plundering and pillage. It was not long before their outrages produced a cycle of violence and retaliation in the allied rear which had little to do with loyalty to Napoleon or feelings of wider patriotism. This smouldering insurrection steadily grew worse as the campaign went on, and caused Schwarzenberg and his colleagues considerable anxiety.

Napoleon drew great comfort from reports of the disturbances in the allied rear, telling Caulaincourt, towards the end of March, that 'With the Burgundians in their present mood, since the looting by [the] Russians and Prussians, a victory will drive the enemy out of France. They will be massacred there — and behold, the means of treating for peace.'[51] It proved a vain hope, but by then the odds were stacked so heavily against him that Napoleon was clutching at straws. After his brilliant string of victories in the middle of February he had rejected the allied peace terms, but had been unable to exploit his military advantage. The allies had fallen back, but then rallied their forces. Bülow was summoned down from Holland in order to reinforce Blücher, who marched north to meet him. Napoleon followed, hoping to defeat Blücher in detail before Bülow could reach him, but the plan failed and he was sharply repulsed at the Battle of Laon (9–10 March).

Meanwhile the peace conference continued its futile meetings at Châtillon, leaving the delegates so bored and frustrated that they felt like murdering each other. By early March even Metternich was beginning to lose hope of peace with Napoleon. But none of the allies now expected an early end to the war, and Castlereagh at last achieved his long-cherished object of uniting the allies in a single formal alliance: the Treaty of Chaumont signed on 9 March 1814 (though dated 1 March). This committed the powers to continue the war until they had achieved their objectives — essentially the terms already presented to Napoleon at Châtillon, the restoration of Ferdinand VII, and the complete independence of Spain, Holland, Italy and Switzerland. Britain pledged to pay £5 million in subsidies over the next twelve months to be divided equally between the three main powers. (This disadvantaged Russia, who lost the disproportionate share she had received of the 1813 subsidies, and Castlereagh agreed to ask Liverpool privately if the British government might not after all consider taking over some of the Russian debt in Holland.)[52] The three Continental Powers each promised to maintain 150,000 men in the field until the end of the war. The treaty was to extend for twenty years after the conclusion of the peace, the parties guaranteeing each other's European possessions against French aggression; and this guarantee was to extend to smaller powers, including Spain, Portugal, Holland and Sweden, who were to be invited to accede to the treaty. Thus it formed a system of collective defence but, as Metternich must have noted with some disappointment, one limited to western Europe and French aggression. It also formalized the division of nations into greater and lesser powers, with the former determining the shape of postwar Europe between themselves, while the latter were limited to issues of immediate concern to them. This division was particularly hard on those lesser states with the greatest pretensions: Portugal did not expect to have a say in the affairs of Germany, but Spain felt the snub keenly, especially when her views were not taken seriously in the settlement of Italy.[53]

Castlereagh used the discussions over the treaty to stake Britain's claim to equality with the other powers. Not only was she contributing £5 million in subsidies to Russia, Prussia and Austria, which was deemed to be the equivalent of 150,000 troops, but, he argued, she had 90,000 men of her own in the field (a slight exaggeration), and was providing a further £6.6 million in subsidies to the smaller powers. On this basis her contribution was the equivalent of 425,000 men — or almost as much as the three

Continental Powers combined. 'What an extraordinary display of power!' Castlereagh exulted to William Hamilton. 'This, I trust, will put an end to any doubts as to the claim we have to an opinion on continental matters.' It is unlikely that the continental statesmen were convinced by his reasoning or quite so impressed, but there was no doubt that Britain was a useful ally.[54]

Castlereagh relied on the Treaty of Chaumont to provide security in the event of peace with Napoleon. But the danger of this was now rapidly diminishing. Napoleon had not accepted the allied terms by 10 March when their offer expired. Metternich managed to keep the conference open until the 19th, but Napoleon, perhaps fearing that his throne would not survive the admission of defeat, placed all his hopes on the slender chance of military victory. With the ending of the Châtillon conference the allies began to receive secret overtures from Paris. Some came from committed royalists, but the most important, veiled and discreet, came from Talleyrand, who wanted to act as midwife to the next regime whatever form it should take.

At the same time, the balance of military operations had begun to swing in favour of the allies. Blücher's army had been paralysed for a week after Laon owing to the mental and physical prostration of its commander, but when Napoleon struck south at Schwarzenberg he was defeated at Arcis-sur-Aube (20–21 March). The allied armies then converged, Schwarzenberg defeating Marmont and Mortier at Fère-Champenoise on the 25th. Napoleon struck boldly at the allied lines of communication, expecting them to retreat while he would be able to collect his garrisons from the fortresses on the Rhine. His sudden move caused confusion in the allied rear, and Castlereagh, Metternich, Hardenberg and the Emperor Francis were cut off from Schwarzenberg and forced to escape to Dijon. Alexander and Frederick William remained with the main army, where they received intercepted dispatches revealing Napoleon's plans and a report to Napoleon from the Minister of Police:

> The treasury, arsenals, and powder stores are empty. We have no resources left. The population is discouraged and discontented. It wants peace at any price. Enemies of the imperial government are sustaining and fomenting popular agitation. Still latent, it will become impossible to suppress unless the Emperor succeeds in keeping the Allies away from Paris.[55]

Schwarzenberg and the other generals wanted to follow Napoleon in order to drive him from their lines of supply and, at least in the case of Gneisenau, seek a decisive battle with the enemy's main force. But Alexander overruled them and ordered the army to advance on Paris, arguing that the threat to the capital would force Napoleon to hurry back, and that even if it did not, the capture of Paris would more than balance any damage Napoleon could do to the army's communications. For once in his life, Alexander's intervention in military affairs was both shrewd and successful. On 28 March

Schwarzenberg and Blücher linked forces, and on the 29th they were before Paris. There was heavy fighting on the 30th as Marmont and Mortier turned at bay on the outskirts of Paris. The troops fought bravely but were so heavily outnumbered that the result was never in doubt. At 2 a.m. on 31 March Marmont signed the capitulation of Paris and withdrew his forces south-east towards Fontainebleau. The Empress Marie Louise and her son, together with many of the officials and prominent citizens who remained loyal to Napoleon, had already left the city, but many others whose loyalty was less certain, including Talleyrand, remained.

Meanwhile at Dijon, on 26 March, Castlereagh and the other ministers received news of the declaration of Bordeaux. This had made an immense sensation in London and had led the government to inform Castlereagh that he must not now make peace with Napoleon unless it was unavoidable, while Liverpool and Bathurst seriously considered continuing the war even if all the allies had made peace.[56] Fortunately this idea was never put to the test. Austria had already accepted the need to continue the war to the bitter end, and the news from Bordeaux removed the last Austrian scruples about recognizing the Bourbons. On 28 March the envoys and ministers of Britain, Prussia, Austria, Russia, Hanover, Holland and Spain drank toasts to Count Lynch, Louis XVIII and the royalist cause, and two days later an Austrian envoy was sent to the Comte d'Artois at Nancy.[57] But Dijon is nearly 200 miles from Paris where the final act of the drama would be played out, and the allied ministers still did not know whether the Czar would support the Bourbons or some other party.

At 11 o'clock in the morning of 31 March 1814, less than two years after Napoleon had launched his invasion of Russia, the Emperor Alexander made his triumphal entry into Paris, the city of his dreams. On one side rode Prince Schwarzenberg, on the other King Frederick William of Prussia; before them went Russia's elite cavalry in full parade uniform, behind came an enormous suite of up to 1,000 officers, followed by the whole army. Among the suite was a handful of British officers including the two military diplomats, 'Lord Cathcart in scarlet regimentals, his low flat cocked hat forming a striking contrast to all the others. Sir Charles Stewart was covered with orders and conspicuous by his fancy dress, evidently composed of what he deemed every army's best.'[58] A huge crowd looked on with mixed emotions: some were sullen and angry, a few were jubilant, while most were immensely relieved that the city had not become a battlefield and were happy to enjoy the spectacle. The allies had called upon the citizens of Paris to emulate the example of Bordeaux and thus bring peace to the world; and in response to this none too subtle hint there was a fair sprinkling of white cockades among the crowd with even a few National Guards wearing them.[59]

After the ceremonies Alexander took up residence as Talleyrand's guest in his palatial house on the corner of rue St Florentin and rue de Rivoli. The

13. The Allied Bakers or The Corsican Toad in the Hole
Design by G. Humphrey, executed by George Cruikshank, 1 April 1814, B.M. Cat. no. 12,206

Three allied generals led by Blücher prepare to thrust a tiny bound Napoleon into the allied oven. The Emperor Francis of Austria (with a weathercock on his hat) pretends to struggle to open the oven door, while in fact he impedes their progress. Wellington comes up from the right carrying two pies, one marked 'Soult pie', the other 'Bourdeaux', and says, 'Shove alltogether [*sic*] Gentlemen! D____ me shove door & all in!'

An interesting satire on allied dissensions in 1814 and Austria's desire for a negotiated peace. The absence of Alexander is surprising.

tide was now running very strongly in favour of the Bourbons, yet even at this late hour, if Alexander had indicated a strong and determined preference for one of the alternatives — a regency, or possibly even Bernadotte — he would probably have carried the day, for Schwarzenberg and Frederick William were too weak to oppose him effectively, while Castlereagh and Metternich were far away. Instead, Alexander allowed Talleyrand to guide him gently from one step to the next, summoning the French senate, or rather those members who could be relied upon, and there discovering that, after all, France was longing for the return of the Bourbons.

As Alexander predicted, Napoleon hurried back to try to save Paris, but he arrived a few hours too late. For a week he remained collecting his army at Fontainebleau. At first he planned to continue the campaign, but in a famous scene Ney, Lefebvre, Moncey, Oudinot and Macdonald informed him that the army would not march, and demanded that he abdicate for the sake of France. On 4 April Napoleon agreed to abdicate in favour of his son, but although Alexander was tempted for a moment, it was now too late, and that night the defection of Marmont and his corps showed that the army was not solid in its opposition to the Bourbons. On 6 April Napoleon abdicated unconditionally. The long war was over.

18

The Year of Revelry,
April 1814–March 1815

Paris in spring, London in summer, Vienna in autumn and winter: 1814 passed in a whirl of gaiety, celebrations and rejoicings, but under the surface the struggle for the spoils of victory continued unabated. Castlereagh, Metternich and Hardenberg did not leave Dijon until 7 April, or reach Paris until the 10th. Perhaps they genuinely believed that the roads were impassable, or perhaps they did not wish to play too obvious a role in the restoration of the Bourbons; but whatever the reason for their tardiness, it left Alexander with a free hand to come to terms with Napoleon and take the lead in laying the foundations of the new regime in France. The allied ministers were not pleased with what they found when they reached Paris. Alexander, continuing to play the part of the magnanimous conqueror, had promised Napoleon the full sovereignty of the island of Elba off the coast of Tuscany, recognition of his title as Emperor, a pension of two million francs a year to be paid by the French government, and an additional settlement on the Empress Marie Louise. Metternich and Castlereagh both protested, but it was important to remove Napoleon from Fontainebleau as quickly as possible, the treaty was ready to be signed, and it was clear that any substantial changes would take time and involve a confrontation with the Czar. Castlereagh therefore merely refused to recognize Napoleon's title as Emperor, which Britain, unlike the Continental Powers, had never acknowledged. He saw all the dangers of giving Napoleon an island so close to both Italy and France, but could not think of an alternative which would be any better. Napoleon himself seriously suggested exile as a private gentleman in England, but a startled Castlereagh did not feel that he could encourage the idea. Fouché suggested exile to America, and Metternich thought an island in the western hemisphere the best solution, but so long as Britain was at war with the United States she was unlikely to agree to such proposals. And so, *faute de mieux*, Elba was accepted, with consequences which are well known.[1]

Alexander assiduously courted popularity in Paris: he praised the army and its generals, encouraged liberal politicians, and, by repeated calls, drew the ex-Empress Josephine from her retirement, for a last glittering hour at the head of society before her sudden death at the end of May. He guaranteed the new French constitution in the name of the allies, before it was drafted, and two of his closest advisers — Nesselrode and Pozzo di Borgo — were on the committee which drew it up. And he encouraged the belief that the allies would grant France significantly more territory than the 'ancient frontiers' of 1792. These attentions succeeded in endearing him to the French public and in irritating the allied ministers, but the Bourbons were unimpressed. They did not forget his lack of sympathy for their claim to the French throne, or forgive his marked attentions to the Bonapartist party, and they resented the imposition of the new constitution which they regarded as excessively liberal. When Louis XVIII left Dover at the end of April there was a hidden barb, which Alexander saw and resented, in his gracious thanks to the Prince Regent: 'It is to the counsels of your Royal Highness, to this glorious country, and to the steadfastness of its inhabitants that I attribute, next after the will of Providence, the re-establishment of my house on the throne of my ancestors.' Events proved that this was no empty courtesy, and that Liverpool was right when he told Castlereagh that Louis was inclined to trust Britain, and after her, Austria, more than any of the other allies. Alexander's playing had pleased the gallery, but failed to convince his most important critic.[2]

Despite the tension between the allies, the peacemaking at Paris proceeded fairly smoothly, delayed less by any real problems than by the social whirl, and by waiting for Louis XVIII, who did not arrive until 3 May. The allies all agreed on the need for a moderate peace to conciliate the French, help establish the new government more securely, and avoid lasting resentment. While the basis of the peace would be the terms offered at Châtillon, the allied ministers went out of their way to soften these terms with concessions, while giving way on other points. Thus while France was to be reduced essentially to the frontiers of 1792 the inclusion of Avignon and some territory in Savoy brought her an additional 500,000 inhabitants. All the conquered French colonies were returned except Mauritius, Tobago and St Lucia, which was being rather more generous than the ministers in London would have liked, though they yielded to Castlereagh's urging on the subject. They even agreed to pay Sweden £1 million to give up her claim to Guadeloupe so that it too could be returned to France. No demand was made for the return of all the works of art, looted on Napoleon's orders from all over Europe, which filled the Louvre and adorned the public squares of Paris; and the financial settlement was equally generous. There were to be no reparations, although Napoleon had always extorted huge sums, and the debts which he owed to the Prussian and other governments for the supplies requisitioned for the campaign of 1812 were cancelled. The British government waived its substantial claim for the cost of maintaining French prisoners of war (which far exceeded the cost of British prisoners in France), so that the only financial obligation imposed on the new government in Paris was to honour debts incurred to private individuals.[3]

The allies got little thanks for their moderation. Possibly because there had been no final, climactic battle outside Paris, many of Napoleon's supporters, especially in the army, did not feel that they had been defeated, and attributed the allied success to scheming politicians in Paris and Marmont's treachery. Even the new French government was inclined to haggle over the allied terms and demanded substantial gains of territory in Belgium. Castlereagh rejected this peremptorily, and warned against the territorial ambitions which had been the cause of so many previous wars. In the end Talleyrand had little choice but to accept the allied terms, and the Peace of Paris was signed on 30 May 1814.[4]

During these negotiations the allies made some progress in settling the wider affairs of Europe, although not on the most difficult issues. The union of Belgium and the Netherlands was agreed, together with the new kingdom's frontier with France, and Britain promised to return many of the Dutch colonies she held, including the fabulously rich Dutch East Indies. Britain retained the Cape of Good Hope, however, paying the Netherlands £2 million in compensation, which was to be used to construct fortresses along the frontier with France. The naval squadron in Antwerp proved to be less formidable than Britain had feared — the ships had been built of unseasoned wood — and Castlereagh persuaded the cabinet to allow France to retain two-thirds of the completed vessels, the remainder going to the Netherlands. There was general agreement that Austria should be the dominant power in northern Italy, receiving Venetia and Lombardy, while Piedmont would absorb Genoa, in part as compensation for the loss of some of Savoy to France. These agreements were all included in the peace treaty. Central and southern Italy remained unsettled. The Pope would be restored to Rome, but the extent of his possessions remained open to negotiation, while a question mark still hung over Murat's possession of Naples. The British government was very pleased with the settlement of the Low Countries and northern Italy, seeing in both the creation of strong checks to future French expansion. The Opposition, however, strongly criticised the fate of Genoa, arguing that the ancient republic, abolished almost twenty years before by Napoleon, should be revived.

But such criticism came later, and the immediate reaction in Britain to the news of Napoleon's downfall and the end of the war was unbridled joy. London celebrated with 'a general and splendid illumination for three successive nights . . . [complete with] every device that the taste and invention of the exhibitors could supply'. In the Strand, for example, was a large transparency of Napoleon 'sitting at a table building towers with cards: while Wellington gives a puff over Napoleon's shoulder that sends the cards flying'.[5] The ministers and the Regent naturally took credit for the success of their policies, while Wilberforce looked back and wished that his old friend Pitt had lived to see the day. The only disappointment was the provision for Napoleon, with Palmerston expressing the common view when he wrote that, 'I am glad we have had nothing to do with that most absurd Treaty with the Ex-Emperor', but this was not enough to mar the pleasures of victory.[6]

The Opposition was divided in its reaction. Grenville was naturally pleased, but Grey had continued to urge a negotiated settlement with Napoleon until well into February, and opposed the return of the Bourbons — although not publicly, as family affairs kept him at home in Northumberland. Brougham characteristically welcomed the peace, not for any national benefit Britain gained, or even for the lessening in human suffering, but because the consequent reduction in the armed forces would curtail Royal patronage and open the way for the Whigs to overthrow the ministers, whom he described — with remarkable lack of acuteness — as 'a good, quiet, easily-beaten set of blockheads'. Lord Auckland, while unable to overcome completely his habitual pessimism, was both more honest and more perceptive: 'It certainly is a blessing of incalculable importance to be freed from the predominating and malignant energies of Buonaparte. But I am not so clearly convinced that "all the rest is plain sailing".'[7] More surprising, but equally creditable, was Whitbread's reaction:

> A Limited Monarchy in France, with Religious Liberty, a Free Press and Legislative Bodies such as have been stipulated for before the Recognition of the Bourbons, leave their Restoration without the possibility of Regret in the Mind of any Man who is a Lover of Liberty and a friend to his kind. Paris safe, Bonaparte suffered to depart, after the experiment had been fully tried of effecting a Peace with him, upon terms such as he was mad to reject — 'Tis more than I dared to hope![8]

Not everyone was satisfied, however, and at Holland House there was much regret both at the dethronement of Napoleon and the restoration of the Bourbons. On receiving an expression of these views from John Allen, the Hollands' librarian, Sydney Smith, replied in a letter which deserves to be quoted at length.

> I cannot enter at all into your feelings about the Bourbons, nor can I attend to so remote an evil as the encoragement [sic] of superstitious attachment to kings when the present evil of a military Monarchy, or of thirty years more of war, is before my eyes. I want to get rid of this great disturber of human happiness, and I scarcely know any price too great to effect it. . . .
> . . . How can any man stop in the midst of the stupendous joy of getting rid of Buonaparte, and prophesy the little piddling evils that will result from restoring the Bourbons? Nor am I quite certain that I don't wish Paris burnt and France laid waste by Cossacks for revenge, and for security. The most important of all objects is the independence of Europe: it has been twice nearly destroyed by the French; it is menaced from no other quarter; and the people must be identified with the sovereign. There is no help for it; it will

teach them in future to hang kings who set up for conquerors. I will not believe that the Bourbons have no party in France. My only knowledge of politics is from the York paper; yet nothing shall convince me that the people are not heartily tired of Buonaparte, and ardently wish for the cessation of the conscription; that is, for the Bourbons.[9]

The mass of the population did not need such arguments to justify their joy: they celebrated the triumphs of their arms and their allies, and the downfall of their enemy, with a patriotism nourished by twenty years of war. The details of the peace terms, with one exception, mattered little to them, for John Bull cared nothing for Genoa and such issues; but his sensitivities had been aroused by the long campaign to abolish the slave trade, and in this respect he found the peace treaty bitterly disappointing. Castlereagh had worked hard in Paris to persuade the French to agree to the immediate abolition of the trade, but without success. Having lived in England, Louis XVIII was aware of the strength of British public opinion on the issue, and Talleyrand was also personally sympathetic, but otherwise French opinion united solidly against the demand, seeing in it nothing more than an underhand British plot to disadvantage the French colonies and commerce. Faced with such intense opposition, Castlereagh agreed to a compromise by which the French promised to abolish the trade within five years. In doing so he totally misjudged the reaction at home despite ample warning, for on 2 May the Commons had unanimously passed a resolution calling on all the Continental Powers to renounce the trade.[10] When Castlereagh returned to England in June he was strongly criticized in Parliament on the issue, and Wilberforce and his supporters organized a campaign which soon produced 800 petitions containing almost one million signatures, urging the government to offer further concessions to secure the immediate abolition of the trade. The government listened and obeyed, and for the next six months or more this is a persistent thread in British diplomacy. Holland, Denmark and Sweden readily agreed to abolition, leaving only France, Portugal and Spain. Castlereagh offered Spain £800,000 to agree to follow the French example and promise to end the trade after five years, but although the Spanish government was desperately short of money, it dared not risk encouraging the independence movements in its American colonies. France rejected an offer of Trinidad or a large sum of money in return for immediate abolition, but by the end of the year had agreed to prohibit slaving north of the equator; and Portugal eventually accepted a similar restriction in return for £300,000 and other substantial concessions. But it was Napoleon in 1815 who finally ended the French trade, and it was not until 1820 that Spain and Portugal followed suit. In all these negotiations the British ministers acted from personal conviction, spurred on by the force of public opinion. They sacrificed tangible national advantages for a humanitarian ideal, but in doing so they reflected the wishes of their countrymen.[11]

The culmination of the peace festivities came in June with the visit of the allied sovereigns to London. On Castlereagh's advice, the Prince Regent had invited the Emperor Alexander early in 1814, and later extended this to all the allied rulers, their ministers and generals. Most were keen to come. London was reputed to be the wealthiest city in the world, the capital of Napoleon's staunchest and most invulnerable enemy, and a much more fitting location for an uninhibited celebration of victory than Paris, where good manners and tact required a certain restraint. Frederick William of Prussia, who has been described as having 'the instincts and interests of a package tourist', happily accepted, and brought with him Marshal Blücher, 'always ready to drink a bumper and make uncouth speeches, which were translated with tact and bonhomie by Sir Charles Stewart'.[12] As a result Blücher soon became the great favourite of the London crowd, displacing their early idol Platov, leader of the Cossacks, who was isolated by his inability to speak anything other than Russian, and whose men were 'so worried by curious intruders, that "they could not bear to be looked at!"'[13]

But Alexander was the greatest star of all, at least at first. A huge crowd turned out to meet him at London Bridge on 7 June, but at the last moment he changed his route to avoid them. It was the first of many graceless and at times perverse actions which soon earned him the bitter enmity of the Prince Regent, and the irritation of the ministers, while diminishing his popularity with the mob. He rejected the Regent's offer of St James's Palace, preferring to stay with his sister, who was already installed in the Pulteney Hotel off Piccadilly. The Grand Duchess Catherine was a strong-minded young woman who had already offended many in London, and who helped prejudice her brother against the Prince Regent. She cultivated a friendship with Princess Charlotte and was credited with an important role in the breakdown of Charlotte's engagement to the Hereditary Prince of Orange at the end of June. (The true reason for the collapse of the marriage plans — Charlotte's infatuation with Prince Frederick of Prussia, nephew of King Frederick William — was only revealed in 1949.)[14] But while Catherine certainly helped lead her brother astray, this hardly explains the extent of his folly. Not content with repeatedly snubbing the Prince Regent, he was rude to the ministers and assiduously courted leading members of the Opposition (who remained unimpressed), and even had to be dissuaded from visiting Princess Caroline — an act which would have earned him the Regent's eternal hatred. Yet the government was eager to pay him every honour and attention, and he was pointedly given priority over all the other visitors, including Frederick William. Whether it was due to lingering resentment at his quarrels with Castlereagh, jealousy at the sight of Britain's prosperity, political miscalculation, or simply that after two years of intense strain he relaxed too completely, the impression he made in London was disastrous. In a few short weeks he squandered the good will which Russia had acquired throughout British society by her role in the defeat of Napoleon in 1812, 1813 and 1814. Castlereagh would now have far less difficulty persuading his colleagues, the Regent, and if necessary the public, of the dangers of Russian ambitions.

This was in marked contrast to the Austrians, whose standing rose considerably during these weeks. The Emperor Francis chose to return to Vienna rather than visit London. He hated public occasions, and probably recognized that he was still regarded by the British public — that sophisticated and well-informed judge of international affairs — as an ogre who had sacrificed his daughter to Napoleon. Instead Metternich represented Austria with grace and discretion, courting the Prince Regent as the architect of Napoleon's downfall and the arbiter of Europe (Metternich's vanity never blinded him to other people's love of flattery), praising the ministers and charming their wives, but shunning the Opposition. Nonetheless, he still had to contend with a great deal of residual distrust even within the cabinet, for none of the other ministers approached Castlereagh in his sympathy for Austria's outlook.

These shifts in perception were far more important than any actual negotiations in London, for the constant round of festivities left little time for serious discussions. It was therefore agreed to postpone the outstanding issues until the Congress which had been announced for Vienna in the autumn.

Wellington played a leading role in the later stages of the victory celebrations. After Napoleon's abdication and Soult's submission he had paid a fleeting visit to Paris to consult with Castlereagh, then to Madrid where he had unsuccessfully attempted to persuade Ferdinand to moderate his hostility to the *liberales*, before returning to Bordeaux where, on 14 June, he paid a cool farewell to his army. He reached Dover on 23 June and was immediately plunged into the whirl of festivities. The crowds cheered, Oxford made him an Honorary Doctor of Laws, and White's held a splendid masked ball in his honour. More formally the Common Council of the City of London held a splendid banquet at the Guildhall and there was a grand thanksgiving service at St Paul's. On 28 June he took his seat in the House of Lords as Viscount, Earl, Marquess and — since 3 May — Duke of Wellington. With the coming of peace the government had given him this final honour, and Parliament added its mite of thanks in the form of a grant of £400,000 — an award which even Whitbread applauded.[15]

Although it was five years since Wellington had been in England, or seen his wife and two young sons, he had no intention of remaining idle in order to taste the dubious pleasures of domestic felicity. Castlereagh had already offered him the Paris embassy which he had accepted with genuine surprise and gratification, commenting with unwonted modesty, 'I should not have thought myself qualified'. Castlereagh, however, believed that Wellington's 'military name would give him and us the greatest ascendency', and certainly Wellington's warm support for the Bourbon cause ensured that he would be most acceptable to Louis XVIII and his court. Nonetheless, it was a strange appointment, and one must question Castlereagh's judgement in making a victorious general the ambassador to the vanquished foe, especially a foe as proud and sensitive as the French.[16]

Wellington took up his position towards the end of August and performed his official functions diligently and well; but in private he was indiscreet, and his liaisons with several women, including at least one of Napoleon's former mistresses, caused a scandal. His presence antagonized old soldiers and conspiring Bonapartists, and added another explosive element to the seething discontent in Paris in the autumn of 1814. The British government soon became concerned both that his presence might be doing more harm than good, and by reports of plots to assassinate him. Liverpool wrote begging him to come home, but Wellington procrastinated and did not leave until January, when Paris was much calmer and he was needed to replace Castlereagh in Vienna.[17]

While Wellington was celebrating in London and enjoying the delights of Paris, much of his army was crossing the Atlantic, for the American war continued, and with the defeat of Napoleon the British were free to take the offensive. Altogether nearly 20,000 British troops headed westward from Europe in the spring and summer of 1814, most, though not all, of them veterans of the Peninsula. About half of this force was directed to Canada, and the first battalions reached Quebec in June. But before the reinforcements could reach Upper Canada, the Americans had launched a determined attack on the Niagara front. They won the Battle of Chippawa on 5 July 1814, but lacking clear naval superiority on Lake Ontario, were unable to exploit their advantage. The British regrouped and counter-attacked, leading to the hard-fought but indecisive Battle of Lundy's Lane on 25 July. The Americans then fell back almost to the frontier, but kept a strong garrison in Fort Erie, beating off a British assault on 15 August. But then, in October, Britain gained complete control of Lake Ontario with the launch of the 102-gun *St Lawrence*, and early in November the Americans blew up Fort Erie and withdrew across the frontier. The fighting around Niagara in 1814 had been as indecisive and fruitless as in earlier years of the war, but the American troops had fought surprisingly well, showing much greater discipline and determination than previously.[18]

Further east, Prevost was under orders to invade the United States and seize either Plattsburg or Sackett's Harbor, which the British government regarded as the obvious American bases for any serious invasion of Canada. The campaign was not an attempt to conquer the United States, but rather to gain positions which might be returned in a peace settlement in exchange for modifications to the U.S.-Canadian border or restrictions on American naval forces on the Lakes. This limited objective reflected British concern at the practical problems facing any extended invasion of the United States. If the *St Lawrence* had been ready sooner, Prevost might have attacked Sackett's Harbor and the campaign could well have been a success; as it was, he had little choice but to advance south down the western shore of Lake

Champlain towards Plattsburg. The great disadvantage of this was that the British naval forces on Lake Champlain were slightly inferior to the Americans, and the campaign soon showed that while Prevost was an able administrator and sound strategist, he was an indifferent and uninspiring commander in the field. The Americans concentrated their defence at Plattsburg and it was there, on 11 September, that their naval squadron completely defeated the British ships. Prevost was convinced that without control of the Lake his campaign would be unsustainable, and he therefore abandoned his attack on Plattsburg and retreated back to Canada. The inglorious end of the campaign ruined Prevost's reputation, but although a more dashing and vigorous commander might have been more successful, the wisdom of advancing without naval superiority was always doubtful, and it seems clear that Prevost would not have done so if it had not been for his orders from London.

The invasion from Canada was only one part of a three-part British attempt to bring the war home to the United States. The second leg of this policy was an escalation in the war of raids on the American coastline which had begun in 1812. The naval squadron had received substantial reinforcements both of ships and of 2,500 troops from Wellington's army. Their most famous exploit was a short campaign in Chesapeake Bay in which they defeated a hastily collected American army at Bladensburg (24 August), occupied Washington and destroyed its public buildings (24–25 August) and were repulsed from Baltimore (13–14 September). The only military benefit of the campaign was the destruction of the virtually useless squadron of gunboats at Benedict, and while the threat to Washington produced some immediate despondency and war-weariness, in the longer run its destruction only hardened American opinion and strengthened the hand of Britain's European critics.[19]

The third British thrust was directed at New Orleans, and British objectives here have been the subject of some debate. New Orleans and Louisiana had been in American hands for only just over a decade and the British government was prepared to countenance, though not encourage, secession if it had strong local support. It has been argued that combined with British support for Indian claims further north, this was intended to create a permanent barrier to the westward expansion of the United States.[20] However, it seems more likely that the British government simply sought a striking victory to drive the Americans to make concessions in the peace negotiations, and to satisfy public opinion. If New Orleans chose to be independent or revert to Spain, the British government would not be displeased to see the United States permanently weakened, but it was seeking an early end to the war, not a vast and troublesome new responsibility. In any case the question is hypothetical, for the expedition was completely mismanaged from the outset, and the army of about 6,000 men was defeated, and its commander Major-General Sir Edward Pakenham (Wellington's brother-in-law) killed, at the Battle of New

Orleans on 8 January 1815. It was the worst British defeat in open battle for many years.

From the middle of 1814, while the fighting continued in America, there were peace negotiations at Ghent in Belgium. At first progress was slow, for the Americans had ludicrously unrealistic instructions — detailing the concessions they were to demand, rather than those they were to make — while the British naturally wished to await the result of their offensives. But by the middle of October the Americans had received fresh instructions, and the British learnt of the failure of Prevost's campaign. Liverpool was concerned with the cost of the war when the clamour in Parliament was for retrenchment, while Castlereagh regarded it as a tiresome embarrassment when he was fully occupied with infinitely more important problems at Vienna. When Wellington was consulted he warned that a decisive military advantage could only be gained with lengthy and expensive preparations, which he evidently did not think were warranted. Liverpool agreed, telling Castlereagh on 18 November that the government had decided not to continue the war with the hope of gaining any territorial advantages. Even so, there were another five weeks of bargaining before the peace was signed, although the final treaty was a remarkably empty document with no mention of impressment or the Orders in Council, no alteration to the U.S.-Canadian border, or restriction on American naval activity on the Lakes, and only token protection for Britain's Indian allies (many of whom had already come to terms with the Americans, often changing sides in the process). Essentially the Peace of Ghent (24 December 1814) confirmed the *status quo ante bellum*; neither side gained anything tangible from the war, though it has been argued that the experience helped unify the American nation. Certainly the United States government escaped very lightly from one of the most foolish and irresponsible wars ever undertaken by a democracy. As one American critic had said in 1812, 'for the Government to go to war in our present unprepared state, would be little short of an act of treason'.[21]

The negotiations at Ghent were overshadowed by the simultaneous negotiations at Vienna for the settlement of Europe. And although there was no formal connection between the two, they could not be completely isolated: problems at Vienna encouraged the British government to make concessions at Ghent, partly to free their hands, and partly to avoid the risk that Russia, or one of the other Continental Powers, might take up the American cause.[22] Similarly, the news of the peace with the United States made a sensation at Vienna and significantly altered the course of the negotiations.

The Congress of Vienna is, of course, famous for its festivities, its glittering pageantry, its balls, its gossip and its amours. The Austrian Emperor spared no expense in providing lavish entertainments for the illustrious visitors who, by one count, included 'the heads of five reigning dynasties and 216 princely families'.[23] There was plenty of time for them to dance and gossip and intrigue, for the vast majority were almost entirely excluded from the inner councils, where the leading statesmen and a few trusted assistants fought out in private the most contentious issues. Not that the leading statesmen avoided the dances, gossip and amours: Metternich and Alexander both indulged themselves at times, apparently even paying court to the same lady. Castlereagh complained, 'We are . . . impeded by the succession of fêtes and private Balls — they waste a great deal of valuable time, and prevent P[rince] Metternich from giving his mind to subjects that ought to engross him.' But it is clear that in general Metternich worked extremely hard and that his other activities did not dissipate his diplomatic energy.[24]

Castlereagh himself was sufficiently prudent and happily married to attract scandal for nothing worse than wearing his diamond George (part of the Garter insignia) around his neck — though even this was enough for Bathurst's son Lord Apsley, who was in Vienna, to inform all and sundry that Castlereagh was Irish not English.[25] Charles Stewart, now Baron Stewart and ambassador to Austria, created much more fun for the gossips with the sort of behaviour which, in more recent times, has made the Anglo-Saxon tourist so beloved on the Continent, including throwing a coachman into the Danube; but it was all put down to high spirits and English eccentricity and no one took lasting offence. The rest of the British delegation were much quieter. Cathcart was there, but played little role in the negotiations. Castlereagh was assisted chiefly by Edward Cooke (under-secretary at the Foreign Office) until his health broke down, and by the diligent and efficient Lord Clancarty. More important than either, however, was Count Münster who, despite having rather different objectives as Hanover's representative, acted as a close ally of Castlereagh.

Castlereagh arrived in Vienna on 13 September with very broad powers and no formal instructions to constrain his discretion. Britain's particular objects on the Continent had already been largely achieved, though there remained some outstanding matters of detail, for example the eastern frontier of the Netherlands, and the question of whether the Scheldt would be open to navigation, in which she felt an interest. There was also the fate of Naples, for the new French and Spanish governments did not conceal their desire to overthrow Murat and reunite the Kingdom of the Two Sicilies. The British government felt some sympathy for this idea, though it did not wish to become directly involved or risk offending Metternich, and it was uneasy at the prospect of a French army returning to Italy so soon. On other matters, including the contentious Polish and Saxon questions, the ministers were content to rely on Castlereagh's judgement, although their preference was to attempt to resolve the problems by conciliation, and certainly to avoid anything which might lead Britain into a fresh war.

But Castlereagh took a more robust view, warning Liverpool in November of the dangers of Alexander's ambition:

his Imperial Majesty does not rise in our estimation, either as a man, or as a politician; and you must make up your mind to watch him, and to resist him if necessary as another Buonaparte . . . acquiescence will not keep him back, nor will opposition accelerate his march. His Imperial Majesty is never more condescending than to those who speak plainly but respectfully to him; and if I were to speculate on the course most likely to save your money, and to give you the longest interval of peace with such a character, I should say that it would lie in never suffering him for a moment to doubt your readiness to support the continental Powers against his ambitious encroachments. . . . With such a personage at the head of between forty and fifty millions of people prone to, and adapted to war, you cannot afford to dissolve your continental relations, unless you are prepared to acquiesce in a domination that would very soon assume the character of that from which we have escaped, and would certainly not degenerate from it in a disposition to circumscribe the power of Great Britain.[26]

Even allowing for some exaggeration in a private letter written to convince a trusted colleague, this shows the extent to which Castlereagh had come to share Metternich's view of the dangers of Russian expansion, and while the two statesmen differed on some questions, they maintained the alliance they had forged at the beginning of the year. Metternich's object remained the same as in 1813: to build up a strong central bloc, excluding both France and Russia from the affairs of Germany. To achieve this he was happy to cooperate with Britain, which had no territorial ambitions on the Continent, but which, through Hanover, had a legitimate but limited interest in the affairs of Germany. Central to Metternich's plans, however, was Prussia, where Hardenberg shared some of his disquiet at Russia's ambitions in Poland, but whose own ambitions in Saxony were unacceptable to many in Vienna. The interplay between these interests, hopes and fears forms the principal, though not the only drama of the Congress. Among the subplots which influenced the final result were Talleyrand's attempts to have France recognized as an equal power by the other four, and conflicting plans put forward by Prussia and Austria for the settlement of Germany. But dozens of other issues competed for the attention of the statesmen, ranging from freedom of the press to the border dispute over Olivenza between Portugal and Spain, from the civil rights of Jews in Lübeck and Hamburg to the abolition of the slave trade.[27]

But despite all the activity which such issues created, there is no doubt that the central problem addressed at Vienna was the settlement of Europe, or that the single most important actor was Alexander. The Czar arrived at Vienna towards the end of September, and finally, after nearly two years of studied reticence, outlined his plans for Poland. He proposed to recreate the Kingdom of Poland, including in it the Polish provinces which Russia had acquired in the partitions, much of Prussian Poland, and that part of Austrian Poland (the Tarnopol circle) which Russia had gained in 1809.

The Kingdom would be granted a constitution and would be bound indissolubly to Russia through a union of the Crowns. Ever since his youth, Alexander had sympathized with the aspirations of Polish patriots, thanks to the influence of his close friend Prince Adam Czartoryski. But it is not clear that his motives were purely idealistic, for his proposals would bring Russia into the heart of central Europe. Alexander's intentions may have been entirely defensive, to secure Russia from a repetition of the invasion of 1812; but good intentions were no guarantee for either Prussia or Austria, and the frontiers which Alexander proposed for them were indefensible, especially as the great strong-points of Thorn and Cracow would be in Russian Poland. Further, if successful, the re-establishment of the Polish Kingdom would give Russia ten million loyal Polish subjects, while leaving five million disaffected ones in Prussia and Austria.[28]

In the face of this threat Hardenberg, Metternich and Castlereagh worked to construct a common front. Hardenberg was the most reluctant to oppose openly Russia's claims, but agreed when Metternich grudgingly promised to support Prussia's claims to Saxony and to the important German fortress of Mainz, provided they succeeded in Poland. Castlereagh warmly supported this arrangement and took a prominent role in the confrontation with Alexander which followed, though he would not give Metternich the assurances he sought of military support if the crisis led to war. But all three ministers underestimated Alexander's determination and strength of feeling on the question. While always relatively civil to Castlereagh, he attacked Metternich in a tirade so violent that the normally assured Austrian — who had plenty of experience of Napoleon's outbursts — left the room deeply shaken. Alexander then launched a campaign to discredit Metternich with the Emperor Francis and secure his dismissal, though without success. Hardenberg was much more vulnerable, for Frederick William felt a loyalty amounting to subservience to the Czar, and not only refused to support his Chancellor, but looked on while Alexander gave Hardenberg a brutal tongue-lashing. With the Prussian King issuing positive orders that his ministers stop conspiring against Russia, the opposition to Alexander's plans appeared to be broken. But the crisis dragged on for another month or more, with Hardenberg now attempting to act as intermediary, while some Austrian soldiers talked of war. Alexander made some concessions, offering to make Thorn and Cracow free cities, and gradually the focus of attention shifted from Poland to Saxony.[29]

The British government was dismayed at the prominent role which Castlereagh had taken in the Polish negotiations. Liverpool believed that Russia would find Poland a very uneasy possession, causing more problems than it was worth. British opinion favoured a restoration of Poland, preferably as a completely independent kingdom, but if the Poles found the Russian solution acceptable, it seemed better than repartition. With little or no chance of a completely satisfactory outcome, Liverpool was 'inclined to think that the less we have to do with it, except as regards giving our opinion, the better'.[30] Talk of war seriously alarmed the ministers in London, and Liverpool cited the American war, the huge debt left after the last war, and the unsettled state of Europe and France in particular, in pleading with Castlereagh for at least a short interval of peace.[31] A letter of a few weeks later shows how far the Prime Minister was from sharing Castlereagh's Continental outlook:

> The more I hear and see of the different Courts of Europe, the more convinced I am that the King of France is (amongst the great Powers) the only Sovereign in whom we can have any real confidence. The Emperor of Russia is profligate from vanity and self-sufficiency, if not from principle. The King of Prussia may be a well-meaning man, but he is the dupe of the Emperor of Russia. The Emperor of Austria I believe to be an honest man, but he has a Minister in whom no one can trust; who considers all policy as consisting in *finesse* and trick; and who has got his government and himself into more difficulties by his devices than could have occurred from a plain course of dealing.[32]

The British government did not accept that Russia's claims in Poland threatened to overturn the entire European equilibrium, or that they affected vital British interests, or that it was necessary to defend Antwerp on the Vistula; and on 27 November Bathurst sent Castlereagh formal instructions stating 'the impossibility of H.R.H. consenting to involve this country in hostilities at this time for any of the objects which have been hitherto under discussion at Vienna'.[33]

By the time this instruction reached Castlereagh, the negotiations at Vienna were approaching their second crisis. The failure of the attempt to curb Russian gains in Poland led Metternich and Castlereagh to withdraw their — always conditional — support for Prussia's claims to Saxony and Mainz. Metternich still favoured an independent central bloc, but Austria's generals were arguing that Prussia's eastern frontier was so weak that she would permanently remain subject to Russian tutelage. More to the point, Austria would not accept a disadvantageous settlement in Saxony as well as in Poland, and there was far more support in the Austrian court and army for a confrontation with Prussia over Saxony than with Russia over Poland. On 10 December Metternich announced his terms to Hardenberg: Austria would agree to Prussia receiving approximately one-fifth of Saxony, 432,000 people out of 2.2 million.

Hardenberg was outraged. He had not expected Metternich to continue to support Prussia's claims to all of Saxony, but he was taken aback by what he regarded as a paltry and insulting offer. As tensions rose, Hardenberg tried to ensure Alexander's support by showing him private letters from Metternich written at the height of the crisis over Poland. The result was a series of violent arguments which further embittered personal relations, delighted the gossips, and ultimately did Hardenberg more harm than good. On 20 December Prussia presented a counteroffer: they would still annex Saxony, but Frederick Augustus, the deposed King, would receive a new state of some 700,000 inhabitants in the Rhineland. Castlereagh objected to this, arguing that such a state would inevitably become a French puppet, while Metternich refused to see Leipzig and Dresden in Prussian hands.

Talleyrand now began to make his presence felt, seriously influencing events for the first time (his earlier interventions had been largely ineffectual). The French government strongly opposed the extinction of Saxony on both legitimist and strategic grounds. Talleyrand indicated to Metternich that France would not expect a quid pro quo in Belgium or the Rhineland in exchange for supporting Austria over Saxony — to be readmitted to the inner councils of the great powers was sufficient — and at the same time reassured Russia that France regarded the Polish question as closed. Nonetheless, there was fierce opposition from Prussia to the idea of French involvement, and Hardenberg talked openly of war, claiming full Russian support. Razumovsky, the Russian delegate, did not dispute this, but in fact Alexander had been cautious and evasive when Hardenberg pressed him for a pledge of military support. Both sides made ostentatious preparations for war: troops were mobilized and marched into position, and plans of campaign widely discussed.

Then, early on 1 January 1815, came the news of the Peace of Ghent, creating a sensation in the tense atmosphere and enormously enhancing Britain's prestige, not because of its terms, which were of no general interest, but because it signalled that Britain would soon be free to intervene with all her resources in any war on the Continent. Later that day Castlereagh presented Metternich and Talleyrand with the outline of a treaty of alliance to resist Prussia's claims to Saxony by all means including war. This was signed on 3 January, with Holland, Hanover and Bavaria acceding later; on the same day Metternich finally accepted Russia's claims in Poland. Although the treaty remained secret, the alliance it codified quickly became apparent, and without solid Russian support Prussia was forced to give ground. Talleyrand was admitted to the allied councils on 4 January, and on the 5th Castlereagh presented a compromise plan by which Prussia would get one-third of Saxony. This became the basis of the settlement, although another month of detailed negotiations followed, in which the Prussian share of Saxony rose to about 900,000 souls. In these negotiations Castlereagh was generally accepted as the mediator and caused Metternich almost as much anguish as Hardenberg by concessions to Prussia in the Rhineland, which disrupted Metternich's carefully laid plans for southern Germany. Strangely, it was Alexander who helped to secure the final agreement, giving Thorn to Prussia and the Tarnopol circle back to Austria, while in return Britain and the Netherlands between them took responsibility for just over half of the much discussed Russian debt in

14. Twelfth Night or What you Will!
George Cruikshank, Jan. 1815, B.M. Cat. no. 12,453

A liberal British reaction to the Congress of Vienna.

The allied sovereigns divide the Twelfth Cake representing Europe. Alexander, on the right, takes Poland and proposes to give it to his brother the Grand Duke Constantine, who stands beside him. On the other side of the cake Frederick William adds Saxony to Prussia, while Francis, taking hold of 'Germany', comments, 'I shall get my peice the the [*sic*] cut as large as I can, I don't think it is large enough.' Between them sits Castlereagh with a large serving knife and fork. He says, 'I have been assisting to divide the Cake but I dont much like my Office the the [*sic*] Gentlemen seem so dissatisfied.' To the right, beyond Alexander and Constantine, four dispossessed figures (possibly including the King of Saxony) beg for a few small pieces, but are ignored. In the background a meretricious-looking Justice is shown with a bandage over one eye and her scales weighed down by avarice and ambition.

In a box to the left of the stage are Bernadotte (delighting in his acquisition of Norway), Louis XVIII, and the Prince of Orange proffering an orange to Princess Charlotte, who disdains him. Below, John Bull welcomes an American Indian.

On the right sit some Turks, and in a box above, Ferdinand gleefully examines a 'List of Prisoners to be Hung for supporting a Free Constitution'; his crown is adorned with tiny gibbets, and behind him stands a figure representing the Inquisition.

Holland. When even this was not quite enough, Castlereagh persuaded Hanover and the Netherlands each to cede Prussia 50,000 souls, and the deal was completed on 6 February 1815.[34]

By then most of the leading ministers and sovereigns were ill, exhausted or embittered, if not all three, while even the social life of the Congress had begun to pall. With the most contentious issues decided, and only matters of detail remaining, Castlereagh at last heeded Liverpool's anxious calls to return to defend the government in the Commons. He left Vienna in the middle of February, leaving Wellington, who had recently arrived from Paris, at the head of the British delegation.

Given Bathurst's instructions of 27 November not to involve Britain in a war over Poland, Castlereagh's act in forming the Triple Alliance of 3 January might be seen as rash, even if it was primarily intended as a bluff. As late as 23 December Liverpool wrote to Castlereagh bluntly stating that the cabinet was 'decidedly and unanimously of opinion that all your endeavours should be directed to the continuance of peace; and that there is no mode in which the arrangements in Poland, Germany, and Italy can be settled, consistently with the stipulations of the Treaty of Paris, which is not to be preferred under present circumstances to a renewal of hostilities between the Continental Powers'. He went on to state that the only grounds on which the British government would consider going to war were 'a clear point of honour', or 'some distinct British interest' such as the defence of the Netherlands.[35] Yet only a few weeks later Liverpool and Bathurst agreed to ratify the Triple Alliance with scarcely a murmur, and without even summoning a full cabinet meeting to consider it.[36] In part this sudden transformation was due to the fact that the deed was done, and to confidence in Castlereagh's judgement. Repudiating the Treaty would humiliate the Foreign Secretary, destroy Britain's international standing as a dependable ally, and quite probably break up the government. But there were other factors which made the ministers more pugnacious in January than in November or December. The most obvious was the end of the American war, but perhaps almost equally important were the growing signs of stability in Paris, and the fact that Castlereagh's Triple Alliance not only included France but bound her to accept the terms of the Peace of Paris, thus protecting the Low Countries on their most vulnerable side. Finally, there was considerable support for the Saxon cause in Britain, even among the Whigs who shared the widespread revulsion at the extinction of an ancient state; while fighting against the revival of Poland, even with the Czar at its head, would have been most unpopular. Even so, it was with heartfelt relief that the ministers greeted the peaceful resolution of the Saxon crisis less than a fortnight after news of the treaty reached London.

Castlereagh could therefore return home without fear of reproach, but his achievements at Vienna were little recognized even by his closest colleagues. In the middle of January Liverpool had warned him, perhaps with a little exaggeration, that 'very few people give themselves any anxiety about what is passing at Vienna, except in as far as it is connected with expense'. The Prime Minister's own praise was tepid, commenting that the Triple Alliance 'will secure the Low Countries for a time and give more éclat to Castlereagh's presence at Vienna, which was certainly wanting'.[37] Ironically, a rather more generous assessment came from Canning, who wrote to Huskisson from Lisbon:

I do not see why he should regret having gone to Vienna, as you seem to think he must. Poland, to be sure, he has not been able to save — but Saxony is arranged — not discreditably to us — and he has done a good job upon the Slave Trade. Naples *I* do not like as it is — but with the Opposition Murat is popular. And then as to the figure which his (Castlereagh's) Colleagues have been making during his absence, that is all clear gain to him — He returns, surely, with great advantages.[38]

There is no doubt that Castlereagh made a serious mistake of policy over the Polish question. Even Sir Charles Webster, his admiring biographer, admits that 'His plans had gone astray and his judgement had been completely at fault. The Cabinet had estimated more correctly than he the weaknesses of the continental Powers. . . .'[39] Whether the dispute over Saxony was really worth the risk of war or not remains debatable, but the policy was a striking success and this success restored Britain's prestige with the Continental statesmen. Liverpool's judgement on the great questions of policy may have been equal or superior to Castlereagh's, and he certainly appreciated the domestic constraints on British action far better; but neither he, nor any of the other ministers, nor even Wellington, could have represented Britain as forcefully and skilfully in the negotiations. The contrast with the middle of 1813 when Britain was largely excluded from the negotiations, and her representatives were obviously ineffectual, shows the true extent of Castlereagh's achievement.

19

The Hundred Days, 1815

What news? *Ma foi!*
The Tiger has broken out of his den.
The Monster was three days at sea.
The Wretch has landed at Fréjus.
The Brigand has arrived at Antibes.
The Invader has reached Grenoble.
The General has entered Lyons.
Napoleon slept last night at Fontainebleau.
The Emperor proceeds to the Tuileries today.
His Imperial Majesty will address his loyal subjects tomorrow.[1]

It was early in February 1815 that Napoleon decided to escape from Elba. He had soon tired of being sovereign of his tiny island kingdom with its limited potential and narrow provincial society. He constantly received reports of discontent in France and Italy, and of the dissension among the allies at Vienna; and he fretted at the apparently permanent separation from his wife and child. The French government refused to pay his promised pension of two million francs per annum and urged the other powers to consent to his removal to some more remote place of exile: St Helena and the Azores were both mentioned. There was little or no chance that Alexander, or even the British government, would agree to the proposal, though Napoleon could not be sure of this, and the danger encouraged him to undertake his desperate venture. But the main reason why Napoleon left Elba was that he had never accepted defeat. He was forty-five years old, at the height of his powers, full of energy and boldness. All his life he had used his phenomenal drive and ability to overcome great odds, to rise from a poor unknown lieutenant of artillery to be Emperor of the French and master of Europe, and now he was expected to spend the rest of his days ruling an island sixteen miles by seven, with a population of 12,000. Of course the odds were heavily stacked against success, but he had overcome such odds before and the reward for success was so great, while death or further exile seemed little worse than stagnating in Elba.[2]

Napoleon sailed from Portoferraio on the evening of 26 February with just over 1,100 companions, including 650 men of the Old Guard and 108 Polish lancers. The flotilla of seven small ships — some no more than fishing boats — avoided the British and French naval vessels in the area and sailed north for France. On 1 March they landed near Fréjus: an attempt to seize Antibes failed, but by midnight they were masters of Cannes. Napoleon decided to avoid the main road through the Rhône Valley, where the people had shown themselves bitterly hostile to him the previous year, and instead strike north on mountain tracks towards Grenoble and the Dauphiné. His small force moved extremely rapidly, giving the local authorities little time to react. By 7 March he was approaching Grenoble and encountered the first serious resistance: a battalion of the 5th Line and some engineers blocked his path at the pass of Laffrey. It was here, in the famous scene, that Napoleon advanced on the French troops, inviting them to shoot their Emperor: old loyalties triumphed over new, and the troops broke ranks and joined Napoleon's cause. Later that day the 7th Regiment of the Line deserted to Napoleon en masse, led by its commander Colonel La Bédoyère; and later still Napoleon entered Grenoble in triumph. Not a shot had been fired and the Emperor's party had grown to over 4,000 men.

News of Napoleon's landing reached Paris on 5 March, and though the French government hoped at first that the report might be false, it immediately set about collecting a force at Lyon to oppose him. Louis XVIII assured foreign diplomats that the news caused him less concern than his gout, while the *Moniteur* described it as 'an act of madness which can be dealt with by a few rural policemen'. But behind the bravado there was real concern. The government knew that it could not depend on the loyalty of the troops, but it had no choice but to rely on them. Marshals Macdonald and St Cyr were sent south to rally the troops and take command at Lyon, while the National Guard was called out. But on the afternoon of the 7th news arrived that Napoleon had entered Gap and been joined by the Commandant with 700 men. The report was false, but it set the scene for what was to come.[3]

It was early on that morning, 7 March, that the first news reached Vienna, in the form of an urgent dispatch from the Austrian consul at Livorno to Metternich, simply stating that Napoleon had disappeared from Elba. Metternich immediately conferred with the other allied ministers and their sovereigns and they agreed to mobilize their forces and take precautions, but until they knew if Napoleon had gone to France, or Naples, or Tuscany, they could do no more. The news was kept secret, but rumours quickly spread.[4] It was not until late on 11 March that the ministers learnt that Napoleon had landed in France. Despite having seen the disaffection in Paris the previous autumn, Wellington was optimistic, telling Castlereagh:

'It is my opinion that Buonaparte has acted upon false or no information, and that the King will destroy him without difficulty, and in a short time.' But he then added more cautiously: 'If he does not, the affair will be a serious one.'[5] Two days later the assembled powers issued a formal declaration that Napoleon's invasion of France was an illegal act which voided the Treaty of Fontainebleau and placed him outside the pale of civil and social relations. The powers declared their support for the French King and offered their assistance to resist the attack upon him. Thus, long before Napoleon had reached Paris, the allies committed themselves to resisting his return from exile.

News of Napoleon's escape and arrival in France reached London together on 10 March. That night Samuel Romilly wrote in his diary:

As I was coming out of the Court of Chancery today, I was told that intelligence had just arrived that Bonaparte had landed in the south of France, on the 1st or 2nd of this month, at the head of about 1,000 men, and was marching towards Grenoble. I gave no credit to the information, but I find that it is but too true. It is in every body's mouth, and has filled every one with consternation. The name of Bonaparte is one

'——at which the world turns pale'.

From all that we have long heard, there can be no doubt that there is great attachment to him in the army, and great indifference for the Bourbons in every part of France; though in many parts of it an earnest desire to remain at peace, whoever may be their sovereign. The defection of the first troops that are called upon to act against Bonaparte will probably be a signal for the revolt of the whole military force of the kingdom.[6]

Romilly's gloomy prognostications were widely shared, and a few days later another radical, H. G. Bennet, wrote, 'If Boney can hold his head up a fortnight, it is our opinion here that the Bourbons are done, which God forbid. Not that I like those personages, but peace with them is better than war with Napoleon.'[7]

The British government expressed its full support for Louis XVIII, and said that it would urge the other powers to act together and assemble a large force on the borders of France to help maintain his authority. However, it would clearly be best if Louis XVIII could deal with the problem without resorting to foreign assistance. But as early as 16 March the reports reaching the Foreign Office were so bad that Castlereagh privately admitted that he could feel little confidence in the French government surviving the crisis. Precautions were taken against demonstrations in favour of Napoleon in Ireland; the British forces in Belgium were mobilized; and Wellington was instructed to take command of them as soon as he could leave Vienna, where Clancarty would replace him as head of the British delegation.[8]

While the allies took precautions, events in France moved with startling speed. The attempt to assemble an army at Lyon was a miserable failure, the

15.   Boney's Return from Elba, or the Devil among the Tailors
Design by G. Humphrey, executed by George Cruikshank, 21 March 1815, B.M. Cat. no. 12,509

Napoleon bursts in among the allied sovereigns, up-ending Louis XVIII onto the floor. John Bull bends to assist Louis, 'Never fear Old Boy I'll help you up again as for that rascal Boney I'll sow [*sic*] him up presently.' Behind John Bull, the Pope seeks to hide under the counter, while the King of Holland is equally terrified by Napoleon's reappearance, exclaiming, 'Donder & Blixen das is de Devil.' But the other allied figures are calm and determined: on the right Alexander reaches for a knout with tape-measures for lashes and says, 'I'll take a few Cossack *measures* to him.' Blücher threatens Napoleon with a huge pair of shears, while behind him Bernadotte comments, 'This looks like another subsidy.'

sullenness of the troops plainly showing where their sympathies lay. The government was confused and leaderless. Soult was dismissed as minister of war on suspicion of treachery, but none of the royalists showed the energy or ability to rally support behind the King. It was not that the country as a whole wanted Napoleon to return, but the great bulk of the population was passive, if not apathetic. No one was willing to die for Louis XVIII, while in the army and in the disbanded officers and soldiers Napoleon had active and zealous partisans. The government's last hope was that Marshal Ney would succeed in blocking Napoleon's path, but not even Ney could inspire the troops to the task, and he himself was soon won over by Napoleon's emotional appeal to his old comrade in arms. Soon after midnight on 20 March Louis XVIII fled from Paris, and on the evening of that same day — the King of Rome's birthday — Napoleon returned to the capital in triumph. The *Moniteur*, reflecting the experience of twenty-five years of political upheaval, calmly reported that 'The King and princes left in the night. H. M. the Emperor arrived this evening at 8 o'clock in his palace of the Tuileries at the head of the same troops which had been sent to block his route this morning.'⁹

Napoleon hastened to assure the world that he was a changed man. He appointed Fouché Minister of Police, and Carnot Minister of the Interior, in an effort to win the support of the newly revived Jacobins who, while they shared some of the names and some of the ideas of twenty years before, were much more moderate and less bloodthirsty than during the Terror. He abolished the slave trade and sent protestations of his peaceful intentions to London and Vienna. But at the same time he prepared for war, and there is little reason to doubt that if he had consolidated his position with a few victories, he would have cast off his liberal pretensions and returned to his old methods of rule. But throughout the Hundred Days his political position in Paris was far from secure. Numerous intrigues were in progress, Fouché corresponded secretly with Metternich and Wellington, and plans were considered to depose Napoleon and install a compromise figure — possibly the Duc d'Orléans or even a regency for Napoleon's son — as an alternative to both Napoleon and Louis XVIII.¹⁰

Even before Napoleon reached Paris, fighting had broken out in Italy, where on 15 March Murat declared war on Austria and proclaimed himself the liberator of Italy. He acted in support of Napoleon, though against the Emperor's injunction to remain quiet for the moment; but Murat knew that his throne was in peril, he was little suited to the waiting game and he hoped to catch the Austrians unprepared. Had he sided with the allies he might, after all, have kept his kingdom, but he was essentially a Gascon cavalier, with all Bernadotte's bravado and none of his cunning. His army of 40,000 ill-trained, ill-equipped men swept north, occupying Rome and then, by early April, Bologna. His proclamations calling on Italian nationalists to join his cause brought much applause but few recruits: just as in 1812 and 1813, the much discussed Italian uprising came to nothing. Soon Murat was forced to fall back and his army became demoralized. On 3 May at Tolentino it was utterly defeated. Murat fled to Naples, arriving on 18 May and leaving the following day by sea; he managed to escape to Cannes. Napoleon, angered by his premature attack and still more by its failure, would not receive him; and Murat remained in Cannes until the news of Waterloo forced him to flee again. He found refuge for a while in Corsica, and at the beginning of October he set off with a few deluded fools in an idiotic attempt to emulate Napoleon and regain his kingdom. The affair was botched from first to last: the populace, far from welcoming their former sovereign, pelted him with fruit and stones until some customs officers arrived to take him into custody. A week later he was court-martialled and shot within the hour. It was a squalid end for one of the most romantic and glittering figures of the era: the innkeeper's son who married Napoleon's sister, led the Emperor's cavalry on a score of battlefields, became Grand Duke of Cleves Berg and King of Naples; the gorgeously uniformed, ringleted, bejewelled Joachim Murat.¹¹

The fighting in Italy had little influence on the Hundred Days. The allied ministers had decided to resist Napoleon's return to power, with force if necessary, before Murat raised his standard; and despite all their disputes and jealousies there was never the least sign of any wavering in this resolution. They knew Napoleon too well to trust his messages promising peace and assumed that he only wanted a breathing space to consolidate his power. The very energy and resourcefulness which he had shown in his return from Elba and the devotion he inspired in the French army naturally aroused their forebodings. As early as 12 March, when they knew little more than that Napoleon had landed in France, they laid the basis of a campaign, though at that time they hoped that this would prove an unnecessary precaution or, at worst, that they would be intervening to aid Louis XVIII in a civil war. The ministers agreed to keep an army of 150,000 Austrians in Italy, where Murat was already viewed with great suspicion, and to form an army of 200,000 Germans and Austrians on the Upper Rhine, and another, almost as large, of British, Hanoverian, Prussian and other contingents on the Lower Rhine. Later this army was divided in two, with Wellington taking command of the British, Hanoverian and Dutch-Belgian troops, while further east a Prussian army was formed under Blücher. A Russian army of 200,000 men was to act as a central reserve at Würzburg, and the ministers had to beat off a determined effort by Alexander to gain the supreme command.[12]

On 18 March — still two days before Napoleon reached Paris — Wellington wrote to Castlereagh from Vienna that the allies had decided to renew the Treaty of Chaumont, and he urged the British government to agree to provide subsidies on the same scale as in 1814. Ironically the Russians, who only a few months before had been threatening to plunge Europe into war over Poland and Saxony, were the most pressing, with Alexander earnestly assuring Wellington that he could not move a man without financial assistance. Castlereagh anticipated these requests, and on 24 March promised the Continental Powers £5 million divided equally between them, and a nominally British army of 150,000 men, at least half of whom would come from the smaller European states in return for further British subsidies. This renewal of the commitment of 1814 was generally satisfactory, though naturally the Continental Powers would have liked an increase in their subsidy, but it led to a protracted and heated dispute between Britain and Prussia over the command of the contingents from the north German states, which delayed the conclusion of the formal agreement until the end of April.[13]

While all the allies agreed on the need to oppose Napoleon with the largest possible force, there was much more doubt over their attitude to the restoration of the Bourbons. As early as 16 March Castlereagh feared that the crumbling support for Louis XVIII might 'leave us [with] no cause to support, except an undisguised dictation to France as to her monarch, which we could not justify or regard as permanent, even if we had [the] power, in a military sense, to give it an existence'. And when the British government ratified the agreement with the allies, it did so with an explicit qualification that the treaty 'is not to be considered as binding his Britannic Majesty to prosecute the war, with a view of imposing upon France any particular Government'.[14]

The other powers agreed with this caution, and Austria made a similar declaration. Both Alexander and Metternich had hopes that the Jacobins, who seemed to wield great influence in Paris, might be encouraged to overthrow Napoleon. This raised the question of what alternative forms of government — excluding Napoleon — might be acceptable to the allies. In a frank interview with Clancarty, Alexander did not conceal his dislike for the Bourbons, but indicated that 'if the French wished for the return of the King, et bien!' Otherwise, 'he did not like Republics, but that a Republican form of Government as being weaker would be less likely to disturb the peace of Europe', while he had no objection if the Duc d'Orléans was preferred. But he would not accept the elevation of a marshal or general to the throne — naming Soult and Eugène as the most obvious possibilities — and hinted that he feared that Metternich might try to press the claims of Marie Louise to a regency. Clancarty was without instructions on the question, but speaking privately told Alexander that he greatly doubted if there was any possibility of an Austrian regency, which he thought would be most unwise, and at the same time deprecated the idea of a republic which, when tried in the 1790s, had been anything but peaceful or stable. The question was thus left open, but Alexander was assured that Britain was not supporting the idea of a regency; and Metternich, in his contacts with Fouché, indicated that while preferable to a republic, he disliked the idea.[15]

In contrast to the Czar, and despite its public declaration, the British government had a strong preference for the restoration of Louis XVIII and believed that the allies should do everything possible to encourage it, short of making it a sine qua non of peace. Castlereagh acknowledged that there was some support for the Duc d'Orléans as a compromise, but believed that if he came to power, 'more especially if brought forward improvidently, his authority would probably soon prove incompetent to repress the factions of the country, and it is not the interest of the Allies, if obliged to enter upon war, to encourage an early and hollow compromise'. Wellington's views fluctuated widely: at one point he believed that 'the great majority of the population in France was decidedly adverse to Buonaparte, and that many Generals and other officers, the whole of the National Guard, and even some regiments of the line, have remained faithful to the King'; while the next day he urged Castlereagh to consider the claims of the Duc d'Orléans. Yet there is little doubt that Wellington, even more than the ministers in London, always regarded the restoration of Louis XVIII as by far the most desirable end to the war. The obvious fragility of the first restoration and the passivity of the King's supporters caused concern, but as in 1814, Wellington and the British government were convinced that Louis XVIII offered the best hope of the peaceful and stable regime in France which was their ultimate goal.[16]

Despite a few rumours to the contrary, the cabinet seems to have been perfectly united both on the question of opposing Napoleon and on the restoration of the Bourbons. The Opposition, however, was divided. From the outset, Lord Grenville believed that war was inevitable if Napoleon was not checked in France, and was inclined to support the government in reviving the alliance. Whitbread, on the other hand, strongly opposed war against an individual and maintained France's right to determine her own government. As his friend H. G. Bennet told Creevey with some exaggeration, 'Sam [Whitbread] is all for Boney, and the Slave Trade decree has done something. We consider the Jacobins are masters at Paris. . . . Leave them to themselves, and quarrel they will, but war will unite every soul.'[17] When the question first came before Parliament at the beginning of April, Ponsonby and the bulk of the Whigs supported the government, but Whitbread's minority of 37 included such respected figures as Tierney, Horner and Romilly. Grey tried to avoid committing himself publicly, in order to avoid an open rift with Grenville, but he too believed that as long as Napoleon's conduct was peaceful and moderate, Britain had no pretext for attacking him. Two more surprising recruits for these views were the Prince's disreputable crony Lord Yarmouth and Lord Wellesley. This last defection baffled Liverpool, but he had the consolation of able and effective support from Grattan and Plunket in the Commons as well as Grenville in the Lords. Wilberforce was more ambivalent, writing in his diary after one debate: 'I spoke ill, because indecisively, as indeed I felt in one sense; for my own judgement would be for treating with Buonaparte if we were free: but we are so committed with the Allies, that we could not honestly separate from them, as agreeing to Whitbread's motion would substantially have been.' A fortnight later memories of 1793 and all that followed preyed on his mind: 'If Buonaparte could be unhorsed, it would, humanly speaking, be a blessing to the European world; indeed to all nations. And government ought to know both his force and their own. Yet I greatly dread their being deceived, remembering how Pitt was.'[18]

During April and May there were a number of debates in the Commons on the issue, and at least three divisions, in which the minority steadily grew as attendance increased; but the government always retained a very comfortable majority (7 April, 37 v. 220; 28 April, 72 v. 273; 25 May, 92 v. 331). In general the ministers were quite satisfied with these results, though Wellington bitterly resented Whitbread's repeated attacks on him and the widespread mistranslation of the allied declaration against Napoleon. Liverpool was complacent, telling Canning (who was still in Lisbon), 'Upon the war, the country, with the exception of the old Opposition, has been nearly unanimous'; while Wilberforce, more impartially, commented, 'It is amazing how little people seem moved. Generally, I think, for war; especially all who used to be friends of Pitt's government.'[19]

All this time, while the politicians debated at Westminster, the armies prepared for war. The allied powers had agreed in 1814 each to keep 75,000 men under arms on the Continent until a final settlement was reached. Britain, burdened by the American war, never achieved this figure, but throughout the winter of 1814–15 she had a substantial force of some 36,000 men (rather more than one-third of whom were Hanoverians) in the Low Countries. The core of this force was the small army which Sir Thomas Graham had led to Holland at the beginning of 1814, and though it had received some reinforcements, the army remained of generally poor quality, with most of the Peninsular regiments going home or being sent to America. The function of the army was to encourage stability, particularly in Belgium, which had just been transferred from French to Dutch rule; and, theoretically at least, to deter a French attack, although it is clear that no one expected it to see any active service. With the breakdown of Princess Charlotte's engagement in June, the British government signalled its continuing close alliance with the Netherlands by appointing the twenty-two-year-old Hereditary Prince of Orange to command the army.

When the news of Napoleon's return reached Brussels the Prince mobilized his army and issued orders to put the Belgian and Dutch fortresses into a state of defence. He also sent an officer, Colonel Tripp, to Paris to offer the French government the assistance of his army against Napoleon and had some idea of occupying the French frontier fortresses. Fortunately the French declined the offer, for the British government greatly disliked the idea, believing that premature foreign intervention would, by arousing nationalist sentiment against the King, be counter-productive; Wellington also disapproved. In any case, the troops could scarcely have done more than cross the frontier before Napoleon reached Paris.[20]

The British ministers were uneasy at leaving their army under the Prince's command, and despite warnings from his staff officers that he had grown proud, Bathurst begged him to consult Lieutenant-General. Sir Henry Clinton, the senior British officer present, about his plans. But the Prince had spent some time at Wellington's headquarters in the Peninsula, and knew that the great man was not in the habit of consulting his subordinates and had a particularly poor opinion of Clinton's ability. He was therefore affronted by the suggestion, and replied coldly, although a little later he unbent sufficiently to explain his (quite sensible) plans in the event of an immediate French offensive — which was Bathurst's chief concern. Fortunately Wellington soon arrived from Vienna to take command of the army, the Prince yielding with good grace to his old chief, while making it clear that he would have greatly resented being superseded by anyone else.[21]

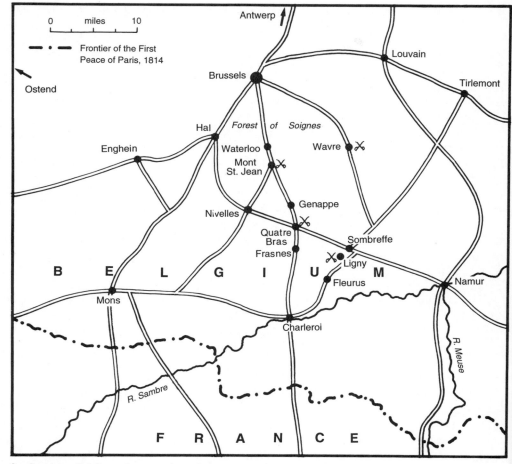

8　Southern Belgium: the campaign of 1815

Wellington had already examined the defences of Belgium in August 1814 on his way to take up the Paris embassy. He arrived in Brussels on 4 April, and took charge of the discussions which the Prince's staff had already begun with the Prussian commanders over how to combine their forces against a French attack. The Prussians suggested that both allied armies retire and unite at Tirlemont, some twenty-five miles east of Brussels. But Wellington, aware of the doubtful loyalty of the Belgian troops and concerned about his communications, felt that it was important to deny Napoleon the éclat of even the temporary occupation of Brussels, and proposed a more forward concentration to the south of the city. Gneisenau, who had recently taken command of the Prussian forces pending Blücher's arrival, and who, contrary to some accounts, showed a great inclination to cooperate closely with the British, readily agreed. This decision, combined with Blücher's eagerness to fight as far forward as possible, shaped the whole course of the campaign; and many of the problems which the allies faced on 15 and 16 June can be attributed to the fact that they were attempting to concentrate their armies too close to the French frontier, so that their troops were having to march great distances across the face of an advancing enemy.[22]

Long before Wellington reached Brussels, reinforcements were on their way to Belgium. Orders were issued to send four good regiments of British infantry (the 52nd, 71st, 91st and 95th) to Ostend as early as 16 March, together with heavy artillery and supplies for the Belgian fortresses. The British government was naturally anxious about the fate of Antwerp, and even before Napoleon had reached Paris it enquired if precautions had been taken for the destruction of ships and naval materials remaining in the dockyards there. By 22 March Castlereagh could announce that 8,000 men were being sent to reinforce the British army, together with 20,000 muskets for the Dutch-Belgian forces. Yet Wellington was far from satisfied, and bluntly told Bathurst on 6 April, 'It appears to me that you have not taken in England a clear view of your situation, that you do not think war certain, and that a great effort must be made, if it is hoped that it should be short.'[23] This was characteristically unfair, and some of Wellington's demands, such as 19,000 cavalry and 150 pieces of British field artillery, were wildly unrealistic; but his complaint does seem to have spurred the ministers on to redouble their efforts. In the month from 25 March to 25 April the British army in the Low Countries showed a net increase of 12,478 rank and file, and this was followed by a further 9,181 between 25 April and 25 May. By the end of May Wellington had over 36,000 British and King's German Legion rank and file present and under arms, compared with only 14,000 two months before, while the total Anglo-Hanoverian army under his command amounted to some 60,000 men, not counting the Dutch-Belgian and other allied contingents. When operations actually began in the middle of June, his whole army, including garrisons and allies, amounted to more than 110,000 men, while his field force was over 90,000 strong.[24]

This excellent performance was achieved largely by stripping Britain and Ireland of their garrisons, despite the vigorous protests of the Irish government, as Peel, the Chief Secretary for Ireland, reported on 15 April:

> The Government here is determined to take [a further] 5,000 men from us, and run any risks. Lord Whitworth and I have laid before Lord Sidmouth the state of the country. His answer is unanswerable by us. 'I know the danger in Ireland, but the Government think it better to take the chance of danger there, for the chance of success which an addition of 5,000 men will give to Lord Wellington.'[25]

The troops withdrawn from Ireland would be replaced in July or August when the regiments which had been sent to Canada in 1814 returned. And it was not only Ireland which was stripped of troops, as Peel acknowledged a few weeks later when he wrote, 'You cannot conceive the denudation of England of troops; there is hardly an effective man in it.'[26]

Nonetheless, some problems remained, and Wellington complained both of a shortage of British artillery and of a 'numerous and very incapable Staff'. Mulgrave did his best to supply Wellington's demands, and despite real problems at the Ordnance he had some success: thus when Wellington requested a siege-train on 5 April, it began to arrive at Ostend on the 20th.[27] The question of the staff was more difficult, with the Horse Guards sending out a number of inexperienced officers without consulting Wellington. Gradually Wellington secured many of the appointments he wanted, yet even after the battle he complained of the inefficiency of his staff and the incompetence of his subordinates, particularly the commander of his artillery. And the British staff did make a number of mistakes during the campaign, as did the French and the Prussian, for although many of the individuals were experienced, they lacked the time to settle down into an efficient team.[28]

Whatever the weaknesses of the British part of Wellington's army, it was undoubtedly better than the allied contingents. Thus, in announcing the departure of a Hanoverian corps of 10,000 men sent to join the army early in April, the Duke of Cambridge, Governor of Hanover, warned Wellington:

> although this corps has been raised about a year, the men have been together hardly above six weeks, having been upon the peace establishment, according to which the greater part of the men are upon furlough for eleven months of the year: they are, therefore, not in that state of drill I could wish them; the officers for the most part have never served. . . . [but] there is the greatest good will in them.[29]

Much the same was true of other contingents, with many of the Dutch-Belgian units, for example, being no more than militia.

This was not the only problem with the Dutch-Belgian troops. Belgium had been incorporated into France since the 1790s, Holland since 1810, and so most of the troops who had any military experience had gained it under, not against, Napoleon, while many Belgians resented their forced union with Holland. There were reports of some soldiers greeting the news of Napoleon's return with enthusiasm, while Sir John Colbourne, who was serving on the staff of the Prince of Orange, warned Bunbury, '*I would not trust the Belgian Troops an inch*'. British officers also suspected a number of senior figures in the Dutch general staff and war office of being inclined to favour France, and this led London to insist on maintaining British garrisons in several of the most important fortresses.[30] Such suspicions naturally did not foster harmony in the alliance, and Wellington frequently complained that the King of the Netherlands (a title assumed on 17 March) was obstinate and hard to work with. The most important bone of contention was the King's desire to have his troops united in a single corps under the command of his son the Prince of Orange, rather than dispersed through the army in divisions and brigades as Wellington wished. Wellington got his way in the end on this question, and in return quietly accepted the need for both the Prince of Orange and his eighteen-year-old brother, Prince Frederick, to hold senior commands.[31]

The weakness of the British force, the poor quality of some of the allied contingents, and the failure to secure more troops from the states of northern Germany all made Wellington look longingly to Portugal for more men. The ministers in London were less enthusiastic, pointing out that it would take three months to organize and transfer a corps of 14–15,000 men from Lisbon to Flanders, even if the Portuguese Regency agreed. But Wellington urged the idea again, and a formal request was made, only to be firmly rejected. The Portuguese government, which was still sore over a number of disputes, including its failure to regain Olivenza from Spain and British pressure on the slave trade, argued that it could not expose the country to the risk of an attack from Spain. Even if it had agreed, it is unlikely that the Portuguese troops would have reached Belgium and been ready to take the field until after Waterloo.[32]

While these preparations and negotiations continued, the allies discussed their plans, trying to balance the desire to strike quickly before Napoleon had consolidated his power with the need to advance with an overwhelming force, leaving nothing to chance, as even a partial defeat would be very dangerous, given the suspicion between the allies and the widespread discontent in their rear, especially in Poland, Saxony and Italy.[33] In the end, caution, and the inevitable delays in preparing a campaign, prevailed, and the allied offensive, which at one stage was intended for May, was postponed until June and then July.

Between March and early May there were repeated reports of French troop movements near the frontier and warnings of an impending French attack on Belgium. Because of the strange state of informal hostilities, the allies would not send their patrols across the frontier (although some intelligence officers did slip into and out of France) and so were vulnerable to such alarms. By 8 May, however, Wellingon felt able to write, 'I say nothing about our defensive operations, because I am inclined to believe Blücher and I are so well united, and so strong, that the enemy cannot do us much mischief.' By June both armies were ready to take the offensive, and Blücher champed at the bit at the need to wait for the Austrian and Russian armies to take up their positions on the Rhine.[34]

In England, April, May and early June was a tense, anxious time: 'a fearful interval, expecting the bursting out of the war', as Wilberforce wrote in his diary. News of the capitulation of Naples, which arrived on 3 June, gave the government's supporters some cheer, but everyone knew that the war would be decided by Napoleon's success or failure and by the French reaction to invasion. Memories and myths of the early 1790s tore at the conscience of many Whigs, so that the liberal Francis Horner could write to an old friend: 'Conceive me to hate Buonaparte as you do, but yet to wish (as I do fervently) for a successful resistance by France to the invasion of the Allies, and you are pretty nearly in possession of all my present politics.'[35]

On 13 June, just before the campaign began, the Prime Minister wrote to his old friend Canning:

> During the twenty years we have passed in political life we have never witnessed a more awful moment than the present. It is impossible ever to answer for the result of military operations; but the chances are certainly all in our favour. The two great problems appear to me to be, whether the authorities at Paris, that is, the Jacobins and Constitutionalists, will endeavour to arrest the progress of the Allies by overthrowing Buonaparte, and by proposing some compromise as to the internal government of France? and whether, if the Allies succeed in again reaching Paris, and in replacing Louis XVIII on the throne, he will be able to maintain himself there?[36]

Napoleon was well aware of the weakness of his political position, and for this as well as military reasons decided to take the initiative and attack the allies. A defensive campaign would evoke memories of the defeat of the previous year, arouse discontent among the population exposed to the allied advance, and open the way for intrigue in Paris. It would also — worst of all — allow the allies to collect all their forces and advance at leisure, so that unless they made some terrible blunders, it would lead to Napoleon's defeat. But by launching an offensive Napoleon had the chance of defeating the allies in detail, breaking the British and Prussian armies before the Austrians and Russians could support them, then advancing into Germany to threaten the flank and rear of the forces on the Rhine. The odds were, of course, still heavily against success, but it was the best chance which Napoleon had.

Ever since his return to Paris, Napoleon had been gathering troops and organizing a new army. The task was much easier than in 1814, for all the prisoners of war and besieged garrisons, which had absorbed so many of his men, had returned to France and many were eager to serve again. By the beginning of June he had a theoretical total of nearly 300,000 men under arms, but many of these were ill-equipped, while others were needed for garrisons and to suppress Royalist sentiment in La Vendée. Small forces had to be left to protect France's southern and eastern frontiers, both because an unopposed allied advance might be politically disastrous and to take part in subsequent operations. Nonetheless, it is surprising that Napoleon's field army amounted to only 124,000 men — no more than Blücher's army, and only about five-eighths of the combined allied field force in Belgium.

The French army's morale was generally excellent, though all the political upheavals and changes of allegiance are said to have led to some suspicion of senior officers among the troops. Napoleon suffered from the absence of Berthier, who had been his chief of staff ever since 1796, but who had followed Louis XVIII into exile. Soult, his replacement, was unaccustomed to the role, though he can hardly be blamed for the fact that his staff officers were less well mounted than those of the Emperor. Ney, who was to command one wing in the campaign, only reached the army as operations began and at first lacked any staff officers of his own, or even details of the units under his command. But despite these problems, the French was probably the best army in the campaign. As we have seen, Wellington's force was a heterogeneous collection of allied contingents, some of very dubious quality, clustered around a fairly small core of British and King's German Legion troops, not all of whom were particularly reliable. The Prussians, while more homogeneous, were weakened by a substantial number of newly raised troops, while others, from western Germany and Saxony, were unhappy at finding themselves under Prussian command. These weaknesses went some way towards offsetting the greater numbers of the allies, although there is no doubt that Napoleon still began the campaign at a significant disadvantage.[37]

The four days of active operations, from 15 to 18 June, have been so closely studied that they appear little more than a comedy of errors. Yet none of the commanders was incompetent, and Napoleon and Wellington were generals of the very finest quality, acting at the height of their powers. Certainly serious mistakes were made on all sides, but it is unlikely that this was worse in 1815 than in the days leading up to Lützen in 1813, Eckmühl in 1809, Jena-Auerstädt in 1806, or Marengo in 1800; or, for that matter, before the Battles of the Pyrenees or the Nive. The very essence of the art of war in the age of Napoleon, and perhaps in any age, consists in the combination of careful planning with rapid improvisation, in a fog of partial, late and inaccurate information. If the great commanders of the past sometimes appear strangely slow or foolish, it is usually because they lacked the leisured hindsight and perfect vision which we use to understand their campaigns.

Since Wellington's lines of communication lay westward to Ostend, while Blücher's were to the east through Liège, Napoleon's plan was to advance rapidly towards Brussels and drive the allied armies apart, and then defeat them in detail. He left Paris on 12 June and joined the army on the 14th — the anniversary of Marengo and Friedland, as he did not fail to remind the troops. Early on the following day the army advanced and attacked the outposts of Zieten's Prussian corps, which occupied a front of some twenty miles along the River Sambre on either side of Charleroi. Zieten was instructed not to attempt any serious defence of the line of the river — his force was too thinly spread for that — but to gain time and to withdraw his force in good order to Sombreffe. This he did with some skill, losing only about 1,200 casualties from his force of just over 31,000 men. He has been criticized for not sending more reports on the progress of the day's operations directly to Wellington, but he informed him when he was first attacked, and sent further reports to his own army's headquarters; he had only the staff of a corps commander; and his brigades (Prussian equivalent to divisions) were widely dispersed, so the failure is really quite understandable.[38]

While Zieten retired towards Sombreffe, the other Prussian corps concentrated their forces and began to move towards the position between Sombreffe and Ligny which the Prussian staff had already selected as suitable for giving battle in the event of a French attack. By the early afternoon of 16 June, three Prussian corps (those of Zieten, Pirch I and Thielmann) were united in the position: together some 83,000 men. Unfortunately the 4th Corps under General Bülow, which was the most distant, was delayed by a misunderstanding of orders and did not reach the battlefield on the 16th, depriving Blücher of another 30,000 men.

Wellington was slower to concentrate his army: he had not issued precautionary orders on the 14th, as had the Prussians, and did not learn of the fighting along the Sambre until the afternoon of the 15th. He then ordered his divisions to concentrate and prepare to march, but still had to guard against the possibility that the first French attacks were a feint and that the real blow would be directed against his communications. So it was not until the evening of the 15th that orders were issued for the army to unite at Quatre Bras. The disadvantage of the allied decision to fight so far forward was now felt, for it meant that there would be serious fighting, and perhaps the deciding battle of the campaign, on the 16th, before either allied army was completely concentrated.

This was the night of the Duchess of Richmond's famous ball, celebrated in every account of the campaign since *Childe Harold*, so that it has now become one of the great clichés of the Hundred Days, along with the thunderstorm on the afternoon and evening of the 17th, and Wellington's pithy, if sometimes apocryphal, remarks ('Humbugged by God!', 'an infamous army', 'Hard pounding this, gentlemen . . .', 'Up Guards and at 'em!', '. . . the playing fields of Eton' and many more). The poor Duke of Richmond little guessed that his wife would thus gain more fame than any of Wellington's subordinates except Lord Uxbridge and, perhaps, Sir Thomas Picton. He had again begged the British government for an active command and again been refused — for his rank was so high that if he were allowed to serve, he would have to be given a senior command, for which he had no experience. Nonetheless, he attended the battle on the 18th, dressed in civilian clothes, but behaving, by his son's account, 'as if he was on service', and is even said to have played a part in initiating the charge of the Union Brigade.[39]

On the morning of the 16th, as the allied armies hurried to concentrate, the French pushed forward. Napoleon did not expect heavy fighting that day. He thought that the Prussians had only a single corps at Sombreffe which he could drive back towards Namur and Liège, while his left wing under Ney cleared Wellington's advance troops from Quatre Bras and Genappe, and prepared for a rapid march on Brussels on the following day. But when it became clear that the Prussians were in strength around Ligny, he was delighted at the prospect of being able to strike a heavy blow against one of the allied armies so early in the campaign. The Battle of Ligny did not begin until about 3 o'clock on the afternoon of the 16th, as many of the French troops had not been able to cross the Sambre on the 15th and took some time to come up. The Prussians had about 83,000 men, the French rather fewer, perhaps 76,000, and the Prussians were occupying a series of villages and enclosures along the Ligny brook. While this greatly strengthened their line, the position had serious disadvantages. The gently rising slopes behind the villages, on which the Prussian reserves were deployed, were exposed both to observation and to French artillery fire; while on the Prussian left, the brook became a serious obstacle which enabled the French to contain most of Thielmann's corps, which was deployed on this side, with a weak force of cavalry. At first Napoleon hoped to envelop the Prussian right flank with Ney's force from Quatre Bras, but when he learnt that Ney was meeting serious opposition, he concentrated his efforts on breaking the centre of the Prussian line. Similarly the Prussians hoped for assistance from Wellington's forces — he visited Blücher's headquarters in the early afternoon and promised to come if he could — but they were equally disappointed. Gneisenau seems to have taken this particularly badly, feeling, unfairly, that the British had betrayed Prussian trust, and showed great suspicion of the British in the following days. The strength of his resentment is surprising, but it may be connected with the fact that it was he, Gneisenau, who bears much of the responsibility for Bülow's failure to reach the battlefield on the 16th. In other words, he naturally preferred to blame the Prussian defeat on her allies rather than on his own mistake.

The fighting at Ligny was intense and generally lacking in tactical finesse. Control of the villages changed hands several times as each side fed fresh reserves into the fray. Late in the day Blücher led a counter-attack in person, but his horse was shot under him and he was ridden over by several waves of French and Prussian cavalry. Although not seriously injured, the seventy-two-year-old Field Marshal was badly bruised and shaken, and the command for the rest of the day devolved on Gneisenau. The French were now making their final attack, Napoleon committing the Imperial Guard and Milhaud's cuirassiers in a last effort to break the Prussian line. The Prussian reserves were exhausted and their troops slowly fell back in the gathering dark, defeated but not broken. Estimates of the losses at Ligny vary widely, but it seems likely that the French lost 10–12,000 casualties, and probable, given the nature of the fighting and the absence of immediate pursuit, that the Prussian loss did not greatly exceed the French, though some estimates put it at over 18,000 men. In addition, a further 8–10,000 Prussian soldiers, mainly from the newly acquired Rhineland and

Westphalian provinces, fled eastwards after the battle, and took no further part in the campaign.[40]

At the same time as the Battle of Ligny, six or seven miles to the north-west, a very different battle was being fought at Quatre Bras. On the 15th the leading troops of Ney's force had reached just beyond Frasnes, a couple of miles south of Quatre Bras, and there had been some slight skirmishing between them and Prince Bernard of Saxe Weimar's Nassau brigade which was quartered at Quatre Bras. But the rest of Ney's troops stretched back to Charleroi and beyond, and it was not until the afternoon of the 16th that sufficient forces had come up to the front to enable him to make a serious attack. The allies were also rapidly concentrating troops at Quatre Bras. The first to arrive were Bijlandt's Dutch-Belgian brigade which, with Prince Bernard's troops, gave the allies rather more than 7,000 men when the battle began. The first French attacks had some success, however, and Bijlandt's battalions were falling back in some disorder when they were rallied by the arrival of Merlen's brigade of Dutch cavalry and Picton's division of British and Hanoverian infantry. And so the battle swayed to and fro, as the arrival of fresh troops gave one side, then the other, the advan-tage. The Duke of Brunswick was killed leading his black-uniformed men into action, and Kellermann's cuirassiers made a splendid and impetuous charge. Gradually the balance swung in Wellington's favour. Ney had rather fewer than 20,000 men, for one of Reille's four divisions had been detached by Napoleon, and D'Erlon's whole corps spent the afternoon marching and counter-marching between the battlefields owing to a famous mix-up of orders. Towards the end of the day Wellington had over 30,000 men on the field, and the French were pushed onto the defensive and were even forced to fall back a short distance. Ney's attacks had been repulsed and Wellington had gained a modest victory — 'modest' since his opponent was in good order and ready to renew the action on the following day. Both armies probably lost 4–5,000 casualties.

The fighting on 16 June might well have decided the campaign. If only D'Erlon . . . , if only Ney . . . , if only Bülow. . . . If events had taken a different course it was quite possible for any of the armies to have struck a fatal blow, but in the actual result Napoleon had gained a significant, but not a decisive, advantage. The Prussian army was shaken, but not broken, and was retiring north, not east; so a junction with Wellington was still possible. On the 17th the Prussians retreated to Wavre, rather more than half way from Ligny to Brussels. When he learnt of the Prussian defeat, Wellington fell back to Mont St Jean, on the direct road from Quatre Bras to Brussels, about ten miles west of Wavre. There he determined to give battle on the following day, having received assurances from Blücher that the Prussians would march to his aid and attack Napoleon in the flank.

Napoleon joined Ney's force with the Imperial Guard, Lobau's small 6th Corps (made smaller by the detachment of one division), and much of the reserve cavalry and artillery, and advanced after Wellington. There was a sharp cavalry skirmish at Genappe, but otherwise no fighting of significance on the 17th. Marshal Grouchy, commanding the French right wing (some 32,000 men), was sent in pursuit of the Prussians, but was unable to regain close contact owing to a late start, and the thunderstorm in the afternoon which turned the fields into thick mud, delaying the march of the troops. Napoleon was surprised but pleased when he saw that Wellington intended to give battle on the 18th, for he was convinced that the Prussians would take no part in the action. Indeed, Blücher's march from Wavre to support Wellington was an extraordinarily bold, even rash, move. He committed his army to a long march on bad country lanes, and if Wellington had been defeated, the Prussians would have been trapped between the forces of Napoleon and Grouchy, with no hope of a secure retreat. It is thus not surprising that Gneisenau begged to be reassured that Wellington really intended to fight, and not merely mount a demonstration before retreating further.[41]

The position Wellington had chosen was far from obvious. The gently rolling countryside presented no great obstacle to the movement of troops, though the reverse slope of the 'ridge' which marked the line held by the allied army protected his troops from observation and, to some extent, from artillery fire. On the far left of the allied line the hamlet of Smohain and the farms of Papelotte and La Haye, with their many enclosures, would slow and impede any French advance. But on the front of the main line, which was very short, barely three miles long, there were only two obstacles: the farms of La Haye Sainte, which was on the Charleroi road a little in front of the allied centre, and Hougoumont, which was well in advance of the allied right wing. Both were strongly built with walled gardens and orchards which made them formidable outposts. For the rest, the army was drawn up behind the ridge with nothing more than a sunken road or a straggling hedge to mark its front.

Wellington had some 74,000 men[42] on the field of battle, while another 17–18,000 were left at Hal and Tubize some eight or ten miles beyond his right flank. The purpose of this detachment has been much discussed and many theories put forward to explain it, the most plausible being that it was intended to guard against an extended attempt to turn Wellington's right flank — a manoeuvre which Napoleon frequently employed.[43]

But Napoleon did not have the men to make any further large detachments: his army at the beginning of the battle was no larger than Wellington's, while from quite early in the day he had to keep back a large force (ultimately more than 15,000 men) to guard against the Prussian advance in his flank and rear. On the other hand, Wellington's army was diluted by unreliable allied contingents, and when the battle began Napoleon had some grounds for his confidence that he could break the allied centre before the Prussians could effectively intervene.

Wellington never wrote a detailed description of the battle, and in his official account of the action, written on the following day, he said little more than that the French made 'repeated attacks of cavalry and infantry, occasionally mixed, but sometimes separate'.[44] A few weeks later, in a famous comparison, he warned J. W. Croker:

> The history of a battle is not unlike the history of a ball. Some individuals may recollect all the little events of which the great result is the battle won or lost; but no individual can recollect the order in which, or the exact moment at which, they occurred, which makes all the difference as to their value or importance.[45]

Contemporary accounts of the battle certainly make confusing reading, and it was many years before the now familiar story, with its orderly succession of events and the different phases of the French attack, emerged. Modern accounts still follow this model, and they are probably as accurate as it is possible to be and remain comprehensible, but it is nonetheless likely that they involve a good deal of oversimplification and that the reality was much more confused than they make it appear.

According to the accepted account, the battle began about 11.30 a.m. with the French artillery bombarding the centre of the allied line and, shortly afterwards, an infantry attack on Hougoumont which continued all day without any success. D'Erlon's corps then advanced to attack the left centre of the British position, i.e. La Haye Sainte and the ground to the east of the Charleroi-Brussels highway. Bijlandt's Dutch-Belgian brigade, which had been left exposed on the forward slope of the ridge, took flight; but the French were then repulsed in great disorder by Picton's division and the charge of the British heavy cavalry (the Union and Household brigades), including the Scots Greys. As was their besetting fault, the British cavalry got out of hand and went too far, and then suffered great loss when the French cavalry reserves advanced against them and forced them to fall back to their original position. A pause now followed while both sides collected and reorganized their forces. The French artillery continued to bombard the allied line, inflicting considerable casualties, despite the protection afforded by being on the reverse slope. Fighting continued at Hougoumont and at La Haye Sainte, and Napoleon began to take serious precautions to protect his right flank and rear from the Prussians. (Leading elements of Bülow's corps had first been observed in the middle of the morning, but due to the long march and difficult nature of the countryside the corps spread back for miles, and it was the middle of the afternoon before sufficient troops were collected to advance further.) Ney now led a succession of cavalry charges against the right centre of Wellington's line (between Hougoumont and La Haye Sainte). The allied infantry formed squares and repulsed the attacks but suffered greatly from the French artillery, while by the close of this stage of the battle the French cavalry were a spent force. Late in the afternoon or in the early evening, La Haye

Sainte fell when its King's German Legion garrison finally ran out of ammunition. From this secure post the French poured a withering fire into the centre of the allied line. Wellington was running short of reserves, and it is sometimes argued that if Napoleon had made his final attack then, he would have carried the day. But the Prussians were advancing through Placenoit and threatening the French rear. Napoleon had already committed first Lobau's corps, and then the Young Guard, to check their advance, which had succeeded for a time, but now they were again being driven back. He drew on his ultimate reserve and committed two battalions of the Old Guard to the struggle, and they recaptured Placenoit and stabilized this front again. But the pause had given Wellington time to rally his forces. Zieten's troops now protected the British left flank, releasing the light cavalry brigades of Vivian and Vandeleur to strengthen the allied centre. The details of the final French attack, led by the Grenadiers and Chasseurs of the Imperial Guard, have been the subject of endless controversy, and many a British officer brightened the long years of retirement on half pay by maintaining, in pamphlets and the columns of Colburn's *United Service Magazine*, that the principal credit for the defeat of the famous Imperial Guard rested with his regiment and his regiment alone.[46] Whoever was right, the Guard fell back in disorder. Napoleon's last reserves were gone, Wellington ordered a general advance all along the line, and the French army broke and fled in confusion. The Prussians took over the pursuit, Blücher and Wellington met, possibly at the inn named La Belle Alliance (though Wellington later denied it, and the story seems too good to be true), and Napoleon barely escaped capture in the rout.

The losses suffered by the armies show the intensity of the fighting at Waterloo. While estimates vary, it seems likely that the French lost at least 30,000 casualties in the battle and about 7,000 unwounded prisoners. Many French regiments appear to have lost more than half their strength. Wellington's army lost more than 15,000 men, of whom about half were British, while the Prussians lost nearly 7,000. Thus 50,000 men were killed or wounded in a few square miles on that single day, along with perhaps 10,000 horses.[47] Wellington was shaken by the losses, which included Sir Thomas Picton, killed at the head of his troops, and Lord Uxbridge who, famously, lost his leg at the very end of the battle, while many of Wellington's own staff had been either killed or wounded. He wrote to the Duke of Beaufort, whose brother, Fitzroy Somerset, was seriously wounded, 'the losses I have sustained have quite broken me down, and I have no feeling for the advantages we have acquired'. And he told Lord Aberdeen, whose brother Alexander Gordon had been killed, 'The glory resulting from such actions, so dearly bought, is no consolation to me, and I cannot suggest it as any to you and his friends.'[48]

Among the wounded was Lady Bessborough's son, Frederick Ponsonby, who commanded the 12th Light Dragoons in Vandeleur's brigade, on the left of the British line. Early in the battle his regiment charged some retreating French infantry (presumably part of D'Erlon's corps) and were counter-attacked by French lancers. Ponsonby was wounded in both arms, his horse ran away with him, and then he was thrown. As he tried to get up, a lancer speared him in the back, piercing his lung. 'My mouth filled with blood', he later wrote, 'and my breathing became very difficult . . . but I did not lose my senses.' He was plundered first by French and later by Prussian soldiers; a French officer gave him brandy and put a knapsack under his head; a skirmisher chatted to him while firing at the British light troops; and, like all the wounded, he was tormented by thirst. Towards evening he was ridden over by Prussian cavalry and finally, in the night, a British soldier, probably looking for plunder, found him and was persuaded to stay. The next morning he was taken to Waterloo, Wellington's physician dressed his wounds, and a week later he was taken to Brussels.[49]

Lady Bessborough was at Schaffhausen when she heard the news on 6 July, and leaving her husband to follow more slowly, she hurried to Brussels, travelling through the midst of the allied armies and making the journey in seven days, two less than the post. Her son 'appears dreadfully weak and helpless, but W. Lamb & the people who saw him ten days ago say the amendment is miraculous'. 'One arm is perfectly useless. Heaven grant it may be restored, but at present it looks terrible. The other, the left, tho' much less bad & with power to move it, is still very sore from the great cuts upon it, the shoulder, the upper part of the arm & below the elbow. The cut on the head is quite well, but it is the wound thro' his lungs I mind most. It is healing however, & I think his voice is stronger even in the few days I have been here.' Thirty-three days after the battle Frederick Ponsonby 'stood up & walked quite accross [sic] the room with scarcely any assistance, & sat up for some time in a chair at the open window'. A few days later the doctor discovered that in addition to his other injuries, the wounded man had a broken rib, but advised that it was already healing well. Soon Lady Bessborough was able to rejoice, 'Is it not wonderfull [sic] . . . that he should be alive! & recovering every day? which he really is, poor fellow.' A few days later she even joked, 'I am grown quite hardened & talk of amputations as rather a pleasure than not', but the ordeal had left its mark on her as well as on her son, and the relief is palpable when, towards the middle of August, the whole family were safely back in England.[50]

According to the well-known story, the first reports of the great victory to reach London were received by Nathan Rothschild on 20 June. He tried to inform the ministers and is said to have taken advantage of his knowledge on the Stock Exchange, though the size of his profit has always been greatly exaggerated.[51] It was not until late on the following day that Major the Honourable Henry Percy, one of Wellington's aides-de-camp, reached London bringing Wellington's official dispatch and two captured French eagles. Percy went first to Downing Street and from there to Lord Harrowby's house in Grosvenor Square where the cabinet were dining.

According to Harrowby's daughter, Percy burst in calling loudly for Lord Bathurst and crying, 'Victory . . . Victory . . . Bonaparte has been beaten'. While he delivered his news a crowd gathered in the Square, and soon Lord Harrowby came to the door and announced the news.[52]

Percy then hurried on to Mrs Boehm's house in St James's Square where the Prince Regent and the Duke of York were attending a ball. According to an unreliable but appealing account, she remembered that

> the first quadrille was in the act of forming, and the Prince was walking to the dais on which his seat was placed, when I saw every one without the slightest sense of decorum rushing to the windows, which had been left wide open because of the extreme sultriness of the weather. The music ceased and the dance stopped; for we heard nothing but the vociferous shouts of an enormous mob who had just entered the square, and were running by the side of a post-chaise and four, out of whose windows were hanging three [*sic*] nasty French eagles. In a second the door of the carriage was flung open and, without waiting for the steps to be let down, out sprang Henry Percy — such a dusty figure — with a flag in each hand — pushing aside everyone who happened to be in his way, darting upstairs, into the ballroom, stepping hastily up to the Regent, dropping on one knee, laying the flags at his feet, and pronouncing the words 'Victory, Sir! Victory!'[53]

The Regent welcomed the news and promoted Percy on the spot, but was soon reduced to tears by the preliminary list of casualties, which included many friends and acquaintances.

While fashionable London celebrated and mourned, and the ministers considered how to reward Wellington (they soon decided to grant him an additional £200,000), the news was rather embarrassing for the Opposition. According to H. G. Bennet's account,

> Nothing could be more droll than the discomfiture of our politicians at Brooks's. The night the news of the battle of Waterloo arrived, Sir Rt. Wilson and Grey demonstrated satisfactorily to a crowded audience that Boney had 200,000 men across [the] Sambre, and that he must then be at Brussels. Wilson read a letter announcing that the English were defiling out of the town by the Antwerp gate; when the shouts in the street drew us to the window, and we saw the chaise and the Eagles. To be sure, we are good people, but sorry prophets! The only consolation I have is in peace, and that we shall have, and have time, too, to look about us, and amend our system at home, and damage royalty, and badger Prinney.[54]

After Waterloo the allied armies advanced into France, meeting little resistance. Napoleon's army was utterly shattered, and though Grouchy was able to extricate his force in a skilful retreat, the war was clearly lost. Napoleon hurried to Paris, but once there hesitated over what to do. He could have dissolved the assembly, imposed martial law, and attempted to rally the army and the people against the allied invasion; but this offered no real prospect of success, his will to resist was broken, and on 22 June he abdicated in favour of his son. A provisional government was appointed, including Fouché, Caulaincourt and Carnot, and on 24 June it asked Wellington and Blücher, whose forces were advancing on Paris, for an armistice. Both generals refused and continued their advance, but contact was maintained and on 29 June Wellington informed the French commissioners, 'before I could stop my operations, I must see some steps taken to re-establish a government in France which should afford the Allies some chance of peace'. When pressed to explain what would satisfy the allies, he denied that he had any authority to speak on the subject, but then informed them that his personal opinion was that

> the best security for Europe was the restoration of the King, and that the establishment of any other government than the King's in France must inevitably lead to new and endless wars; that Buonaparte and the army having overturned the King's government, the simple and natural measure, after Buonaparte was prisoner or out of the way, and the army defeated, was to recall the King to his authority, and that it was a much more dignified proceeding to recall him without conditions, and to trust to the energy of their constitution for any reforms they wished to make either in the government or the constitution, than now to make conditions with their Sovereign; and that, above all, it was important that they should recall the King without loss of time, as it would not then appear that the measure had been forced upon them by the Allies.[55]

Wellington went on explicitly to rule out allied acceptance of Napoleon II and to indicate his personal opposition to the Duc d'Orléans. He exchanged letters and had several meetings with Fouché, and the two men got on remarkably well, with Wellington continuing to champion Fouché's interests well after the restoration had been achieved. And while Fouché managed the actual transition in Paris, it was largely owing to Wellington's bluntness that the allies and the Bourbons were spared any serious intrigue to support an alternative government.[56]

Paris formally capitulated on 3 July. The British and Prussian armies occupied the barriers on the 6th and entered the city on the following day, with Louis XVIII arriving on the 8th, one hundred and eleven days after he had fled in the night. Wellington reported that the city was 'perfectly quiet', but later there were such reports of enthusiasm that Bathurst commented, 'they are quite wild with rapture at having been conquered again'.[57] The French army withdrew behind the Loire, and Marshal Davout struggled hard to keep it in order, hoping to demand concessions from the new regime, including an amnesty for all political offences committed during Napoleon's return and a pledge that the army would not be purged. The government, however, would not negotiate and the troops deserted in large numbers, leaving Davout with no choice but to make his submission to the King on 14 July.[58]

The Convention of Paris contained a clause promising immunity to the citizens for their past political behaviour, and this raised concern in London that it might be construed as a general amnesty. Wellington replied by pointing out that the Convention only bound the parties to it, that is the allied armies, but could not hinder the French government from prosecuting traitors. The British government was extremely anxious for Louis XVIII to do so, Liverpool arguing that the restored regime could only establish its authority by showing that it dared to spill blood. 'It is a curious circumstance,' he told Canning, 'that after the sanguinary scenes which we recollect at the beginning of the French Revolution, all parties appear now to have an insuperable repugnance to executions. This arises not from mercy, but from fear.'[59] Liverpool's diagnosis was true of Paris, but not some of the provinces, where ultra-royalist mobs were soon taking vengeance on their local Bonapartist opponents in what has been called the 'White Terror'. Such behaviour appalled Talleyrand, Fouché and other 'liberal' ministers in Louis XVIII's first government, and it was only considerable pressure both from the allies and from the royalists that produced a list of fifty-seven exclusions from the general amnesty issued by the King. Fouché, who was still Minister of Police despite being at least as guilty as any of the fifty-seven, ensured that they all received ample warning and opportunities to escape. Only three were arrested and tried, Marshal Ney, General La Bédoyère and Count Lavalette, but they were all sentenced to death. This produced an outcry among the Whigs in England, and Sir Robert Wilson helped Lavalette to escape, but La Bédoyère and Ney were shot by firing squads in August and December. And so the intrepid Michel Ney, the most heroic and probably the most popular of all the marshals, died in the end at the hands of French soldiers.

The great outstanding problem of this kind was what to do with Napoleon, and here too the experience of 1814 warned against leniency. Blücher favoured a summary execution if the ex-Emperor should be captured by Prussian troops, but Wellington urged him 'to have nothing to do with so foul a transaction', and argued, 'that he [Blücher] and I had acted too distinguished parts in these transactions to become executioners; and that I was determined that if the Sovereigns wished to put him to death they should appoint an executioner, which should not be me'.[60] But Wellington had no wish to see Napoleon go free and refused to give him passports to the United States, as did the British admiral off Rochefort where Napoleon had taken refuge. Seeing that there was no hope of escape, the fugitive Emperor surrendered to Captain Maitland of H.M.S. *Bellerophon* on 16 July, sending the Prince Regent a grandiloquent appeal:

Exposed to the factions which distract my country and to the enmity of the greatest powers of Europe, I have closed my political career, and I come, like Themistocles, to throw myself upon the hospitality of the British people. I put myself under the protection of their laws, which I claim from your Royal

Highness, as the most powerful, the most constant, and the most generous of my enemies.[61]

This blatant appeal to the Regent's vanity caused much comment and discussion in England, with one wag suggesting that it would earn Napoleon the Garter at least, while Lady Holland was reported to be 'very cross and absurd about Buonaparte, "poor dear man", as she calls him'.[62]

The *Bellerophon* brought Napoleon to England, but he was not allowed to land, and huge crowds of spectators thronged out in small boats to catch a glimpse of him; some were passionately enthusiastic, others merely curious. Sir Francis Burdett had to be dissuaded by Romilly from moving a writ of habeas corpus for Napoleon's release; and a subpoena was actually issued requiring Napoleon's testimony in a libel case in London — a manoeuvre which was only defeated by Lord Keith and the *Bellerophon* making strenuous efforts to avoid the man who came to serve the subpoena.[63] In general, though, the mood of the country was still very hostile to Napoleon, an attitude encouraged by a virulent press full of cheap abuse and derisive jeers. The ministers felt little sympathy or sentiment for their fallen opponent, and Croker's reaction to Napoleon's appeal probably expresses the most common reaction of country and cabinet alike:

I could not help bursting out into a loud laugh, which astonished the French, who thought all beautiful, but '*Thémistocle*' sublime and pathetic. I called the whole letter a base flattery, and said Buonaparte should have died rather than have written such a one; the only proper answer to it would have been to have enclosed him a copy of one of his *Moniteurs*, in which he accused England of assassination and every other horror.[64]

The government still had to decide what to do with their troublesome prisoner. With some exasperation Liverpool told Castlereagh, 'we wish that the King of France would hang or shoot Bonaparte as the best termination of the business', but this was clearly no longer practical, and Liverpool may not have been altogether serious. The allies were happy to let Britain take charge of the prisoner, and Castlereagh suggested that he be detained in a fortress in Scotland, but Liverpool objected. There were legal difficulties with detaining him in Great Britain and he would attract too much public attention, and in any case it was desirable to send him far away, so that his presence would no longer 'contribute to keep up a certain degree of ferment in France'.[65] So the decision was taken to send him to St Helena, a small island in the middle of the South Atlantic, with a healthy climate, and which was secure enough to enable him to live with a reasonable degree of freedom. The story of his unhappy exile and descent into petty quarrels with the Governor, which exacerbated his rapidly deteriorating health, is too well known to need repeating here. And while we may regret that the British government did not act with greater generosity, particularly on small points of little consequence which touched the Emperor's pride, we

Buonaparte on the 17th of JUNE

Buonaparte on the 17th of JULY — 1815

16. Buonaparte on the 17th of June
Buonaparte on the 17th of July — 1815
George Cruikshank, Aug. 1815, B.M. Cat. no. 12,592

Napoleon did not actually reach Torbay until 24 July, but Cruikshank alters the date to stress the speed and completeness of his fall. Napoleon's speech in the second frame parodies his letter to the Prince Regent:

> O! good Mr Bull I wish you to know,
> (Although you are my greatest foe)
> That my Career is at an end:
> And I wish you now to stand my Friend
> For tho' at the Battle of Waterloo,
> I was by you beat black & blue
> Yet you see I wish to live with you
> For I'm sure what is said of your goodness is true
> And now if in England you'll let me remain
> I ne'er will be guilty of bad Tricks again.

must recognize that its prime responsibility was to help establish and maintain the peace and stability of the new European settlement which Napoleon had already once disrupted.

The greatest threat to that settlement still appeared to come from France. Liverpool and his colleagues in London feared that even with Napoleon in safe custody the restored Bourbons would be unable to establish a stable regime. 'For what is a King unsupported by opinion, by an army, or by a national party?' Feeling in Britain was running high, inflamed by the press which demanded that France suffer. The Prince Regent agreed, urging the Austrian Emperor, through his ambassador in London, to revive his ancient claims to Alsace Lorraine. (The ambassador replied by sarcastically enquiring if the Regent intended to revive the English claim to Aquitaine and Normandy, to which the Prince responded that he desired nothing for himself.) This climate of opinion influenced the views of the cabinet, and Liverpool told Castlereagh, 'I am satisfied that we must look for security in [the] frontier, and in really weakening the power of France'.[66] A few days later he was more specific:

> The prevailing idea in this country is, that we are fairly entitled to avail ourselves of the present moment to take back from France the principal conquests of Louis XIV. It is argued with much force that France will never forgive the humiliation which she has already received — that she will take the first convenient opportunity of endeavouring to redeem her military glory — and that it is our duty, therefore, to take advantage of the present moment to prevent the evil consequences which may flow from the greatness of our own success.

And he warned, 'we shall never be forgiven if we leave France without securing a sufficient frontier for the protection of the adjoining countries.'[67]

But Castlereagh and Wellington strongly disagreed with this approach, the latter complaining to Beresford that the government 'are taking up a little too much the tone of their rascally newspapers. They are shifting their objects; and, having got their cake, they want to both eat it and keep it.' Castlereagh firmly told the Prime Minister, 'it is not our business to collect trophies, but to try if we can bring back the world to peaceful habits. I do not believe this to be compatible with any attempt now materially and permanently to affect the territorial character of France, as settled by the Peace of Paris.'[68]

Gradually, after many letters were exchanged, their views converged in a compromise, though the ministers in London yielded more ground. By 23 August Liverpool had accepted Castlereagh's revised ideas, asking only for the addition of the destruction of the French fortresses of Lille and Strasbourg as a sop to public opinion; and when Liverpool was told that even this demand would be an embarrassment, it was dropped, and he sent his Foreign Secretary a formal assurance that 'Whatever may be the first popular impression on the result of the negotiation according to the principles which have been agreed upon . . . you will be most cordially and zealously supported and upheld by all your colleagues in this country.'[69]

While these exchanges were crossing the Channel, Castlereagh was holding talks with the allies. Relations with Alexander had taken a surprising turn. The Czar had at first felt some chagrin at the news of Waterloo, recognizing that it meant that he could not dominate the scene as he had in 1814. And he was reported as arguing that the allies 'must not mar our own existence again by too much lenity; and having shown the French what it was to be merciful, we must now make them feel what it is to be just'. But by the time he reached Paris on 10 July, his attitude had changed, so that

Castlereagh said that he had never seen him 'in a more cordial, contented, and at the same time reasonable disposition'.[70] He made no objection to the restoration of Louis XVIII, and went out of his way to court the royal government while shunning the Jacobins and Bonapartists. He worked hard to conciliate Castlereagh, even half-apologizing for his behaviour in London, and helped persuade the French government to confirm Napoleon's abolition of the slave trade. As a result Castlereagh, who had struggled in 1814 to arouse his colleagues' suspicion of Russia, now sought to allay them. The only danger was that Alexander, who was strongly defending French interests in the peace negotiations, might be seeking to establish a close Franco-Russian axis. This had always been Metternich's nightmare, and it gave him some anxiety now, but it came to nothing.[71]

Metternich himself kept a remarkably low profile in the negotiations. This may have been calculated, and it did Austria no harm, but there are hints that he was still jaded with exhaustion by the long months of the Congress, and had temporarily lost his zest for diplomacy and for the other diversions which Paris offered in abundance.[72]

Alexander and Metternich both broadly supported Castlereagh's approach to the peace settlement, though with many differences on details. The Prussians violently opposed it. Opinion in Prussia, particularly in the army, had been bitterly disappointed by the First Peace of Paris and the settlement at Vienna. The hatred of France, which had inspired Blücher's army in the campaigns of 1813, 1814 and 1815, led it to commit great excesses in its advance on Paris after Waterloo. The other allied armies committed similar faults, though not on the same scale as the Prussians, whose depredations made Wellington fear a popular uprising by the French people.[73] Prussian behaviour in Paris was equally heavy-handed and provocative, and Wellington had to intervene to prevent the destruction of the Pont Jena. Hardenberg deplored such behaviour and the pretensions of the Prussian generals to dictate to their own government (even complaining to Lord Clancarty that he felt himself in the midst of Praetorian bands), but he did not fundamentally disagree with their desire for large swathes of French territory.[74] Prussia would not annex this territory directly: rather the Netherlands and some of the smaller German states would be the immediate beneficiaries, but they in turn would be expected to yield territory to Prussia, all of Luxembourg in the case of the Netherlands.[75]

These plans received considerable support from the smaller states, who were moved by a mixture of greed, and fear and hatred of France. Even Count Münster, the Hanoverian minister, favoured a harsh peace, and when it became clear that his differences with Castlereagh were irreconcilable, he left Paris. The policy of the smaller powers, even more than the Prussians, seems to have annoyed Castlereagh, for at least Prussia might hope to defend her acquisitions in a future war, while the smaller powers would inevitably appeal to Britain and the other allies. He sent Clancarty to the Netherlands to speak to the King, and asked the Dutch envoy in Paris how he 'would relish having these fortresses without the guarantee of England. . . . This view of the question appeared altogether to damp His Excellency's appetite for such acquisitions.'[76]

Prussia was less easily dealt with, and as the negotiations dragged on tempers frayed, but Castlereagh had the support of Alexander and, less actively, Metternich. In the end it was agreed to reduce France to the frontiers she had held in 1790. This involved the loss of some territory to Belgium and Switzerland, Savoy reverting to Piedmont, which also received the suzerainty of Monaco, while the Saar basin, including Saarbrücken and Saarlouis, was added to Prussia's Rhineland territory. In addition, France had to pay an indemnity of 700 million francs (a compromise between the 600 million proposed by Castlereagh and the 1,200 million wanted by Prussia) and had to return all the looted art treasures in the Louvre. This produced great ill-feeling among the Parisians, and Wellington was hissed and booed in the theatre, although in fact he and Castlereagh privately opposed the measure.[77] The stability of the French government and the security of Europe were to be protected by the presence of an Army of Occupation of 150,000 men, under the command of the Duke of Wellington, which was to have possession of all the fortresses of northern and eastern France for between three and five years. It was this proposal which reconciled the ministers in London to the comparatively mild terms of the peace, Mulgrave, for example, commenting that the popularity of the French government would depend, not on the terms of the peace, but 'on the number of foreign bayonets that glitter for some years in the eyes of the French population, either to awe the disaffected or protect the loyal'.[78]

The allies also concluded two alliances, the Czar's Holy Alliance, whose high moral pretensions Castlereagh and Metternich found risible, and the Quadruple Alliance, which was little more than a renewal of the Treaty of Chaumont, with the four powers pledging to maintain the terms of the peace in the face of any future aggression by France, and to consult each other in the event of another revolution in Paris. It also made provision for periodic meetings of the allied ministers to discuss matters of common concern, thus laying the foundation for future congresses. Both the Quadruple Alliance and the Second Peace of Paris were signed on 20 November 1815, more than five months after Waterloo, a delay which Castlereagh suspected had as much to do with the desire of the allies to maintain their armies — over 900,000 men in all — at French expense while continuing to pocket British subsidies as with the intricacies of the negotiations.[79]

But at last the peace was signed, and on the whole it proved remarkably successful. Having endured a generation of almost continuous war, Europe now enjoyed a generation of almost continuous peace. Neither the Bourbon government in France nor the union of Belgium and Holland survived the events of 1830, but the resulting crisis was resolved by diplomacy rather than force of arms (though there was some fighting); and the establishment

of Belgium as an independent country under international guarantee satisfied Britain's need for a barrier to French expansion northwards. In any case
the balance of power in Europe was shifting. Partly because of economic
and demographic causes, but also because the peace settlement of 1814–15
reduced the size of France while increasing that of her rivals, France was no
longer the threat to the rest of Europe that she had been for the previous 150
years. It would be another century before Britons would again be called
upon to fight to preserve that disunion in Europe which was so essential to
Britain's security and independence.

Conclusion

How important was Waterloo? Few battles are so immediately decisive, with a war being won on a single bloody afternoon. Yet if Napoleon had won, would history have been very different? It has become customary to say that it mattered little who won the battle, and that even if Napoleon had triumphed he would soon have been overthrown by the vast Austrian and Russian armies which were gathering against him. Perhaps so, but there seems little reason for confidence on such a hypothetical question. If Napoleon had defeated Wellington and Blücher, he might well have gone on to defeat the Russians and Austrians, and even consolidate his power permanently in France. The odds would still have been against him, but they were rapidly shortening. And only those who view the past in quasi-geological terms — happily taking the long view of 500 years, where no individuals matter much — can fairly argue that Napoleon's success or failure was of little consequence.

But there is another sense in which Waterloo is important, for as well as being a French defeat, it was a British victory, the crowning glory which brought the long war to a fitting close. The war as a whole, and Waterloo in particular, gave Britain a sense of uniqueness, an inner confidence, which lasted a full century until it was shattered on the Somme. Alone of the European powers, she had withstood the whirlwind unleashed by the French Revolution unscathed. French troops had never marched in triumph through London as they had through Vienna, Rome, Madrid, Lisbon, Brussels, Amsterdam, Berlin, Warsaw and Moscow. Britain had not tasted the bitter humiliation of defeat and had prospered while her allies had collapsed. In 1783, only ten years before the war began, Britain had been defeated and divided by the American war; now that memory was expunged, not only by the victory over France, but by the defeat of the United States in the war of 1812. The loss of the American colonies had been offset by the acquisition of a new colonial empire, and by unprecedented dominance of international trade and the high seas. Waterloo set the seal on this achievement. Britain triumphed on land, as she had long done on the sea, and had overthrown the all-conquering enemy. Popular memory soon forgot Napoleon's first abdication: Waterloo was the last and greatest of Sir Edward Creasy's *Fifteen Decisive Battles of the World*, while eighty years after the battle an Australian clergyman expressed the mood of the time when he called his four-volume history of the French wars *How England Saved Europe*.[1]

Nelson and Trafalgar, Moore and Coruña, Wellington and Waterloo, thus became the focus for popular British patriotism throughout the nineteenth century. The war and its memory gave the British people a taste for military glory and greatly eroded the traditional distrust of standing armies.[2] At the same time the war had seen a great increase in the power and size of the state, ranging from the treatment of enemy aliens and working-class radicals to the far more pervasive effect of the income (or 'property') tax. It is hard for us to recognize what an innovation this was, but Alexander Baring, speaking in Parliament, gives a sense of the resentment it aroused:

> In theory, it might be very beautiful to tax every man according to his property, but nothing could be more odious than that a man should be catechised by persons who possessed more than inquisitorial powers; for his own part, he would much rather be summoned before the bench of bishops, to be questioned as to his belief in doctrinal points of religion, than appear before the commissioners under the property tax.[3]

These changes in British society were not accepted without opposition. Pressure in Parliament forced the prompt abolition of the property tax against the wishes of the ministers, while the modest peace establishment which they proposed was denounced as an attempt to make Britain a military, and hence a despotic, state. Throughout the nineteenth century, liberals continued to oppose government spending, particularly on the armed forces, but not all the speeches of Gladstone, Bright and Cobden could restore the lost innocence of a world which had never known income tax.

Of course the property tax represented not only the intrusion of the state into previously private affairs, but also the crude financial demands of the war, and these even surpassed military operations in reaching new heights in 1813, 1814 and 1815. Total government spending grew rapidly from £82 million in 1811, £87 million in 1812, and £95 million in 1813, to £111 million in 1814 and £113 million in 1815. The increases of 1814 and 1815 were paid for by a revival of trade (with America in 1815, as well as Europe in 1814), some new taxes, and very heavy borrowing, particularly in 1815 when the emergency was seen as temporary. The budget presented on 14 June 1815 shows how heavily Britain had become committed to military operations, for while the navy was allocated £18.6 million, the army was promised £39.1 million, with a further £15 million reserved for foreign payments and the vote of credit, and no less than £30 million for servicing the national debt.[4]

By the end of 1815 there was some reason for politicians and economists to be appalled at the unprecedented growth in the national debt. In 1793 it had been £245 million; by 1807 it had reached £618 million, and by 1815 it had climbed to £834 million, or £43 for every man, woman and child in Great Britain and Ireland. Yet even this by no means represents the whole cost of the war, for the government, after the 1790s, paid as much as possible out of taxation. Modern estimates of the total cost of the war vary widely, depending on the method of calculation (for example, should the cost of servicing debt raised for military purposes be included, or should a deduction be made for the cost of peace-establishments in order to obtain a net figure?), but Professor O'Brien's cautious estimate of £1,039 million gives some idea of the burden Britain faced at a time when her economy was still in its infancy.[5]

The effect of this enormous demand for funds on the economy as a whole is also the subject of debate. Most economic historians argue that the effect was disruptive and harmful, but C. H. Lee has concluded more cautiously that

> There is no evidence that industry was deprived of investment by increased government demand for funds. . . . It seems likely that the increased government borrowing in the Napoleonic Wars . . . absorbed idle funds and did not crowd out any industrial growth. Without the quarter of a century of warfare, the development path of the British economy would have been rather different, but it is by no means certain that its rate of growth would have been any greater.[6]

Whatever the overall effect on the economy, individuals felt that they were paying a high price for the war, and they were not mistaken. Between 1808 and 1815 government spending grew to over 25 per cent of national income, compared with only 6 per cent before 1793. And the great bulk of the increase in government revenue came not from economic growth but from new and higher taxes.[7] Nor was peace followed by the longed-for plenty. Rather there was a severe and prolonged recession as the economy adjusted to the return of peace and Britain's markets regained their prosperity. Many an old soldier, like the anonymous memoirist of the 71st who had gone through the war repenting his impulsive enlistment, found himself working the roads for a pittance and regretting his discharge.[8] Yet in the longer run, when memories of the property tax and the postwar recession had faded, bellicose Britons could reflect that their country had emerged from the long war with her position relative to her economic rivals enormously enhanced.

Memories of the human cost of the war also faded, and in time were replaced by the image of the cheerful Chelsea pensioner with his rattling tales of youthful adventure in the Peninsula under 'the Duke'. Here too the statistics are uncertain and need to be handled with care. There are no figures for the total number of British soldiers who died in the Peninsular War, but there is good authority for saying that from Christmas 1810 until 25 May 1814 just over 35,000 British officers and men in Wellington's army died, of whom 24,000 succumbed to sickness and disease, and rather more than 11,000 were killed in action or died from wounds. This would suggest that the total figure for British deaths in the Peninsula was 50–60,000, although this is no more than a rough estimate. Figures for the whole war, from 1793 to 1815, are even more uncertain. British troops saw far less action in the years before 1808, and it appears that only one in nine of the soldiers and sailors who died did so owing to enemy action (which compares with five in every six in the First World War). Overall, the excess mortality suffered by Britain during the whole war has been estimated at between 200,000 and 250,000, with the army suffering more than twice the losses of the navy. This is the net loss, that is the total number of deaths attributable to the war, minus those who could be expected to have died anyway, and so a more precise figure would be misleading. Allowing for the smaller population, this represents a loss on the same scale as Britain suffered in the First World War, though the impact of the later conflict was much greater, being compressed into only four years.[9]

Such figures give no clue to the suffering they represent, and even Frederick Ponsonby's ordeal, which gives some food for the imagination, was less bad than that of many of the Waterloo wounded. He was British and he was a senior officer, both of which afforded him some protection from the soldiers, camp-followers and peasants who wandered the field after the battle, plundering the fallen, stripping the dead of their clothes, and sometimes killing the defenceless wounded in order to strip and plunder them too. Ponsonby spent half a day and one night lying with his wounds undressed, tormented by thirst. But it was four days before the last British wounded were collected from the field and attended to, and for many of the French it was even longer. Once rescued, he had his wounds dressed by the best doctor, and he received devoted and careful nursing in comfortable clean quarters in Brussels, without which he would probably have died. The common soldiers, particularly the French, were treated in vast, makeshift infirmaries in the churches, the private houses and the very streets and squares of Brussels. They were given every care and attention possible, but their numbers were so great that they overwhelmed the available resources, for no one had prepared for carnage on such a scale. There are stories of great kindness and compassion, as the inhabitants ignored the danger of fever and pestilence and took the wounded into their own homes; and stories of grief and terrible suffering, such as Lady De Lancy's account of her husband's last days. One surgeon recalls performing operation after operation for thirteen hours at a stretch until 'my clothes [were] stiff with blood, and my arms powerless with the exertion of using the knife!' Around him 'lay at one time thirteen [wounded men], all beseeching to be taken next; one full of entreaty, one calling upon me to remember my promise to take him, another execrating'; and this was a fortnight after the battle, and there were no anaesthetics and no antiseptics.[10]

Whether any reasons of state could possibly justify such suffering is a moral question lying essentially outside the scope of this work, but a few observations can be made. The great majority of the British population in 1815 were not, and never had been, pacifists, despite the example of the Quakers in their midst. Unlike other nations of the period, Britain made little use of conscription for foreign service: some militiamen were coerced into 'volunteering' into the line, and the navy used the press gang to gain recruits, but, by and large, Wellington's army consisted of men who had chosen to serve. Nor was civil life free from similar pains and hardships, as anyone who has read Fanny Burney's harrowing account of her operation will realize. None of this justifies or excuses the additional suffering caused by war, but it places it in context. And there was no obviously preferable alternative, for neutrality offered no escape from the war, which touched almost every corner of Europe. Compare the experience of Britain and Holland. The Dutch entered the war with reluctance, and fought without enthusiasm until they were conquered by France in early 1795. But defeat did not bring repose. Holland was bled white by taxes, its trade was ruined, its colonies lost, and its fleet destroyed by Duncan at Camperdown. Dutch as well as British sailors continued to fight and die horribly throughout the war, and Dutch soldiers were forced to fight from Spain to Moscow. Without the Channel, without determination, and without good fortune, this might have been Britain's fate, and simply denouncing war as a great evil scarcely begins the argument. It is a debate which has been going on since before the days of Christ, and which seems set to continue until the end of the world; for there has never been a shortage of people willing to kill — and die, but mostly kill — for what they hold to be their own or believe to be right.

Britain's object in entering the war in 1793 had been defensive — to prevent France gaining control of the Low Countries and to preserve the balance of power in Europe — and though it took more than twenty years, this object was finally achieved in 1814 and consolidated in 1815. The restoration of the Bourbons was a secondary issue, and while it was always regarded as desirable (at least by Pittites), for much of the war it was considered totally impractical; and when it was revived in late 1813, it was seen primarily as a means to the end of taming France. During the war Britain conquered almost all the colonies of France and her allies, and it says a great deal about the priorities and outlook of her government that in the peace negotiations she insisted on retaining poor, but strategically important, colonies such as St Lucia and the Cape of Good Hope, while returning the fabulously wealthy Dutch East Indies. Similarly, despite the great financial cost of the war to Britain, she opposed the imposition of an indemnity on France in 1814 and sought to minimize it in 1815.

The war had been won and Britain's role in the victory was undeniable. She alone had continued the struggle when Napoleon dominated central Europe and even Russia was reduced to a compliant ally. The Channel and Britain's command of the sea were central to this success, giving her defences such an advantage that Napoleon never risked putting them to the test. Equally important was the resilience and strength of her financial system, which was able to survive Napoleon's attacks and still provide the funds needed for British expeditions and subsidies to the allies. But although Britain could defend herself, for many years all her attempts to take the offensive ended in defeat and recrimination, the wars of the first three coalitions serving only to strengthen French power.

The Spanish uprising of 1808 began a new and more promising era. Napoleon was forced to try to occupy and hold down a large, poor, difficult country against the wishes of its inhabitants. The Spanish resistance was sustained less by loyalty to Ferdinand VII and the Bourbons than by resentment at the French occupation and the misconduct, looting and brutality which Napoleon's armies brought with them. This created a vicious circle whereby attempts to suppress the insurrection only gave it more fuel. It also provided the ideal opportunity for the British army to return to the Continent. Napoleon could not put an end to the Spanish war with a single decisive campaign as he had destroyed previous coalitions, while the need to maintain a large army in central Europe and to disperse his troops throughout Spain prevented him from concentrating an over-whelming force against the British. Even as late as the Vitoria campaign the French could have held their own against Wellington, if it had not been for the diversion created by the insurrection in the northern provinces of Spain.

But while the war in Spain created the opportunity for British action, it did not ensure its success; and much of the credit for this success must go to Wellington. It seems most unlikely that any other British soldier of the period had the stamina and skill, the tactical brilliance, strategic insight and organizational ability to sustain the enterprise for the five demanding years from 1809 to 1814. Wellington had all these qualities together with the self-confidence to carry on even when, as in early 1810, much of the army was despondent and lacked confidence in him. His coolness in action was superb, but not unusual among senior commanders; more outstanding was his forethought, meticulous preparation and 'two o'clock in the morning courage', which were shown at their best in the defence of Portugal in 1810 and the capture of Ciudad Rodrigo and Badajoz in 1812. Like all generals, he made some mistakes, and his quick temper and propensity to grumble made him a difficult subordinate, but he never lost a battle or an army, and he was the one irreplaceable ingredient in Britain's success in Portugal and Spain.

The role of the Peninsular War in Napoleon's defeat has been much discussed. Napoleon himself, and his admirers, like to emphasize it, for it diverts attention from disasters such as the Russian campaign, with which he was more closely associated. National pride encourages British, Spanish and Portuguese historians to rate it highly, while Germans and Russians, equally naturally, are less impressed. Unfortunately there is little hard evidence against which to test these assessments. For example, there are no reliable figures for the total number of French soldiers who died in the Peninsula and the few published estimates vary wildly.[11] Nonetheless, it seems clear that the Peninsula was a great but sustainable drain on Napoleon's army and finances. In 1812, four years after the war in Spain began, he collected the largest army Europe had ever seen for the invasion of Russia. Without the war in Spain the quality of this army would certainly have been higher, and its numbers might have been still larger, but it is drawing the long bow to suggest that the Peninsula was a decisive factor in the Russian disaster. In 1813 the veteran troops in Spain might well have turned the tide in Germany; but if there had been no war in Spain, these same veterans would probably have marched on Moscow in 1812, and so been unavailable for service in 1813.

But Britain's war effort was not limited to the Peninsula. Her continued resistance encouraged Napoleon's enemies throughout Europe, while the Orders in Council caused considerable economic dislocation across the Continent, adding to discontent and depriving Napoleon of tax and customs revenue. Wellington's victories shattered the myth of French invincibility, and British subsidies helped finance allied campaigns. Over the whole course of the war, from 1793, Britain paid £65,830,228 in subsidies, and a disproportionate amount of this, almost half, came in the last three years, 1813–15.[12] These subsidies were never enough to pay more than a fraction of the cost of the war, and they produced relatively little influence or gratitude. But their importance should not be underestimated, especially for the final campaigns when the Continental Powers, although nearly exhausted by the long war and previous defeats, were making a last gigantic effort.

In the end it is impossible to disentangle one aspect of the war, whether it is the Peninsula, the economic war or Britain's role, and fairly assess in isolation its importance in Napoleon's fall. From Portugal to Poland it was one conflict, and the allies in 1813 benefited as much from Wellington's campaigns as he did from their operations. Napoleon was finally overthrown by the combined efforts of almost all the powers of Europe. Not all were equally important or necessary: Hesse-Cassel's contribution would have been little missed; Bavaria's scarcely more so; even Sweden's was probably not essential. But Russia, Prussia, Austria, Britain, Spain and Portugal all played roles which would have been difficult, perhaps impossible, to replace. And of these, one can fairly say that there could have been no victory without Russia; while without Britain, defeat might have been accepted and become permanent.

The ultimate responsibility for the conduct of the war lay with the government in London. It was the cabinet which determined strategic priorities, balancing the needs of one theatre with those of another, and selecting the soldiers and diplomats who were to implement the policy. The ministers of the Portland, Perceval and Liverpool governments were blessed by good fortune, but also showed much determination, sound sense and good judgement. They seized the opportunity of the war in Spain with alacrity, provided generous aid to the Spanish patriots, and dispatched the largest British army to the Continent for many years. They did not despair when the high hopes of 1808 came crashing to the ground; and they gave way to Canning's persuasion and made a further effort to save Portugal. They recognized Sir Arthur Wellesley's talents and persevered with him, despite the embarrassment of Cintra and the opposition of the King. They generously supported his campaigns with men, money and *matériel*, defended him against the Opposition's attacks, and entrusted him with the broadest discretion in the conduct of his operations. At the same time, they watched the wider European scene, quietly maintaining unofficial contacts with the Continental Powers, while discouraging premature attempts to overthrow Napoleon. Naturally they made some mistakes, persisting with the Orders in Council for too long, failing to conciliate the United States, mounting the Walcheren expedition, and possibly in not giving more aid directly to Russia in 1812. But in general their judgement was remarkably good, and when the great crisis came in 1813–14, they broke all precedents, and ignored all warnings, to make the greatest possible effort to bring the war to a successful conclusion. Finally, in Castlereagh they found a statesman who could protect Britain's interests in the peace negotiations and, building on Wellington's success, give her a powerful voice in the affairs of Europe.

Yet the ministers have never received much recognition. Liverpool was long remembered chiefly as the butt of Disraeli's jibe 'the Arch-Mediocrity'; Bathurst receives a scant column in the *Dictionary of National Biography*; and even Canning and Castlereagh are famous more for their rivalry and their duel, for their postwar diplomacy and for Castlereagh's peacemaking, than for their part in the defeat of Napoleon. The war in the Peninsula has usually been viewed in isolation, and it is no surprise to see Wellington emerge as the hero of that story. But if we step back and view the war as a whole, we can see the importance of the ministers. They lack the glamour of the marvellous glittering figure in the foreground, but that is no reason to neglect their achievement.

Abbreviations

Adm.	Admiralty
British Diplomacy	*British Diplomacy: Select Documents dealing with the Reconstruction of Europe*, edited by C. K. Webster (London, G. Bell, 1921)
Castlereagh Correspondence	*Correspondence, Despatches, and Other Papers of Viscount Castlereagh, Second Marquis of Londonderry*, edited by his brother, Charles William Vane, Marquis of Londonderry, 12 vols (London, William Shoberl, 1848–53)
D.N.B.	*Dictionary of National Biography*
F.O.	Foreign Office
Fortescue	*A History of the British Army*, by the Hon. J. W. Fortescue, 13 vols (London, Macmillan, 1899–1930)
H.M.C.	Historical Manuscripts Commission
J.S.A.H.R.	*Journal of the Society for Army Historical Research*
N.R.A.	National Register of Archives
N.R.S.	Navy Record Society
Oman	*A History of the Peninsular War*, by Sir Charles Oman, 7 vols (Oxford, Clarendon Press, 1902–30)
P.R.O.	Public Record Office
P.R.O.N.I.	Public Record Office of Northern Ireland
W.D.	*The Dispatches of Field Marshal The Duke of Wellington, during his various campaigns in India, Denmark, Portugal, Spain, the Low Countries and France...*, compiled by Colonel Gurwood, 8 vols (London, Parker, Furnivall and Parker, 1944)
W.O.	War Office
W.P.	The Wellington Papers at the University of Southampton Library
W.S.D.	*Supplementary Despatches, Correspondence and Memoranda of Field Marshal Arthur, Duke of Wellington, K. G.*, edited by his son, The Duke of Wellington, 15 vols (London, John Murray, 1858–72)

Notes

Where possible I have used the published version of a letter, often adding the superscription (e.g. 'private', or 'private and confidential') from the manuscript, since it is easier for most readers, should they wish to follow up a point at issue, to consult a published source rather than to visit an archive.

Introduction

1. Richard Glover, *Britain at Bay: Defence against Bonaparte, 1803–14* (London, George Allen and Unwin, 1973), pp. 83–9.
2. Canning to Granville Leveson Gower, 'Private', 2 Oct. 1807, P.R.O. 30/29, 8/4, ff. 460–4.
3. E.g. Grey to Grenville, 8 May 1812, *Historical Manuscripts Commission: Report on the Manuscripts of J. B. Fortescue, Esq. preserved at Dropmore*, 10 vols (London, H.M.S.O., 1892–1915; henceforth cited as *H.M.C. Dropmore*), vol. 10, pp. 243–4.
4. John M. Sherwig, *Guineas and Gunpowder: British Foreign Aid in the Wars with France, 1793–1815* (Harvard University Press, 1969), pp. 176–81; Christopher D. Hall, *British Strategy in the Napoleonic War, 1803–1815* (Manchester University Press, 1992), pp. 134–7.
5. Peter Jupp, *Lord Grenville, 1759–1834* (Oxford, Clarendon Press, 1985), pp. 402–10.
6. Hawkesbury to the King, 23 March 1807, in A. Aspinall (ed.), *The Later Correspondence of George III*, 5 vols (Cambridge University Press, 1962–70), vol. 4, no. 3408, p. 535. The implied comparison with Canning in this letter is obvious.
7. Henry, Lord Brougham, *Statesmen of the Time of George III and IV*, 3 vols (Edinburgh, Adam and Charles Black, 1872), vol. 2, p. 50.
8. C. R. Middleton quoting Cornwallis to Ross, 25 Dec. 1800, *The Administration of British Foreign Policy, 1782–1846* (Durham N.C., Duke University Press, 1977), p. 130.
9. Richard Glover, *Peninsular Preparation: The Reform of the British Army, 1795–1809* (Cambridge University Press, 1963), pp. 35–6.
10. Figures from the Hon. J. W. Fortescue, *The County Lieutenancies and the Army, 1803–1814* (London, Macmillan, 1909), pp. 291–3. These figures include deaths (about half the total), desertions and men discharged, and are slightly inflated as some men recorded as being discharged were in fact transferred to other units; see W. B. Hodge, 'On the Mortality arising from Military Operations', *Quarterly Journal of the Statistical Society*, vol. 19, Sept. 1856, pp. 228–30, 264–5.

11. Fortescue, *County Lieutenancies*, pp. 196–7.
12. Figures from Fortescue, *County Lieutenancies*, p. 304.
13. Draft 'Memorandum for the Cabinet, relative to the State of the Military Force', by Lord Castlereagh, March 1807, *Correspondence, Despatches and Other Papers of Viscount Castlereagh, Second Marquis of Londonderry*, edited by Charles William Vane, Marquis of Londonderry, 12 vols (London, William Shoberl, 1848–53; henceforth cited as *Castlereagh Correspondence*), vol. 8, pp. 46–52. See also below, chapter 1, p. 22.
14. I am unconvinced by Richard Glover's argument in 'The French Fleet, 1807–14: Britain's Problem; and Madison's Opportunity', *Journal of Modern History*, vol. 39, 1967, pp. 233–52.
15. Paul Webb, 'Construction, repair and maintenance in the battlefleet of the Royal Navy, 1793–1815', in *The British Navy and the Use of Naval Power in the Eighteenth Century*, ed. Jeremy Black and Philip Woodfine (Leicester University Press, 1988), pp. 207–19.

1   The First Year of the Portland Government, 1807–8

1. H. Butterfield, *The Peace Tactics of Napoleon, 1806–1808* (Cambridge University Press, 1929), pp. 94–7, 187–94; Patricia K. Grimsted, *The Foreign Ministers of Alexander I: Political Attitudes and the Conduct of Russian Diplomacy, 1801–1825* (Berkeley, University of California Press, 1969), pp. 160–1.
2. Sherwig, *Guineas and Gunpowder*, pp. 186–7.
3. Raymond Carr, 'Gustavus IV and the British Government, 1804–9', *English Historical Review*, vol. 60, 1945, p. 54.
4. 'Memorandum respecting the State of the Military Force', by Lord Castlereagh, 26 May 1807, *Castlereagh Correspondence*, vol. 8, pp. 62–6; Castlereagh to the King, 1 June 1807,

enclosing Cabinet Minute of the same day, *Later Correspondence of George III*, vol. 4, no. 3471, pp. 587–8; Canning to Granville Leveson Gower, 'Private', 9 June 1807, P.R.O. 30/29, 8/4, ff. 420–5, gives reasons for not sending the force to Hanover; the Hon. J. W. Fortescue, A *History of the British Army*, 13 vols (London, Macmillan, 1899–1930; henceforth cited simply as Fortescue), vol. 6, pp. 8–9.
5. A. N. Ryan, 'Causes of the British Attack upon Copenhagen', *English Historical Review*, vol. 68, Jan. 1953, pp. 47–9; Lady Bessborough to Granville Leveson Gower, [12] July 1807, *Lord Granville Leveson Gower (First Earl Granville), Private Correspondence, 1781–1821*, ed. Castalia Countess Granville, 2 vols (London, John Murray, 1916; henceforth cited as *Private Correspondence of Granville Leveson Gower*), vol. 2, p. 261.
6. Canning to Granville Leveson Gower, 9 June 1807, P.R.O. 30/29, 8/4, ff. 420–5. This letter is partially printed by A. N. Ryan in his useful collection 'Documents Relating to the Copenhagen Operation, 1807', in *The Naval Miscellany*, vol. 5, ed. N. A. M. Rodger (London, Allen and Unwin for the Navy Records Society, 1984), pp. 297–329; see also Ryan, 'Causes of the British Attack on Copenhagen', pp. 40–7.
7. Mulgrave to the King and reply, 14 July 1807; Castlereagh to the King and reply, 17 and 18 July 1807, *Later Correspondence of George III*, vol. 4, nos 3497, 3501, pp. 604, 606–7.
8. J. H. Rose, 'A British Agent at Tilsit', in his *Napoleonic Studies* (London, Geo. Bell & Sons, 1904), pp. 153–65, is probably still the best discussion of this question.
9. Canning to Granville Leveson Gower, 'Private', 8.30 p.m., 5 August 1807, P.R.O. 30/29, 8/4, ff. 438–44.
10. J. H. Rose, 'Canning and Denmark in 1807', in his *Napoleonic Studies*, pp. 133–52; Jackson's own private account of his conduct supports this interpretation: Francis Jackson to George

Jackson, Kiel, 7 August 1807, *Diaries and Letters of Sir George Jackson, K.C.H.*, ed. Lady Jackson, 2 vols (London, Richard Bentley, 1872), vol. 2, pp. 192–4.

11. Fortescue, vol. 6, pp. 64–73; C. T. Atkinson (ed.), 'Gleanings from the Cathcart Mss. Part VI — The "Conjoint" Expedition to Copenhagen, 1807', *J.S.A.H.R.*, vol. 30, no. 122, Spring 1952, pp. 80–7.

12. R. C. Anderson, *Naval Wars in the Baltic* (London, Wood, 1910), p. 319.

13. The King is quoted in Canning to Mrs Canning, 26 August 1807, *The Later Correspondence of George III*, vol. 4, p. 607n; on Canning's role in the expedition see Boringdon to Granville Leveson Gower, 18 Sept. 1807, P.R.O. 30/29, 9/1, ff. 202–3.

14. *Parliamentary Debates*, vol. 10, cols 382–3 (Sidmouth) and 1288–9 (Wilberforce); Canning to Mrs Canning, 1 Aug. 1807, quoted in *The Later Correspondence of George III*, vol. 4, p. 613n.

15. Castlereagh to Cathcart, 22 Sept. 1807, *Castlereagh Correspondence*, vol. 6, pp. 182–6.

16. Canning to Granville Leveson Gower, 'Private', 29 Sept. 1807, P.R.O. 30/29, 8/4, ff. 454–7; M. S. Anderson, 'The Continental System and Russo-British Relations during the Napoleonic Wars', in K. Bourne and D. C. Watt (eds), *Studies in International History* (London, Longmans, 1967), pp. 70–1.

17. A. N. Ryan, 'An Ambassador afloat: Vice-Admiral Sir James Saumarez and the Swedish Court, 1808–1812', in Black and Woodfine (eds), *The British Navy and the Use of Naval Power in the 18th Century*, pp. 239–40.

18. Ryan, 'An Ambassador Afloat . . .', pp. 240–2; Carr, 'Gustavus IV and the British Government', pp. 58–62; Castlereagh to the King, 17 April 1808, *Later Correspondence of George III*, vol. 5, 3646, pp. 65–6.

19. Canning to Sir A. Paget, no. 1, 16 May 1807, and same to same, 'Private', 26 May 1807, *The Paget Papers: Diplomatic and Other Correspondence of the Rt. Hon. Sir Arthur Paget*, ed. Sir Augustus Paget, 2 vols (London, Heinemann, 1896), vol. 2, pp. 290–93, 295–8.

20. Castlereagh to the King and reply, 22 and 23 May 1807, *Later Correspondence of George III*, vol. 4, no. 3463, p. 583.

21. Piers Mackesy, *The War in the Mediterranean, 1803–1810* (Westport, Greenwood, 1981; first published by Harvard University Press, 1957), pp. 206–7.

22. Robert W. Daly, 'Operations of the Russian Navy during the Reign of Napoleon I', *Mariner's Mirror*, vol. 34, July 1948, pp. 176–9; Canning to Granville Leveson Gower, 'Private', 29 Sept. 1807, P.R.O. 30/29, 8/4, ff. 454–7; *Select Speeches of the Right Honourable George Canning . . .*, ed. Robert Walsh (Philadelphia, Key and Biddle, 1835), pp. 65–6 (for the Russian ambassador's preparations); Mackesy, *War in the Mediterranean*, p. 227 (for Admiral Purvis); R. C. Anderson, *Naval Wars in the Levant* (Liverpool University Press, 1952), pp. 456–7 (for Siniavin's orders).

23. John Rosselli, *Lord William Bentinck and the British Occupation of Sicily, 1811–1814* (Cambridge University Press, 1956), pp. 158–63.

24. Canning to Chatham, 'Private & Secret', 14 Nov. 1807, Canning Papers, bundle 31; Canning to Lord Wellesley, 'Private', 26 Nov. 1807, ibid., bundle 39.

25. Canning to Granville Leveson Gower, 'Private', 5 Nov. 1807, P.R.O. 30/29, 8/4, ff. 466–70.

26. Canning to Granville Leveson Gower, 'Private', 5 Nov. 1807, P.R.O. 30/29, 8/4, ff. 466–70.

27. Strangford to Canning, 29 Nov. 1807, and Sir Sidney Smith to William Wellesley-Pole, 1 Dec. 1807, both in John Barrow, *Life and Correspondence of Admiral Sir William Sidney Smith*, 2 vols (London, Richard Bentley, 1848), vol. 2, pp. 261–9; see also Rose Macaulay, *They Went to Portugal* (London, Cape, 1946), pp. 359–78.

28. Eli F. Heckscher, *The Continental System: An Economic Interpretation* (Oxford, Clarendon Press, 1922), p. 245.

29. Herbert J. Wood, 'England, China and the Napoleonic Wars', *Pacific Historical Journal*, vol. 9, June 1940, pp. 139–56.
30. Canning to Boringdon, 12 Sept. 1807, in A. G. Stapleton, *George Canning and His Times* (London, Parker, 1859), pp. 128–9; Castlereagh to Sir A. Wellesley, 16 Sept. 1807, P.R.O.N.I., D3030/2533/2.
31. Liverpool to Hawkesbury, 25 Apr. 1808, B. L. Loan Ms 72, vol. 56, ff. 68–70; Duke of York to Col. J. W. Gordon, 20 Dec. 1807, B. L. Add. Ms 49, 472, f. 123.
32. 'Memorandum for Cabinet Measures suggested respecting South America' by Lord Castlereagh, 21 Dec. 1807, *Castlereagh Correspondence*, vol. 8, pp. 96–100.

2   From Bayonne to Cintra: The First Months of the Peninsular War

1. Charles Esdaile, 'War and Politics in Spain, 1808–1814', *Historical Journal*, vol. 31, no. 2, 1988, p. 300.
2. Dalrymple's letters are in C.O. 91/47; Hunter's in F.O. 72/62; on Vaughan and Archdekin, see F.O. 72/64, esp. ff. 42–53, 153–4. On the spies: Col. James Burke's extraordinary adventures are described in F.O. 72/81. They are hardly credible, but gain some credence from references to him in W.O. 1/237, ff. 5–7, 9–10. Sir Arthur Wellesley sent a private agent — one John Duggan — to Spain, but no more is heard of him. Sir A. Wellesley to John Beckett, 'Secret', 26 June 1808, Wellington Papers, W.P. 1/206, printed with the name deleted in *Supplementary Despatches, Correspondence and Memoranda of Field Marshal Arthur Duke of Wellington K.G.*, edited by his son the Duke of Wellington, 15 vols (London, John Murray, 1858–72; henceforth cited as *W.S.D.*), vol. 5, p. 462.
3. Castlereagh to Spencer, 16 Jan. and 17 May 1808, W.O. 6/185, pp. 6–13, 17–20. Spencer's letters to Castlereagh are in W.O. 1/226.
4. Portland to the King and reply, 21 and 22 Apr. 1808, *Later Correspondence of George III*, vol. 5, no. 3649, pp. 67–9. Castlereagh to Portland, 'Secret', n.d. [22 and 24 Apr. 1808], and enclosures, Portland Papers, PwF 8583, 8584 + a, b, c.
5. Dalrymple to Castlereagh, 31 May, 2 and 9 June 1808, B.L. Add. Ms 38, 242, ff. 231–3, 235–9, 263–4 and enclosures.
6. Herrara to Dalrymple and reply, 8 and 9 June 1808, B.L. Add. Ms 38, 242, ff. 268, 272; Castlereagh to Dalrymple, 25 May 1808, W.O. 6/185, pp. 22–7.
7. Précis of Spencer's letters to Castlereagh, *Castlereagh Correspondence*, vol. 7, pp. 151–7; Spencer to Castlereagh, 24 June 1808, W.O. 6/185, pp. 174–8.
8. Castlereagh to Dalrymple, 25 May 1808, W.O. 6/185, pp. 22–7.
9. Castlereagh to Dalrymple, 'private', 25 May 1808, W.O. 6/185, pp. 27–32.
10. Castlereagh to the King and reply, 1 and 2 June 1808, *Later Correspondence of George III*, vol. 5, no. 3667, p. 82. Mackesy, *War in the Mediterranean*, p. 266.
11. There is remarkable confusion about the date on which the messengers reached London, but it is clearly established by Canning to the King, 8 June 1808, *Later Correspondence of George III*, vol. 5, no. 3669, p. 84, and *The Times*, 9 June 1808. The declaration granting them full powers is in F.O. 72/65, ff. 10–11, and is printed in *Castlereagh Correspondence*, vol. 6, pp. 363–4. The appeal to Britain is in F.O. 72/65, ff. 13–14.
12. Campbell is quoted in Denis Gray, *Spencer Perceval: The Evangelical Prime Minister, 1762–1812* (Manchester University Press, 1963), p. 179; on the Royal Dukes see *The Correspondence of George, Prince of Wales, 1770–1812*, ed. A. Aspinall, 8 vols (London, Cassell, 1963–71), vol. 6, pp. 247–8.
13. *The Times*, 9 June 1808; *The Morning Chronicle*, 15 June 1808, quoted in Michael Roberts, *The Whig Party, 1807–1817* (London, Cass, 1965; first published 1939), p. 119; Cobbett

quoted by Joseph Farington, *The Farington Diary*, ed. James Grieg, 8 vols (London, Hutchinson, 1922–8), vol. 5, p. 84, entry for 2 July 1808.

14. Frederick George Stephens and Mary Dorothy George, *Catalogue of Political and Personal Satires, Preserved in the Department of Prints and Drawings in the British Museum*, 11 vols (London, British Museum Publications, 1978; first published 1870–1954), vol. 8, nos 10,994, 10,996–11,001, 11,003–6 (the 11 Spanish prints for July).

15. R. I. and S. Wilberforce, *The Life of William Wilberforce*, 5 vols (London, John Murray, 1838), vol. 3, p. 367, quoting Wilberforce's diary incorrectly dated 14 June 1808.

16. Whitbread to Grey, n.d. [16 June 1808], printed in Cecil Price (ed.), *The Letters of Richard Brinsley Sheridan*, 3 vols (Oxford, Clarendon Press, 1966), vol. 3, p. 38n.

17. Grey is quoted in Roberts, *The Whig Party*, p. 119n; Whitbread to Creevey, 29 June 1808, in *The Creevey Papers*, ed. Sir Herbert Maxwell (London, John Murray, 1923), p. 88. On Auckland see his letters to Grenville of 12 July, 4 and 7 Aug. 1808 in *H.M.C. Dropmore*, vol. 9, pp. 208–9, 210–12, 212–13; on Norfolk see Lord Holland, *Further Memoirs of the Whig Party, 1807–1821*, ed. Lord Stavordale (London, John Murray, 1905), p. 15.

18. *Parliamentary Debates*, vol. 11, cols 890–1.

19. Lord Holland, *Further Memoirs of the Whig Party, 1807–1821*, p. 13.

20. Eldon to [Canning], 10 June 1808, Canning Papers, bundle 31A. George III to Canning, 8 June 1808, *Later Correspondence of George III*, vol. 5, no. 3669, p. 84. Canning to the King, 11 June 1808, ibid., vol. 5, no. 3672, pp. 85–6.

21. Printed on pp. 321–2 of 'State Papers' section of the *Annual Register* for 1808.

22. George III to Canning, 12 June 1808, *Later Correspondence of George III*, vol. 5, no. 3672, p. 86.

23. Castlereagh to Col. Dyer, Maj. Roche and Capt. Patrick, 19 June 1808, *Castlereagh Correspondence*, vol. 6, pp. 371–3.

24. Herrera to Dalrymple, Cadiz, 8 June 1808, B.L. Add. Ms 38,242, f. 268; Asturian Junta to Mr Hunter, 18 June 1808, F.O. 72/65, ff. 90–2; on the attitude of the Asturian and Galician representatives in London see Castlereagh to Sir A. Wellesley, 30 June 1808, *The Dispatches of Field Marshal the Duke of Wellington . . .*, compiled by Col. Gurwood, 8 vols (London, Parker, Furnivall and Parker, 1844; henceforth cited as *W.D.*), *W.D.* III, p. 19n. On the Galician Junta, Sir A. Wellesley to Castlereagh, 21 July 1808, *W.D.* III, pp. 31–4.

25. Castlereagh to Sir A. Wellesley, 'Private', 26 June 1808, W.P. 1/205; Castlereagh to Lt-Col. Browne, 21 June 1808, Great Britain, *Parliamentary Papers*, vol. XI, 1809, p. 7; Castlereagh to Sir A. Wellesley, 30 June 1808, *W.D.* III, pp. 19n–20n.

26. Castlereagh to Sir A. Wellesley, 30 June 1808, *W.D.* III, pp. 19n–20n.

27. Cotton to William Wellesley-Pole (Secretary of the Admiralty), 'Secret', 12 June 1808, W.O. 1/237, ff. 89–90; the King to Mulgrave, 1 July 1808, *Later Correspondence of George III*, vol. 5, no. 3682, p. 94; Castlereagh to Sir A. Wellesley, 30 June 1808, *W.D.* III, p. 21n.

28. Sir A. Wellesley's evidence to the Enquiry into the Convention of Cintra printed in *W.D.* III, pp. 135–79; quote from p. 143.

29. Return of the force embarked 13 July 1808, *W.D.* III, p. 27n, lists 10,728 all ranks (9,505r and f).

30. Cooke to Sir A. Wellesley, 2 July 1808, with enclosed Memorandum in W.P. 1/207; Memorandum on Spain by 'J.W.G.', Horse Guards, 28 June 1808, W.O. 1/638, ff. 495–9.

31. George, *B.M. Catalogue of Satires . . .*, vol. 8, no. 11,023, pp. 670–1; Col. J.W. Gordon to Sir D. Dundas, 15 Oct. 1808, B.L. Add. Ms 49,512A, ff. 31–4.

32. Castlereagh to Sir A. Wellesley, 'Private', 30 June 1808, W.P. 1/205; Thomas Graham to Lady Asgill, 24 July 1808, in Cecil Aspinall-Oglander, *Freshly Remembered: The Story of Thomas Graham, Lord*

Lynedoch (London, Hogarth Press, 1956), p. 196.

33. Spencer to Castlereagh, 24 June 1808, W.O. 6/185, pp. 174–8 (see above, p. 36); Castlereagh to Sir A. Wellesley, 15 July 1808, *W.D.* III, p. 25n; Charles Stewart to Castlereagh, n.d., Durham Record Office, D/Lo/C17/3.

34. Castlereagh to the King, 14 July 1808, *Later Correspondence of George III*, vol. 5, no. 3693, pp. 103–4; *The Diary of Sir John Moore*, ed. Maj.-Gen. Sir J. F. Maurice, 2 vols (London, Edward Arnold, 1904), vol. 2, p. 239, entry for 23 July 1808; Charles Stewart to Castlereagh, n.d., Durham Record Office, D/Lo/C17/3.

35. Castlereagh to Dalrymple, 15 July 1808, *Parliamentary Papers*, vol. XI 1809, no. 22, p. 18; Castlereagh to the King, 14 July 1808, *Later Correspondence of George III*, vol. 5, no. 3693, pp. 103–4.

36. Castlereagh to Dalrymple, 15 July 1808, *W.D.* III, p. 27n.

37. On Burrard see Michael Glover, *Britannia Sickens: Sir Arther Wellesley and the Convention of Cintra* (London, Leo Cooper, 1970), pp. 65–6; and Fortescue, vol. 6, p. 195.

38. *Diary of Sir John Moore*, vol. 2, pp. 240–3, 250–2, which includes the letters. Moore's interpretation is on p. 250.

39. Sir A. Wellesley to Castlereagh, 21 July 1808, *W.D.* III, pp. 28–34.

40. Wellesley to Castlereagh, 21 and 25 July 1808, *W.D.* III, pp. 28–34, 36–7.

41. Wellesley to Spencer, 26 July 1808 (4 letters), *W.D.* III, pp. 37–40; Wellesley's evidence to the Cintra Enquiry, *W.D.* III, p. 183.

42. Spencer to Castlereagh, 24 June 1808, W.O. 6/185, pp. 74–8. See above, p. 36. Wellesley to Castlereagh, 1 Aug. 1808, *W.D.* III, pp. 42–6.

43. Wellesley to Castlereagh, 1 Aug. 1808, *W.D.* III, p. 46.

44. Wellesley to Castlereagh, 1 Aug. 1808, *W.D.* III, pp. 42–6; Wellesley's evidence to the Cintra Enquiry, *W.D.* III, p. 139.

45. For accounts of Roliça see Sir Charles Oman, *A History of the Peninsular War*, 7 vols (Oxford, Clarendon Press, 1902–30; henceforth cited as Oman), vol. 1, pp. 236–40; Fortescue, vol. 6, pp. 207–14. Casualty figures: Oman, vol. 1, p. 239 (for the French); Fortescue, vol. 6, p. 213 (for the British).

46. Wellesley to Castlereagh, 17 Aug. 1808, *W.D.* III, pp. 80–3 (the Roliça despatch); Wellesley to Castlereagh, 18 Aug. 1808, *W.D.* III, p. 85 (the 1,500 men). As the British gained possession of the battlefield they should have been able to make a reasonably accurate estimate of the French losses.

47. Fortescue, vol. 6, pp. 215–16, argues cogently that this was a mistake; but Burrard's arguments were quite reasonable and his decision is defensible.

48. French forces: Oman, vol. 1, pp. 246n–7n; Lisbon garrison: ibid., pp. 242–3; British army: Fortescue, vol. 6, p. 219n.

49. Burrard's evidence to the Cintra Enquiry quoted in Glover, *Britannia Sickens*, p. 123.

50. Wellesley to Castlereagh, 22 Aug. 1808, *W.D.* III, pp. 94–5; Wellesley to Richmond, 27 Aug. 1808, *W.D.* III, pp. 102–3; cf. Fortescue, vol. 6, p. 234 — who says that the French lost 1,800 casualties and 300–400 prisoners.

51. Dalrymple's evidence to the Cintra Enquiry quoted in Glover, *Britannia Sickens*, p. 128.

52. Wellesley's evidence to the Cintra Enquiry, *W.D.* III, pp. 153–4.

53. Yet Sir Charles Oman and most other historians of the campaign have accepted that the basis of the Convention was reasonable and that a prolongation of the campaign would have been detrimental to British interests. While these arguments have some merit I believe that Wellesley's opinion has had undue influence and that some of the arguments used to support it smack of special pleading, e.g. Oman's claim that 'The loss of 25,000 soldiers would be nothing to Napoleon', vol. 1, p. 268; see also pp. 274–5.

Junot himself admitted later that his

army could not have escaped to Elvas, and though he claimed that he could have held out in Lisbon for at least a month inflicting 5–6,000 British casualties, I am inclined to agree with Charles Stewart that this was 'mere brag' (Charles Stewart to Castlereagh, 17–18 Sept. 1808, P.R.O.N.I. D3030/P/213/1). The British generals could not *know* any of this, but it was their job to assess what a defeated army was capable of achieving.

Nor can the Convention be defended by comparing it with the agreement for the repatriation of the defeated French army from Egypt in 1801, for while the terms were similar the context was not. In 1801 Britain was already engaged in peace talks with France and had no Continental allies who would be disadvantaged by the return of the French troops, while in 1808 Junot's corps was freed to join immediately in Napoleon's new campaign against Spain.

Still, it is hard to run counter to the considered opinions of such weighty authorities as Oman, Fortescue and Napier.

54. Wellesley's evidence, in *W.D.* III, p. 156.

55. Cotton had objected to letting the Russian fleet go, and by a compromise it was agreed that Britain would hold the Russian ships until six months after a peace and immediately repatriate the sailors.

56. Castlereagh to Stewart, 10 Aug. 1808, P.R.O.N.I. D3030/Q2/2, p. 49; Edward Cooke to Stewart, 10 Aug. 1808, P.R.O.N.I. D3030/AA/1.

57. Castlereagh to the King, 12 p.m. [1 Sept. 1808], *Later Correspondence of George III*, no. 3711, p. 119.

58. Castlereagh to Sir A. Wellesley, 4 Sept. 1808, *Castlereagh Correspondence*, vol. 6, pp. 420–1.

59. Portland to Castlereagh, and Castlereagh to Stewart, both 4 Sept. 1808, *Castlereagh Correspondence*, vol. 6, pp. 421–4.

60. George, *BM Catalogue of Satires . . .*, vol. 8, pp. 676–7, no. 11,034.

61. *The Farington Diary*, vol. 5, pp. 98–9.

62. On the King see: Auckland to Grenville, 20 Sept. 1808, *H.M.C. Dropmore*, vol. 9, pp. 215–16; Wilberforce to Babington, 28 Sept. 1808, Wilberforce, *Life of Wilberforce*, vol. 3, pp. 379–80; Lady Bessborough to Granville Leveson Gower, 24 Sept. 1808, in *Private Correspondence of Granville Leveson Gower*, vol. 2, p. 329; Moira to McMahon, 26 Oct. 1808, in *Correspondence of George, Prince of Wales*, vol. 6, pp. 334–5; Auckland to Grenville, 29 Sept. 1808, *H.M.C. Dropmore*, vol. 9, p. 220; and for the suggestion about a riot see Roberts, *The Whig Party*, p. 120n.

63. *The Farington Diary*, vol. 5, p. 100; *The Times*, 16 Sept. 1808.

64. Castlereagh to the King, 6 p.m., 15 Sept. 1808, in *Later Correspondence of George III*, vol. 5, no. 3720, pp. 124–5.

65. Canning to Perceval, 'Private', Sat. morn., 17 Sept. 1808, Canning Papers, bundle 32/1. There is an inaccurate and wrongly dated version of this letter in Spencer Walpole, *The Life of the Rt. Hon. Spencer Perceval*, 2 vols (London, Hurst and Blackett, 1874) vol. 1, pp. 294–6.

66. Canning to Perceval, 'Private', 5 p.m., 17 Sept. 1808, Canning Papers, bundle 32/1.

67. Canning to Castlereagh, 'Private', 6 p.m., 17 Sept. 1808, Canning Papers, bundle 32/3.

68. Castlereagh to Canning, 'Private', n.d., 'Sunday Even.' [18 Sept. 1808], Canning Papers, bundle 34.

69. Canning to Castlereagh, 'Private and Secret', 17 Sept. 1808, Canning Papers, bundle 32/3.

70. Hawkesbury to Canning, 'Private', 18 Sept. 1808, Canning Papers, bundle 69; Harrowby to Countess Harrowby, Tiverton, 24 [Sept. 1808], Harrowby Papers, vol. LVII, ff. 256–7; Castlereagh to Perceval, n.d. [18 Sept. 1808], Perceval Papers, 8/VII/6.

71. Sir A. Wellesley to Castlereagh, 14 Oct. 1809, *W.S.D.*, vol. 6, pp. 401–3.

72. Lady Bessborough to Granville Leveson Gower, 27–29 Sept. 1808,

Private Correspondence of Granville Leveson Gower, vol. 2, pp. 329–31.

73. Granville Leveson Gower to Lady Bessborough, n.d., *Private Correspondence of Granville Leveson Gower*, vol. 2, pp. 331–2. In a marvellous understatement in the same letter Leveson Gower says that Canning — a close friend — 'is really quite unhappy about the detested Convention', *The Times*, 29 Sept. 1808; Richard M. Schneer, 'Arthur Wellesley and the Cintra Convention: a New Look at an Old Puzzle', *Journal of British Studies*, vol. 19, no. 2, 1980, pp. 93–119, gives a most interesting account of the controversy, although not all his conclusions are convincing.

74. Moira's opinion, dated 27 Dec. 1808, is printed in Oman, vol. 1, pp. 628–30.

75. Canning to Villiers, 'Private and Confidential', 27 Sept. 1809, Canning Papers, bundle 48.

3   The Road to Coruña, August 1808–January 1809

1. Oman, vol. 1, p. 339. To this must be added Junot's corps with an effective strength of 20,000 men, ibid., pp. 644–5.

2. Cuesta, the most senior Spanish General, openly talked of staging a coup, and was finally dismissed for arresting some members of the Supreme Junta, Oman, vol. 1, p. 357 and n, 359. The political ambitions of other generals were less glaringly obvious, but no less dangerous.

3. Oman, vol. 1, p. 347; pp. 363–4 on central Spain; Oman's criticism of the Supreme Junta (p. 365) is quite unfair.

4. Ibid., p. 365, cites Charles Vaughan's papers for the figure of 122,000 muskets received before 16 Nov. Canning writing to Frere on 16 Nov. 1808 (*Parliamentary Papers*, 1810, vol. 15, pt N, no. 13, pp. 16–17) claimed that over 160,000 muskets had been sent.

5. *Parliamentary Papers*, 1809, vol. XI, p. 247. Charles Vaughan acknowledged the arrival of approximately £1.2

million by 16 Nov., Oman, vol. 1, p. 365.

6. Extract of Canning to Mr Duff, 27 July 1808, Canning Papers, bundle 46. There is a most interesting and well-documented account of this arrangement in D. W. Davies, *Sir John Moore's Peninsular Campaign, 1808–1809* (The Hague, Martinus Nijhoff, 1974), pp. 67–9.

7. Rev. James Robertson, *Narrative of a Secret Mission to the Danish Islands in 1808* (London, Longmans, 1863), passim, and Oman, vol. 1, pp. 367–75.

8. E.g. Castlereagh to Romana, 1 Oct. 1808, *Castlereagh Correspondence*, vol. 6, pp. 460–1; Canning to Romana, 7 April 1809, Canning Papers, bundle 45.

9. Bentinck's correspondence is in W.O. 1/230 — see especially Bentinck to Castlereagh, 14 Nov. 1808, W.O. 1/230, p. 163.

10. Margaret Drabble (ed.), *The Oxford Companion to English Literature* (Oxford, O.U.P., 1985), p. 369.

11. Castlereagh to Maj.-Gen. Leith, 26 Aug. 1808, *Castlereagh Correspondence*, vol. 6, pp. 413–15.

12. Canning to Castlereagh, 17 and 23 July, and 5 Aug. 1808, all 'Private and Secret', Canning Papers, bundle 32/3.

13. 'Memorandum for consideration, on Measures projected in the present State of Affairs in Spain and Portugal', '[by Lord Castlereagh]', 10 Aug. 1808, *Castlereagh Correspondence*, vol. 6, pp. 399–401. Castlereagh to Stewart, 10 Aug. 1808, P.R.O.N.I. D3030/Q2/2, p. 49.

14. Cooke to Stewart, 19 Aug. 1808, P.R.O.N.I. D3030/AA/2.

15. Camden to Bathurst, 1 Sept. 1808, Bathurst Papers, B.L. Loan 57, vol. 3, no. 248.

16. Castlereagh to the King, 1 Sept. 1808, *Later Correspondence of George III*, vol. 5, no. 3711, pp. 118–19.

17. Castlereagh to Dalrymple, 2 Sept. 1808, *Parliamentary Papers*, 1809, vol. XI, p. 43.

18. Castlereagh to Bentinck, 30 Sept. 1808, in James Moore, *A Narrative of the Campaign of the British Army in*

Spain, commanded by . . . Sir John Moore (London, Johnson, 1809; henceforth cited as Moore, *Narrative . . .*), pp. 241–3, although Wellesley, when he arrived in England in October, strongly disapproved of the choice of Coruña, saying that the British infantry at least should be landed at Santander. Sir A. Wellesley to Castlereagh, 19 Oct. 1808, *Castlereagh Correspondence*, vol. 6, pp. 476–81.

19. *Later Correspondence of George III*, vol. 5, no. 3726, pp. 128–30.

20. Castlereagh to the King and reply, 23 and 24 Sept. 1808, *Later Correspondence of George III*, vol. 5, nos 3725, 3727, pp. 127–8, 131. Canning to Portland, 24 March 1809, Canning Papers, bundle 33A.

21. Castlereagh to Moore, 25 Sept. 1808, Moore, *Narrative . . .*, pp. 237–40.

22. *Diary of Sir John Moore*, 14 Oct. 1808, vol. 2, p. 272.

23. *Diary of Sir John Moore*, 27 Oct. 1808, vol. 2, pp. 273–4; Moore to Castlereagh, 27 Oct. 1808, Moore, *Narrative . . .*, pp. 250–2. Davies, *Sir John Moore's Peninsular Campaign*, pp. 61, 71, points out that strictly speaking Castlereagh's instructions obliged Moore to send at least part of the infantry and artillery by sea. This is true, but Davies does not give equal weight to the fact that the instructions also obliged Moore to send the cavalry by land. Castlereagh to Moore, 25 Sept. 1808, Moore, *Narrative . . .*, pp. 237–40. Castlereagh himself did not interpret his orders so strictly: he wrote to the Duke of York that Moore was to go by land or sea 'as he may find more eligible'. Castlereagh to the Duke of York, 26 Sept. 1808, P.R.O.N.I. D3030/2884.

24. Moore to Castlereagh, 24 and 25 Nov. 1808, Moore, *Narrative*, pp. 257–64.

25. Oman, vol. 1, pp. 466–70.

26. Moore to Frere, 19 Nov. 1808, Moore, *Narrative . . .*, pp. 38–40.

27. Moore to Frere and replies, 27 and 30 Nov. 1808, Moore, *Narrative . . .*, pp. 63–5, 79, 80–4. See also Moore to Frere, 6 Dec. 1808, printed in *Diary of Sir John Moore*, vol. 2, pp. 349–52. Moore's other letters on and around 27 Nov. confirm that he was seriously intending to take the offensive.

28. Davies, *Sir John Moore's Peninsular Campaign*, pp. 123–6, gives a good account of the Charmilly episode and shows that by his own account Charmilly was in Madrid for only three hours on a winter's night, and that much of his time was spent in talks. Moore suspected the value of Charmilly's evidence but could not completely discount it.

29. Moore to Baird, 6 Dec. 1808, Moore, *Narrative . . .*, pp. 92–3.

30. Frere to Moore, 8 Dec. 1808, Moore, *Narrative . . .*, pp. 138–9.

31. Oman, vol. 1, p. 536.

32. Oman, vol. 1, pp. 559–61. The irony is, of course, that if Napoleon had continued the pursuit he would have found the British with their backs to the sea at Coruña. Whether or not he could have defeated and destroyed Moore's army would largely have depended on the proportion of his army he had kept in the chase. Certainly the whole army could not advance through Galicia owing to the shortage of supplies.

33. Fortescue, vol. 6, p. 380n. Soult's army had just over 16,000 men compared with approximately 15,000 in Moore's army.

34. Oman, vol. 1, pp. 583–95; Fortescue vol. 6, pp. 380–9. The British appear to have suffered some 700–800 casualties in the battle, while estimates of the French loss range from 600 to 1,500.

35. Moore to Castlereagh, 24 Nov. 1808, Moore, *Narrative . . .*, pp. 257–60.

36. Moore to Castlereagh, 24 Nov. 1808, Moore, *Narrative . . .*, pp. 260–4.

37. Castlereagh to Moore, 10 Dec. 1808, *Parliamentary Papers*, 1809, vol. XI, pp. 77–9; Canning to Frere, 9 Dec. 1808, F.O. 72/60, ff. 147–56.

38. Canning to Castlereagh, 'Private and Secret', 3 p.m., 10 Dec., and 'Private and Confidential', 11 Dec. 1808, Canning Papers, bundle 32/3.

Canning to Frere, 'Private and Most Confidential', 11 Dec. 1808, Canning Papers, bundle 45.

39. Canning to Castlereagh, 'Private and Confidential', 30 Dec. 1808, Canning Papers, bundle 32/3; Canning to Portland, 'Private and Confidential', 30 and 31 Dec. 1808, Canning Papers, bundle 32/4.

40. Portland to Canning, 'Private and Confidential', 31 Dec. 1808, Canning Papers, bundle 33/A.

41. Portland to Canning, 'Private and Confidential', 1 Jan. 1809, Canning Papers, bundle 33/A.

42. Col. J. W. Gordon to Moore, 'Secret', Horse Guards, 9 Jan. 1809, B. L. Add. Ms 49,512A, ff. 36–7; Sir A. Wellesley to Col. H. M. Gordon [Military Secretary to the Commander-in-Chief in Ireland], 'Private & Confidential', London, 22 Jan. 1809, W.P. 1/233.

43. Wendy Hinde, *George Canning* (London, Collins, 1973), p. 213.

4   In Search of a Strategy, December 1808–April 1809

1. Canning to Frere, 'Secret', 14 Jan. 1809, F.O. 72/71, ff. 1–5, and Canning to Frere, 'Private and Secret', 14 Jan. 1809, Canning Papers, bundle 45.

2. Frere to Canning, 'Private and Secret', 27? Dec. 1808, and 13 Jan. 1809, Canning Papers, bundle 45.

3. Sir G. Smith to Cradock, 19 Jan. 1809; Cradock to Castlereagh, 31 Jan. 1809; both in W.O. 1/232, pp. 505–11, 351–61.

4. Canning to Frere, 'Private and Confidential', 25 Jan. 1809, Canning Papers, bundle 45.

5. J. A. Vann, 'Hapsburg Policy and the Austrian War of 1809', *Central European History*, vol. 7, no. 4, Dec. 1974, pp. 291–310; Gunther E. Rothenberg, *Napoleon's Great Adversaries: The Archduke Charles and the Austrian Army, 1792–1814* (London, Batsford, 1982), pp. 121–2.

6. Palmerston to Miss Temple, n.d. [c. 9 Aug. 1808], Palmerston Papers, BR 24/1.

7. Mackesy, *War in the Mediterranean*, pp. 306–9.

8. 'Substance of a Communication', Vienna, 11 Oct. 1808 (received 2 Dec. 1808); and draft of reply, 24 Dec. 1808, both in F.O. 7/89.

9. Canning to Chatham, 'Private & Secret', 21 Nov. 1808, Canning Papers, bundle 31, Mackesy, *War in the Mediterranean*, p. 309.

10. Francis Jackson to George Jackson, 8 Nov. 1808, *Diaries and Letters of Sir George Jackson*, vol. 2, pp. 300–3.

11. Canning to Villiers, 22 Nov. 1808 (2 letters), F.O. 63/74, ff. 1–16, 17–20; Villiers to Freire, 4 March 1809, F.O. 63/75, f. 182.

12. Cradock's dispatches to Castlereagh are in W.O. 1/232; see especially his letters of 14 Dec., 4 Jan. and 12 Feb., pp. 65–8, 191–203, 429–38.

13. Freire to Villiers, 26 Dec. 1808, F.O. 63/75, f. 36; Villiers to Canning, 26 or 27 Dec. 1808, F.O. 63/75, ff. 22–4; Villiers to Canning, 'Private', 26 Dec. 1808, and 'Private & Confidential', 3 Jan. 1809, Canning Papers, bundle 48.

14. Canning to Villiers, 'Private', 14 and 28 Jan. 1809, Canning Papers, bundle 48.

15. Duke of York to Col. J. W. Gordon, 27 Jan. 1809, B. L. Add. Ms 49, 473, f. 3; *Dictionary of National Biography*, vol. 5, p. 1318. It is possible that the command was also offered, informally, to Thomas Graham, but declined as he did not choose to serve except with British troops; however, Graham did not receive his permanent rank until March 1809, after Beresford had been appointed. See A. M. Delavoye, *The Life of Thomas Graham, Lord Lynedoch* (London, Richardson and Marchant Singer, 1880), pp. 803–4, and Aspinall-Oglander, *Freshly Remembered*, p. 197.

16. Circular to the Cabinet by Canning, 10 Feb. 1809, Canning Papers, bundle 41; Castlereagh to Charles Stewart, 22 Sept. 1809, P.R.O.N.I. D3030/3295, where he admits opposing Wellesley's appointment.

17. Fortescue, vol. 7, p. 128.

18. On Beresford and his reforms see Samuel E. Vichness, 'Marshal of Por-

tugal: The Military Career of William Carr Beresford, 1785–1814' (unpublished PhD thesis submitted to Florida State University in 1976), passim.

19. Circular to the Cabinet by Canning, 24 Feb. 1809, Canning Papers, bundle 41A.

20. Canning to Villiers, 'Private and Confidential', 28 Feb. 1809, Canning Papers, bundle 48.

21. Castlereagh to Cradock, 27 Feb. 1809, *Castlereagh Correspondence*, vol. 7, pp. 37–9; cf. same to same, 28 Jan. 1809, W.O. 1/232, pp. 287–91.

22. Moore to Castlereagh, 25 Nov. 1808, in Moore, *Narrative* . . . , pp. 265–6; Donkin to Cradock, 1 Jan. 1809, W.O. 1/232, pp. 231–8, enclosed in Cradock to Castlereagh, 4 Jan. 1809, W.O. 1/232, pp. 191–203. Donkin's reputation was later tarnished by his involvement in Sir John Murray's failure on the east coast of Spain in 1813.

23. 'Memorandum on the defence of Portugal', London, 7 March 1809, *W.D.* III, pp. 181–3; cf. Sir A. Wellesley to Castlereagh, 'Private', 1 Aug. 1808, *W.D.* III, pp. 46–7.

24. Canning to Portland, 'Private and Secret', 21 March 1809, Canning Papers, bundle 33A. Castlereagh to the King, 26 March, and reply, 27 March 1809, *The Later Correspondence of George III*, vol. 5, no. 3844, pp. 246–7.

25. The King to Portland, 18 March 1809, *Later Correspondence of George III*, vol. 5, no. 3837, p. 237.

26. Canning to the King, 13 Feb. 1809, *Later Correspondence of George III*, vol. 5, no. 3814, p. 194.

27. Sherwig, *Guineas and Gunpowder*, pp. 208–9.

28. Ibid., pp. 208–13; Canning to Frere, 10 April 1809, F.O. 72/71, ff. 78–81.

29. Mackesy, *War in the Mediterranean*, pp. 311–34.

30. Sherwig, *Guineas and Gunpowder*, p. 209.

31. Fortescue, vol. 7, pp. 45–55; Gordon C. Bond, *The Grand Expedition* (Athens, University of Georgia Press, 1979), pp. 7–20; Castlereagh to Chatham, 18 May 1809, Chatham Papers, P.R.O. 30/8/366, ff. 58–9;

and reply, 18 May 1809, *Castlereagh Correspondence*, vol. 6, p. 256–7.

32. 'Memorandum respecting the intended expedition' by Sir David Dundas, 3 June 1809, *Castlereagh Correspondence*, vol. 6, pp. 270–3, where the replies of the other senior officers are also printed; Bond, *The Grand Expedition*, pp. 7–20.

33. Hugh Popham, *A Damned Cunning Fellow: The Eventful Life of Rear-Admiral Sir Home Popham . . . 1762–1820* (Tywardreath, Old Ferry Press, 1991), pp. 184–5; Fortescue, vol. 7, pp. 49–50; Castlereagh to the King, 15 and 21 June 1809, and reply, 22 June 1809, *Later Correspondence of George III*, vol. 5, nos 3905 and 3910, pp. 298, 302–3.

5 The Military Campaigns of 1809, April–September

1. Castlereagh to Sir A. Wellesley, 2 and 3 April 1809, *W.S.D.*, vol. 6, pp. 210–13.

2. Sir A. Wellesley to Villiers, 17 May 1809, *W.D.* III, pp. 238–9; on the operations see Oman, vol. 2, pp. 332–42, and Fortescue, vol. 7, pp. 158–63.

3. Castlereagh to Stewart, 26 May 1809, and Londonderry to Stewart, 25 May 1809, both in P.R.O.N.I. D 3030/Q2/2, pp. 67–9; Grey to Grenville, 25 May 1809, *H.M.C. Dropmore*, vol. IX, p. 308.

4. Sir A. Wellesley to Castlereagh, 7 May 1809, *W.D.* III, pp. 219–20; Frere to Canning, 25 April 1809, *Parliamentary Papers*, 1810, vol. XV, part A, no. 2, pp. 5–7.

5. Canning to Frere, 'Private', 19 April 1809, Canning Papers, bundle 45; the King to Castlereagh, 3 Oct. 1809, *The Later Correspondence of George III*, vol. 5, no. 3986, pp. 387–8.

6. Canning to Frere, 'Private', 19 April 1809, Canning Papers, bundle 45.

7. Castlereagh to Sir Arthur Wellesley, 25 May 1809, *Castlereagh Correspondence*, vol. 7, p. 71.

8. Castlereagh to the King, 25 May 1809, and reply (26 May), *Later Correspon-*

dence of George III, vol. 5, no. 3887, pp. 284–5.

9. Castlereagh to Sir A. Wellesley, 11 July 1809, *Castlereagh Correspondence*, vol. 7, pp. 95–6. Wellesley also received £100,000 from Cadiz: see Fortescue, vol. 7, p. 196.

10. Sir A. Wellesley to Villiers, 31 May 1809, and to Castlereagh, 11 June 1809, both in *W.D.* III, pp. 262–3, 289.

11. Sir A. Wellesley to Lt-Col. Carroll, 19 June 1809, *W.S.D.*, vol. 6, pp. 289–90; Sir A. Wellesley to Lt-Col. Bourke, 21 June 1809, *W.D.* III, pp. 310–11.

12. Sir A. Wellesley to Lt-Col. Roche (liaison officer at Cuesta's headquarters), 4 and 8 July 1809, *W.D.* III, pp. 342, 347–8.

13. Sir A. Wellesley to Frere, Plasencia, 13 July 1809, *W.D.* III, pp. 353–4; Frere to Canning, 'Private, secret and confidential', 19 July 1809, Canning Papers, bundle 45.

14. Sir A. Wellesley to Col. O'Donoju, Plasencia, 16 July 1809, *W.D.* III, p. 360; Frere to Canning, 22 July 1809, *Parliamentary Papers*, 1810, vol. XV, pt A, p. 38.

15. Sir A. Wellesley to Frere, 24 July 1809, and to Castlereagh, 24 July 1809, both in *W.D.* III, pp. 366–7, 368–9.

16. Sir A. Wellesley to Frere, Talavera, 24 July 1809, *W.D.* III, pp. 367–8.

17. Casualty figures from Fortescue, vol. 7, pp. 256–8. The account of the battle is largely based on Fortescue, vol. 7, pp. 223–61, and Oman, vol. 2, pp. 507–58.

18. Fortescue, vol. 7, p. 268; see also Sir A. Wellesley's letters to Beresford, 29 July 1809, Frere and O'Donoju, both 3 Aug. 1809, *W.D.* III, pp. 379–80, 389–91.

19. Castlereagh to Charles Stewart, 5 and 21 Aug. 1809, P.R.O.N.I. D 3030/Q2/2, pp. 77, 79; Canning to Bagot, 14 Aug. 1809, *George Canning and His Friends*, ed. Capt. Josceline Bagot, 2 vols (London, John Murray, 1909), vol. 1, p. 318.

20. The King to Portland, 16 Aug. 1809, *Later Correspondence of George III*, vol. 5, no. 3934, p. 324 — the Duke of York shared this view: Duke of York

to Col. J. W. Gordon, 14 Aug. 1809, B.L. Add. Ms 49,473, f.20. Castlereagh to Sir A. Wellesley, 26 Aug. 1809, *Castlereagh Correspondence*, vol. 7, p. 117; the title was gazetted on 4 Sept.

21. Thomas Graham to Robert Graham of Fintry, 27 Sept. 1809, quoted in Aspinall-Oglander, *Freshly Remembered*, p. 196.

22. Fortescue, vol. 7, pp. 56–7.

23. Wellington to Liverpool, 20 March 1812, *W.D.* V, p. 554; cf. same to same, 11 Sept. 1811, ibid., p. 270. This account of the expedition and its consequences is based largely on Bond, *The Grand Expedition*, passim, and Fortescue, vol. 7, pp. 47–96. Fortescue concluded that the expedition had only a 'very precarious' chance of success, even if everything had gone according to plan (pp. 93–6), and this judgement is supported by Carl A. Christie, 'The Royal Navy and the Walcheren Expedition of 1809', in *New Aspects of Naval History*, ed. Craig L. Symonds et al. (Annapolis, Naval Institute Press, 1981), pp. 190–200, esp. p. 193. Gordon Bond, however, disagrees, arguing that an attack on Antwerp between 6 and 8 Aug. had a good chance of success (p. 161).

24. Liverpool to Wellington, 26 June 1810, *W.S.D.*, vol. 6, pp. 547–8.

6   Old Wine in New Bottles:
The Perceval Government,
September 1809–June 1810

1. Canning to Portland, 24 March 1809, enclosed in same to same, 'Private', 2 April 1809, Canning Papers, bundle 33, Granville Leveson Gower to Lord Boringdon, 10 April 1809, quoted by Aspinall in *Later Correspondence of George III*, vol. 5, p. xviii. There is a more detailed account of the political crisis in Rory Muir, 'The British Government and the Peninsular War, 1801 to June 1811' (unpublished PhD thesis presented to the University of Adelaide in 1988), pp. 158–68, 220–9.

2. Perceval to Canning and reply, 28 and 31 Aug. 1809, Walpole, *Life of Perceval*, vol. 1, pp. 358–9, 362–3; Gray, *Perceval*, pp. 223–4.

3. Holland, *Further Memoirs*, p. 35; Hinde, *Canning*, p. 227.

4. Charles Ellis to Lord Binning, 2 Oct. 1809, quoted by Aspinall in *Later Correspondence of George III*, vol. 5, p. 368n; Canning to Huskisson, 13 Oct. 1809, *The Huskisson Papers*, ed. Lewis Melville (London, Constable, 1931), pp. 69–71.

5. Cabinet Minute, 18 Sept. 1809, *Later Correspondence of George III*, vol. 5, pp. 357–62; the King to Perceval, 22 Sept. 1809, Walpole, *Life of Perceval*, vol. 2, pp. 27–30; cf. *Later Correspondence of George III*, vol. 5, p. 371.

6. Memorandum by [Col. Meyrick Shawe], Jan. 1814, *W.S.D.*, vol. 7, pp. 258–9. This memorandum is printed with a number of substantial deletions. The manuscript is in W.P. 1/445. The memorandum was intended as a justification of Lord Wellesley's part in the Perceval government by a close friend and admirer. As such it must be used with caution, but it gives a far franker insight into the attitudes of Lord Wellesley and his coterie than any other document that I have seen.

7. Eldon to Sir William Scott, n.d., c.4 Oct. 1809, Horace Twiss, *The Public and Private Life of Lord Chancellor Eldon*, 2 vols (London, John Murray, 1846), vol. 1, pp. 421–2.

8. —— [Mr Dardis] to the Marquess of Buckingham, 26 March and 2 April 1810, *Memoirs of the Courts and Cabinets of George III*, ed. the Duke of Buckingham and Chandos, 4 vols (London, Hurst and Blackett, 1855), vol. 4, pp. 427–33; Iris Butler, *The Eldest Brother: The Marquess Wellesley, 1760–1842* (London, Hodder and Stoughton, 1973), p. 441.

9. [Huskisson's Memorandum on the War], 13 Aug. 1809, B.L. Add. Ms 37,416, ff. 355–68, cited in the rest of this section as 'Huskisson's Memorandum'. Covering letters: Huskisson to Canning, 'Private & Confidential', 18 Aug. 1809, B.L. Add. Ms 37,416, ff. 107–8; Huskisson to Perceval, 'Private & Confidential', 18 Aug. [1809], Perceval Papers, 9/XIV/9 N.R.A., no. 196. Unless specified, quotes from Huskisson come from the Memorandum.

10. Elizabeth B. Schumpeter, 'English Prices and Public Finance, 1660–1822', *Review of Economic Statistics*, vol. XX, 1938, table 7, p. 37.

11. N.J. Silberling, 'Financial and Monetary Policy of Great Britain during the Napoleonic Wars', *Quarterly Journal of Economics*, vol. 38, 1924, table 1, p. 215. These figures appear tiny to us, so it is worth noting that according to one modern estimate, in 1811 Britain spent 16 per cent of her Gross National Income on the war: the same proportion as in 1915! A. D. Harvey, *Britain in the Early Nineteenth Century* (London, Batsford, 1978), p. 334.

12. Huskisson to Perceval, 'Private & Confidential', 24 Aug. 1809, Perceval Papers, 9/XIV/II N.R.A., no. 200.

13. Col. J. W. Gordon to Huskisson, 25 Sept. 1809, quoted in Gray, *Perceval*, p. 359.

14. [Notes on Finance by George Rose], 11 Nov. 1809, B.L. Add. Ms 31,237, ff. 192–201; Perceval's 'Memorandum on Financial Affairs of Britain', n.d. [late Aug. or early Sept. 1809], Portland Papers, University of Nottingham, Pw F no. 7635, p. 25.

15. The King to Perceval, 6 Dec. 1809, *Later Correspondence of George III*, vol. 5, no. 4041, pp. 465–6; Wellesley to Perceval, 'Private & Confidential', 2 Dec. 1809, Perceval Papers, 7/I/11, N.R.A., no. 353.

16. Perceval to [Marquess Wellesley], n.d. [Jan. 1810], B.L. Add. Ms 37,295, f. 227.

17. Lt-Gen. Sir W. Napier, *The Life and Opinions of General Sir Charles James Napier*, 4 vols (London, John Murray, 1857), vol. 1, pp. 126–7; John Aitchison, *An Ensign in the Peninsular War: The Letters of John Aitchison*, ed. W.F.K. Thompson (London, Michael Joseph, 1981), pp. 65–8; Charles

Stewart to Castlereagh, 12 Dec. 1809, P.R.O.N.I. D 3030/P/236.

18. Canning to Lord Wellesley, 12 Aug. 1809, B.L. Add. Ms 37,286, ff. 257–72 (partly printed in *W.S.D.*, vol. 6, pp. 350–3); Sir A. Wellesley, 'Observations on Mr. Sec. Canning's Dispatch of the 12th August to Marquis Wellesley', 5 Sept. 1809, *W.D.* III, pp. 477–8. For a more detailed account of the issues involved in this question see Muir, 'The British Government and the Peninsular War', pp. 212–19, 254–7.

19. Liverpool to Wellington, 15 Dec. 1809, *W.S.D.*, vol. 6, pp. 438–41.

20. Liverpool to Wellington, 'Private', 15 Dec. 1809, B. L. Add. Ms 38,244, ff. 112–18.

21. Liverpool to Wellington, 2 Jan. 1810, *W.S.D.*, vol. 6, p. 464.

22. Wellington to Liverpool, 31 Jan. and 9 Feb. 1810, *W.D.* III, pp. 719–22, 729–31.

23. Liverpool to Wellington, 27 Feb. 1810, W.O. 6/50, pp. 40–3.

24. Wellington to Liverpool, 24 Jan. 1810, *W.D.* III, pp. 698–700; Liverpool to Wellington, 'Private & Confidential', 13 March 1810, *W.S.D.*, vol. 6, pp. 493–4.

25. Wellington to Charles Stuart, 21 April 1810, *W.D.* IV, pp. 27–9; Wellington to Wellesley-Pole, 9 May 1810, 'Some Letters of the Duke of Wellington to his brother William Wellesley-Pole', ed. Sir Charles Webster, *Camden Miscellany*, vol. XVIII (Camden, third series, vol. 79, 1948; henceforth cited as *Letters to Wellesley-Pole*), pp. 33–4; Wellington to Liverpool, 2 April 1810, *W.D.* III, pp. 809–12; Liverpool to Wellington, 'Private', n.d. [April 1810], *W.S.D.*, vol. 6, p. 517.

26. Charles Stewart to Castlereagh, n.d. [23 May 1810], P.R.O.N.I. D 3030/P/8.

27. Wellington to Liverpool, 21 March, 14 March and 23 May 1810, *W.D.* III, pp. 791–2, 781; *W.D.* IV, p. 87.

28. Sherwig, *Guineas and Gunpowder*, p. 232n.

29. Wellington to Lord Wellesley, 14 Oct. 1809, B. L. Add. Ms 37,415, f. 56.

30. Wellington to Wellesley-Pole, 22 Oct. 1809, *Letters to Wellesley-Pole*, pp. 26–7.

31. Wellington to Liverpool, 1 March 1810, *W.D.* III, pp. 759–62; Wellington to Craufurd, 4 April 1810, *W.D.* IV, pp. 1–2; Wellington to Wellesley-Pole, 9 May 1810, *Letters to Wellesley-Pole*, pp. 33–4.

32. Wellington to Villiers 5 June 1810; to Admiral Berkeley, 7 April 1810; and to Charles Stuart, 21 April 1810, *W.D.* IV, pp. 103–4, 7–8, 27–9.

33. Memorandum by [Col. Meyrick Shawe], Jan. 1814, *W.S.D.*, vol. 7, p. 262; see above, p. 406n6.

34. Memorandum by [Col. Meyrick Shawe], Jan. 1814, *W.S.D.*, vol. 7, p. 259.

35. 'Memorandum by the Marquess Wellesley on a Spanish Army', n.d., *W.S.D.*, vol. 6, pp. 550–2.

36. Memorandum by [Col. Meyrick Shawe], Jan. 1814, *W.S.D.*, vol. 7, p. 262.

37. Liverpool to Wellington, 10 Sept. 1810, *W.S.D.*, vol. 6, pp. 591–3.

38. Perceval to Wellesley, 19 April 1810, Perceval Papers, 7/I/19 N.R.A., no. 433.

39. Perceval to Wellesley, 14 and 23 July 1810, and Wellesley to Perceval, 22 July 1810, Walpole, *Life of Perceval*, vol. 2, pp. 124–8.

40. Sherwig, *Guineas and Gunpowder*, p. 228.

41. Memorandum by [Col. Meyrick Shawe], Jan. 1814, *W.S.D.*, vol. 7, p. 265.

42. Quoted by Aspinall in *The Later Correspondence of George III*, vol. 5, p. xlix.

43. Wellesley-Pole to Wellington, 'Confidential', 7 March 1810, Raglan Ms no. 101. *A Persian at the Court of King George, 1809–10: The Journal of Mirza Abul Hassan Khan*, trans. and ed. Margaret Morris Cloake (London, Barrie and Jenkins, 1988), p. 37. Francis Jackson to George Jackson, 1 May 1810, *The Bath Archives: A further selection from the Diaries and Letters of Sir George Jackson K.C.H. from 1809 to 1816*, ed. Lady Jackson, 2 vols (London, Richard Bentley, 1873),

vol. 1, p. 108; Harvey, *Britain in the Early Nineteenth Century*, p. 266 (on Stratford Canning); Mildred L. Fryman, 'Charles Stuart and the "Common Cause": The Anglo-Portuguese Alliance, 1810–1814' (unpublished PhD thesis submitted to Florida State University in 1974), pp. 177–8.

44. Wellington to Wellesley-Pole, 6 April 1810, *Letters to Wellesley-Pole*, pp. 31–2.

7   The French Invasion of Portugal, July–December 1810

1. Napoleon to Berthier, 29 May 1810, quoted in Oman, vol. 3, p. 227, and ('poor troops') Napoleon to Masséna, 18 April 1810, quoted in Horward, *Napoleon and Iberia: The Twin Sieges of Ciudad Rodrigo and Almeida, 1810* (Tallahassee, Florida State University Press, 1984), p. 52.
2. Returns in W.O. 17/2465 (unpaginated) for 25 June 1810 and 25 Oct. 1810. These figures cover all arms, including waggon train and artillery, the King's German Legion and sick, but exclude officers, sergeants, drummers, etc.
3. Wellington's 'Memorandum for Lieut. Col. Fletcher, commanding Royal Engineers', 20 Oct. 1809, *W.D.* III, pp. 556–60. See also Oman, vol. 3, p. 157.
4. Wellington to Liverpool, 27 Oct. 1810, *W.D.* IV, pp. 362–3.
5. Wellington to Liverpool, 14 July 1810, *W.D.* IV, pp. 168–9.
6. Wellington to Graham, 3 May 1810, *W.D.* IV, pp. 49–50.
7. Maj.-Gen. Sir W.F.P. Napier, *History of the War in the Peninsula and in the South of France* . . . , 6 vols (London, Boone, 1853), vol. 3, p. 49.
8. Wellington to Liverpool, 14 Nov. 1809, *W.D.* III, pp. 587–8.
9. Sir David Dundas to Liverpool, 8 June 1810, W.O. 25/3224 (unfoliated).
10. W.O. 17/2465 (unpaginated). The precise figures are: 25 Jan., 31,824; 25 March, 34,631; 25 June, 32,774; 25

Aug., 35,564; 25 Sept., 38,743; 25 Oct., 40,991; 25 Nov., 42,824.
11. W.O. 17/2465 (unpaginated). Precise number of sick rank and file: 25 Feb., 6,533; 25 March, 6,273; 25 April, 6,075; 25 May, 5,473; 25 June, 4,017; 25 Aug., 5,297; 25 Sept., 7,079; 25 Oct., 9,405; 25 Nov., 8,294; 25 Dec., 7,783.
12. Wellington to Wellesley-Pole, 5 Sept. 1810, *W.S.D.*, vol. 6, pp. 587–9.
13. Liverpool to Wellington, 10 Sept. 1810, *W.S.D.*, vol. 6, pp. 591–4.
14. Wellington to Admiral Berkeley, 15 June 1810, *W.D.* IV, pp. 120–1; and to Herrasti, 7 May, 6 and 19 June 1810, *W.D.* IV, pp. 55, 105, 125.
15. There is a very full and scholarly account of the sieges of Ciudad Rodrigo and Almeida in Horward, *Napoleon and Iberia*, passim.
16. Francisco A. De La Fuente, 'Dom Miguel Pereira Forjaz: His Early Career and Role in the Mobilization and Defense of Portugal During the Peninsular War, 1807–1814' (unpublished PhD thesis submitted to Florida State University, 1980), pp. 133–6. Fryman, 'Charles Stuart and the "Common Cause"', pp. 224–5, 231.
17. Wellington to Charles Stuart, 7 Sept. 1810, *W.D.* IV, pp. 263–4.
18. It has sometimes been suggested that Wellington fought at Bussaco for political reasons, but his correspondence makes it clear that he really hoped to decide the campaign there and then: see, for example, Wellington to Liverpool, 30 Sept. 1810, *W.D.* IV, pp. 304–8, and also Donald D. Horward, *The Battle of Bussaco: Massena vs. Wellington* (Tallahassee, Florida State University Studies no. 44, 1965), pp. 142–3.
19. Masséna's orders are printed in Oman, vol. 3, p. 549, and discussed on p. 347. See also Horward, *Battle of Bussaco*, pp. 79–83.
20. Wellington to Liverpool, 30 Sept. 1810, *W.D.* IV, pp. 304–8; Lt Rice Jones, *An Engineer Officer under Wellington in the Peninsula*, ed. Capt. the Hon. H.V. Shore (Cambridge, Trotman, 1986), diary entry for 27

Sept. 1810, p. 73; Cocks to the Hon. John Somers Cocks, 5 Oct. 1810, in *Intelligence Officer in the Peninsula: The Letters and Diaries of Maj. the Hon. Edward Charles Cocks, 1786–1812*, ed. Julia Page (New York, Hippocrene, 1986), pp. 84–5; and Colbourne to his sister, 29 Sept. 1810; in G.C. Moore Smith, *The Life of John Colbourne, Field-Marshal Lord Seaton . . .* (New York, Dutton, 1903), p. 141.

21. Horward, *The Battle of Bussaco*, p. 175.

22. Wellington to Liverpool, 30 Sept. 1810, *W.D.* IV, pp. 304–8; *The Times*, 18 Oct. 1810; Horward, *The Battle of Bussaco*, p. 173: 515 killed, 3,608 wounded, 364 prisoners = 4,487 total.

23. On 21 Sept., two days after ordering Trant to Sardão, Wellington wrote that he had 'not yet give[n] up hopes of discovering a remedy for this . . . misfortune'. He later attempted to put all the blame for the retreat from Bussaco on Trant's immediate superior, who had delayed his march, but as Oman and Horward point out, this is implausible. Wellington to Liverpool, 30 Sept. 1810, *W.D.* IV, pp. 304–8; Memorandum of Operations in 1810, by Wellington, 23 Feb. 1811, *W.D.* IV, pp. 619–34, esp. p. 629. Oman, vol. 3, pp. 394–5; Horward, *The Battle of Bussaco*, p. 140.

24. Cocks's Journal, 1 Aug. 1810, Page, *Intelligence Officer in the Peninsula*, p. 71; Rice Jones's Journal, 3 Oct. 1810, *An Engineer Officer under Wellington*, p. 78. Wellington, however, wrote, 'With few exceptions, the troops have continued to conduct themselves with great regularity', Wellington to Liverpool, 5 Oct. 1810, *W.D.* IV, pp. 315–16.

25. Wellington to Charles Stuart, Henry Wellesley and Liverpool, 30 Sept., 7 and 13 Oct. 1810, *W.D.* IV, pp. 309–10, 321, 329–32.

26. Aitchison to his father, 13 Oct. 1810, *An Ensign in the Peninsular War*, p. 120; and F. Boverick (Cocks's servant) to Mrs Gardener, 13 Oct. 1810, Page, *Intelligence Officer in the Peninsula*, p. 87.

27. Wellington to Liverpool, 27 Oct. 1810, *W.D.* IV, p. 364; George D. Knight, 'Lord Liverpool and the Peninsular War, 1809–1812' (unpublished PhD, thesis submitted to Florida State University in 1976), p. 120.

28. Liverpool to Craig (Private), 11 Sept. 1810, B.L. Add. Ms 38,233, ff. 79–85; Lady Bessborough to Granville Leveson Gower, 19 Sept. 1810, *Private Correspondence of Granville Leveson Gower*, vol. 2, pp. 366–7; Auckland to Grenville, 2 Oct. 1810, *H.M.C. Dropmore*, vol. X, pp. 52–3.

29. Lady Holland, *The Journal of Elizabeth Lady Holland (1791–1811)*, ed. the Earl of Ilchester, 2 vols (London, Longmans, 1908), vol. 2, p. 264; Grey to Col. J. W. Gordon, 15 Oct. 1810, B.L. Add. Ms 49,477, ff. 101–2; T. Grenville to Grenville, 17 Oct. 1810, *H.M.C. Dropmore*, vol. X, pp. 55–6; Auckland to Grenville, 16 Oct. 1810, ibid., vol. X, p. 54.

30. *The Courier* is quoted by Auckland: Auckland to Grenville, 16 Oct. 1810, *H.M.C. Dropmore*, vol. X, p. 54; Liverpool to Wellington, 17 Oct. 1810, *W.S.D.*, vol. 6, p. 618; General Charles Craufurd to Brigadier Robert Craufurd, 19 Oct. 1810, in Rev. A. Craufurd, *General Craufurd and His Light Division* (Cambridge, Trotman, 1987), pp. 161–3.

31. Palmerston to Miss Temple, 14 Oct. 1810, Palmerston Papers, BR 24/1.

32. *The Times*, 18 Oct. 1810.

33. *The Times*, 24 Oct. 1810.

34. Harrowby to Countess Harrowby, 10 and 12 Nov. 1810, Harrowby Papers, vol. LVII, ff. 291–6.

35. Grenville to Grey, 1 Nov. 1810, *H.M.C. Dropmore*, vol. 10, pp. 61–2.

36. Grey to Grenville, 9 Nov. 1810, *H.M.C. Dropmore*, vol. 10, pp. 66–8.

37. Ida Macalpine and Richard Hunter, *George III and the Mad-Business* (London, Allen Lane, 1969), pp. 143–51.

38. Lady Bessborough to Granville Leveson Gower, n.d., 'Saturday', Dec. [1810], *Private Correspondence of Granville Leveson Gower*, vol. 2, pp. 372–3.

8   The Turn of the Tide: Britain and the Peninsula, 1811

1. Holland, *Further Memoirs of the Whig Party*, p. 88.
2. *Journal of Lady Holland*, vol. 2, p. 282.
3. The Prince to Perceval, 4 Feb. 1811, *The Correspondence of George, Prince of Wales*, vol. 7, no. 2836, pp. 200–1.
4. Quoted in Gray, *Perceval*, p. 412.
5. Liverpool to Wellington, 10 Sept. 1810, *W.S.D.*, vol. 6, pp. 591–3; Wellington to Liverpool, 29 Dec. 1810, *W.D.* IV, pp. 485–6; Liverpool to Wellington, 17 Jan. 1811, W.O. 6/29, pp. 19–23.
6. Liverpool to Wellington, 20 Feb. 1811, *W.S.D.*, vol. 7, pp. 69–70.
7. Wellington to Lord Wellesley, 26 Jan. 1811, *W.D.* IV, pp. 553–6; Col. Bunbury to Liverpool, 8 March 1811[?], B.L. Add. Ms 38,246, ff. 53–4; rumour quoted in Walpole, *Life of Perceval*, vol. 2, p. 204n. The decision to increase the Portuguese subsidy was made by 6 March, i.e. before news of Masséna's retreat reached London: Liverpool to Wellington, 6 March 1811, W.O. 6/50, pp. 188–91.
8. Wellington to Charles Stuart, 28 Jan. 1811, *W.D.* IV, pp. 559–60.
9. Wellington to William Wellesley-Pole, 11 Jan. 1811, Raglan Papers, Wellington A, no. 39. This letter is printed, with an important silent deletion including the part quoted here, in *W.S.D.*, vol. 7, pp. 40–3.
10. William Wellesley-Pole to Wellington, 1 Feb. 1811, Raglan Papers, Wellington B, no. 111.
11. Wellington to Beresford, 4 Feb. 1811, *W.D.* IV, pp. 577–8.
12. Wellington to Henry Wellesley, 31 Dec. 1810, *W.S.D.*, vol. 7, pp. 11–12.
13. Cocks to Miss Margaret Maria Cocks, 3 Nov. 1810, Page, *Intelligence Officer in the Peninsula*, pp. 91–2.
14. Oman, vol. 4, pp. 13–14, 608–10.
15. Wellington to Charles Stuart, 6 Feb. 1811, *W.D.* IV, p. 583.
16. Wellington to Beresford, 29 Jan., and to Lord Wellesley, 16 March 1811, *W.D.* IV, pp. 563, 674. Oman, vol. 4, pp. 23–63.

17. Oman, vol. 4, pp. 202–5.
18. Ibid., pp. 306–48, 622–4, 630.
19. Wellington to William Wellesley-Pole, 15 May 1811, *W.S.D.*, vol. 7, pp. 123–4.
20. Wellington to Wellesley-Pole, 2 July 1811, *W.S.D.*, vol. 7, pp. 175–7. Beresford's behaviour at Albuera has been successfully obfuscated, but see Vichness, 'Marshal of Portugal', p. 424, and Fortescue, vol. 8, pp. 202–3. A month after the battle, Wellesley-Pole wrote to Wellington from London: 'Beresford's Action is considered here as a proof of the astonishing Bravery of the British Troops, which appears to have saved him and his Army — there are so many Letters in London from the Army detailing particulars that every body knows the whole Story, even to the General's loss of Head and ordering the Retreat etc etc . . . the truth is Beresford has entirely lost all hope of being considered by *us lookers on* as a General and I think it most fortunate that you did not leave him longer to himself. . . .' William Wellesley-Pole to Wellington, 16 June 1811, Raglan Mss, Wellington B, no. 114.
21. Fortescue, vol. 8, p. 226n.
22. Liverpool to Wellington, 11 April 1811 (3 letters), *W.S.D.*, vol. 7, pp. 102, 104–5; and W.O. 6/50, pp. 203–6.
23. Liverpool to Wellington, 11 April 1811, *W.S.D.*, vol. 7, pp. 104–5.
24. Liverpool to Wellington, 29 and 30 May 1811, W.O. 6/50, pp. 219–22, 222–3.
25. Liverpool to Wellington, 28, 29 and 30 (2 letters) May 1811, W. O. 6/50, pp. 217–24; Liverpool to Wellington, 29 May 1811, *W.S.D.*, vol. 7, pp. 114–15. The original draft of the instructions, dated 29 May, with the qualifying passages crossed out, is in B.L. Loan Ms 72, vol. 21, ff. 63–4.
26. Wellington to Liverpool, 23 March 1811, *W.D.* IV, pp. 691–3.
27. Wellington to Wellesley-Pole, 2 July 1811, *W.S.D.*, vol. 7, pp. 175–7; Wellington to Liverpool, 1 Aug. 1811, *W.D.* V, pp. 194–5.

28. Figures from W.O. 17/2467 and 2468 (both unfoliated).
29. Wellington to Liverpool, 8 May 1811, *W.D.* IV, pp. 790–1.
30. Henry Wellesley to Lord Wellesley, 'Private', 12 Jan. 1811, B.L. Add. Ms 37,292, ff. 250–1. This letter is printed without date in *W.S.D.*, vol. 7, p. 52.
31. Henry Wellesley to Wellington, 25 Jan. 1811, *W.S.D.*, vol. 7, pp. 47–8; Wellington to Lord Wellesley, 26 Jan. 1811, *W.D.* IV, pp. 553–6; Wellington to Liverpool, 2 Feb. 1811, *W. D.* IV, p. 575.
32. Liverpool to Lord Wellesley, 'Private', 'Saturday', n.d. [Feb. 1811], B.L. Add. Ms 37,310, ff. 43–4.
33. Lord Wellesley to Henry Wellesley, 18 April 1811, *W.S.D.*, vol. 7, pp. 140–2; Henry Wellesley to Bardaxi, 15 March 1811, and reply, 25 March 1811, W. P. 1/341. Henry Wellesley to Wellington, 25 May 1811, *W. S. D.*, vol. 7, pp. 139–40, and reply, 29 May 1811, *W.D.* V, pp. 57–8.
34. Wellington to Liverpool, 4 Dec. 1811, *W.D.* V, pp. 389–91.
35. *Parliamentary Debates*, vol. 19, cols 394–8, 450–7.
36. *Parliamentary Debates*, vol. 19, cols 766–8.
37. Grey to Grenville, 1 Sept. 1811, and Grenville to Grey, 28 Jan. 1812, *H.M.C. Dropmore*, vol. 10, pp. 167–9, 197–200.
38. Perceval to Croker, 11 Nov. 1810, *The Correspondence and Diaries of the late Right Honourable John Wilson Croker . . .*, ed. Louis J. Jennings, 3 vols (London, John Murray, 1884; henceforth cited as *Croker Papers*), vol. 1, pp. 34–5; *Parliamentary Debates*, vol. 19, cols 1063–76.
39. Figures from the tables of bankruptcies in the *Annual Register*.
40. Torrens to Bunbury, 'Private', 15 July 1812, *Historical Manuscripts Commission: Report on the Manuscripts of Earl Bathurst . . .* (London, H.M.S.O., 1923; henceforth cited as *H.M.C. Bathurst*), p. 188. In 1811 the home garrison was at its lowest level since the Peace of Amiens, and was further reduced in the following year. Hodge,

'On the Mortality of Military Operations', pp. 264–5.
41. William Wellesley-Pole to Wellington, [London], 16 June 1811, Raglan Ms no. 114; Wellington to Torrens, 20 June 1811, *W.S.D.*, vol. 7, p. 163.
42. The Hon. Edmund Phipps, *Memoirs of the Political and Literary Life of Robert Plumer Ward Esq.*, 2 vols (London, John Murray, 1850), vol. 1, p. 394.
43. Macalpine and Hunter, *George III and the Mad-Business*, pp. 158–60; Gray, *Perceval*, p. 424.
44. Huskisson to Gordon, 'Private', 19 July [1811], B.L. Add. Ms 49,480, ff. 120–1, quoting the *Morning Chronicle*; Lord Wellesley to Thomas Tyrwhitt, 'Private and Secret', 20 July 1811, *Correspondence of George, Prince of Wales*, vol. 8, no. 3104, pp. 50–1; Wellesley to Perceval, 'Private and Secret', 28 July 1811, *The Wellesley Papers*, 2 vols (London, Herbert Jenkins, 1914), vol. 2, pp. 55–6; Arbuthnot to Herries, 6 Aug. 1811, B.L. Add. Ms 57,370, ff. 3–6.
45. Grey to Grenville, 23 May 1811, *H.M.C. Dropmore*, vol. 10, pp. 136–8.
46. Creevey to Mrs Creevey, 20 July 1811, *Creevey Papers*, pp. 145–6.
47. Arbuthnot to Herries, 5 Aug. 1811, B.L. Add. Ms 57,370, ff. 3–6.
48. E.g. the Prince Regent to Lady Hertford, 23 Nov. 1811, *Correspondence of George, Prince of Wales*, vol. 8, pp. 232.

9 Sicily and the Mediterranean, 1810–12

1. Mackesy, *The War in the Mediterranean, 1803–1810*, pp. 353–5.
2. B.R. Mitchell and Phyllis Deane, *Abstract of British Historical Statistics* (Cambridge University Press, 1962), p. 311.
3. Richard Glover, 'The French Fleet . . .', p. 242.
4. Ann Parry, *The Admirals Fremantle* (London, Chatto and Windus, 1971), pp. 86–9; Liverpool to Bentinck, 23 Aug. 1811, W.O. 6/61, pp. 61–3.

5. Mackesy, *The War in the Mediterranean, 1803–1810*, pp. 231–58.

6. On Anglo-Sicilian relations see in particular: John Rosselli, *Lord William Bentinck and the British Occupation of Sicily, 1811–1814* (Cambridge University Press, 1956, which for the rest of this chapter will be cited as *Bentinck and Sicily*); and Desmond Gregory, *Sicily: The Insecure Base: A History of the British Occupation of Sicily, 1806–1815* (Fairleigh Dickinson University Press, 1988).

7. Rosselli, *Bentinck and Sicily*, pp. 158–63.

8. Fortescue, who was no great admirer of Stuart, concluded that his decision was correct, but Liverpool was furious, Fortescue, vol. 7, pp. 315, 441–2. On Napoleon's attitude to the conquest of Sicily see Albert Espitalier, *Napoleon and King Murat* (London, Bodley Head, 1912), ch. 4.

9. Rosselli, *Bentinck and Sicily*, pp. 12–15.

10. [Perceval to Lord Wellesley, 13 April 1811], B.L. Add. Ms 37,292, ff. 356–61.

11. Details of Bentinck's character and career from John Rosselli, *Lord William Bentinck, 1774–1839* (London, Chatto and Windus for Sussex University, 1974), esp. part 1, chs 2, 3 and 5.

12. Bentinck to Lord Wellesley, London, 4 April 1811, B.L. Add. Ms 37,292, ff. 313–36; [Perceval to Lord Wellesley, 13 April 1811], ibid., ff. 356–61; [Lord Wellesley to Harrowby, n.d.], ibid., ff. 354–5.

13. Lord Wellesley to Bentinck, 'Secret', no. 12, 7 Oct. 1811, F.O. 70/44 (unfoliated).

14. The memorandum on the defence of Sicily is printed, with its covering letter (Liverpool to the Prince Regent, 8 Oct. 1811), in *Correspondence of George, Prince of Wales*, vol. 8, no. 3200, pp. 164–5.

15. C.S.B. Buckland, *Metternich and the British Government from 1809 to 1813* (London, Macmillan, 1932), pp. 231–45; cf. ibid., pp. 223–5.

16. Three memoranda from Nugent, n.d. [March 1811], F.O. 7/100 (unfoliated).

17. Memorandum on Archduke Francis by Bentinck, 'Secret', n.d. [July? 1811], F.O. 70/44 (unfoliated).

18. Rosselli, *Lord William Bentinck*, pp. 121–2, 171.

19. Wellesley to Bentinck, 'Secret', no. 17, 21 Oct. 1811, F.O. 70/44.

20. Rosselli, *Bentinck and Sicily*, pp. 44–53.

21. Bentinck to Liverpool, 25 Jan. 1812, and reply, 4 March 1812, *W.S.D.*, vol. 7, pp. 289–91, 300–1; Wellington to Bentinck, 24 March, and to Sir Henry Wellesley, 11 April 1812, *W.D.* V, pp. 556–7, 588–9.

22. Bentinck to Liverpool, no. 22, 'Secret', 29 June 1812, W.O. 1/311, pp. 437–43; see also Bentinck's earlier letters of 19 May and 9 June in the same volume (pp. 281–4, 355–66).

23. Wellington to Sir Henry Wellesley, 15 July 1812, *W.D.* V, p. 745; Mulgrave to Bathurst, n.d., *H.M.C. Bathurst* pp. 223–4; Bathurst to Bentinck, 'Secret', 22 July 1812, W.O. 6/61, pp. 201–4.

24. For an account of its operations, see Oman, vol. 5, pp. 565–75, and vol. 6, pp. 161–6.

25. [Bathurst] to Bentinck, 'Secret', 11 Aug. 1812, W.O. 6/61, pp. 205–12.

26. Fortescue, vol. 8, pp. 450, 555–6; C.K. Webster, *The Foreign Policy of Castlereagh, 1812–15* (London, G. Bell, 1931), p. 75.

10   Britain and the Continental Powers, 1810–11

1. There is a very full account of confidential British contacts with the Austrian government and the background of her agents in Buckland, *Metternich and the British Government*, see esp. pp. 79–86 (Johnson), 86–96 (Horn) and 261–77 (King).

2. Buckland, *Metternich and the British Government*, pp. 172–3, 181 (P.O.W.s).

3. Quoted ibid., p. 185.

4. On Mills see an excellent article in R. G. Thorne, *The House of Commons, 1790–1820*, 5 vols (London, Secker

and Warburg for the History of Parliament Trust, 1986), vol. 4, pp. 591-3, and Buckland, *Metternich and the British Government*, pp. 99-106. C. C. Smith to Mills, 8 Nov. 1811, F.O. 64/83, f. 2.

5. Ryan, 'An Ambassador Afloat: Vice-Admiral Sir James Saumarez and the Swedish Court, 1808-1812', pp. 250-3.

6. Grimsted, *The Foreign Ministers of Alexander I*, p. 176.

7. The decline of the Tilsit alliance is charted in Alexander C. Niven, *Napoleon and Alexander I: A Study in Franco-Russian Relations, 1807-1812* (Washington, University Press of America, 1978).

8. Alexander's letters to Czartoryski, which contain many of his military calculations, are printed, with one reply, in *The Memoirs of Prince Adam Czartoryski...*, ed. Adam Gielgud, 2 vols (London, Remington, 1888), vol. 2, pp. 222-8. See also Alan Palmer, *Alexander I* (London, Weidenfeld and Nicolson, 1974), pp. 199-203, and Buckland, *Metternich and the British Government*, pp. 162-8.

9. Palmer, *Alexander I*, p. 201.

10. Quoted in J. R. Seeley, *Life and Times of Stein...*, 3 vols (Cambridge University Press, 1878), vol. 2, p. 442. See also R. B. Mowat, *The Diplomacy of Napoleon* (London, Edward Arnold, 1924), p. 254n; Gordon A. Craig, *The Politics of the Prussian Army, 1640-1945* (Oxford University Press, 1978), p. 56.

11. Quoted in Alan Palmer, *Napoleon in Russia* (London, Andre Deutsch, 1967), p. 26.

12. *The Diaries and Correspondence of the Right Hon. George Rose...*, ed. Rev. Leveson Vernon Harcourt, 2 vols (London, Richard Bentley, 1860), vol. 2, p. 475, quoting Rose's diary for 19 Nov. 1810; Mills to [Foreign Office?], 5 Jan. 1811, F.O. 64/83, ff. 4-8; Maj.-Gen. F. Decken to Charles Culling Smith, 'Private and Confidential', 18 March 1811, F.O. 64/84, ff. 10-12.

13. Liverpool to Wellington, 11 April 1811, *W.S.D.*, vol. 7, p. 102; 'Mem. of Communications from Russia', 2 April 1811, F.O. 65/77, ff. 1-7.

14. This and following paragraphs are based on Lord Wellesley, 'Notes on the General State of Europe', 15 May 1811, *The Wellesley Papers*, vol. 2, pp. 44-55.

15. Wellington to Arbuthnot, 28 May 1811, *The Correspondence of Charles Arbuthnot*, ed. A. Aspinall, Camden, third series, vol. 65 (London, 1941), pp. 6-7.

16. Yorke to Saumarez, Admiralty, 14 June 1811, *The Saumarez Papers: Selections from the Baltic Correspondence of Vice-Admiral Sir James Saumarez, 1808-1812*, ed. A. N. Ryan (Navy Records Society, vol. 110, 1968), pp. 183-4.

17. The memorandum, dated 17 Aug. 1811, is in F.O. 65/76, ff. 149-66.

18. On the Russian P.O.W.s and British civilians, see F.O. 65/76, ff. 185, 189; on the export of saltpetre, F.O. 65/76, ff. 15, 18, 20, 30, 51-62, 203, and also Perceval to Wellesley, n.d. [late 1811?], B.L. Add. Ms 37,296, ff. 155-8, and Sherwig, *Guineas and Gunpowder*, p. 273. On trade and licences see A. N. Ryan, 'Trade with the Enemy in the Scandinavian and Baltic Ports during the Napoleonic War: For and Against', in *Trans. Royal Historical Soc.*, vol. 12, 1961, pp. 123-40, esp. 133-4. On the Portuguese and Spanish diplomats see F.O. 65/76, ff. 169-70, and F.O. 65/77 passim, esp. ff. 66, 219-30.

19. Buckland, *Metternich and the British Government*, pp. 220, 260. Wellesley to the Prince Regent, 16 Sept. 1811, *Correspondence of George, Prince of Wales*, vol. 8, p. 134.

20. Buckland, *Metternich and the British Government*, pp. 208-9 (quoting Johnson), 256-9, 303.

21. Fournier, *Napoleon I: A Biography*, 2 vols (London, Longmans, 1912), vol. 2, p. 166; Craig, *Politics of the Prussian Army*, p. 57; Münster to Wellesley, 'most secret', 22 Oct. 1811, *The Wellesley Papers*, vol. 2, pp. 60-5.

22. Fournier, *Napoleon I*, vol. 2, p. 167; Enno E. Kraehe, *Metternich's German Policy*, 2 vols (Princeton University

Press, 1963, 1983), vol. 1, pp. 140–1.

23. Craig, *Politics of the Prussian Army*, pp. 56–8; Fournier, *Napoleon I*, vol. 2, pp. 166–7.

24. Mills to Smith, 20 July 1811, F.O. 64/83, ff. 126–9; Decken to [Foreign Office?], 7 Sept. 1811, F.O. 64/84, ff. 83–4; Smith to R.H. Crewe, 'secret', 8 Sept. 1811, F.O. 64/84, f. 85.

25. Draft of C. C. Smith to Lords of the Admiralty, 'most secret', 12 Sept. 1811, F.O. 64/84, ff. 90–2; Barrow to Saumarez, 14 Sept. 1811, and Wellesley to the Lords Commissioners of the Admiralty, 13 Sept. 1811, both in *The Saumarez Papers*, pp. 190–1. [Notes of a conversation with Lord Wellesley by Edward Thornton], 'secret', 14 Sept. 1811, B.L. Add. Ms 37,293, ff. 107–14.

26. Mills to C. C. Smith, 26 Aug. 1811, F.O. 64/83, ff. 138–40; Gneisenau to Saumarez, 8 Sept. 1811, *The Saumarez Papers*, pp. 189–90; Gneisenau to Decken, 10 Sept. 1811, enclosed in Decken to C. C. Smith, 5 Oct. 1811, F.O. 64/84, ff. 127–8. The quote is from Gneisenau's letter to Decken.

27. On Ompteda see Baron Ompteda, *A Hanoverian-English Officer a Hundred Years Ago . . .* (London, H. Grevel, 1892), pp. 260–2. Münster to the Prince Regent, 10 Oct. 1811, enclosing [Memorandum by Ompteda], 8 Oct. 1811, both in *The Correspondence of George, Prince of Wales*, vol. 8, pp. 167–173.

28. F.O. 64/84, ff. 114–20, 138, 161, 167 (correspondence with the Ordnance); Croker to Saumarez, 5 Oct. 1811, *The Saumarez Papers*, pp. 194–6.

29. Yorke to Saumarez, 5 Oct. 1811, Ibid., pp. 196–8.

30. [Notes by Thornton of a conference with Lord Wellesley, 5 Oct. 1811], B.L. Add. Ms 37,293, ff. 133–8; Wellesley to Thornton, 'Secret', 9 Oct. 1811, F.O. 73/70 (unfoliated).

31. Mills to Smith, 7, 17 and 19 Sept. 1811, F.O. 64/83, ff. 141–9; Münster to Wellesley, 'most secret', 22 Oct. 1811, *The Wellesley Papers*, vol. 2, pp. 60–5.

32. Wellesley to the Prince Regent, 22 Oct. 1811, *The Correspondence of*

George, Prince of Wales, vol. 8, p. 195; Buckland, *Metternich and the British Government*, pp. 277–85.

33. Buckland, *Metternich and the British Government*, p. 304; Kraehe, *Metternich's German Policy*, vol. 1, pp. 136–42.

34. Thornton's dispatches to Wellesley are in F.O. 73/70 (unfoliated).

11 The Triumphs and Tribulations of 1812

1. Richard Ryder to Harrowby, 21 Dec. 1811, Harrowby Papers, vol. 5, ff. 79–80.

2. Prince Regent to Duke of York, 13 Feb. 1812, *Correspondence of George, Prince of Wales*, vol. 8, pp. 370–1: the draft of this letter is printed in *The Letters of King George IV*, ed. A. Aspinall, 3 vols (Cambridge University Press, 1938), vol. 1, pp. 2–4.

3. Bathurst, 'Notes concerning Lord Wellesley's Resignation', 17 Feb. [1812], *H. M. C. Bathurst*, pp. 164–6; Wellesley to the Prince Regent, 17 Feb. 1812, *Letters of George IV*, vol. 1, p. 9.

4. Holland, *Further Memoirs . . .*, p. 113; Münster to Lord Wellesley, 9 March 1812, B.L. Add. Ms 37,293, f. 232; Bentinck to Wellesley, 7 May 1812, ibid., ff. 238–9; for more on relations between Wellington, Henry Wellesley and the British government at this time, see below, pp. 207–12.

5. 'Memorandum delivered by Lords Grenville and Grey to Lord Wellesley at Apsley House', 24 May 1812, *H.M.C. Dropmore*, vol. 10, pp. 271–2.

6. 'Memorandum intended for Lord Moira' [by Huskisson?], [8] June 1812, printed in Michael Roberts, 'The Ministerial Crisis of May-June 1812', *English Historical Review*, vol. 51, July 1936, pp. 485–6. This article gives more details of Moira's government than are available elsewhere.

7. Quote from Hinde, *Canning*, p. 252; for Arbuthnot's role, see Thorne, *The Commons, 1790–1820*, vol. 5, p. 289.

8. *Annual Register* for 1812, pp. 95–110; Gray, *Spencer Perceval*, pp. 389–90;

Mitchell and Deane, *Abstract of British Historical Statistics*, pp. 392, 396.

9. P. Coquelle, *Napoleon and England, 1803–1810* (London, G. Bell, 1904), pp. 270–71; the letters from Maret and Castlereagh are printed in the *Annual Register* for 1812, pp. 420–23.

10. Oman, vol. 4, pp. 638–42; vol. 5, pp. 82–4; vol. 6, pp. 741–5. These figures are for gross strength; the equivalent figures for effectives are 291,000 in July 1811, falling to 214,000 in October 1812.

11. Fortescue, vol. 8, pp. 349–67, esp. 366 for losses in the storm. Casualties for the siege as a whole were rather more than double this; see Oman, vol. 5, pp. 587–8.

12. Unfortunately this experiment proved unhappy, with the naval officers displaying little eagerness to cooperate, and providing inferior captured Russian pieces. Fortescue, vol. 8, pp. 374–5; Oman, vol. 5, p. 224.

13. Wellington to Sir Henry Wellesley, 14 March 1812, *W.D.* V, p. 550.

14. Oman, vol. 5, pp. 202–16, 279–89, and Fortescue, vol. 8, pp. 415–18, 420, both severely censure Napoleon's orders while providing evidence that Marmont's operations might have proved much more fruitful if pursued with more energy.

15. Figures from Oman, vol. 5, pp. 594–5.

16. Fortescue, vol. 8, p. 405; David Gates, *The Spanish Ulcer: A History of the Peninsular War* (London, George Allen and Unwin, 1986), p. 339, says 29 hours.

17. Wellington to Liverpool, 22 April and 26 May 1812, *W.D.* V, pp. 606–8, 670–73.

18. Wellington to Bathurst, 21 July 1812, *W.D.* V, pp. 749–52.

19. There are no reliable figures for French losses at Salamanca. Oman, vol. 5, pp. 469–71, and Fortescue, vol. 8, pp. 504–6, discuss the problem.

20. 'Return of the Corps and Detachments of Cavalry and Infantry embarked for the Peninsula between 1st January 1812 and the Present Period', Adjutant General's Office, 27 Nov. 1812, P.R.O.N.I. D3030/3387; 'Return of

the Regiments arrived in the Peninsula in the Year ended 15th December 1812', W.P. 1/359; Fortescue, vol. 8, pp. 571–2 (for Skerrett's force).

21. Duke of York to Bathurst, 22 Dec. 1812, W.P. 1/354; 'Return of the Casualties suffered by the Army under Wellington's command, 15th December 1811 to 14th December 1812', W.P. 1/359. Figures for the sick based on the Returns in W.O. 17/2469 and 2470. Morning states for Wellington's army give different raw figures, but reflect the same trends.

22. Liverpool to Wellington, 'Private', 5 March 1812, B.L. Add. Ms 38,326, ff. 20–1; Wellington to Bathurst, 4 July 1812, *W.D.* V, p. 733. On the proposed sale of Exchequer Bills see T.M.O. Redgrave, 'Wellington's Logistical Arrangements in the Peninsular War, 1809–1814' (unpublished PhD thesis presented to the University of London, n.d.), pp. 124–5.

23. 'Memorandum for Lord Bathurst on Lord Wellington's private letter', n.a., n.d., W.P. 1/342; E. Herries, *Memoir of the Public and Private Life of the Rt. Hon. John Charles Herries*, 2 vols (London, John Murray, 1880), vol. 1, p. 84n; Sir John Clapham, *The Bank of England: A History, 1694–1914*, 2 vols (Cambridge University Press, 1966), vol. 2, p. 35.

24. Bathurst to Wellington, 31 Aug., 9 Sept. and 13 Oct. 1812, *W.S.D.*, vol. 7, pp. 412–13, 415–16, 457–8; Liverpool and Vansittart to the Governors of the Bank of England, 11 Sept. 1812, B.L. Add. Ms 38,249, ff. 155–6.

25. Bathurst to Harrowby, 16 Sept. 1812, Harrowby Papers, vol. XIV, ff. 59–60; Harrowby to Bathurst, 17 Sept. 1812, *H.M.C. Bathurst*, pp. 213–14.

26. Wellington to Bathurst 13 Aug. 1812, *W.D.* VI, p. 25, and reply, 10 Sept. 1812, enclosing Melville to Bathurst, 7 Sept. 1812, *W.S.D.*, vol. 7, pp. 418–19.

27. Oman, vol. 5, pp. 548–58, and Popham, *Damned Cunning Fellow*, pp. 197–211, give accounts of Popham's campaign, while many relevant letters are printed in *The Keith Papers*, ed. C.

Lloyd, 3 vols (Navy Record Society, vol. 96, 1956), vol. 3, pp. 259–89.

28. Liverpool to Wellington, 20 Jan. 1812, *W.S.D.*, vol. 7, pp. 256–7; Perceval to Wellington, 22 Jan. 1812, and Perceval to Henry Wellesley, n.d., both in Walpole, *Life of Perceval*, vol. 2, pp. 261, 242.

29. Wellington to Lord Wellesley, 20 March 1812, *W.S.D.*, vol. 7, pp. 307–8; Wellington to Charles Stewart, 14 March 1812, Durham Record Office, D/Lo/C 113 (18).

30. Pole to Wellington, 12 Feb. and 12 April 1812, Raglan Mss, Wellington B, nos 116 and 118.

31. Wellington to Pole, 29 June 1812, Raglan Mss, Wellington A, no. 47.

32. Wellington to Liverpool, 9 and 29 June 1812, *W.S.D.*, vol. 7, p. 343, and B.L. Loan Ms 72, vol. 21, ff. 187–8.

33. Wellington to Pole, 29 June and 27 Aug. 1812, Raglan Mss, Wellington A, nos 47, 50; Wellington to Liverpool, 7 Sept. 1812, *W.D.* VI, p. 59; Liverpool to Wellington, 'Private', 7 Oct. 1812, W.P. 1/352.

34. Wellington to Pole, 7 July and 7 Sept. 1812, Raglan Mss, Wellington A, nos 48, 51.

35. Sir Henry Wellesley to Charles Arbuthnot, 'Private', 5 July 1812, *Correspondence of Charles Arbuthnot*, p. 7.

36. T. Sydenham to Sir H. Wellesley, 14 Sept. 1812, and enclosure, W.P. 1/361; Wellington to Liverpool, 23 Nov. 1812, *W.D.* VI, pp. 172–5; Wellington to Pole, 26 Dec. 1812, Raglan Mss, Wellington A, no. 52.

37. Wellington to Bathurst, 26 Jan. 1813, *W.D.* VI, p. 247; Wellington to the Prince Regent, 27 Jan. 1813, *Letters of George IV*, vol. 1, pp. 215–16; Wellington to——M.P., 14 Feb. 1813, *W.D.* VI, p. 303.

38. 'The Political Notebook of Richard Wellesley II', unpaginated, Carver Ms 54.

39. Richard Ryder to Harrowby, 26[?] Oct. 1811, Harrowby Papers, vol. V, ff. 67–70. [Harrowby?] to Castlereagh, 3 Aug. 1812, and enclosure, *Castlereagh Correspondence*, vol. 8, pp. 270–2.

40. Sir H. Wellesley to Lord Wellesley, no. 112, 28 Oct. 1811, F.O. 72/114, ff. 83–7. In this whole section I draw deeply on Charles Esdaile's admirable study, *The Duke of Wellington and the Command of the Spanish Army, 1812–1814* (Basingstoke, Macmillan, 1990), although I sometimes differ from his interpretation of events, especially in relation to the policy of the British government.

41. Lord Wellesley to Sir H. Wellesley, no. 5, 'Secret',17 Jan. 1812, F.O. 72/127, ff. 9–21.

42. Wellington to Sir H. Wellesley, 3 May, and to Liverpool, 6 May 1812, *W.D.* V, pp. 625–9, 637–8; Castlereagh to Sir H. Wellesley, 2 and 3 June 1812, F.O. 72/127, ff. 157–62, 165–6; Sir H. Wellesley to Wellington, 12 May 1812, *W.S.D.*, vol. 7, pp. 329–31; Wellington to Sir H. Wellesley, 27 May 1812, *W.S.D.*, vol. 7, pp. 337–8.

43. Esdaile, *Wellington and the Spanish Army*, ch. 2 passim, esp. pp. 50–6.

44. Oman, vol. 6, p. 178.

45. Ibid., vol. 5, pp. 494, 537–8.

46. Ibid., vol. 6, pp. 18–20, and Fortescue, vol. 8, pp. 564–5, both censure, but cannot explain, the slowness of Wellington's advance.

47. Fortescue, vol. 8, p. 583. Popham's cannon never reached Burgos. Wellington did not request them at the outset of the siege and ordered them to return to the coast when he decided to give the operation up, so all the effort was in vain. However, a much needed supply of gunpowder did reach him from Popham. Popham, *Damned Cunning Fellow*, p. 206.

48. Wellington to the Officers commanding Divisions and Brigades, 28 Nov. 1812, *W.D.* VI, pp. 180–2. This letter was widely published throughout the army. See also his General Order of 16 Nov. 1812, *W.S.D.*, vol. 7, p. 470.

49. *Parliamentary Debates*, vol. 21, cols 707–13, 869–83.

50. Auckland to Grenville, 25 Aug. 1812; Grey to Grenville, 19 Aug. 1812, both in *H.M.C. Dropmore*, vol. 10, pp. 293–4, 291–2. Lady Bessborough to Granville Leveson Gower, 7 Sept.

[1812], *Private Correspondence of Granville Leveson Gower*, vol. 2, p. 454.

51. Frederick Robinson to Catherine Harris, 20 Aug. 1812, *Memoirs of Sir Lowry Cole*, ed. M. L. Cole and S. Gwynn (London, Macmillan, 1934), p. 92.

52. Liverpool to Peel, 10 Sept. 1812, Parker, *Peel*, vol. 1, p. 37; Lady Bessborough to Granville Leveson Gower, 23 Sept. 1812, and n.d. [c. 16 Aug. 1812], both in *Private Correspondence of Granville Leveson Gower*, vol. 2, pp. 457–8, 449.

53. Peel to Liverpool, 14 Sept. 1812, C. S. Parker, *Sir Robert Peel...*, 3 vols (London, John Murray, 1891), vol. 1, p. 37.

54. This was Liverpool's estimate: Liverpool to Peel, 1 and 7 Nov. 1812, Parker, *Peel*, vol. 1, pp. 44–5.

55. Canning to Wellesley, 19 Nov. 1812, *Wellesley Papers*, vol. 2, pp. 125–8; cf. Political Notebook of Richard Wellesley II (unfoliated), undated entry, c. Nov. 1812, Carver, 54.

56. Peel to Fitzgerald, 5 Dec. 1812, Parker, *Peel*, vol. 1, p. 64.

12   Britain and Napoleon's Invasion of Russia

1. Wellesley to the Prince Regent, 22 Oct. 1811, *Correspondence of George, Prince of Wales*, vol. 8, p. 195.

2. Mills to [Foreign Office], no. 9, 23 March 1812, F.O. 64/85 (unfoliated); see also H. von Treitschke, *History of Germany in the Nineteenth Century* (London, Jarrold, 1915), vol. 1, p. 459. The number of Prussian officers who resigned is sometimes greatly overstated: for the correct figure see P. Paret, *Yorck and the Era of Prussian Reform* (Princeton University Press, 1966), p. 171.

3. Michael and Diana Josselson, *The Commander: A Life of Barclay de Tolly* (Oxford University Press, 1980), pp. 87, 93.

4. Liverpool to Wellington, 'Private', 2 April 1802 [*sic* for 1812], B. L.

Add. Ms 38,326, ff. 26–9; cf. Castlereagh to Charles Stewart, 15 April 1812, P.R.O.N.I. D3030/Q2/2 (typescript).

5. Castlereagh to Thornton, no. 1, 13 March 1812; and same to same, 'Private & Separate', 13 March 1812, both in F.O. 73/71 (unfoliated).

6. Thornton's dispatches to Castlereagh are in F.O. 73/72 and 73. On the Spanish offer to subsidize Russia see [Castlereagh] to Thornton, unnumbered, 31 May 1812, F.O. 73/71.

7. [Castlereagh] to Thornton, no. 18, 18 July 1812, F.O. 73/71; Thornton to Castlereagh, no. 53, 18 July; no. 60, 30 July, and no. 65, 2 Aug. 1812, F.O. 73/73 and 74 (both unfoliated).

8. *Parliamentary Debates*, vol. 23, col. 1147.

9. Wellington to Bathurst, 21 July 1812, *W.D.* V, p. 761; Liverpool to Wellington, 19 Aug. 1812, *W.S.D.*, vol. 7, pp. 401–2.

10. Sherwig, *Guineas and Gunpowder*, pp. 280–2; extensive correspondence on naval cooperation in the defence of Riga in both *Letters and Papers of Admiral of the Fleet Sir Thos. Byam Martin*, ed. Sir Richard Vesey Hamilton, 3 vols (Navy Record Society, 1898), vol. 2, and *The Saumarez Papers*; Bathurst to Wellington, 20 Aug. 1812, *W.S.D.*, vol. 7, pp. 403–4.

11. Thornton to Castlereagh, 'Separate, Secret & Confidential', 3 May 1812; and same to same, no. 18, 6 May 1812, F.O. 73/72.

12. So the *Dictionary of National Biography*, vol. 3, pp. 1196–8, implies.

13. C.K. Webster (ed.), *British Diplomacy, 1813–1815: Select Documents dealing with the Reconstruction of Europe* (London, G. Bell, 1921), p. xxxiii; cf. Webster, *Foreign Policy of Castlereagh*, pp. 96–7.

14. [Castlereagh] to Cathcart, nos 1 and 3, 24 July 1812, F.O. 65/78, ff. 1–11, 15–16.

15. Cathcart to Castlereagh, nos 3 and 4, 14 August 1812, F.O. 65/79, ff. 11–19.

16. Cathcart to Castlereagh, nos 9, 10, 11, 12, all 30 Aug. 1812, F.O. 65/79, ff. 35–53.

17. Palmer, *Alexander I*, pp. 246–7.
18. Cathcart to Castlereagh, nos 20 and 35, 30 Sept. and 30 Oct. 1812, F.O. 65/79, ff. 115–18, and F.O. 65/80, f. 30; Cathcart to Saumarez, 6 Oct. 1812, *The Saumarez Papers*, pp. 255–7; Liverpool to Cathcart, 'Private & Confidential', 22 Oct. 1812, C. D. Yonge, *The Life and Administration of Robert Banks, Second Earl of Liverpool K.G.*, 3 vols (London, Macmillan, 1868), vol. 1, pp. 442–4; Sidmouth to [Bragge Bathurst], 24 Oct. 1812, Sidmouth Papers, 152M/C 1812/OZ. It is possible that Alexander's offer was prompted by memories of the pre-emptive British attack on the Danish fleet at Copenhagen in 1807.
19. Cathcart to Castlereagh, no. 19, 22 Sept. 1812, and enclosure in same to same, no. 26, 18 Oct. 1812, F.O. 65/ 79, ff. 109–14, 144–5.
20. Russian claims in A. A. Lobanov-Rostovsky, *Russia and Europe, 1789– 1825* (Durham N. C., 1947), pp. 240–1; modern estimates: David Chandler, *The Campaigns of Napoleon* (New York, Macmillan, 1974), pp. 852–3, and Richard Riehn, *1812: Napoleon's Russian Campaign* (New York, Wiley, 1991), p. 395.
21. Bunbury to Bathurst, 'Private', 7 Oct. 1812, *H.M.C. Bathurst*, pp. 216–17; Liverpool to Peel, 7 Oct. 1812, and Robinson to Peel, 18 Oct. 1812, both in Parker, *Peel*, vol. 1, pp. 41, 61–2.
22. Torrens to Lt-Col. Campbell, 'P[rivate]', 16 Sept. 1812, W.O. 3/ 603, pp. 80–2; Bathurst to Wellington, 22 Aug. 1812 and 12 Oct. 1812, and Liverpool to Wellington, 27 Oct. and 22 Dec. 1812, *W.S.D.*, vol. 7, pp. 408, 455–6, 462–4, 502–3.
23. Grey to Grenville, 1 Nov. 1812, *H.M.C. Dropmore*, vol. 10, pp. 298– 300; see also M.S. Anderson, 'British Public Opinion and the Russian Campaign of 1812', in *Slavonic and Eastern European Review*, vol. 34, 1956, pp. 408–25, esp. 419–22.
24. George Jackson's diary for 13 Nov. and 19 Dec. 1812, *The Bath Archives*, vol. 1, pp. 436–7, 445–6.

13   A Foolish and Unnecessary War: Britain and the United States, 1811–13

1. Bradford Perkins, *Prologue to War: England and the United States, 1805– 1812* (University of California Press, 1968), p. 399. This is a detailed and scholarly account of the road to war, while the same author's *Castlereagh and Adams: England and the United States, 1812–1823* (University of California Press, 1964) describes the diplomatic contacts during the war, the peace negotiations and postwar relations with equal skill.
2. Perkins, *Prologue to War*, p. 29.
3. Ibid., pp. 392–6.
4. Harry L. Coles, *The War of 1812* (University of Chicago Press, 1965), p. 43. Throughout this chapter I have drawn heavily on this excellent short account of the war, supplemented by Reginald Horsman's *The War of 1812* (London, Eyre and Spottiswoode, 1969), which, while narrower in focus, gives a more detailed account of the military and naval operations, based on considerable original research.
5. Quoted in Perkins, *Castlereagh and Adams*, p. 11.
6. Bathurst to Wellington, 6 Oct. 1812, *W.S.D.*, vol. 7, p. 442.
7. Fortescue, vol. 8, pp. 515–16, 524; 'Statement of the British Naval Force on the North American Stations, in the Years 1810–13', in *Castlereagh Correspondence*, vol. 8, pp. 286–92.
8. Coles, *War of 1812*, pp. 41–4. This and the following paragraphs are based on Coles, ch. 2.
9. Peel to Goulburn, 30 Dec. 1812, Parker, *Peel*, vol. 1, p. 65; Coles, *War of 1812*, pp. 78–84.
10. Mulgrave to Canning, 'Private & Secret', 18 July 1808, Canning Papers, bundle 31; see also Melville to Wellington, 28 July 1813, *W.S.D.*, vol. 8, pp. 144–7.
11. Charles Wright and Ernest Fayle, *A History of Lloyds* (London, Macmillan, 1928), p. 191; the £600,000 taken by the *Essex*, ibid., p. 177; 1,300 prizes in all, Coles, *War of 1812*, p. 98; ibid., p. 105, says that half were retaken; but Horsman, *War of 1812*, says that one

third were, as does Perkins, *Castle-reagh and Adams*, p. 37.

12. British figures: Mitchell and Deane, *Abstract of British Historical Statistics*, p. 282; U.S. figures: Coles, *War of 1812*, p. 89.

13. Figures quoted from W.F. Galpin, 'The American Grain Trade to the Spanish Peninsula', *American Historical Review*, vol. 28, 1922, p. 25n; Jefferson, quoted in Perkins, *Castlereagh and Adams*, p. 8; see also Redgrave, 'Wellington's Logistical Arrangements', pp. 60–2.

14. Returns in W.O. 17/1517, General Returns, Canada, 1813.

15. J. W. Ward, *Letters to Ivy from the first Earl of Dudley*, ed. S. H. Romilly (London, Longmans, 1905), n.d. [c. July 1813], pp. 210–12; Wellington to Bathurst, 10 Feb. 1813, *W.D.* VI, pp. 296–7.

16. Perkins, *Castlereagh and Adams*, p. 63 (*The Times*); pp. 68–9, 76 (British objectives).

14   From Tauroggen to the Armistice: Britain and the Continental Powers, December 1812–June 1813

1. Castlereagh to Cathcart, 15 Jan. [1813], *Castlereagh Correspondence*, vol. 8, pp. 301–5.

2. Quoted in Muriel E. Chamberlain, *Lord Aberdeen: A Political Biography* (London, Longman, 1983), p. 136.

3. Franklin D. Scott, *Bernadotte and the Fall of Napoleon* (Harvard Historical Monograph, no. 7, 1935), pp. 31–4; this interpretation of the treaty is confirmed by Castlereagh to Cathcart, no. 26, 28 April 1813, F.O. 65/83.

4. Quoted in Paul R. Sweet, *Wilhelm von Humboldt: A Biography*, 2 vols (Ohio State University Press, 1980), vol. 2, p. 120.

5. Paret, *Yorck and the Era of Prussian Reform*, pp. 191–6.

6. Kraehe, *Metternich's German Policy*, vol. 1, pp. 154–6.

7. Bunbury to Bathurst, 'Private and Secret', 19 Jan. 1813, B.L. Loan 57, vol. 7, no. 637, partly printed in *H.M.C. Bathurst*, pp. 226–7; Webster, *Foreign Policy of Castlereagh*, p. 121; Sherwig, *Guineas and Gunpowder*, p. 287.

8. Torrens to Wellington, 'Private', 14 April 1813, W.P. 1/368; *Croker Papers* quoted in the *D.N.B.*, vol. 18, p. 1166. Stewart had been made a K.B. on 1 Feb. 1813.

9. Liverpool to Wellington, 'Private and Confidential', 22 Dec. 1812, *W.S.D.*, vol. 7, pp. 502–3.

10. Walpole to Cathcart, [Private], 28 Dec. 1812, F.O. 65/88. (There is a full account of Walpole's mission in Buckland, *Metternich and the British Government*, pp. 407–38.) King to Castlereagh, 'Secret', no. 26, 5 Feb. 1813, printed in the *English Historical Review*, vol. 39, 1924, pp. 256–8, by C.S.B. Buckland as 'An English Estimate of Metternich'.

11. Kraehe, *Metternich's German Policy*, vol. 1, p. 153, whose interpretation of Metternich's policy I generally follow in this and the following paragraphs.

12. Ibid., vol. 1, p. 167.

13. These figures, which are only rough approximations, from F. L. Petre, *Napoleon's Last Campaign in Germany, 1813* (London, Arms and Armour, 1977; first published 1912), pp. 21–6.

14. Kraehe, *Metternich's German Policy*, vol. 1, pp. 169–71.

15. Stewart to Castlereagh, 19 April 1813, *Castlereagh Correspondence*, vol. 8, pp. 360–6.

16. [Castlereagh] to Cathcart, no. 11, 9 April 1813, F.O. 65/83; Cathcart to Castlereagh, no. 37, 27 April 1813, F.O. 65/85. Sherwig, *Guineas and Gunpowder*, pp. 289–95, 301–4, expertly unravels the tangled issue of Federative Paper.

17. Memoir by Münster, 30 March 1813; Castlereagh to Stewart, 'Private', 4 May 1813, both in P.R.O.N.I. D 3030/3454 and 3478; Cathcart to Castlereagh, no. 37, 27 April 1813, F.O. 65/85; Webster, *Foreign Policy of Castlereagh*, pp. 132–3.

18. Cathcart to Castlereagh, 'Most Secret & Confidential', 8 July 1813, F.O. 65/86; Chandler, *Campaigns of Napoleon*, pp. 866–9; Petre, *Last Campaign in Germany*, pp. 9–20.

19. Frederick William is quoted in Palmer, *Alexander I*, p. 265.

20. Chandler, *Campaigns of Napoleon*, p. 898; on allied problems see Josselson, *The Commander*, pp. 172–4.

21. Stewart to Castlereagh, 6 June 1813, *Castlereagh Correspondence*, vol. 9, pp. 22–3; Cathcart to Castlereagh, no. 57, 6 June 1813, and no. 61, 'Most Secret', 16 June 1813, F.O. 65/85.

22. H. A. Kissinger, *A World Restored: Metternich, Castlereagh and the Problems of Peace, 1812–1822* (London, Weidenfeld and Nicolson, 1957), p. 86, and Kraehe, *Metternich's German Policy*, vol. 1, p. 179n, make much of the point that Britain was only excluded from the preliminary, not the final peace. But what hope would she have of obtaining acceptable terms if Napoleon had already satisfied the other powers by concessions? Negotiating separately destroyed the strength of the Coalition, while Metternich, the mediator, did not support British objectives in Spain and the Low Countries.

23. Stewart to Cooke, 16 June 1813, quoted in Webster, *Foreign Policy of Castlereagh*, p. 140n; Cathcart to Stewart, 'Most Confidential', 10 June 1813, P.R.O.N.I. D3030/3506.

24. Cathcart to Castlereagh, no. 61, 'Most Secret', 16 June 1813, F.O. 65/85.

25. *Parliamentary Debates*, vol. 26, col. 957.

26. *Parliamentary Debates*, vol. 26, cols 998–1003.

27. E. A. Smith, *Lord Grey, 1764–1845* (Oxford, Clarendon, 1990), pp. 174–6; Jupp, *Lord Grenville*, pp. 440–2. Grey to Grenville, 12 Nov., and reply, 24 Nov. 1813, *H.M.C. Dropmore*, vol. 10, pp. 355–8, 360–3.

28. Lady Bessborough to Granville Leveson Gower, n.d., *Private Correspondence of Granville Leveson Gower*, vol. 2, p. 485.

29. Castlereagh to General Hope, 22 June 1813, quoted in Webster, *Foreign Policy of Castlereagh*, p. 145.

30. Ward, *Letters to Ivy*, pp. 206–8.

31. Quoted in Thorne (ed.), *The Commons, 1790–1820*, vol. 3, p. 399.

32. The figures for estimated spending do not include the cost of servicing the accumulated debt. *Annual Register*, 1812, p. 96; *Annual Register*, 1813, pp. 42–5, 66–84; William Smart, *Economic Annals of the Nineteenth Century*, 2 vols (London, Macmillan, 1910–17), vol. 1, pp. 359–63; there is an account of Vansittart's modifications to the sinking fund in E. L. Hargreaves, *The National Debt* (London, 1930), pp. 126–30.

33. Schumpeter, 'English Prices and Public Finance', p. 36.

15 Wellington Victorious: The Liberation of Spain, January–October 1813

1. Oman, vol. 6, pp. 250–51.

2. Bathurst to Wellington, 12 Oct. 1812, *W.S.D.*, vol. 7, pp. 455–6; Liverpool to Wellington, 27 Oct. 1812, *W.S.D.*, vol. 7, pp. 462–4; Wellington to Bathurst, 7 Nov. 1812, *W.D.* VI, pp. 153–4; 'Memorandum on the Present State of Affairs, and the Military Operations which might be pursued', by H. E. B[unbury], 31 Dec. 1813 [*sic* for 1812], *W.S.D.*, vol. 8, pp. 457–62.

3. Bathurst to Wellington, 23 June 1813, Liverpool to Wellington, 'Private', 3 July 1813, and same to same, 'Private and Confidential', 7 July 1813, *W.S.D.*, vol. 8, pp. 16–18, 49–50, 64–5; Wellington to Bathurst, 12 July 1813, and Wellington to Liverpool, 25 July 1813, *W.D.* VI, pp. 594–5, 627–8; Bathurst to Wellington, 14 July 1813, *W.S.D.*, vol. 8, pp. 73–4. I believe that Oman (vol. 6, pp. 558–61) greatly overstates the significance of this exchange.

4. Bathurst to Wellington, 2 July 1813, *W.S.D.*, vol. 8, pp. 46–7.

5. All this from Oman, vol. 6, pp. 376–9, 384–91.

6. Oman, vol. 6, pp. 391–450, esp. 395–8, 446–50, for Oman's discussion of Wellington's plans. Fortescue, vol. 9, p. 189, goes so far as to say 'the results of the day were very far from satisfactory', which I think is rather too strong.

7. The Prince Regent to Wellington, 3 July 1813, *W.D.* VI, p. 600n; Col. Torrens to the Duke of York, P[rivate], 22 Aug. 1812, W.O. 3/603, pp. 9–10; Wellington to the Duke of York, 16 July 1813, *W.D.* VI, p. 600; Torrens to Wellington, 21 July 1813 and enclosures, *W.S.D.*, vol. 8, pp. 95–7; Bathurst to Wellington, 9 Sept. 1813, *W.S.D.*, vol. 8, p. 246; Wellington to Bathurst, 25 Sept. 1813, *W.D.* VII, pp. 22–3.

8. *Parliamentary Debates*, vol. 26, col. 1132.

9. In addition to Oman (vol. 6, pp. 587–741) and Fortescue (vol. 9, pp. 241–305) there is an excellent account of the Battles of the Pyrenees in F. C. Beatson, *With Wellington in the Pyrenees* (London, Tom Donovan, 1993; first published 1914), passim — which despite its title is neither a memoir nor a boy's book.

10. Quoted in Oman, vol. 6, p. 641.

11. Ibid., vol. 7, pp. 154–5.

12. Wellington to Sir H. Wellesley, 17 June, and to Bathurst, 14 August 1813, *W.D.* VI, pp. 532–3, 680–2.

13. Wellington to Lord William Bentinck, 20 July 1813, *W.D.* VI, pp. 614–15; see also Oman, vol. 6, pp. 523–7, 737–8.

14. Liverpool to Wellington, 'Private and Confidential', 7 July 1813, *W.S.D.*, vol. 8, pp. 64–5; Wellington to Liverpool, 25 July 1813, *W.D.* VI, pp. 627–8.

15. Wellington to Bathurst, 19 Sept. 1813, *W.D.* VII, p. 10.

16. Oman, vol. 7, pp. 216–18.

17. Wellington to Bathurst, 19 Sept. 1813, *W.D.* VII, p. 10.

18. Brougham to Grey, 22 Aug. 1813, Brougham, *Life and Times of Henry Lord Brougham written by himself . . .*, 3 vols (Edinburgh, Blackwoods, 1871), vol. 2, pp. 82–4. The account of the 1813 campaign given above is based primarily on the relevant chapters in Oman, vols 6 and 7, supplemented by Fortescue, vol. 9, and Wellington's correspondence.

19. Figures from Oman, vol. 6, pp. 276–9, 308, 763–5. These figures appear to be more than normally doubtful, but give a rough indication of the size of the armies involved. Oman's statement (p. 279) that Suchet had a gross strength of 75,000 evidently must include Decaen. Elio's 15,000 men does not include about another 15,000 guerrillas operating in Aragon who were nominally under his command.

20. Rosselli, *Bentinck and the British Occupation of Sicily*, pp. 86–100.

21. Oman, vol. 6, pp. 308–13, 488–522.

22. Ibid., vol. 7, pp. 70–71.

23. Ibid., p. 90.

24. Rosselli, *Bentinck and the British Occupation of Sicily*, pp. 102–34; Bathurst to Bentinck, 16 Sept. 1813, Portland (Bentinck) Papers, Pw Jd 576.

25. Bathurst to Wellington, 23 June 1813, *W.S.D.*, vol. 8, pp. 16–18; Wellington to Bathurst, 29 June and 12 July 1813, *W.D.* VI, pp. 559–60, 594–5.

26. Sir H. Wellesley to Castlereagh, 3 July 1813, *W.S.D.*, vol. 8, pp. 56–7; for a full account of Anglo-Spanish relations in 1813 see Esdaile, *Wellington and the Spanish Armies*, chs 5 and 6.

27. Picton to Sir Charles [Hastings], 26 July 1813, *Historical Manuscripts Commission: Report on the Manuscripts of the Late Reginald Rawdon Hastings, Esq*, ed. Francis Bickley, 4 vols (London, H.M.S.O., 1934–47), vol. 3, pp. 302–4; Wellington to Liverpool, 25 July 1813, *W.D.* VI, pp. 627–8.

28. De la Fuente 'Forjaz', pp. 379–80; Sherwig, *Guineas and Gunpowder*, p. 367.

29. De la Fuente 'Forjaz', pp. 379–80, 393–6, 424–8, Fryman, 'Charles Stuart', pp. 347–56.

30. Figures based on Returns in W.O. 17/2471–4 and Morning States in W.O. 1/276: while the two sets of returns give slightly different figures (the totals in the morning states being

about 10 per cent lower), they show the same trends and are generally consistent.

31. Fortescue, vol. 9, pp. 78–83; Oman, vol. 6, pp. 231–5.

32. Redgrave, 'Wellington's Logistical Arrangements', pp. 126–30; Herries, *Memoir*, vol. 1, p. 79; examples of pleasant letters from Wellington to Bathurst praising the supply of specie, 3 March, 30 March, 9 Aug. 1813, *W.D.* VI, pp. 334–5, 391–2, 670; shortage later in the year, Wellington to Bathurst, 21 Nov., 8 and 21 Dec. 1813, *W.D.* VII, pp. 150–51, 189, 213–16.

33. Bathurst to Wellington, 22 July 1813, and Torrens to Wellington, 'Private', 19 Aug. 1813, *W.S.D.*, vol. 8, pp. 109, 198–9.

34. Fortescue, vol. 9, p. 104n.

35. Bathurst to Wellington, 12 May 1813, *W.S.D.*, vol. 7, p. 619.

36. Bathurst to Wellington, 9 Oct. 1813, W.P. 1/378.

37. Wellington to William Wellesley-Pole, 2 Dec. 1813, Raglan Mss, Wellington A, no. 66.

38. Wellington to William Wellesley-Pole, 18 Aug., 24 Sept., 2 Dec. 1813, and 9 Jan. 1813 [*sic* for 1814], Raglan Mss, Wellington A, nos 57, 59, 66, 67.

39. Wellington to William Wellesley-Pole, 24 Sept. 1813, Raglan Mss, Wellington A, no. 59; Norman Gash, *Lord Liverpool* (London, Weidenfeld and Nicolson, 1984), pp. 203–4; Neville Thompson, *Wellington After Waterloo* (London, Routledge and Kegan Paul, 1986), pp. 54–5. In 1826 Liverpool refused to make Gerald Wellesley a bishop because he had been living separately from his wife, although not divorced, since 1819. The details of the 1813 incident remain obscure.

40. William Wellesley-Pole to Wellington, 2 Feb. 1814, Raglan Mss, Wellington B, no. 125; see also Pole's earlier letters of 28 July, 1 Sept. and 18 Dec. 1813 (Raglan Mss, Wellington B, nos 120, 121, 124) and Wellington's letters cited above.

16 From the Armistice to Frankfort: Britain and the Continental Powers, June–November 1813

1. Bathurst to Wellington, 23 June 1813, *W.S.D.*, vol. 8, pp. 16–18; Wellington to Bathurst, 12 July 1813, *W.D.* VI, pp. 594–5.

2. Castlereagh to Cathcart, no. 42, 5 July 1813, *British Diplomacy*, pp. 6–10.

3. Castlereagh to Cathcart, 6 July 1813, *British Diplomacy*, pp. 10–11. Full text in *Castlereagh Correspondence*, vol. 9, p. 30.

4. Liverpool to Wellington, 'Private', 3 July 1813; Bathurst to Wellington, 27 July 1813, *W.S.D.*, vol. 8, pp. 49–50, 134–5.

5. For example, Castlereagh to Cathcart, 6 and 9 April 1813, F.O. 65/83. It is only fair to add that this latent hostility to Britain was matched or exceeded by similar feelings felt by the Continental Courts for each other.

6. Kraehe, *Metternich's German Policy*, vol. 1, pp. 174–7.

7. Cathcart to Castlereagh, no. 57, 6 June 1813; same to same, no. 61, 'Most Secret', 16 June 1813, F.O. 65/85; Stewart to Castlereagh, 16 June 1813, *British Diplomacy*, pp. 66–9.

8. Kraehe, *Metternich's German Policy*, vol. 1, pp. 188–9.

9. Castlereagh to Cathcart, 1 Sept. 1813, *British Diplomacy*, pp. 18–19; Webster, *Foreign Policy of Castlereagh*, p. 159.

10. Castlereagh to Cathcart, 30 June 1813, *Castlereagh Correspondence*, vol. 8, pp. 411–12; see also Castlereagh to Cathcart, 30 June 1813, *British Diplomacy*, pp. 5–6 (different letter).

11. For some recent, but I think unconvincing, defences of Aberdeen's performance on the Continent see: Chamberlain, *Lord Aberdeen*; Lucille Iremonger, *Lord Aberdeen* (London, Collins, 1978); and P. Schroeder, 'An Unnatural "Natural Alliance": Castlereagh, Metternich and Aberdeen in 1813', *International History Review*, vol. 10, Nov. 1988, pp. 521–40.

12. Scott, *Bernadotte and the Fall of Napoleon*, pp. 83–91.

13. Reaction to Vitoria: Thornton to Castlereagh, 'Private and Secret', 12 July 1813, P.R.O.N.I. D 3030/3541; Jackson to Stewart, 27 July 1813, *British Diplomacy*, pp. 72–3. Offer of the command: Nugent to Wellington, Prague, 27 July 1813, *W.S.D.*, vol. 8, pp. 132–3; Wellington to Bathurst, 12 July 1813, *W.D.* VI, pp. 594–5.

14. Kraehe, *Metternich's German Policy*, vol. 1, p. 192; Josselson, *The Commander*, pp. 177–81.

15. Quoted in Josselson, *The Commander*, p. 177.

16. Figures from Chandler, *Campaigns of Napoleon*, pp. 900–1.

17. Quoted in Josselson, *The Commander*, p. 181.

18. Chandler, *Campaigns of Napoleon*, p. 906.

19. Figures from ibid., pp. 938–9; dates, ibid., p. 939, and from V. J. Esposito and J. R. Etling, *A Military History and Atlas of the Napoleonic Wars* (London, Arms and Armour, 1980; first published 1964), p. 127.

20. On the Prussian experience see Dennis E. Showalter, 'The Prussian *Landwehr* and its Critics, 1813–1819', *Central European History*, vol. 4, no. 1, March 1971, pp. 3–33, esp. 9–11. On the wider question see Hans Kohn, *Prelude to Nation States* (Princeton, Van Nostrand, 1967), pp. 279–88, and Esdaile, *The Wars of Napoleon* (forthcoming), ch. 8.

21. Aberdeen to Castlereagh, no. 2, 12 Sept., and no. 3, 13 Sept. 1813, F.O. 7/102; 23 Sept. 1813, 'Private', printed in Lady Frances Balfour, *The Life of George, Fourth Earl of Aberdeen*, 2 vols (London, Hodder and Stoughton, n.d. [1922]), vol. 1, pp. 105–7.

22. Aberdeen to Castlereagh, 12 Nov. 1813, printed in Balfour, *Life of Aberdeen*, vol. 1, pp. 153–8.

23. Aberdeen to Castlereagh, no. 3, 13 Sept., and no. 15, 9 Oct. 1813, F.O. 7/102.

24. Castlereagh to Aberdeen, no. 3, 6 Aug., and 'Most Secret and Separate',

6 Aug. 1813, *British Diplomacy*, pp. 94–6, 96–7; Aberdeen to Castlereagh, no. 4, 14 Sept. 1813, and enclosure, F.O. 7/102.

25. Kraehe, *Metternich's German Policy*, vol. 1, pp. 202–7.

26. Sherwig, *Guineas and Gunpowder*, pp. 287, 300. 'An Account of the Value of All Arms, Ammunition and other Articles supplied by the Ordnance Department to any Foreign Power or State, between 31st December 1812 and 31st December 1813 . . .', B.L. Add. Ms 31,231, f. 30. Scott, *Bernadotte and the Fall of Napoleon*, pp. 117–18.

27. Sherwig, *Guineas and Gunpowder*, pp. 305–6.

28. Castlereagh to Cathcart, nos 65, 66 and 'Private', all 18 Sept. 1813, with the enclosed 'Projet of a Treaty of Alliance Offensive and Defensive against France', all printed in *British Diplomacy*, pp. 19–29.

29. Cathcart to Castlereagh, 'Private', 30 Oct., 'Secret', 11 Nov., and 'Secret', 17 Nov. 1813, all in *British Diplomacy*, pp. 35–41; Kissinger, *World Restored*, p. 95.

30. Stewart to Castlereagh, 24 Nov. 1813, *British Diplomacy*, p. 88; Aberdeen to Castlereagh, no. 37, 'Most Secret', 14 Nov., and no. 51, 'Most Secret', 5 Dec. 1813, F.O. 7/103.

31. Grimsted, *Foreign Ministers of Alexander I*, pp. 206–8; Kraehe, *Metternich's German Policy*, vol. 1, p. 250.

32. Sweet, *Humboldt*, vol. 2, pp. 152–3; cf. Kraehe, *Metternich's German Policy*, vol. 1, p. 250.

33. Kraehe, *Metternich's German Policy*, vol. 1, pp. 250–63, deftly untangles the complications surrounding the overture, though much remains unclear. On Belgium see Aberdeen to Castlereagh, no. 48, 'Secret and Confidential', 2 Dec. 1813, F.O. 7/103.

34. Webster, *Foreign Policy of Castlereagh*, pp. 177, 187–9.

35. Wellington to Bathurst, 9 Nov. 1813, *W.D.* VII, p. 125; [Castlereagh] to Cathcart, no. 85, 29 Nov. 1813, F.O. 65/83.

36. Kraehe, *Metternich's German Policy*, vol. 1, pp. 260–1.

17   The Invasion of France,
November 1813–April 1814

1. Wellington to Bathurst, 10 Jan. 1814,
    W.D. VII, pp. 252–4; see also same to
    same, 21 Nov. 1813, ibid., pp. 151–3.
2. Wellington to Bathurst, 27 Nov. 1813,
    W.D. VII, pp. 166–8.
3. Oman, vol. 7, pp. 297–313.
4. Wellington to Sir Henry Wellesley, 16
    Jan. 1814, *W.D.* VII, pp. 267–8.
5. Wellington to Sir Henry Wellesley, 5
    Feb. 1814, *W.D.* VII, pp. 304–5.
6. Castlereagh to Liverpool, no. 18, 23
    Feb. 1814, F.O. 92/2, ff. 197–200.
7. Figures for Soult's army in the
    autumn of 1813 from Joseph A. Clerc,
    *Campagne du Maréchal Soult dans les
    Pyrénées Occidentales en 1813–1814*
    (Paris, Librairie Militaire de L.
    Baudoin, 1894), pp 382–3; those for
    the spring contain some guesswork
    based on figures in Oman. Most of
    the appendices in Oman, vol. 7, give
    the forces at particular actions, not
    the total army including garrisons.
    For Suchet see Oman, vol. 7, pp. 406,
    550–1.
8. Returns for Wellington's army in
    W.O. 17/2475–6.
9. Oman, vol. 7, p. 286; Richard Davis,
    The English Rothschilds (London,
    Collins, 1983), p. 30; Lord Rothschild,
    The Shadow of a Great Man (London,
    privately printed, 1982), pp. 15–24.
10. Clive Emsley, *Longman Companion
    to Napoleonic Europe* (London,
    Longman, 1993), p. 140: Paris had
    547,000 inhabitants; Marseilles
    111,000; Lyon 110,000; and Bordeaux
    91,000.
11. Wellington to Liverpool, 4 March
    1814, *W.D.* VII, p. 345; see also
    Wellington to Burghersh, 14 Jan.
    1814, ibid., pp. 264–5.
12. Wellington to Beresford, 7 March
    1814, *W.D.* VII, pp. 352–5.
13. Oman, vol. 7, pp. 388–405; Dalhousie
    to the Quartermaster-General, 19
    March 1814, *W.S.D.*, vol. 8, pp.
    667–8; Wellington to the Duc
    d'Angoulême, 29 March 1814, *W.D.*
    VII, pp. 399–401.
14. Rosselli, *Bentinck and the British
    Occupation of Sicily*, pp. 131–42; the
    proclamation quoted on p. 138;
    Castlereagh to Liverpool, 5 May 1814,
    quoted on p. 142. Rosselli's comment,
    p. 139. See also R. M. Johnston, 'Lord
    William Bentinck and Murat', *English
    Historical Review*, vol. 19, 1904, pp.
    263–80.
15. Bathurst to Maj.-Gen. Dunlop, 'Most
    Secret', 28 May 1813, B.L. Add. Ms
    37,051, ff. 31–4; Scott, *Bernadotte and
    the Fall of Napoleon*, p. 55 (on
    Dolgorouki); G. J. Renier, *Great
    Britain and the Establishment of the
    Kingdom of the Netherlands, 1813–1815*
    (London, Allen and Unwin, 1930), pp.
    65–75.
16. Renier, *Britain and the . . . Nether-
    lands, 1813–1815*, p. 98 (for the sema-
    phore message); Wilberforce, *Life of
    Wilberforce*, vol. 4, p. 151; Auckland to
    Grenville, 22 Nov. 1813, *H.M.C.
    Dropmore*, vol. 10, p. 359. Auckland
    had, of course, been British ambassa-
    dor at the Hague between 1790 and
    1794, which may partly explain his un-
    characteristic exuberance.
17. Lady Bessborough to Granville
    Leveson Gower, n.d., *Private Corre-
    spondence of Granville Leveson Gower*,
    vol. 2, p. 491.
18. Bathurst to Wellington, 31 Dec. 1813,
    W.S.D., vol. 8, pp. 450–2.
19. Castlereagh to Cathcart, 'Private', 30
    Nov. 1813, F.O. 97/343; Harrowby to
    Bathurst, 16 Jan. 1814, *H.M.C.
    Bathurst*, pp. 260–3; Fournier,
    Napoleon I, vol. 2, p. 364 (the overture
    through Wessenberg on 28 March).
20. Scott, *Bernadotte and the Fall of
    Napoleon*, pp. 119–45; Liverpool to
    Castlereagh, 26 Jan. 1814, printed in
    Webster, *Foreign Policy of Castlereagh*,
    p. 518; Castlereagh to Liverpool,
    no. 7, 3 Feb. 1814, F.O. 92/2, ff.
    86–7.
21. Bathurst to Wellington, 31 Dec. 1813,
    W.S.D., vol. 8, pp. 450–2; Castlereagh
    to Liverpool, no. 7, 3 Feb. 1814, F.O.
    92/2, ff. 86–7; T. I. Leiren,
    'Norwegian Independence and British
    Opinion, January to August 1814',
    Scandinavian Studies, vol. 47, 1975,
    pp. 364–82.
22. Cabinet Memorandum, 26 Dec. 1813,
    British Diplomacy, pp. 123–6.

23. Memorandum for the Comte de Gramont [by Wellington], 20 Dec. 1813, and Wellington to Bathurst, 21 Dec. 1813, *W.D.* VII, pp. 212–13, 213–16.

24. Memorandum by Liverpool, 4 Jan. 1814, *W.S.D.*, vol. 8, pp. 486–9; Webster, *Foreign Policy of Castlereagh*, p. 236.

25. Liverpool to Castlereagh, 29 Dec. 1813, printed in Webster, *Foreign Policy of Castlereagh*, pp. 510–11, conveys Bathurst's view; Harrowby to Bathurst, 16 Jan. 1814, and Mulgrave to Bathurst, 'Private and Secret', 6 Jan. 1814, both in *H.M.C. Bathurst*, pp. 260–3, 255–8; Castlereagh to Liverpool, 30 Dec. 1813, *British Diplomacy*, pp. 128–9.

26. There is a full account of the proposed marriage in Ch. 3 of Renier's *Britain and the . . . Netherlands, 1813–1815*; for Russian hopes of Holland see Kraehe, *Metternich's German Policy*, vol. 1, p. 304.

27. Romilly, *Memoirs of the Life of Sir Samuel Romilly written by himself . . .*, 3 vols (London, John Murray, 1840), vol. 3, p. 126n; Webster, *Foreign Policy of Castlereagh*, p. 198n.

28. The account of military operations in this and subsequent paragraphs in this chapter is based largely on Henry Houssaye, *Napoleon and the Campaign of 1814* (London, Rees, 1914); F. L. Petre, *Napoleon at Bay, 1814* (London, Arms and Armour, 1977; first published 1914) and Chandler, *The Campaigns of Napoleon*. The figure of nearly 900,000 men comes from Petre, p. 12.

29. Quoted in Kraehe, *Metternich's German Policy*, vol. 1, p. 284.

30. Castlereagh to Liverpool, 22 Jan. 1814, *W.S.D.*, vol. 8, pp. 535–40.

31. Castlereagh to Liverpool, 'Most Secret', 22 Jan. 1814, *W.S.D.*, vol. 8, pp. 534–5.

32. Sweet, *Humboldt*, vol. 2, p. 159, quoting a letter of Humboldt's of 4 Feb. 1814.

33. Quoted in Webster, *Foreign Policy of Castlereagh*, p. 200.

34. Lady Burghersh, quoted in Wendy Hinde, *Castlereagh* (London, Collins, 1981), p. 204.

35. Castlereagh to Liverpool, [28] and 29 Jan. and 29 Jan. 1814, *British Diplomacy*, pp. 138–40, 141–4. The quotation comes from the second letter.

36. Castlereagh to Liverpool, 29 Jan. 1814, *British Diplomacy*, pp. 141–4.

37. Castlereagh to Sir Charles Stewart, 31 Jan. [1814], *Castlereagh Correspondence*, vol. 9, pp. 216–17.

38. A. A. L. de Caulaincourt, *No Peace With Napoleon!* (New York, Morrow, 1936), p. 14.

39. Castlereagh to Liverpool, 16 and 18 Feb. 1814, *British Diplomacy*, pp. 147–56; and *Castlereagh Correspondence*, vol. 9, pp. 266–7.

40. Castlereagh to Liverpool, no. 17, 21 Feb. 1814, F.O. 92/2; same to the same, 'Most Secret and Confidential', 26 Feb. 1814, *British Diplomacy*, pp. 160–1.

41. Liverpool to Castlereagh, 27 Feb. 1814, printed in Webster, *Foreign Policy of Castlereagh*, pp. 523–4.

42. Cooke to Castlereagh, 5 Jan. 1814, *Castlereagh Correspondence*, vol. 9, pp. 136–9; Liverpool to Castlereagh, 12 Jan. and 12 Feb. 1814, printed in Webster, *Foreign Policy of Castlereagh*, pp. 514–15, 520–2; Hamilton to Castlereagh, 12 Feb. 1814, *Castlereagh Correspondence*, vol. 9, pp. 261–2.

43. Ward, *Letters to Ivy*, p. 230 (letter undated).

44. Castlereagh to Liverpool, 16 Feb. 1814, *British Diplomacy*, pp. 147–55 (quote on p. 152).

45. Liverpool to Castlereagh, 12 Feb. 1814, printed in Webster, *Foreign Policy of Castlereagh*, pp. 520–2; on Wellesley see Webster, *Foreign Policy of Castlereagh*, p. 237.

46. Liverpool to Castlereagh, 6 Jan. 1814, printed in Webster, *Foreign Policy of Castlereagh*, pp. 512–13.

47. Liverpool to Castlereagh, 12 Feb. 1814, printed in Webster, *Foreign Policy of Castlereagh*, pp. 520–2.

48. Liverpool to Castlereagh, 20 Jan. 1814, printed in Webster, *Foreign Policy of Castlereagh*, pp. 515–16.

49. Napoleon to Joseph, 18 Feb. 1814, quoted in Fournier, *Napoleon*, vol. 2, p. 350; Caulaincourt, *No Peace with Napoleon!*, p. 19.

50. Castlereagh to Liverpool, 30 Jan. 1814, *Castlereagh Correspondence*, vol. 9, pp. 212–14.

51. Caulaincourt, *No Peace with Napoleon!*, pp. 18–19.

52. Castlereagh to Liverpool, 8 March 1814, *Castlereagh Correspondence*, vol. 9, pp. 327–9.

53. The Treaty of Chaumont is well discussed from different perspectives in Sherwig, *Guineas and Gunpowder*, pp. 318–21, Kraehe, *Metternich's German Policy*, vol. 1, pp. 303–7, and Webster, *Foreign Policy of Castlereagh*, pp. 226–9. Liverpool at least was keenly aware of Spanish sensitivity: Liverpool to Castlereagh, 21 March 1814, printed in Webster, *Foreign Policy of Castlereagh*, p. 529.

54. Castlereagh to Hamilton, 10 March 1814, *British Diplomacy*, pp. 165–6; Castlereagh's calculations are in his letter to Liverpool, no. 33, 'Most Secret', 10 March 1814, F.O. 92/3.

55. Quoted in Barbara Norman, *Napoleon and Talleyrand: The Last Two Weeks* (New York, Stein and Day, 1970), p. 76.

56. Bathurst to Castlereagh, 22 March 1814, *British Diplomacy*, pp. 171–2; Liverpool to Wellington, 24 March 1814, and Bathurst to Wellington, 29 March 1814, both in *W.S.D.*, vol. 8, pp. 680–2, 702–3.

57. Webster, *Foreign Policy of Castlereagh*, pp. 243–4.

58. Quoted in ibid., p. 247.

59. Sir Charles Stewart to Castlereagh, 1 April 1814, *Castlereagh Correspondence*, vol. 9, pp. 418–21; the allied proclamation, issued on the night of 29 March, is quoted in Houssaye, *Napoleon and the Campaign of 1814*, p. 382.

18   The Year of Revelry, April 1814–March 1815

1. Castlereagh to Liverpool, 14 April 1814, *British Diplomacy*, pp. 175–7;

Kraehe, *Metternich's German Policy*, vol. 2, pp. 9–10.

2. Louis XVIII quoted in Webster, *Foreign Policy of Castlereagh*, pp. 251–2; Liverpool to Castlereagh, 26 April 1814, printed, ibid., pp. 537–8; Palmer, *Alexander*, p. 289.

3. Webster, *Foreign Policy of Castlereagh*, pp. 264–76.

4. Castlereagh to Liverpool, 19 May 1814, *British Diplomacy*, pp. 183–5. The Treaty, with its secret articles, is printed in Edward Hertslet (comp.) *Map of Europe by Treaty . . . Since 1814*, 4 vols (London, 1875–91), vol. 1 pp. 1–28.

5. The first quote is from *Annual Register*, 1814 Chronicle, p. 29; the second from the reminiscences of Georgiana McCrae, who was a child at the time, quoted in Brenda Niall, *Georgiana: A Biography of Georgiana McCrae, Painter, Diarist, Pioneer* (Melbourne University Press, 1994), p. 25.

6. Wilberforce to Hannah More, 9 April 1814, *Life of Wilberforce*, vol. 4, p. 171; Palmerston to Temple, 6 May 1814, Palmerston Papers GC/TE/139.

7. Smith, *Lord Grey*, pp. 176–7; Brougham to Creevey, n.d., 1814, *Creevey Papers*, pp. 192–3; Auckland to Grenville, 'Private', 12 April 1814, *H.M.C. Dropmore*, vol. 10, pp. 385–6.

8. Whitbread to Thomas Sheridan, 10 April 1814, *Creevey Papers*, pp. 190–91.

9. Smith to Allen, 10 March [*sic* for April] 1814, *The Letters of Sydney Smith*, ed. Nowell C. Smith, 2 vols (Oxford, Clarendon, 1953), vol. 1, pp. 245–6.

10. *Parliamentary Debates*, vol. 27, cols 636–47. Webster, however, is wrong to state (*Foreign Policy of Castlereagh*, p. 272) that on 3 May it resolved 'against the surrender of the colonies without Abolition'.

11. Webster, *Foreign Policy of Castlereagh*, pp. 271–2, 413–24; *Life of Wilberforce*, vol. 4, pp. 186–97; Jerome Reich, 'The Slave Trade at the Congress of Vienna — a Study in English Public Opinion', *Journal of Negro History*, vol. 53, April 1968, pp. 129–43.

12. Frederick William described by Palmer, *Alexander*, p. 283; Blücher by Webster in *Foreign Policy of Castlereagh*, p. 291. Both give excellent and complementary accounts of the visit of the allied sovereigns to London, Palmer describing the celebrations most enjoyably, while Webster concentrates on the diplomacy.

13. *Life of Wilberforce*, vol. 4, p. 198; Creevey to Mrs Creevey, 14 June 1814, *Creevey Papers*, pp. 195–7.

14. Aspinall, 'The Rupture of the Orange Marriage Negotiations, 1814', *History*, vol. 34, 1949, pp. 44–60.

15. Elizabeth Longford, *Wellington: The Years of the Sword* (London, Weidenfeld and Nicolson, 1968), pp. 350–52, 362–6.

16. Wellington to Castlereagh, 21 April 1814, *W.D.* VII, p. 461; Castlereagh to Liverpool, 13 April 1814, *Castlereagh Correspondence*, vol. 9, pp. 458–9.

17. Liverpool to Wellington, 13 November 1814, *W.S.D.*, vol. 9, pp. 430–1; see also Rory Muir, 'From Soldier to Statesman: Wellington in Paris and Vienna, 1814–15', in Alan J. Guy (ed.), *The Road to Waterloo* (London, National Army Museum, 1990), pp. 155–63.

18. This and following paragraphs are based on Horsman, *War of 1812*, chs 7–9, and Coles, *War of 1812*, chs 5 and 6. See also Bathurst to Prevost, 3 June 1814, printed in J. M. Hitsman, *The Incredible War of 1812* (University of Toronto Press, 1965), pp. 249–51.

19. Perkins, *Castlereagh and Adams*, pp. 94–6.

20. Coles, *War of 1812*, pp. 233–6.

21. Harmanus Bleecker quoted in Perkins, *Prologue to War*, p. 388. On the negotiations at Ghent see Perkins, *Castlereagh and Adams*, chs 4–7; Wellington to Liverpool, 9 Nov., and Liverpool to Castlereagh, 18 Nov. 1814, *W.S.D.*, vol. 9, pp. 424–6, 438–9.

22. Liverpool to Castlereagh, 28 Oct. 1814, *British Diplomacy*, pp. 219–20.

23. Alan Palmer, *Metternich: Councillor of Europe* (London, Weidenfeld and Nicolson, 1972), p. 130.

24. Castlereagh to the Prince Regent, 20 Oct. 1814, *Letters of George IV*, vol. 1, no. 494, pp. 501–2; Kraehe, *Metternich's German Policy*, vol. 2, pp. 118–326 passim.

25. Apsley to Bathurst, 22 Jan. 1815, *H.M.C. Bathurst*, pp. 327–8. The Viennese were probably more shocked by the Castlereaghs' sabbatarianism, though on one occasion Beethoven conducted a concert of his own music on a weekday, rather than the traditional Sunday, to accommodate them. Palmer, *Metternich*, p. 140.

26. Castlereagh to Liverpool, 'Private', n.d., Nov. 1814, Yonge, *Life of Liverpool*, vol. 2, pp. 52–3.

27. There is no comprehensive, scholarly account of the Congress in English. Kraehe's *Metternich's German Policy*, vol. 2, is detailed, erudite and persuasive, but naturally does not attempt to cover all aspects of the Congress. The British role is best covered in Webster's *Foreign Policy of Castlereagh*, supplemented by his *The Congress of Vienna, 1814–15* (London, Thames and Hudson, 1965; first published 1919), rather than vice versa. Harold Nicolson's *Congress of Vienna* (London, Constable, 1946) has long been popular but is now dated. The greatest absence is any full account of Russian policy.

28. Castlereagh to Liverpool, 2 Oct. 1814, *British Diplomacy*, pp. 197–9; Kraehe, *Metternich's German Policy*, vol. 2, pp. 131–7; Grimsted, *Foreign Ministers of Alexander I*, pp. 33, 54. Kraehe is much less inclined than Grimsted to accept Alexander's idealism at face value.

29. Kraehe, *Metternich's German Policy*, vol. 2, pp. 158–263.

30. Liverpool to Castlereagh, 14 Oct. 1814, *W.S.D.*, vol. 9, pp. 342–3; see also Liverpool to Bathurst, 15 Dec. 1814, ibid., p. 480, on Poland proving a burden to Russia.

31. Liverpool to Castlereagh, 28 Oct., 2 and 25 Nov. 1814, *British Diplomacy*, pp. 219–22, 244–6; see also Liverpool to Wellington, 26 Nov. 1814, *W.S.D.*, vol. 9, pp. 455–6.

32. Liverpool to Wellington, 23 Dec. 1814, *W.S.D.*, vol. 9, p. 494.

33. Bathurst to Castlereagh, 27 Nov. 1814, *British Diplomacy*, pp. 247–8.

34. Kraehe, *Metternich's German Policy*, vol. 2, pp. 264–307 (reaction to Ghent, pp. 292–3).

35. Liverpool to Castlereagh, 23 Dec. 1814, *British Diplomacy*, pp. 265–7.

36. Liverpool had, however, consulted sufficient colleagues to be able to state that ten out of thirteen supported it, and that though Mulgrave was expected to oppose it, he was unlikely to press his objection. Liverpool to Bathurst, 21 Jan. 1815, *H.M.C. Bathurst*, pp. 326–7. Westmorland also opposed the Treaty: précis of Westmorland to Bathurst, 19 Jan. 1815, ibid., p. 326. Bathurst to Castlereagh, 18 Jan. 1815, *British Diplomacy*, p. 291.

37. Liverpool to Castlereagh, 16 Jan. 1815, *Castlereagh Correspondence*, vol. 10, pp. 240–2; Liverpool to Bathurst, 18 Jan. 1815, *H.M.C. Bathurst*, pp. 325–6.

38. C[anning] to Huskisson, Lisbon, 17 March 1815, B.L. Add. Ms 38,740, ff. 91–3.

39. Webster, *Foreign Policy of Castlereagh*, p. 361.

19   The Hundred Days, 1815

1. Anon., 'On Napoleon's Return from Elba', quoted in Norman, *Napoleon and Talleyrand*, p. 262.

2. There is a good account of Napoleon's exile in Elba and escape in Norman Mackenzie, *The Escape from Elba: The Fall and Flight of Napoleon, 1814–1815* (O.U.P., 1982), passim.

3. *Moniteur* quoted in Vincent Cronin, *Napoleon* (Harmondsworth, Penguin, 1976), p. 487; Fitzroy Somerset (British chargé d'affaires in Paris) to Castlereagh, no. 23, 'Secret & Confidential', 6 March 1815; nos 24, 25 and [private], all 7 March 1815, F.O. 27/113.

4. Kraehe, *Metternich's German Policy*, vol. 2, pp. 326–8. Kraehe endorses Metternich's own account while correcting some details.

5. Wellington to Castlereagh, 'Private', 12 March 1815, W.P. 1/453. The version of this letter printed in *W.D.* VIII, pp. 2–3, has significant silent deletions.

6. Romilly, diary, 10 March 1815, Romilly, *Memoirs and Correspondence*, vol. 3, pp. 158–9.

7. Bennet to Creevey, 16 March 1815, *Creevey's Life and Times . . .* , ed. John Gore (London, John Murray, 1934), p. 74.

8. Castlereagh to Fitzroy Somerset, 12 March, and to Wellington, 16 March 1815, *W.S.D.*, vol. 9, pp. 591–2, 597; Peel to Gregory, 16 and 22 March 1815, Parker, *Peel*, vol. 1, pp. 171–3.

9. Quoted in Philip Mansel, *Louis XVIII* (London, Blond and Briggs, 1981), p. 227.

10. Hubert Cole, *Fouché: The Unprincipled Patriot* (London, Eyre and Spottiswoode, 1971), pp. 251–7.

11. A. Hilliard Atteridge, *Marshal Murat* (London, Nelson, n.d., c. 1912), pp. 351–74.

12. Wellington to Castlereagh, 'Private', 12 March 1815, W.P. 1/453. The version of this letter printed in *W.D.* VIII, pp. 2–3, has significant silent deletions.

13. Wellington to Castlereagh, 18 March 1815, *W.D.* VIII, pp. 4–5; Castlereagh to Wellington, 'Private', 24 March 1815, *W.S.D.*, vol. 9, pp. 608–9; Enno E. Kraehe, 'Wellington and the Reconstruction of the Allied Armies during the Hundred Days', *International History Review*, vol. XI, Feb. 1989, pp. 84–97, gives a detailed account of the dispute.

14. Castlereagh to Wellington, 'Private', 16 March 1815, *W.S.D.*, vol. 9, p. 597; declaration printed in *Annual Register* for 1815, p. 369, of which a draft is in F.O. 92/13, ff. 63–4.

15. Clancarty to Castlereagh, 'Private and Secret', 15 April 1815, *British Diplomacy*, pp. 325–30; R. E. Cubberly, *The Role of Fouché during the Hundred Days* (Madison, 1969), pp. 53–70, esp. 58.

16. Castlereagh to Wellington, 'Secret & Private', 16 April 1815, *W.S.D.*, vol. 10, pp. 80–1; Wellington to Clancarty, 10 April 1815, *W.D.* VIII, pp. 21–3, and Wellington to Castlereagh, 'Private & Confidential', 11 April 1815, *W.S.D.*, vol. 10, pp. 60–2.

17. Bennet to Creevey, 3 April 1815, *Creevey Papers*, pp. 213–15; Bennet suggests in this letter that Liverpool and Sidmouth favoured peace, but their correspondence shows that he was mistaken.

18. Grey to Lord Wellesley, 2 and 6 April 1815, B.L. Add. Ms 37,297, ff. 236–7, 238–9; Bennet to Creevey, 3 April 1815, *Creevey Papers*, pp. 213–15 (for Yarmouth); Liverpool to Canning, 13 June 1815, *W.S.D.*, vol. 10, pp. 464–5 (on Lord Wellesley); Wilberforce diary, 27 April and 10 May 1815, *Life of Wilberforce*, vol. 4, pp. 258–9.

19. Wellington to Wellesley-Pole, 5 May 1815, W.P. 1/464 (printed with name deleted in *W.D.* VIII, pp. 61–2); Castlereagh to Wellington, 8 April 1815, *W.S.D.*, vol. 10, pp. 44–5; Liverpool to Canning, 13 June 1815, ibid., pp. 464–5; Wilberforce diary, 10 May 1815, *Life of Wilberforce*, vol. 4, p. 259.

20. Fitzroy Somerset to Castlereagh, 'Private', Paris, 17 and 18 March 1815, both F.O. 27/113 (re Col. Tripp); Stuart to Castlereagh, no. 45, 21 March 1815, F.O. 37/78; Bathurst to the Hereditary Prince of Orange, 21 March 1815, W.O. 6/16, pp. 146–7; Wellington to the Hereditary Prince of Orange, 22 March 1815, W.P. 1/453.

21. Colbourne to Bunbury, 'Private', Brussels, 21, 24 and 31 March 1815, B.L. Add. Ms 37,052, ff. 77–80, 91–4, 115–16; Hereditary Prince of Orange to Bathurst, 31 March 1815, *H.M.C. Bathurst*, pp. 343–4; same to same, 'Secret', 3 April 1815, W.O. 1/205, pp. 13–16 (his plans); same to same, 17 March 1815, *W.S.D.*, vol. 9, p. 600 (resupersession).

22. J. H. Rose, 'Sir Hudson Lowe and the beginnings of the Campaign of 1815', *English Historical Review*, vol. 16, July 1901, pp. 517–27, prints the relevant

correspondence; see also Wellington to Clancarty, 6 April 1815, W.P. 1/457.

23. [Bunbury] to Colbourne, 'Private', 16 March 1815, W.O. 6/16, pp. 141–4; [Castlereagh to Stuart], no. 11, 22 March 1815, F.O. 37/76; Wellington to Bathurst, 'Private', 6 April 1815, W.P. 1/457, printed with deletions in *W.D.* VIII, pp. 17–18.

24. Strength of the Anglo-Hanoverian forces based on General Returns in W.O. 17/1760, which are broadly confirmed by other returns such as that in *W.S.D.*, vol. 10, p. 716. For the army at the beginning of the campaign: Scott Bowden, *Armies at Waterloo* (Arlington, Empire Games, 1983), p. 319; see also Lt-Col. W. H. James, *The Campaign of 1815* (Edinburgh, Blackwood, 1908), pp. 323–4.

25. Peel to Gregory, 15 April 1815, Parker, *Peel*, vol. 1, pp. 175–6.

26. Peel to Gregory, 3 May 1815, Parker, *Peel*, vol. 1, p. 176.

27. On staff: Wellington to Torrens, 14 April 1815, WP 1/458 (printed with this passage deleted in *W.D.* VIII, p. 31); on siege-train: Wellington to Bathurst, 5 May, and to Hardinge, 20 May 1815, *W.D.* VIII, pp. 62, 97.

28. Wellington to Bathurst, 25 June 1815, W.P. 1/471 (printed with silent deletion which singles out the commanding officer of the artillery for special criticism, in *W.D.* VIII, pp. 168–9). Sir James Edmonds, 'Wellington's Staff at Waterloo', *Journal of the Society for Army Historical Research*, vol. 12, 1933, pp. 239–47, demonstrates that many of the staff had wide experience.

29. Duke of Cambridge to Wellington, 7 April 1815, *W.S.D.*, vol. 10, pp. 26–7.

30. Colbourne to Bunbury, 'Private', 21 March 1815, B.L. Add. Ms 37,052, ff. 77–80; Bathurst to Wellington, 2 May 1815 (2 letters), *W.S.D.*, vol. 10, pp. 215–16.

31. Stuart to Castlereagh, nos 75 and 87, 11 and 17 April 1815, F.O. 37/78; Wellington to Bathurst, 'Private', 28 April 1815, *W.S.D.*, vol. 10, pp. 167–8.

32. Wellington to Castlereagh, 26 March 1815, *W.D.* VIII, pp. 11–12; Bathurst

to Wellington, 7 April; Torrens to Bathurst, 8 April; Bathurst to Wellington, 14 April; Beresford to Wellington, 28 April and 12 May 1815; all *W.S.D.*, vol. 10, pp. 27–8, 41–3, 75–6, 170–71, 276. Sherwig, *Guineas and Gunpowder*, p. 337.

33. Castlereagh to Wellington, 'Private', 26 March 1815, *British Diplomacy*, pp. 317–18.

34. Wellington to Stewart, 8 May 1815, *W.D.* VIII, pp. 66–9; Wellington to Prince of Orange, 11 May 1815, ibid., p. 78 (on problems with reconnaissance); Hardinge to Somerset, 2 June 1815, *W.S.D.*, vol. 10, p. 413 (on Blücher).

35. Wilberforce diary, 13 May 1815, *Life of Wilberforce*, vol. 4, p. 259; Horner to Francis Jeffrey, 13 June 1815, *Memoirs and Correspondence of Francis Horner M.P.*, ed. Leonard Horner, 2 vols (London, John Murray, 1843), vol. 2, pp. 257–9.

36. Liverpool to Canning, 13 June 1815, *W.S.D.*, vol. 10, pp. 464–5.

37. James, *Campaign of 1815*, pp. 12–40, 106 (Ney), 111 (Soult's aides-decamp).

38. For Zieten's operations see Col. F. Maurice, 'Waterloo, Part VI, Zieten's Defence on the 15th', *United Service Magazine*, Jan. 1891, pp. 73–9; for the criticism, see James, *Campaign of 1815*, p. 93.

39. Richmond to Bathurst, 10 April 1815, *H.M.C. Bathurst*, pp. 344–5; Torrens to Wellington, 16 April 1815, *W.S.D.*, vol. 10, p. 83; *Waterloo Letters*, ed. Maj.-Gen. H. T. Siborne (Cambridge, Trotman, 1983; first published 1891), pp. 36, 89.

40. Sir Charles Oman, 'French Losses in the Waterloo Campaign', *English Historical Review*, vol. 19, Oct. 1904, pp. 681–93, and vol. 21, Jan. 1906, pp. 132–5, esp. the former, p. 688. J. C. Ropes, *The Campaign of Waterloo* (London, Putnam's, 1893), p. 159, and Bowden, *Armies at Waterloo*, p. 324, both put the Prussian loss at 18,000 or over, while James, *Campaign of 1815*, p. 136, puts it at 6,000.

41. Some British writers make this the basis for wild and unfounded accusations of disloyalty and worse, which

reflect more the poor state of Anglo-German relations in the years before and after the First World War, and in particular the controversy aroused by some very foolish remarks by the Kaiser, than the events of 1815. For examples see James, *Campaign of 1815*, pp. 203–6, and Fortescue, vol. 10, pp. 341–2.

42. Bowden, *Armies at Waterloo*, pp. 227, 271–2, corrects Siborne's misreading of the return in *W.D.* VIII, pp. 392–3, which has been generally copied by later writers and which underlies the traditional figure of 68,000 men.

43. Dorsey Gardner, *Quatre Bras, Ligny and Waterloo* (London, 1882), pp. 208–10, and Maurice, 'Waterloo, Part V, Historical Difficulties: The Three Staffs', *United Service Magazine*, vol. 1, new series, 1890, pp. 538–9, discuss virtually all the theories.

44. Wellington to Bathurst, 19 June 1815, *W.D.* VIII, pp. 146–50.

45. Wellington to Croker, 8 August 1815, *W.P.* 1/478 (printed in *W.D.* VIII, pp. 231–2, with Croker's name deleted).

46. The quintessential example of the genre is Rev. William Leeke, *The History of Lord Seaton's Regiment (the 52nd Light Infantry) at the Battle of Waterloo*, 2 vols (London, 1866), but see also George Gawler's *The Crisis and Close of the Action at Waterloo* (Dublin, 1833) and the resulting correspondence in the *United Service Magazine*, vols 5–8, 1833 to 1836.

47. Oman, 'French Losses', p. 690; Bowden, *Armies at Waterloo*, pp. 323–5; Return of killed, wounded and missing on 18 June 1815, *W.D.* VIII, p. 151. This last includes a column on horses: 10,000 is a rough extrapolation from this.

48. Wellington to Beaufort, 19 June, and to Aberdeen, 19 June 1815, both *W.D.* VIII, pp. 154–5.

49. Ponsonby's undated account of his experiences in *Lady Bessborough and Her Family Circle*, ed. the Earl of Bessborough (London, John Murray, 1940), pp. 240–3; a more colourful and detailed version is printed in Gardner, *Quatre Bras, Ligny and Waterloo*,

pp. 268–70, but no source is given. Ponsonby's account in *Waterloo Letters*, pp. 112–14, is much less personal.

50. Lady Bessborough's letters, 16 July to 11 Aug. 1815, in Bessborough, *Lady Bessborough and Her Family Circle*, pp. 247–53.

51. Rothschild, *Shadow of a Great Man*, pp. 24–39, discusses the question at length, showing how slight is the evidence.

52. R. Colby, *The Waterloo Despatch* (London, H.M.S.O., 1965), passim.

53. Julian Young's account, as quoted in Michael Glover, *A Very Slippery Fellow* (Oxford University Press, 1978), p. 150.

54. Bennet to Creevey, n.d., *Creevey Papers*, pp. 240–1.

55. Wellington to Bathurst, 2 July 1815, *W.D.* VIII, pp. 188–93.

56. Cole, *Fouché*, pp. 265–82, 289–93.

57. Wellington to Bathurst, 8 July 1815, *W.D.* VIII, p. 202; Bathurst quoted in Harriet, Countess Granville to Lady G. Morpeth, 13 July 1815, *Letters of Harriet, Countess Granville*, ed. F. Leveson Gower, 2 vols (London, Longmans, 1894), vol. 1, pp. 54–5; Mansel, *Louis XVIII*, p. 257, says that Louis XVIII was received rapturously, but Cole, *Fouché*, p. 292, says that Fouché ensured that there was only a small crowd to greet the King.

58. John G. Gallaher, 'Marshal Davout and the Second Bourbon Restoration', *French Historical Studies*, vol. 6, 1970, pp. 350–64.

59. Liverpool to Canning, 4 Aug. 1815, *W.S.D.*, vol. 11, pp. 94–6; Bathurst to Wellington, 7 July, and reply, 13 July 1815, *W.D.* VIII, p. 206 and n.

60. Wellington to Sir C. Stuart, 28 June 1815, *W.D.* VIII, pp. 175–6.

61. Quoted in J. H. Rose, *Life of Napoleon I*, 2 vols (London, G. Bell, 1904), vol. 2, p. 520.

62. Major Hamilton to Creevey, 28 July 1815, Creevey, *Life and Times*, p. 96 (the Garter); Harriet Countess Granville to Lady G. Morpeth, 21 July 1815, *Letters of Harriet Countess Granville*, vol. 1, p. 57 (Lady Holland).

63. Romilly, diary, 3 Aug. 1815, Romilly, *Memoirs and Correspondence*, vol. 3, pp. 191–2; Jean Duhamel, *The Fifty Days: Napoleon in England* (London, Hart-Davis, 1969), pp. 86–94.

64. Croker to Mrs Croker, 20 July 1815, *Croker Papers*, vol. 1, pp. 68–9.

65. Both quotes from Liverpool to Castlereagh, 21 July 1815, *W.S.D.*, vol. 11, p. 47.

66. Both quotes from Liverpool to Castlereagh, 10 July 1815, *W.S.D.*, vol. 11, pp. 24–5; see Webster, *Foreign Policy of Castlereagh*, p. 464 and n, for the Regent and the Austrian ambassador.

67. Liverpool to Castlereagh, 15 July 1815, *W.S.D.*, vol. 11, pp. 32–3.

68. Wellington to Beresford, 7 Aug. 1815, *W.D.* VIII, p. 231; Castlereagh to Liverpool, 'Private and Confidential', 17 Aug. 1815, *British Diplomacy*, pp. 362–7.

69. Liverpool to Castlereagh, 23 and 28 Aug. 1815, *British Diplomacy*, pp. 368–9, 372–3; the quote is from the latter.

70. Stewart to Castlereagh, 26 June 1815, *W.S.D.*, vol. 10, pp. 592–3; Castlereagh to Liverpool, 12 July 1815, *British Diplomacy*, pp. 341–2.

71. Castlereagh to Liverpool, 'Most Secret and Confidential', 24 July, and same to same, 24 Aug. 1815, both in *British Diplomacy*, pp. 350–1, 370–1.

72. Palmer, *Metternich*, pp. 150–3. Unfortunately we lack the expert guidance of Enno E. Kraehe, whose *Metternich's German Policy*, vol. 2, ends with the conclusion of the Congress of Vienna.

73. Wellington to Castlereagh, 14 July 1815, *W.D.* VIII, pp. 207–8; Craig, *Politics of the Prussian Army*, pp. 66–7.

74. Sweet, *Humboldt*, vol. 2, p. 212; Castlereagh to Liverpool, 24 Aug. 1815, *British Diplomacy*, pp. 370–1.

75. Webster, *Foreign Policy of Castlereagh*, p. 467.

76. Castlereagh to Liverpool, 4 Sept. 1815, *British Diplomacy*, pp. 375–6; Renier, *Great Britain and the Establishment of the Kingdom of the Netherlands*, pp. 309–14; Webster, *Foreign Policy of Castlereagh*, p. 468 (on Münster).

77. Castlereagh to Liverpool, 24 July 1815, *W.S.D.*, vol. 11, pp. 54–5; Webster, *Foreign Policy of Castlereagh*, p. 473.

78. Mulgrave to Bathurst, 6 Oct. 1815, *H.M.C. Bathurst*, p. 387.

79. Castlereagh to Liverpool, 'Private and Confidential', 17 Aug. 1815, *British Diplomacy*, pp. 362–7.

Conclusion

1. W. H. Fitchett, *How England Saved Europe*, 4 vols (London, Smith Elder, 1899–1900).

2. See Linda Colley, *Britons* (Yale University Press, 1992), ch. 7, for the role of mass participation in the Volunteers in the development of popular British patriotism.

3. Quoted in Smart, *Economic Annals*, vol. 1, p. 426.

4. Budget of 1815 from ibid., pp. 432–3, except the figure on servicing the debt which, like figures on total government expenditure, is from Mitchell and Deane, *Abstract of British Historical Statistics*, p. 396.

5. P. K. O'Brien, 'Public Finance in the Wars with France, 1793–1815', in H. T. Dickinson (ed.), *Britain and the French Revolution* (Basingstoke, Macmillan, 1989), p. 176; figures on national debt from Schumpeter, 'English Prices and Public Finance, 1660–1822', table 7, p. 37; see also S. Dowell, *Hstory of Taxation and Taxes in England*, 4 vols (London, Longmans, Green, 1888), vol. 2, p. 257.

6. C. H. Lee, *The British Economy Since 1700* (Cambridge, C.U.P., 1986), pp. 68–9. A. D. Harvey argues that overall the British economy benefited from the war, *Britain in the Early Nineteenth Century*, pp. 323–39, and *Collision of Empires: Britain in three world wars, 1793–1945* (Hambledon, 1992), ch. 2 passim.

7. O'Brien, 'Public Finance in the Wars with France, 1793–1815', pp. 177, 182.

8. Anon., *A Soldier of the Seventy-First*, ed. Christopher Hibbert (London, Leo Cooper, 1975).

9. Hodge, 'On the Mortality of Military Operations . . .', pp. 237, 241; Major Greenwood, 'British loss of life in the Wars of 1794–1815 and 1914–18 with discussion', *Journal of the Royal Statistical Society*, vol. 105, 1942, pp. 1–16, esp. 5–7, 12. A return printed in *W.S.D.*, vol. 7, p. 249, which shows that 14,737 British soldiers under Wellington's command died between 29 April 1809 and 15 Dec. 1811, though unknown to Hodge, generally supports his conclusions. If we estimate 5–6,000 deaths between Aug. 1808 and April 1809 (remembering the rigours of the Coruña campaign) we get a total of 50–51,000, to which must be added some allowance for the forces on the east coast and at Gibraltar. Note that the figure for deaths in the Peninsula is a gross total, while that for the whole war is net; they are therefore *not* directly comparable.

10. Charles Bell's account quoted in Antony Brett-James, *The Hundred Days* (London, Macmillan, 1964), pp. 202–3; other details from ibid., pp. 198–202, C. A. Eaton, *Waterloo Days* (London, George Bell & Sons, 1888), pp. 152–4, and R. L. Blanco, *Wellington's Surgeon General: Sir James McGrigor* (Durham N. C., Duke University Press, 1974), pp. 148–61. See also Lady De Lancey, *A Week at Waterloo* (London, John Murray, 1906).

11. David Chandler, *On the Napoleonic Wars: Collected Essays* (London, Greenhill, 1994), p. 172, quotes an estimate of 240,000 'casualties'; Michael Glover, *Legacy of Glory: The Bonaparte Kingdom of Spain* (New York, Scribners, 1971), p. x, states that 'the Spanish venture cost France, in dead, disabled and troops who could not be withdrawn, more than six hundred thousand men, almost all of them native Frenchmen'. Neither indicates his source, and Dumas and Vedel-Petersen state that 'No official statistics have been compiled showing the losses sustained by France in these

wars [of 1792–1815]. In fact, it would even seem that the documents on which to base them were destroyed': Samuel Dumas and K. O. Vedel-Petersen, *Losses of Life Caused by War* (Oxford, Clarendon Press for the Carnegie Endowment for International Peace, 1923), p. 27. Harvey, *Collision of Empires*, p. 145, quotes two contemporary estimates of losses, including prisoners, up until 1 June 1812 and 30 April 1813, of 488,924 and 473,000, respectively: obviously they are incompatible, though one or both may lie behind Glover's estimate. These figures would indicate a total of at least 600,000 for the whole war in the Peninsula, which seems too high, for it implies that on average between one-third and half of the French troops in the Peninsula died, were permanently incapacitated, or captured *each year*, and had to be replaced. Chandler's figure is more plausible (assuming that by 'casualties' he means deaths), but it would imply that despite deprivation and the activities of the guerrillas French troops did not die at a significantly greater rate than the British. As this seems unlikely I would be inclined to guess that the real figure is in the region of 300,000 or perhaps a little higher. This would mean that on average about one in five French soldiers serving in Spain and Portugal died each year. But it is only a guess.

12. Sherwig, *Guineas and Gunpowder*, pp. 345, 353–4.

Bibliographical Essay

There is a great abundance of sources on Britain's war against Napoleon. The Public Record Office has a wealth of official correspondence, including the reports of generals and ambassadors, which often contain extensive enclosures, as well as the letters and instructions which they were sent from the ministers in London. This is particularly useful for aspects of the war which are less well documented elsewhere, for example operations in the Mediterranean after 1810 and relations with the Continental Powers, particularly between 1810 and 1812. I cannot claim to have examined all the relevant material in the P.R.O., for it is almost inexhaustible, and in time one reaches and passes the point of diminishing returns.

The Public Records usually give a full account of what happened, and even what was expected to happen, but they seldom reveal much about the underlying hopes and fears of the cabinet. Unfortunately no cabinet minister in this period seems to have kept a diary — at least none is known to have survived — but the private correspondence of most of the ministers is extant and available to scholars. The most rewarding collection, especially for 1807–9, is the Canning Papers, which are largely unpublished and give a vivid picture of the views of the energetic Foreign Secretary and of his struggles in cabinet. Unlike many other ministers, Canning kept copies of his own letters as well those he received. The Castlereagh Papers also contain a great deal of interest, including copies of many out-going letters, official papers, and the lively correspondence between Edward Cooke and Charles Stewart. The collection is very extensive, but a good deal of it has been published in the twelve volumes of *Castlereagh Correspondence*. Of the rest, the Liverpool and Wellesley Papers at the British Library are large, important collections, while the Harrowby Papers at Sandon Hall yield many glimpses behind the façade of cabinet solidarity, especially for the period of the Perceval government.

The Wellington Papers at the University of Southampton form an immense collection of documents which have been extensively published in *Wellington's Dispatches* and *Supplementary Despatches*. However, the editors of those volumes made many deletions, sometimes simply replacing names with asterisks or dashes, but sometimes suppressing long passages with no indication that there have been cuts. To give a single example, the long memorandum by Meyrick Shawe explaining Lord Wellesley's grievances against his cabinet colleagues, printed in *W.S.D.*, vol. 7, pp. 257–88, appears so indiscreet, and provides such evidence to damn Wellesley's conduct, that one assumes that it is complete, but in fact many wilder or more personal passages are suppressed and can be found in the manuscript (in W.P. 1/445). The papers also contain a number of letters to and from Wellington which have not been published and much ancillary material; but as at the P.R.O., one can easily get the feeling that one is drowning in a sea of paper long before the further shore comes into sight.

Two other manuscript sources deserve mention. First, Wellington's letters to William Wellesley-Pole, which although partly published, contain some of his most violent denunciations of the government and — almost equally interesting — Pole's replies. (These letters are owned by Lord Raglan, and I was fortunate enough to see them when they were on temporary loan to the Royal Military Academy, Sandhurst. They are now at the county Record Office at Gwent.) And second, the correspondence of Colonel J. W. Gordon at the British Library, which is a particularly rich fund of gossip, rumour and opinion about politics and the war.

Of the published primary sources, *Wellington's Dispatches* and *Supplementary Despatches* and Castlereagh's *Correspondence* are — with all their faults — fundamental to any detailed understanding of Britain's part in the war. Almost equally important is *The Later Correspondence of George III*, which has been magnificently edited by Professor Aspinall, whose sometimes lengthy footnotes double the value of the work by quoting many previously unpublished letters to illuminate obscure points. His editions of the *Correspondence of George Prince of Wales* and *Letters of King George IV* (which begins in February 1812) are also useful, although less so, as far less important material has survived in the Royal Archives, reflecting the contrast between the old King's promptness and efficiency in doing business, and his son's self-indulgence and laziness.

James Moore's *Narrative . . .* and Sir John Moore's *Diary* are essential for the Coruña campaign, while the latter is also useful for his earlier services (including Sicily and Sweden) and provides ample evidence of Moore's character. *H. M. C. Bathurst* and the *Wellesley Papers* print many interesting papers: the originals are now in the British Library, but it is an immense advantage to have the full text constantly available rather than to have to rely on one's often hasty and sometimes scarcely legible notes. Webster's *British Diplomacy* is a convenient and helpful selection, though it naturally reflects his own interests and priorities. George Jackson's *Diaries and Letters* and the *Bath Archives* give a vivid picture of the frustrations of diplomacy in the field and preserve much interesting contemporary gossip. The Victorian lives of politicians vary widely in quality (none are particularly readable) and the reliability with which they print documents, but they can be quite useful. Parker's *Peel* and Yonge's *Liverpool* are well worth looking at, as, to a lesser extent, are Pellew's *Sidmouth* and Twiss's *Eldon*. So too is Walpole's *Perceval*, even though its transcriptions are noticeably unreliable.

There are plentiful sources for opinion beyond the inner circle of ministers. Lady Bessborough's letters (chiefly in the *Private Correspondence of Granville Leveson Gower*) are delightful, remaining as fresh and amusing today as when they were written. Sydney Smith's letters are almost equally good, living up to his reputation for wit and sound sense, though they have much less on the war. Wilberforce's moral stature and political independence make his letters and diaries (printed in the *Life* by his sons) most interesting, even though the editing is sometimes worse than inaccurate. Palmerston's letters to the Sulivans, J. W. Ward's *Letters to Ivy*, Plumer Ward's parliamentary diary (which covers much of the period of the Perceval government and is printed in the *Memoir* by Phipps), Charles Abbot's diary (he was Speaker of the Commons throughout this period) and Farington's diary are all helpful on occasion. With all these sources one is looking for the passing comment on the events of the day, the otherwise unreported but significant rumour, or the revealing thumbnail sketch of a politician, soldier or diplomat, while the writers are chiefly concerned with their own everyday affairs and will often fail to mention great events, either because they are otherwise occupied, or because their correspondents are at hand and their discussions can be face to face and not through the post.

For the Opposition view of events and much political gossip, *H.M.C. Dropmore* is invaluable, printing Lord Grenville's correspondence (mostly letters to him, particularly from those doughty pessimists, Lord Auckland and Tom Grenville). Buckingham's *Memoirs of the Court and Cabinets of George III* and *Memoirs of the . . . Regency* complete the Grenville family view, while the *Memoirs of the . . . Regency* includes some most interesting, if unreliable, reports from a member of Lord Wellesley's entourage. Creevey — gossip and backbiter par excellence — gives the views of the more radical Whigs, while the correspondence of Horner and Romilly, Lord Holland's *Further Memoirs*, Lady Holland's *Journal* and Brougham's autobiography are all sometimes useful, though the last must be used with great care, for Brougham doctored many of the documents he printed — on which see Professor Aspinall's article.

By far the most important secondary sources for this study were Sir Charles Oman's magnificent *A History of the Peninsular War* and Sir John Fortescue's comprehensive *A History of the British Army*. Each has its particular virtues. Oman is a pleasure to read and gives a full account of the war, not neglecting the Spanish campaigns. He shows a complete mastery of the subject — particularly after volume one — and he is fair in his opinions, though his desire to correct Napier's bias makes him stress the faults of Napoleon, Soult and — to a lesser extent — Moore. Fortescue has the great advantage of covering campaigns outside the Peninsula, though naturally he covers only British campaigns. He combines scrupulous accuracy in military details with strong prejudices on broader matters which unduly influence his judgement — and like Wellington he was blessed, or cursed, with a sharp pen. His opinions of politicians should be treated with great care: Pitt, Dundas and Canning were among his villains, Canning was not even a gentleman, while Castlereagh was a paragon, except when he quarrelled with Sir John Moore, for whom Fortescue, like Napier but less accountably, felt the greatest veneration. His accounts of the campaigns of 1814 and 1815, written after the First World War, also display a violent anti-German bias. But these defects are slight compared with the wide reading and deep research which enabled both Oman and Fortescue to describe meticulously the course of military operations in the last years of the war against Napoleon. Their work builds upon and largely supersedes Napier, whose famous *History* laid the foundation for all subsequent accounts of the war in the Peninsula.

In the last twenty or thirty years a number of important monographs have appeared: D. W. Davies gives an excellent account of Sir John Moore's campaign and asks some provocative questions; Charles Esdaile sheds much new light on the Spanish side of the war and expertly untangles the knotty question of Wellington's command of the Spanish armies and Anglo-Spanish relations in general; T. M. O. Redgrave's thesis on Wellington's logistics is most useful, as are the three overlapping theses on Anglo-Portuguese relations by De la Fuente, Vichness and Fryman. Donald Horward's valuable account of the Bussaco campaign is based on a great deal of original research; while Richard Schneer's article and Michael Glover's *Britannia Sickens* are both interesting on Cintra (the former is more original, though I think many of its conclusions are misguided). But one great yawning gap remains — there is no scholarly account of the war as a whole from the French perspective, which might explain Napoleon's policies and show the constraints of manpower and finance which he faced.

Christopher Hall's *British Strategy in the Napoleonic War* has an excellent discussion of the mechanics of warfare and a good account of operations between 1803 and 1807 (including Copenhagen); but the treatment of the Peninsular War is perfunctory, and by 1813 the pace of the narrative has accelerated to a headlong gallop. *The Grand Expedition* by Gordon Bond is a good account of the Walcheren Expedition, although the chapters on the broad strategic context and British politics are less convincing. Questions of manpower are discussed with great authority by Fortescue in his *County Lieutenancies and the Army*, while Hodge's immensely thorough and learned article on statistics provides much food for thought.

On the wider war, one immediately notices the absence of any broad-ranging study of the naval war after Trafalgar: Piers Mackesy on the Mediterranean and A. N. Ryan on the Baltic are both good (the former indeed gives a superb account of his subject), but naturally limited to their fields. Two brief articles by Paul Webb hint at the approach which might be taken and discuss some of the problems it would face. There is a similar gap for Britain's financial policies: P. K. O'Brien's article in *Britain and the French Revolution* whets the appetite, but his promised full treatment of the subject is yet to appear.

British diplomacy is not well covered until 1812, when there is the sure hand of Professor Webster to guide us. His *Foreign Policy of Castlereagh 1812–15* ranks immediately after Oman and Fortescue in importance for this study. It has long been acknowledged as the definitive work on the subject and occasionally, I think, its conclusions have been accepted a little too uncritically. Webster's own commitment to Britain's close involvement in the affairs of Europe sometimes coloured his judgement, while at times his biographical zeal and desire to rehabilitate his subject led him to be a little overgenerous in his praise. His coverage of issues peripheral to his theme — which was the reconstruction of Europe, not winning the war — can also be rather thin, for example Britain's relations with Sicily and Spain. But these are quibbles; his work has stood the test of time and successive generations of scholars and remains definitive; without it, this book would have been infinitely poorer — indeed it could not have been written in its present form.

After Webster, pride of place in this field must go to J. M. Sherwig, whose *Guineas and Gunpowder: British Foreign Aid in the Wars with France, 1793–1815* covers an immense, intricate and unappealing subject with exemplary skill. Three more specialized works, each excellent in its field, come next: Rosselli's *Lord William Bentinck and the British Occupation of Sicily*, Renier's *Great Britain and the Establishment of the Kingdom of the Netherlands* and Buckland's *Metternich and the British Government*. Rosselli explores a previously neglected facet of the war and explains Bentinck's behaviour without attempting to whitewash his faults or exaggerate his follies. The monograph can be supplemented by Rosselli's biography, which gives a fuller account of Bentinck's Italian plans, and by Gregory's *Sicily: The Insecure Base*, which is thorough but pedestrian. Renier is almost equally useful, though far from exciting. Buckland has written an extraordinary book, very long and scholarly, yet with no index and so deeply enmeshed in the details of the subject that individual letters are often discussed and paraphrased for pages, while the wider picture is only rarely glimpsed; but for all that, it is a revelation of the subterranean diplomacy which went on at a time when Napoleon appeared to dominate Central Europe.

Accounts of the policies of the Continental Powers vary widely in quality. Enno Kraehe's *Metternich's German Policy* is much broader than its title implies and, particularly from the end of 1812 onwards, it provides by far the best account of Metternich's policy in English. Occasionally I felt that Kraehe's interpretation was a little over-intricate, but that fault — if it is a fault — appears peculiarly appropriate in a Metternich scholar. Dorothy McGuigan's *Metternich and the Duchess* concentrates on Metternich's love affair with the Duchess of Sagan, but unlike many such books it is serious and scholarly, quotes extensively from contemporary documents, and provides a wealth of detail on the events of 1813–15. Paul Sweet's *Wilhelm von Humboldt* gives much interesting information on Prussian policy, though the lack of a formal history, or even an English life of Hardenberg, is regrettable. By contrast there are three good English lives of Bernadotte: Alan Palmer's is the most recent, and as with all his books combines wide reading with a pleasant style; Barton's is the most detailed — though he is fiercely partisan in favour of his subject — but the best for Bernadotte's role in the defeat of Napoleon is Franklin Scott's scholarly monograph. Unfortunately there is little on Russian policy: Lobanov-Rostovsky is disappointing; Grimsted has many useful insights, but her subject is the Foreign Ministers, not the policy they pursued (though she does confirm the Czar's overwhelming domination of policymaking); Palmer's *Alexander I* is excellent, the best of all his biographies, entertaining and well-informed, with a sure grasp of both the details and the broad context of policy — but still, it is such an important topic that one wishes there were a specialized monograph which could thoroughly explore the issues.

Finally, on international relations, I must mention Paul Schroeder's *The Transformation of European Politics, 1763–1848*, which only appeared after the main text of *Britain and the Defeat of Napoleon* was substantially finished. Anyone reading both works will notice numerous differences of opinion and interpretation of the same events, but although I was not convinced by all Schroeder's arguments, his book is one of the most stimulating, intelligent and thought-provoking studies to have appeared on the subject in many years. It fills an enormous void by providing an excellent account of the whole period set in an even wider chronological frame, and it is animated by an original thesis. The breadth of reading and scholarship it contains is enormous.

The best general history of Britain in the period is A. D. Harvey's *Britain in the Early Nineteenth Century*, which has a lively and detailed account of politics up until Perceval's death. Clive Emsley's *British Society and the French Wars, 1793–1815* is an excellent introduction to the subject, while there are some stimulating essays by leading specialists in their field in *Britain and the French Revolution*, edited by H. T. Dickinson, which, despite its title, covers the whole period 1793–1815. The five volumes of the *History of Parliament* which cover 1790–1820 (edited by R. G. Thorne) are meticulous and thorough, equally useful for an obscure and egregious backbencher who made a single ill-judged contribution to a debate on the war, and for masterly essays on major political figures such as Castlereagh and Perceval. The emphasis is always on their performance in the Commons, rather than their contribution to policy or their life outside Parliament, but that is the purpose of the work and often is an advantage, revealing a familiar figure (e.g. Sir A. Wellesley or Charles Stewart) from a fresh perspective. One's only serious complaint is the absence of a companion volume on the Lords. An even more impressive achievement — for it was largely the work of one scholar — is Dorothy George's magnificent *Catalogue of Personal and Political Satires* and her two-volume introduction to the field, *English Political Caricature*. These works add another dimension to the subject while displaying an extraordinary knowledge of the day-to-day politics of the period. The publication on microfilm by Chadwyck-Healey of all the caricatures described in the catalogue (over 17,000) adds immensely to its value.

Most political history, however, seems to be written in the form of biographies, and some of these are very good indeed. Denis Gray's *Spencer Perceval* is scholarly and thorough, based on a great deal of original research. Wendy Hinde's *George Canning* is an excellent example of how to make scholarship entertaining and enjoyable without sacrificing detail or analysis. Her *Castlereagh* does not quite reach the same standard, but it is still the best of the many biographies available. After long neglect there is now an attractive sketch of Lord Liverpool by Norman Gash, and a most stimulating article on his 'Political Arts' by Boyd Hilton. It is fascinating to compare their differing interpretations of this most underrated of Prime Ministers. George Knight's unpublished thesis on Liverpool and the Peninsular War is rather disappointing. On the other side of politics there are excellent biographies of Lord Grenville (by Peter Jupp) and Lord Grey (by E. A. Smith), while Michael Roberts's *The Whig Party, 1807–1812* is still very useful. It seems extraordinary that there is no biography, either modern or Victorian, of Lord Bathurst, but although he was a genial man and an efficient minister who was at the centre of government for twenty years, it is possible that he did not impress his character on events in a way which suits a biographer — certainly he was less flamboyant than Canning or Wellesley. Unfortunately Iris Butler's *The Eldest Brother* is an example of 'popular' biography, and is more concerned with Lord Wellesley's marital and extramarital affairs than with his role in cabinet. John Severn's 'Richard Marquess Wellesley and the Conduct of Anglo–Spanish Diplomacy' is more serious but lacks a grasp of wider events and is far too inclined to accept Wellesley's own interpretation, though I must add that I have not seen the published version of this thesis. Even more unfortunate is the lack of a good, full life of Wellington. Elizabeth Longford's *Wellington* is certainly long enough, and her style, with its emphasis on anecdotes and colour, has proved very popular, but some readers will wish for more analysis and a more critical approach — that this need not become arid or boring is shown by the success of Alan Palmer and Wendy Hinde. But perhaps Wellington, like Napoleon, is not really a suitable subject for a biography, for much of his *Life* must inevitably become a history of his times. Yet it would be churlish to end on a note of complaint when so many of the contemporary letters and so much of the subsequent scholarship combine literary excellence, historical acumen, and wit. It is a wonderful period to study.

Bibliography

I UNPUBLISHED SOURCES

a) At the Public Record Office, Kew

Admiralty Papers
Adm. 1/339: In letters from Lisbon, 1807–8, /340: In letters from Lisbon, 1808, /4354: Secret letters; Adm. 2/1365: Secret Orders and Instructions

Colonial Office Papers
C.O. 91/47: Gibraltar, 1807, 173/2: Letters from Admiral Collingwood

Foreign Office Papers
F.O. 7 Austria 7/89: Austria, 1809 [1808], /99: Mr King, 1810–13, /100: General Nugent, March 1811–Nov. 1813, /101: Drafts to Aberdeen, Aug.–Dec. 1813, /102: Letters from Aberdeen, Sept.–Nov. 1813, /103: Letters from Aberdeen, Nov.–Dec. 1813; F.O. 27 France 27/113: France, 1815: Fitzroy Somerset; F.O. 34 Hanover 34/3: 1811, /4: 1812; F.O. 37 Holland 37/76: To Clancarty, Charles Stuart, Jan.–July 1815, /77: From Sir C. Stuart, Feb.–March 1815, /78: From Sir C. Stuart, March-May 1815; F.O. 63 Portugal 63/74: To Villiers, Nov. 1808–Jan. 1810, /75: From Villiers, Dec. 1808–March 1809, /76: From Villiers, April 1809–Aug. 1809, /77: From Villiers, Sept. 1809–Nov. 1809, /78: From Villiers, Dec. 1809–Feb. 1810, /80: De Sousa, 1809, /88: To Stuart, 1810, /93: From Stuart, Sept.–Oct. 1810, /94: From Stuart, Oct.–Nov. 1810, /105: To Stuart, 1811; F.O. 64 Prussia 64/83: G. Mills, 1811, /84: Domestic Various, Jan. 1811–Jan. 1812, /85: G. Mills, 1812, /86: Drafts to Sir C. Stewart, April–Dec. 1813, /92, 1812–13: Mills, Jackson, Hope, etc.; F.O. 65 Russia 65/76: Foreign and domestic, 1811, /77: Secret, 1811, /78: To Cathcart, July–Dec. 1812, /79: From Cathcart, July–Nov. 1812, /80: From Cathcart, Nov.–Dec. 1812, /81: Domestic various, Jan.–Aug. 1812, /83: Drafts to Cathcart, 1813, /84: From Cathcart, Jan.–March 1813, /85: From Cathcart, April–June 1813, /86: From Cathcart, July–Sept. 1813, /87: From Cathcart, Sept.–Dec. 1813, /88: 1812–13: Lord Walpole, Sir R. Wilson, etc., /89: 1812–13: domestic various; F.O. 67 Sardinia 67/41 (or 42: the two volumes had been transposed): Sardinia: Mr Hill, 1811; F.O. 70 Sicily 70/39: Lord

Amherst, 1810, /42: Lord Amherst, Feb.–March 1811, /44: Lord William Bentinck, 1811, /50: Foreign Secretary to Bentinck, 1812, /56: To Bentinck and Montgomerie, 1813, /63: Lord William Bentinck, Jan.–April 1814; **F.O. 72 Spain** 72/60: To Frere, 1808, /62: Mr Hunter, 1808, /64: Duff, Dalrymple, etc., April–Dec. 1808, /65: 'Foreign Various', 1808, /66: Spanish representatives, 1808, /71:To Frere, 1809, /81: Secret, Col. James Burke, /93: To Henry Wellesley, 1809–10, /108: To Henry Wellesley, 1811, /111: From Henry Wellesley, May–June 1811, /114: From Henry Wellesley, Oct.–Nov. 1811, /127: To Sir Henry Wellesley, Jan.–June 1812, /128: To Sir Henry Wellesley, July–Dec. 1812, /132: From Sir Henry Wellesley, Sept.–Dec.1812, /142: To Sir Henry Wellesley, 1813; **F.O. 73 Sweden** 73/70: Mr Thornton, Oct. 1811–March 1812, /71: To Thornton, March–Dec. 1812, /72: From Thornton, April–May 1812, /73: From Thornton, May–July 1812, /74: From Thornton, Aug.–Dec. 1812, /76: Domestic various, 1811–12; **F.O. 78 Turkey** 78/79: Mr Liston, March–Dec. 1812; **F.O. 92 Continent** 92/1: Jan.–March 1814 drafts, /2: Castlereagh to Liverpool, Jan.–Feb. 1814, /3: Castlereagh to Liverpool, Feb.–Mar. 1814, /4: Castlereagh to Liverpool, Mar.–May 1814, /13: To Wellington, 1815, /14: From Wellington, Feb.–May 1815; **F.O. 95** 95/378: Confidential letter book, 1810–12, /656: Royal Letters, 1810–13; **F.O. 97** 97/343: Viscount Castlereagh (Supplementary), 1813

War Office Papers

W.O. 1 In Letters 1/199: British Army in Holland, 1813–14, /205: Belgium, Jan.–June 1815, /226: Spencer, 1808, /230: Lord William Bentinck, 1808, /232: Sir J. Cradock, 1808–9, /234: Sir Hew Dalrymple, 1808, /237: Miscellaneous, 1808–9, /239: Beresford, 1809, /240: Sir J. Cradock, 1809, /244: Wellington, 1810, /276: Morning States, 1813, /310: In Letters, Sicily, 1811, /311: Bentinck to Liverpool, Jan.–June 1812, /312: Bentinck to Sec. of State, July–Dec. 1812, /638: From Commander-in-Chief, /752: From Foreign Office; **W.O. 3** 3/595: Private Correspondence of the Commander-in-Chief, 1809, /603: Out Letters of Commander-in-Chief (Private), Aug.–Dec. 1812; **W.O. 6 Out Letters from the Secretary of State of War and the Colonies** 6/16: Holland, Flanders, France, 1813–18, /29: To Wellington, 1810–11, /34: Drafts to Wellington, 1809–10, /36: Sec. for War to Wellington, 1812, /44: Cadiz, 1810–14, /45: Out Letters to Cadiz, 1810, /46, 1808: Spain and Portugal, Drafts, /49: 1808–9 Spain and Portugal, Drafts, /50: Out Letters: Spain and Portugal, 1810–12, /51: Out Letters: Spain and Portugal, 1812–13, /61: Out Letters: Sicily, 1811–12, /134: Sec. of State to C.-in-C., /164: To Foreign Office, 1807–10, /166: To Foreign Office, 1810–14, /167: To Foreign Office, 1814–15, /185: Secret letters, 1807–15, /205: To Wellington, June–Sept. 1810; **W.O. 17 Returns** 17/1486: Cadiz, 1810–11, /1516–7: Canada, 1812–13, /1760: France, 1815, /1773: North of Germany and Flanders, 1813–14, /1797: Gibraltar, 1810–11, /1934–7: Sicily, Mediterranean and E. Spain, /2464–5: Spain and Portugal, 1808–9, 1810, /2467–76: Spain and Portugal, 1811–14; **W.O. 25/3224–5** Establishment of the British Army and Means of Recruiting, 1809–11, 1813–15; **W.O. 30/51 and 52** Intelligence from Spain and Portugal; **W.O. 133/13** Private Letter book of Maj.-Gen. Robert Brownrigg, Quartermaster-General

Private Papers
P.R.O. 30/8 Chatham Papers: vols 260, 365–9; **P.R.O. 30/29 Granville Leveson Gower Papers**: 8/4, 8/5, 9/1, 9/3; **P.R.O. 30/58 Dacre Adams Papers**: Bundle 10

b) British Library, London
Aberdeen Papers: Add. Ms 43,223–5; **Bathurst Papers**: Loan Ms 57, vols. 3–7, 20, 21, 57, 60 and 95; **Bunbury Papers**: Add. Ms 37,050–2; **Canning Papers**: Add. Ms 38,833, 46,841; **Col. J. W. Gordon Papers**: Add. Ms 49,472–3, 49,476–7, 49,480–2, 49,484–5, 49,488, 49,494, 49,502, 49,510, 49,512A; **Herries Papers**: Add. Ms 57,367–8, 57,370, 57,372; **Huskisson Papers**: Add. Ms 38,737–40, 38,759–60, 39,948; **Liverpool Papers**: Add. Ms 38,190–1, 38,193–6, 38,242–51, 38,255, 38,320, 38,323, 38,325–8, 38,360–4, 38,366, 38,378–9, 38,382, 38,473–4, 38,564, 38,566, 38,571–3, 38,580, 59,772, Loan Ms 72, vols 6, 9, 12, 16, 17, 18, 20, 21, 22, 24, 27, 28, 31, 33, 34, 35 and 56; **Miscellany**: Add. Ms 45,498; **Perceval Papers**: Add. Mss 49,177, 49,185, 49,188; **Robinson Papers**: Add. Ms 40,862; **Rose Papers**: Add. Ms 31,237, 42,773, 42,774B; **Vansittart Papers**: Add. Ms 31,230–1, 31,250; **Wellesley Papers**: Add. Ms 13,804, 13,806, 37,286–9, 37,292–7, 37,309–10, 37,314–15, 37,415–16; **Wellington Papers**: Add. Ms 64,131; **Yorke Papers**: Add. Ms 35,894, 45,036, 45,038, 45,042, 45,044–5

c) Public Record Office of Northern Ireland, Belfast
Castlereagh Papers: D3030/2477–3985 (some of these letters were being treated for conservation, and hence were unavailable), D3030/H1–44: Correspondence with his father (Typescripts), D3030/P1–40; 205–39: Letters of Charles Stewart, 1808–11, D3030/AA1–25: Letters of Edward Cooke to Charles Stewart, 1808–14, D3030/GG/5: Bound volume of letters of Charles Stewart, D3030/Q2/2: Volume of typescript letters, mostly Castlereagh to Charles Stewart, D3030/Q3/3: Another volume of typescript letters

d) Durham County Record Office, Durham
Papers of Charles Stewart: D/LO/C 17 (2–3) (I am grateful to the Durham Record Office for supplying me with photocopies of these two important letters from Charles Stewart to Castlereagh which I had seen calendared at the Public Record Office of Northern Ireland.)

e) West Yorkshire Archive Service, Leeds District Archives, Leeds
Canning Papers: Bundles 22: Letters to Mrs Canning, 1807–8, 23: Letters to Mrs Canning, 1809, 31: Miscellaneous official, 1808–9, 32: Canning to Perceval, Hawkesbury, Castlereagh and Portland, 1807–8, 33A: Canning-Portland Correspondence,1807–9, 33B: Canning-Perceval Correspondence, 34: Miscellaneous Correspondence, 34A: Miscellaneous Correspondence, 39: Miscellaneous, 1807, 40: Miscellaneous Letters of Canning, 1808, 41A: Cabinet Minutes etc., 45: Correspondence re Spain, 1808–9, 46: Spain and Spanish America, 1807–9, 46A: Correspondence with Spain, 47: Correspondence with Chevalier de Sousa,

432   Bibliography

48: Correspondence re Portugal and Brazil, 63: Miscellaneous Correspondence, 67: Correspondence with Huskisson, 69: Correspondence with Liverpool

f) House of Lords Record Office, Westminster
Microfilm Copy of the **Papers of Spencer Perceval**, held by D.C.L. Holland Esq., Microfilm Reels 7–10, Bundles I, II, VII, XIV, XXI, XXII, C

g) Southampton University Library, Southampton
Wellington Papers: W.P. 1: Correspondence of Sir Arthur Wellesley, Duke of Wellington, Bundles 201–2, 204–7, 210, 212–13, 222–9, 231, 233, 235, 237, 238, 240, 242, 244, 246, 248, 250, 252, 254, 257, 259–61, 273, 276, 278, 280, 281, 291–5, 297–302, 311, 313, 316, 332, 334–46, 348–50, 352–4, 356, 358–64, 366–9, 371–2, 374, 376, 378–80, 382, 387–94, 397–400, 403, 439, 443, 445, 447, 452–5, 457–8, 464–5, 470–71, 476, 478, W.P. 12: Papers of Henry Wellesley, W.P. 12/1/1, /2/1, /2/2; Carver Papers (Papers of Richard, Marquess Wellesley, and his son Richard Wellesley) Carver 7–9, 34, 44–7, 50–4, 61, 74, 91, 99, 100, 102–3, 115–16; **Palmerston Papers**: BR 22(i) and 24/1, GC [General Correspondence] / GO [Goulburn], / MA [Malmesbury], / MU [Mulgrave], / SH [Sir George Shee], / SU [Sulivan], / TE [William Temple], / WA [Plumer Ward]

h) County, Record Office, Gwent (papers seen when on loan at the library of the Royal Military College, Camberley)
Raglan Papers: Wellington A: 89 Letters of Wellington to his brother William Wellesley-Pole, 1807–17, Wellington B: 40 Copies of letters from William Wellesley-Pole to Wellington, 1808–16

i) Sandon Hall, Stafford
Harrowby Papers: Volumes V, IX, XI, XIII, XIV, XVII, XVIII, LVII and LVIII

j) Kent Archives Office, Maidstone
Camden Papers: U 840 Papers of John Jeffreys Pratt, 1st Marquess of Camden, Bundles C86, 87, 88, 90, 98, 203, 226, 229, 256 and 258

k) University of Nottingham Library, Nottingham
Portland Papers: Papers of the 3rd Duke of Portland, Pw. F. 3061, 3503, 4119, 5854, 7635, 5855, 8580, 8582a,b+c, 8583, 8584, 8585, 8586, Papers of Lord William Bentinck: Pw Jc

l) National Library of Ireland
Richmond Papers: Mss 58, 59, 60 and 61 (each number represents a bound volume of manuscripts)

m) Devon Record Office, Exeter
Sidmouth Papers: 152M C 1811/ OM, OR, OZ, C 1812/ OM, OZ, C 1813/ OF, OZ, C 1814/OZ

II   PUBLISHED PRIMARY SOURCES
(arranged alphabetically by subject, not editor)

Abbot, Charles: *The Diary and Correspondence of Charles Abbot, Lord Colchester*, edited by Charles, Lord Colchester, 3 vols (London, John Murray, 1861).

Aitchison, John: *An Ensign in the Peninsular War: The Letters of John Aitchison*, edited by W.F.K. Thompson (London, Michael Joseph, 1981).

Arbuthnot, Charles: *The Correspondence of Charles Arbuthnot*, edited by A. Aspinall, Camden Third Series, vol. LXV (London, 1941).

Auckland, Lord: *The Journal and Correspondence of William, Lord Auckland*, 4 vols (London, Richard Bentley, 1862).

Bathurst, Earl: *Historical Manuscripts Commission: Report on the Manuscripts of Earl Bathurst, Preserved at Cirencester Park* (London, H.M.S.O., 1923; H.M.C. Series 76).

Bessborough, Lady, *Lady Bessborough and Her Family Circle*, edited by the Earl of Bessborough (London, John Murray, 1940).

Brougham, Lord: *The Life and Times of Henry Lord Brougham*, written by Himself, 3 vols (Edinburgh and London, Blackwoods, 1871).

Browne, Thomas: *The Napoleonic War Journal of Captain Thomas Henry Browne, 1807–1816*, edited by Roger Norman Buckley (London, Bodley Head for the Army Records Society, 1987).

Buckingham and Chandos, Duke of: *Memoirs of the Court and Cabinets of George III*, 4 vols (London, Hurst and Blackett, 1853–5).

——: *Memoirs of the Court of England during the Regency, 1811–1820*, 2 vols (London, Hurst and Blackett, 1856).

Burghersh, Lady: *Letters of Lady Burghersh . . . From Germany and France during the Campaign of 1813–14*, edited by Lady Rose Weigall (London, John Murray, 1893).

Burghersh, Lord: *Correspondence of Lord Burghersh, afterwards Eleventh Earl of Westmorland, 1808–1840*, edited by his grand-daughter Rachel Weigall (London, John Murray, 1912).

Canning, George: *George Canning and His Friends*, edited by Captain Josceline Bagot, 2 vols (London, John Murray, 1909).

——: *Select Speeches of the Right Honourable George Canning . . .* , edited by Robert Walsh (Philadelphia, Key and Biddle, 1835).

Castlereagh, Lord: *Correspondence, Despatches, and other Papers of Viscount Castlereagh, Second Marquess of Londonderry*, edited by his brother, Charles William Vane, Marquess of Londonderry, 12 vols (London, William Shoberl, 1848–53). (N.B. The first four volumes were published as *Memoirs and Correspondence of Viscount Castlereagh . . .*)

Cathcart, Lord: 'Gleanings from the Cathcart Mss, Part VI — The "Conjoint" Expedition to Copenhagen, 1807', edited by C. T. Atkinson, *Journal of the Society for Army Historical Research*, vol. 30, no. 122, Spring 1952, pp. 80–7.

Caulaincourt, A. A. L. de: *No Peace with Napoleon!* (New York, William Morrow, 1936).

Cocks, Edward: *Intelligence Officer in the Peninsula: Letters and Diaries of Major The Hon. Edward Charles Cocks, 1786–1812*, edited by Julia Page (New York, Hippocrene/Tunbridge Wells, Spellmount, 1986).

Cole, Sir Lowry: *Memoirs of Sir Lowry Cole*, edited by M. L. Cole and S. Gwynn (London, Macmillan, 1934).

Collingwood, Lord: *A Selection from the Public and Private Correspondence of Vice-Admiral Lord Collingwood . . .*, edited by G.L. Newnham Collingwood (London, James Ridgeway, 1829).

Creevey, Thomas: *The Creevey Papers*, edited by Sir Herbert Maxwell (London, John Murray, 1923).

——: *Creevey's Life and Times: A Further Selection from the Correspondence of Thomas Creevey*, edited by John Gore (London, John Murray, 1934).

Croker, John Wilson: *The Correspondence and Diaries of the late Right Honourable John Wilson Croker . . .*, edited by Louis J. Jennings, 3 vols (London, John Murray, 1884).

Czartoryski, Prince Adam: *Memoirs of Prince Adam Czartoryski and his Correspondence with Alexander I . . .*, edited by Adam Gielgud, 2 vols (London, Remington, 1888).

Dalrymple, Sir Hew: *Memoir written by General Sir Hew Dalrymple, Bart. of His Proceedings as Connected with the Affairs of Spain, at the Commencement of the Peninsular War* (London, Thomas and William Boone, 1830).

DeLancey, Lady: *A Week at Waterloo in 1815*, edited by Major B. R. Ward (London, John Murray, 1906).

Dropmore: *Historical Manuscripts Commission: Report on the Manuscripts of J. B. Fortescue, Esq. Preserved at Dropmore*, 10 vols (London, H.M.S.O., 1892–1927).

Eaton, Charlotte A: *Waterloo Days: The Narrative of an Englishwoman resident at Brussels in June 1815* (London, G. Bell, 1888).

Eldon, Lord: *Lord Eldon's Anecdote Book*, edited by A. L. J. Lincoln and R. L. McEwen (London, Stevens & Sons, 1960).

Farington, Joseph: *The Farington Diary*, edited by James Grieg, 8 vols (London, Hutchinson, 1922–8).

Gawler, George: *The Crisis and Close of the Action at Waterloo* (Dublin, 1833).

George III: *The Later Correspondence of George III*, edited by A. Aspinall, 5 vols (Cambridge University Press, 1962–70).

George IV: *The Correspondence of George, Prince of Wales, 1770–1812*, edited by A. Aspinall, 8 vols (London, Cassell, 1963–71).

——: *The Letters of King George IV*, edited by A. Aspinall, 3 vols (Cambridge University Press, 1938).

Glenbervie, Lord: *The Diaries of Sylvester Douglas, Lord Glenbervie*, edited by Francis Bickley, 2 vols (London, Constable, 1928).

——: *The Glenbervie Journals*, edited and arranged by Walter Sichel (London, Constable, 1910).

Gower, Lord Granville Leveson: *Lord Granville Leveson Gower (First Earl Granville), Private Correspondence, 1781–1821*, edited by his daughter-in-law Castalia Countess Granville, 2 vols (London, John Murray, 1916).

Granville, Harriet Countess: *The Letters of Harriet, Countess Granville, 1810–1845,*

2 vols, edited by her son Hon. F. Leveson Gower (London, Longmans, Green, 1894).

Hastings: *Historical Manuscripts Commission: Report on the Manuscripts of the Late Reginald Rawdon Hastings, Esq., of the Manor House, Ashby de la Zouch*, edited by Francis Bickley, 4 vols (London, H.M.S.O., 1934–47).

Heathcote, Ralph: *Ralph Heathcote: Letters of a Young Diplomatist and Soldier during the Time of Napoleon . . .*, edited by Countess Gröben (London, John Lane, The Bodley Head, 1907).

Hertslet, Edward (comp.): *A Map of Europe by Treaty . . . since 1814*, 4 vols (London, 1875–91).

Holland, Lady: *The Journal of Elizabeth Lady Holland (1791–1811)*, edited by the Earl of Ilchester, 2 vols (London, Longmans, 1908).

Holland, Lord: *Further Memoirs of the Whig Party, 1807–1821, with some Miscellaneous Reminiscences*, edited by Lord Stavordale (London, John Murray, 1905).

Horner, Francis: *Memoirs and Correspondence of Francis Horner, M.P.*, edited by Leonard Horner, 2 vols (London, John Murray, 1843).

Huskisson, William: *The Huskisson Papers*, edited by Lewis Melville (London, Constable, 1931).

Jackson, Sir George: *The Diaries and Letters of Sir George Jackson . . .*, edited by Lady Jackson, 2 vols (London, Richard Bentley, 1872).

———: *The Bath Archives: A further selection from the Diaries and Letters of Sir George Jackson, K.C.H. from 1809 to 1816*, edited by Lady Jackson, 2 vols (London, Richard Bentley, 1873).

Jones, Lt Rice: *An Engineer Officer under Wellington in the Peninsula*, by Lt Rice Jones, edited by Capt. the Hon. H.V. Shore (Cambridge, Ken Trotman, 1986).

Keith, Lord: *The Keith Papers*, vol. 3, edited by C. Llyod, Navy Records Society, vol. 96 (1955).

Kennedy, Sir J.: *Notes on the Battle of Waterloo* (London, 1865).

Khan, Mirza Abul Hassan: *A Persian at the Court of King George, 1809–1810: The Journal of Mirza Abul Hassan Khan*, translated and edited by Margaret Morris Cloake (London, Barrie and Jenkins, 1988).

Leeke, Rev. William: *The History of Lord Seaton's Regiment (the 52nd Light Infantry) at the Battle of Waterloo*, 2 vols (London, 1866).

Leveson Gower: see Gower.

Malmesbury, Earl of: *Diaries and Correspondence of James Harris, First Earl of Malmesbury . . .*, edited by his grandson, the third Earl, 4 vols (London, Richard Bentley, 1844).

Martin, Sir Thomas Byam: *Letters and Papers of Admiral of the Fleet Sir Thos. Byam Martin*, edited by Sir Richard Vesey Hamilton, vol. 2, Navy Record Society, vol. 12 (1898).

Moore, James: *A Narrative of the Campaign of the British Army in Spain, commanded by his Excellency Lieut.-General Sir John Moore, K.B. . . .* (London, Joseph Johnson, 1809).

Moore, Sir John: *The Diary of Sir John Moore*, edited by Maj.-Gen. Sir J.F. Maurice, 2 vols (London, Edward Arnold, 1904).

Ompteda, Baron: *A Hanoverian-English Officer a Hundred Years Ago: Memoirs of Baron Ompteda* (London, H. Grevel, 1892).

Paget, Sir Arthur: *The Paget Papers: Diplomatic and Other Correspondence of the*

Rt. Hon. Sir Arthur Paget, edited by Sir Augustus Paget, 2 vols (London, Heinemann, 1896).

Paget Brothers: *The Paget Brothers*, edited by Lord Hylton (London, John Murray, 1918).

Palmerston, Third Viscount: *The Letters of the Third Viscount Palmerston to Laurence and Elizabeth Sulivan, 1804–1863*, edited by Kenneth Bourne, Camden Fourth Series, vol. 23 (London, Royal Historical Society, 1979).

Pelet, Jean Jacques: *The French Campaign in Portugal, 1810–1811: An Account by Jean Jacques Pelet*, edited and translated by Donald D. Horward (Minneapolis, University of Minnesota Press, 1973).

Robertson, Rev. James: *Narrative of a Secret Mission to the Danish Islands in 1808 by the Rev. James Robertson*, edited by Alexander Clinton Fraser (London, Longman, 1863).

Romilly, Sir Samuel: *Memoirs of the Life of Sir Samuel Romilly, written by Himself: with a selection from His Correspondence*, edited by his sons, 3 vols (London, John Murray, 1840).

Rose, George: *The Diaries and Correspondence of the Right Hon. George Rose . . .*, edited by Rev. Leveson Vernon Harcourt, 2 vols (London, Richard Bentley, 1860).

Ryan, A. N. (ed.): 'Documents Relating to the Copenhagen Operation, 1807', in *The Naval Miscellany*, vol. 5, edited by N. A. M. Rodger (London, Allen and Unwin for the Navy Record Society, 1984), pp. 297–324.

Saumarez, Sir James: *The Saumarez Papers: Selections from the Baltic Correspondence of Vice-Admiral Sir James Saumarez, 1808–1812*, edited by A. N. Ryan (Navy Record Society, vol. 110, 1968).

Scott, Sir Walter: *The Letters of Sir Walter Scott, 1787–1832*, edited by H. J. C. Grierson, 12 vols (London, Constable, 1932–7).

Sheridan, R. B.: *The Letters of Richard Brinsley Sheridan*, edited by Cecil Price, 3 vols (Oxford, Clarendon Press, 1966).

Siborne, Maj.-Gen. H. T.: *Waterloo Letters*, edited by Major-General H. T. Siborne (London, Cassell, 1891; reprinted, Cambridge, Trotman, 1983).

Smith, Rev. Sydney: *The Letters of Sydney Smith*, edited by Nowell C. Smith, 2 vols (Oxford, Clarendon Press, 1953).

Soldier: *A Soldier of the Seventy-First* [anonymous memoir], edited by Christopher Hibbert (London, Leo Cooper, 1975; first published 1819).

Tomkinson, Lt-Col.: *The Diary of a Cavalry Officer in the Peninsular War and Waterloo Campaign, 1809–1815*, edited by James Tomkinson (London, Swan Sonnenschein, 1895).

Ward, J. W.: *Letters to Ivy from the first Earl of Dudley*, [edited] by S. H. Romilly (London, Longmans, Green & Co., 1905).

Ward, Robert Plumer: *Memoirs of the Political and Literary Life of Robert Plumer Ward Esq.*, by the Hon. Edmund Phipps, 2 vols (London, John Murray, 1850).

Webster, C. K.: *British Diplomacy, 1813–1815: Select Documents dealing with the Reconstruction of Europe*, edited by C. K. Webster (London, G. Bell, 1921).

Wellesley, Henry: *The Diary and Correspondence of Henry Wellesley, First Lord Cowley, 1790–1846*, edited by his grandson, Colonel the Hon. F. A. Wellesley (London, Hutchinson & Co., [1930]).

Wellesley, Richard Marquess: *The Despatches and Correspondence of the Marquess Wellesley, K. G. During His Lordship's Mission to Spain as Ambassador Extraordi-*

nary to the Supreme Junta in 1809, edited by Montgomery Martin (London, John Murray, 1838).

——: *The Wellesley Papers*, 'by the editor of "The Windham Papers"', 2 vols (London, Herbert Jenkins, 1914).

Wellington, Arthur Wellesley, First Duke of: *The Dispatches of Field Marshal The Duke of Wellington, during his various campaigns in India, Denmark, Portugal, Spain, the Low Countries, and France*, compiled by Colonel Gurwood, 8 vols (London, Parker Furnivall and Parker, 1844).

——: *Supplementary Despatches, Correspondence and Memoranda of Field Marshal Arthur, Duke of Wellington, K. G.*, edited by his son, The Duke of Wellington, 15 vols (London, John Murray, 1858–72). (The title varies slightly from volume to volume.)

——: 'Some letters of the Duke of Wellington to his brother William Wellesley-Pole', edited by Sir Charles Webster, *Camden Miscellany*, vol. XVIII (Camden, Third Series, vol. LXXIX; London, Royal Historical Society, 1948).

——: 'Unpublished Letters of Wellington, July–August 1812', edited by I. J. Rousseau, *Cambridge Historical Journal*, vol. 3, 1929, pp. 96–101.

Wilberforce, William: *The Life of William Wilberforce*, by his sons Robert Isaac Wilberforce and Samuel Wilberforce, 5 vols (London, John Murray, 1838).

Wilson, Sir Robert: *General Wilson's Journal, 1812–14*, edited by Antony Brett-James (London, Kimber, 1964).

III   NEWSPAPERS, JOURNALS AND OFFICIAL PUBLICATIONS

The Annual Register, 1807–15.

Cobbett's Parliamentary Debates.

Dictionary of National Biography, 22 vols (Oxford University Press, 1921–2).

Great Britain, *Parliamentary Papers*. Presented in pursuance of the address of 15 February 1808; 1809, vol. XI, and 1810, vol. XV.

The Times.

IV   SECONDARY SOURCES

Anderson, M. S.: *The Eastern Question, 1774–1923* (London, Macmillan, 1966).

——: *Britain's Discovery of Russia, 1553–1815* (London, Macmillan, 1958).

——: 'The Continental System and Russo-British Relations during the Napoleonic Wars', in K. Bourne and D. C. Watt (eds), *Studies in International History* (London, Longmans, 1967).

——: 'British Publish Opinion and the Russian Campaign of 1812', *Slavonic and Eastern European Review*, vol. 34, 1956, pp. 408–25.

Anderson, R. C.: *Naval Wars in the Baltic* (London, Wood, 1910).

——: *Naval Wars in the Levant* (Liverpool University Press, 1952).

Anglesey, Lord: *One-Leg: The Life and Letters of Henry William Paget, first Marquess of Anglesey, K. G., 1768–1854* (London, Cape, 1961).

Ashley, the Hon. Evelyn: *The Life and Correspondence of Henry John Temple Viscount Palmerston*, 2 vols (London, Richard Bentley, 1879).

Aspinall, Prof. Arthur: *Politics and the Press, c.1780–1850* (London, Home and Thal, 1949).

——: 'The Cabinet Council, 1783–1835', The Raleigh Lecture on History, British Academy, 1952, published in the *Proceedings of the British Academy*, vol. XXXVIII.

——: 'The Canningite Party', *Transactions of the Royal Historical Society*, 4th series, vol. XVII, 1934, pp. 177–226.

——: 'Lord Brougham's *Life and Times*', *English Historical Review*, vol. LIX, 1944, pp. 87–112.

——: 'The Rupture of the Orange Marriage Negotiations', *History*, vol. 34, 1949, pp. 44–60.

——: 'The Reporting and Publishing of the House of Commons Debates, 1771–1834', in R. Pares and A. J. P. Taylor (eds), *Essays Presented to Sir Lewis Namier* (London, Macmillan, 1956).

Aspinall-Oglander, Cecil: *Freshly Remembered: The Story of Thomas Graham, Lord Lynedoch* (London, The Hogarth Press, 1956).

Atteridge, A. Hilliard: *Marshal Murat* (London, Nelson, n.d., c.1912).

Baggally, J. W.: *Ali Pasha and Great Britain* (Oxford, Blackwell, 1938).

Balfour, Lady Frances: *The Life of George, Fourth Earl of Aberdeen*, 2 vols (London, Hodder and Stoughton, n.d. [1922]).

Barnes, Hilary: 'Canning and the Danes, 1807', *History Today*, vol. 15, Aug. 1965, pp. 530–8.

Barrow, John: *The Life and Correspondence of Admiral Sir William Sidney Smith*, 2 vols (London, Richard Bentley, 1848).

Bartlett, C. J.: *Castlereagh* (London, Macmillan, 1966).

Barton, Sir Dunbar Plunkett: *Bernadotte. Prince and King, 1810–1844* (London, John Murray, 1925).

Barton, H. A.: 'Late Gustavian Autocracy in Sweden: Gustavus IV Adolf and His Opponents, 1792–1809', *Scandinavian Studies*, vol. 46, 1974, pp. 265–84.

Beatson, Brig.-Gen. F. C.: *With Wellington in the Pyrenees* (London, Tom Donovan, 1993; first published 1914).

Berkeley, Alison D. (ed.): *New Lights on the Peninsular War . . .* (Lisbon, British Historical Society of Portugal, 1991).

Bindoff, S. T., et al.: *British Diplomatic Representatives, 1789–1852*, Camden Third Series, vol. 50 (London, Camden Society, 1934).

Black, Jeremy, and Philip Woodfine (eds): *The British Navy and the Use of Naval Power in the Eighteenth Century* (Leicester University Press, 1988).

Blanco, Richard, L.: *Wellington's Surgeon General: Sir James McGrigor* (Duke University Press, 1974).

Blanning, T. C. W.: *The Origins of the French Revolutionary Wars* (London and New York, Longman, 1987).

Bond, Gordon C.: *The Grand Expedition* (Athens, University of Georgia Press, 1979).

Bourne, Kenneth: *Palmerston: The Early Years, 1784–1841* (London, Allen Lane, 1982).

——, and D. C. Watt (eds): *Studies in International History* (London, Longmans, 1967).

Bowden, Scott: *Armies at Waterloo* (Arlington, Empire Games, 1983).

Brett-James, Antony: *The Hundred Days: Napoleon's Last Campaign from eye-witness accounts* (London, Macmillan, 1964).

Brougham, Lord: *Statesmen of the Time of George III and IV* (Edinburgh, Adam and Charles Black, 1872), 3 vols.

Brownrigg, Beatrice: *The Life and Letters of Sir John Moore* (New York, Appleton, 1923).

Buckland, C. S. B.: *Metternich and the British Government from 1809 to 1813* (London, Macmillan, 1932).

——: 'An English Estimate of Metternich in 1813', *English Historical Review*, vol. 39, 1924, pp. 256–8.

Burne, A. H.: *The Noble Duke of York* (London, Staples Press, 1949).

Butler, Iris: *The Eldest Brother: The Marquess Wellesley, the Duke of Wellington's Eldest Brother* (London, Hodder and Stoughton, 1973).

Butterfield, H.: *The Peace Tactics of Napoleon, 1806–1808* (Cambridge University Press, 1929).

Canadian: *Dictionary of Canadian Biography*, vol. 5, 1801–20 (essays on Prevost and Brock; University of Toronto Press, 1983).

Carr, Raymond: *Spain 1808–1939* (Oxford, Clarendon Press, 1966).

——: 'Gustavus IV and the British Government, 1804–9', *English Historical Review*, vol. 60, 1945, pp. 36–66.

Carver, Field-Marshal Lord: *Wellington and His Brothers*, The First Wellington Lecture (University of Southampton, 1989).

Cate, Curtis: *The War of the Two Emperors: The Duel between Napoleon and Alexander: Russia, 1812* (New York, Random House, 1985).

Chamberlain, Muriel E.: *Lord Aberdeen: A Political Biography* (London, Longman, 1983).

Chandler, David: *The Campaigns of Napoleon* (New York, Macmillan, 1974).

——: *Dictionary of the Napoleonic Wars* (London, Arms and Armour, 1979).

——: *On the Napoleonic Wars: Collected Essays* (London, Greenhill, 1994).

Christie, Carl A.: 'The Royal Navy and the Walcheren Expedition of 1809', in *New Aspects of Naval History*, edited by Craig L. Symonds et al. (Annapolis, Naval Institute Press, 1981), pp. 190–200.

Christie, Ian R.: *Wars and Revolutions: Britain, 1760–1815* (London, Edward Arnold, 1982).

——: 'George III and the historians — thirty years on', *History*, vol. 71, no. 232, June 1986, pp. 205–21.

Clapham, Sir John: *The Bank of England: A History, 1694–1914*, 2 vols (Cambridge University Press, 1966).

Clarke, John: *British Diplomacy and Foreign Policy, 1782–1865: The National Interest* (London, Unwin Hyman, 1989).

Clerc, Joseph C. A.: *Campagne de Maréchal Soult dans les Pyrénées occidentales en 1813–14* (Paris, Librairie Militaire de L. Boudoin, 1894).

Colby, Reginald: *The Waterloo Despatch* (London, H.M.S.O., 1965).

Cole, Hubert: *Fouché: The Unprincipled Patriot* (London, Eyre and Spottiswoode, 1971).

Coles, Harry L.: *The War of 1812* (University of Chicago Press, 1965).

Colley, Linda: *Britons: Forging the Nation, 1707–1837* (Yale University Press, 1992).

Collyer, Cedric: 'Canning and the Napoleonic Wars', *History Today*, vol. 11, April 1961, pp. 227–35.

Connelly, Owen: *The Gentle Bonaparte* (New York, Macmillan, 1968).

——: *Napoleon's Satellite Kingdoms* (New York, Free Press, 1969).

Cookson, J. E.: 'Political Arithmetic and War in Britain, 1793–1815', *War and Society*, vol. 1, no. 2, 1983, pp. 37–60.

——: *The Friends of Peace: Anti-War Liberalism in England, 1793–1815* (Cambridge University Press, 1982).

——: *Lord Liverpool's Administration: The Crucial Years, 1815–1822* (Edinburgh, Scottish Academic Press, 1975).

Coquelle, P.: *Napoleon & England, 1803–1813* (London, G. Bell, 1904).

Corbett, Sir J. S.: 'Napoleon and the British Navy after Trafalgar', *Quarterly Review*, April 1922, pp. 238–55.

Corti, Count: *The Rise of the House of Rothschild* (London, Gollancz, 1928).

Craig, Gordon A.: *The Politics of the Prussian Army, 1640–1945* (Oxford University Press, 1978; first published 1955).

——: 'Problems of Coalition Warfare: The Military Alliance against Napoleon, 1813–14', in his *War Politics and Diplomacy* (London, Weidenfeld and Nicolson, 1966).

Craufurd, Rev. Alexander: *General Craufurd and His Light Division* (Cambridge, Ken Trotman, 1987; first published 1891).

Crawley, C. W.: 'French and English Influence in the Cortes of Cadiz, 1810–14', *Cambridge Historical Journal*, vol. VI, 1939, pp. 176–206.

——: 'England and the Sicilian Constitution of 1812', *English Historical Review*, vol. 55, April 1940, pp. 251–74.

Cronin, Vincent: *Napoleon* (Harmondsworth, Penguin, 1976).

Cubberly, Ray E.: *The Role of Fouché during the Hundred Days* (Madison, 1969).

Cunningham, Audrey: *British Credit in the Last Napoleonic War* (Cambridge University Press, 1910).

Daly, Robert W.: 'Operations of the Russian Navy during the reign of Napoleon I', *Mariner's Mirror*, vol. 34, July 1948, pp. 169–183.

Darvall, F. O.: *Popular Disturbances and Public Order in Regency England* (Oxford University Press, 1934).

Davies, D. W.: *Sir John Moore's Peninsular Campaign, 1808–1809* (The Hague, Martinus Nijhoff, 1974).

Davies, Godfrey: 'The Whigs and the Peninsular War, 1808–1814', *Transactions of the Royal Historical Society*, 2nd series, vol. 4, 1919, pp. 114–31.

Davis, Richard: *The English Rothschilds* (London, Collins, 1983).

De La Fuente, Francisco A.: 'Dom Miguel Pereira Forjaz: His Early Career and Role in the Mobilization and Defence of Portugal . . . 1807–1814' (unpublished PhD thesis submitted to Florida State University, 1980).

Delavoye, A. M.: *Life of Thomas Graham, Lord Lynedoch* (London, Richardson and Marchant Singer, 1880).

Derry, John W.: *Castlereagh* (London, Allen Lane, 1976).

Dickinson, H. T. (ed.): *Britain and the French Revolution, 1789–1815* (Basingstoke, Macmillan Education, 1989).

Dixon, P.: *Canning: Politician and Statesman* (London, Weidenfeld and Nicolson, 1976).

Dowell, S.: *History of Taxation and Taxes in England*, 4 vols (London, Longmans, Green, 1888).

Drabble, Margaret (ed.): *The Oxford Companion to English Literature* (Oxford University Press, 1985).

Duhamel, Jean: *The Fifty Days: Napoleon in England* (London, Hart-Davis, 1969).

Dumas, Samuel, and K. O. Vedel-Petersen: *Losses of Life Caused by War* (Oxford, Clarendon Press for the Carnegie Endowment for International Peace, 1923).

Edmonds, Sir James E.: 'Wellington's Staff at Waterloo', *Journal of the Society for Army Historical Research*, vol. 12, 1933, pp. 239–47.

Ehrman, John: *The Younger Pitt*, vol. 2, *The Reluctant Transition* (London, Constable, 1983).

Emsley, Clive: *British Society and the French Wars, 1793–1815* (London and Basingstoke, Macmillan, 1979).

——: *The Longman Companion to Napoleonic Europe* (London, Longman, 1993).

Esdaile, Charles J.: *The Spanish Army in the Peninsular War* (Manchester University Press, 1988).

——: *The Duke of Wellington and the Command of the Spanish Army, 1812–14* (Basingstoke, Macmillan, 1990).

——: 'War and Politics in Spain, 1808–1814', *The Historical Journal*, vol. 31, no. 2, 1988, pp. 295–317.

——: 'Wellington and the Military Eclipse of Spain, 1808–1814', *International History Review*, vol. XI, Feb. 1989, pp. 55–67.

——: *The Wars of Napoleon* (forthcoming).

Espitalier, Albert: *Napoleon and King Murat* (London, Bodley Head, 1912).

Esposito, V. J., and J. R. Etling: *A Military History and Atlas of the Napoleonic Wars* (London, Arms and Armour, 1980; first published 1964).

Fanshawe, Admiral Sir E. G.: *Sir Hew Dalrymple at Gibraltar and in Portugal in 1808* (London, Simpkin, Marshall, Hamilton, Kent & Co. [1900]).

Festing, Gabrielle: *John Hookham Frere and his Friends* (London, James Nisbet, 1899).

Fitchett, W. H.: *How England Saved Europe*, 4 vols (London, Smith Elder, 1899–1900).

Fortescue, The Hon. J. W.: *A History of the British Army*, 13 vols (London, Macmillan, 1899–1930).

——: *The County Lieutenancies and the Army, 1803–14* (London, Macmillan, 1909).

——: *British Statesmen of the Great War, 1793–1814* (Oxford, Clarendon Press, 1911).

Fournier: *Napoleon I: A Biography*, 2 vols (London, Longmans, 1912).

Fregosi, Paul: *Dreams of Empire: Napoleon and the First World War, 1792–1815* (London, Hutchinson, 1989).

French, David: *The British Way in Warfare, 1688–2000* (London, Unwin Hyman, 1990).

Frere, W. E., and Sir Bartle: 'Memoir of John Hookham Frere', in vol. 1 of *The Works of John Hookham Frere*, 2 vols (London, Basil Montagu Pickering, 1872).

Fryman, Mildred L.: 'Charles Stuart and the "Common Cause": The Anglo-Portuguese Alliance, 1810–1814' (unpublished PhD thesis submitted to Florida State University in 1974).

Fulford, Roger: *Samuel Whitbread* (London, Macmillan, 1967).

——: *Royal Dukes* (London, Duckworth, 1933).

Gallaher, John G.: 'Marshal Davout and the Second Bourbon Restoration', *French Historical Studies*, vol. VI, 1970 , pp. 350–64.

Galpin, W. F.: 'The American Grain Trade to the Spanish Peninsula', *American Historical Review*, vol. 28, 1922, pp. 24–44.

Gardner, Dorsey: *Quatre Bras, Ligny and Waterloo: A Narrative of the Campaign in Belgium in 1815* (London, 1882).

Gash, Norman: *Lord Liverpool* (London, Weidenfeld and Nicolson, 1984).

——: *Mr. Secretary Peel: The Life of Sir Robert Peel to 1830* (London, Longmans, 1961).

—— (ed.): *Wellington: Studies in the Military and Political Career of the First Duke of Wellington* (1990).

——: *Wellington Anecdotes: A Critical Survey*, The Fourth Wellington Lecture (University of Southampton, 1992)

Gates, David: *The Spanish Ulcer: A History of the Peninsular War* (London, George Allen and Unwin, 1986).

George, M. Dorothy: *English Political Caricature*, 2 vols (Oxford, Clarendon Press, 1959).

——: see also Stephens below.

Glover, Michael: *Britannia Sickens: Sir Arthur Wellesley and the Convention of Cintra* (London, Leo Cooper, 1970).

——: *Wellington's Army. In the Peninsula, 1808–1814* (Newton Abbot, David and Charles, 1977).

——: *Wellington's Peninsular Victories* (London, Pan, 1963).

——: *Legacy of Glory: The Bonaparte Kingdom of Spain* (New York, Scribners, 1971).

——: *Wellington as a Military Commander* (London, Sphere, 1973).

——: *A Very Slippery Fellow: The Life of Sir Robert Wilson, 1777–1849* (Oxford University Press, 1978).

Glover, Richard: *Britain at Bay: Defence against Bonaparte, 1803–1814* (London, George Allen and Unwin, 1973).

——: *Peninsular Preparation: The Reform of the British Army, 1795–1809* (Cambridge University Press, 1963).

——: 'The French Fleet, 1807–1814: Britain's Problem and Madison's Opportunity', *Journal of Modern History*, vol. 39, 1967, pp. 233–52.

Goebel, Dorothy B.: 'British Trade to the Spanish Colonies, 1796–1823', *American Historical Review*, vol. XLIII, 1937–8, pp. 288–320.

Goldenberg, Joseph A.: 'The Royal Navy's Blockade in New England Waters, 1812–1815', *International History Review*, vol. 6, Aug. 1984, pp. 424–39.

Graham, G. S.: *Great Britain in the Indian Ocean, 1810–1850* (Oxford, Clarendon Press, 1967).

Graubard, S. R.: 'Castlereagh and the Peace of Europe', *Journal of British Studies*, vol. 3, 1963, pp. 79–87.

Gray, Denis: *Spencer Perceval: The Evangelical Prime Minister, 1762–1812* (Manchester University Press, 1963).

Greenwood, Major: 'British Loss of Life in the Wars of 1794–1815 and 1914–18: with a Discussion', *Journal of the Royal Statistical Society*, vol. 105, 1942, pp. 1–16.

Gregory, Desmond: *Sicily: The Insecure Base: A History of the British Occupation of Sicily, 1806–15* (Fairleigh Dickinson University Press, 1988).

——: 'British Occupations of Madeira during the Wars against Napoleon', *Journal of the Society for Army Historical Research*, vol. LXVI, no. 266, Summer 1988, pp. 80–96.

Grimsted, Patricia K.: *The Foreign Ministers of Alexander I: Political Attitudes and the Conduct of Russian Diplomacy, 1801–1825* (Berkeley, University of California Press, 1969).

Grunwald, Constantin de: *Baron Stein: Enemy of Napoleon* (London, Cape, 1940).

Gulick, E. V.: *Europe's Classical Balance of Power* (New York, Norton, 1967; first published 1955).

Guy, Alan J. (ed.): *The Road to Waterloo: The British Army and the Struggle against Revolutionary and Napoleonic France, 1793–1815* (London, National Army Museum, 1990).

Haley, A. H.: *Our Davy: General Sir David Baird, K.B., 1757–1829* (Liverpool, Bullfinch, n.d. [c.1991]).

Hall, Christopher D.: *British Strategy in the Napoleonic War, 1803–15* (Manchester University Press, 1992).

Hamilton-Williams, David: *Waterloo: New Perspectives: The Great Battle Re-appraised* (London, Arms and Armour, 1993).

Hargreaves, E. L.: *The National Debt* (London, 1930).

Harvey, A. D.: *Britain in the Early Nineteenth Century* (London, Batsford, 1978).

——: *Collision of Empires: Britain in Three World Wars, 1793–1945* (Hambledon, 1992).

——: 'European Attitudes to Britain during the French Revolutionary and Napoleonic Era', *History*, vol. 63, 1978, pp. 356–65.

Hayman, Sir Peter: *Soult: Napoleon's Maligned Marshal* (London, Arms and Armour, 1990).

Heckscher, Eli F.: *The Continental System: An Economic Interpretation* (Oxford, Clarendon Press, 1922).

Herries, E.: *Memoir of the Public and Private Life of the Rt. Hon. John Charles Herries* (London, John Murray, 1880).

Hibbert, Christopher: *George IV*, 2 vols (London, Longman, 1972, and Allen Lane, 1973).

Hickey, Donald R.: *The War of 1812: A Forgotten Conflict* (Illinois University Press, 1989).

Hill, Draper: *Mr. Gillray: The Caricaturist* (London, Phaidon, 1965).

Hilton, Boyd: 'The Political Arts of Lord Liverpool', *Transactions of the Royal Historical Society*, 5th series, vol. 38, 1988, pp. 147–70.

Hinde, Wendy: *George Canning* (London, Collins, 1973).

——: *Castlereagh* (London, Collins, 1981).

Hitsman, J. M.: *The Incredible War of 1812* (University of Toronto Press, 1965).

Hodge, William Barwick: 'On the Mortality Arising from Military Operations', *Quarterly Journal of the Statistical Society*, vol. 19, Sept. 1856, pp. 219–71.

Hook, Theodore: *The Life of General, the Right Honourable, Sir David Baird*, 2 vols (London, Richard Bentley, 1833).

Horsman, Reginald: *The War of 1812* (London, Eyre and Spottiswoode, 1969).

Horward, Donald D.: *The Battle of Bussaco: Masséna vs. Wellington* (Tallahassee, Florida State University, Florida State University Studies, no. 44, 1965).

——: *Napoleon and Iberia: The Twin Sieges of Ciudad Rodrigo and Almeida, 1810* (Tallahassee, Florida State University Press, 1984).

——: 'British Seapower and its Influence upon the Peninsular War (1808–1814)', *The Naval War College Review*, vol. 31, no. 2, Fall 1978, pp. 54–71.

Houssaye, Henry: *Napoleon and the Campaign of 1814* (London, Hugh Rees, 1914).

——: *The Return of Napoleon* (London, Longmans, 1934).

——: *1815: Waterloo* (London, A. & C. Black, 1900).

Ingram, Edward: *In Defence of British India: Great Britain and the Middle East, 1775–1842* (London, Cass, 1984).

Iremonger, Lucille: *Lord Aberdeen* (London, Collins, 1978).

James, Lawrence: *The Iron Duke: A Military Biography of Wellington* (London, Weidenfeld and Nicolson, 1992).

James, Lt-Col. W. H.: *The Campaign of 1815: Chiefly in Flanders* (Edinburgh, Blackwood, 1908).

Johnston, Otto W.: 'British Espionage and Prussian Politics in the Age of Napoleon', *Intelligence and National Security: An Interdisciplinary Journal*, vol. 2, 1987, pp. 230–44.

Johnston, Robert M.: 'Lord William Bentinck and Murat', *English Historical Review*, vol. 19, 1904, pp. 263–80.

Jones, W. D.: *'Prosperity' Robinson: The Life of Viscount Goderich, 1782–1859* (London, Macmillan, 1967).

Josselson, Michael and Diana: *The Commander: A Life of Barclay de Tolly* (Oxford University Press, 1980).

Jupp, Peter: *Lord Grenville, 1759–1834* (Oxford, Clarendon Press, 1985).

Kaufmann, William W.: *British Policy and the Independence of Latin America, 1804–1824* (Archon Books, 1967).

Kennedy, Paul M.: *The Rise and Fall of British Naval Mastery* (London, Allen Lane, 1976).

Kissinger, H. A.: *A World Restored: Metternich, Castlereagh and the Problems of Peace, 1812–1822* (London, Weidenfeld and Nicolson, 1957).

Knapton, E. J.: 'Some Aspects of the Bourbon Restoration of 1814', *Journal of Modern History*, 1934, vol. 6, pp. 405–25.

Knight, George D.: 'Lord Liverpool and the Peninsular War, 1809–1812' (unpublished PhD thesis submitted to Florida State University in 1976).

Kohn, Hans: *Prelude to Nation States: The French and German Experience, 1789–1815* (Princeton, Van Nostrand, 1967).

Kraehe, Enno E.: *Metternich's German Policy*, 2 vols (Princeton University Press, 1963, 1983).

——: 'Wellington and the Reconstruction of the Allied Armies during the Hundred Days', *International History Review*, vol. XI, Feb. 1989, pp. 84–97.

Kukiel, Marian: *Czartoryski and European Unity, 1770–1861* (Princeton University Press, 1955).

Lackland, H. M.: 'Lord William Bentinck in Sicily, 1811–12', *English Historical Review*, vol. 42, 1927, pp. 371–96.

——: 'The Failure of the Constitutional Experiment in Sicily, 1813–14', *English Historical Review*, vol. 41, 1926, pp. 210–35.

Lane-Poole, Stanley: *The Life of the Right Honourable Stratford Canning . . .* , 2 vols (London, Longmans, 1888).

Lee, C. H.: *The British Economy since 1700* (Cambridge University Press, 1986).

Lefebvre, Georges: *Napoleon: From Tilsit to Waterloo* (New York, Columbia University Press, 1970).

Leiren, T. I.: 'Norwegian Independence and British Opinion: January to August 1814', *Scandinavian Studies*, vol. 47, 1975, pp. 364–82.

Lobanov-Rostovsky, A. A.: *Russia and Europe, 1789–1825* (Durham N.C., 1947).

Longford, Elizabeth: *Wellington: The Years of the Sword* (London, Weidenfeld and Nicolson, 1969).

Lovett, Gabriel H.: *Napoleon and the Birth of Modern Spain*, 2 vols (New York University Press, 1965).

Lynch, J.: 'British Policy and Spanish America, 1783–1808', *Journal of Latin American Studies*, vol. 1, 1969.

Macalpine, Ida, and Richard Hunter, *George III and the Mad-Business* (London, Allen Lane the Penguin Press, 1969).

Macartney, C. A.: *The Hapsburg Empire, 1790–1918* (London, Weidenfeld and Nicolson, 1968).

Macaulay, Rose: *They Went to Portugal* (London, Cape, 1946).

Macdonell, A. G.: *Napoleon and His Marshals* (London, Macmillan, 1934).

McGuigan, Dorothy G.: *Metternich and the Duchess* (New York, Doubleday, 1975).

Mackenzie, Norman: *The Escape from Elba: The Fall and Flight of Napoleon, 1814–1815* (Oxford University Press, 1982).

Mackesy, Piers: *The War in the Mediterranean, 1803–1810* (Westport, Greenwood Press, 1981; first published in 1957 by Harvard University Press).

——: *Statesmen at War: The Strategy of Overthrow* (London, Longmans, 1974).

——: *War Without Victory: The Downfall of Pitt, 1799–1802* (Oxford, Clarendon Press, 1984).

McQuiston, Julian R.: 'Rose and Canning in Opposition, 1806–7', *The Historical Journal*, vol. XIV, 1971, pp. 503–27.

Mansel, Philip: *Louis XVIII* (London, Blond and Briggs, 1981).

——: 'How Forgotten were the Bourbons in France between 1812 and 1814?', *European Studies Review*, vol. 13, 1983, pp. 13–37.

——: 'Wellington and the French Restoration', *International History Review*, vol. XI, Feb. 1989, pp. 76–83.

Marcus, G. J.: *A Naval History of England*, 2 vols (London, Longmans, 1961, 1971).

Marlowe, John: *Anglo-Egyptian Relations, 1800–1956* (London, Frank Cass, 1965).

Marshall-Cornwall, James: *Marshal Masséna* (Oxford University Press, 1965).

Maurice, Col. J. F.: 'Waterloo', six parts in *United Service Magazine*, new series, vol. 1, April 1890 to January 1891.

Maxwell, Sir Herbert: *The Life of Wellington: The Restoration of the Martial Power of Great Britain*, 2 vols (London, Sampson Low, Marston & Co., 1900).

Middleton, C. R.: *The Administration of British Foreign Policy, 1782–1846* (Durham N.C., Duke University Press, 1977).

Mitchell, B. R., and Phyllis Deane: *Abstract of British Historical Statistics* (Cambridge University Press, 1962).

Mitchell, Leslie: *Holland House* (London, Duckworth, 1980).

Morley, Charles: 'Alexander I and Czartoryski: The Polish Question from 1801 to 1813', *Slavonic and East European Review*, vol. 25, April 1947, pp. 405–26.

Mowat, R. B.: *The Diplomacy of Napoleon* (London, Edward Arnold, 1924).

Muir, R. J. B.: 'The British Government and the Peninsular War, 1808 to June

1811' (unpublished PhD thesis submitted to the University of Adelaide in 1988).

Napier, Maj.-Gen. Sir W. F. P.: *History of the War in the Peninsula and in the South of France, from the Year 1807 to the Year 1814*, 6 vols (London, Thomas and William Boone, 1853).

——: *The Life and Opinions of General Sir Charles James Napier, G.C.B.*, 4 vols (London, John Murray, 1857).

New, Chester: *Life of Henry Brougham to 1830* (Oxford, Clarendon Press, 1961).

Niall, Brenda: *Georgiana: A Biography of Georgiana McCrae, Painter, Diarist, Pioneer* (Melbourne University Press, 1994).

Nicolson, Harold: *The Congress of Vienna: A Study in Allied Unity, 1812–1822* (London, Constable, 1946).

Niven, Alexander C.: *Napoleon and Alexander I: A Study in Franco-Russian Relations, 1807–1812* (Washington, University Press of America, 1978).

Norman, Barbara: *Napoleon and Talleyrand: The Last Two Weeks* (New York, Stein and Day, 1976).

O'Brien, P. K.: 'Public Finance in the Wars with France, 1793–1815', in H. T. Dickinson (ed.), *Britain and the French Revolution, 1789–1815* (Basingstoke, Macmillan Education, 1989).

——: 'The Political Economy of British Taxation, 1660–1815', *Economic History Review*, vol. XLI, 1988, pp. 1–32.

O'Gorman, F.: *The Emergence of the British Two Party System, 1760–1832* (London, Edward Arnold, 1982).

Olphin, H. K.: *George Tierney* (London, George Allen and Unwin, 1934).

Olson, Mancur: *The Economics of Wartime Shortage: A History of British Food Supplies in the Napoleonic War and in World Wars One and Two* (Durham N.C., Duke University Press, 1963).

Oman, Carola: *Sir John Moore* (London, Hodder and Stoughton, 1953).

Oman, Sir Charles: *A History of the Peninsular War*, 7 vols (Oxford, Clarendon Press, 1902–30).

——: *Studies in the Napoleonic Wars* (London, Methuen, 1929).

——: *Wellington's Army, 1809–1814* (London, Greenhill, 1986; first published by Edward Arnold in 1913).

——: 'French Losses in the Waterloo Campaign', *English Historical Review*, October 1904 and January 1906, pp. 680–93, 132–5.

Page, Julia: see Cocks in Published Primary Sources.

Palmer, Alan: *Alexander I: Tsar of War and Peace* (London, Weidenfeld and Nicolson, 1974).

——: *Metternich* (London, Weidenfeld and Nicolson, 1972).

——: *Bernadotte: Napoleon's Marshal, Swedish King* (London, John Murray, 1990).

——: *An Encyclopedia of Napoleon's Europe* (London, Weidenfeld and Nicolson, 1984).

——: *Napoleon in Russia* (London, Andre Deutsch, 1967).

Pares, Richard: *King George III and the Politicians* (Oxford, Clarendon Press, 1953).

Pares and Taylor: see above under Aspinall.

Paret, P.: *Yorck and the Era of Prussian Reform* (Princeton University Press, 1966).

Parker, Charles Stuart: *Sir Robert Peel . . .*, 3 vols (London, John Murray, 1891).

Parkinson, C. Northcote: *Britannia Rules: The Classic Age of Naval History, 1793–1815* (London, Weidenfeld and Nicolson, 1977).

Parkinson, Roger: *The Hussar General* (London, Peter Davies, 1975).

——: *The Fox of the North* (New York, McKay, 1976).

——: *Clausewitz* (London, Wayland Publishers, 1970).

Parry, Ann: *The Admirals Fremantle, 1788–1920* (London, Chatto and Windus, 1971).

Patterson, M. W.: *Sir Francis Burdett and His Times, 1770–1844*, 2 vols (London, Macmillan, 1931).

Pearce, Robert R.: *Memoirs and Correspondence of . . . Richard Marquess Wellesley*, 3 vols (London, Richard Bentley, 1843).

Pellew, George: *Life and Correspondence of the Rt. Hon. Henry Addington, first Viscount Sidmouth*, 3 vols (London, John Murray, 1847).

Perkins, Bradford: *Prologue to War: England and the United States, 1805–1812* (University of California Press, 1968; first published 1961).

——: *Castlereagh and Adams: England and the United States, 1812–1823* (University of California Press, 1964).

Petre, F. L.: *Napoleon and the Archduke Charles* (London, Arms and Armour Press, 1976; first published 1909).

——: *Napoleon's Last Campaign in Germany, 1813* (London, Arms and Armour Press, 1977; first published 1912).

——: *Napoleon at Bay, 1814* (London, Arms and Armour Press, 1977; first published 1914).

Platt, D. C. M.: *Latin America and British Trade, 1806–1914* (London, A. & C. Black, 1972).

Popham, Hugh: *A Damned Cunning Fellow: The Eventful Life of Rear-Admiral Sir Home Popham . . . , 1762–1820* (Tywardreath, Old Ferry Press, 1991).

Putney, M.: 'The Slave Trade in French Diplomacy from 1814 to 1815', *Journal of Negro History*, vol. 60, July 1975, pp. 411–27.

Raack, R. C.: *The Fall of Stein* (Harvard Historical Monographs, no. 58, Harvard University Press, 1965).

Redgrave, T. M. O.: 'Wellington's Logistical Arrangements in the Peninsular War, 1809–1814' (unpublished PhD thesis presented to the University of London, no date).

Reich, Jerome: 'The Slave Trade at the Congress of Vienna — A Study of English Public Opinion', *Journal of Negro History*, vol. 53, April 1968, pp. 129–43.

Reilly, Robin: *William Pitt the Younger* (New York, G.P. Putnam's Sons, 1979).

Renier, G. J.: *Great Britain and the Establishment of the Kingdom of the Netherlands, 1813–15. A Study in British Foreign Policy* (London, Allen and Unwin, 1930).

Riehn, Richard K.: *1812: Napoleon's Russian Campaign* (New York, Wiley, 1991).

Roberts, Michael: *The Whig Party, 1807–1812* (London, Frank Cass, 1965; first published 1939).

——: 'The Ministerial Crisis of May–June 1812', *English Historical Review*, vol. 51, 1936, pp. 466–87.

Robertson, William Spence: 'The Juntas of 1808 and the Spanish Colonies', *English Historical Review*, vol. 31, 1916, pp. 573–85.

Robson, William H.: 'New Light on Lord Castlereagh's Diplomacy', *Journal of Modern History*, vol. 3, 1931, pp. 198–218.

Rolo, P. J. V.: *George Canning: Three Biographical Studies* (London, Macmillan, 1965).

Ropes, J. C.: *The Campaign of Waterloo* (London, Putnam's, 1893).

Rose, J. H.: *Life of Napoleon I*, 2 vols (London, Geo. Bell & Sons, 1904).

——: *Napoleonic Studies* (London, Geo. Bell & Sons, 1904).

——: 'Canning and the Spanish Patriots in 1808', *American Historical Review*, vol. 12, 1906–7.

——: 'Sir Hudson Lowe and the Beginnings of the Campaign of 1815', *English Historical Review*, vol. 16, July 1901, pp. 517–27.

Ross, Steven T.: *European Diplomatic History, 1789–1815* (Malabar, Florida, Krieger, 1981).

Rosselli, John: *Lord William Bentinck and the British Occupation of Sicily, 1811–1814* (Cambridge University Press, 1956).

——: *Lord William Bentinck: The Making of a Liberal Imperialist, 1774–1839* (London, Chatto and Windus for Sussex University Press, 1974).

Rothenberg, Gunther E.: *Napoleon's Great Adversaries: The Archduke Charles and the Austrian Army, 1792–1814* (London, Batsford, 1982).

Rothschild, Lord: *The Shadow of a Great Man* (London, privately printed, 1982).

Ruppenthal, R.: 'Denmark and the Continental System', *Journal of Modern History*, vol. 15, March 1943, pp. 7–23.

Ryan, A. N.: 'Trade with the Enemy in Scandinavian and Baltic Ports during the Napoleonic Wars: for and against', *Transactions of the Royal Historical Society*, vol. 12, 1961, pp. 123–40.

——: 'Causes of the British Attack on Copenhagen in 1807', *English Historical Review*, vol. 68, January 1953, pp. 37–55.

——: 'An Ambassador Afloat: Vice-Admiral Sir James Saumarez and the Swedish Court, 1808–1812', in Jeremy Black and Philip Woodfine (eds), *The British Navy and the Use of Naval Power in the Eighteenth Century* (Leicester University Press, 1988).

Rydjord, J.: 'British Mediation between Spain and her Colonies, 1811–13', *Hispanic American Historical Review*, vol. 21, Feb. 1941, pp. 29–50.

Sack, James J.: *The Grenvillites, 1801–1829* (University of Illinois Press, 1979).

Saul, Norman E.: *Russia and the Mediterranean, 1797–1807* (University of Chicago Press, 1970).

——: *Distant Friends: The United States and Russia, 1763–1867* (University Press of Kansas, 1991).

Schneer, Richard M.: 'Arthur Wellesley and the Cintra Convention: A New Look at an Old Puzzle', *Journal of British Studies*, vol. 19, no. 2, Spring 1980, pp. 93–119.

Schroeder, P.: 'An unnatural "natural alliance": Castlereagh, Metternich and Aberdeen in 1813', *International History Review*, vol. X, 1988, pp. 522–40.

——: *The Transformation of European Politics, 1763–1848* (Oxford, Clarendon Press, 1994).

Schumpeter, Elizabeth B.: 'English Prices and Public Finance, 1660–1822', *Review of Economic Statistics*, vol. XX, 1938, pp. 21–37.

Scott, Franklin D.: *Bernadotte and the Fall of Napoleon* (Harvard Historical Monographs no. 7, Harvard University Press, 1935).

——: 'Bernadotte and the throne of France in 1814', *Journal of Modern History*, vol. 5, Dec. 1933, pp. 465–78.

Seeley, J. R.: *The Life and Times of Stein*, 3 vols (Cambridge University Press, 1878).

Severn, John K.: 'Richard Marquess Wellesley and the Conduct of Anglo-Spanish Diplomacy, 1809–1812' (unpublished PhD thesis submitted to Florida State University in 1975). (This has been published as *A Wellesley Affair*, University of Florida Press, 1981, but I have not seen the published version.)

Sherwig, John M.: *Guineas and Gunpowder: British Foreign Aid in the Wars with France, 1793–1815* (Harvard University Press, 1969).

Shore, H. N.: 'The Navy in the Peninsular War', series of 15 articles in the *United Service Magazine*, 1912–14.

Showalter, Dennis E.: 'The Prussian *Landwehr* and its Critics, 1813–19', *Central European History*, vol. 4, no. 1, March 1971, pp. 3–33.

Silberling, N. J.: 'Financial and Monetary Policy of Great Britain during the Napoleonic Wars', *Quarterly Journal of Economics*, vol. 38, 1924, pp. 214–33, 397–439.

Smart, William: *Economic Annals of the Nineteenth Century*, 2 vols (London, Macmillan, 1910–17).

Smith, E. A.: *Lord Grey, 1764–1845* (Oxford, Clarendon Press, 1990).

Smith, G. C. Moore: *The Life of John Colborne, Field Marshal Lord Seaton* (New York, E.P. Dutton & Co., 1903).

Stapleton, Augustus Granville: *George Canning and His Times* (London, John W. Parker & Son, 1859).

Stephens, Frederick George, and Mary Dorothy George: *Catalogue of Political and Personal Satires, Preserved in the Department of Prints and Drawings in the British Museum*, 11 vols (London, British Museum Publications, 1978; first published 1870–1954).

Sweet, Paul R.: *Wilhelm von Humboldt: A Biography*, 2 vols (Ohio State University Press, 1980).

Symonds: see Christie, Carl A.

Thompson, Neville: *Wellington after Waterloo* (London, Routledge and Kegan Paul, 1986).

Thorne, R. G.: *The House of Commons, 1790–1820*, 5 vols, part of *The History of Parliament* (London, Secker and Warburg for The History of Parliament Trust, 1986).

Trietschke, Heinrich von: *History of Germany in the Nineteenth Century*, vol. 1 (London, Jarrold and Allen & Unwin, 1915).

Trulsson, Sven G.: *British and Swedish Policies and Strategies in the Baltic after the Peace of Tilsit in 1807* (C.W.K. Gleerup, Bibliotheca Historica Lundensis XL, Sweden, 1976).

Twiss, Horace: *The Public and Private Life of Lord Chancellor Eldon . . .* , 2 vols (London, John Murray, 1846).

Vann, J. A.: 'Hapsburg Policy and the Austrian War of 1809', *Central European History*, vol. 7, 1974, pp. 291–310.

Vichness, Samuel E.: 'Marshal of Portugal: The Military Career of William Carr Beresford, 1785–1814' (unpublished PhD thesis submitted to Florida State University in 1976).

Walpole, Spencer: *The Life of the Rt. Hon. Spencer Perceval*, 2 vols (London, Hurst and Blackett, 1874).

Ward, A. W., and G. P. Gooch: *The Cambridge History of British Foreign Policy*, 3 vols (Cambridge University Press, 1922).

Ward, S. G. P.: 'Fresh Light on the Corunna Campaign', *Journal of the Society for Army Historical Research*, vol. 28, no. 115, 1950, pp. 107–26.

Watson, G. E.: 'The United States and the Peninsular War', *The Historical Journal*, vol. 19, December 1976, pp. 859–76.

Watson, J. Steven: *The Reign of George III, 1760–1815* (Oxford, Clarendon Press, 1960).

Webb, P. L. C.: 'The Rebuilding and Repair of the Fleet, 1783–1793', *Bulletin of the Institute of Historical Research*, vol. 50, 1977, pp. 194–209.

——: 'Construction, repair and maintenance in the battlefleet of the Royal Navy, 1793–1815', in Jeremy Black and Philip Woodfine (eds), *The British Navy and the Use of Naval Power in the Eighteenth Century* (Leicester University Press, 1988).

Webster, C. K.: *The Foreign Policy of Castlereagh, 1812–1815* (London, G. Bell, 1931).

——: *The Congress of Vienna, 1814–15* (London, Thames and Hudson, 1965; first published 1919).

——: 'The Duel between Castlereagh and Canning in 1809', *Cambridge Historical Journal*, vol. 3, 1929, pp. 83–95, 314.

White, D. Fedotoff: 'The Russian Navy in Trieste during the Wars of the Revolution and the Empire', *American Slavic and East European Review*, vol. 6, Dec. 1947, pp. 25–41.

Wilson, Joan: *A Soldier's Wife: Wellington's Marriage* (London, Weidenfeld and Nicolson, 1987).

Wood, Herbert J.: 'England, China, and the Napoleonic Wars', *Pacific Historical Journal*, vol. 9, 1940, pp. 139–56.

Wortley, Mrs Edward Stuart: *Highcliffe and the Stuarts* (London, John Murray, 1927).

Wright, Charles, and C. Ernest Fayle: *A History of Lloyd's: From the Founding of Lloyd's Coffee House to the Present Day* (London, Macmillan, 1928).

Yonge, Charles Duke: *The Life and Administration of Robert Banks, Second Earl of Liverpool, K.G.*, 3 vols (London, Macmillan, 1868).

Young, Peter, and J. P. Lawford: *Wellington's Masterpiece: The Battle and Campaign of Salamanca* (London, Allen and Unwin, 1973).

Ziegler, Philip: *Addington* (London, Collins, 1965).

Index